# business

# business

O.C. Ferrell
University of New Mexico

Geoffrey Hirt
DePaul University

Linda Ferrell
University of New Mexico

 McGraw-Hill
Irwin

Boston   Burr Ridge, IL   Dubuque, IA   New York   San Francisco   St. Louis
Bangkok   Bogotá   Caracas   Kuala Lumpur   Lisbon   London   Madrid   Mexico City
Milan   Montreal   New Delhi   Santiago   Seoul   Singapore   Sydney   Taipei   Toronto

BUSINESS

Published by McGraw-Hill/Irwin, a business unit of The McGraw-Hill Companies, Inc., 1221 Avenue of the Americas, New York, NY, 10020. Copyright © 2009 by The McGraw-Hill Companies, Inc. All rights reserved. No part of this publication may be reproduced or distributed in any form or by any means, or stored in a database or retrieval system, without the prior written consent of The McGraw-Hill Companies, Inc., including, but not limited to, in any network or other electronic storage or transmission, or broadcast for distance learning.

Some ancillaries, including electronic and print components, may not be available to customers outside the United States.

This book is printed on acid-free paper.
1 2 3 4 5 6 7 8 9 0 WCK/WCK 0 9 8

ISBN 978-0-07-351171-9
MHID 0-07-351171-4

Publisher: *Paul Ducham*
Executive editor: *Doug Hughes*
Senior developmental editor: *Christine Scheid*
Editorial assistant: *Kelly Pekelder*
Marketing manager: *Sarah Schuessler*
Marketing director: *Krista Bettino*
Senior project manager: *Susanne Riedell*
Lead production supervisor: *Carol A. Bielski*
Senior designer: *Cara David*
Senior photo research coordinator: *Jeremy Cheshareck*
Photo researcher: *Mike Hruby*
Media project manager: *Srikanth Potluri, Hurix Systems Pvt. Ltd.*
Interior design: *Jillian Lindner and Cara David*
Typeface: *10/12 Minion Pro Regular*
Compositor: *Laserwords Private Limited*
Printer: *Quebecor World Versailles Inc.*

**Library of Congress Cataloging-in-Publication Data**

Ferrell, O. C.
    Business / O.C. Ferrell, Geoffrey Hirt, Linda Ferrell.—1st ed.
        p. cm.
    A scaled-down "magazine" version of: Business : a changing world / O. C. Ferrell, Geoffrey Hirt, Linda Ferrell. 6th ed. c2008. With no preface or introduction.
    Includes index.
    ISBN-13: 978-0-07-351171-9 (alk. paper)
    ISBN-10: 0-07-351171-4 (alk. paper)
    1. Business. 2. Management—United States. I. Hirt, Geoffrey A. II. Ferrell, Linda. III. Title.
HF1008.F472 2009
650—dc22
                                                                                    2007044165

# business

# business

O.C. Ferrell
University of New Mexico

Geoffrey Hirt
DePaul University

Linda Ferrell
University of New Mexico

 McGraw-Hill
Irwin

Boston   Burr Ridge, IL   Dubuque, IA   New York   San Francisco   St. Louis
Bangkok   Bogotá   Caracas   Kuala Lumpur   Lisbon   London   Madrid   Mexico City
Milan   Montreal   New Delhi   Santiago   Seoul   Singapore   Sydney   Taipei   Toronto

BUSINESS

Published by McGraw-Hill/Irwin, a business unit of The McGraw-Hill Companies, Inc., 1221 Avenue of the Americas, New York, NY, 10020. Copyright © 2009 by The McGraw-Hill Companies, Inc. All rights reserved. No part of this publication may be reproduced or distributed in any form or by any means, or stored in a database or retrieval system, without the prior written consent of The McGraw-Hill Companies, Inc., including, but not limited to, in any network or other electronic storage or transmission, or broadcast for distance learning.

Some ancillaries, including electronic and print components, may not be available to customers outside the United States.

This book is printed on acid-free paper.
1 2 3 4 5 6 7 8 9 0 WCK/WCK 0 9 8

ISBN 978-0-07-351171-9
MHID 0-07-351171-4

Publisher: *Paul Ducham*
Executive editor: *Doug Hughes*
Senior developmental editor: *Christine Scheid*
Editorial assistant: *Kelly Pekelder*
Marketing manager: *Sarah Schuessler*
Marketing director: *Krista Bettino*
Senior project manager: *Susanne Riedell*
Lead production supervisor: *Carol A. Bielski*
Senior designer: *Cara David*
Senior photo research coordinator: *Jeremy Cheshareck*
Photo researcher: *Mike Hruby*
Media project manager: *Srikanth Potluri, Hurix Systems Pvt. Ltd.*
Interior design: *Jillian Lindner and Cara David*
Typeface: *10/12 Minion Pro Regular*
Compositor: *Laserwords Private Limited*
Printer: *Quebecor World Versailles Inc.*

### Library of Congress Cataloging-in-Publication Data

Ferrell, O. C.
  Business / O.C. Ferrell, Geoffrey Hirt, Linda Ferrell.—1st ed.
    p. cm.
    A scaled-down "magazine" version of: Business : a changing world / O. C. Ferrell, Geoffrey Hirt, Linda Ferrell. 6th ed. c2008. With no preface or introduction.
  Includes index.
  ISBN-13: 978-0-07-351171-9 (alk. paper)
  ISBN-10: 0-07-351171-4 (alk. paper)
  1. Business. 2. Management—United States. I. Hirt, Geoffrey A. II. Ferrell, Linda. III. Title.
HF1008.F472 2009
650—dc22
                                                                2007044165

www.mhhe.com

# brief contents

v

# contents

## part 3  ●○
## Managing for Quality and Competitiveness

## part 4  ●●
## Creating the Human Resource Advantage

# business

# the dynamics of
# BUSINESS
# A N D
# ECONOMICS

## INTRODUCTION
We begin our study of business by examining the fundamentals of business and economics in this chapter. First, we introduce the nature of business, including its goals, activities, and participants. Next, we describe the basics of economics and apply them to the United States' economy. Finally, we establish a framework for studying business in this text.

### ● ● LO1
Define basic concepts such as business, product, and profit.

## THE NATURE OF BUSINESS

A business tries to earn a profit by providing products that satisfy people's needs. The outcome of its efforts are products that have both tangible and intangible characteristics that provide satisfaction and benefits. When you purchase a product, what you are buying is the benefits and satisfaction you think the product will provide. A Subway sandwich, for example, may be purchased to satisfy hunger; a Porsche Cayenne sport utility vehicle, to satisfy the need for transportation and the desire to present a certain image.

Most people associate the word *product* with tangible goods—an automobile, computer, loaf of bread, coat, or some other tangible item. However, a product can also be a service, which results when people or machines provide or process something of value to customers. Dry cleaning, photo processing, a checkup by a doctor, a performance by a movie star or basketball player—these are examples of services. A product can also be an idea. Consultants and attorneys, for example, generate ideas for solving problems.

### The Goal of Business

The primary goal of all businesses is to earn a profit, the difference between what it costs to make and sell a product and what a customer pays for it. If a company spends $2.00 to manufacture, finance, promote, and distribute a product that it sells for $2.75, the business earns a profit of 75 cents on each product sold. Businesses have the right to keep and use their profits as they choose—within legal limits—because profit is the reward for the risks they take in providing products. Not all organizations are businesses. Nonprofit organizations, such as Greenpeace, Special Olympics, and other charities and social causes, do not have the fundamental purpose of earning profits, although they may provide goods or services.

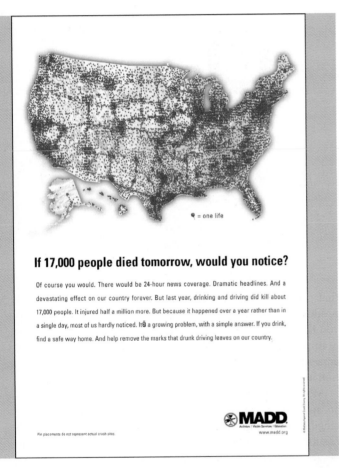

If 17,000 people died tomorrow, would you notice?

Of course you would. There would be 24-hour news coverage. Dramatic headlines. And a devastating effect on our country forever. But last year, drinking and driving did kill about 17,000 people. It injured half a million more. But because it happened over a year rather than in a single day, most of us hardly noticed. It's a growing problem, with a simple answer. If you drink, find a safe way home. And help remove the marks that drunk driving leaves on our country.

*Nonprofit organization MADD (Mothers Against Drunk Driving).*

To earn a profit, a person or organization needs management skills to plan, organize, and control the activities of the business and to find and develop employees so that it can make products consumers will buy. A business also needs marketing expertise to learn what products consumers need and want and to develop, manufacture, price, promote, and distribute those products. Additionally, a business needs financial resources and skills to fund, maintain, and expand its operations. Other challenges for businesspeople include abiding by laws and government regulations; acting in an ethical and socially responsible manner; and adapting to economic, technological, and social changes. Even nonprofit organizations engage in management, marketing, and finance activities to help reach their goals.

To achieve and maintain profitability, businesses have found that they must produce quality products, operate efficiently, and be socially responsible and ethical in dealing with customers, employees, investors, government regulators, the community, and society. Because these groups have a stake in the success and outcomes of a business, they are sometimes called stakeholders. Many businesses, for example, are concerned about how the production and distribution of their products affect the environment. In one year, Hewlett-Packard Company recycled more than 70,000 tons of product, which was equivalent to 10 percent of the company's sales. Concerns about landfills becoming high-tech graveyards plague many electronics firms. Television manufacturers worry as consumers trade their bulky TVs for high-definition, flat-screen versions.[1] Other businesses are concerned about the quality of life in the communities in which they operate. Cummins Inc., an Indiana-based manufacturing firm with operations around the world has helped to develop a technical school in Soweto, South Africa, to aid with education and skill development in a previously disadvantaged community.[2] Others are concerned with promoting business careers among African American, Hispanic, and Native American students. The Diversity Pipeline Alliance plans an aggressive advertising campaign to show minority students ages 12 to 24 how a business education can lead to career opportunities.[3] Still other businesses are concerned with social responsibility in times of natural disasters. With extensive damage to the U.S. Gulf Coast from hurricanes in the mid 2000s, Home Depot has committed $10 million to rebuilding storm-ravaged communities. The Home Depot also publishes a "Hurricane Guide" with the Weather Channel, which contains information on preparing for a hurricane and what to do before, during, and after a hurricane.[4]

●● **LO2**

Identify the main participants and activities of business, and explain why studying business is important.

## The People and Activities of Business

Figure 1.1 shows the people and activities involved in business. At the center of the figure are owners, employees, and customers; the outer circle includes the primary business

FIGURE 1.1 Overview of the Business World

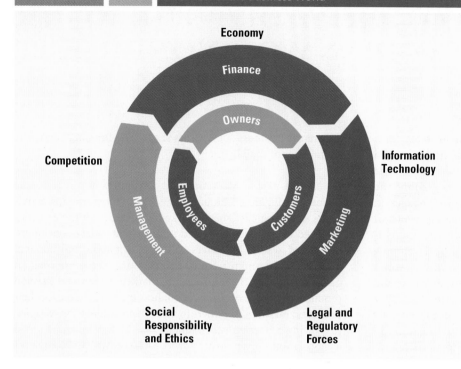

technology, and ethical and social concerns—all have an impact on the daily operations of businesses. You will learn more about these participants in business activities throughout this book. Next, we will examine the major activities of business.

**management.** Notice that in Figure 1.1 management and employees are in the same segment of the circle. This is because management involves coordinating employees' actions to achieve the firm's goals, organizing people to work efficiently, and motivating them to achieve the business's goals. NASCAR has been a family-run business since its inception. Brian France, current chairman and CEO, is following in the footsteps of his father and grandfather in providing leadership for the sport. NASCAR is now the second most popular spectator sport in the country outperforming fan numbers and viewership for the IRL (Indianapolis Racing League).[6] Management is also concerned with acquiring, developing, and using resources (including people) effectively and efficiently. Under CEO Eric Schmidt's leadership, Google will continue to advance broadband adoption in all forms, knowing that broadband users visit Google sites more often. In a partnership with Dell, Google will be preloaded on tool bars and as desktop search software to generate more traffic and, consequently, ad revenue for Google.[7]

activities—management, marketing, and finance. Owners have to put up resources—money or credit—to start a business. Employees are responsible for the work that goes on within a business. Owners can manage the business themselves or hire employees to accomplish this task. The president of General Motors, for example, does not own GM but is an employee who is responsible for managing all the other employees in a way that earns a profit for investors, who are the real owners. Finally, and most importantly, a business's major role is to satisfy the customers who buy its goods or services. Note also that people and forces beyond an organization's control—such as legal and regulatory forces, the economy, competition,

A nationally recognized, environmentally efficient wind-powered brewery, New Belgium Brewery in Fort Collins, Colorado, eliminates 1,800 metric tons of $CO_2$ emissions per year. (From www.newbelgium.com)

Production and manufacturing is another element of management. In essence, managers plan, organize, staff, and control the tasks required to carry out the work of the company or nonprofit organization. We take a closer look at management activities in Parts 3 and 4 of this text.

> # "MANAGERS PLAN, ORGANIZE, STAFF, AND CONTROL THE TASKS REQUIRED TO CARRY OUT THE WORK OF THE COMPANY OR NONPROFIT ORGANIZATION."

To illustrate the importance of management, consider a small hypothetical Mexican restaurant, owned and managed by the Lopez family, that provides traditional home-style recipes and excellent service in the community. Among the many management activities the Lopez family engages in are finding, training, scheduling, and motivating waitstaff and cooks; locating and purchasing high-quality ingredients and equipment; planning daily meals and developing new recipes; and deciding what local community charities it wants to support. If a large corporate restaurant chain, such as On the Border, opens a restaurant nearby, the Lopez family will have to decide how to respond to the new competition—change prices or the menu, advertise, or make some other response. Consequently, making decisions to ensure the business achieves its short- and long-term goals is a vital part of management.

**marketing.** Marketing and consumers are in the same segment of Figure 1.1 because the focus of all marketing activities is satisfying customers. Marketing includes all the activities designed to provide goods and services that satisfy consumers' needs and wants. Marketers gather information and conduct research to determine what customers want. Using information gathered from marketing research, marketers plan and develop products and make decisions about how much to charge for their products and when and where to make them available. In response to growing concerns over childhood obesity, McDonald's formed a "global mom's panel" to meet twice each year with the company's

## Frontier Airlines—A Whole Different Animal

Frontier Airlines started out in 1946 as Monarch Airlines, became Frontier Airlines, and 40 years later was taken over by Continental Airlines. In 1994, former Frontier president M. C. "Hank" Lund and investors revived Frontier as a new air carrier. Current CEO Jeff Potter has been instrumental in helping Frontier flourish while other airlines are facing bankruptcy proceedings.

Potter first worked for the old Frontier Airlines cleaning jets. He later landed a job at Frontier's ticket counter—and that's when a love for the airline business began. Potter worked at a number of airlines—climbing his way up the ladder—until he returned to Frontier in 1995 as vice president of marketing. In the five years he held this position, the airline's revenues increased fivefold. Potter briefly left Frontier in 2000 to run another airline but returned a year later to be groomed as CEO. Since Potter has taken over as CEO, he has been able to either turn a profit or limit the company's losses in what is currently a highly challenging time for the airline industry.

Experts credit Potter with much of Frontier's success. He is known as an informal, respectful leader who considers himself simply to be part of the Frontier team. He views all employee contributions as being on par with his own and believes in empowering employees.

Previous CEO Sam Addoms believed strongly in a family-inspired work culture, and Potter has embraced this idea. All of this makes Frontier a strong company, and, as a result, customers are treated to enjoyable, comfortable experiences.

Some of Frontier's success is because the airline's fleet is relatively new. This means that the planes are more efficient to maintain, which cuts down on costs and repair time. Another fact in Frontier's favor is the carrier's location in Denver, Colorado. Denver International Airport is the country's fifth most used airport, and its location practically in the middle of the country means that the airline gets year-round business. Frontier started by providing flights to North Dakota and Montana and grew to flying in eight markets. Frontier now flies to 48 cities in 29 states plus seven locations in Mexico.

Despite Frontier's success, the airline does face challenges. Southwest Airlines, another and perhaps better-known discount carrier, started operations in Denver and is a direct competitor. However, analysts predict that Frontier will come out on top based on its high-quality customer service. Frontier and Jet Blue are the only U.S. domestic carriers with DirectTV. Televisions on the back of each seat make 25 channels of live TV available for free while on the ground and for $5 once in the air. Frontier can waive the fee when flights are delayed or other service problems occur.

While Frontier's clever marketing campaign (using talking animal spokesmascots such as Griswald the Bear and Flip the Dolphin) and low-key corporate culture are helpful, its success for the future rests on its continued ability to provide on-time flights, quality service, and low-priced fares in a fun environment for employees and customers.[5] ❖

### Q: Discussion Questions

1. What are the key elements that affect consumers' decisions as to which airline to fly?

2. Compare Frontier's advertising with that of other airlines you are familiar with. How are they alike? Different?

3. Why is Frontier so successful?

top executives to talk about menu items and nutrition. McDonald's has worked to improve the nutritional value of its menu options, expanding salads and adding french fry alternatives for children, such as carrot sticks. McDonald's chicken McNuggets, which are a Happy Meal favorite among children, are now made with 100 percent white meat.[8] Other food producers have responded to consumer health concerns by modifying their products to make them healthier. Pepsico, for example, has eliminated all transfats from its line of snack chips through a full conversion to nonhydrogenated oils. Such a move reduces consumers' risk of coronary disease.[9] Marketers use promotion—advertising, personal selling, sales promotion (coupons, games, sweepstakes, movie tie-ins), and publicity—to communicate the benefits and advantages of their products to consumers and increase sales. Nonprofit organizations also use promotion. For example, the National Fluid Milk Processor Promotion Board's "milk mustache" advertising campaign has featured Mischa Barton, Jeff Gordon, Tony Hawk, Peyton and Eli Manning, and Gisele Bunschen, as well as animated "celebrities" such as Garfield.[10] We will examine marketing activities in Part 5 of this text.

finance.   Owners and finance are in the same part of Figure 1.1 because, although management and marketing have to deal with financial considerations, it is the primary responsibility of the owners to provide financial resources for the operation of the business. Moreover, the owners have the most to lose if the business fails to make a profit. Finance refers to all activities concerned with obtaining money and using it effectively. People who work as accountants, stockbrokers, investment advisors, or bankers are all part of the financial world. Owners sometimes have to borrow money to get started or attract additional owners who become partners or stockholders. A mentoring group called 8 Wings helps women entrepreneurs obtain funding by assisting them in perfecting their business plan, preparing their presentation to potential funding sources, and introducing them to potential investors and other business contacts. The 8 Wings partners typically take stock or options in the companies they help.[11] Owners of small businesses in particular often rely on bank loans for funding. Part 6 of this text discusses financial management.

## Why Study Business?

Studying business can help you develop skills and acquire knowledge to prepare for your future career, regardless of whether you plan to work for a multinational *Fortune* 500 firm, start your own business, work for a government agency, or manage or volunteer at a nonprofit organization. The field of business offers a variety of interesting and challenging career opportunities throughout the world, such as human resources management, information technology, finance, production and operations, wholesaling and retailing, and many more.

Studying business can also help you better understand the many business activities that are necessary to provide satisfying goods and services—and that these activities carry a price tag. For example, if you buy a new compact disk, about half of the price goes toward activities related to distribution and the

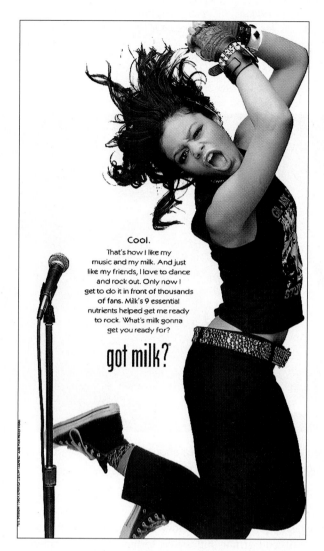

*Did the "Got Milk?" campaign with famous celebrities and their milk mustaches get you to drink more milk?*

retailer's expenses and profit margins. The production (pressing) of the CD represents about $1, or a small percentage of its price. Most businesses charge a reasonable price for their products to ensure that they cover their production costs, pay their employees, provide their owners with a return on their investment, and perhaps give something back to their local communities. Magic Johnson, through his Magic Johnson Foundation, has successfully worked to bring entertainment, retailing, housing, and jobs to New York, Chicago, Atlanta, Miami, San Diego, Houston, and many more downtown and diverse urban areas. By bringing Burger King, and TGI Friday's restaurants, Starbucks, Loew's movie theatres, and 24 Hour Fitness centers, as well as commercial and residential real estate, he has revitalized neighborhoods and provided support for the social needs of children, young adults, and inner-city communities throughout the nation.[12] Thus, learning about business can help you become a well-informed consumer and member of society.

Business activities help generate the profits that are essential not only to individual businesses and local economies but also

*When you buy a Coldplay CD, about half of the price goes toward activities related to distribution, retail expenses, and profit margins.*

**Economics** is the study of how resources are distributed for the production of goods and services within a social system. You are already familiar with the types of resources available. Land, forests, minerals, water, and other things that are not made by people are **natural resources.** **Human resources,** or labor, refers to the physical and mental abilities that people use to produce goods and services. **Financial resources,** or capital, are the funds used to acquire the natural and human resources needed to provide products. Because natural, human, and financial resources are used to produce goods and services, they are sometimes called *factors of production.*

to the health of the global economy. Without profits, businesses find it difficult, if not impossible, to buy more raw materials, hire more employees, attract more capital, and create additional products that in turn make more profits and fuel the world economy. Understanding how our free-enterprise economic system allocates resources and provides incentives for industry and the workplace is important to everyone.

 **L03**

Define economics and compare the four types of economic systems.

# THE ECONOMIC FOUNDATIONS OF BUSINESS

To continue our introduction to business, it is useful to explore the economic environment in which business is conducted. In this section, we examine economic systems, the free-enterprise system, the concepts of supply and demand, and the role of competition. These concepts play important roles in determining how businesses operate in a particular society.

## Economic Systems

An **economic system** describes how a particular society distributes its resources to produce goods and services. A central issue of economics is how to fulfill an unlimited demand for goods and services in a world with a limited supply of resources. Different economic systems attempt to resolve this central issue in numerous ways, as we shall see.

Although economic systems handle the distribution of resources in different ways, all economic systems must address three important issues:

1. What goods and services, and how much of each, will satisfy consumers' needs?
2. How will goods and services be produced, who will produce them, and with what resources will they be produced?
3. How are the goods and services to be distributed to consumers?

Communism, socialism, and capitalism, the basic economic systems found in the world today (Table 1.1), have fundamental differences in the way they address these issues.

**communism.** Karl Marx (1818–1883) first described **communism** as a society in which the people, without regard to class, own all the nation's resources. In his ideal political-economic system, everyone contributes according to ability and receives benefits according to need. In a communist economy, the people (through the government) own and operate all businesses and factors of production. Central government planning determines what goods and services satisfy citizens' needs, how the goods and services are produced, and how they are distributed. However, no true communist economy exists today that satisfies Marx's ideal.

On paper, communism appears to be efficient and equitable, producing less of a gap between rich and poor. In practice, however, communist economies have been marked by low standards of living, critical shortages of consumer goods, high prices, and little freedom. Russia, Poland, Hungary, and other Eastern European nations have turned away from communism and toward economic systems governed by supply and demand rather than by central planning. However, their experiments with alternative economic systems have been fraught with difficulty and hardship. China, North Korea, and Cuba continue to apply communist principles to their economies, but these countries are also enduring economic and political change. Consequently, communism is declining and its future as an economic system is uncertain.

## socialism.
Closely related to communism is socialism, an economic system in which the government owns and operates basic industries—postal service, telephone, utilities, transportation, health care, banking, and some manufacturing—but individuals own most businesses. Central planning determines what basic goods and services are produced, how they are produced, and how they are distributed. Individuals and small businesses provide other goods and services based on consumer demand and the availability of resources. As with communism, citizens are dependent on the government for many goods and services.

Most socialist nations, such as Sweden, India, and Israel, are democratic and recognize basic individual freedoms. Citizens can vote for political offices, but central government planners usually make decisions about what is best for the nation. People are free to go into the occupation of their choice, but they often work in government-operated organizations. Socialists believe their system permits a higher standard of living than other economic systems, but the difference often applies to the nation as a whole rather than to its individual citizens. Socialist economies profess egalitarianism—equal distribution of income and social services. They believe their economies are more stable than those of other nations. Although this may be true, taxes and unemployment are generally higher in socialist countries. Perhaps as a result, many socialist countries are also experiencing economic turmoil.

## capitalism.
Capitalism, or free enterprise, is an economic system in which individuals own and operate the majority of businesses that provide goods and services. Competition, supply, and demand determine which goods and services are produced, how they are produced, and how they are distributed. The United States, Canada, Japan, and Australia are examples of economic systems based on capitalism.

There are two forms of capitalism: pure capitalism and modified capitalism. In pure capitalism, also called a free-market system, all economic decisions are made without government intervention. This economic system was first described by Adam Smith in *The Wealth of Nations* (1776). Smith, often called the father of capitalism, believed that the "invisible hand of competition" best regulates the economy. He argued that competition should determine what goods and services people need. Smith's system is also called *laissez-faire* ("to leave alone") *capitalism* because the government does not interfere in business.

**TABLE 1.1** Comparison of Communism, Socialism, and Capitalism

|  | Communism | Socialism | Capitalism |
| --- | --- | --- | --- |
| Business ownership | Most businesses are owned and operated by the government. | The government owns and operates major industries; individuals own small businesses. | Individuals own and operate all businesses. |
| Competition | None. The government owns and operates everything. | Restricted in major industries; encouraged in small business. | Encouraged by market forces and government regulations. |
| Profits | Excess income goes to the government. | Profits earned by small businesses may be reinvested in the business; profits from government-owned industries go to the government. | Individuals are free to keep profits and use them as they wish. |
| Product availability and price | Consumers have a limited choice of goods and services; prices are usually high. | Consumers have some choice of goods and services; prices are determined by supply and demand. | Consumers have a wide choice of goods and services; prices are determined by supply and demand. |
| Employment options | Little choice in choosing a career; most people work for government-owned industries or farms. | Some choice of careers; many people work in government jobs. | Unlimited choice of careers. |

Source: "Gross Domestic Product or Expenditure, 1930–2002," *InfoPlease* (n.d.), www.infoplease.com/ipa/A0104575.html (accessed February 16, 2004).

● **FREE-MARKET SYS-TEM** pure capitalism, in which all economic decisions are made without government intervention

● **MIXED ECONO-MIES** economies made up of elements from more than one economic system

● **DEMAND** the number of goods and services that consumers are willing to buy at different prices at a specific time

● **SUPPLY** the number of products—goods and services—that businesses are willing to sell at different prices at a specific time

● **EQUILIBRIUM PRICE** the price at which the number of products that businesses are willing to supply equals the amount of products that consumers are willing to buy at a specific point in time

Modified capitalism differs from pure capitalism in that the government intervenes and regulates business to some extent. One of the ways in which the United States and Canadian governments regulate business is through laws. Laws such as the Federal Trade Commission Act, which created the Federal Trade Commission to enforce antitrust laws, illustrate the importance of the government's role in the economy.

**mixed economies.** No country practices a pure form of communism, socialism, or capitalism, although most tend to favor one system over the others. Most nations operate as mixed economies, which have elements from more than one economic system. In socialist Sweden, most businesses are owned and operated by private individuals. In capitalist United States, the federal government owns and operates the postal service and the Tennessee Valley Authority, an electric utility. In Great Britain and Mexico, the

A number of basic individual and business rights must exist for free enterprise to work. These rights are the goals of many countries that have recently embraced free enterprise.

1. Individuals must have the right to own property and to pass this property on to their heirs. This right motivates people to work hard and save to buy property.

2. Individuals and businesses must have the right to earn profits and to use the profits as they wish, within the constraints of their society's laws and values.

3. Individuals and businesses must have the right to make decisions that determine the way the business operates. Although there is government regulation, the philosophy in countries like the United States and Australia is to permit maximum freedom within a set of rules of fairness.

4. Individuals must have the right to choose what career to pursue, where to live, what goods and services to purchase, and

[ **"Demand is the number of goods and services that consumers are willing to buy at different prices at a specific time."** ]

governments are attempting to sell many state-run businesses to private individuals and companies. In once-communist Russia, Hungary, Poland, and other Eastern European nations, capitalist ideas have been implemented, including private ownership of businesses.

## The Free-Enterprise System

Many economies—including those of the United States, Canada,and Japan—are based on free enterprise, and many communist and socialist countries, such as China and Russia, are applying more principles of free enterprise to their own economic systems. Free enterprise provides an opportunity for a business to succeed or fail on the basis of market demand. In a free-enterprise system, companies that can efficiently manufacture and sell products that consumers desire will probably succeed. Inefficient businesses and those that sell products that do not offer needed benefits will likely fail as consumers take their business to firms that have more competitive products.

more. Businesses must have the right to choose where to locate, what goods and services to produce, what resources to use in the production process, and so on.

Without these rights, businesses cannot function effectively because they are not motivated to succeed. Thus, these rights make possible the open exchange of goods and services.

## ● ● LO4

Describe the role of supply, demand, and competition in a free enterprise system.

## The Forces of Supply and Demand

In the United States and in other free-enterprise systems, the distribution of resources and products is determined by supply and demand. Demand is the number of goods and services that consumers are willing to buy at different prices at a specific time. From your own experience, you probably recognize that consumers are usually willing to buy more of an item as its price

*Consumers are less sensitive to the price of milk (left) than to steak (right). When the price of milk goes up, demand does not fall significantly because people still need to buy milk. However, if the price of steak rises beyond a certain point, people will buy less because they can turn to the many substitutes for steak.*

falls because they want to save money. Consider handmade rugs, for example. Consumers may be willing to buy six rugs at $350 each, four at $500 each, but only two at $650 each. The relationship between the price and the number of rugs consumers are willing to buy can be shown graphically, with a *demand curve* (see Figure 1.2).

**Supply** is the number of products that businesses are willing to sell at different prices at a specific time. In general, because the potential for profits is higher, businesses are willing to supply more of a good or service at higher prices. For example, a company that sells rugs may be willing to sell six at $650 each, four at $500 each, but just two at $350 each. The relationship between the price of rugs and the quantity the

company is willing to supply can be shown graphically with a *supply curve* (see Figure 1.2).

In Figure 1.2, the supply and demand curves intersect at the point where supply and demand are equal. The price at which the number of products that businesses are willing to supply equals the amount of products that consumers are willing to buy at a specific point in time is the **equilibrium price.** In our rug example, the company is willing to supply four rugs at $500 each, and consumers are willing to buy four rugs at $500 each. Therefore, $500 is the equilibrium price for a rug at that point in time, and most rug companies will price their rugs at $500. As you might imagine, a business that charges more than $500 (or whatever the current equilibrium price is) for its rugs will not sell many and might not earn a profit. On the other hand, a business that charges less than $500 accepts a lower profit per rug than could be made at the equilibrium price.

If the cost of making rugs goes up, businesses will not offer as many at the old price. Changing the price alters the supply curve, and a new equilibrium price results. This is an ongoing process, with supply and demand constantly changing in response to changes in economic conditions, availability of resources, and degree of competition. For example, gasoline prices rose sharply in 2006 in response to a shrinking supply of gasoline and crude oil and rising demand.[13] On the other hand, the world's largest music company, Universal Music Group, slashed the suggested retail price for CDs of popular artists like 50 Cent and Shania Twain to around

| FIGURE | 1.2 | Equilibrium Price of Handmade Rugs |
| --- | --- | --- |

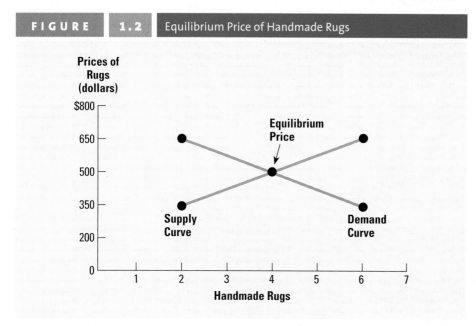

$10.00 in response to declining demand for music CDs. Sales of CDs have declined by 30 percent over the last few years, partly due to increased downloading of music from the Internet and increased competition from companies such as Apple and Wal-Mart, which sell individual songs for $0.99 or lower.[14] Prices for goods and services vary according to these changes in supply and demand. This concept is the force that drives the distribution of resources (goods and services, labor, and money) in a free-enterprise economy.

Critics of supply and demand say the system does not distribute resources equally. The forces of supply and demand prevent sellers who have to sell at higher prices (because their costs are high) and buyers who cannot afford to buy goods at the equilibrium price from participating in the market. According to critics, the wealthy can afford to buy more than they need, but the poor are unable to buy enough of what they need to survive.

## The Nature of Competition

**Competition,** the rivalry among businesses for consumers' dollars, is another vital element in free enterprise. According to Adam Smith, competition fosters efficiency and low prices by forcing producers to offer the best products at the most reasonable price; those who fail to do so are not able to stay in business. Thus, competition should improve the quality of the goods and services available or reduce prices. For example, thanks to smart design and excellent timing, Apple dominates the market for downloadable music with its iTunes online service and iPod MP3 player. However, many companies have set their sights on capturing some of the firm's market share with new products of their own. Wal-Mart and Napster have launched online music services, while many rival computer firms have introduced MP3 players with new features and/or lower prices.

Within a free-enterprise system, there are four types of competitive environments: pure competition, monopolistic competition, oligopoly, and monopoly.

**Pure competition** exists when there are many small businesses selling one standardized product, such as agricultural commodities like wheat, corn, and cotton. No one business sells enough of the product to influence the product's price. And,

● ● **Competition, the rivalry among businesses for consumers' dollars, is another vital element in free enterprise.**

because there is no difference in the products, prices are determined solely by the forces of supply and demand.

**Monopolistic competition** exists when there are fewer businesses than in a pure-competition environment and the differences among the goods they sell is small. Aspirin, soft drinks, and vacuum cleaners are examples of such goods. These products differ slightly in packaging, warranty, name, and other characteristics, but all satisfy the same consumer need. Businesses have some power over the price they charge in monopolistic competition because they can make consumers aware of product differences through advertising. Consumers value some features more than others and are often willing to pay higher prices for a product with the features they want. For example, Advil, a nonprescription pain reliever, contains ibuprofen instead of aspirin. Consumers who cannot take aspirin or who believe ibuprofen is a more effective pain reliever may not mind paying a little extra for the ibuprofen in Advil.

An **oligopoly** exists when there are very few businesses selling a product. In an oligopoly, individual businesses have control over their products' price because each business supplies a large portion of the products sold in the marketplace. Nonetheless, the prices charged by different firms stay fairly close because a price cut or increase by one company will trigger a similar response from another company. In the airline industry, for example, when one airline cuts fares to boost sales, other airlines quickly follow with rate decreases to remain competitive. Oligopolies exist when it is expensive for new firms to enter the marketplace. Not just anyone can acquire enough financial capital to build an automobile production facility or purchase enough airplanes and related resources to build an airline.

When there is one business providing a product in a given market, a **monopoly** exists. Utility companies that supply electricity, natural gas, and water are monopolies. The government permits such monopolies because the cost of creating the good or supplying the service is so great that new producers cannot compete for sales. Government-granted monopolies are subject to government-regulated prices. Some monopolies exist because of technological developments that are protected by patent laws. Patent laws grant the developer of new technology a period of time (usually 17 years) during which no other producer can use the same technology without the agreement of the original developer. The United States granted the first patent in 1790, and the patent office received 440,000 patent applications in 2006.[15] This monopoly allows the developer to recover research, development, and production expenses and to earn a reasonable profit. Examples of this type of monopoly are the dry-copier process developed by Xerox and the self-developing photographic technology created by Polaroid. Both companies operated for years without competition and could charge premium prices because no alternative products existed to compete with their products. Through continuous development, Polaroid maintains market dominance. Xerox's patents have expired, however, and many imitators have forced market prices to decline.

 **L05**

Specify why and how the health of the economy is measured.

## Economic Cycles and Productivity

**expansion and contraction.** Economies are not stagnant; they expand and contract. **Economic expansion** occurs when an economy is growing and people are spending more money. Their purchases stimulate the production of goods and services, which in turn stimulates employment. The standard of living rises because more people are employed and have money to spend. Rapid expansions of the economy, however, may result in **inflation,** a continuing rise in prices. Inflation can be harmful if individuals' incomes do not increase at the same pace as rising prices, reducing their buying power. Zimbabwe has the highest inflation rate at over 1,000 percent.[16]

**Economic contraction** occurs when spending declines. Businesses cut back on production and lay off workers, and the economy as a whole slows down. Contractions of the economy lead to **recession**—a decline in production, employment, and income. Recessions are often characterized by rising levels of **unemployment,** which is measured as the percentage of the population that wants to work but is unable to find jobs. Figure 1.3 shows the overall unemployment rate in the civilian labor force over the past 80 years. Rising unemployment levels tend to stifle demand for goods and services, which can have the effect of forcing prices downward, a condition known as *deflation.* The United States has experienced numerous recessions, the most recent being 1990–1991 and

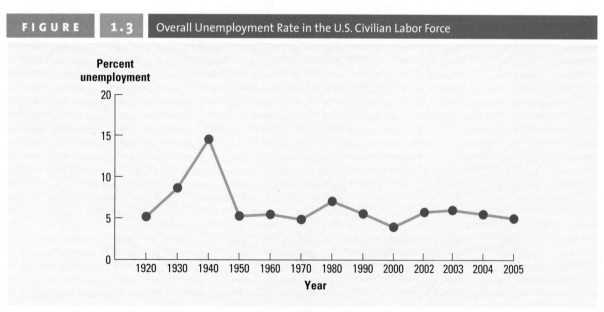

**FIGURE 1.3** Overall Unemployment Rate in the U.S. Civilian Labor Force

Source: "Overall Unemployment Rate in the Civilian Labor Force, 1920–2006," *InfoPlease* (n.d.), http://www.infoplease.com/ipa/A0104719.html (accessed May 29, 2007).

2001–2002; Japan has also experienced numerous recessions in the last decade. A severe recession may turn into a **depression,** in which unemployment is very high, consumer spending is low, and business output is sharply reduced, such as occurred in the United States in the early 1930s.

Economies expand and contract in response to changes in consumer, business, and government spending. War also can affect an economy, sometimes stimulating it (as in the United States during World Wars I and II) and sometimes stifling it (as during the Vietnam and Persian Gulf wars). Although fluctuations in the economy are inevitable and to a certain extent predictable, their effects—inflation and unemployment—disrupt lives and thus governments try to minimize them.

**measuring the economy.** Countries measure the state of their economies to determine whether they are expanding or contracting and whether corrective action is necessary to minimize the fluctuations. One commonly used measure is **gross domestic product (GDP)**—the sum of all goods and services produced in a country during a year. GDP measures only those goods and services made within a country and therefore does not include profits from companies' overseas operations; it does include profits earned by foreign companies within the country being measured. However, it does not take into account the concept of GDP in relation to population (GDP per capita). Figure 1.4 shows the increase in GDP over several years, while Table 1.2 compares a number of economic statistics for a sampling of countries.

Another important indicator of a nation's economic health is the relationship between its spending and income (from taxes). When a nation spends more than it takes in from taxes, it has a **budget deficit.** In the 1990s, the U.S. government eliminated its long-standing budget deficit by balancing the money spent for social, defense, and other programs with the amount of money taken in from taxes.

## Bingham Hill: Who Moved My Cheese?

The Bingham Hill Cheese Company, founded in Fort Collins, Colorado, by Tom and Kristi Johnson in 1999, closed its doors in February 2006 after going through successes and major challenges in its six-year life. Tom, with a background in environmental science, and Kristi, a former patent lawyer, took cheesemaking courses in college. Inspired by the fact that many artisan cheeses widely available in Europe were not available in the United States, the Johnsons eventually began the Bingham Hill Cheese Company. Bingham Hill was modeled after the microbreweries of Colorado and was called a "microcheesery." The company's first cheese, Rustic Blue, was an instant hit and, upon first entrance, won first place in the blue cheese class of the American Cheese Society's annual competition. The Johnsons sent samples of Rustic Blue to a number of stores and were immediately greeted by orders.

After much local success, California natural foods retailer Trader Joe's began stocking Bingham Hill cheeses. This was by far the largest success Bingham Hill had experienced. However, the cheese was so popular that, despite an attempt at quick expansion, Bingham Hill simply could not supply the 200 stores carrying the brand with enough cheese to keep the products on the shelves. Trader Joe's eventually quit carrying the brand, but the Johnsons learned from the experience and began expanding to accommodate the new large accounts they had lined up such as Kroger grocery stores and Super Target. One thing that allowed the Bingham Hill brand to stand out was the fact that the cheese was handmade. The cheese was stirred, cut, ladled, turned, and inspected daily by the owners and their employees. Even in the midst of growth, the Johnsons intended to continue making the cheese by hand.

To handle large accounts and remain competitive in the market, Bingham Hill expanded its building size from 2,000 to 14,000 square feet, added employees, and increased its output from 30,000 pounds of cheese in 2000 to around 250,000 pounds in 2005. It became well known for making spreadable cheeses such as those purchased by Kroger and Super Target. Spreadable cheeses are not aged, which cut down on costs for space and time. The Johnsons also created new products made with goat's milk and sheep's milk as well as cow's milk. By constantly refocusing, the Johnsons were able to learn and benefit from past mistakes and to find the best markets for their brands; however, this simply was not enough.

In 2005, Bingham Hill cheeses won 10 medals at the annual World Cheese Awards in London. The company was one of three national specialty cheese makers, and top restaurants and chefs were requesting their products regularly. Each of the 20 cheeses produced by the company won awards. Still, in spite of (or perhaps due to) the high quality and popularity of the products, the company could not deal with rising expenses. In 2005, the costs of milk, fuel, shipping, and labor became too much. On top of financial struggles, the landlords of Bingham Hill's cheese production facility planned to demolish the building, and the company was not able to invest in a new location. Officials in Wisconsin offered the Johnsons incentives to move the company to that state, but ultimately the Johnsons chose to remain in Colorado close to family.

Once Bingham Hill's doors were closed, the Johnsons auctioned recipes, artisan instructions, packaging, equipment, and supplies on eBay. As for the Johnsons—Kristi will return to work as an attorney and Tom plans to work as a freelance writer.[18] ❖

## Q: Discussion Questions

1. How does a highly successful small company like Bingham Hill fail?

2. Why was Bingham Hill so successful?

3. What could have been done to save Bingham Hill?

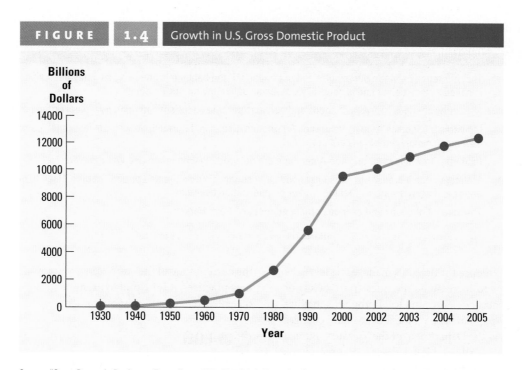

**FIGURE 1.4**  Growth in U.S. Gross Domestic Product

Source: "Gross Domestic Product or Expenditure, 1930–2005," *InfoPlease* (n.d.), http://www.infoplease.com/ipa/A0104575.html (accessed May 29, 2007).

In recent years, however, the budget deficit has reemerged and grown to record levels, partly due to defense spending in the aftermath of the terrorist attacks of September 11, 2001. Because Americans do not want their taxes increased, it is difficult for the federal government to bring in more revenue and reduce the deficit. Like consumers and businesses, when the government needs money, it borrows from the public, banks, and other institutions. The national debt (the amount of money the nation owes its lenders) exceeded $8.8 billion in 2007,[17] due largely to increased spending by the government. This figure is especially

**TABLE 1.2**  A Comparative Analysis of a Sampling of Countries

| Country | GDP (in billions of U.S. dollars) | GDP per capita (in U.S. dollars) | Unemployment Rate (%) | Inflation Rate (%) |
|---|---|---|---|---|
| Argentina | $599.1 | 15,000 | 10.2 | 10 |
| Australia | 666.3 | 32,900 | 4.9 | 3.8 |
| Brazil | 1.616 (trillion) | 8,600 | 9.6 | 3 |
| Canada | 1.165 (t) | 35,200 | 6.4 | 2 |
| China | 10 (t) | 7,600 | 4.2 | 1.5 |
| France | 1.871 (t) | 30,100 | 8.7 | 1.5 |
| Germany | 2.585 (t) | 31,400 | 7.1 | 1.7 |
| India | 4.042 (t) | 3,700 | 7.8 | 5.3 |
| Israel | 166.3 | 26,200 | 8.3 | −0.1 |
| Japan | 34.22 (t) | 33,100 | 4.1 | 0.3 |
| Mexico | 1.134 (t) | 10,600 | 3.2* | 3.4 |
| Russia | 1.723 (t) | 12,100 | 6.6 | 9.8 |
| South Africa | 576.4 | 13,000 | 25.5 | 5 |
| United Kingdom | 1.903 (t) | 31,400 | 2.9 | 3 |
| United States | 12.98 (t) | 43,500 | 4.8 | 2.5 |

*Estimated for urban areas; unemployment rates in rural areas may be higher.

Source: CIA, "Country Listing," *The World Fact Book 2007* (n.d.), https://www.cia.gov/library/publications/the-world-factbook/index.html (accessed May 29, 2007).

**TABLE 1.3**  How Do We Evaluate Our Nation's Economy?

| Unit of Measure | Description |
| --- | --- |
| Trade balance | The difference between our exports and our imports. If the balance is negative, as it has been since the mid-1980s, it is called a trade deficit and is generally viewed as unhealthy for our economy. |
| Consumer Price Index | Measures changes in prices of goods and services purchased for consumption by typical urban households. |
| Per capita income | Indicates the income level of "average" Americans. Useful in determing how much "average" consumers spend and how much money Americans are earning. |
| Unemployment rate | Indicates how many working age Americans are not working who otherwise want to work.* |
| Inflation | Monitors price increases in consumer goods and services over specified periods of time. Used to determine if costs of goods and services are exceeding worker compensation over time. |
| Worker productivity | The amount of goods and services produced for each hour worked. |

*Americans who do not want to work in a traditional sense, such as househusbands/housewives, are not counted as unemployed.

worrisome because, to reduce the debt to a manageable level, the government either has to increase its revenues (raise taxes) or reduce spending on social, defense, and legal programs, neither of which is politically popular. The national debt figure changes daily and can be seen at the Department of the Treasury, Bureau of the Public Debt, Web site. Table 1.3 describes some of the other ways we evaluate our nation's economy.

# THE AMERICAN ECONOMY

As we said previously, the United States is a mixed economy based on capitalism. The answers to the three basic economic issues are determined primarily by competition and the forces of supply and demand, although the federal government does intervene in economic decisions to a certain extent. To understand the current state of the American economy and its effect on business practices, it is helpful to examine its history and the roles of the entrepreneur and the government.

## ● ● L06

Trace the evolution of the American economy, and discuss the role of the entrepreneur in the economy.

## A Brief History of the American Economy

**the early economy.**  Before the colonization of North America, Native Americans lived as hunter/gatherers and farmers, with some trade among tribes. The colonists who came later operated primarily as an *agricultural economy.* People were self-sufficient and produced everything they needed at home, including food, clothing, and furniture. Abundant natural resources and a moderate climate nourished industries such as farming, fishing, shipping, and fur trading. A few manufactured goods and money for the colonies' burgeoning industries came from England and other countries.

As the nation expanded slowly toward the West, people found natural resources such as coal, copper, and iron ore and used them to produce goods such as horseshoes, farm implements, and kitchen utensils. Farm families who produced surplus goods sold or traded them for things they could not produce themselves, such as fine furniture and window glass. Some families also spent time turning raw materials into clothes and household goods. Because these goods were produced at home, this system was called the domestic system.

**the industrial revolution.**  The 19th century and the Industrial Revolution brought the development of new technology and factories. The factory brought together all the resources needed to make a product—materials, machines, and workers. Work in factories became specialized as workers

American Eli Whitney is credited with creating the cotton gin in 1793. The device removed the seeds from cotton, which was much more efficient than removing them by hand. But the machine was so easy to copy that Whitney's cotton-gin-producing company was driven out of business by competitors just four years after he had invented the device.

focused on one or two tasks. As work became more efficient, productivity increased, making more goods available at lower prices. Railroads brought major changes, allowing farmers to send their surplus crops and goods all over the nation for barter or for sale.

Factories began to spring up along the railways to manufacture farm equipment and a variety of other goods to be shipped by rail. Samuel Slater set up the first American textile factory after he memorized the plans for an English factory and emigrated to the United States. Eli Whitney revolutionized the cotton industry with his cotton gin. Francis Cabot Lowell's factory organized all the steps in manufacturing cotton cloth for maximum efficiency and productivity. John Deere's farm equipment increased farm production and reduced the number of farmers required to feed the young nation. Farmers began to move to cities to find jobs in factories and a higher standard of living. Henry Ford developed the assembly-line system to produce automobiles. Workers focused on one part of an automobile and then pushed it to the next stage until it rolled off the assembly line as a finished automobile. Ford's assembly line could manufacture many automobiles efficiently, and the price of his cars was $200, making them affordable to many Americans.

### the manufacturing and marketing economies.

Industrialization brought increased prosperity, and the United States gradually became a *manufacturing economy*—one devoted to manufacturing goods and providing services rather than producing agricultural products. The assembly line was applied to more industries, increasing the variety of goods available to the consumer. Businesses became more concerned with the needs of the consumer and entered the *marketing economy*. Expensive goods such as cars and appliances could be purchased on a time-payment plan. Companies conducted research to find out what products consumers needed and wanted. Advertising made consumers aware of differences in products and prices.

Because these developments occurred in a free-enterprise system, consumers determined what goods and services were produced. They did this by purchasing the products they liked at prices they were willing to pay. The United States prospered, and American citizens had one of the highest standards of living in the world.

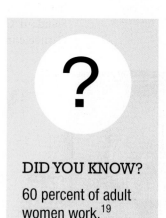

**?**

**DID YOU KNOW?**

60 percent of adult women work.[19]

### the service and internet-based economy.

After World War II, with the increased standard of living, Americans had more money and more time. They began to pay others to perform services that made their lives easier. Beginning in the 1960s, more and more women entered the workforce. The profile of the family changed: Today there are more single-parent families and individuals living alone, and in two-parent families, both parents often work. One result of this trend is that time-pressed Americans are increasingly paying others to do tasks they used to do at home, like cooking, laundry, landscaping, and child care. These trends have gradually changed the United States to a *service economy*—one devoted to the production of services that make life easier for busy consumers. Service industries such as restaurants, banking, medicine, child care, auto repair, leisure-related industries, and even education are growing rapidly and may account for as much as 80 percent of the U.S. economy. These trends continue with advanced technology contributing to new service products such as overnight mail, electronic banking, and shopping through cable television networks and the Internet. Table 1.4 provides an overview of e-commerce in the United States. More about the Internet and e-commerce can be found in Chapter 4.

WHAT A GREAT LOCATION FOR AN E-MARKETPLACE.

Introducing the e-marketplace alliance: IBM, i2 and Ariba. Three of the biggest names in e-business working together to help make your business work more efficiently — whether you buy or sell ships, sleds or seafood. It's b2b>3.

ibm i2 ariba

www.ibm-i2-ariba.com or call 877 426 2676; priority code: emarket1

*As this IBM ad demonstrates, the Internet has made it possible for people and firms to do business with one another just about any place in the world.*

**TABLE 1.4** U.S. e-Commerce Overview

| | |
|---|---|
| Total retail sales of all types | $3,905 billion |
| Total e-commerce sales | $104 billion |
| Total travel sales online | $77.7 billion |
| Online advertising | $13 billion |
| Number of VOIP subscribers, U.S. | $10.3 million |
| Active home Internet users in the U.S. | 210 million |
| Number of high speed Internet connections | 60 million |
| Number of Web logs | 66.6 million |
| Percent of U.S. adults online | 70 |

Source: "E-Commerce & Internet Industry Overview," Plunkett Research, Ltd., http://www.plunkettresearch.com/industries/ecommerceinternet/ecommerceinternetstatistics/tabid/167/default.aspx (accessed May 29, 2007).

*Burt's Bees began as an endeavor to sell products made from beeswax at craft fairs in Maine.*

## The Role of the Entrepreneur

An **entrepreneur** is an individual who risks his or her wealth, time, and effort to develop for profit an innovative product or way of doing something. While pregnant, Laurie McCartney realized there was no "one-stop shopping" for those expecting and new mothers. Out of her frustration came Babystyle. Today, Babystyle sells $50 million in products annually, including Bugaboo strollers, classic wood toys, stylish maternity clothing, baby clothes, diaper bags, and more. The company employs 280 employees in seven states with 18 retail stores.

The free-enterprise system provides the conditions necessary for entrepreneurs to succeed. In the past, entrepreneurs were often inventors who brought all the factors of production together to produce a new product. Thomas Edison, whose inventions include the record player and light bulb, was an early American entrepreneur. Henry Ford was one of the first persons to develop mass assembly methods in the automobile industry. Other entrepreneurs, so-called captains of industry, invested in the country's growth. John D. Rockefeller built Standard Oil out of the fledgling oil industry, and Andrew Carnegie invested in railroads and founded the United States Steel Corporation. Andrew Mellon built the Aluminum Company of America and Gulf Oil. J. P. Morgan started financial institutions to fund the business activities of other entrepreneurs. Although these entrepreneurs were born in another century, their legacy to the American economy lives on in the companies they started, many of which still operate today. Milton Hershey began producing chocolate in 1894 in Lancaster, Pennsylvania. In 1900, the company was mass producing chocolate in many forms, lowering the cost of chocolate and making it more affordable to the masses whereas it has once been a high-priced, luxury good. Early advertising touted chocolate as "a palatable confection and most nourishing food." Today, the Hershey Company employs more than 15,000 employees and sells almost $5 billion in chocolates and candies throughout the world.[21]

Entrepreneurs are constantly changing American business practices with new technology and innovative management

# Planet Bluegrass Keeps the Party Alive!

Craig Ferguson

Founded: 1988

The Business: Planet Bluegrass

Success: Now managing the popular Telluride Bluegrass Festival for a second year, the company has managed to double attendance to almost 10,000 people a day.

The Telluride Bluegrass Festival, founded in 1974 by a small group of hippies, was floundering when Craig Ferguson, a Denver-based attorney, rounded up a group of about 10 investors to purchase the festival. Ferguson, president of the company, and the investors founded Planet Bluegrass in 1988. Since managing the festival, the company has increased capacity and attracted big names to the event. Previous headliners include Arlo Guthrie, Barenaked Ladies, and Bonnie Raitt. In addition to the Telluride Bluegrass Festival, Planet Bluegrass has developed an annual Folks Festival and a Celtic-inspired musical event in Lyons, Colorado. The company also revived RockyGrass—another bluegrass festival held in Lyons. Planet Bluegrass has also implemented a one-week music school prior to the festivals in Lyons—headliners offer workshops in picking, singing, songwriting, and instrument building. Another way Planet Bluegrass profits is by offering clothing and CDs featuring past festival musicians. Festivarians, as festival fans are called, flock to the festivals by the thousands, inspiring Planet Bluegrass to continue to expand its offerings.[20] ❖

# "BUSINESS ETHICS GENERALLY REFERS TO THE STANDARDS AND PRINCIPLES USED BY SOCIETY TO DEFINE APPROPRIATE AND INAPPROPRIATE CONDUCT IN THE WORKPLACE."

techniques. Bill Gates, for example, built Microsoft, a software company whose products include MS-DOS (a disk operating system), Word, and Windows, into a multibillion-dollar enterprise. Frederick Smith had an idea to deliver packages overnight, and now his FedEx Company plays an important role in getting documents and packages delivered all over the world for businesses and individuals. Entrepreneurs have been associated with such uniquely American concepts as Dell Computers, Ben & Jerry's, Levi's, Holiday Inns, McDonald's, Dr Pepper, and Wal-Mart. Wal-Mart, founded by entrepreneur Sam Walton, was the first retailer to reach $100 billion in sales in one year and now routinely passes that mark. Wal-Mart has more than 1.9 million employees and operates more than 6,775 stores in the United States, Canada, Mexico, Asia, Europe, and South America. San Walton's heirs own about 40 percent of the company.[22] We will examine the importance of entrepreneurship further in Chapter 6.

## The Role of Government in the American Economy

The American economic system is best described as modified capitalism because the government regulates business to preserve competition and protect consumers and employees. Federal, state, and local governments intervene in the economy with laws and regulations designed to promote competition and to protect consumers, employees, and the environment. Many of these laws are discussed in Appendix A.

Additionally, government agencies such as the U.S. Department of Commerce measure the health of the economy (GDP, productivity, etc.) and, when necessary, take steps to minimize the disruptive effects of economic fluctuations and reduce unemployment. When the economy is contracting and unemployment is rising, the federal government through the Federal Reserve Board (see Chapter 14) tries to spur growth so that consumers will spend more money and businesses will hire more employees. To accomplish this, it may reduce interest rates or increase its own spending for goods and services. When the economy expands so fast that inflation results, the government may intervene to reduce inflation by slowing down economic growth. This can be accomplished by raising interest rates to discourage spending by businesses and consumers. Techniques used to control the economy are discussed in Chapter 14.

## The Role of Ethics and Social Responsibility in Business

In the last few years, you may have read about a number of scandals at a number of well-known corporations, including Enron, WorldCom, Tyco, and Arthur Andersen. In many cases, misconduct by individuals within these firms had an adverse effect on current and retired employees, investors, and others associated with these firms. In some cases, individuals went to jail for their actions. Martha Stewart was convicted of obstructing justice and lying to federal investigators. She was sentenced to five months in jail and five months of home detention for making false statements. Martha Stewart agreed to pay $195,000 and accept a five-year ban on serving as a director of a public company to settle civil insider-trading charges with the Securities and Exchange Commission.[23] These scandals undermined public confidence in Corporate America and sparked a new debate about ethics in business. Business ethics generally refers to the standards and principles used by society to define appropriate and inappropriate conduct in the workplace. In many cases, these standards have been codified as laws prohibiting actions deemed unacceptable.

Society is increasingly demanding that businesspeople behave ethically and socially responsibly toward not only their customers but also their employees, investors, government regulators, communities, and the natural environment. Green Mountain Coffee Roasters, which ranked number one on the *Business Ethics* 100 Best Corporate citizens list in 2007, for example, has pledged to pay above-market prices for coffee beans to farmer cooperatives in Central and South America in order to help boost the quality of life in those regions. General Mills supports minority-owned suppliers and charities that target women and minorities.[24] Thus, social responsibility relates to the impact of business on society.

One of the primary lessons of the scandals of the early 2000s has been that the reputation of business organizations depends not just on bottom-line profits but also on ethical conduct and concern for the welfare of others. Consider that in the aftermath of these scandals, the reputations of every U.S. company suffered regardless of their association with the scandals.[25] While

# DESTINATION CEO

**Jim McCann (BWTV)** Mother's Day is coming and millions of flowers will have to be delivered "at the last minute." The largest florist in the country is able to satisfy customers around the globe through the Internet florist, 1-800-Flowers. Jim McCann is the CEO of 1-800-Flowers, shown in the video on your student DVD. The road to a business career, no less executive management, was not typical for Jim McCann. He did not experience a traditional "climb up the corporate ladder." Looking for a career as a police officer, McCann attended the John Jay College of Criminal Justice in New York City. His career path led him to a career in social services. A chance meeting with a friend provided McCann a chance to buy his first flower shop. It cost him $10,000 for his original shop located on 1st Avenue and 62nd Street in New York. Initially, Jim's passion and interest in the floral business was more of a part-time hobby. However, that soon changed as he began to grow and expand the business.

There were many "firsts" pioneered by McCann in this industry. For example, he was the first to introduce the innovation of a 24-hour ordering service (that was 28 years ago). As time went on, he purchased 10 additional flower shops. Looking for an opportunity to broaden his markets, he visited the Dallas-based 800 Flowers to pursue partnership opportunities. What he found, however, was a company in dire straights. Rather than collaborating with the company, he purchased them.

He views his firm as a both a leader in business innovation and as a change agent—24-hour ordering capabilities, the first to accept credit cards over the phone, and the first to have an Internet presence on AOL. Now, 70 percent of his sales are from the Internet. Total sales this year reached $650 million, up 8 percent from the previous year. McCann credits his success as a business leader to his family roots that emphasized hard work and diligence. Prior to becoming CEO of this multimillion-dollar enterprise, Jim McCann was a social service worker. He credits much of his innovative and creative abilities to working with his clients in that sector.

## >>DISCUSSION QUESTIONS

1. Identify four central business terms that would directly apply to the Jim McCann story.

2. What type of business model did McCann develop as he moved from his hobby to a multimillion dollar business?

3. Based on the facts presented in the video, how would you determine whether the company has used its productive resources to create valuable goods and services?

>>To see the complete video about Jim McCann, go to our Web site at **www.mhhe.com/FerrellM** and look for the link to the Destination CEO videos.

The only thing certain anymore is that the world is constantly changing, and this applies to future career options for you and your classmates. The traditional career track that earlier generations followed, in which a person started working at one company upon graduation and worked his or her way up until retirement, is passé. In fact, the average large corporation replaces the equivalent of its entire workforce every four years. Moreover, constantly evolving technology means today's graduates and workers need to be computer literate and able to adapt to new technologies. The globalization of business suggests that you be fluent in a second or even third language, for there is a good chance that you'll be working with people from around the world, and you may even do a stint overseas yourself. Changes in the makeup of the workforce mean more doors opening for women and minorities as companies recognize the need to understand and cater to the desires of a diverse customer base. Changes in organizational structure may require you to work in teams, where communication is a crucial skill, or they may leave you out of the corporate hierarchy altogether, and instead put you in an entrepreneurial role as a self-employed contractor or small-business owner.

Because of these and other changes taking place in the business world that we discuss throughout this book, when you enter the workforce full time, you are far more likely to define yourself by what you do ("I design RISC chips") than by your employer ("I work for Motorola"). And, you're more likely to think in terms of short-term projects, such as launching a product or reengineering a process, rather than a long-term career track like the one your grandfather may have followed.

This business course and textbook, including the boxes, cases, and skills-building exercises, will help you learn the basic knowledge, skills, and trends that you can use whether you work for a corporation or run your own small business, whether you work in upper management or on the shop floor. Along the way, we'll introduce you to some specific careers and offer advice on developing your own job opportunities in career boxes in each chapter. We also present salary range information for different types/levels of jobs. According to the 2000 Census, the average U.S. family earned $63,410 annually, and the breakdown of earnings was:

| | |
|---|---|
| Less than $15,000 | 10.4% |
| $15,000–$34,999 | 23.3 |
| $35,000–$49,999 | 16.8 |
| $50,000–$74,999 | 22.0 |
| $75,000–$99,999 | 12.3 |
| $100,000–$149,999 | 9.7 |
| $150,000+ | 5.5[26] |

progress is being made in business ethics, as employees become more sensitive to ethical issues, reporting of ethical misconduct has increased over the past few years. The fact that employees continue to report observing misconduct and experiencing pressure to engage in unethical or illegal acts remains troubling and suggests that companies need to continue their efforts to raise ethical standards. We take a closer look at ethics and social responsibility in business in Chapter 2.

## CAN YOU LEARN BUSINESS IN A CLASSROOM?

Obviously, the answer is yes, or there would be no purpose for this textbook! To be successful in business, you need knowledge, skills, experience, and good judgment. The topics covered in this chapter and throughout this book provide some of the knowledge you need to understand the world of business. The boxes, and examples within each chapter describe experiences to help you develop good business judgment. The interactive exercises and assignments found in our Web site at www.mhhe.com/inbus will help you develop skills that may be useful in your future

*U.S. mortgage giant Fannie Mae owned numerous awards for corporate excellence in the 1990s and early 2000s. But later it was discovered that the company's executives, led by CEO Franklin Raines, had manipulated Fannie Mae's accounting records to line their own pockets. Raines was swept out of office in 2004, and in 2006, the U.S. Securities and Exchange Commission fined Fannie Mae $400 million.*

career. However, good judgment is based on knowledge and experience plus personal insight and understanding. Therefore, you need more courses in business, along with some practical experience in the business world, to help you develop the special insight necessary to put your personal stamp on knowledge as you apply it. The challenge in business is in the area of judgment, and judgment does not develop from memorizing an introductory business textbook. If you are observant in your daily experiences as an employee, as a student, and as a consumer, you will improve your ability to make good business judgments.

Figure 1.5 is an overview of how the chapters in this book are linked together and how the chapters relate to the participants, the activities, and the environmental factors found in the business world. The topics presented in the chapters that follow are those that will give you the best opportunity to begin the process of understanding the world of business. ■

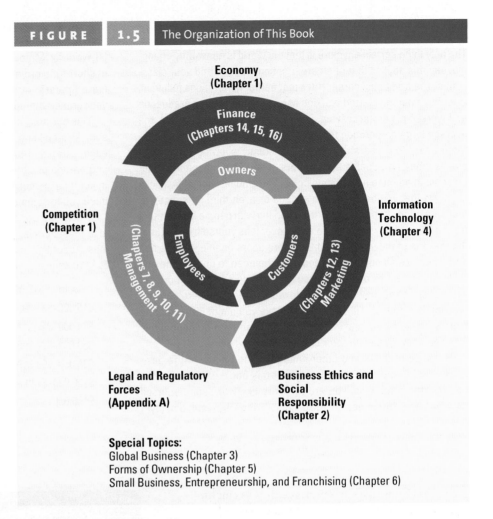

**FIGURE 1.5** The Organization of This Book

Economy (Chapter 1)

Finance (Chapters 14, 15, 16)

Owners

Competition (Chapter 1)

(Chapters 7, 8, 9, 10, 11) Management

Employees

Customers

(Chapters 12, 13) Marketing

Information Technology (Chapter 4)

Legal and Regulatory Forces (Appendix A)

Business Ethics and Social Responsibility (Chapter 2)

Special Topics:
Global Business (Chapter 3)
Forms of Ownership (Chapter 5)
Small Business, Entrepreneurship, and Franchising (Chapter 6)

## Build Your Business Plan

### The Dynamics of Business and Economics

Have you ever thought about owning your business? If you have, how did your idea come about? Is it your experience with this particular field? Or might it be an idea that evolved from your desires for a particular product or service not being offered in your community. For example, perhaps you and your friends have yearned for a place to go have coffee, relax, and talk. Now is an opportunity to create the café bar you have been thinking of!

Whether you consider yourself as a visionary or a practical thinker, think about your community. What needs are not being met? While it is tempting to suggest a new restaurant (maybe one even near campus), easier-to-implement business plans can range from a lawn care business or a designated driver business, to a placement service agency for teenagers.

Once you have an idea for a business plan, think about how profitable this idea might be. Is there sufficient demand for this business? How large is the market for this particular business? What about competitors? How many are there?

To learn about your industry you should do a thorough search of your initial ideas of a product/service on the Internet.

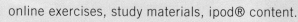

# BUSINESS PLAN DEVELOPMENT

## GUIDELINES FOR THE DEVELOPMENT OF THE BUSINESS PLAN

These guidelines are for students to create a hypothetical business plan for a product/service/business of their choice. Students should assume to have $25,000 to start this new business in their community.

At the end of every chapter there will be a section entitled "Build Your Business Plan" to assist you in the development of the business plan.

## PHASE 1: DEVELOPMENT OF THE BUSINESS PROPOSAL

You are encouraged to submit your idea for approval to your instructor as soon as possible. This will eliminate wasted effort on an idea that is not feasible in the instructor's view. Business plan proposals will be evaluated based on their thoroughness and your ability to provide support for the idea.

The business proposal consists of:

**Business Description.** This consists of an overview of the existing product/service or the product/service/business you will be starting (manufacturer, merchandiser, or service provider). This includes developing a mission (reason for existence; overall purpose of the firm) and a rationale for why you believe this business will be a success. What is your vision for this proposed product/business?

**Brief Marketing Plan.** (The marketing plan will be further developed as the plan evolves.) A description of your business/product/service is required. Identify the target market and develop a strategy for appealing to it. Justify your proposed location for this business. Describe how you will promote the new business and provide a rationale for your pricing strategy. Select a name for this business. The name should be catchy yet relate to the competencies of the business.

**Competitive Analysis.** Identify the competition as broadly as possible. Indicate why this business will be successful given the market.

# PHASE 2: FINAL WRITTEN BUSINESS PLAN

**Executive Summary.** The executive summary appears first, but should be written last.

**Business Description.** This section requires fleshing out the body of the business plan including material from your revised preliminary proposal with more data, charts, appendices. Include a description of the proposed form of organization, either a partnership or corporation, and the rationalization of the form chosen.

**Industry and Market Analysis.** An analysis of the industry including the growth rate of the industry and number of new entrants into this field is necessary. Identify uncontrollable variables within the industry. Determine an estimate of the proposed realistic size of the potential market. This will require interpretation of statistics from U.S. Census, as well as local sources such as the Chamber of Commerce.

**Competitive Analysis.** Include an exhaustive list of the primary and secondary competition, along with the competitive advantage of each.

**Marketing Strategy.** Target market specifics need to be developed.

Decisions on the marketing mix variables need to be made:

- Price (at the market, below market, above market).
- Promotion (sales associates, advertising budget, use of sales promotions, and publicity/goodwill).
- Distribution—Rationale of choice and level of distribution.
- Product/Service—A detailed rationale of the perceived differential advantage of your product service offering.

**Operational Issues.** How will you make or provide your product/service? Location rationale, facility type, leasing considerations and sources of suppliers needs to be detailed. Software/hardware requirements necessary to maintain operations determined.

**Human Resource Requirement.** Number and description of personnel needed including realistic required education and skills.

**Financial Projections.** Statement of cash flows must be prepared for the first twelve months of the business. This must include start-up costs, opening expenses, estimation of cash inflows and outflows. A breakeven analysis should be included and an explanation of all financial assumptions.

## Appendices

# PHASE 3: ORAL PRESENTATION

Specific separate guidelines on the oral presentation will be provided. ■

## learning OBJECTIVES

**LO1** Define business ethics and social responsibility, and examine their importance.

**LO2** Detect some of the ethical issues that may arise in business.

**LO3** Specify how businesses can promote ethical behavior.

**LO4** Explain the four dimensions of social responsibility.

**LO5** Debate an organization's social responsibilities to owners, employees, consumers, the environment, and the community.

# business ethics and social responsibility

2

**introduction**   Auto manufacturers that make hybrid cars have taken on the challenge of contributing to society through its business activities. At the other extreme, wrongdoing by some businesses has focused public attention and government involvement to encourage more acceptable business conduct. Any business decision may be judged as right or wrong, ethical or unethical, legal or illegal.

In this chapter, we take a look at the role of ethics and social responsibility in business decision making. First we define business ethics and examine why it is important to understand ethics' role in business. Next we explore a number of business ethics issues to help you learn to recognize such issues when they arise. Finally, we consider steps businesses can take to improve ethical behavior in their organizations. The second half of the chapter focuses on social responsibility. We survey some important responsibility issues and detail how companies have responded to them.

## LO1

Define business ethics and social responsibility, and examine their importance.

# BUSINESS ETHICS AND SOCIAL RESPONSIBILITY

In this chapter, we define business ethics as the principles and standards that determine acceptable conduct in business organizations. The acceptability of behavior in business is determined by customers, competitors, government regulators, interest groups, and the public, as well as each individual's personal moral principles and values. Enron is an example of one of the largest ethical disasters in the 21st century. Two former Enron CEOs, Ken Lay and Jeff Skilling, were found guilty on all

Many consumers and social advocates believe that businesses should not only make a profit but also consider the social implications of their activities. We define social responsibility as a business's obligation to maximize its positive impact and minimize its negative impact on society. Although many people use the terms *social responsibility* and *ethics* interchangeably, they do not mean the same thing. Business ethics relates to an *individual's* or a *work group's* decisions that society evaluates as right or wrong, whereas social responsibility is a broader concept that concerns the impact of the *entire business's* activities on society. From an ethical perspective, for example, we may be concerned about a health care organization overcharging the government for Medicare services. From a social responsibility perspective, we might be concerned about the impact that this overcharging will have on the ability of the health care system to provide adequate services for all citizens.

The most basic ethical and social responsibility concerns have been codified as laws and regulations that encourage businesses to conform to society's standards, values, and attitudes. For example, after accounting scandals at a number of well-known firms in the early 2000s shook public confidence in the integrity of Corporate America, the reputations of every U.S. company suffered regardless of their association with the

> ## "Many consumers and social advocates believe that businesses should not only make a profit but also consider the social implications of their activities."

counts of conspiring to hide the company's financial condition. The judge in the case said the defendants could be found guilty of consciously avoiding knowing about wrongdoing at the company. Many other top executives including Andy Fastow, the chief financial officer, were found guilty of misconduct and are serving time in prison. The fall of Enron took many layers of management pushing the envelope and a great deal of complacency on the part of employees who saw wrongdoing and ignored it. Most unethical activities within organizations are supported by an organizational culture that encourages employees to bend the rules.[1]

scandals.[2] To help restore confidence in corporations and markets, Congress passed the Sarbanes-Oxley Act, which criminalized securities fraud and stiffened penalties for corporate fraud. At a minimum, managers are expected to obey all laws and regulations. Most legal issues arise as choices that society deems unethical, irresponsible, or otherwise unacceptable. However, all actions deemed unethical by society are not necessarily illegal, and both legal and ethical concerns change over time (see Table 2.1). Business law refers to the laws and regulations that govern the conduct of business. Many problems and

**TABLE 2.1** A Timeline of Ethical and Socially Responsible Concerns

| 1960s | 1970s | 1980s | 1990s | 2000s |
|---|---|---|---|---|
| • Environmental issues | • Employee militancy | • Bribes and illegal contracting practices | • Sweatshops and unsafe working conditions in third-world countries | • Employee benefits |
| • Civil rights issues | • Human rights issues | • Influence peddling | | • Privacy issues |
| • Increased employee-employer tension | • Covering up rather than correcting issues | • Deceptive advertising | • Rising corporate liability for personal damages (e.g., cigarette companies) | • Financial mismanagement |
| • Honesty | • Discrimination | • Financial fraud (e.g., savings and loan scandal) | | • Abusive behavior |
| • Changing work ethic | • Harassment | | • Financial mismanagement and fraud | • Cyber crime |
| • Rising drug use | | • Transparency issues | | • Intellectual property theft |

Source: Adapted from "Business Ethics Timeline," Copyright © 2003, *Ethics Resource Center* (n.d.), www.ethics.org, updated 2006. Used with permission.

# ETHICAL CONDUCT BUILDS TRUST AMONG INDIVIDUALS AND IN BUSINESS RELATIONSHIPS, WHICH VALIDATES AND PROMOTES CONFIDENCE IN BUSINESS RELATIONSHIPS.

conflicts in business can be avoided if owners, managers, and employees know more about business law and the legal system. Business ethics, social responsibility, and laws together act as a compliance system requiring that businesses and employees act responsibly in society. In this chapter, we explore ethics and social responsibility; Appendix A addresses business law, including the Sarbanes-Oxley Act.

## THE ROLE OF ETHICS IN BUSINESS

You have only to pick up *The Wall Street Journal* or *USA Today* to see examples of the growing concern about legal and ethical issues in business. HealthSouth, for example, has joined the growing list of companies tarnished by accounting improprieties and securities fraud. Former CEO Richard Scrushy was indicted for allegedly conspiring to inflate the health care firm's reported revenues by $2.7 billion to meet shareholder expectations. Although Scrushy pleaded "not guilty" to the 85 criminal charges, 15 former HealthSouth executives have admitted to participating in the deception. Scrushy was acquitted by a jury trial in the first attempt to hold a chief executive accountable under the Sarbanes-Oxley Act. The defense called the star witness, former HealthSouth finance chief William T. Owens, a big rat.[3] In 2006, Scrushy was found guilty on six counts of bribery and mail fraud by Alabama court for making payments to an Alabama governor to be on the state hospital regulatory board. He plans to appeal the conviction. Regardless of what an individual believes about a particular action, if society judges it to be unethical or wrong, whether correctly or not, that judgment directly affects the organization's ability to achieve its business goals.[4]

Well-publicized incidents of unethical and illegal activity—ranging from accounting fraud to using the Internet to steal another person's credit-card number, from deceptive advertising of food and diet products to unfair competitive practices in the computer software industry—strengthen the public's perceptions that ethical standards and the level of trust in business need to be raised. Author David Callahan has commented, "Americans who wouldn't so much as shoplift a pack of chewing gum are committing felonies at tax time, betraying the trust of their patients, misleading investors, ripping off their insurance companies, lying to their clients, and much more."[5] Often, such charges start as ethical conflicts but evolve into legal disputes when cooperative conflict resolution cannot be accomplished. For example, Shirley Slesinger Lasswell, whose late husband acquired the rights to Winnie the Pooh and his friends from

creator A. A. Milne in 1930, filed a lawsuit against the Walt Disney Company over merchandising rights to the characters. Although Lasswell granted rights to use the character to Walt Disney, she contended that the company cheated her and her family out of millions of dollars in royalties on video sales for two decades. Disney asserted that video sales were not specified in its agreement with Lasswell and declined to pay her a percentage of those sales. A California Superior Court judge dismissed the case after 13 years of negotiations and proceedings, effectively siding with Disney.[6] Indeed, many activities deemed unethical by society have been outlawed through legislation.

California Congressman Duke Cunningham resigned after pleading guilty to accepting millions of dollars in bribes and underreporting his income to the federal government. In 2006, Cunningham was sentenced to prison for more than eight years and ordered to pay $2 million in restitution.

However, it is important to understand that business ethics goes beyond legal issues. Ethical conduct builds trust among individuals and in business relationships, which validates and promotes confidence in business relationships. Establishing trust and confidence is much more difficult in organizations that have established reputations for acting unethically. If you were to discover, for example, that a manager had misled you about company benefits when you were hired, your trust and confidence in that company would probably diminish. And, if you learned that a colleague had lied to you about something, you probably would not trust or rely on that person in the future.

Ethical issues are not limited to for-profit organizations. In government, several politicians and some high-ranking officials have been forced to resign in disgrace over ethical indiscretions. Irv Lewis "Scooter" Libby, a White House advisor, was indicted on five counts of criminal charges: one count of obstruction of justice, two counts of perjury, and two counts of making false statements. In 2007 he was convicted on four of those counts. Each count carries a $250,000 fine and maximum prison term of 30 years.[7] Several scientists have been accused of falsifying research data, which could invalidate later research based on their data and jeopardize trust in all scientific research. Hwang Woo-Suk was found to have faked some of his famous stem cell research, in which he claimed to have created 30 cloned human

## LO2

Detect some of the ethical issues that may arise in business.

## Recognizing Ethical Issues in Business

Learning to recognize ethical issues is the most important step in understanding business ethics. An ethical issue is an identifiable problem, situation, or opportunity that requires a person to choose from among several actions that may be evaluated as right or wrong, ethical or unethical. In business, such a choice often involves weighing monetary profit against what a person considers appropriate conduct. The best way to judge the ethics of a decision is to look at a situation from a customer's or competitor's viewpoint: Should liquid-diet manufacturers make unsubstantiated claims about their products? Should an engineer agree to divulge her former employer's trade secrets to ensure that she gets a better job with a competitor? Should a salesperson omit facts about a product's poor

> " **Many business issues may seem straightforward and easy to resolve, but in reality, a person often needs several years of experience in business to understand what is acceptable or ethical.** "

embryos and made stem cell lines from skin cells of 11 people, as well as producing the world's first cloned dog. He also apologized for using eggs from his own female researchers, which was in breach of guidelines, but he still denies fabricating his research.[8] Even sports can be subject to ethical lapses. At many universities, for example, coaches and athletic administrators have been put on administrative leave after allegations of improper recruiting practices by team members came to light.[9] Jimmy Johnson's crew chief, Chad Knaus, was thrown out of the Daytona 500 for illegal modifications made to Johnson's car during NASCAR pole qualifying. Although Johnson finished fifth in qualifying, he had to start from the rear of the field and then went on to win the 2006 Daytona 500.[10] Thus, whether made in science, politics, sports, or business, most decisions are judged as right or wrong, ethical or unethical. Negative judgments can affect an organization's ability to build relationships with customers and suppliers, attract investors, and retain employees.[11]

Although we will not tell you in this chapter what you ought to do, others—your superiors, co-workers, and family—will make judgments about the ethics of your actions and decisions. Learning how to recognize and resolve ethical issues is an important step in evaluating ethical decisions in business.

safety record in his presentation to a customer? Such questions require the decision maker to evaluate the ethics of his or her choice.

Many business issues may seem straightforward and easy to resolve, but in reality, a person often needs several years of experience in business to understand what is acceptable or ethical. For example, if you are a salesperson, when does offering a gift—such as season basketball tickets—to a customer become a bribe rather than just a sales practice? Clearly, there are no easy answers to such a question. But the size of the transaction, the history of personal relationships within the particular company, as well as many other factors may determine whether an action will be judged as right or wrong by others.

Ethics is also related to the culture in which a business operates. In the United States, for example, it would be inappropriate for a businessperson to bring an elaborately wrapped gift to a prospective client on their first meeting—the gift could be viewed as a bribe. In Japan, however, it is considered impolite *not* to bring a gift. Experience with the culture in which a business operates is critical to understanding what is ethical or unethical.

To help you understand ethical issues that perplex businesspeople today, we will take a brief look at some of them in this section. The vast number of news-format investigative programs

# BULLYING IS ASSOCIATED WITH A HOSTILE WORKPLACE WHEN SOMEONE CONSIDERED A TARGET (OR A GROUP) IS THREATENED, HARASSED, BELITTLED, OR VERBALLY ABUSED OR OVERLY CRITICIZED.

has increased consumer and employee awareness of organizational misconduct. In addition, the multitude of cable channels and Internet resources has improved the awareness of ethical problems among the general public. The National Business Ethics Survey of more than 3,000 U.S. employees found that workers witness many instances of ethical misconduct in their organizations (see Table 2.2). The most common types of observed misconduct were abusive/intimidating behavior, lying, and placing employee interests over organizational interests.[12]

One of the principal causes of unethical behavior in organizations is overly aggressive financial or business objectives. Many of these issues relate to decisions and concerns that managers have to deal with daily. It is not possible to discuss every issue, of course. However, a discussion of a few issues can help you begin to recognize the ethical problems with which businesspersons must deal. Many ethical issues in business can be categorized in the context of their relation with abusive and intimidating behavior, conflicts of interest, fairness and honesty, communications, and business associations.

## abusive and intimidating behavior.

Abusive or intimidating behavior is the most common ethical problem for employees. The concepts can mean anything from physical threats, false accusations, being annoying, profanity, insults, yelling, harshness, or ignoring someone, to unreasonableness, and the meaning of these words can differ by person—you probably have some ideas of your own. Abusive behavior can be placed on a continuum from a minor distraction to disrupting the workplace. For example, what one person may define as yelling might be another's definition of normal speech. Civility in our society has been a concern, and the workplace is no exception. The productivity level of many organizations has been damaged by the time spent unraveling abusive relationships.

Abusive behavior is difficult to assess and manage because of diversity in culture and lifestyle. What does it mean to speak profanely? Is profanity only related to specific words or other such terms that are common in today's business world? If you are using words that are normal in your language but others consider profanity, have you just insulted, abused, or disrespected them?

Within the concept of abusive behavior, intent should be a consideration. If the employee was trying to convey a compliment but the comment was considered abusive, then it was probably a mistake. The way a word is said (voice inflection) can be important. Add to this the fact that we now live in a multicultural environment—doing business and working with many different cultural groups—and the businessperson soon realizes the depth of the ethical and legal issues that may arise. There are problems of word meanings by age and within cultures. For example an expression such as "Did you guys hook up last night?" can have various meanings, including some that could be considered offensive in a work environment.

Bullying is associated with a hostile workplace when someone considered a target (or a group) is threatened, harassed, belittled, or verbally abused or overly criticized. While bullying may create what some may call a hostile environment, this term is generally associated with sexual harassment. Although sexual harassment has legal recourse, bullying has little legal recourse at this time. Bullying can cause psychological damage that can result in health endangering consequences to the target. As Table 2.3 indicates, bullying can use a mix of

**TABLE 2.2** Types and Incidences of Observed Misconduct

| Type of Conduct Observed | Employees Observing It |
|---|---|
| Abusive or intimidating behavior toward employees | 21% |
| Lying to employees, customers, vendors, or the public | 19 |
| Situations placing employee interests over organizational interests | 18 |
| Violations of safety regulations | 16 |
| Misreporting of actual time worked | 16 |
| Discrimination on the basis of race, color, gender, age, or similar categories | 12 |
| Stealing or theft | 11 |
| Sexual harassment | 9 |

Source: "National Business Ethics Survey 2005," "Survey Documents State of Ethics in the Workplace," and "Misconduct," Ethics Resource Center (n.d.), www.ethics.org/nbes/2005/release.html (accessed April 11, 2006).

● **BRIBES** payments, gifts, or special favors intended to influence the outcome of a decision

verbal, nonverbal, and manipulative threatening expressions to damage workplace productivity. One may wonder why workers tolerate such activities, the problem is that 81 percent of workplace bullies are supervisors. A top officer at Boeing cited an employee survey indicating 26 percent had observed abusive or intimidating behavior by management.[13]

### conflict of interest.

A conflict of interest exists when a person must choose whether to advance his or her own personal interests or those of others. For example, a manager in a corporation is supposed to ensure that the company is profitable so that its stockholder-owners receive a return on their investment. In other words, the manager has a responsibility to investors. If she instead makes decisions that give her more power or money but do not help the company, then she has a conflict of interest—she is acting to benefit herself at the expense of her company and is not fulfilling her responsibilities. To avoid conflicts of interest, employees must be able to separate their personal financial interests from their business dealings. For example, a $1 million donation by Citigroup to the 92nd Street Y nursery school represents a possible conflict of interest. Jack Grubman, an analyst for Salomon Smith Barney, upgraded his rating for AT&T stock after Sanford Weill, the CEO of Citigroup (the parent company of Salomon Smith Barney), agreed to use his influence to help Grubman's twins gain admission to the elite Manhattan nursery school. During the late 1990s, Weill, an AT&T board member, had been upset

In 2005, former WorldCom CEO Bernard Ebbers was sentenced to 25 years in prison, one of the longest sentences ever received by a former chief executive. The stiff sentence stemmed in large part from the estimated $2 billion investor losses prosecutors attributed to Ebber's fraud at WorldCom.

**TABLE 2.3** Actions Associated with Bullies

1. Spreading rumors to damage others
2. Blocking others' communication in the workplace
3. Flaunting status or authority to take advantage of others
4. Discrediting others' ideas and opinions
5. Use of e-mails to demean others
6. Failing to communicate or return communication
7. Insults, yelling, and shouting
8. Using terminology to discriminate by gender, race, or age
9. Using eye or body language to hurt others or their reputation
10. Taking credit for others' work or ideas

Source: © O. C. Ferrell, 2006.

that Citigroup wasn't getting any of AT&T's business. Grubman changed his AT&T rating to buy. A year later he bragged in an e-mail that he had made the switch to placate Weill in exchange for Weill's help in getting Grubman's children into the exclusive 92nd Street Y nursery school. Grubman has denied elevating his rating for AT&T's stock to gain admission to the school, but his children were enrolled. Industry leaders still avoid him, publicly anyway, but on the fringes of telecom, Grubman has had no trouble finding people who are willing to overlook his past or are simply unaware of it. According to a *Fortune* article, although Grubman was "banned from Wall Street, the former Telecom King wants to prove that he wasn't a huckster".[14]

As mentioned earlier, it is considered improper to give or accept bribes—payments, gifts, or special favors intended to influence the outcome of a decision. A bribe is a conflict of interest because it benefits an individual at the expense of an organization or society. Companies that do business overseas should be aware that bribes are a significant ethical issue and are in fact illegal in many countries. For example, three former executives of IBM Korea went to jail in Seoul after being convicted of using bribes to win orders for computer parts.[15] Bribery is more prevalent in some countries than in others. Transparency International has developed a Corruption Perceptions Index (Table 2.4). Note there are 19 countries perceived as less corrupt than the United States.[16]

### fairness and honesty.

Fairness and honesty are at the heart of business ethics and relate to the general values of decision makers. At a minimum, businesspersons are expected to follow all applicable laws and regulations. But beyond obeying the law, they are expected not to harm customers, employees, clients, or competitors knowingly through deception, misrepresentation, coercion, or discrimination. Honesty and fairness can relate to how the employees uses the resources of the organization. Vault.com found that 67 percent of employees have taken office supplies from work to use for matters unrelated to their job. Most employees do not view taking office supplies as stealing or dishonest, with 97 percent saying they have never gotten caught and it would not matter if they were found out. In

**TABLE 2.4**  Corruption Perceptions Index

| Rank | Country | 2006 CPI Score* |
|---|---|---|
| 1 | Finland/Iceland/New Zealand | 9.6 |
| 4 | Denmark | 9.5 |
| 5 | Singapore | 9.4 |
| 6 | Sweden | 9.2 |
| 7 | Switzerland | 9.1 |
| 8 | Norway | 8.8 |
| 9 | Australia/Netherlands | 8.7 |
| 11 | Austria/Luxembourg/United Kingdom | 8.6 |
| 14 | Canada | 8.5 |
| 15 | Hong Kong | 8.3 |
| 16 | Germany | 8.0 |
| 17 | Japan | 7.6 |
| 18 | France/Ireland | 7.4 |
| 20 | Belgium/Chile/USA | 7.3 |

*CPI score relates to perceptions of the degree of corruption as seen by businesspeople and country analysts and ranges between 10 (highly clean) and 0 (highly corrupt).

Source: "Transparency International 2006 Corruption Perception Index," Transparency International, (n.d.), http://www.transparency.org/policy_research/surveys_indices/cpi/2006 (accessed June 1, 2007).

addition, only 3.7 percent say they have taken items like keyboards, software, and memory sticks. Still, an employee should be aware of policies on taking items and recognize how these decisions relate to ethical behavior.[17] Figure 2.1 below provides an overview of the most pilfered office supplies.

One aspect of fairness relates to competition. Although numerous laws have been passed to foster competition and make monopolistic practices illegal, companies sometimes gain control over markets by using questionable practices that harm competition. Bullying can also occur between companies that are in intense competition. Even respected companies such as Intel have been accused of monopolistic bullying. A competitor, Advanced Micro Devices (AMD), claimed in a lawsuit that 38 companies, including Dell and Sony, were strong-arming customers (such as Apple) into buying Intel chips rather than those marketed by AMD. The AMD lawsuit seeks billions of dollars and will take years to litigate. In many cases, the alleged misconduct can have not only monetary and legal implications but can threaten reputation, investor confidence, and customer loyalty. A front-cover *Forbes* headline stated "Intel to ADM: Drop Dead." An example of the intense competition and Intel's ability to use its large size won it the high-profile Apple account, displacing IBM and Freescale. ADM said it had no opportunity to bid because Intel offered to deploy 600 Indian engineers to help Apple software run more smoothly on Intel chips.[18]

Another aspect of fairness and honesty relates to disclosure of potential harm caused by product use. Mitsubishi Motors, Japan's number-four automaker, faced criminal charges and negative publicity after executives admitted that the company had systematically covered up customer complaints about tens of thousands of defective automobiles over a 20-year period to avoid expensive and embarrassing product recalls.[19]

Dishonesty has become a significant problem in the United States. As reported earlier in this chapter, lying was the second most observed form of misconduct in the National Business Ethics Survey. Dishonesty is not found only in business, however.

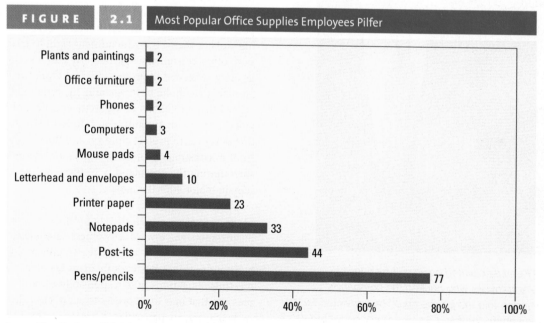

**FIGURE 2.1**  Most Popular Office Supplies Employees Pilfer

| | |
|---|---|
| Plants and paintings | 2 |
| Office furniture | 2 |
| Phones | 2 |
| Computers | 3 |
| Mouse pads | 4 |
| Letterhead and envelopes | 10 |
| Printer paper | 23 |
| Notepads | 33 |
| Post-its | 44 |
| Pens/pencils | 77 |

Source: "More Employees Taking Supplies," *The (Wilmington, Del.) News Journal,* using data from Lawyers.com, April 1, 2007, http://www.usatoday.com/money/industries/retail/2007-03-30-supply_N.htm (accessed June 1, 2007).

A survey of nearly 25,000 high school students revealed that 62 percent of the students admitted to cheating on an exam at least once, 35 percent confessed to copying documents from the Internet, 27 percent admitted to shoplifting, and 23 percent owned up to cheating to win in sports.[20] If today's students are tomorrow's leaders, there is likely to be a correlation between acceptable behavior today and tomorrow, adding to the argument that the leaders of today must be prepared for the ethical risks associated with this downward trend. According to a poll by Deloitte and Touche of teenagers aged 13 to 18, when asked if people who practice good business ethics are more successful than those who don't, 69 percent of teenagers agreed.[21] The same poll found only 12 percent of teens think business leaders today are ethical. On the other hand, another survey indicated that many students do not define copying answers from another students' paper or downloading music or content for classroom work as cheating.[22]

**communications.** Communications is another area in which ethical concerns may arise. False and misleading advertising, as well as deceptive personal-selling tactics, anger

*Ex-Enron CEO Ken Lay claimed he wasn't responsible for a few rogue employees who cooked the company's books. But the judge told the jury he could be convicted for avoiding knowing about the fraud. Lay was later convicted of conspiracy to commit securities and wire fraud but died before he was sentenced.*

consumers and can lead to the failure of a business. Truthfulness about product safety and quality are also important to consumers. Claims about dietary supplements and weight-loss products can be particularly problematic. For example, the Fountain of Youth Group, LLC, and its founder, Edita Kaye, settled charges brought by the Federal Trade Commission that the company made unsubstantiated claims about its weight-loss products. Under the settlement, the firm agreed to stop making specific weight-loss and health claims about its products without competent scientific proof. It was also fined $6 million, but that fine was suspended because the firm lacked the resources to pay it.[23]

Some companies fail to provide enough information for consumers about differences or similarities between products. For example, driven by high prices for medicines, many consumers are turning to Canadian, Mexican, and overseas Internet sources for drugs to treat a variety of illnesses and conditions. However, research suggests that a significant percentage of these imported pharmaceuticals may not actually contain the labeled drug, and the counterfeit drugs could even be harmful to those who take them.[24]

Another important aspect of communications that may raise ethical concerns relates to product labeling. The U.S. Surgeon General currently requires cigarette manufacturers to indicate clearly on cigarette packaging that smoking cigarettes is harmful to the smoker's health. In Europe, at least 30 percent of the front side of product packaging and 40 percent of the back needs to be taken up by the warning. The use of descriptors such as "light" or "mild" has been banned.[25] However, labeling of other products raises ethical questions when it threatens basic rights, such as freedom of speech and expression. This is the heart of the controversy surrounding the movement to require warning labels on movies and videogames, rating their content, language, and appropriate audience age. Although people in the entertainment industry believe that such labeling violates their First Amendment right to freedom of expression, other consumers—particularly parents—believe that such labeling is needed to protect children from harmful influences. Similarly, alcoholic beverage and cigarette manufacturers have argued that a total ban on cigarette and alcohol advertisements violates the First Amendment. Internet regulation, particularly that designed to protect children and the elderly, is on the forefront in consumer protection legislation. Because of the debate surrounding the acceptability of these business activities, they remain major ethical issues.

**business relationships.** The behavior of businesspersons toward customers, suppliers, and others in their workplace may also generate ethical concerns. Ethical behavior within a business involves keeping company secrets, meeting obligations and responsibilities, and avoiding undue pressure that may force others to act unethically.

Managers, in particular, because of the authority of their position, have the opportunity to influence employees' actions. For example, a manager can influence employees to use pirated computer software to save costs. The use of illegal software puts the employee and the company at legal risk, but employees may feel pressured to do so by their superior's authority. The National Business Ethics Survey found that employees who feel pressure to compromise ethical standards view top and middle managers as the greatest source of such pressure.[26]

It is the responsibility of managers to create a work environment that helps the organization achieve its objectives and fulfill its responsibilities. However, the methods that managers use to enforce these responsibilities should not compromise employee rights. Organizational pressures may encourage a person to engage in activities that he or she might otherwise view as unethical, such as invading others' privacy or stealing a competitor's secrets. For example, Betty Vinson, an accounting executive at WorldCom, protested when her superiors asked her to make improper accounting entries to cover up the company's deteriorating financial condition. She acquiesced only after being told that it was the only way to save the troubled company. She, along with several other WorldCom accountants, pleaded guilty to conspiracy and fraud charges related to WorldCom's bankruptcy after the accounting improprieties came to light.[27] Or the firm may provide only vague or lax supervision

Although it stood by the safety of its product, Bausch & Lomb recalled its ReNu with MoistureLoc contact lens solution in 2006 following reports that some consumers experienced eye infections after using the product.

fabricated significant portions of at least eight major stories and conspired to cover up his lapses in judgment. The newspaper later apologized to its readers, and Kelley resigned.[28] A manager attempting to take credit for a subordinate's ideas is engaging in another type of plagiarism.

## Making Decisions about Ethical Issues

Although we've presented a variety of ethical issues that may arise in business, it can be difficult to recognize specific ethical issues in practice. Whether a decision maker recognizes an issue as an ethical one often depends on the issue itself. Managers, for example, tend to be more concerned about issues that affect those close to them, as well as issues that have immediate rather than long-term consequences. Thus, the perceived importance of an ethical issue substantially affects choices, and only a few issues receive scrutiny, while most receive no attention at all.[29]

Table 2.5 lists some questions you may want to ask yourself and others when trying to determine whether an action is ethical. Open discussion of ethical issues

> ## "It is the responsibility of managers to create a work environment that helps the organization achieve its objectives and fulfill its responsibilities."

on ethical issues, providing the opportunity for misconduct. Managers who offer no ethical direction to employees create many opportunities for manipulation, dishonesty, and conflicts of interest.

Plagiarism—taking someone else's work and presenting it as your own without mentioning the source—is another ethical issue. As a student, you may be familiar with plagiarism in school; for example, copying someone else's term paper or quoting from a published work or Internet source without acknowledging it. In business, an ethical issue arises when an employee copies reports or takes the work or ideas of others and presents it as his or her own. At *USA Today,* for example, an internal investigation into the work of veteran reporter Jack Kelley identified dozens of stories in which Kelley appeared to have plagiarized material from competing newspapers. The investigation also uncovered evidence Kelley

does not eliminate ethical problems, but it does promote both trust and learning in an organization.[30] When people feel that they cannot discuss what they are doing with their co-workers or superiors, there is a good chance that an ethical issue

**TABLE 2.5**  Questions to Consider in Determining Whether an Action Is Ethical

Are there any potential legal restrictions or violations that could result from the action?

Does your company have a specific code of ethics or policy on the action?

Is this activity customary in your industry? Are there any industry trade groups that provide guidelines or codes of conduct that address this issue?

Would this activity be accepted by your co-workers? Will your decision or action withstand open discussion with co-workers and managers and survive untarnished?

How does this activity fit with your own beliefs and values?

● **CODES OF ETHICS**
formalized rules and standards that describe what a company expects of its employees

● **WHISTLEBLOWING** the act of an employee exposing an employer's wrongdoing to outsiders, such as the media or government regulatory agencies

exists. Once a person has recognized an ethical issue and can openly discuss it with others, he or she has begun the process of resolving an ethical issue.

 **L03**

Specify how businesses can promote ethical behavior.

## Improving Ethical Behavior in Business

Understanding how people make ethical choices and what prompts a person to act unethically may reverse the current trend toward unethical behavior in business. Ethical decisions in an organization are influenced by three key factors: individual moral standards, the influence of managers and co-workers, and the opportunity to engage in misconduct (Figure 2.2). While you have great control over your personal ethics outside the workplace, your co-workers and superiors exert significant control over your choices at work through authority and example. In fact, the activities and examples set by co-workers, along with rules and policies established by the firm, are critical in gaining consistent ethical compliance in an organization. If the company fails to provide good examples and direction for appropriate conduct, confusion and conflict will develop and result in the opportunity for misconduct. If your boss or co-workers leave work early, you may be tempted to do so as well. If you see co-workers making personal long-distance phone calls at work and charging them to the company, then you may be more likely to do so also. In addition, having sound personal values contributes to an ethical workplace.

Because ethical issues often emerge from conflict, it is useful to examine the causes of ethical conflict. Business managers and employees often experience some tension between their

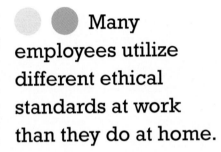

**Many employees utilize different ethical standards at work than they do at home.**

own ethical beliefs and their obligations to the organizations in which they work. Many employees utilize different ethical standards at work than they do at home. This conflict increases when employees feel that their company is encouraging unethical conduct or exerting pressure on them to engage in it.

It is difficult for employees to determine what conduct is acceptable within a company if the firm does not have ethics policies and standards. And without such policies and standards, employees may base decisions on how their peers and superiors behave. Professional codes of ethics are formalized rules and standards that describe what the company expects of its employees. Codes of ethics do not have to be so detailed that they take into account every situation, but they should provide guidelines and principles that can help employees achieve organizational objectives and address risks in an acceptable and ethical way. The development of a code of ethics should include not only a firm's executives and board of directors, but also legal staff and employees from all areas of a firm.[31] Table 2.6 lists some key things to consider when developing a code of ethics.

Codes of ethics, policies on ethics, and ethics training programs advance ethical behavior because they prescribe which activities are acceptable and which are not, and they limit the opportunity for misconduct by providing punishments for violations of the rules and standards. According to the National Business Ethics Survey (NBES), employees in organizations that have written standards of conduct, ethics training, ethics offices or hotlines, and systems for anonymous reporting of misconduct are more likely to report misconduct when they observe it. The survey also found that such programs are associated with higher employee perceptions that they will be held accountable for ethical infractions.[32] The enforcement of such codes and policies through rewards and punishments increases the acceptance of ethical standards by employees.

One of the most important components of an ethics program is a means through which employees can report observed misconduct anonymously. The NBES found that although employees are increasingly reporting illegal and unethical activities they observe in the workplace, 59 percent of surveyed employees indicated they are unwilling to report misconduct because they fear that no corrective action will be taken or that their report will not remain confidential.[33] The lack of anonymous reporting mechanisms may encourage whistleblowing, which occurs when an employee exposes an employer's wrongdoing to outsiders, such as the media or government regulatory agencies. However, more companies are

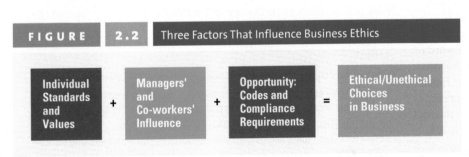

| FIGURE | 2.2 | Three Factors That Influence Business Ethics |
|---|---|---|

Individual Standards and Values + Managers' and Co-workers' Influence + Opportunity: Codes and Compliance Requirements = Ethical/Unethical Choices in Business

**TABLE 2.6**   Key Things to Consider in Developing a Code of Ethics

- Create a team to assist with the process of developing the code (include management and nonmanagement employees from across departments and functions).
- Solicit input from employees from different departments, functions, and regions to compile a list of common questions and answers to include in the code document.
- Make certain that the headings of the code sections can be easily understood by all employees.
- Avoid referencing specific U.S. laws and regulations or those of specific countries, particularly for codes that will be distributed to employees in multiple regions.
- Hold employee group meetings on a complete draft version (including graphics and pictures) of the text using language that everyone can understand.
- Inform employees that they will receive a copy of the code during an introduction session.
- Let all employees know that they will receive future ethics training which will, in part, cover the important information contained in the code document.

Source: Adapted from William Miller, "Implementing an Organizational Code of Ethics," *International Business Ethics Review* 7 (Winter 2004), pp. 1, 6–10.

> # "Organizations recognize that effective business ethics programs are good for business performance."

establishing programs to encourage employees to report illegal or unethical practices internally so that they can take steps to remedy problems before they result in legal action or generate negative publicity. In recent years, whistleblowers have provided crucial evidence documenting illegal actions at a number of companies. At Enron, for example, Sherron Watkins, a vice president, warned the firm's CEO, Ken Lay, that the energy company was using improper accounting procedures. Lay forwarded Watkins's concerns to Vinson and Elkins, Enron's outside lawyers, and they provided opinion letters approving the questionable transactions. Watkins also took her concerns to senior accountants at Arthur Andersen, and it is unclear if any action was taken. Watkins sold some of her Enron stock based on her knowledge, but was not indicted for insider trading. Soon after, Watkins testified before Congress that Enron had concealed billions of dollars in debt through a complex scheme of off-balance sheet partnerships.[34] Enron ultimately went bankrupt when its improprieties and high levels of debt were exposed. Unfortunately, whistleblowers are

Sherron Watkins, Colleen Rowley, and Cynthia Cooper (right to left) jeopardized their careers by blowing the whistle at Enron, the FBI, and WorldCom, respectively. The three women later ended up on the cover of Time after being named the magazine's "persons of the year."

often treated negatively in organizations. The government is rewarding firms that encourage employees to report misconduct—with reduced fines and penalties when violations occur.

The current trend is to move away from legally based ethical initiatives in organizations to cultural- or integrity-based initiatives that make ethics a part of core organizational values. Organizations recognize that effective business ethics programs are good for business performance. Firms that develop higher levels of trust function more efficiently and effectively and avoid damaged company reputations and product images. Organizational ethics initiatives have been supportive of many positive and diverse organizational objectives, such as profitability, hiring, employee satisfaction, and customer loyalty.[35] Conversely, lack of organizational ethics initiatives and the absence of workplace values such as honesty, trust, and integrity can have a negative impact on organizational objectives. According to one report on employee loyalty and work practices, 79 percent of employees who questioned their bosses' integrity indicated that they felt uncommitted or were likely to quit soon.[36]

● ● **LO4**

Explain the four dimensions of social responsibility.

# THE NATURE OF SOCIAL RESPONSIBILITY

There are four dimensions of social responsibility: economic, legal, ethical, and voluntary (including philanthropic) (Figure 2.3).[37] Earning profits is the economic foundation of the pyramid in Figure 2.3, and complying with the law is the next step. However a business whose *sole* objective is to maximize profits is not likely to consider its social responsibility, although its activities will probably be legal. (We looked at ethical responsibilities in the first half of this chapter.) Finally, voluntary responsibilities are additional activities that may not be required but which promote human welfare or goodwill. Legal and economic concerns have long been acknowledged in business, but voluntary and ethical issues are more recent concerns.

**Corporate citizenship** is the extent to which businesses meet the legal, ethical, economic, and voluntary responsibilities placed on them by their various stake-holders. It involves the activities and organizational processes adopted by businesses to meet their social responsibilities. A commitment to corporate citizenship by a firm indicates a strategic focus on fulfilling the social responsibilities expected of it by its stakeholders. Corporate citizenship involves action and measurement of the extent to which a firm embraces the corporate citizenship philosophy and then follows through by implementing citizenship and social responsibility initiatives. For example, ChevronTexaco, a multinational provider of petroleum and energy products, communicates its values in a document called "The ChevronTexaco Way." This document serves as an ethical foundation and guides the company's conduct around the world. For example, the firm has signed the Global Sullivan Principles, an international, voluntary code of conduct for corporations around the world; contributed to environmental causes such as the World Wildlife Fund and The Nature Conservancy; and donated funds and resources to important social causes around the world. The corporation also publishes a regular report on its social responsibility conduct and initiatives.[38]

Most companies today consider being socially responsible a cost of doing business. Eddie Bauer created a Corporate Social Responsibility (CSR) department to coordinate its social responsibility efforts. The department focuses on five areas: global labor practices, environmental affairs, sustainable business practices, governmental affairs, and public affairs (including philanthropy and volunteerism). The company's good corporate citizenship enhances its bottom line. According to John Thomas, vice president of the CSR department, "Customers are making more learned decisions today on how they shop and who they make their purchases from. Those decisions, I believe, are made on the basis of what a company stands for, what its values are, as well as what its contributions to the community are."[39] *Corporate Responsibility Officer* magazine

| FIGURE | 2.3 | The Pyramid of Social Responsibility |

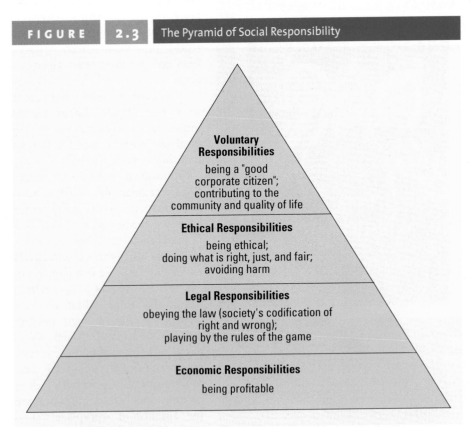

Source: Reprinted with permission from A. B. Carroll, "The Pyramid of Corporate Social Responsibility: Toward the Moral Management of Organizational Stakeholders," *Business Horizons*, July/August 1991. Copyright © 1991 by the Board of Trustees at Indiana University, Kelley School of Business.

publishes an annual list of the 100 best American corporate citizens based on service to seven stakeholder groups: stockholders, local communities, minorities, employees, global stakeholders, customers, and the environment. Table 2.7 shows the top 20 from that list.

Although the concept of social responsibility is receiving more and more attention, it is still not universally accepted. Table 2.8 lists some of the arguments for and against social responsibility.

## Social Responsibility Issues

As with ethics, managers consider social responsibility on a daily basis as they deal with real issues. Among the many social issues that managers must consider are their firms' relations with owners and stockholders, employees, consumers, the environment, and the community.

Social responsibility is a dynamic area with issues changing constantly in response to society's desires. There is much evidence that social responsibility is associated with improved business performance. Consumers are refusing to buy from businesses that receive publicity about misconduct. A number of studies have found a direct relationship between social responsibility and profitability, as well as that social responsibility is linked to employee commitment and customer loyalty—major concerns of any firm trying to increase profits.[40] This section highlights a few of the many social responsibility issues that managers face; as managers become aware of and work toward the solution of current social problems, new ones will certainly emerge.

 **LO5**

Debate an organization's social responsibilities to owners, employees, consumers, the environment, and the community.

**relations with owners and stockholders.** Businesses must first be responsible to their owners, who are primarily concerned with earning a profit or a return on their investment in a company. In a small business, this responsibility is fairly easy to fulfill because the owner(s) personally manages the business or knows the managers well. In larger businesses, particularly corporations owned by thousands of stockholders, assuring responsibility to the owners becomes a more difficult task.

A business's responsibilities to its owners and investors, as well as to the financial community at large, include maintaining proper accounting procedures, providing all relevant information to investors about the current and projected performance of the firm, and protecting the owners' rights and investments. In short, the business must maximize the owners' investment in the firm.

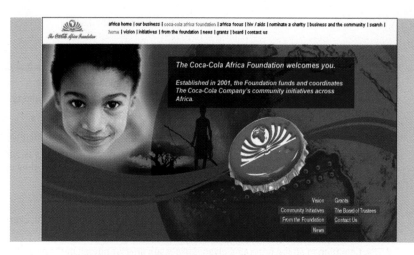

*The Coca-Cola Africa Foundation Provides millions of dollars each year to reduce the impact of HIV/AIDS on Coca-Cola's employees and independent bottlers in Africa.*

**employee relations.** Another issue of importance to a business is its responsibilities to employees, for without employees a business cannot carry out its goals. Employees expect businesses to provide a safe workplace, pay them adequately for their work, and tell them what is happening in their company. They want employers to listen to their grievances and

**TABLE 2.7** Best Corporate Citizens

| | |
|---|---|
| 1 | Green Mountain Coffee Roasters Inc. |
| 2 | Advanced Micro Devices Inc. |
| 3 | NIKE Inc. |
| 4 | Motorola Inc. |
| 5 | Intel Corp. |
| 6 | International Business Machines Corp. |
| 7 | Agilent Technologies Inc. |
| 8 | Timberland Co. (The) |
| 9 | Starbucks Coffee Co. |
| 10 | General Mills Inc. |
| 11 | Salesforce.com.Inc. |
| 12 | Applied Materials Inc. |
| 13 | Texas Instruments Inc. |
| 14 | Herman Miller Inc. |
| 15 | Rockwell Collins |
| 16 | Interface Inc. |
| 17 | Steelcase Inc. |
| 18 | Dell Inc. |
| 19 | Cisco Systems Inc. |
| 20 | Lam Research Corp. |

Source: Abby Schultz, "100 Best Corporate Citizens 2007," *Corporate Responsibility Officer* (n.d), http://www.thecro.com/files/100BestGatefold.pdf (accessed June 1, 2007).

**TABLE 2.8** The Arguments For and Against Social Responsibility

**For:**

1. Business helped to create many of the social problems that exist today, so it should play a significant role in solving them, especially in the areas of pollution reduction and cleanup.

2. Businesses should be more responsible because they have the financial and technical resources to help solve social problems.

3. As members of society, businesses should do their fair share to help others.

4. Socially responsible decision making by businesses can prevent increased government regulation.

5. Social responsibility is necessary to ensure economic survival: If businesses want educated and healthy employees, customers with money to spend, and suppliers with quality goods and services in years to come, they must take steps to help solve the social and environmental problems that exist today.

**Against:**

1. It sidetracks managers from the primary goal of business—earning profits. Every dollar donated to social causes or otherwise spent on society's problems is a dollar less for owners and investors.

2. Participation in social programs gives businesses greater power, perhaps at the expense of particular segments of society.

3. Some people question whether business has the expertise needed to assess and make decisions about social problems.

4. Many people believe that social problems are the responsibility of government agencies and officials, who can be held accountable by voters.

treat them fairly. When employees at Ramtech Building Systems Inc. approached management with their concerns about cursing used in the company's manufacturing facilities, a Language Code of Ethics was instituted. Many employees indicate that obscene language is common in the workplace, particularly in high-stress jobs. For example, 43 percent of the 12,000 U.S. Postal Service employees surveyed recently reported being cursed at in the workplace.[41] Companies are adjusting their policies and offering training to clean up employee language.

Of a more serious nature, a growing employee-relations concern for multinational companies is the spread of AIDS and its effect on the workforce. Daimler-Chrysler South Africa (DCSA), for example, provides HIV/AIDS testing, free anti-AIDS drugs, and additional treatment and support for its 6,000 South African employees and their families in an effort to combat the disease, which has infected about 9 percent of DCSA's employees there. The company spends an estimated $420,000 a year on antiretroviral drugs. Other German automakers, including

# Nestlé's Commitment to Africa

If you search the Internet for information regarding Nestlé, you are likely to come across a large amount of documentation referring to a 30-year-old scandal involving infant formula and poor handling of the resolution of debt owed by Ethiopia. Critics argue that Nestlé's socially responsible activities serve only as coverups for these scandals. Whatever the truth may be, Nestlé appears to be a company learning from its past mistakes—sometimes, the errors of the past can be great motivators to do good in the future. In the past few years, Nestlé has been working to promote itself as a company focused more on wellness, and for many years—although perhaps overshadowed by negative publicity—the company has been heavily focused on helping to improve the lives of people in Africa.

Nestlé opened the first of 27 African factories in South Africa in 1927. Since that time, African consumers have come to view Nestlé products as familiar parts of their lives. The company employs around 11,500 people in Africa; only 120 of those people are from other countries. Companies working with Nestlé provide about 50,000 additional jobs. In 2004, dean of the University of Ibadan's Faculty of Social Sciences found that in Nigeria, Nestlé employees earn above-average manufacturing wages. It was noted that more than 75 percent of those employees would decline to change jobs if given the option. Nestlé is reputed to be a large supporter of bettering the standard of living in African communities.

Nestlé does not own farmland in Africa, but it does work to help local farmers improve the quality of their crops and often their incomes. For example, Nestlé is the largest direct buyer of coffee in the world. The company also invests highly in research on how to help farmers improve the quality of their coffee crops. By improving the quality, the farmers can become more competitive in the global market.

In Africa, Nestlé is committed to improving the labor standards of farming, promoting local African products, preserving water, creating less waste, and offering nutritional education. Nestlé is also contributing to the United Nations' Millennium Development Goals in Africa to wipe out extreme poverty and hunger; ensure universal primary education; promote gender equality and empower women; reduce child mortality; improve maternal health; fight HIV/AIDS, malaria, and other diseases; and work toward environmental sustainability. Nestlé is committed, in a wide variety of ways, to helping people in Africa lead high-quality, healthy lives.[42] ❖

# Q: Discussion Questions

1. Do you think that Nestlé's socially responsible activities today have made up for possible mistakes involving infant formula in the past?

2. What has Nestlé done to improve its image in Africa?

3. What can Nestlé do to improve its commitment to Africa?

Volkswagen and BMW, have launched similar programs to cover their employees in South Africa, where 600 people die every day from the disease. Many U.S. companies have set up AIDS prevention and treatment programs for their employees in Africa as well. Companies as diverse as Coca-Cola (the largest private employer on the African continent), MTV, American Express, Nike, and ExxonMobil have also joined the Global Business Coalition to help fight the epidemic.[43]

Congress has passed several laws regulating safety in the workplace, many of which are enforced by OSHA. Labor unions have also made significant contributions to achieving safety in the workplace and improving wages and benefits. Most organizations now recognize that the safety and satisfaction of their employees are a critical ingredient in their success, and many strive to go beyond what is expected of them by the law. Healthy, satisfied employees supply more than just labor to their employers, however. Employers are beginning to realize the importance of obtaining input from even the lowest-level employees to help the company reach its objectives.

A major social responsibility for business is providing equal opportunities for all employees regardless of their sex, age, race, religion, or nationality. Women and minorities have been slighted in the past in terms of education, employment, and advancement opportunities; additionally, many of their needs have not been addressed by business. For example, as many as 1.6 million current and former female Wal-Mart employees filed a class-action discrimination lawsuit accusing the giant retailer of paying them lower wages and salaries than it does men in comparable positions. Pretrial proceedings not only uncovered discrepancies between the pay of men and women but also the fact that men dominate higher-paying store manager positions while women occupy more than 90 percent of cashier jobs, most of which pay about $14,000 a year. Wal-Mart faces fines and penalties in the millions of dollars if found guilty of sexual discrimination.[44] Women, who continue to bear most child-rearing responsibilities, often experience conflict between those responsibilities and their duties as employees. Consequently, day care has become a major employment issue for women, and more companies are providing day care facilities as part of their effort to recruit and advance women in the workforce. In addition, companies are considering alternative scheduling such as flex-time and job sharing to accommodate employee concerns. Telecommuting has grown significantly over the past 5 to 10 years, as well. Many Americans today believe business has a social obligation to provide special opportunities for women and minorities to improve their standing in society.

● CONSUMERISM the activities that independent individuals, groups, and organizations undertake to protect their rights as consumers

**consumer relations.** A critical issue in business today is business's responsibility to customers, who look to business to provide them with satisfying, safe products and to respect their rights as consumers. The activities that independent individuals, groups, and organizations undertake to protect their rights as consumers are known as consumerism. To achieve their objectives, consumers and their advocates write letters to companies, lobby government agencies, make public service announcements, and boycott companies whose activities they deem irresponsible.

Many of the desires of those involved in the consumer movement have a foundation in John F. Kennedy's 1962 consumer bill of rights, which highlighted four rights. The *right to safety* means that a business must not knowingly sell anything that could result in personal injury or harm to consumers. Defective or dangerous products erode public confidence in the ability of business to serve society. They also result in expensive litigation that ultimately increases the cost of products for all consumers. The right to safety also means businesses must provide a safe place for consumers to shop. In

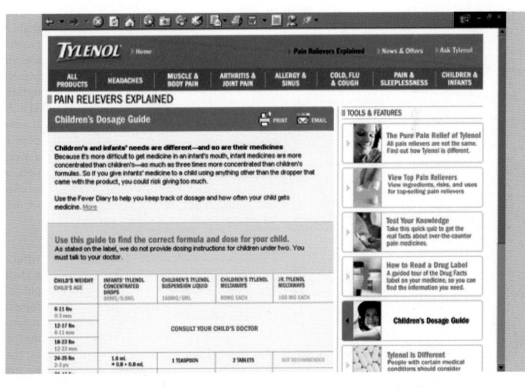

J&J's Tylenol wants to make sure that parents know how to use its products for their children.

recent years, many large retailers have been under increasing pressure to improve safety in their large warehouse-type stores. At Home Depot, for example, three consumer deaths and numerous serious injuries have been caused by falling merchandise. One lawsuit brought against the company over injuries received in one of its stores resulted in a $1.5 million judgment. To help prevent further deaths, injuries, and litigation, Home Depot now has a corporate safety officer and has hired 130 safety managers to monitor store compliance with new safety measures.[45]

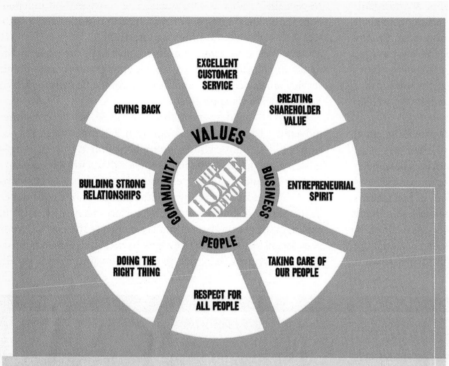

**EXCELLENT CUSTOMER SERVICE**
Along with our quality products, service, price and selection, we must go the extra mile to give customers knowledgeable advice about merchandise and to help them use those products to their maximum benefit.

**CREATING SHAREHOLDER VALUE**
The investors who provide the capital necessary to allow our Company to grow need and expect a return on their investment. We are committed to providing it.

**ENTREPRENEURIAL SPIRIT**
The Home Depot associates are encouraged to initiate creative and innovative ways of serving our customers and improving the business, as well as to adopt good ideas from others.

**TAKING CARE OF OUR PEOPLE**
The key to our success is treating people well. We do this by encouraging associates to speak up and take risks, by recognizing and rewarding good performance and by leading and developing people so they may grow.

**RESPECT FOR ALL PEOPLE**
In order to remain successful, our associates must work in an environment of mutual respect where each associate is regarded as part of The Home Depot team.

**DOING THE RIGHT THING**
We exercise good judgment by "doing the right thing" instead of just "doing things right." We strive to understand the impact of our decisions, and we accept responsibility for our actions.

**BUILDING STRONG RELATIONSHIPS**
Strong relationships are built on trust, honesty and integrity. We listen and respond to the needs of customers, associates, communities and vendors, treating them as partners.

**GIVING BACK**
An important part of the fabric of The Home Depot is in giving our time, talents, energy and resources to worthwhile causes in our communities and society.

*Home Depot acknowledges the importance of all stakeholders in operating its business.*

The *right to be informed* gives consumers the freedom to review complete information about a product before they buy it. This means that detailed information about ingredients, risks, and instructions for use are to be printed on labels and packages. The *right to choose* ensures that consumers have access to a variety of products and services at competitive prices. The assurance of both satisfactory quality and service at a fair price is also a part of the consumer's right to choose. Some consumers are not being given the right to choose. Many are being billed for products and services they never ordered. According to the Federal Trade Commission, complaints about unordered merchandise and services jumped 169 percent over a two-year period. Burdine's, a department store chain, was investigated for failing to notify customers it was enrolling them in a company buying club. Fleet Mortgage was sued for adding fees for unrequested insurance to customers' mortgage bills, and HCI Direct was sued by 11 states for charging customers for panty hose samples they had never ordered.[46] The *right to be heard* assures consumers that their interests will receive full and sympathetic consideration when the government formulates policy. It also assures the fair treatment of consumers who voice complaints about a purchased product.

The role of the Federal Trade Commission's Bureau of Consumer Protection is to protect consumers against unfair, deceptive, or fraudulent practices. The bureau, which enforces a variety of consumer protection laws, is divided into five divisions. The Division of Enforcement monitors compliance with and investigates violations of laws, including unfulfilled holiday delivery promises by online shopping sites, employment opportunities fraud, scholarship scams, misleading advertising for health care products, and more.

**environmental issues.** Environmental responsibility has become a leading issue as both business and the public acknowledge the damage done to the environment in the past. Today's consumers are increasingly demanding that businesses take a greater responsibility for their actions and how they impact the environment.

**Animal Rights.** One area of environmental concern in society today is animal rights. Probably the most controversial business practice in this area is the testing of cosmetics and drugs on animals who may be injured or killed as a result. Animal-rights activists, such as People for the Ethical Treatment of Animals, say such research is morally wrong because it harms living creatures. Consumers who share this sentiment may boycott companies that test products on animals and take their business instead to companies such as The Body Shop and John Paul Mitchell Systems, which do not use animal testing. However, researchers in the cosmetics and pharmaceutical industries argue that animal testing is necessary to prevent harm to human beings who will eventually use the products. Business practices that harm endangered wildlife and their habitats are another environmental issue.

**pollution.** Another major issue in the area of environmental responsibility is pollution. Water pollution results from dumping toxic chemicals and raw sewage into rivers and oceans, oil spills, and the burial of industrial waste in the ground where it may filter into underground water supplies. Fertilizers and insecticides used in farming and grounds maintenance also run off into water supplies with each rainfall. Water pollution problems are especially notable in heavily industrialized areas. Medical waste—such as used syringes, vials of blood, and AIDS-contaminated materials—has turned up on beaches in New York, New Jersey,

Organizations such as PETA address animal rights issues.

and Massachusetts, as well as other places. Society is demanding that water supplies be clean and healthful to reduce the potential danger from these substances.

Air pollution is usually the result of smoke and other pollutants emitted by manufacturing facilities, as well as carbon monoxide and hydrocarbons emitted by motor vehicles. In addition to the health risks posed by air pollution, when some chemical compounds emitted by manufacturing facilities react with air and rain, acid rain results. Acid rain has contributed to the deaths of many valuable forests and lakes in North America as well as in Europe. Air pollution may also contribute to global warming, in which carbon dioxide collects in the earth's atmosphere, trapping the sun's heat and preventing the earth's surface from cooling. As a result, the automobile industry is facing increasing pressure to develop affordable, fuel-efficient automobiles that do not contribute to air pollution problems. Urbanization and industrialization has led to more energy consumption, raising carbon monoxide emissions and higher temperatures. The global surface temperature has been increasing over the past 35 years. Worldwide passenger vehicle ownership has been growing due to rapid industrialization and consumer purchasing power in China, India, and other developing countries with large populations. On the positive side, there are more than 100 million bicycles produced worldwide, more than double the passenger vehicles produced annually.[48]

# Texas Screams for Ice Cream

Amy Simmons

The Business: Amy's Ice Cream

Founded: 1984

Success: $5 million in sales through 13 stores and a wholesale business

After a large corporation bought out Amy Simmons's employer, she decided the traditional corporate life was not for her. With a partner, Scott Shaw, she wrote a hot check to open the first Amy's Ice Cream in Austin, Texas. The

duo raised money by selling shares in the business to their friends and a former co-worker. The store's high-quality ingredients and creative flavors, coupled with the zany antics of its behind-the-counter "scoopers," quickly gained it a loyal following and made Amy an Austin icon. Recently, Amy's Ice Cream was featured in its own chapter in *Inc.* writer Donna Fenn's book *Alpha Dogs—How Your Small Business Can Become a Leader of the Pack.* With about 160 employees, Amy's Ice Cream—which now includes catering and a

wholesale business—eschews advertising in favor of spending money supporting local events and charities such as local public television, Candlelighter's Childhood Cancer Foundation, Austin Partners in Education, and Fiesta at Laguna Gloria. The company has also worked with national charities such as the Ronald McDonald House and the Make a Wish Foundation. The company's brand new, state-of-the-art 6,000-square-foot factory, which includes numerous energy-saving devices, was recycled from an old post office.[47] ❖

> # RELATED TO THE PROBLEM OF LAND POLLUTION IS THE LARGER ISSUE OF HOW TO DISPOSE OF WASTE IN AN ENVIRONMENTALLY RESPONSIBLE MANNER.

Land pollution is tied directly to water pollution because many of the chemicals and toxic wastes that are dumped on the land eventually work their way into the water supply. Land pollution results from the dumping of residential and industrial waste, strip mining, forest fires, and poor forest conservation. In Brazil and other South American countries, rain forests are being destroyed—at a rate of one acre per minute—to make way for farms and ranches, at a cost of the extinction of the many animals and plants (some endangered species) that call the rain forest home. Large-scale deforestation also depletes the oxygen supply available to humans and other animals.

Related to the problem of land pollution is the larger issue of how to dispose of waste in an environmentally responsible manner. Americans are producing more trash, with the average person producing about 5 pounds of trash every day up from about 3.3 pounds in 1970. At the same time, more than 30 percent of Americans recycle, up from 8 percent in 1970.[49] One specific solid waste problem is being created by rapid innovations in computer hardware that make many computers obsolete after just 18 months. By 2005, 350 million computers reached obsolescence, and at least 55 million ended up in landfills.[50] Computers contain such toxic substances as lead, mercury, and polyvinyl chloride, which can leach into the soil and contaminate groundwater when disposed of improperly. Dell Computer, the leading seller of personal computers, has come under increasing criticism from environmental groups for failing to adopt a leadership role in reducing the use of toxic materials in the manufacture of computers and in recycling used computer parts. The company has also encountered criticism for using prison labor to handle the recycling it does do. Several states are considering legislation that would require computers to be recycled at the same levels as in Europe.[51] Dell has started a free recycling program, which recycles old Dell computers when you buy a new Dell computer.

### Response to Environmental Issues.
Partly in response to federal legislation such as the National Environmental Policy Act of 1969 and partly due to consumer concerns, businesses are responding to environmental issues. Many small and large companies, including Walt Disney Company, Chevron, and Scott Paper, have created a new executive position—a vice

**DID YOU KNOW?**

In one year, Americans generated 230 million tons of trash and recycled 23.5 percent of it.[55]

president of environmental affairs—to help them achieve their business goals in an environmentally responsible manner. A survey indicated that 83.5 percent of *Fortune* 500 companies have a written environmental policy, 74.7 percent engage in recycling efforts, and 69.7 percent have made investments in waste-reduction efforts.[52] Many companies, including Alcoa, Dow Chemical, Phillips Petroleum, and Raytheon, now link executive pay to environmental performance.[53] Some companies are finding that environmental consciousness can save them money. DuPont saved more than $3 billion through energy conservation by replacing natural gas with methane in its industrial boilers in many of its plants.[54]

Many firms are trying to eliminate wasteful practices, the emission of pollutants, and/or the use of harmful chemicals from their manufacturing processes. Other companies are seeking ways to improve their products. Utility providers, for example, are increasingly supplementing their services with alternative energy sources, including solar, wind, and geothermal power. In many places, local utility customers can even elect to purchase electricity from green sources—primarily wind power—for a few extra dollars a month. The Austin, Texas, city-owned utility's award-winning GreenChoice program includes many small and large businesses among its customers.[56] Indeed, a growing number of businesses and consumers are choosing "green power" sources where available. New Belgium Brewing, the third largest craft brewer, is the first all-wind-powered brewery in the United States. Many businesses have turned to *recycling*, the reprocessing of materials—aluminum, paper, glass, and some plastic—for reuse. Such efforts to make products, packaging, and processes more environmentally friendly have been labeled "green" business or marketing by the public and media. Lumber products at Home Depot may carry a seal from the Forest Stewardship Council to indicate that they were harvested from sustainable forests using environmentally friendly methods.[57] Likewise, most Chiquita bananas are certified through the Better Banana Project as having been grown with more environmentally and labor-friendly practices.[58]

It is important to recognize that, with current technology, environmental responsibility requires trade-offs. Society must weigh the huge costs of limiting or eliminating pollution against the health threat posed by the pollution. Environmental responsibility imposes costs on both business and the public. Although people certainly do not want oil fouling beautiful waterways and killing wildlife, they insist on low-cost, readily available gasoline and heating oil. People do not want to contribute to the growing garbage-disposal problem, but they often refuse to pay more for "green" products packaged in an environmentally friendly manner, to recycle as much of their own waste as possible, or to permit the building of additional waste-disposal facilities (the "not in my backyard," or NIMBY, syndrome). Managers must coordinate environmental goals with other social and economic ones.

## community relations.

A final, yet very significant, issue for businesses concerns their responsibilities to the general welfare of the communities and societies in which they operate. Many businesses simply want to make their communities better places for everyone to live and work. The most common way that businesses exercise their community responsibility is through donations to local and national charitable organizations. Corporations contributed more than $12 billion to environmental and social causes last year.[59] For example, Safeway, the nation's fourth-largest grocer, has donated millions of dollars to organizations involved in medical research, such as Easter Seals and the Juvenile Diabetes Research Foundation International. The company's employees have also raised funds to support social causes of interest.[60] Avon's Breast Cancer Awareness Crusade has helped raise $300 million to fund community-based breast cancer education and

Whole Foods Market acts in Socially responsible ways by using solar energy to generate 25 percent of its power.

early detection services. Avon, a marketer of women's cosmetics, is also known for employing a large number of women and promoting them to top management; the firm has more female top managers (86 percent) than any other *Fortune* 500 company.[61] Even small companies participate in philanthropy through donations and volunteer support of local causes and national charities, such as the Red Cross and the United Way.

After realizing that the current pool of prospective employees lacks many basic skills necessary to work, many companies have become concerned about the quality of education in the United States. Recognizing that today's students are tomorrow's employees and customers, firms such as Kroger, Campbell's Soup, Kodak, American Express, Apple Computer, Xerox, and Coca-Cola are donating money, equipment, and employee time to help improve schools in their communities and around the nation. They provide scholarship money, support for teachers, and computers for students, and they send employees out to tutor and motivate young students to stay in school and succeed. Target, for example, contributes significant resources to education, including direct donations of $100 million to schools as well as fund-raising and scholarship programs that assist teachers and students. Through the retailer's Take Charge of Education program, customers using a Target Guest Card can designate a specific school to which Target donates 1 percent of their total purchase. This program is designed to make customers feel that

*Funded by The Tobacco Tax Initiative, the California Department of Health Services promotes the negative effects of smoking.*

Many career opportunities are emerging today in the field of business ethics and social responsibility. Approximately one-third of *Fortune* 1,000 firms have an ethics officer, a position that most companies have created only in the last few years. The ethics officer is typically responsible for (1) meeting with employees, the board of directors, and top management to discuss and provide advice about ethics issues; (2) distributing a code of ethics; (3) creating and maintaining an anonymous, confidential service to answer questions about ethical issues; (4) taking actions on possible ethics code violations; and (5) reviewing and modifying the code of ethics. Entry-level jobs in ethics involve assisting with communications programs or training.

If you are interested in a career in the area of business ethics and social responsibility, take courses in business ethics, legal environment, and business and society. Many ethics officers have law degrees due to the interrelationship of many legal and ethical issues. Some elective courses in moral philosophy or sociology may also be useful. Subscribe to a magazine such as *Business Ethics,* a popular trade journal that provides information about companies that have ethics programs or are involved with socially responsible activities. By learning more about how real companies are carrying out the ethics/social responsibility function, you will be better prepared to apply for a job and be knowledgeable in matching your interests with a company's needs. Although there are only a small number of jobs available today in this emerging area, you could be in the forefront of a developing concern that has much potential for career advancement. If you prepare yourself properly through education and possibly a part-time job or internship in a large firm with an ethics department, you will greatly enhance the probability of developing a successful career in business ethics and social responsibility.[63]

> ["Business is also beginning to take more responsibility for the hard-core unemployed."]

their purchases are benefiting their community while increasing the use of Target Guest Cards.[62]

Hewlett-Packard's Diversity in Education Initiative focuses on math and science in four minority communities and works with students from elementary school to the university level. The program provides hands-on science kits to elementary and middle schools and gives 40 high school students (10 from each community) annual $3,000 college scholarships. A mentor is assigned to each student, who is given a paid summer internship at Hewlett-Packard and taught how to conduct a job search.[64] Although some members of the public fear business involvement in education, others believe that if business wants educated employees and customers in the future, it must help educate them now.

Business is also beginning to take more responsibility for the hard-core unemployed. Some are mentally or physically handicapped; some are homeless. Organizations such as the National Alliance of Businessmen fund programs to train the hard-core unemployed so that they can find jobs and support themselves. In addition to fostering self-support, such opportunities enhance self-esteem and help people become productive members of society. ∎

## CHECK OUT

www.mhhe.com/FerrellM

for study materials including Interactive Exercises, Quizzes, iPod downloads, and video.

# Build Your Business Plan

**Business Ethics And Social Responsibility** Think about which industry you are considering competing in with your product/service. Is there any kind of questionable practices in the way the product has been traditionally sold? Produced? Advertised? Have there been any recent accusations regarding safety within the industry? What about any environmental concerns?

For example, if you are thinking of opening a lawn care business, you need to be thinking about what possible effects the chemicals you are using will have on the client and the environment. You have a responsibility to keep your customers safe and healthy. You also have the social responsibility to let the community know of any damaging effect you may be directly or indirectly responsible for.

M IS WANTING MORE, GETTING MORE, ACHIEVING MORE

www.mhhe.com/FerrellIM    start here.

# APPENDIX A

## THE LEGAL AND REGULATORY ENVIRONMENT

**Business law** refers to the rules and regulations that govern the conduct of business. Problems in this area come from the failure to keep promises, misunderstandings, disagreements about expectations, or, in some cases, attempts to take advantage of others. The regulatory environment offers a framework and enforcement system in order to provide a fair playing field for all businesses. The regulatory environment is created based on inputs from competitors, customers, employees, special interest groups, and the public's elected representatives. Lobbying by pressure groups who try to influence legislation often shapes the legal and regulatory environment.

### SOURCES OF LAW

Laws are classified as either criminal or civil. *Criminal law* not only prohibits a specific kind of action, such as unfair competition or mail fraud, but also imposes a fine or imprisonment as punishment for violating the law. A violation of a criminal law is thus called a

> "The primary method of resolving conflicts and business disputes is through lawsuits, where one individual or organization takes another to court using civil laws."

crime. *Civil law* defines all the laws not classified as criminal, and it specifies the rights and duties of individuals and organizations (including businesses). Violations of civil law may result in fines but not imprisonment. The primary difference between criminal and civil law is that criminal laws are enforced by the state or nation, whereas civil laws are enforced through the court system by individuals or organizations.

Criminal and civil laws are derived from four sources: the Constitution (constitutional law), precedents established by judges (common law), federal and state statutes (statutory law), and federal and state administrative agencies (administrative law). Federal administrative agencies established by Congress control and influence business by enforcing laws and regulations to encourage competition and protect consumers, workers, and the environment. The Supreme Court is the ultimate authority on legal and regulatory decisions for appropriate conduct in business.

### COURTS AND THE RESOLUTION OF DISPUTES

The primary method of resolving conflicts and business disputes is through **lawsuits,** where one individual or organization takes another to court using civil laws. The legal system, therefore, provides a forum for businesspeople to resolve disputes based on our legal foundations. The courts may decide when harm or damage results from the actions of others.

Because lawsuits are so frequent in the world of business, it is important to understand more about the court system where such disputes are resolved. Both financial restitution and specific actions to undo wrongdoing can result from going before a court to resolve a conflict. All decisions made in the courts are based on criminal and civil laws derived from the legal and regulatory system.

A businessperson may win a lawsuit in court and receive a judgment, or court order, requiring the loser of the suit to pay monetary damages. However, this does not guarantee the victor will be able to collect those damages. If the loser of the suit lacks the financial resources to pay the judgment—for example, if the loser is a bankrupt business—the winner of the suit may not be able to collect the award. Most business lawsuits involve a request for a sum of money, but some lawsuits request that a court specifically order a person or organization to do or to refrain from doing a certain act, such as slamming telephone customers.

## The Court System

**Jurisdiction** is the legal power of a court, through a judge, to interpret and apply the law and make a binding decision in a particular case. In some instances, other courts will not enforce the decision of a prior court because it lacked jurisdiction. Federal courts are granted jurisdiction by the Constitution or by Congress. State legislatures and constitutions determine which state courts hear certain types of cases. Courts of general jurisdiction hear all types of cases; those of limited jurisdiction hear only specific types of cases. The Federal Bankruptcy Court, for example, hears only cases involving bankruptcy. There is some combination of limited and general jurisdiction courts in every state.

In a **trial court** (whether in a court of general or limited jurisdiction and whether in the state or the federal system), two tasks must be completed. First, the court (acting through the judge or a jury) must determine the facts of the case. In other words, if there is conflicting evidence, the judge or jury must decide who to believe. Second, the judge must decide which law or set of laws is pertinent to the case and must then apply those laws to resolve the dispute.

*Marcia & Bill Baker found Heinz was underfilling their 20-oz. ketchup bottles by 1.5 oz. Heinz paid civil penalties and costs of $180,000 and had to overfill all ketchup bottles in California by 1/8 oz. for a year.*

An **appellate court,** on the other hand, deals solely with appeals relating to the interpretation of law. Thus, when you hear about a case being appealed, it is not retried, but rather reevaluated. Appellate judges do not hear witnesses but instead base their decisions on a written transcript of the original trial. Moreover, appellate courts do not draw factual conclusions; the appellate judge is limited to deciding whether the trial judge made a mistake in interpreting the law that probably affected the outcome of the trial. If the trial judge made no mistake (or if mistakes would not have changed the result of the trial), the appellate court will let the trial court's decision stand. If the appellate court finds a mistake, it usually sends the case back to the trial court so that the mistake can be corrected. Correction may involve the granting of a new trial. On occasion, appellate courts modify the verdict of the trial court without sending the case back to the trial court.

## Alternative Dispute Resolution Methods

Although the main remedy for business disputes is a lawsuit, other dispute resolution methods are becoming popular. The schedules of state and federal trial courts are often crowded; long delays between the filing of a case and the trial date are common. Further, complex cases can become quite expensive to pursue. As a result, many businesspeople are turning to alternative methods of resolving business arguments: mediation and arbitration, the mini-trial, and litigation in a private court.

**Mediation** is a form of negotiation to resolve a dispute by bringing in one or more third-party mediators, usually chosen by the disputing parties, to help reach a settlement. The mediator suggests different ways to resolve a dispute between the parties. The mediator's resolution is nonbinding—that is, the parties do not have to accept the mediator's suggestions; they are strictly voluntary.

**Arbitration** involves submission of a dispute to one or more third-party arbitrators, usually chosen by the disputing parties, whose decision usually is final. Arbitration differs from

## The Trials of Martha Stewart

Martha Stewart is arguably America's most famous homemaker and one of its richest women executives. She left a position as a successful stockbroker to start a gourmet-food shop and catering business that evolved into Martha Stewart Living Omnimedia Inc. (MSLO), a company with interests in publishing, television, merchandising, electronic commerce, and related international partnerships. In 2001, however, Stewart became the center of headlines, speculation, and eventually a much-publicized trial on criminal charges related to her sales of 4,000 shares of ImClone stock one day before that firm's stock price plummeted.

On December 27, 2001, Martha Stewart sold 3,928 shares of ImClone stock, one day before the Food and Drug Administration refused to review ImClone System's cancer drug Erbitux; the company's stock tumbled following the announcement. Stewart later told investigators that she sold the stock after her broker, Peter Bacanovic, informed her that ImClone's stock had fallen below a $60 threshold they had previously arranged. However, Bacanovic's assistant, Douglas Faneuil, who handled the sale for Stewart, later told Merrill Lynch lawyers that Bacanovic had pressured him to lie about the stop-loss order.

In June 2003, a federal grand jury indicted Stewart on charges of securities fraud, conspiracy (together with Peter Bacanovic), making false statements, and obstruction of justice, but not insider trading. The 41-page indictment alleged that she lied to federal investigators about the stock sale, attempted to cover up her activities, and defrauded Martha Stewart Living Omnimedia shareholders by misleading them about the gravity of the situation and thereby keeping the stock price from falling. The indictment further accused Stewart of deleting a computer log of the telephone message from Bacanovic informing her that he thought ImClone's stock "was going to start trading downward." Bacanovic was indicted on similar charges. Both Stewart and

Bacanovic pleaded "not guilty" to all charges, but Stewart resigned her positions as chief executive officer and chairman of the board of Martha Stewart Living Omnimedia just hours after the indictment.

In February 2004, U.S. District Judge Miriam Goldman Cedarbaum threw out the most serious of the charges against Stewart—securities fraud. However, just one week later, a jury convicted Stewart on four remaining charges of making false statements and conspiracy to obstruct justice. Her broker, Peter Bacanovic, was also found guilty on four out of five charges including making false statements, conspiracy to obstruct justice, and perjury. Stewart was sentenced to five months in jail and five months in at-home detention. She finished her jail time in March 2005.

Shares of MSLO surged since the company reported better than expected 2005 results. *Martha Stewart Living* magazine also had strong ad sale gains, and the company is hoping to take advantage of Martha's rebound by launching a new magazine, *Blueprint,* a publication targeted at 25- to 45-year-old women. The first issue was available on May 1, 2006. The company announced a deal with homebuilder KB Home in 2005 to build "Martha Stewart–inspired" homes in the Southeast, and due to the success of the first community in Cary, North Carolina, the companies announced that they were expanding the partnership across the country.

Shortly after her prison release, Martha Stewart decided to fight rather than settle civil insider-trading charges from the Securities and Exchange Commission. In June 2003, the SEC civil complaint was stayed until criminal proceedings were completed. In response to the SEC complaint filed in May 2006 with the U.S. District Court in Manhattan, Stewart denied the allegations that she used nonpublic information when she sold 3,928 shares of ImClone stock in December 2001. Instead, she said she "acted in good faith." Fighting the

charges offers Stewart the chance to reclaim her chief executive and chairman titles, but another public trial could deal a blow to the company and reverse the turnaround that it has made so far since her release. In 2006 Martha Stwart reversed previous statements and settled the civil charges by paying a fine. ❖

# Q: Discussion Questions

1. Why do you think Martha Stewart was convicted of lying about insider trading—a charge that was later thrown out?

2. Do you think the legal system was fair to Martha Stewart given her gender and her celebrity status? Was she used as an example?

3. What do you think Martha Stewart would suggest to others to avoid the legal problems that changed her life?

**Sources:** Krysten Crawford, "Stewart Considers Serving Time Now," *CNN/Money,* July 20, 2004, http://money.cnn.com; O. C. Ferrell, John Fraedrich, and Linda Ferrell, "Martha Stewart: Insider-Trading Scandal," in *Business Ethics: Ethical Decision Making and Cases,* 6th ed. (Boston: Houghton Mifflin, 2005), pp. 300–6; Sarah Rush, "Kmart Suing Stewart's Company," *The Coloradoan,* February 14, 2004, p. D10; Kara Scannell and Matthew Rose, "Stewart Lawyer Says the Case Wasn't Proved," *The Wall Street Journal,* March 3, 2004, http://online.wsj.com; "Stewart Convicted on All Charges," *CNN/Money,* March 5, 2004, http://money.cnn.com/2004/03/05/news/companies/martha_verdict/; "Martha Stewart to Settle with SEC," gautier.com June 7, 2006 (accessed Aug 2, 2006).

mediation in that an arbitrator's decision must be followed, whereas a mediator merely offers suggestions and facilitates negotiations. Cases may be submitted to arbitration because a contract—such as a labor contract—requires it or because the parties agree to do so. Some consumers are barred from taking claims to court by agreements drafted by banks, brokers, health plans, and others. Instead, they are required to take complaints to mandatory arbitration. Arbitration can be an attractive alternative to a lawsuit because it is often cheaper and quicker, and the parties frequently can choose arbitrators who are knowledgeable about the particular area of business at issue.

A method of dispute resolution that may become increasingly important in settling complex disputes is the **mini-trial**, in which both parties agree to present a summarized version of their case to an independent third party. That person then advises them of his or her impression of the probable outcome if the case were to be tried. Representatives of both sides then attempt to negotiate a settlement based on the advisor's recommendations. For example, employees in a large corporation who believe they have muscular or skeletal stress injuries caused by the strain of repetitive motion in using a computer could agree to a mini-trial to address a dispute related to damages. Although the mini-trial itself does not resolve the dispute, it can help the parties resolve the case before going to court. Because the mini-trial is not subject to formal court rules, it can save companies a

great deal of money, allowing them to recognize the weaknesses in a particular case.

In some areas of the country, disputes can be submitted to a private nongovernmental court for resolution. In a sense, a **private court system** is similar to arbitration in that an independent third party resolves the case after hearing both sides of the story. Trials in private courts may be either informal or highly formal, depending on the people involved. Businesses typically agree to have their disputes decided in private courts to save time and money.

# REGULATORY ADMINISTRATIVE AGENCIES

Federal and state administrative agencies (listed in Table A.1) also have some judicial powers. Many administrative agencies, such as the Federal Trade Commission, decide disputes that involve their regulations. In such disputes, the resolution process is usually called a "hearing" rather than a trial. In these cases, an administrative law judge decides all issues.

Federal regulatory agencies influence many business activities and cover product liability, safety, and the regulation or deregulation of public utilities. Usually, these bodies have the power to enforce specific laws, such as the Federal Trade

**TABLE A.1**   The Major Regulatory Agencies

| Agency | Major Areas of Responsibility |
| --- | --- |
| Federal Trade Commission (FTC) | Enforces laws and guidelines regarding business practices; takes action to stop false and deceptive advertising and labeling. |
| Food and Drug Administration (FDA) | Enforces laws and regulations to prevent distribution of adulterated or misbranded foods, drugs, medical devices, cosmetics, veterinary products, and particularly hazardous consumer products. |
| Consumer Product Safety Commission (CPSC) | Ensures compliance with the Consumer Product Safety Act; protects the public from unreasonable risk of injury from any consumer product not covered by other regulatory agencies. |
| Interstate Commerce Commission (ICC) | Regulates franchises, rates, and finances of interstate rail, bus, truck, and water carriers. |
| Federal Communications Commission (FCC) | Regulates communication by wire, radio, and television in interstate and foreign commerce. |
| Environmental Protection Agency (EPA) | Develops and enforces environmental protection standards and conducts research into the adverse effects of pollution. |
| Federal Energy Regulatory Commission (FERC) | Regulates rates and sales of natural gas products, thereby affecting the supply and price of gas available to consumers; also regulates wholesale rates for electricity and gas, pipeline construction, and U.S. imports and exports of natural gas and electricity. |
| Equal Employment Opportunity Commission (EEOC) | Investigates and resolves discrimination in employment practices. |
| Federal Aviation Administration (FAA) | Oversees the policies and regulations of the airline industry. |
| Federal Highway Administration (FHA) | Regulates vehicle safety requirements. |
| Occupational Safety and Health Administration (OSHA) | Develops policy to promote worker safety and health and investigates infractions. |
| Securities and Exchange Commission (SEC) | Regulates corporate securities trading and develops protection from fraud and other abuses; provides an accounting oversight board. |

Commission Act, and have some discretion in establishing operating rules and regulations to guide certain types of industry practices. Because of this discretion and overlapping areas of responsibility, confusion or conflict regarding which agencies have jurisdiction over which activities is common.

Of all the federal regulatory units, the **Federal Trade Commission (FTC)** most influences business activities related to questionable practices that create disputes between businesses and their customers. Although the FTC regulates a variety of business practices, it allocates a large portion of resources to curbing false advertising, misleading pricing, and deceptive packaging and labeling. When it receives a complaint or otherwise has reason to believe that a firm is violating a law, the FTC issues a complaint stating that the business is in violation.

If a company continues the questionable practice, the FTC can issue a cease-and-desist order, which is an order for the business to stop doing whatever has caused the complaint. In such cases, the charged firm can appeal to the federal courts to have the order rescinded. However, the FTC can seek civil penalties in court—up to a maximum penalty of $10,000 a day for each infraction—if a cease-and-desist order is violated. In its battle against unfair pricing, the FTC has issued consent decrees alleging that corporate attempts to engage in price fixing or invitations to competitors to collude are violations even when the competitors in question refuse the invitations. The commission can also require companies to run corrective advertising in response to previous ads considered misleading.

The FTC also assists businesses in complying with laws. New marketing methods are evaluated every year. When general sets of guidelines are needed to improve business practices in a particular industry, the FTC sometimes encourages firms within that industry to establish a set of trade practices voluntarily. The FTC may even sponsor a conference bringing together industry leaders and consumers for the purpose of establishing acceptable trade practices.

Unlike the FTC, other regulatory units are limited to dealing with specific products, services, or business activities. The Food and Drug Administration (FDA) enforces regulations prohibiting the sale and distribution of adulterated, misbranded, or hazardous food and drug products. For example, the FDA outlawed the sale and distribution of most over-the-counter hair-loss remedies after research indicated that few of the products were effective in restoring hair growth.

The Environmental Protection Agency (EPA) develops and enforces environmental protection standards and conducts research into the adverse effects of pollution. The Consumer Product Safety Commission recalls about 300 products a year, ranging from small, inexpensive toys to major appliances. The Consumer Product Safety Commission's Web site provides details regarding current recalls.

## IMPORTANT ELEMENTS OF BUSINESS LAW

To avoid violating criminal and civil laws, as well as discouraging lawsuits from consumers, employees, suppliers, and others, businesspeople need to be familiar with laws that address business practices.

### The Uniform Commercial Code

At one time, states had their own specific laws governing various business practices, and transacting business across state lines was difficult because of the variation in the laws from state to state. To simplify commerce, every state—except Louisiana—has enacted the Uniform Commercial Code (Louisiana has enacted portions of the code). The **Uniform Commercial Code (UCC)** is a set of statutory laws covering several business law topics. Article II of the Uniform Commercial Code, which is discussed in the following paragraphs, has significant impact on business.

**Sales Agreements.** Article II of the Uniform Commercial Code covers sales agreements for goods and services such as installation but does not cover stocks, bonds, or real estate, or personal services. Among its many provisions, Article II stipulates that a sales agreement can be enforced even though it does not specify the selling price or the time or place of delivery. It also requires that a buyer pay a reasonable price for goods at the time of delivery if the buyer and seller have not reached an agreement on price. Specifically, Article II addresses the rights of buyers and sellers, transfers of ownership, warranties, and the legal placement of risk during manufacture and delivery.

Article II also deals with express and implied warranties. An **express warranty** stipulates the specific terms the seller will honor. Many automobile manufacturers, for example, provide three-year or 36,000-mile warranties on their vehicles, during which period they will fix any and all defects specified in the warranty. An **implied warranty** is imposed on the producer or seller by law, although it may not be a written document provided at the time of sale. Under Article II, a consumer may assume that the product for sale has a clear title (in other words, that it is not stolen) and that the product will both serve the purpose for which it was made and sold as well as function as advertised.

## The Law of Torts and Fraud

A **tort** is a private or civil wrong other than breach of contract. For example, a tort can result if the driver of a Domino's Pizza delivery car loses control of the vehicle and damages property or injures a person. In the case of the delivery car accident, the injured persons might sue the driver and the owner of the company—Domino's in this case—for damages resulting from the accident.

**Fraud** is a purposeful unlawful act to deceive or manipulate in order to damage others. Thus, in some cases, a tort may also represent a violation of criminal law. Health care fraud has become a major issue in the courts.

An important aspect of tort law involves **product liability**—businesses' legal responsibility for any negligence in the design, production, sale, and consumption of products. Product liability laws have evolved from both common and statutory law. Some states have expanded the concept of product liability to include injuries by products whether or not the producer is proven negligent. Under this strict product liability, a consumer who files suit because of an injury has to prove only that the product was defective, that the defect caused the injury, and that the defect made the product unreasonably dangerous. For example, a carving knife is expected to be sharp and is not considered defective if you cut your finger using it. But an electric knife could be considered defective and unreasonably dangerous if it continued to operate after being switched off.

Reforming tort law, particularly in regard to product liability, has become a hot political issue as businesses look for relief from huge judgments in lawsuits. Although many lawsuits are warranted—few would disagree that a wrong has occurred when a patient dies because of negligence during a medical procedure or when a child is seriously injured by a defective toy, and that the families deserve some compensation—many suits are not. Because of multimillion-dollar judgments, companies are trying to minimize their liability, and sometimes they pass on the costs of the damage awards to their customers in the form of higher prices. Some states have passed laws limiting damage awards and some tort reform is occurring at the federal level. Table A.2 lists the state courts systems the U.S. Chamber of Commerce's Institute for Legal Reform has identified as

New car buyers receive express warranties stating what is covered for repair or replacement over a specific period of time.

being "friendliest" and "least friendly" to business in terms of juries' fairness, judges' competence and impartiality, and other factors.

## The Law of Contracts

Virtually every business transaction is carried out by means of a **contract,** a mutual agreement between two or more parties that can be enforced in a court if one party chooses not to comply with the terms of the contract. If you rent an apartment or house, for example, your lease is a contract. If you have borrowed money under a student loan program, you have a contractual agreement to repay the money. Many aspects of contract law are covered under the Uniform Commercial Code.

A "handshake deal" is in most cases as fully and completely binding as a written, signed contract agreement. Indeed, many oil-drilling and construction contractors have for years agreed

**TABLE A.2** State Court Systems' Reputations for Supporting Business

| Most Friendly to Business | Least Friendly to Business |
| --- | --- |
| Delaware | Mississippi |
| Nebraska | West Virginia |
| Virginia | Alabama |
| Iowa | Louisiana |
| Idaho | California |
| Utah | Texas |
| New Hampshire | Illinois |
| Minnesota | Montana |
| Kansas | Arkansas |
| Wisconsin | Missouri |

Source: U.S. Chamber of Commerce Institute for Legal Reform, in Martin Kasindorf, "Robin Hood Is Alive in Court, Say Those Seeking Lawsuit Limits," *USA Today,* March 8, 2004, p. 4A.

to take on projects on the basis of such handshake deals. However, individual states require that some contracts be in writing to be enforceable. Most states require that at least some of the following contracts be in writing:

- Contracts involving the sale of land or an interest in land.
- Contracts to pay somebody else's debt.
- Contracts that cannot be fulfilled within one year.
- Contracts for the sale of goods that cost more than $500 (required by the Uniform Commercial Code).

Only those contracts that meet certain requirements—called *elements*—are enforceable by the courts. A person or business seeking to enforce a contract must show that it contains the following elements: voluntary agreement, consideration, contractual capacity of the parties, and legality.

For any agreement to be considered a legal contract, all persons involved must agree to be bound by the terms of the contract. *Voluntary agreement* typically comes about when one party makes an offer and the other accepts. If both the offer and the acceptance are freely, voluntarily, and knowingly made, the acceptance forms the basis for the contract. If, however, either the offer or the acceptance are the result of fraud or force, the individual or organization subject to the fraud or force can void, or invalidate, the resulting agreement or receive compensation for damages.

The second requirement for enforcement of a contract is that it must be supported by *consideration*—that is, money or something of value must be given in return for fulfilling a contract. As a general rule, a person cannot be forced to abide by the terms of a promise unless that person receives a consideration. The something-of-value could be money, goods, services, or even a promise to do or not to do something.

*Contractual capacity* is the legal ability to enter into a contract. As a general rule, a court cannot enforce a contract if either party to the agreement lacks contractual capacity. A person's contractual capacity may be limited or nonexistent if he or she is a minor (under the age of 18), mentally unstable, retarded, insane, or intoxicated.

*Legality* is the state or condition of being lawful. For an otherwise binding contract to be enforceable, both the purpose of and the consideration for the contract must be legal. A contract in which a bank loans money at a rate of interest prohibited by law, a practice known as usury, would be an illegal contract, for example. The fact that one of the parties may commit an illegal act while performing a contract does not render the contract itself illegal, however.

**Breach of contract** is the failure or refusal of a party to a contract to live up to his or her promises. In the case of an apartment lease, failure to pay rent would be considered breach of contract. The breaching party—the one who fails to comply—may be liable for monetary damages that he or she causes the other person.

## The Law of Agency

An **agency** is a common business relationship created when one person acts on behalf of another and under that person's control. Two parties are involved in an agency relationship: The **principal** is the one who wishes to have a specific task accomplished; the **agent** is the one who acts on behalf of the principal to accomplish the task. Authors, movie stars, and athletes often employ agents to help them obtain the best contract terms.

An agency relationship is created by the mutual agreement of the principal and the agent. It is usually not necessary that such an agreement be in writing, although putting it in writing is certainly advisable. An agency relationship continues as long as both the principal and the agent so desire. It can be terminated by mutual agreement, by fulfillment of the purpose of the agency, by the refusal of either party to continue in the relationship, or by the death of either the principal or the agent. In most cases, a principal grants authority to the agent through a formal *power of attorney,* which is a legal document authorizing a person to act as someone else's agent. The power of attorney can be used for any agency relationship, and its use is not limited to lawyers. For instance, in real estate transactions, often a lawyer or real estate agent is given power of attorney with the authority to purchase real estate for the buyer. Accounting firms often give employees agency relationships in making financial transactions.

> **An agency is a common business relationship created when one person acts on behalf of another and under that person's control.**

Both officers and directors of corporations are fiduciaries, or people of trust, who use due care and loyalty as an agent in making decisions on behalf of the organization. This relationship creates a duty of care, also called duty of diligence, to make informed decisions. These agents of the corporation are not held responsible for negative outcomes if they are informed and diligent in their decisions. The duty of loyalty means that all decisions should be in the interests of the corporation and its stakeholders. Scandals at Enron, Tyco, and WorldCom are associated with officers and directors who failed to carry out their fiduciary duties. Lawsuits from shareholders called for the officers and directors to pay large sums of money from their own pockets.

## The Law of Property

Property law is extremely broad in scope because it covers the ownership and transfer of all kinds of real, personal, and intellectual property. **Real property** consists of real estate and everything permanently attached to it; **personal property** basically is everything else. Personal property can be further subdivided into tangible and intangible property. *Tangible property* refers to items that have a physical existence, such as automobiles, business inventory, and clothing. *Intangible property* consists of rights and duties; its existence may be represented by a document or by some other tangible item. For example, accounts receivable, stock in a corporation, goodwill, and trademarks are all examples of intangible personal property. **Intellectual property** refers to property, such as musical works, artwork, books, and computer software, that is generated by a person's creative activities.

Copyrights, patents, and trademarks provide protection to the owners of property by giving them the exclusive right to use it. *Copyrights* protect the ownership rights on material (often intellectual property) such as books, music, videos, photos, and computer software. The creators of such works, or their heirs, generally have exclusive rights to the published or unpublished works for the creator's lifetime, plus 50 years. *Patents* give inventors exclusive rights to their invention for 17 years. The most intense competition for patents is in the pharmaceutical industry. Most patents take a minimum of 18 months to secure.

A *trademark* is a brand (name, mark, or symbol) that is registered with the U.S. Patent and Trademark Office and is thus legally protected from use by any other firm. Among the symbols that have been so protected are McDonald's golden arches and Coca-Cola's distinctive bottle shape. It is estimated that large multinational firms may have as many as 15,000 conflicts related to trademarks. Companies are diligent about protecting their trademarks both to avoid confusion in consumers' minds and because a term that becomes part of everyday language can no longer be trademarked. The names *aspirin* and *nylon,* for example, were once the exclusive property of their creators but became so widely used as product names (rather than brand names) that now anyone can use them.

As the trend toward globalization of trade continues, and more and more businesses trade across national boundaries, protecting property rights, particularly intellectual property such as computer software, has become an increasing challenge. While a company may be able to register as a trademark a brand name or symbol in its home country, it may not be able to secure that protection abroad. Some countries have copyright and patent laws that are less strict than those of the United States; some countries will not enforce U.S. laws. China, for example, has often been criticized for permitting U.S. goods to be counterfeited there. Such counterfeiting harms not only the sales of U.S. companies but also their reputations if the knockoffs are of poor quality. Thus, businesses engaging in foreign trade may have to take extra steps to protect their property because local laws may be insufficient to protect them.

## The Law of Bankruptcy

Although few businesses and individuals intentionally fail to repay (or default on) their debts, sometimes they cannot fulfill their financial obligations. Individuals may charge goods and services beyond their ability to pay for them. Businesses may take on too much debt in order to finance growth or business events such as an increase in the cost of commodities can bankrupt a company. An option of last resort in these cases is bankruptcy, or legal insolvency. Major airlines such as United, Northwest, and Delta filed for chapter 11 bankruptcy in the last few years due to increases in fuel costs and intense competition that kept prices low.

Individuals or companies may ask a bankruptcy court to declare them unable to pay their debts and thus release them from the obligation of repaying those debts. The debtor's assets may then be sold to pay off as much of the debt as possible. In the case of a personal bankruptcy, although the individual is released from repaying debts and can start over with a clean slate, obtaining credit after bankruptcy proceedings is very difficult. About 2 million households in the United States filed for bankruptcy in 2005, the most ever. However, a new, more restrictive law went into effect in late 2005, and fewer consumers are using bankruptcy to eliminate their debts. The law makes it harder for consumers to prove that they should be allowed to clear their debts for what is called a "fresh start" or Chapter 7 bankruptcy. Although the person or company in debt usually initiates bankruptcy proceedings, creditors may also initiate them. Table A.3 describes the various levels of bankruptcy protection a business or individual may seek.

**TABLE A.3**  Types of Bankruptcy

| | |
|---|---|
| Chapter 7 | Requires that the business be dissolved and its assets liquidated, or sold, to pay off the debts. Individuals declaring Chapter 7 retain a limited amount of exempt assets, the amount of which may be determined by state or federal law, at the debtor's option. Although the type and value of exempt assets varies from state to state, most states' laws allow a bankrupt individual to keep an automobile, some household goods, clothing, furnishings, and at least some of the value of the debtor's residence. All nonexempt assets must be sold to pay debts. |
| Chapter 11 | Temporarily frees a business from its financial obligations while it reorganizes and works out a payment plan with its creditors. The indebted company continues to operate its business during bankruptcy proceedings. Often, the business sells off assets and less-profitable subsidiaries to raise cash to pay off its immediate obligations. |
| Chapter 13 | Similar to Chapter 11 but limited to individuals. This proceeding allows an individual to establish a three- to five-year plan for repaying his or her debt. Under this plan, an individual ultimately may repay as little as 10 percent of his or her debt. |

# LAWS AFFECTING BUSINESS PRACTICES

One of the government's many roles is to act as a watchdog to ensure that businesses behave in accordance with the wishes of society. Congress has enacted a number of laws that affect business practices; some of the most important of these are summarized in Table A.4. Many state legislatures have enacted similar laws governing business within specific states.

The **Sherman Antitrust Act,** passed in 1890 to prevent businesses from restraining trade and monopolizing markets, condemns "every contract, combination, or conspiracy in restraint of trade." For example, a request that a competitor agree to fix prices or divide markets would, if accepted, result in a violation of the Sherman Act. Proof of intent plays an important role in attempted monopolization cases under the Sherman Act. Enforced by the Antitrust Division of the Department of Justice, the Sherman Antitrust Act applies

**TABLE A.4**   Major Federal Laws Affecting Business Practices

| Act (Date Enacted) | Purpose |
| --- | --- |
| Sherman Antitrust Act (1890) | Prohibits contracts, combinations, or conspiracies to restrain trade; establishes as a misdemeanor monopolizing or attempting to monopolize. |
| Clayton Act (1914) | Prohibits specific practices such as price discrimination, exclusive dealer arrangements, and stock acquisitions in which the effect may notably lessen competition or tend to create a monopoly. |
| Federal Trade Commission Act (1914) | Created the Federal Trade Commission; also gives the FTC investigatory powers to be used in preventing unfair methods of competition. |
| Robinson-Patman Act (1936) | Prohibits price discrimination that lessens competition among wholesalers or retailers; prohibits producers from giving disproportionate services or facilities to large buyers. |
| Wheeler-Lea Act (1938) | Prohibits unfair and deceptive acts and practices regardless of whether competition is injured; places advertising of foods and drugs under the jurisdiction of the FTC. |
| Lanham Act (1946) | Provides protections and regulation of brand names, brand marks, trade names, and trademarks. |
| Celler-Kefauver Act (1950) | Prohibits any corporation engaged in commerce from acquiring the whole or any part of the stock or other share of the capital assets of another corporation when the effect substantially lessens competition or tends to create a monopoly. |
| Fair Packaging and Labeling Act (1966) | Makes illegal the unfair or deceptive packaging or labeling of consumer products. |
| Magnuson-Moss Warranty (FTC) Act (1975) | Provides for minimum disclosure standards for written consumer product warranties; defines minimum consent standards for written warranties; allows the FTC to prescribe interpretive rules in policy statements regarding unfair or deceptive practices. |
| Consumer Goods Pricing Act (1975) | Prohibits the use of price maintenance agreements among manufacturers and resellers in interstate commerce. |
| Antitrust Improvements Act (1976) | Requires large corporations to inform federal regulators of prospective mergers or acquisitions so that they can be studied for any possible violations of the law. |
| Trademark Counterfeiting Act (1980) | Provides civil and criminal penalties against those who deal in counterfeit consumer goods or any counterfeit goods that can threaten health or safety. |
| Trademark Law Revision Act (1988) | Amends the Lanham Act to allow brands not yet introduced to be protected through registration with the Patent and Trademark Office. |
| Nutrition Labeling and Education Act (1990) | Prohibits exaggerated health claims and requires all processed foods to contain labels with nutritional information. |
| Telephone Consumer Protection Act (1991) | Establishes procedures to avoid unwanted telephone solicitations; prohibits marketers from using automated telephone dialing system or an artificial or prerecorded voice to certain telephone lines. |
| Federal Trademark Dilution Act (1995) | Provides trademark owners the right to protect trademarks and requires relinquishment of names that match or parallel existing trademarks. |
| Digital Millennium Copyright Act (1998) | Refined copyright laws to protect digital versions of copyrighted materials, including music and movies. |
| Children's Online Privacy Protection Act (2000) | Regulates the collection of personally identifiable information (name, address, e-mail address, hobbies, interests, or information collected through cookies) online from children under age 13. |
| Sarbanes-Oxley Act (2002) | Made securities fraud a criminal offense; stiffened penalties for corporate fraud; created an accounting oversight board; and instituted numerous other provisions designed to increase corporate transparency and compliance. |
| Do Not Call Implementation Act (2003) | Directs FCC and FTC to coordinate so their rules are consistent regarding telemarketing call practices, including the Do Not Call Registry. |

to firms operating in interstate commerce and to U.S. firms operating in foreign commerce. The Sherman Antitrust Act, still highly relevant 100 years after its passage, is being copied throughout the world as the basis for regulating fair competition.

Because the provisions of the Sherman Antitrust Act are rather vague, courts have not always interpreted it as its creators intended. The Clayton Act was passed in 1914 to limit specific activities that can reduce competition. The **Clayton Act** prohibits price discrimination, tying and exclusive agreements, and the acquisition of stock in another corporation where the effect may be to substantially lessen competition or tend to create a monopoly. In addition, the Clayton Act prohibits members of one company's board of directors from holding seats on the boards of competing corporations. The act also exempts farm cooperatives and labor organizations from antitrust laws.

In spite of these laws regulating business practices, there are still many questions about the regulation of business. For instance, it is difficult to determine what constitutes an acceptable degree of competition and whether a monopoly is harmful to a particular market. Many mergers were permitted in the 1990s that resulted in less competition in the banking, publishing, and automobile industries. In some industries, such as utilities, it is not cost effective to have too many competitors. For this reason, the government permits utility monopolies, although recently, the telephone, electricity, and communications industries have been deregulated. Furthermore, the antitrust laws are often rather vague and require interpretation, which may vary from judge to judge and court to court. Thus, what one judge defines as a monopoly or trust today may be permitted by another judge a few years from now. Businesspeople need to understand what the law says on these issues and try to conduct their affairs within the bounds of these laws.

## THE INTERNET: LEGAL AND REGULATORY ISSUES

Our use and dependence on the Internet is increasingly creating a potential legal problem for businesses. With this growing use come questions of maintaining an acceptable level of privacy for consumers and proper competitive use of the medium. Some might consider that tracking individuals who visit or "hit" their Web site by attaching a "cookie" (identifying

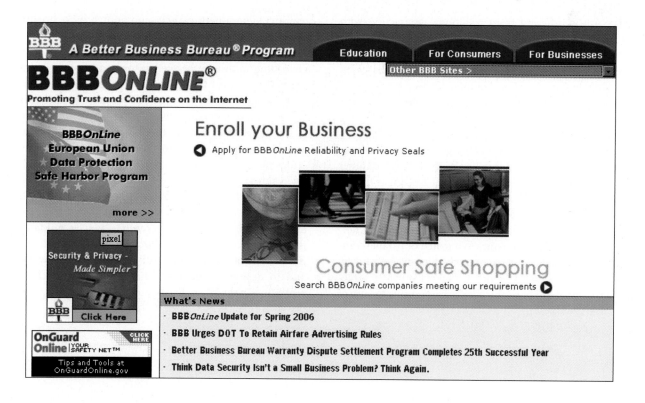

you as a Web site visitor for potential recontact and tracking your movement throughout the site) is an improper use of the Internet for business purposes. Others may find such practices acceptable and similar to the practices of non-Internet retailers who copy information from checks or ask customers for their name, address, or phone number before they will process a transaction. There are few specific laws that regulate business on the Internet, but the standards for acceptable behavior that are reflected in the basic laws and regulations designed for traditional businesses can be applied to business on the Internet as well.

The central focus for future legislation of business conducted on the Internet is the protection of personal privacy. The present basis of personal privacy protection is the U.S. Constitution, various Supreme Court rulings, and laws such as the 1971 Fair Credit Reporting Act, the 1978 Right to Financial Privacy Act, and the 1974 Privacy Act, which deals with the release of government records. With few regulations on the use of information by businesses, companies legally buy and sell information on customers to gain competitive advantage. It has been suggested that the treatment of personal data as property will ensure privacy rights by recognizing that customers have a right to control the use of their personal data.

trademark-protected entities, and requires the relinquishment of names that match or closely parallel company trademarks. The reduction of geographic barriers, speed of response, and memory capability of the Internet will continue to create new challenges for the legal and regulatory environment in the future.

## LEGAL PRESSURE FOR RESPONSIBLE BUSINESS CONDUCT

To ensure greater compliance with society's desires, both federal and state governments are moving toward increased organizational accountability for misconduct. Before 1991, laws mainly punished those employees directly responsible for an offense. Under new guidelines established by the Federal Sentencing Guidelines for Organizations (FSGO), however, both the responsible employees and the firms that employ them are held accountable for violations of federal law. Thus, the government now places responsibility for controlling and preventing misconduct squarely on the shoulders of top management. The main objectives of the federal guidelines are to train employees, self-monitor and supervise employee

> ## "Internet has also created a copyright dilemma for some organizations"

Internet use is different from traditional interaction with businesses in that it is readily accessible, and most online businesses are able to develop databases of information on customers. Congress has restricted the development of databases on children using the Internet. The Children's Online Privacy Protection Act of 2000 prohibits Web sites and Internet providers from seeking personal information from children under age 13 without parental consent.

The Internet has also created a copyright dilemma for some organizations that have found that the Web addresses of other online firms either match or are very similar to their company trademark. "Cybersquatters" attempt to sell back the registration of these matching sites to the trademark owner. Companies such as Taco Bell, MTC, and KFC have paid thousands of dollars to gain control of domain names that match or parallel company trademarks. The Federal Trademark Dilution Act of 1995 helps companies address this conflict. The act provides trademark owners the right to protect trademarks, prevents the use of

conduct, deter unethical acts, and punish those organizational members who engage in illegal acts.

A 2004 amendment to the FSGO requires that a business's governing authority be well informed about its ethics program with respect to content, implementation, and effectiveness. This places the responsibility squarely on the shoulders of the firm's leadership, usually the board of directors. The board must ensure that there is a high-ranking manager accountable for the day-to-day operational oversight of the ethics program. The board must provide for adequate authority, resources, and access to the board or an appropriate subcommittee of the board. The board must ensure that there are confidential mechanisms available so that the organization's employees and agents may report or seek guidance about potential or actual misconduct without fear of retaliation. Finally, the board is required to oversee the discovery of risks and to design, implement, and modify approaches to deal with those risks.

# DESTINATION CEO

## Michael Critelli—Pitney Bowes

**Summary:** Pitney Bowes touches our lives in significant ways every day. The company is the primary provider of postal equipment in the world. In fact, more than 10 billion pieces of mail are processed on Pitney Bowes equipment each year.

Michael Critelli has been the CEO of the company since 1996. He started out as a dishwasher in a family bakery business in Rochester, New York, in the 1960s. From these humble beginnings, he went on to major in communications and earned a law degree. His educational background in communications has helped in every facet of his professional career from his trial lawyer experiences through his position as CEO.

Critielli was selected as CEO, he feels, based on his ability to be flexible and sensitive to the needs of regulators and politicians and to the overall complexity of the regulatory environment in which the core mail business of the company is situated. Pitney Bowes, under Critelli, has excelled in their core mail-processing business and has expanded the reach of the company to a variety of other areas. These include personalized postal products, a broader Web presence, partnerships with e-Bay, and retailing kiosks for postal products. Critelli notes that they are in businesses today that were unimaginable five years ago.

The complexity and rapidly changing legal, regulatory, and political environment characterizes the context of the operations of Pitney Bowes. The company has been responsive to stakeholders, including customers, and it shows in its performance. Revenue for the last consecutive 19 quarters has been up.

## >> DISCUSSION QUESTIONS

1. How did Michael Critelli's undergraduate education prepare him for his current position as CEO?

2. What are the essential characteristics of the legal and regulatory environment in which Pitney Bowes operates?

3. What is the core business of Pitney Bowes? What other related businesses have they developed under Critelli's leadership?

>>To see the complete video about Michael Critelli, go to our Web site at **www.mhhe.com/FerrellM** and look for the link to the Destination CEO videos.

**TABLE A.5**  Seven Steps to Compliance

1. Develop standards and procedures to reduce the propensity for criminal conduct.
2. Designate a high-level compliance manager or ethics officer to oversee the compliance program.
3. Avoid delegating authority to people known to have a propensity to engage in misconduct.
4. Communicate standards and procedures to employees, other agents, and independent contractors through training programs and publications.
5. Establish systems to monitor and audit misconduct and to allow employees and agents to report criminal activity.
6. Enforce standards and punishments consistently across all employees in the organization.
7. Respond immediately to misconduct and take reasonable steps to prevent further criminal conduct.

Source: United States Sentencing Commission, *Federal Sentencing Guidelines for Organizations,* 1991.

If an organization's culture and policies reward or provide opportunities to engage in misconduct through lack of managerial concern or failure to comply with the seven minimum requirements of the FSGO (provided in Table A.5), then the organization may incur not only penalties but also the loss of customer trust, public confidence, and other intangible assets. For this reason, organizations cannot succeed solely through a legalistic approach to compliance with the sentencing guidelines; top management must cultivate high ethical standards that will serve as barriers to illegal conduct. The organization must want to be a good citizen and recognize the importance of compliance to successful workplace activities and relationships.

The federal guidelines also require businesses to develop programs that can detect—and that will deter employees from engaging in—misconduct. To be considered effective, such compliance programs must include disclosure of any wrongdoing, cooperation with the government, and acceptance of responsibility for the misconduct. Codes of ethics, employee ethics training, hotlines (direct 800 phone numbers), compliance directors, newsletters, brochures, and other communication methods are typical components of a compliance program. The ethics component, discussed in Chapter 2, acts as a buffer, keeping firms away from the thin line that separates unethical and illegal conduct.

Despite the existing legislation, a number of ethics scandals in the early 2000s led Congress to pass—almost unanimously—the **Sarbanes-Oxley Act,** which criminalized securities fraud

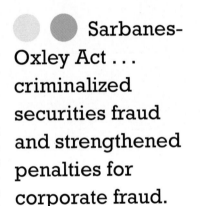 **Sarbanes-Oxley Act ... criminalized securities fraud and strengthened penalties for corporate fraud.**

and strengthened penalties for corporate fraud. It also created an accounting oversight board that requires corporations to establish codes of ethics for financial reporting and to develop greater transparency in financial reports to investors and other interested parties. Additionally, the law requires top corporate executives to sign off on their firms' financial reports, and they risk fines and jail sentences if they misrepresent their companies' financial position. Table A.6 summarizes the major provisions of the Sarbanes-Oxley Act.

The Sarbanes-Oxley Act has created a number of concerns and is considered burdensome and expensive to corporations. Large corporations report spending more than $4 million each year to comply with the Act according to Financial Executives International. The Act has caused more than 500 public companies a year to report problems in their accounting systems. More than 1,000 businesspersons have been convicted of corporate crimes since the law was passed in 2002. This means that the overwhelming majority of businesses are in compliance with the law.

On the other hand, there are many benefits, including greater accountability of top managers and boards of directors, that improve investor confidence and protect employees, especially their retirement plans. It is believed that the law has more benefits than drawbacks—with the greatest benefit being that boards of directors and top managers are better informed. Some companies such as Cisco and Pitney Bowes report improved efficiency and cost savings from better financial information. ∎

**TABLE A.6**  Major Provisions of the Sarbanes-Oxley Act

1. Requires the establishment of a Public Company Accounting Oversight Board in charge of regulations administered by the Securities and Exchange Commission.

2. Requires CEOs and CFOs to certify that their companies' financial statements are true and without misleading statements.

3. Requires that corporate boards of directors' audit committees consist of independent members who have no material interests in the company.

4. Prohibits corporations from making or offering loans to officers and board members.

5. Requires codes of ethics for senior financial officers; code must be registered with the SEC.

6. Prohibits accounting firms from providing both auditing and consulting services to the same client without the approval of the client firm's audit committee.

7. Requires company attorneys to report wrongdoing to top managers and, if necessary, to the board of directors; if managers and directors fail to respond to reports of wrongdoing, the attorney should stop representing the company.

8. Mandates "whistleblower protection" for persons who disclose wrongdoing to authorities.

9. Requires financial securities analysts to certify that their recommendations are based on objective reports.

10. Requires mutual fund managers to disclose how they vote shareholder proxies, giving investors information about how their shares influence decisions.

11. Establishes a 10-year penalty for mail/wire fraud.

12. Prohibits the two senior auditors from working on a corporation's account for more than five years; other auditors are prohibited from working on an account for more than seven years. In other words, accounting firms must rotate individual auditors from one account to another from time to time.

Source: O. C. Ferrell, John Fraedrich, and Linda Ferrell, *Business Ethics: Ethical Decision Making and Cases,* 6th ed. (Boston: Houghton Mifflin, 2005), p. 63.

**LO1** Explore some of the factors within the international trade environment that influence business.

**LO2** Investigate some of the economic, legal-political, social, cultural, and technological barriers to international business.

**LO3** Specify some of the agreements, alliances, and organizations that may encourage trade across international boundaries.

**LO4** Summarize the different levels of organizational involvement in international trade.

**LO5** Contrast two basic strategies used in international business.

# business in a borderless world

## 3

**introduction** Consumers around the world can drink Coca-Cola and Pepsi; eat at McDonald's and Pizza Hut; see movies from Mexico, England, France, Australia, and China; and watch CNN and MTV on Toshiba and Sony televisions. The products you consume today are just as likely to have been made in China, Korea, or Germany as in the United States. Likewise, consumers in other countries buy Western electrical equipment, clothing, rock music, cosmetics, and toiletries, as well as computers, robots, and earth-moving equipment.

Many U.S. firms are finding that international markets provide tremendous opportunities for growth. Accessing these markets can promote innovation, while intensifying global competition spurs companies to market better and less expensive products. Today, the 6.5 billion people that inhibit the earth create one tremendous marketplace.

In this chapter, we explore business in this exciting global marketplace. First, we'll look at the nature of international business, including barriers and promoters of trade across international boundaries. Next, we consider the levels of organizational involvement in international business. Finally, we briefly discuss strategies for trading across national borders.

Mexico, the sale affects the economies of the countries involved. To begin our study of international business, we must first consider some economic issues: why nations trade, exporting and importing, and the balance of trade.

## Why Nations Trade

Nations and businesses engage in international trade to obtain raw materials and goods that are otherwise unavailable to them or are available elsewhere at a lower price than that at which they themselves can produce. A nation, or individuals and organizations from a nation, sell surplus materials and goods to acquire funds to buy the goods, services, and ideas its people need. Poland and Hungary, for example, want to trade with Western nations so that they can acquire new technology and techniques to revitalize their formerly communist economies. Which goods and services a nation sells depends on what resources it has available.

Some nations have a monopoly on the production of a particular resource or product. Such a monopoly, or **absolute advantage,** exists when a country is the only source of an item, the only producer of an item, or the most efficient producer of an item. Because South Africa has the largest deposits of diamonds in the world, one company, De Beers Consolidated Mines, Ltd., controls a major portion of the world's diamond trade and uses its control to maintain high prices for gem-quality diamonds. The United States, until recently, held an absolute advantage in oil-drilling equipment. But an absolute advantage not based on the availability of natural resources rarely lasts, and Japan and Russia are now challenging the United States in the production of oil-drilling equipment.

Most international trade is based on **comparative advantage,** which occurs when a country specializes in products that it can supply more efficiently or at a lower cost than it can produce other items. The United States has a

## ●● LO1

Explore some of the factors within the international trade environment that influence business.

# THE ROLE OF INTERNATIONAL BUSINESS

**International business** refers to the buying, selling, and trading of goods and services across national boundaries. Falling political barriers and new technology are making it possible for more and more companies to sell their products overseas as well as at home. And, as differences among nations continue to narrow, the trend toward the globalization of business is becoming increasingly important. Starbucks, for example, serves 20 million customers a week at more than 11,000 coffee shops in 36 countries.[2] Amazon.com, an online retailer, has distribution centers from Nevada to Germany that fill millions of orders a day and ship them to customers in every corner of the world. In China, Procter & Gamble has developed bargain-priced versions of Tide, Crest, and Oil of Olay, and it regularly relies on groups that live in the countryside for consumer information.[3] Indeed, most of the world's population and two-thirds of its total purchasing power are outside the United States.

**DID YOU KNOW?**

McDonald's serves 46 million customers a day at 31,000 restaurants in 119 countries.[1]

> ## Falling political barriers and new technology are making it possible for more and more companies to sell their products overseas as well as at home.

When McDonald's sells a Big Mac in Moscow, Sony sells a stereo in Detroit, or a small Swiss medical supply company sells a shipment of orthopedic devices to a hospital in Monterrey,

comparative advantage in producing agricultural commodities such as corn and wheat. Until recently, the United States had a comparative advantage in manufacturing automobiles, heavy machinery, airplanes, and weapons; other countries now hold the comparative advantage for many of these products. Other countries, particularly India and Ireland, are also gaining a comparative advantage over the United States in the provision of some services, such as call-center operations, engineering, and software programming. As a result, U.S. companies are increasingly **outsourcing,** or transferring manufacturing and other tasks to countries where labor and supplies are less expensive. Outsourcing has become a controversial practice in the United States because many jobs have moved overseas where those tasks can be accomplished for lower costs. For example, India is a popular choice for call centers for U.S. firms. As call centers are the first

● **OUTSOURCING** the transferring of manufacturing or other tasks—such as data processing—to countries where labor and supplies are less expensive

● **EXPORTING** the sale of goods and services to foreign markets

● **IMPORTING** the purchase of goods and services from foreign sources

goods and services, particularly agricultural, entertainment (movies, television shows, etc.), and technological products. **Importing** is the purchase of goods and services from foreign sources. Many of the goods you buy in the United States are likely to be imports or to have some imported components. Sometimes, you may not even realize they are imports. The United States imported more than *$2.2 trillion* in goods and services last year.[7]

# "Outsourcing has become a controversial practice in the United States"

job choice for millions of young Indians, employers are getting choosier about the people they hire, and it is difficult to train Indians to speak the kind of colloquial English, French, Spanish, German, or Dutch that customers want, although there are estimates that by 2010 more than 160,000 workers with excellent English and foreign-language skills will be needed. Many foreigners are beginning to see India and the call-center jobs as a way to travel the world. They typically earn about $350 a month and work the phones for six months or a year before chilling on the beaches of Goa or trekking the Himalayas. There are more than 30,000 foreigners working at Indian info tech and outsourcing companies, which is triple the number of two years ago.[4]

## Trade between Countries

To obtain needed goods and services and the funds to pay for them, nations trade by exporting and importing. **Exporting** is the sale of goods and services to foreign markets. The United States exported more than *$1.4 trillion in goods* and services last year.[5] In China, General Motors is targeting wealthier customers with the Cadillac, middle management with the Buick Excelle, office workers with the Chevrolet Spark, and rural consumers with the Wuling minivan.[6] U.S. businesses export many

## Balance of Trade

You have probably read or heard about the fact that the United States has a trade deficit, but what is a trade deficit? A nation's

*Because of saturation of the U.S. market, many businesses that seek additional growth are looking beyond U.S. borders for potential new customers and worldwide sales. This Starbucks in Tokyo was its first to open overseas. What other relatively "new" companies do you think would benefit by capturing international markets?*

**BALANCE OF TRADE** the difference in value between a nation's exports and its imports

**TRADE DEFICIT** a nation's negative balance of trade, which exists when that country imports more products than it exports

**BALANCE OF PAYMENTS** the difference between the flow of money into and out of a country

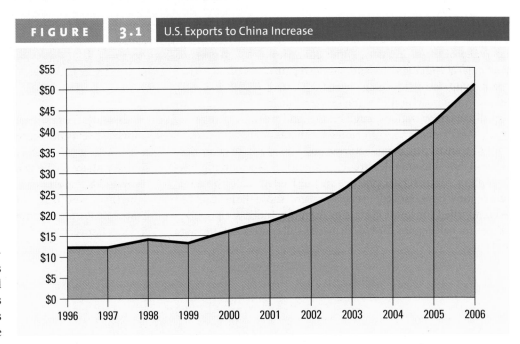

| FIGURE | 3.1 | U.S. Exports to China Increase |

Sources: David J. Lynch, "Building Explosion in China Pumps Up Exports from USA," *USA Today,* April 20, 2006. p. B1.s; "U.S. Domestic Exports for Selected World Areas and the Top Ten Countries- 2006," *U.S. Census Bureau, Foreign Trade Statistics* (n.d.), http://www.census.gov/foreign-trade/Press-Release/2006pr/aip/related_party/ (accessed June 7, 2007).

balance of trade is the difference in value between its exports and imports. Because the United States (and some other nations as well) imports more products than it exports, it has a negative balance of trade, or trade deficit. In 2006 the United States had a $763 billion trade deficit, an 65 percent increase over 2004. China accounted for most of this deficit increase. Total U.S. imports reached $2.2 trillion in 2006, 56 percent more than the $1.4 trillion in exports (see Table 3.1).[8] The trade deficit fluctuates according to such factors as the health of the United States and other economies, productivity, perceived quality, and exchange rates. In 2006 the U.S. had a $232.5 billion deficit with China. As Figure 3.1 indicates, U.S. exports to China have been rapidly increasing but not fast enough to offset the imports from China. Trade deficits are harmful because they can mean the failure of businesses, the loss of jobs, and a lowered standard of living.

Of course, when a nation exports more goods than it imports, it has a favorable balance of trade, or trade surplus. Until about 1970, the United States had a trade surplus due to an abundance of natural resources and the relative efficiency of its manufacturing systems. Table 3.2 shows the top 10 countries with which the United States has a trade deficit and a trade surplus.

The difference between the flow of money into and out of a country is called its balance of payments. A country's balance of trade, foreign investments, foreign aid, loans, military expenditures, and money spent by tourists comprise its balance of payments. As you might expect, a country with a trade surplus generally has a favorable balance of payments because it is receiving more money from trade with foreign countries than it is paying out. When a country has a trade deficit, more

**TABLE 3.2** Top 10 Countries Maintaining Trade Deficits/Surpluses with the United States

| Trade Deficit | Trade Surplus |
| --- | --- |
| 1. China | Netherlands |
| 2. Japan | Hong Kong |
| 3. Mexico | United Arab Emirates |
| 4. Canada | Australia |
| 5. Germany | Singapore |
| 6. Nigeria | Belgium |
| 7. Venezuela | United Kingdom |
| 8. Ireland | Panama |
| 9. Italy | Greece |
| 10. Malaysia | Turkey |

Source: "Top Ten Countries with Which the U.S. has a Trade Deficit." www.census.gov/foreign-trade/top/dst/current/deficit.html (accessed June 7, 2007); "Top Ten Countries with Which the U.S. has a Trade Surplus." www.census.gov/foreign-trade/top/dst/current/surplus.html (accessed June 7, 2007).

**TABLE 3.1** U.S. Trade Deficit, 1980–2006 (in billions of dollars)

| | 1980 | 1990 | 2000 | 2006 |
| --- | --- | --- | --- | --- |
| Exports | $333 | $576 | $1,133 | $1,437.8 |
| Imports | 326 | 632 | 1,532 | 2,201.4 |
| Trade Surplus/Deficit | 7 | −57 | −399 | −763.6 |

Sources: Department of Commerce and Robert E. Scott and David Ratner, "Trade Picture," The Economic Policy Institute, February 10, 2006, http://www.epinet.org/content.cfm/webfeatures_econindicators_tradepich20060210 (accessed June 5, 2006); "2006 Annual Trade Highlights, Dollar Change from Prior Year," *U.S. Census Bureau, Foreign Trade Statistics* (n.d.), http://www.census.gov/foreign-trade/statistics/highlights/annual.html (accessed June 7, 2007).

money flows out of the country than into it. If more money flows out of the country than into it from tourism and other sources, the country may experience declining production and higher unemployment, because there is less money available for spending.

## ●● LO2

Investigate some of the economic, legal-political, social, cultural, and technological barriers to international business.

# INTERNATIONAL TRADE BARRIERS

Completely free trade seldom exists. When a company decides to do business outside its own country, it will encounter a number of barriers to international trade. Any firm considering international business must research the other country's economic, legal, political, social, cultural, and technological background. Such research will help the company choose an appropriate level of involvement and operating strategies, as we will see later in this chapter.

hard-wired telephone systems. Consequently, opportunities for growth in the cell phone market remain strong in Southeast Asia, Africa, and the Middle East. Haier, China's top appliance maker, makes larger washing machines for Chinese cities, but has also developed a smaller model costing just $37 for poorer areas.[9]

A country's level of development is determined in part by its **infrastructure,** the physical facilities that support its economic activities, such as railroads, highways, ports, airfields, utilities and power plants, schools, hospitals, communication systems, and commercial distribution systems. When doing business in LDCs, for example, a business may need to compensate for rudimentary distribution and communication systems, or even a lack of technology.

**exchange rates.**  The ratio at which one nation's currency can be exchanged for another nation's currency is the **exchange rate.** Exchange rates vary daily and can be found

## "Devaluation decreases the value of currency in relation to other currencies."

## Economic Barriers

When looking at doing business in another country, managers must consider a number of basic economic factors, such as economic development, infrastructure, and exchange rates.

**economic development.**  When considering doing business abroad, U.S. businesspeople need to recognize that they cannot take for granted that other countries offer the same things as are found in *industrialized nations*—economically advanced countries such as the United States, Japan, Great Britain, and Canada. Many countries in Africa, Asia, and South America, for example, are in general poorer and less economically advanced than those in North America and Europe; they are often called *less-developed countries* (LDCs). LDCs are characterized by low per-capita income (income generated by the nation's production of goods and services divided by the population), which means that consumers are less likely to purchase nonessential products. Nonetheless, LDCs represent a potentially huge and profitable market for many businesses because they may be buying technology to improve their infrastructures, and much of the population may desire consumer products. For example, cellular and wireless phone technology is reaching many countries at less expense than traditional

in newspapers and through many sites on the Internet. Familiarity with exchange rates is important because they affect the cost of imports and exports.

Occasionally, a government may alter the value of its national currency. Devaluation decreases the value of currency in relation to other currencies. If the U.S. government were to devalue the dollar, it would lower the cost of American goods abroad and make trips to the United States less expensive for foreign tourists. Thus, devaluation encourages the sale of domestic goods and tourism. Mexico has repeatedly devalued the peso for this reason. Revaluation, which increases the value of a currency in relation to other currencies, occurs rarely.

## Legal and Political Barriers

A company that decides to enter the international marketplace must contend with potentially complex relationships among the different laws of its own nation, international laws, and the laws of the nation with which it will be trading; various trade restrictions imposed on international trade; and changing political climates. Many companies provide assistance in this area. MyCustoms.com helps companies comply with local trade rules, and NextLinx Corp. provides business advice about international commerce laws.[10]

CMAR0297  Brazil: Avon lady delivers Avon products to Amazon region jungle in a canoe. May 1994 #3767 ©John Maier, Jr. / The Image Works

*Because the transportation infrastructure is inadequate in the Amazon jungle in Brazil, Avon products are sometimes delivered by canoe.*

**laws and regulations.** The United States has a number of laws and regulations that govern the activities of U.S. firms engaged in international trade. For example, the Webb-Pomerene Export Trade Act of 1918 exempts American firms from antitrust laws if those firms are acting together to enter international trade. This law allows selected U.S. firms to form monopolies to compete with foreign monopolistic organizations, although they are not allowed to limit free trade and competition within the United States or to use unfair methods of competition in international trade. The United States also has a variety of friendship, commerce, and navigation treaties with other nations. These treaties allow business to be transacted between citizens of the specified countries.

Once outside U.S. borders, businesspeople are likely to find that the laws of other nations differ from those of the United States. Many of the legal rights that Americans take for granted do not exist in other countries, and a firm doing business abroad must understand and obey the laws of the host country. Many countries forbid foreigners from owning real property outright; others have strict laws limiting the amount of local currency that can be taken out of the country and the amount of foreign currency that can be brought in.

Some countries have copyright and patent laws that are less strict than those of the United States, and some countries fail

## Mexican Coke Is a Legal Alien

Mexican Coke, different in formulation from American Coke, is rapidly gaining U.S. popularity due to both the growing number of Mexican immigrants living in the United States and the interest of soda connoisseurs. In the 1980s, U.S. bottlers of Coke began using high-fructose corn syrup to sweeten the soda as a cost-cutting measure. The Mexican version is still sweetened with the original cane sugar. Those who have tasted both versions notice a distinct difference, although the Coca-Cola Company insists there is no real discrepancy between the two formulas. Fans of Mexican Coke note a cleaner taste and a longer lasting fizz. Mexican Coke still comes in the old-fashioned glass bottles. But perhaps the most important reason many Mexican immigrants buy Mexican Coke is that the taste reminds them of home.

Erik Carvallo, owner of the Latino supermarket Las Tarascas in Lawrenceville, Georgia, repeatedly sells 20 cases of Mexican Coke per week—almost always leaving his shelf bare—while the American version collects dust. Mexican Coke sells for about $1.25 per 12-ounce bottle. In many places, a 20-ounce bottle of American Coke sells for around $1, but Mexican Coke devotees are willing to pay the price to drink what they call "the real thing."

As the market for Mexican Coke grows, the Coca-Cola Company is looking into how to block its arrival in the U.S. market. Coca-Cola sets up distribution in terms of territories. American bottlers do not profit from the sale of imported Coke, which is bottled by independent Mexican companies and brought across the border by third-party distributors and retailers. Although Coke appears concerned about violating bottling territorial rights, some suspect that the company's concern lies in the fact that Americans might begin to demand a formula that costs more to produce. Many American bottling companies are not as concerned, feeling that it has little impact on their profits. Importing Mexican Coke is perfectly legal, but the fact that the Coca-Cola Company may produce a superior product in another country could have a negative impact on its U.S. market.

Although the Coca-Cola Company frowns on the importation of Mexican Coke to the United States, it is pleased by Coke's popularity in Mexico. It is estimated that, on average, an individual in Mexico drinks 500 bottles of Coke per year—the average American drinks about 410 bottles per year. Coca-Cola has been producing beverages in Mexico for 80 years, and local bottlers have helped make Coke part of Mexican culture. Regardless of the controversy surrounding Mexican Coke's importation, fans of the drink are fans for life. There is no doubt that feelings for Mexican Coke run strong throughout the United States.[11] ❖

**Q:** Discussion Questions

1. What challenges does the importing of Mexican Coke to the United States create for the Coca-Cola Company?

2. Why is Mexican Coke so popular with Mexican immigrants in the United States?

3. What should the Coca-Cola company do in response to Mexican Coke's success in the United States?

to honor U.S. laws. Because copying is a tradition in China and Vietnam and laws protecting copyrights and intellectual property are weak and minimally enforced, those countries are flooded with counterfeit videos, movies, CDs, computer software, furniture, and clothing. Companies are angry because the counterfeits harm not only their sales, but also their reputations if the knockoffs are of poor quality. Such counterfeiting is not limited to China or Vietnam. Thirty-five percent of the packaged software installed on personal computers worldwide in 2006 was illegal, amounting to $40 billion in global losses due to software piracy. However, some improvements in a number of markets indicate education, enforcement, and policy efforts are beginning to pay off in emerging economies such as China, Russia, and India and in Central/Eastern Europe and in the Middle East and Africa.[12] In countries where these activities occur, laws against them may not be sufficiently enforced, if counterfeiting is in fact deemed illegal. Thus, businesses engaging in foreign trade may have to take extra steps to protect their products because local laws may be insufficient to do so.

### tariffs and trade restrictions.

Tariffs and other trade restrictions are part of a country's legal structure but may be established or removed for political reasons. An **import tariff** is a tax levied by a nation on goods imported into the country. A *fixed tariff* is a specific amount of money levied on each unit of a product brought into the country, while an *ad valorem tariff* is based on the value of the item. Most countries allow citizens traveling abroad to bring home a certain amount of merchandise without paying an import tariff. A U.S. citizen may bring $200 worth of merchandise into the United States duty free. After that, U.S. citizens must pay an ad valorem tariff based on the cost of the item and the country of origin. Thus, identical items purchased in different countries might have different tariffs.

Countries sometimes levy tariffs for political reasons, as when they impose sanctions against other countries to protest their actions. However, import tariffs are more commonly imposed to protect domestic products by raising the price of imported ones. Such protective tariffs have become controversial, as Americans become increasingly concerned over the U.S. trade deficit. Protective tariffs allow more expensive domestic goods to compete with foreign ones. Many advocate the imposition of tariffs on products imported from Japan, particularly luxury automobiles, audio components, and computers. However, Congress fears economic reprisals from Japan if the tariffs are levied on Japanese products.

Critics of protective tariffs argue that their use inhibits free trade and competition. Supporters of protective tariffs say they insulate domestic industries, particularly new ones, against well-established foreign competitors. Once an industry matures, however, its advocates may be reluctant to let go of the tariff that protected it. Tariffs also help when, because of low labor costs and other advantages, foreign competitors can afford to sell their products at prices lower than those charged by domestic companies. Some Americans argue that tariffs should be used to keep domestic wages high and unemployment low.

**Exchange controls** restrict the amount of currency that can be bought or sold. Some countries control their foreign trade by forcing businesspeople to buy and sell foreign products through a central bank. If John Deere, for example, receives payments for its tractors in a foreign currency, it may be required to sell the currency to that nation's central bank. When foreign currency is in short supply, as it is in many Third World and Eastern European countries, the government uses foreign currency to purchase necessities and capital goods and produces other products locally, thus limiting its need for foreign imports.

A **quota** limits the number of units of a particular product that can be imported into a country. A quota may be established by voluntary agreement or by government decree. After U.S. yarn suppliers complained that cotton yarn (used in underwear, socks, and T-shirts) from Pakistan was flooding the market, a quota was imposed. Pakistan complained, and a textile-monitoring panel recommended that the United States lift the restrictions. The United States refused. However, in 2001, the quota was ruled a violation of global trade rules, and the United States was ordered to remove it.[13]

Because laws protecting copyrights and intellectual property are weak in many Southeast Asian countries, like China, counterfeit goods, like these Louis Vuitton handbags, can often be found to purchase on the street.

● **IMPORT TARIFF** a tax levied by a nation on goods imported into the country

● **EXCHANGE CONTROLS** regulations that restrict the amount of currency that can be bought or sold

● **QUOTA** a restriction on the number of units of a particular product that can be imported into a country

● **EMBARGO** a prohibition on trade in a particular product

● **DUMPING** the act of a country or business selling products at less than what it costs to produce them

● **CARTEL** a group of firms or nations that agrees to act as a monopoly and not compete with each other, in order to generate a competitive advantage in world markets

An embargo prohibits trade in a particular product. Embargoes are generally directed at specific goods or countries and may be established for political, economic, health, or religious reasons. The United States forbids the importation of cigars from Cuba for political reasons. Health embargoes prevent the importing of various pharmaceuticals, animals, plants, and agricultural products. Muslim nations forbid the importation of alcoholic beverages on religious grounds.

One common reason for setting quotas or tariffs is to prohibit dumping, which occurs when a country or business sells products at less than what it costs to produce them. The United States, for example, levied extra import duties against some types of Canadian lumber after the U.S. International Trade Commission found evidence that lower prices on the partially subsidized Canadian lumber threatened to harm the domestic lumber industry. However, some of the antidumping tariffs were later found to be in violation of global trade rules, and the United States was ordered to rescind them.[14] A company may dump its products for several reasons. Dumping permits quick entry into a market. Sometimes dumping occurs when the domestic market for a firm's product is too small to support an efficient level of production. In other cases, technologically obsolete products that are no longer salable in the country of origin are dumped overseas. Dumping is relatively difficult to prove, but even the suspicion of dumping can lead to the imposition of quotas or tariffs.

**political barriers.** Unlike legal issues, political considerations are seldom written down and often change rapidly.

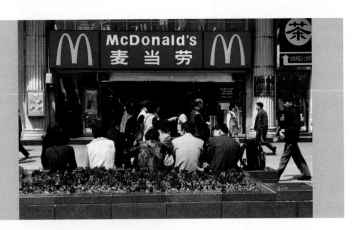

*Understanding the differences among the cultures of a country is important for firms doing international business. Consider McDonald's, like this one in Shanghai, China, or one in India, where cows are considered sacred and few people eat beef. What other cultural differences might affect a company like McDonald's? How should these differences be dealt with?*

Nations that have been subject to economic sanctions for political reasons in recent years include Cuba, Iran, Syria, and North Korea. While these were dramatic events, political considerations affect international business daily as governments enact tariffs, embargoes, or other types of trade restrictions in response to political events.

Businesses engaged in international trade must consider the relative instability of countries such as Colombia, Haiti, and Honduras. Political unrest in countries such as Peru, Somalia, and Russia may create a hostile or even dangerous environment for foreign businesses. Civil war, as in Chechnya and Bosnia, may disrupt business activities and place lives in danger. And, a sudden change in power can result in a regime that is hostile to foreign investment. Some businesses have been forced out of a country altogether, as they were when Fidel Castro closed Cuba to American business. Whether they like it or not, companies are often involved directly or indirectly in international politics.

Political concerns may lead a group of nations to form a cartel, a group of firms or nations that agrees to act as a monopoly and not compete with each other, to generate a competitive advantage in world markets. Probably the most famous cartel is OPEC, the Organization of Petroleum Exporting Countries, founded in the 1960s to increase the price of petroleum throughout the world and to maintain high prices. By working to ensure stable oil prices, OPEC hopes to enhance the economies of its member nations.

## Social and Cultural Barriers

Most businesspeople engaged in international trade underestimate the importance of social and cultural differences; but these differences can derail an important transaction. For example, when Big Boy opened a restaurant in Bangkok, it quickly became popular with European and American tourists, but the local Thais refused to eat there. Instead, they placed gifts of rice and incense at the feet of the Big Boy statue (a chubby boy holding a hamburger) because it reminded them of Buddha. In Japan, customers were forced to tiptoe around a logo painted on the floor at the entrance to an Athlete's Foot store because in Japan, it is considered taboo to step on a crest.[15] And in Russia, consumers found the American-style energetic happiness of McDonald's employees insincere and offensive when the company opened its first stores there.[16] Unfortunately, cultural norms are rarely written down, and what is written down may well be inaccurate.

Cultural differences include differences in spoken and written language. Although it is certainly possible to translate words from one language to another, the true meaning is sometimes misinterpreted or lost. Consider some translations that went awry in foreign markets:

- A Scandinavian vacuum manufacturer Electrolux used the following in an American campaign: "Nothing sucks like an Electrolux."

**TABLE 3.3**  Cultural Behavioral Differences

| Region | Gestures Viewed as Rude or Unacceptable |
| --- | --- |
| Japan, Hong Kong, Middle East | Summoning with the index finger |
| Middle and Far East | Pointing with index finger |
| Thailand, Japan, France | Sitting with soles of shoes showing |
| Brazil, Germany | Forming a circle with fingers (e.g., the "O.K." sign in the United States) |
| Japan | Winking means "I love you" |
| Buddhist countries | Patting someone on the head |

Source: Adapted from Judie Haynes, "Communicating with Gestures," *EverythingESL* (n.d.), www.everythingesl.net/inservice/body_language.php (accessed March 2, 2004).

- The Coca-Cola name in China was first read as "Ke-kou-ke-la," meaning "bite the wax tadpole."
- In Italy, a campaign for Schweppes Tonic Water translated the name into Schweppes Toilet Water.[17]

Translators cannot just translate slogans, advertising campaigns, and Web site language; they must know the cultural differences that could affect a company's success.

Differences in body language and personal space also affect international trade. Body language is nonverbal, usually unconscious communication through gestures, posture, and facial expression. Personal space is the distance at which one person feels comfortable talking to another. Americans tend to stand a moderate distance away from the person with whom they are speaking. Arab businessmen tend to stand face-to-face with the object of their conversation. Additionally, gestures vary from culture to culture, and gestures considered acceptable in American society—pointing, for example—may be considered rude in others. Table 3.3 shows some of the behaviors considered rude or unacceptable in other countries. Such cultural differences may generate uncomfortable feelings or misunderstandings when business people of different countries negotiate with each other.

Family roles also influence marketing activities. Many countries do not allow children to be used in advertising, for example. Advertising that features people in nontraditional social roles may or may not be successful either. The California Milk Processor Board aired a commercial in which a father and his young daughter shop at a supermarket for sugar, flour, cinnamon, and milk for a cake to be baked when they get home. The ad does not seem unusual except that when it was aired on Spanish-language television, the concept was striking. It is rare

# Bosch Provides Global Innovation and Social Responsibility

How many of us today rely on antilock brakes and take them for granted? Although they come standard on most of today's cars, this is a relatively new phenomenon. In 1978, when Bosch introduced the first mass-produced antilock braking system on the Mercedes S-class, it was an expensive novelty that made most automakers skeptical. Today, Bosch supplies 30 percent of the 46 million antilock braking systems installed worldwide. This is a typical pattern for Bosch—design something innovative and unique and wait for the general public to embrace it. Back in 1931, Robert Bosch—the company's founder—declared that the automobile ought to be available to everyone and set out to make this possible. As a first step, the creation of the Bosch spark plug helped bring about the mass production of automobile components. Recently, Bosch created a set of features that allow a car to parallel park itself—necessary? Perhaps not, but at one time people thought antilock brakes weren't necessary either.

The German company, started by 25-year-old Robert Bosch in 1886, is now the largest international auto parts company, with $49.7 billion in revenue. Bosch is a private company and, since the foundation's opening in 1964, 92 percent is owned by the family charitable foundation while the Bosch family owns the rest. In 2004, Bosch reported a profit of $2.1 billion. Of the $2.1 billion, $72 million went to the Bosch foundation and $6 million went to the Bosch family. Bosch then put 96 percent of the remaining profit back into the company. Lavish spending on research and development can take its toll on a company. Therefore, Bosch relies on more than auto components to make a profit. The company also runs consumer goods and building technology and industrial technology units. In the United States, there are dishwashers and ranges marketed under the Bosch, Siemens, Thermador, and Gaggenau brand names; the Bosch Aquastar tankless gas water heater; and Bosch, Skil, and Dremel power tools. However, Bosch still believes that creating innovative automotive technology is, while perhaps not the most profitable, the heart of its business.

Ever focused on innovation, Bosch intends to move beyond creating components that make cars safer and better for the environment to creating components that help people become better drivers. The company speaks of the "sensitive car"—one that has blind spot detection, night vision, a lane departure warning system, and adaptive cruise control capable of bringing the car to a complete stop. Some of these features are set to appear on cars in the next few years. What may sound revolutionary in automotive technology today may be standard tomorrow—and for the foreseeable future we can count on Bosch to be a part of bringing this revolutionary technology to our attention.[20] ❖

# Q: Discussion Questions

1. Why is Bosch so innovative?

2. Why do you believe Bosch has 30 percent of the world market for antilock braking systems?

3. How is Bosch socially responsible operating as a private company?

for Latino men to appear along with their daughters in Spanish-language ads and even rarer for the commercials to be set outside the home. The Hispanic culture typically reinforces how little boys need their fathers, not how little girls do.[18]

The people of other nations quite often have a different perception of time as well. Americans value promptness; a business meeting scheduled for a specific time seldom starts more than a few minutes late. In Mexico and Spain, however, it is not unusual for a meeting to be delayed half an hour or more. Such a late start might produce resentment in an American negotiating in Spain for the first time.

Companies engaged in foreign trade must observe the national and religious holidays and local customs of the host country. In many Islamic countries, for example, workers expect to take a break at certain times of the day to observe religious rites. Companies also must monitor their advertising to guard against offending customers. In Thailand and many other countries, public displays of affection between the sexes are unacceptable in advertising messages; in many Middle Eastern nations, it is unacceptable to show the soles of one's feet. In the Muslim world, exposure of a woman's skin, even her arms, is considered offensive.[19]

Fly fishing isn't common in Chiang Mai, Thailand, but lure manufacturers have flocked there in recent years. Having made handicrafts for centuries, Chiang Mai residents have developed a high level of finger dexterity that enables them to produce superior lures. "Chiang Mai is to fly tying what Silicon Valley is to computers," says an executive at Targus Fly & Feather, a Mesa, Arizona, company with large lure-making operations in Thailand.

With the exception of the United States, most nations use the metric system. This lack of uniformity creates problems for both buyers and sellers in the international marketplace. American sellers, for instance, must package goods destined for foreign markets in liters or meters, and Japanese sellers must convert to the English system if they plan to sell a product in the United States. Tools also must be calibrated in the correct system if they are to function correctly. Hyundai and Honda service technicians need metric tools to make repairs on those cars.

The literature dealing with international business is filled with accounts of sometimes humorous but often costly mistakes that occurred because of a lack of understanding of the social and cultural differences between buyers and sellers. Such problems cannot always be avoided, but they can be minimized through research on the cultural and social differences of the host country.

## Technological Barriers

Many countries lack the technological infrastructure found in the United States, and some marketers are viewing such barriers as opportunities. For instance, marketers are targeting many countries such as India and China and some African countries where there are few private phone lines. Citizens of these countries are turning instead to wireless communication through cell phones. Technological advances, such as the Internet, are creating additional global marketing opportunities. In some countries, broadband access to the Internet is spreading much faster than in the United States. In fact, 10 nations, including South Korea, Hong Kong, and Canada, outrank the United States in terms of subscribers to broadband Internet access. The growth of high-speed Internet access should facilitate online commerce.[21]

## ●● LO3

Specify some of the agreements, alliances, and organizations that may encourage trade across international boundaries.

# TRADE AGREEMENTS, ALLIANCES, AND ORGANIZATIONS

Although these economic, political, legal, and sociocultural issues may seem like daunting barriers to international trade, there are also organizations and agreements—such as the General Agreement on Tariffs and Trade, the World Bank, and the International Monetary Fund—that foster international trade and can help companies get involved in and succeed in global markets. Various regional trade agreements, such as the North American Free Trade Agreement and the European Union, also promote trade among member nations by eliminating tariffs and trade restrictions. In this section, we'll look briefly at these agreements and organizations.

# DESTINATION CEO

**Nigel Travis—Papa John's** After burgers and fries, pizza is the most popular restaurant food in the United States. Papa John's Pizza is the third largest pizza franchise in the world. Currently, there are 3,000 Papa John's storefronts in the United States and 400 storefronts globally. There are an additional 800 storefronts in the pipeline for global expansion. It is clear that growth will only continue through global expansion of the franchise.

Nigel Travis was born in Great Britain and received his degree in human resources management. His early career was spent with Kraft Foods in the labor relations function. His HR career took him to Rolls Royce, Massey-Ferguson, and Blockbuster. At age 55, after spending a successful 11 years at Blockbuster Video, Travis decided that he wanted to serve in the role of CEO. After considering several offers, he selected Papa John's. Since assuming the CEO position with the pizza maker, they have opened 400 stores globally and have plans to introduce 800 more. Travis's management style emphasizes communication, and he attributes his early success as a manager to his role as a soccer coach as a young man.

Travis sees that future growth for the pizza chain will be outside of the U.S. market. He also sees technology as an important element of expansion. For example, to enhance the brand, Papa John's has launched a Web presence where consumers can order and reorder their pizzas well in advance.

## >>DISCUSSION QUESTIONS

1. Why do you think that expansion opportunities for the Papa John's franchise are global rather than domestic?

2. To what does Nigel Travis attribute his success as a global manager?

3. How does technology play a role in the global expansion of Papa John's?

>>To see the complete video about Nigel Travis, go to our Web site at **www.mhhe.com/FerrellM** and look for the link to the Destination CEO videos.

## General Agreement on Tariffs and Trade (GATT)

During the Great Depression of the 1930s, nations established so many protective tariffs covering so many products that international trade became virtually impossible. By the end of World War II, there was considerable international momentum to liberalize trade and minimize the effects of tariffs. The General Agreement on Tariffs and Trade (GATT), originally signed by 23 nations in 1947, provided a forum for tariff negotiations and a place where international trade problems could be discussed and resolved. More than 100 nations abided by its rules. GATT sponsored rounds of negotiations aimed at reducing trade restrictions. The most recent round, the Uruguay Round (1988–1994), further reduced trade barriers for most products and provided new rules to prevent dumping.

The World Trade Organization (WTO), an international organization dealing with the rules of trade between nations, was created in 1995 by the Uruguay Round. Key to the World Trade Organization are the WTO agreements, which are the legal ground rules for international commerce. The agreements were negotiated and signed by most of the world's trading nations and ratified by their parliaments. The goal is to help producers of goods and services and exporters and importers conduct their business. In addition to administering the WTO trade agreements, the WTO presents a forum for trade negotiations, monitors national trade policies, provides technical assistance and training for developing countries, and cooperates with other international organizations. Based in Geneva, Switzerland, the WTO has also adopted a leadership role in negotiating trade disputes among nations.[22] For example, the WTO investigated complaints from the European Union and seven countries about a U.S. tariff on imported steel and ultimately ruled the U.S. duties illegal under international trade rules. The United States had imposed the tariffs to protect domestic steel producers from less expensive imported steel, but the WTO found that the United States had failed to prove that its steel industry had been harmed by dumping.[23] Facing the prospect of retaliatory sanctions against American goods, the U.S. dropped the tariffs 16 months early after the ruling.[24]

> **NAFTA makes it easier for U.S. businesses to invest in Mexico and Canada**

## The North American Free Trade Agreement (NAFTA)

The North American Free Trade Agreement (NAFTA), which went into effect on January 1, 1994, effectively merged Canada, the United States, and Mexico into one market of more than 421 million consumers.[25] NAFTA will eliminate virtually all tariffs on goods produced and traded among Canada, Mexico, and the United States to create a free trade area by 2009. The estimated annual output for this trade alliance is $11 trillion.[26] NAFTA makes it easier for U.S. businesses to invest in Mexico and Canada; provides protection for intellectual property (of special interest to high-technology and entertainment industries); expands trade by requiring equal treatment of U.S. firms in both countries; and simplifies country-of-origin rules, hindering Japan's use of Mexico as a staging ground for further penetration into U.S. markets. Although most tariffs on products coming to the United States are being lifted, duties on more sensitive products, such as household glassware, footware, and some fruits and vegetables, are being phased out over a 15-year period.

Canada's 33 million consumers are relatively affluent, with a per-capita GDP of $32,900.[27] Trade between the United States and Canada totals approximately $680 billion.[28] Canada's trade with the United States is responsible for more than half (52 percent) of Canada's GDP. The United States represents roughly 80 percent of Canada's exports and 60 percent of their imports. Canada, in return, represents 23.5 percent of U.S. exports and 17.4 percent of its imports. Canada is the number-one foreign market for goods exports for 39 of the 50 states. In fact, Canada is a larger market for U.S. goods than all 25 countries of the European Union combined, which has 15 times the population of Canada.[29]

With a per capita GDP of $10,100, Mexico's 107 million consumers are less affluent than Canadian consumers. However, they bought $120 billion worth of U.S. products last year, making Mexico the United States' second-largest trading market, after Canada.[30] Many U.S. companies have taken advantage of Mexico's low labor costs and proximity to the United States to set up production facilities, sometimes called *maquiladoras.* Production at the *maquiladoras,* especially in the automotive, electronics, and apparel industries, tripled between 1994 and 2000 as companies as diverse as Ford, John Deere, Motorola, Sara Lee, Kimberly-Clark, and VF Corporation set up facilities in north-central Mexican states. With the *maquiladoras* accounting for roughly half of Mexico's exports, Mexico has risen to become the world's ninth-largest economy.[31]

Mexico's membership in NAFTA links the United States and Canada with other Latin American countries, providing additional opportunities to integrate trade among all the nations in the Western Hemisphere. Indeed, efforts to create a free trade agreement among the 34 nations of North and South America was expected to be completed by 2005. Like NAFTA, the *Free Trade Area of the Americas (FTAA)* will progressively eliminate trade barriers and create the world's largest free trade zone with 800 million people.[32] However, opposition and demonstrations have hampered efforts to move forward with the proposed plan. Although the deadline was missed and it is not in place yet, there is still a chance for the FTAA to become a reality. A trade dispute between the United States and Brazil over investment, intellectual property rights, antidumping tariffs, and agriculture subsidies may also delay the final agreement.[33]

Despite its benefits, NAFTA has been controversial and disputes continue to arise over the implementation of the trade agreement. Archer Daniels Midland, for example, filed a claim against the Mexican government for losses resulting from a tax on soft drinks containing high-fructose corn syrup, which the company believes violates the provisions of NAFTA.[34] While many Americans feared the agreement would erase jobs in the United States, Mexicans have been disappointed that the agreement failed to create more jobs. Moreover, Mexico's rising standard of living has increased the cost of doing business there; some 850 *maquiladoras* have closed their doors and transferred work to China and other nations where labor costs are cheaper. Indeed, China has become the United States' second largest importer.[35]

Although NAFTA has been controversial, it has become a positive factor for U.S. firms wishing to engage in international marketing. Because licensing requirements have been relaxed under the pact, smaller businesses that previously could not afford to invest in Mexico and Canada will be able to do business in those markets without having to locate there. NAFTA's long phase-in period provides ample time for adjustment by those firms affected by reduced tariffs on imports. Furthermore, increased competition should lead to a more efficient market, and the long-term prospects of including most countries in the Western Hemisphere in the alliance promise additional opportunities for U.S. marketers.

## The European Union (EU)

The **European Union (EU)**, also called the *European Community* or *Common Market,* was established in 1958 to promote trade among its members, which initially included Belgium, France, Italy, West Germany, Luxembourg, and the Netherlands. East and West Germany united in 1991, and by 1995 the United Kingdom, Spain, Denmark, Greece, Portugal, Ireland, Austria, Finland, and Sweden had joined as well. Cyprus, the Czech Republic, Estonia, Hungary, Latvia, Lithuania, Malta, Poland, Slovakia, and Slovenia joined in 2004. In 2007 Bulgaria and Romania also became members, which brought total membership to 27. Croatia, the former Yugoslav Republic of Macedonia, and Turkey are candidate countries that hope to join the European Union soon.[36] Until 1993 each nation functioned as a separate market, but at that time the members officially unified into one of the largest single world markets, which today includes 390 million consumers.

To facilitate free trade among members, the EU is working toward standardization of business regulations and requirements, import duties, and value-added taxes; the elimination of customs checks; and the creation of a standardized currency for use by all members. Many European nations (Austria, Belgium, Finland, France, Germany, Ireland, Italy, Luxembourg, the Netherlands, Portugal, and Spain) link their exchange rates together to a common currency, the *euro;* however, several EU members have rejected use of the euro in their countries. Although the common currency requires many marketers to modify their pricing strategies and will subject them to increased competition, the use of a single currency frees companies that sell goods among

Although both the United States and most Central American countries have passed the Central America Free Trade Agreement (CAFTA), there is still a great deal of opposition to CAFTA's full implementation. Those critical of the agreement claim it will harm small farmers in Central America, will erode workers' rights, and protect pharmaceutical companies at the expense of the poor. Proponents argue that on balance, participating countries will be made better off.

accounts for more than 48 percent of global trade. APEC differs from other international trade alliances in its commitment to facilitating business and its practice of allowing the business/private sector to participate in a wide range of APEC activities.[39]

Despite economic turmoil and a recession in Asia in recent years, companies of the APEC have become increasingly competitive and sophisticated in global business in the last three decades. The Japanese and South Koreans in particular have made tremendous inroads on world markets for automobiles, motorcycles, watches, cameras, and audio and video equipment. Products from Samsung, Sony, Sanyo, Toyota, Daewoo, Mitsubishi, Suzuki, and Toshiba are sold all over the world and have set standards of quality by which other products are often judged. The People's Republic of China, a country of 1.3 billion people, has launched a program of economic reform to stimulate its economy by privatizing many industries, restructuring its banking system, and increasing public spending on infrastructure (including railways and telecommunications).[40] As a result, China has become a manufacturing powerhouse with an economy growing at a rate of more than 10 percent a year.[41] Less visible and sometimes less stable Pacific Rim regions, such as Thailand, Singapore, Taiwan, Vietnam, and Hong Kong, have also become major manufacturing and financial centers.

European countries from the nuisance of dealing with complex exchange rates.[37] The long-term goals are to eliminate all trade barriers within the EU, improve the economic efficiency of the EU nations, and stimulate economic growth, thus making the union's economy more competitive in global markets, particularly against Japan and other Pacific Rim nations, and North America. However, several disputes and debates still divide the member nations, and many barriers to completely free trade remain. Consequently, it may take many years before the EU is truly one deregulated market.

The EU has enacted some of the world's strictest laws concerning antitrust issues, which have had unexpected consequences for some non-European firms. For example, after a five-year investigation, the union fined U.S.-based Microsoft a record 497 million euros ($627 million U.S.) for exploiting its "near-monopoly" in computer operating systems in Europe by including a free media player with Windows to the detriment

> ## "The IMF is the closest thing the world has to an international central bank."

of software offered by European makers. Microsoft denied the charges and appealed. Microsoft lost its appeal in the courts. In addition to the fine, the European Commission insisted that Microsoft release its programming codes to European rivals to allow them to make their competing products compatible with computers relying on Microsoft's Windows operating system.[38]

## Asia-Pacific Economic Cooperation (APEC)

The Asia-Pacific Economic Cooperation (APEC), established in 1989, promotes open trade and economic and technical cooperation among member nations, which initially included Australia, Brunei Darussalam, Canada, Indonesia, Japan, Korea, Malaysia, New Zealand, the Philippines, Singapore, Thailand, and the United States. Since then the alliance has grown to include China, Hong Kong, Chinese Taipei, Mexico, Papua New Guinea, Chile, Peru, Russia, and Vietnam. The 21-member alliance represents 2.6 billion consumers, has a combined gross domestic product of (U.S.) $24 trillion, and

## World Bank

The World Bank, more formally known as the International Bank for Reconstruction and Development, was established by the industrialized nations, including the United States, in 1946 to loan money to underdeveloped and developing countries.

It loans its own funds or borrows funds from member countries to finance projects ranging from road and factory construction to the building of medical and educational facilities. The World Bank and other multilateral development banks (banks with international support that provide loans to developing countries) are the largest source of advice and assistance for developing nations. The International Development Association and the International Finance Corporation are associated with the World Bank and provide loans to private businesses and member countries.

## International Monetary Fund

The International Monetary Fund (IMF) was established in 1947 to promote trade among member nations by eliminating trade barriers and fostering financial cooperation. It also makes short-term loans to member countries that have balance-of-payment deficits and provides foreign currencies to member nations. The International Monetary Fund also tries to avoid financial crises and panics by alerting the international community about countries that will not be able to repay their debts. The IMF's Internet site provides additional information about the organization, including news releases, frequently asked questions, and members.

The IMF is the closest thing the world has to an international central bank. If countries get into financial trouble, they can borrow from the World Bank. The IMF has bailed out Thailand, Russia, and Argentina and, in recent years, has focused on loans to developing countries. The usefulness of the IMF for developed countries is limited because these countries use private markets as a major source of capital.[42]

 **L04**

Summarize the different levels of organizational involvement in international trade.

# GETTING INVOLVED IN INTERNATIONAL BUSINESS

Businesses may get involved in international trade at many levels—from a small Kenyan firm that occasionally exports African crafts to a huge multinational corporation such as Shell Oil that sells products around the globe. The degree of commitment of resources and effort required increases according to the level at which a business involves itself in international trade. This section examines exporting and importing, trading companies, licensing and franchising, contract manufacturing, joint ventures, direct investment, and multinational corporations.

## Exporting and Importing

Many companies first get involved in international trade when they import goods from other countries for resale in their own businesses. For example, a grocery store chain may import bananas from Honduras and coffee from Colombia. A business may get involved in exporting when it is called upon to supply a foreign company with a particular product. Such exporting enables enterprises of all sizes to participate in international business. Table 3.4 shows the number of U.S. exporters and the export value by company size, while Figure 3.2 shows the major export markets for U.S. companies.

Exporting sometimes takes place through countertrade agreements, which involve bartering products for other products instead of for currency. Such arrangements are fairly common in international trade, especially between Western companies and Eastern European nations. An estimated 40 percent or more of all international trade agreements contain countertrade provisions.

*The key difference between the IMF and the World Bank is that the IMF focuses primarily on maintaining the international monetary system, whereas the World Bank concentrates on poverty reduction through low-interest loans and other programs. In this photo, outgoing World Bank President James D. Wolfensohn (right); Development Committee Chairman. Trevor Manuel, the Finance Minister of South Africa (center); and IMF Managing Director Rodrigo de Rato (far left) speak with reporters at the IMF headquarters in Washington.*

Although a company may export its wares overseas directly or import goods directly from their manufacturer, many choose to deal with an intermediary, commonly called an *export agent*. Export agents seldom produce goods themselves; instead, they usually handle international transactions for other firms. Export agents either purchase products outright or take them on consignment. If they purchase them outright, they generally mark up the price they have paid and attempt to sell the product in the international marketplace. They are also responsible for storage and transportation.

An advantage of trading through an agent instead of directly is that the company does not have to deal with foreign currencies or the red tape (paying tariffs and handling

**TABLE 3.4** U.S. Exporters and Value by Company Size

| | Number of Exporters | % | Value (Dollars and Billions) | % |
|---|---|---|---|---|
| Small (<100 employees) | 215,991 | 90.3 | 151.3 | 19.3 |
| Medium (100–499 employees) | 16,621 | 7 | 77.1 | 9.9 |
| Large (500+ employees) | 6,482 | 2.7 | 556 | 70.9 |

Source: "Profile of U.S. Exporting Companies, 2004-2005," U.S. Census Bureau, press release, January 10, 2007, http://www.census.gov/foreign-trade/Press-Release/edb/2005/ (accessed June 7, 2007)

paperwork) of international business. A major disadvantage is that, because the export agent must make a profit, either the price of the product must be increased or the domestic company must provide a larger discount than it would in a domestic transaction.

## Trading Companies

A **trading company** buys goods in one country and sells them to buyers in another country. Trading companies handle all activities required to move products from one country to another, including consulting, marketing research, advertising, insurance, product research and design, warehousing, and foreign exchange services to companies interested in selling their products in foreign markets. Trading companies are similar to export agents, but their role in international trade is larger. By linking sellers and buyers of goods in different countries, trading companies promote international trade. The best known U.S. trading company is Sears World Trade, which specializes in consumer goods, light industrial items, and processed foods.

## Licensing and Franchising

**Licensing** is a trade arrangement in which one company—the *licensor*—allows another company—the *licensee*—to use its company name, products, patents, brands, trademarks, raw materials, and/or production processes in exchange for a fee or royalty. The Coca-Cola Company and PepsiCo frequently use licensing as a means to market their soft drinks, apparel, and other merchandise in other countries. Licensing is an attractive alternative to direct investment when the political stability of a foreign country is in doubt or when resources are unavailable for direct investment. Licensing is especially advantageous for small manufacturers wanting to launch a well-known brand internationally. Yoplait is a French yogurt that is licensed for production in the United States.

**Franchising** is a form of licensing in which a company—the *franchiser*—agrees to provide a *franchisee* a name, logo, methods of operation, advertising, products, and other elements associated with the franchiser's business, in return for a financial commitment and the agreement to conduct business in accordance with the franchiser's standard of operations. Wendy's, McDonald's, Pizza Hut, and Holiday Inn are well-known franchisers with international visibility. Twenty percent of all U.S. franchise systems have foreign operations. The majority of these were located in developed markets such as Canada, Japan, Europe, and Australia.[43] Table 3.5 lists the top 10 global franchises as ranked by *Entrepreneur* magazine.

Licensing and franchising enable a company to enter the international marketplace without spending large sums of money abroad or hiring or transferring personnel to handle overseas affairs. They also minimize problems associated

**FIGURE 3.2** U.S. Exporters and Value by Company Size

Number of Exporters:
- Canada: 83,727
- Mexico: 43,158
- Japan: 26,933
- China: 23,923
- United Kingdom: 39,786

Source: "Profile of U.S. Exporting Companies, 2004–2005," U.S. Census Bureau, press release, January 10, 2007, http://www.census.gov/foreign-trade/Press-Release/edb/2005/ (accessed June 7, 2007).

**TABLE 3.5** Top 10 Global Franchise Operations

1. Subway
2. Dunkin' Donuts
3. Domino's Pizza LLC
4. McDonald's
5. The UPS Store/Mail Boxes Etc.
6. Re/Max Int'l. Inc.
7. Curves
8. Sonic Drive In Restaurants
9. InterContinental Hotels Group
10. Century 21 Real Estate LLC

Source: "Top 10 Global Franchises for 2007," *Entrepreneur* (n.d.), http://www.entrepreneur.com/topglobal/index.html (accessed June 7, 2007).

with shipping costs, tariffs, and trade restrictions. And, they allow the firm to establish goodwill for its products in a foreign market, which will help the company if it decides to produce or market its products directly in the foreign country at some future date. However, if the licensee (or franchisee) does not maintain high standards of quality, the product's image may be hurt; therefore, it is important for the licensor to monitor its products overseas and to enforce its quality standards.

## Contract Manufacturing

Contract manufacturing occurs when a company hires a foreign company to produce a specified volume of the firm's product to specification; the final product carries the domestic firm's name. Spalding, for example, relies on contract manufacturing for its sports equipment; Reebok uses Korean contract manufacturers to manufacture many of its athletic shoes.

## Outsourcing

Earlier, we defined outsourcing as transferring manufacturing or other tasks (such as information technology operations) to companies in countries where labor and supplies are less expensive. Many U.S. firms have outsourced tasks to India, Ireland, Mexico, and the Philippines, where there are many well-educated workers and significantly lower labor costs. Experts estimate that 20 percent of manufacturers and financial-service firms have outsourced some information-technology tasks and project that figure will double.[44] Bank of America, for example, set up a subsidiary in India to outsource 1,000 back-office support jobs. The bank also contracts with several Indian firms to provide software services. Experts believe that two-thirds of U.S. banks outsource services to China, India, and Russia.[45] Even small firms can outsource. For example, Avalon, an Irish manufacturer of high-end guitars played by musicians like Eric Clapton, contracted with Cort Musical Instruments Company in South Korea to augment the firm's production and help it build a global brand. The outsourcing arrangement helped the small business boost output from 1,500 guitars a year to 8,000 annually, helping it become more competitive with larger manufacturers.[46]

Although outsourcing has become politically controversial in recent years amid concerns over jobs lost to overseas workers, foreign companies transfer tasks and jobs to U.S. companies—sometimes called *insourcing*—far more often than U.S. companies outsource tasks and jobs abroad.[47] For example, Indian-based Bharti TeleVentures, a cell-phone operator, signed a 10-year contract to insource its software, hardware, and other information-technology tasks to IBM in the United States.[48] However, some firms are bringing their outsourced jobs back after concerns that foreign workers were not adding enough value.

Domino's Pizza has expanded its operations into more than 50 international markets via franchising. In Asia, the chain's stores serve up pizzas with toppings such as squid, sweet mayonnaise, and duck gizzards.

## Joint Ventures and Alliances

Many countries, particularly LDCs, do not permit direct investment by foreign companies or individuals. Or, a company may lack sufficient resources or expertise to operate in another country. In such cases, a company that wants to do business in another country may set up a joint venture by finding a local partner (occasionally, the host nation itself) to share the costs and operation of the business. General Motors, for example, has a joint venture with Russian automaker Avtovaz in Togliatti, which manufactures four-wheel-drive Chevrolet Nivas and Opel Astras for the Russian market. Demand for the relatively pricey Astra has grown along with Russian household incomes.[49]

In some industries, such as automobiles and computers, strategic alliances are becoming the predominant means of competing. A strategic alliance is a partnership formed to create competitive advantage on a worldwide basis. In such industries, international competition is so fierce and the costs of competing on a global basis are so high that few firms have the resources to go it alone, so they collaborate with other companies. An example of such an alliance is New United Motor

● **CONTRACT MANUFACTURING** the hiring of a foreign company to produce a specified volume of the initiating company's product to specification; the final product carries the domestic firm's name

● **JOINT VENTURE** the sharing of the costs and operation of a business between a foreign company and a local partner

● **STRATEGIC ALLIANCE** a partnership formed to create competitive advantage on a worldwide basis

Manufacturing Inc. (NUMMI), formed by Toyota and General Motors in 1984 to make automobiles for both firms. This alliance joined the quality engineering of Japanese cars with the marketing expertise and market access of General Motors. Today, NUMMI manufactures the popular Toyota Tacoma compact pick-up truck as well as the Toyota Corolla, Pontiac Vibe, and a right-hand drive Toyota Voltz for sale in Japan.[50]

## Direct Investment

Companies that want more control and are willing to invest considerable resources in international business may consider **direct investment,** the ownership of overseas facilities. Direct investment may involve the development and operation of new facilities—such as when Starbucks opens a new coffee shop in Japan—or the purchase of all or part of an existing operation in a foreign country. General Motors, for example, owns nearly 45 percent of Korean-based Daewoo, 12 percent in Japanese-based Isuzu, and 20 percent of Japanese-based Fuji Heavy Industries.[51]

The highest level of international business involvement is the **multinational corporation (MNC),** a corporation, such as IBM or ExxonMobil, that operates on a worldwide scale, without significant ties to any one nation or region. Table 3.6 lists the 10 largest multinational corporations. MNCs are more than simple corporations. They often have greater assets than some of the countries in which they do business. General Motors, ExxonMobil, Ford Motors, and General Electric, for example, have sales higher than the GDP of many of the countries in which they operate. Nestlé, with headquarters in Switzerland, operates more than 300 plants around the world and receives revenues from Europe; North, Central, and South America; Africa; and Asia. The Royal Dutch/Shell Group, one of the world's major oil producers, is another MNC. Its main offices are located in The Hague and London. Other MNCs include BASF, British Petroleum, Cadbury Schweppes, Matsushita, Mitsubishi, Siemens, Texaco, Toyota, and Unilever. Many MNCs have been targeted by antiglobalization activists at global business forums, and some protests have turned violent. The activists contend that MNCs increase the gap between rich and poor nations, misuse and misallocate scarce resources, exploit the labor markets in LDCs, and harm their natural environments.[52]

*Tesco, the U.K. supermarket chain, has a joint venture in China in which it has purchased a 50 percent share in Ting Hsin—which owns and operates the 25-store hypermark chain Hymall.*

**TABLE 3.6**   The 10 Largest Global Corporations

| Rank | Company | Revenues (in millions) |
|------|---------|------------------------|
| 1 | ExxonMobil | $339,938 |
| 2 | Wal-Mart Stores | 315,654 |
| 3 | Royal Dutch Shell | 306,731 |
| 4 | BP | 267,600 |
| 5 | General Motors | 192,604 |
| 6 | Chevron | 189,481 |
| 7 | DaimlerChrysler | 186,106 |
| 8 | Toyota Motor | 185,805 |
| 9 | Ford Motor | 177,210 |
| 10 | ConocoPhillips | 166,683 |

Source: "Global 500: Fortune's Annual Ranking of the World's Largest Corporations," *Fortune,* http://money.cnn.com/magazines/fortune/global500 (accessed June 8, 2007).

# INTERNATIONAL BUSINESS STRATEGIES

Planning in a global economy requires businesspeople to understand the economic, legal, political, and sociocultural realities of the countries in which they will operate. These factors will affect the strategy a business chooses to use outside its own borders.

## Developing Strategies

Companies doing business internationally have traditionally used a **multinational strategy,** customizing their products, promotion, and distribution according to cultural, technological, regional, and national differences. In France, for example, South Korean–owned AmorePacific Corporation marketed its Lolita Lempicka perfume, with a decidedly French accent. Named for a French fashion designer, the fifth-best-selling fragrance in France was formulated by French experts and marketed in a bottle designed by a French artist. Indeed, few French consumers realize the popular perfume is owned by a Korean firm.[53] Many soap and detergent manufacturers have adapted their products to local water conditions, washing equipment, and washing habits. For customers in some less-developed countries, Colgate-Palmolive Co. has developed an inexpensive, plastic, hand-powered washing machine for use in households that have no electricity. Even when products are standardized, advertising often has to be modified to adapt to language and cultural differences. Also, celebrities used in advertising in the United States may be unfamiliar to foreign consumers and thus would not be effective in advertising products in other countries.

More and more companies are moving from this customization strategy to a **global strategy (globalization),** which involves standardizing products (and, as much as possible, their promotion and distribution) for the whole world, as if it were a single entity. Examples of globalized products are American clothing, movies, music, and cosmetics. ExxonMobil launched a $150 million marketing effort to promote its brands: Exxon, Esso, Mobil, and General. The ads have the same look and feel regardless of the country in which they appear. The ad's message was the same for all countries except the story was told in one of 25 languages.[55]

Before moving outside their own borders, companies must conduct environmental analyses to evaluate the potential of and problems associated with various markets and to determine what strategy is best for doing business in those markets. Failure to do so may result in losses and even negative publicity. Some companies rely on local managers to gain greater insights and faster response to changes within a country. Astute businesspeople today "think globally, act locally." That is, while constantly being aware of the total picture, they adjust their firms' strategies to conform to local needs and tastes.

## Managing the Challenges of Global Business

As we've pointed out in this chapter, many past political barriers to trade have fallen or been minimized, expanding and opening new market opportunities. Managers who can meet the challenges of creating and implementing effective and sensitive business strategies for the global marketplace can help

● **MULTINATIONAL STRATEGY** a plan, used by international companies, that involves customizing products, promotion, and distribution according to cultural, technological, regional, and national differences

● **GLOBAL STRATEGY (GLOBALIZATION)** a strategy that involves standardizing products (and, as much as possible, their promotion and distribution) for the whole world, as if it were a single entity

---

## Tag, You're It! Flickr—The Hot New Thing in Online Photo Sharing

Stewart Butterfield & Caterina Fake

Business: Flickr

Founded: 2004

Success: In 2005, Yahoo! bought Flickr for an undisclosed sum.

Flickr, an innovative online photo sharing site, has become popular globally in two short years. Using Flickr, members can do much more than simply download digital photos to online photo albums. In addition to the traditional downloading, photos taken by camera

phone can immediately be sent from the phone to a member's Flickr site for instant viewing—providing friends and family a glimpse into what is going on as things are happening. One of the most interesting features of Flickr is that photos can be "tagged" by the member uploading them to his/her site. This tagging then links one member's photos to any other photos sporting the same tag—thereby creating a series of communities based on tags. For example, if a member tags pictures of his/her dog with "St. Bernard," those pictures will then be linked to any others on the site

also tagged "St. Bernard." Flickr has become a social site—a way to meet and converse in pictures. Although Flickr was originally a sideline idea developed by online game designers Stewart Butterfield and Caterina Fake, they soon realized, after sharing the concept with a blogging group, that people were looking for something like Flickr. In Flickr's first year, the site went from having zero members to more than 170,000. At the end of 2005, the site had 1.5 million members worldwide, about 60 million photos, and was purchased by Yahoo![54] ❖

To be a successful businessperson in the 21st century, you will need to be globally aware, looking beyond your own region or country to the whole world. Being globally aware requires objectivity, tolerance, and knowledge. Objectivity is crucial in assessing opportunities, evaluating potential markets and opportunities, and resolving problems. Tolerance of cultural differences does not mean that you have to accept as your own the cultural ways of other countries, but it does mean that you must permit others to be different but equal. Being globally aware requires staying informed about social and economic trends because a country's prospects can change, sometimes almost overnight, as social, political, and economic trends change direction or accelerate.

Both trade agreements like NAFTA and new technologies are reducing borders among nations and creating many exciting career opportunities. Most new jobs will have at least some global component. Examples of exciting careers in global business include export and import management, product management and distribution, and advertising. An export manager is responsible for managing all of a large company's exporting activities and supervises the activities of foreign sales representatives who live and work abroad. Since products may be sold in many countries, product management and distribution transcends national boundaries, but may have to be customized for a particular country or region. Students interested in advertising will find an exciting career meeting the challenges of communicating information to people of diverse languages and needs.

While the likelihood of receiving a foreign assignment in your first job is low, the possibility of developing and implementing global strategies is high. Today, many colleges and universities are encouraging study in international business, foreign languages, cross-cultural communications, and related areas to prepare students for the borderless world. In the future, you can expect that it will be a requirement, not an option, to have global business skills.[57]

lead their companies to success. For example, the Commercial Service is the global business solutions unit of the U.S. Department of Commerce that offers U.S. firms wide and deep practical knowledge of international markets and industries, a unique global network, inventive use of information technology, and a focus on small and mid-sized businesses. Another example is the benchmarking of best international practices that benefits U.S. firms, which is conducted by the network of CIBERs (Centers for International Business Education and Research) at leading business schools in the United States. These 30 CIBERs are funded by the U.S. government to help U.S. firms become more competitive globally. A major element of the assistance that these governmental organizations can provide firms (especially for small and medium-sized firms) is knowledge of the internationalization process.[56] Small businesses, too, can succeed in foreign markets when their managers have carefully studied those markets and prepared and implemented appropriate strategies. Being globally aware is therefore an important quality for today's managers and will become a critical attribute for managers of the 21st century. ■

# CHECK OUT

## www.mhhe.com/FerrellM

# for study materials including Interactive Exercises, Quizzes, iPod downloads, and video.

# Build Your Business Plan

**Business in a Borderless World** Think about the product/service you are contemplating for your business plan. If it is an already established product or service, try to find out if the product is currently being sold internationally. If not, can you identify opportunities to do so in the future? What countries do you think would respond most favorably to your product? What problems would you encounter if you attempted to export your product to those countries?

If you are thinking of creating a new product or service for your business plan, think about the possibility of eventually marketing that product in another country. What countries or areas of the world do you think would be most responsive to your product?

Are there countries that the U.S. has trade agreements or alliances with which would make your entry into the market easier? What would be the economic, social, cultural, and technological barriers you would have to recognize before entering the prospective country (ies)? Think about the specific cultural differences that would have to be taken into consideration before entering the prospective country.

M IS FOR MOMENTUM

are you M-powered?
www.mhhe.com/FerrellM

# Managing Information Technology & E-Business

4

# Introduction

The technology behind computers, the Internet, and their applications has changed the face of business over the past few decades. Information technology (IT) relates to processes and applications that create new methods to solve problems, perform tasks, and manage communication. Information technology has been associated with using computers to obtain and process information as well as using application software and the Internet to organize and communicate information. Information technology's impact on the economy is very powerful especially with regard to productivity, employment, and working environments. Technology has resulted in social issues related to privacy, intellectual property, quality of life, and the ability of the legal system to respond to this environment. Most businesses are using information technology to develop new strategies, enhance employee productivity, and improve services to customers.

In this chapter we first examine the role and impact of technology in our information-driven economy. Next, we discuss the need to manage information. We then analyze management information systems and take a look at information technology applications. Then we provide an overview of the Internet and examine e-business as a strategy to improve business performance and create competitive advantage. Finally, we examine the legal and social issues associated with information technology and e-business.

●● **LO1**

Summarize the role and impact of technology in the global economy.

# THE IMPACT OF TECHNOLOGY ON OUR LIVES

**Technology** relates to the application of knowledge, including the processes and procedures to solve problems, perform tasks, and create new methods to obtain desired outcomes. IT includes intellectual knowledge as well as the computer systems devised to achieve business objectives. Technology has been a driving force in the advancement of economic systems and the quality of life. Today, our economic productivity is based more on technology than on any other advance. Information technology is important because our economy is service based. Technology has changed the way consumers take vacations, make purchases, drive cars, and obtain entertainment. Consider the

encyclopedia. Thanks to the ever-growing amount of information available on the Internet, sales of traditional hard-bound encyclopedias have plummeted as more people turn to Internet search engines to help them with research for school, work, or fun. Sales of *Encyclopedia Britannica,* first published in 1768, have declined rapidly over the last decade, while other publishers went out of business. The firms that survived did so by adapting and providing computerized encyclopedia or online access to encyclopedia content. In the workplace, technology has improved productivity and efficiency, reduced costs, and enhanced customer service. The Department of Homeland Security, for example, created a secure Web-based network that lets emergency services share information and coordinate responses to disasters. The Disaster Management Interoperability Services system facilitates vital communications during disasters and may benefit the country during a terrorist attack.[2] The economy of the 21st century is based on these dynamic changes in our society.

Information technology also is changing many traditional products. AFE Cosmetics and Skincare operates www.cosmetics.com, which provides customized cosmetics and skin care products. Lip gloss can be customized to match a specific

> [ "Today, our economic productivity is based more on technology than on any other advance." ]

outfit. Foundation can be matched to skin tone. From the time an order is received, there is a flow of information to achieve this one-to-one fulfillment strategy. A similar company, Reflect.com, was launched by Procter & Gamble to provide customized

---

## Hey, Hey, We're the Arctic Monkeys

Alex Turner, Jamie Cook, Andy Nicholson, and Matt Helders

Business: Arctic Monkeys

Founded: 2002

Success: In all of British chart history, no debut album has sold faster than the Arctic Monkeys' *Whatever People Say I Am, That's What I'm Not.*

The Arctic Monkeys, from Sheffield, England, have skyrocketed to fame in three short years thanks in great part to the Internet. About a year after the band's formation, demo CDs—handed out at small concert gigs—were downloaded to the Internet. Loyal

fans shared the music via cyberspace, people began to take notice, and the band's fan base increased tremendously. In 2004, the band began to receive attention from BBC Radio 1 and the British press based on the offerings floating around the Internet. The Arctic Monkeys resisted the idea of signing with a record label for quite some time—even going as far as forbidding record company scouts from their concerts. Given that they had a large number of sold-out shows across the United Kingdom—thanks primarily to Internet word-of-mouth—they weren't sure they needed representation. However, in 2005 they did sign with Domino Records owner Laurence

Bell—a representative who only signs artists whose music he likes and can truly promote. The Arctic Monkeys' debut album, released in 2006, has made history by becoming the fastest selling debut album in U.K. chart history, and the album is outselling all the other top 20 albums combined. The band won "Best New Act" at the 2006 Brit Awards and made history yet again by being named both "Best New Band" and "Best British Band" in the same year at the 2006 NME Awards. The Arctic Monkeys' quick rise to fame has astounded those in the music business, some of whom say they haven't seen anything like it since The Beatles rose to fame.[1] ❖

beauty products. The company is no longer in business.[3] Keeping pace with new information technology is a challenge for businesses adjusting to new competitive environments.

Information technology has improved global access by linking people in businesses through telecommunications. Satellites permit instant visual and electronic voice connections almost anywhere in the world. The self-sustaining nature of technology acts as a catalyst to spur even faster development. As new innovations are introduced, they stimulate the need for more technology to facilitate further development. Technologies begin a process that creates new opportunities in every industry segment or customer area that is affected.

Productivity, the amount of output per hour of work, is a key ingredient in determining the standard of living. For the past eight years, the United States has enjoyed significantly faster productivity growth than it did over the preceding two decades. Some analysts believe that the potential gains in productivity from technological advances associated with the computer revolution are far from over.[4] In recent years, economic and productivity growth has resulted in the annual addition of 2 million jobs.[5] For example, the ability to access information in "real time" through the electronic data interface between retailers, wholesalers, and manufacturers has reduced delivery lead times, as well as the hours required to produce and deliver products. Product design times and costs have decreased because technology has minimized the need for architectural drafters and some engineers required for building projects. Consider Autodesk Buzzsaw on-demand, which provides a secure, Web-based collaboration and project management service that helps project teams interact, store, manage, and share documents from any Internet connection. This service enhances productivity by reducing costs for architectural firms, builders, engineering companies, and educational institutions as well as those in the hospitality, manufacturing, and retail industries.[6] Medical diagnoses have become faster, more thorough, and more accurate, thanks to access to information and records, hastening treatment and eliminating unnecessary procedures.[7] Some medical services are even offered online to patients.

## ●● LO2

Specify how information is managed, and explain a management information system.

# MANAGING INFORMATION

Data refers to numerical or verbal descriptions related to statistics or other items that have not been analyzed or summarized. Data can exist in a variety of forms—as patterns of numbers or letters printed on paper, stored in electronic memory, or accumulated as facts in a person's mind.[8] Knowledge is usually referred to as an understanding of data gained through study or experience. Information then includes meaningful and useful interpretation of data and knowledge that can be used in making decisions. The less information available, the more risk associated with a decision. For example, when a manager purchases a new computer without conducting any research, the risk of a poor decision is great. A more informed decision could be made after determining existing, and likely, computing needs and the price, capability, and quality of available computers from a number of sources. Information is necessary for good decision making. When information is properly understood, guidelines can be developed that help simplify and improve decisions in future similar circumstances. Therefore, effective information management is crucial.

Businesses often engage in data processing efforts to improve data flow and the usefulness of information. Often, computers are communicating this data without the direct

Handheld devices such as the BlackBerry and Palm Pilot are improving the productivity of workers by letting them access their e-mail and real-time information on the go.

interface or help of an individual. Goods can be ordered when inventories drop or a previous customer can be notified automatically when new product information is available. All of this depends on software and equipment that has been put in place to make data more useful based on established decision criteria.

## Management Information Systems

Because information is a major business resource, it should be viewed as an asset that must be developed and distributed to managers. Technology has been used to develop systems that provide managers with the information needed to make decisions. A management information system (MIS) is used for organizing and transmitting data into information that can be used for decision making. The purpose of the MIS is to obtain data from both internal and external sources to create information that is easily accessible and structured for user-friendly communication to managers. The MIS can range from a simple system in which information is delivered through e-mail to a complex system of records and data that is delivered through sophisticated communications software. At Anheuser-Busch, for example, a system called BudNet compiles information about past sales at individual stores, inventory, competitors' displays and prices, and a host of other information collected by distributors' sales representatives on handheld computers. The system allows company executives to respond quickly to changes in demographic or social trends or competitors' strategies with an appropriate promotional message, package, display, or discount. The system also helps the company pinpoint demographic consumption trends, craft promotional messages, and even develop new products such as Tilt, an innovative malt beverage with caffeine, guarana, and ginseng.[9]

The MIS breaks down time and location barriers, making information available when and where it is needed to solve problems. An effective MIS can make information available around the globe in seconds, and with wireless communications, it is possible for users to carry the system in a briefcase or pocket. Wireless devices in use today include computers, personal data assistants, cell phones, pagers, and GPS positioning devices found in cars. For example, General Motors provides OnStar Telematics that provide advanced satellite-based communication to pinpoint a car's location. The system can put the car's driver in touch with an adviser for emergency assistance or requests for directions, or connect with an online concierge for entertainment, restaurant, and shopping information. When an airbag deploys in a vehicle equipped with OnStar, the system automatically alerts an adviser, who calls immediately to discern the nature of the emergency.[10]

## Collecting Data

To be effective, an MIS must be able to collect data, store and update data, and process and present information. Much of the data that is useful for managers typically comes from sources inside the organization. Such internal data can be obtained from company records, reports, and operations. The data may relate to customers, suppliers, expenses, and sales. Information about employees such as salaries, benefits, and turnover can be of great value and is usually incorporated into the system. External sources of data include customers, suppliers, industry publications, the mass media, and firms that gather data for sale.

A database is a collection of data stored in one place and accessible throughout the network. A database management program permits participants to electronically store information and organize the data into usable categories that are arranged by decision requirements. For example, if management needs to know the 20 top customers by sales volume, then the system can quickly access the database and print a list of the customers in a matter of moments. This same type of information retrieval can occur throughout the functional areas of the business with the appropriate database management software.

Databases developed by Information Resources Inc. (IRI) allow businesses to tap into an abundance of information on sales, pricing, and promotion for hundreds of consumer product categories using data from scanners at the checkouts in stores.

*Scheid Vineyards produces premium wine grapes and operates approximately 5,700 acres of vineyards, primarily in Monterey County, California. The company sells most of its grapes to wineries that produce high-quality table wines. Scheid's clients can get real-time information about the specific grape blocks they're purchasing via the company's "Vit Watch" information system, accessible on the Web. Vit Watch allows both Scheid and its client to keep abreast of what is happening "in the field"—literally.*

IRI can track new products to assess their performance and gauge competitors' reactions. Once new products are on store shelves, IRI monitors related information, including the prices and market share of competing products. IRI can also help companies assess customers' reactions to changes in a product's price, packaging, and display. By tracking a product's sales in relation to promotional efforts, the effect of a company's advertising as well as that of competitors can be known.[11] Nearly all of the consumer package goods firms in the *Fortune* Global 500 use Information Resources Inc.'s services.[12]

## ● ● **LO3**

Describe the Internet and explore its main uses.

# THE INTERNET

The Internet, the global information system that links many computer networks together, has profoundly altered the way people communicate, learn, do business, and find entertainment.

Although many people believe the Internet began in the early 1990s, its origins can actually be traced to the late 1950s (see Table 4.1). Over the past four decades, the network evolved from a system for government and university researchers into a tool used by millions around the globe for communication, information, entertainment, and e-business. With the development of the World Wide Web, a collection of interconnected Web sites or "pages" of text, graphics, audio, and video within the Internet, use of the Internet exploded in the early 1990s.

An intranet is a network of computers similar to the Internet that is available only to people inside an organization. Businesses establish intranets to make the MIS available for employees and to create interactive communication about data. The intranet allows employees to participate in creating

> ● **INTERNET** global information system that links many computer networks together
>
> ● **WORLD WIDE WEB** a collection of interconnected Web sites or pages of text, graphics, audio, and video within the Internet
>
> ● **INTRANET** a network of computers similar to the Internet that is available only to people inside an organization

**TABLE 4.1** History of Information Technology

| Year | Event | Significance |
|---|---|---|
| 1836 | Telegraph | The telegraph revolutionized human (tele)communications with Morse code, a series of dots and dashes used to communicate between humans. |
| 1858–1866 | Transatlantic cable | Transatlantic cable allowed direct instantaneous communication across the Atlantic Ocean. |
| 1876 | Telephone | The telephone created voice communication, and telephone exchanges provide the backbone of Internet connections today. |
| 1957 | USSR launches Sputnik | Sputnik was the first artificial earth satellite and the start of global communications. |
| 1962–1968 | Packet switching networks developed | The Internet relies on packet switching networks, which split data into tiny packets that may take different routes to a destination. |
| 1971 | Beginning of the Internet | People communicate over the Internet with a program to send messages across a distributed network. |
| 1973 | Global networking becomes a reality | Ethernet outlined—this is how local networks are basically connected today, and gateways define how large networks (maybe of different architecture) can be connected together. |
| 1991 | World Wide Web established | User-friendly interface to World Wide Web established with text-based, menu-driven interface to access Internet resources. |
| 1992 | Multimedia changes the face of the Internet | The term "surfing the Internet" is coined. |
| 1993 | World Wide Web revolution begins | Mosaic, user-friendly Graphical Front End to the World Wide Web, makes the Internet more accessible and evolves into Netscape. |
| 1995 | Internet service providers advance | Online dial-up systems (CompuServe, America Online, Prodigy) begin to provide Internet access. |
| 2000 | Broadband connections to the Internet emerge | Provides fast access to multimedia and large text files. |
| 2002 | Advances in wireless | Mobile phones, handheld computers, and personal data assistants provide wireless access to the Internet. |
| 2004 | Wireless technology expands | Use of radio waves to send e-mail, Web pages, and other information through the air (Wi-Fi). |
| 2006 | Wireless expands globally | Worldwide expansion of smart phones and Wi-Fi in developing countries. |

information useful throughout the organization. The development of an intranet saves money and time because paper is eliminated and data becomes available on an almost instantaneous basis. More than half

In the next few pages, we will take a brief look at who uses the Internet and ways the Internet is used.

## Internet Users

The first Internet users were overwhelmingly male, young, and college-educated, and they resided in the United States.

## "More than half of all businesses are running some type of intranet."

of all businesses are running some type of intranet. Even universities are capturing the benefits of intranets. Duke University has introduced an intranet system to help students manage their on-campus recruiting work. With this system, Duke MBA students can apply for jobs, sign up for career counseling, bid on interview slots, post job leads, and network with other students.[13]

Some businesses open up their intranets to other selected individuals or companies through an **extranet,** a network of computers that permits selected companies and other organizations to access the same information and may allow different managers in various organizations to collaborate and communicate about the information. For example, one of the most common uses of an extranet is for a company such as Wal-Mart to permit suppliers such as Procter & Gamble or Kraft to access the Wal-Mart MIS to determine inventory levels and product availability. An extranet allows users to share data, process orders, and manage information.

In the mid-1990s, Mark Cuban, now the owner of the Dallas Mavericks, figured out a way to broadcast live sporting games over the Internet and made a fortune doing so. In 1998, Cuban sold his company, Broadcast.com, to Yahoo! for $5.7 billion.

With increased access, the demographics of Internet users are changing. Men are still slightly more intense Internet users than women; however, women under 30 and black women outpace their male counterparts. Table 4.2 shows Internet use by selected country. Worldwide Internet use has surpassed the 1 billion mark. Much of the world growth in Internet use is coming from countries such as China, India, Brazil, Russia and Indonesia. Future growth is likely to come from smart phone and mobile Internet use.[14]

An increasing number of Americans have high-speed Internet access at home. According to the Organization for Economic Cooperation and Development, the United States has the largest total number of broadband subscribers at 58.1 million. More than 70 percent of U.S. adults have Internet access at home. A large percentage of Internet users are between the ages of 2 and 17. Web sites such as Disney.com and Nickjr.com are popular among children, whereas teenagers frequent sites such as myspace.com.[15]

**TABLE 4.2**  Internet Use, by Selected Country

| Country | Users (in millions) | Estimated Percentage of the Population |
|---|---|---|
| Australia | 14.7 | 70.2 |
| United States | 208.9 | 69.2 |
| Canada | 22 | 67.8 |
| Japan | 86.3 | 67.1 |
| United Kingdom | 37.6 | 62.3 |
| Germany | 50.5 | 61.2 |
| Israel | 3.7 | 51.1 |
| Chile | 6.7 | 42.4 |
| Argentina | 13.0 | 34 |
| Mexico | 20.2 | 19 |
| Russia | 23.7 | 16.5 |
| China | 137 | 10.4 |
| South Africa | 5.1 | 10.3 |
| India | 40 | 3.5 |
| Iraq | 0.036 | 0.1 |

Source: "Internet World Stats, Usage and Population Statistics," Internet World Stats, March 19, 2007, http://www.internetworldstats.com/stats.htm (accessed June 12, 2007).

## Internet Uses

The Internet is used mainly for communication, information, entertainment, and e-business. The most popular use of the Internet in the United States for both individuals and businesses is communication or e-mail. E-mail is fast, easy to use, and convenient. Internet sales in the past year were more than $80 billion. Figure 4.1 shows the likelihood that teens and adults engage in online activities. E-mail has been criticized as diverting employees' attention away from pertinent daily business. One employee noted that of the 250 e-mails he received, around 85 percent were unrelated to his job. According to one study, in 2007 the total volume of spam reached its highest peak even. Users now receive 8 spam messages for every 10 e-mails they receive in their inbox. It is projected that by 2008, 90 percent of all e-mail will be spam.[16]

An adaptation of e-mail is instant messaging (IM), which allows users to carry on one or more real-time conversations simultaneously. Companies such as America Online, Time Warner Inc.,

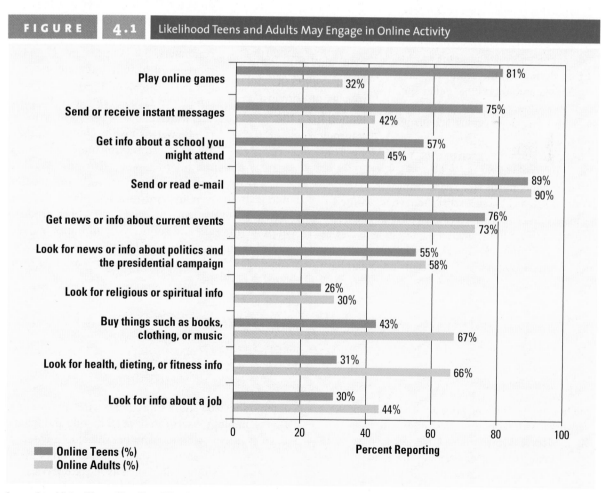

**FIGURE 4.1**  Likelihood Teens and Adults May Engage in Online Activity

Play online games — Online Teens 81%, Online Adults 32%
Send or receive instant messages — Online Teens 75%, Online Adults 42%
Get info about a school you might attend — Online Teens 57%, Online Adults 45%
Send or read e-mail — Online Teens 89%, Online Adults 90%
Get news or info about current events — Online Teens 76%, Online Adults 73%
Look for news or info about politics and the presidential campaign — Online Teens 55%, Online Adults 58%
Look for religious or spiritual info — Online Teens 26%, Online Adults 30%
Buy things such as books, clothing, or music — Online Teens 43%, Online Adults 67%
Look for health, dieting, or fitness info — Online Teens 31%, Online Adults 66%
Look for info about a job — Online Teens 30%, Online Adults 44%

Percent Reporting

■ Online Teens (%)
■ Online Adults (%)

Source: Sean Michael Kerner, "Teen Use of Web, Online Technologies Growing," Pew Internet & American Life Project, July 27, 2005, www.clickz.com/stats/sectors/demographics/print.php/3523376 (accessed April 7, 2006).

and Yahoo! provide free IM services to millions of customers. Like most Internet innovations, IM is letting people communicate faster and more efficiently than ever. Once the realm of teenagers, IM is becoming more widespread in the workplace—although the content is not necessarily work related. Instant messaging allows employees in large firms to communicate quickly and inexpensively, but of the more than 20 percent of instant message users who report doing so at work, 33 percent use the technology to primarily communicate with friends and family and 21 percent indicate they use it for both work and personal messages.[17]

Many users turn to the Net for information on a vast array of topics. Search engines, such as Google, provide access to information on just about every imaginable subject. The user simply enters a word or phrase, and the search engine returns links to Web sites that potentially contain information the user is seeking. There are also many online reference materials, including encyclopedias, atlases, and almanacs. Other Web sites provide information on one specific topic, such as the weather, tourist/travel information, health/fitness, a particular sport, or any of a limitless number of topics. There are also online publications such as *Business Week, The Wall Street Journal,* the *New York Times,* and hundreds more. There are also sites that provide current and practical information on equipment and technological tools (e.g., www.howstuffworks.com). Many businesses provide online information on their products even if they do not sell the products online or sell only a limited amount online. Other sites provide photos (www.photovault.com). It is likely there is a site with information on just about anything you can think of.

Other users find entertainment on the Net. You can listen to and download music; read books; track your favorite band, movie star, sports team, or local gas prices; watch video clips; chat about your favorite TV show; play games; build your own crossword puzzles; enter contests and sweepstakes; and find something interesting to do this weekend in your community. At Apple's iTunes Music Store, for example, legal downloads of music (at 99 cents per song) have

**DID YOU KNOW?**

Every day, 600,000 illegal copies of movies are downloaded from the Internet.[18]

## Emerging Technologies

The growth of information and communication technologies has exploded in recent years. Consider that the number of subscribers to mobile phone services surpassed the number of fixed-line subscribers in 2002, and cellular has become the dominant technology for voice communications.[20] Internet browsing by a mobile phone is growing throughout the world as cell phone penetration increases. In South Korea, Japan, and urban China, at least 90 percent of the households have at least one mobile phone. In the United States, 75 percent of households own a mobile phone. Globally, around one-fourth of cell phone owners have used their phone to browse the Web.[21] Indeed, the number of digital photos taken by cell phones has outstripped the number taken by digital cameras. Camera phones are so popular in Japan that funeral attendees are now using the phones to take pictures of deceased friends and relatives. A funeral director in Tokyo stated, "I get the sense that people no longer respect the dead. It's disturbing."[22]

Wireless fidelity (Wi-Fi) networks are changing the way individuals and businesses use the Internet. Wi-Fi sends Web pages and other information to your laptop computer or other electronic device using radio waves. In the not-too-distant future, experts expect Wi-Fi to link all sorts of devices—not just computers, but lamps, stereos, appliances, and more—and to fully integrate the Internet into our lives. Cooks using wireless notebook computers can take advantage of Epicuriuos's Web site, which allows access to "how to" videos that can be watched while cooking in the kitchen.[23] Wi-Fi is also transforming how companies use the Internet. Some firms use Wi-Fi to replace expensive wired networks or to maintain communications even in hard-to-reach places like warehouses. As such, investments in Wi-Fi can boost productivity and improve the ease and connectivity of multiple devices. Bluetooth technology allows mobile phones, computers, and personal digital assistants (PDAs), as well as other devices, to be

> "Search engines, such as Google, provide access to information on just about every imaginable subject."

exceeded 2 billion songs since the program launched four years ago. Real Networks, with more than 300 million users, provides digital media services and software to allow viewing of sporting events, news, or entertainment or listening to music. Interestingly, only 5 percent of music sales occur digitally.[19]

interconnected using a short-range wireless connection. Using this technology, users can have all mobile and fixed computer devices in sync with one another. Bluetooth wireless technology is installed on more than 5 million units every week as well as some automobiles, such as select BMWs.[24]

Wireless mesh networks are answering the need for more product differentiation and diverse technological advancements. One of the big "killer applications" of wireless technologies will be the establishment of "plug and play" mesh networks, which provide optimized cost, benefit, and reliability ratios. Mesh networks avoid the central switching points found in the current Internet network structure and thus eliminates centralized failure. The mesh networks are self-healing and self-organizing, requiring no manual configuration, thus improving the reliability of communication between points.[25]

Internet Voice, also known as Voice over Internet Protocol (VoIP), allows you to make telephone calls using broadband Internet connections instead of traditional hard-wired, land lines. While some services only work through your computer, others allow you to use your traditional phone line with an adapter. Companies operating in this market include Vonage, Skype, Sunrocket, Time Warner Cable, and Net Zero, to name a few.[26]

Another emerging technology of great importance to business is radio frequency identification (RFID) systems, which use radio waves to identify and track resources and products within the distribution channel. Goods tagged with an RFID tag can be tracked electronically from supplier to factory floor, from warehouse to retail store. Companies are also increasingly employing global positioning systems (GPS) to facilitate shipping and inventory management tasks. Wal-Mart is a leader in the use of RFID technology, getting its suppliers to use RFID chips in the pallets and cases shipped to stores. This helps minimize one of the most costly problems in retailing—empty shelves with replacement product hiding in the storeroom. In a study by the University of Arkansas, stores using this technology and process saw a 16 percent reduction in product missing from shelves.[27]

The growth of wireless voice communications and their increasing integration with Internet technologies generates opportunities for further innovations and applications. For

example, location-based wireless technologies already aid police and parents in protecting children from kidnapping and other crimes. Multimedia messaging services (MMS) and streaming mobile video raise exciting possibilities for more person-to-person services and even personalized entertainment.[28] However, these possibilities also raise privacy questions, as we shall see later in this chapter.

## ● ● L04

Define e-business, and discuss the e-business models.

## E-BUSINESS

Because the phenomenal growth of the Internet and the World Wide Web have provided the opportunity for e-business to grow faster than any other innovation in recent years, we have devoted an entire section to this subject. E-business growth has not been without some setbacks as businesses experimented with new approaches to utilizing information technology and the Internet. Because e-business is based on an interactive model to conduct business, it has expanded the methods for maintaining business relationships. The nature of the Internet has created tremendous opportunities for businesses to forge relationships with consumers and business customers, target markets more precisely, and even reach previously inaccessible markets. The Internet also facilitates business transactions, allowing companies to network with manufacturers, wholesalers, retailers, suppliers, and outsource firms to serve customers more efficiently. Traditional methods included conducting business personally, through the mail (package document delivery service), and via telephone. The telecommunication opportunities created by the Internet have set the stage for e-business development and growth.

In 2006, Nike and Apple® announced the launch of the Nike + iPod Sport Kit, a wireless system that allows Nike + shoes to "talk" iPod® nanos. A sensor in the kit measures a Nike + shoe wearer's activity level and then wirelessly transfers the data to his or her iPod nano.

## The Nature of E-Business

In general, e-business has the same goal as traditional business. All businesses try to earn a profit by providing products that satisfy people's needs. E-business can be distinguished from traditional business as carrying out the goals of business through utilization of the Internet. There are many different areas of e-business that use familiar terms. For

*Jeff Bezos, founder, CEO, and chairman of Amazon.com, holds the company's first sign, quickly spray-painted prior to an interview with a Japanese television station in 1995.*

the public. The Otto Group is the world's number-two online retailer, behind Amazon.com. The company generated around $3.8 billion in online sales in one year through its Crate & Barrel stores and other companies. In Japan, the Otto Sumisho, a catalog retailer, is pioneering the use of mobile technology to buy online, with 30 percent of sales being generated by cell phone orders.[29] Other online companies, such as booksellers, other computer dealers, and even some car companies, are trying to duplicate Otto Group's success.

E-commerce includes activities such as conducting marketing research, providing and obtaining price and product information, and advertising, as well as online selling. Even the U.S. government engages in e-commerce activities—marketing everything from bonds and other financial instruments to oil-drilling leases and wild horses. Procter & Gamble uses the Internet as a fast, cost-effective means for marketing research, judging consumer demand for potential new products by inviting online consumers to sample new prototype products and provide feedback. If a product gets rave reviews from the samplers, the company might decide to introduce it. Procter & Gamble already conducts nearly 100 percent of its concept testing and 40 percent of its 6,000 product tests and other studies online, saving the company significant time and money in getting new products to market.[30]

E-business has changed our economy with companies that could not exist without the technology available through the Internet. For example, DoubleClick is an Internet advertising firm that was founded in 1996 as an agency for advertising for Web sites. The company recognized the value of new information technology and created a priority ad-placement technology, DART, that is used to manage marketing e-mails as well as place banner advertising on Web sites. The firm could not have existed without the development of the Internet.[31]

Many companies that attempted to transact business on the Internet, often called dot-coms, had problems making a profit. Most of the early dot-coms, such as eToys.com, Pets.com, Garden.com, Hardware.com, and BigWords.com, found that no single technology could completely change the nature of business, and many failed. Some dot-coms failed because they thought the only thing that mattered was the brand awareness they created through advertising. The reality, however, is that Internet markets are more similar to traditional markets than they are different.

> " **e-commerce uses the Internet to carry out marketing activities, including buying and selling activities conducted online.** "

example, e-commerce uses the Internet to carry out marketing activities, including buying and selling activities conducted online. These activities include communicating and fostering exchanges and relationships with customers, suppliers, and

Thus, successful e-business strategies, like traditional business strategies, depend on creating products that customers need or want, not merely developing a brand name or reducing the costs associated with online transactions. Consider Amazon.com,

# IN THE FUTURE, MOST BENEFITS AND SIGNIFICANT GAINS WILL COME FROM RESTRUCTURING THE WAY WORK IS DONE WITHIN BUSINESSES.

which struggled for years to earn a profit, but finally moved into the black and currently operates with profits of $359 million on sales near $8.5 billion.[32] Some of the reasons behind the online retailer's success include the fact that it offers 10 times the selection of a typical "big-box" electronics store and more than 500 top clothing brands. The company's attention to customer satisfaction earned it an 88 on the American Customer Satisfaction Index, the highest score ever recorded on that survey.[33]

Instead of e-business changing all industries, it has had much more impact in certain industries where the cost of business and customer transactions is very high. For example, investment trading is less expensive online because customers can buy and sell investments, such as stocks and mutual funds, on their own. Firms such as E* Trade and Charles Schwab Corp, the biggest online brokerage firm, have been innovators in online trading. Traditional brokers such as Merrill Lynch have had to follow these companies and provide online trading for their customers.

E-business can use many benefits of the Internet to reduce the cost of both customer and business transactions. Because the Internet lowers the cost of communication, it can contribute significantly in any industry or activity that depends on the flow of information. Opportunities exist for information-intensive industries such as entertainment, health care, government services, education, and computer services such as software.[34] For example, some insurance companies now pay for doctor–patient e-visits. Computer-literate patients can now consult their doctors through many Web sites, including Superior Health Medical Group. Patients of Superior Health can access e-Visit to obtain diagnoses, advice, and prescriptions without ever leaving their homes. Visitors can expect a response within 24 hours, and the approximate cost is $35.00 versus $63.00 for an office visit. During the first four months the service was offered, there was no charge for using e-Visit to familiarize consumers with the service and to encourage use.[36]

A recent trend to help companies control the rising labor costs associated with providing customer service and support is the practice of outsourcing service jobs. The federal government does not keep track of how many U.S. jobs have moved to companies overseas, but there are estimates that 300,000 to 400,000 jobs have gone to places like China, Russia, and India in the last three years. Whether U.S. citizens are aware or not, they may be talking to an employee in India whenever they call the technical support number for Delta Airlines, American Express, Sprint, CitiBank, IBM, or Hewlett-Packard, even McDonald's is outsourcing drive-through orders.

In the future, most benefits and significant gains will come from restructuring the way work is done within businesses.

## Online Dating: Be Careful What You Wish For

The dating scene has changed drastically in recent years thanks to technological innovations. Gone are the days where you actually had to venture out and strike up a conversation face-to-face to meet someone. Case in point—online dating services are more popular than ever. Research shows that there are more than 90 million single adults in the United States; many of them are willing to do what it takes or spend what it takes to find love. However, the top online dating services are losing ground. An Internet tracking company, monitors 836 dating sites—an increase from 611 a few years ago.

A reason for the slowdown is that 61 percent of users fear that people on online dating sites may misrepresent themselves. In fact, more than 30 percent of those visiting online sites confess to being married or in a committed relationship—so the fear appears to be founded. True.com and other online dating sites are now offering background checks, looking into both criminal and marital history/ backgrounds. This may very well be a service members will pay more to receive.

Throwing a new wrench into the online dating game after about 2 million successful marriages, are the divorces among these couples that are beginning to occur. In a number of divorce proceedings, spouses are citing false claims made on profiles as well as the fact that they neglected to get to know each other as people much beyond their dating site profiles. This turn of events has dating sites rushing to offer new services aimed at helping these couples stay together. EHarmony.com is set to launch a "relationship lab": The site will follow a selection of couples who met on the site for about five years to find out how they fare in marriage. The site is also offering a $240 package that includes 12 sessions with in-house psychologists. JDate.com, a site for Jewish singles, has brought in a dating coach to assist customer service representatives with relationship counseling. The traditional online dating site may be slowing down, but there are always new ways to enter the market and boost revenue. New and veteran companies alike are coming up with inventive ways to entice those looking for love right in to the cyberspace dating game.[35] ❖

## Q: Discussion Questions

1. Why do you think online dating Web sites are so popular?

2. What are some of the ethical issues related to the operation of an online dating site?

3. How do you think online dating sites could be improved to increase their business success?

● BUSINESS-TO-
BUSINESS (B2B) use of
the Internet for transac-
tions and communications
between organizations

While e-business can reduce the cost of both customer and business transactions, it can also improve coordination within and across businesses. E-business systems can become the communications backbone linking traditional relationships and storing employee knowledge in management information systems so that co-workers can access this knowledge instead of starting from the ground up. Leading experts suggest that most e-business benefits will come from changes in business practices and the way organizations function. With the crucial role of communication and information in business, the long-term impact of e-business on economic growth could be substantial.[37]

One area where e-business may have promised too much is in the area of manufacturing. Intranets can be important in reducing inventories and in eliminating costs in purchasing and other supply chain activities, as well as in eliminating unnecessary transactions. The Internet can be useful in determining the cost of components and other supplies and detailed information on customers to help customize products. Still the Internet mainly helps in moving information, while most manufacturing involves making things and motivating employees to maintain quality. Manufacturers still need to move truckloads of materials through congested highways and maintain a labor force that can get the job done. E-business can help manage manufacturing operations but is only one component that can provide quality and productivity.

## E-Business Models

There are three major e-business models or markets with unique challenges and opportunities that represent areas with shared characteristics and decisions related to organizational structure, job requirements, and financial needs. The models are based on e-business customer profiles and how the Internet is used to maintain relationships.

busines-to-business. **Business-to-business (B2B)** e-business, sometimes called collaborative commerce, is the use of the Internet for transactions and communications between organizations. B2B activities are the largest and fastest growing area of e-business, with one-fourth of all B2B transactions taking place on the Internet. Typical ways that a company might join the B2B world range from the easiest—going online with an electronic catalog—to the more complex—creating a private trading network, using collaborative design, engaging in supply chain management, and creating a public exchange.[38]

Many B2B companies combine these to be successful. For example, Internet infrastructure maker Cisco Systems receives 68 percent of its orders online, and 70 percent of its service calls are resolved online. Cisco is in the process of linking all of its contract manufacturers and key suppliers into an advanced Web supply-chain management system called the e-HUB. This advanced Internet communication system speeds up the information about demand and is distributed to suppliers.[39] Ford Motor Company links 30,000 auto parts suppliers and its 6,900-member dealer network for transactions. Ford expects to save $8.9 billion a year on costs and earn approximately $3 million a year from fees it charges for the use of its supplier network.[40]

The forces unleashed by the Internet are particularly important in B2B relationships, where uncertainties are being reduced by improving the quantity, reliability, and timeliness of information. General Motors, IBM, and Procter & Gamble are learning to consolidate and rationalize their supply chains using the Internet. Covisint is a leading provider of services that provide linkages between partners, customers, and suppliers. There are more than 266,000 users in more than 30,000 companies in 96 countries using their services. Users of these services include DaimlerChrysler, Delphi, Ford Motor Company, General Motors, Lear Automotive, Mitsubishi, Johnson Controls, and Visteon.

Volkswagen's software system, iPad, has cut order processing time from two hours to nine minutes since VW's purchasing agents receive product descriptions directly from suppliers online.

The goal of the alliance is to provide time and cost-saving efficiencies in the automotive and health care industries.[41]

## business-to-consumer.

Business-to-consumer (B2C) e-business means delivering products and services directly to individual consumers through the Internet. The Internet provides an opportunity for mass customization, meaning that individuals can communicate electronically over the Internet and receive responses that satisfy their individual needs. If products and communication can be customized to fit the individual, then long-term relationships can be nurtured. For example, after a consumer makes a purchase at Amazon. com, the site provides recommendations for books, music, DVD, and toys, as well as electronics and software on future site visits by that consumer. Dell Computer is a leading B2C e-business that not only custom-builds computers for consumers but also provides customer service online.

U.S. e-tailers generated more than $80 billion in sales in 2005—a figure expected to grow by a compound annual growth rate of 17 percent through 2008 to exceed $117 billion. Experts believe the escalation of online retail sales will come primarily from first-time Internet buyers and that the online buying population will continue to grow to include one-half the adult population by 2008.[42]

Services provided in e-business relationships are often referred to as e-services. E-services are efforts to enhance the value of

Internet provide additional opportunities for enhancing the value to the consumer. Some examples of e-services include MapQuest's driving direction service and travel services provided by Travelocity.com and Expedia. A majority of travelers use the Internet for booking travel. Nearly 80 percent use the Internet for travel information or planning.[43] Table 4.3 summarizes other findings of the Travel Industry Association of America. The key to the success of e-service sites is creating and nurturing one-to-one relationships with consumers. For example, some e-service travel sites also sell books/maps, apparel, insurance, and bags/luggage.[44]

## consumer-to-consumer.

One market that is sometimes overlooked is the consumer-to-consumer (C2C) market, where consumers market goods and services to each other through the Internet. C2C e-business has become very popular thanks to eBay and other online auctions through which consumers can sell goods, often for higher prices than they might receive through newspaper classified ads or garage sales. Some consumers have even turned their passion for trading online into successful businesses. For example, a collector of

> ## "Services provided in e-business relationships are often referred to as e-services."

products through an experience that is created for the consumer. While traditional retailers provide many services, e-business companies have discovered that the unique characteristics of the

vintage guitars might find items in local markets, such as pawnshops or flea markets, and then sell them for a higher price on eBay. Others use Zshops at Amazon.com for selling used

---

**TABLE 4.3**  Trends in the Online Travel Business

Most popular Web sites used for travel planning:

| | |
|---|---|
| Expedia, Travelocity, and Priceline | 67% |
| Google or Yahoo! | 64 |
| Airline and hotel Web sites | 54 |

The use of travel agents is declining with 31% reporting use of a travel agent versus 39% the previous year.

Airline tickets, lodging, and rental cars are the top-three travel items booked online; however, other areas such as cultural event tickets, theme/amusement park tickets, travel packages, and tickets for sporting events showed significant growth.

Leisure travelers spend an average of $1,288 when booking online, whereas business travelers spend an average of $1,357 when booking their travel online.

When it comes to leisure travel, women are more likely to be online travel planners (56%) and bookers (55%).

Source: Travel Industry Association of America, "Leading Travel Industry Consumer Survey Reports Significantly More Travelers Plan and Book Trips Online," November 16, 2005, http://www.tia.org/pressmedia/pressrec.asp?Item=689 (accessed June 14, 2006).

items. The growing C2C market may threaten some traditional businesses if consumers find it more efficient to sell their books, CDs, and other used items through online auctions or other C2C venues.[45]

## Customer Relationship Management (CRM)[46]

One characteristic of companies engaged in e-business is a renewed focus on building customer loyalty and retaining customers. Customer relationship management (CRM) focuses on using information about customers to create strategies that develop and sustain desirable long-term customer relationships. This focus is possible because today's technology helps companies target customers more precisely and accurately than ever before. CRM technology allows businesses to identify specific customers, establish interactive dialogs with them to learn about their needs, and combine this information with their purchase histories to customize products to meet those needs. Procter & Gamble, for example, encourages Oil of Olay customers to join their Club Olay. Members receive special offers, free samples, and skin type/product pairings. In addition, Procter & Gamble is able to collect information on products registrants use as well as reactions to P&G products.[47]

Advances in technology and data collection techniques now permit firms to profile customers in real time. The goal is to assess the

simply be too expensive to retain given the low level of profits they generate. Companies can discourage these unprofitable customers by requiring them to pay higher fees for additional services. For example, many banks and brokerages charge sizable maintenance fees on small accounts. Such practices allow firms to focus their resources on developing and managing long-term relationships with more profitable customers.[48]

CRM focuses on building satisfying relationships with customers by gathering useful data at all customer-contact points—telephone, fax, online, and personal—and analyzing those data to better understand customers' needs and desires. Companies are increasingly automating and managing customer relationships through technology. Indeed, one fast-growing area of CRM is customer-support and call-center software, which helps companies capture information about all interactions with customers and provides a profile of the most important aspects of the customer experience on the Web and on the phone. Customer-support and call-center software can focus on those aspects of customer interaction that are most relevant to performance, such as how long customers have to wait on the phone to ask a question of a service representative or how long they must wait to receive a response from an online request. This technology can also help marketers determine whether call-center personnel are missing opportunities to promote additional products or to provide better service. For example, after buying a new Saab automobile, the customer is supposed to meet a service mechanic who can answer any technical questions about the new car during the first service visit.

Lands' End promotes its online shopping experience by enticing customers with the benefit of not having to stand in line.

> ## "Companies are increasingly automating and managing customer relationships through technology."

worth of individual customers and thus estimate their lifetime value (LTV) to the firm. Some customers—those that require considerable coddling or who return products frequently—may

Saab follows up this visit with a telephone survey to determine whether the new car buyer met the Saab mechanic and to learn about the buyer's experience with the first service call.

Sales automation software can link a firm's sales force to applications that facilitate selling and providing service to customers. Often these applications enable customers to assist themselves instead of using traditional sales and service organizations. Salesforce.com provides salesforce automation for clients such as Accenture, Cisco, Deloitte, and Intel. Systems such as Salesforce make tracking and forecasting sales more efficient and effective.[49] In addition, CRM systems can provide sales managers with information that helps provide the best product solution for customers and thus maximize service. Dell Computer, for example, employs CRM data to identify those customers with the greatest needs for computer hardware and then provides these select customers with additional value in the form of free, secure, customized Web sites. These "premier pages" allow customers—typically large companies—to check their order status, arrange deliveries, and troubleshoot problems. Although Dell collects considerable data about its customers from its online sales transactions, the company avoids selling customer lists to outside vendors.[50]

*Fashion designers for Zara, the Spain-based fashion retailer, collect purchase information and research customer trends to determine what their customers will want to wear in the next few weeks. They share this information with other departments to forecast sales and coordinate deliveries.*

 **LO5**

Identify the legal and social issues of information technology and e-business.

# LEGAL AND SOCIAL ISSUES

The extraordinary growth of information technology, the Internet, and e-business has generated many legal and social issues for consumers and businesses. These issues include privacy concerns, identity theft, and protection of intellectual property and copyrights. Each of these is discussed in this section, as well as steps taken by individuals, companies, and the government to address the issues.

## Privacy

Businesses have long tracked consumers' shopping habits with little controversy. However, observing the contents of a consumer's shopping cart or the process a consumer goes through when choosing a box of cereal generally does not result in specific, personally identifying data. Although consumers' use of credit cards, shopping cards, and coupons involves giving up a certain degree of anonymity in the traditional shopping process, consumers can still choose to remain anonymous by paying cash. Shopping on the Internet, however, allows businesses to track consumers on a far more personal level, from their online purchases to the Web sites they favor.[51] Current technology has made it possible to amass vast quantities of personal information, often without consumers' knowledge, and allows for the collection, sharing, and selling of this information to interested third parties. Privacy has, therefore, become one of Web users' biggest concerns.

How is personal information collected on the Web? Many sites follow users' online "tracks" by storing a "cookie," or identifying string of text, on their computers. Cookies permit Web site operators to track how often a user visits the site, what he or she looks at while there, and in what sequence. Cookies allow Web site visitors to customize services, such as virtual shopping carts, as well as the particular content they see when they log onto a Web page, but the potential for misuse has left many consumers uncomfortable with this technology.

> **The extraordinary growth of information technology, the Internet, and e-business has generated many legal and social issues for consumers and businesses.**

# "SOME MEASURE OF PROTECTION OF PERSONAL PRIVACY IS PROVIDED BY THE U.S. CONSTITUTION, AS WELL AS SUPREME COURT RULINGS AND FEDERAL LAWS"

Some measure of protection of personal privacy is provided by the U.S. Constitution, as well as Supreme Court rulings and federal laws (see Table 4.4). Some of these laws relate specifically to Internet privacy while others protect privacy both on and off the Internet. The U.S. Federal Trade Commission (FTC) also regulates and enforces privacy standards and monitors Web sites to ensure compliance.

Businesses are beginning to recognize that the only way to circumvent further government regulation with respect to privacy is to develop systems and policies to protect consumers' interests. Several nonprofit organizations have also stepped in to help companies develop privacy policies. Among the best known of these are TRUSTe and the Better Business Bureau Online. TRUSTe is a nonprofit organization devoted to promoting global trust in Internet technology. Companies that agree to abide by TRUSTe's privacy standards may display a "trustmark" on their Web sites. Almost 2,000 Web sites display the trustmark seal of approval from TRUSTe.[52] The BBBOn-Line program provides verification, monitoring and review, consumer dispute resolution, a compliance seal, enforcement mechanisms, and an educational component. It is managed by the Council of Better Business Bureaus, an organization with

**TABLE 4.4** Privacy Laws

| Act (Date Enacted) | Purpose |
|---|---|
| Privacy Act (1974) | Requires federal agencies to adopt minimum standards for collecting and processing personal information; limits the disclosure of such records to other public or private parties; requires agencies to make records on individuals available to them on request, subject to certain conditions. |
| Right to Financial Privacy Act (1978) | Protects the rights of financial-institution customers to keep their financial records private and free from unjust government investigation. |
| Computer Security Act (1987) | Brought greater confidentiality and integrity to the regulation of information in the public realm by assigning responsibility for standardization of communication protocols, data structures, and interfaces in telecommunications and computer systems to the National Institute of Standards and Technology (NIST), which also announces security and privacy guidelines for federal computer systems. |
| Computer Matching and Privacy Protection Act (1988) | Amended the Privacy Act by adding provisions regulating the use of computer matching, the computerized comparison of individual information for purposes of determining eligibility for federal benefits programs. |
| Video Privacy Protection Act (1988) | Specifies the circumstances under which a business that rents or sells videos can disclose personally identifiable information about a consumer or reveal an individual's video rental or sales records. |
| Telephone Consumer Protection Act (1991) | Regulates the activities of telemarketers by limiting the hours during which they can solicit residential subscribers, outlawing the use of artificial or prerecorded voice messages to residences without prior consent, prohibiting unsolicited advertisements by telephone facsimile machines, and requiring telemarketers to maintain a "do not call list" of any consumers who request not to receive further solicitation. |
| Driver Privacy Protection Act (1993) | Restricts the circumstances under which state departments of motor vehicles may disclose personal information about any individual obtained by the department in connection with a motor vehicle record. |
| Fair Credit Reporting Act (amended in 1997) | Promotes accuracy, fairness, and privacy of information in the files of consumer reporting agencies (e.g., credit bureaus); grants consumers the right to see their personal credit reports, to find out who has requested access to their reports, to dispute any inaccurate information with the consumer reporting agency, and to have inaccurate information corrected or deleted. |
| Children's Online Privacy Protection Act (2000) | Regulates the online collection of personally identifiable information (name, address, e-mail address, hobbies, interests, or information collected through cookies) from children under age 13 by specifying what a Web site operator must include in a privacy policy, when and how to seek consent from a parent, and what responsibilities an operator has to protect children's privacy and safety online. |
| Do Not Call Implementation Act (2003) | Directs the FCC and FTC to coordinate so that their rules are consistent regarding telemarketing call practices, including the Do Not Call Registry and other lists, as well as call abandonment. |

considerable experience in conducting self-regulation and dispute-resolution programs, and it employs guidelines and requirements outlined by the Federal Trade Commission and the U.S. Department of Commerce.[53]

## Spam

Spam, or unsolicited commercial e-mail (UCE), has become a major source of discontent with the Internet. Many Internet users believe spam violates their privacy and steals their resources. Many companies despise spam because it costs them $50 billion a year in lost productivity, new equipment, antispam filters, and manpower. By some estimates, spam accounts for or deceptive unsolicited commercial e-mail and requires senders to provide information on how recipients can opt out of receiving additional messages. However, spammers appear to be ignoring the law and finding creative ways to get around spam filters.[57] Although North America is believed to be the source of 80 percent of spam, the European Union ordered eight member nations to enact antispam and privacy-protection legislation. The EU already has strict regulations concerning electronic communications and bans all unsolicited commercial e-mail, but not all member nations have ratified the regulations.[58] Figure 4.2 shows the volume of spam by country.

> "By some estimates, spam accounts for 94 percent of all e-mail."

94 percent of all e-mail. However, it is not just the rising volume of spam that is a problem, but also the size of the spam messages. To defeat content filters, spammers are increasingly using images, which means that unsolicited bulk e-mail is getting bulkier.[54] Spam has been likened to receiving a direct-mail promotional piece with postage due. Some angry recipients of spam have even organized boycotts against companies that advertise in this manner. Other recipients, however, appreciate the opportunity to learn about new products. Table 4.5 shows how spam volume has changed in personal and corporate e-mail accounts.

Most commercial online services (e.g., AmericaOnline) and Internet service providers offer their subscribers the option to filter out e-mail from certain Internet addresses that generate a large volume of spam. In 2005 AOL alone blocked an average of 1.5 billion spam messages each day (in 2005, half a trillion spam messages were blocked).[55] Businesses are installing software to filter out spam from outside their networks. Some companies have filed suit against spammers under the Controlling the Assault of Non-Solicited Pornography and Marketing (CAN-SPAM) Law, which went into effect in 2004 and bans fraudulent

## Identity Theft

Another area of growing concern is identity theft, which occurs when criminals obtain personal information that allows them to impersonate someone else in order to use their credit to obtain financial accounts and make purchases. The Federal Trade Commission reported 246,035 consumer complaints about identity theft in 2006. The most common complaints related to credit-card fraud, as well as utility fraud, bank fraud, employment-related fraud, government document fraud, and loan fraud.[59] Because of the Internet's relative anonymity and speed, it fosters legal and illegal access to databases containing Social Security numbers, drivers' license numbers, dates of birth, mothers' maiden names, and other information that can be used to establish a credit card or bank account in another person's name in order to make transactions. One growing scam used to initiate identity theft fraud is the practice of *phishing*, whereby con artists counterfeit a genuine well-known Web site and send out e-mails directing victims to the fake Web site where they find instructions to reveal sensitive information such as credit card numbers. Phishing scams

**TABLE 4.5** How Spam Volume has changed

| How Spam Volume Changed? | Users (%) |
|---|---|
| Getting more spam in personal e-mail account | 37 |
| Getting less spam in personal e-mail account | 10 |
| Have not noticed a change | 51 |
| Getting more spam in work e-mail account | 29 |
| Getting less spam in work e-mail account | 8 |
| Have not noticed a change | 55 |

Source: Enid Burnes, "Computer Users More Savvy About E-mail Spam," *ClickZ Stats,* May 25, 2007, http://www.clickz.com/showPage.html?page=3625976 (accessed June 12, 2007).

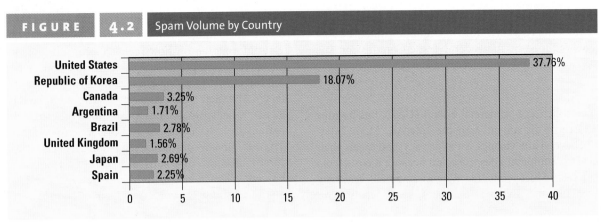

**FIGURE 4.2** Spam Volume by Country

Source: "Messaging Security Resources: Percentage of Total Spam Volumes by Country," *Secure Computing* (n.d.), http://www.ciphertrust.com/resources/statistics/spam_sources.php (accessed June 11, 2007).

have faked Web sites for PayPal, AOL, and the Federal Deposit Insurance Corporation.[60]

Typically, it takes 14 months before a victim discovers identity theft, and in 45 percent of the cases, it took nearly two years to resolve the theft.[61] According to the National Fraud Center, arrests for identity theft fraud have increased to nearly 10,000 a year, with losses from such fraud reaching $745 million, 9.3 million adults are victims of identity fraud on an annual

# My Space Is Your Space

Today's teens and young adults have grown up with the Internet—a tool allowing people to remain completely connected around the world 24/7. Young men and women nationwide use e-mail, instant messaging, and online gathering sites every day. Online socializing is incredibly popular and common among teens and young adults, many of whom simply don't remember a time without it. Among the most visited Web sites for socializing are MySpace and Facebook.

By 2005, MySpace was the fourth most viewed site on the Internet. Chris DeWolfe and Tom Anderson created MySpace.com in 2003 for the music industry, hoping to create a site on which musicians could post bios, songs, and gig dates/locations and on which they could network. Although many musicians still use the site, it has become highly popular with the teenage/young adult crowd—the average user is between 14 and 34 years of age. In two years, membership increased from zero to 47.3 million. At MySpace, you create a profile and begin to acquire friends—people who join your networking group via your approval. Friending, as it's called, is what keeps many users loyal to MySpace. Many people measure social status based on how many "friends" they have. Members spend hours each day instant messaging and writing bulletins to their MySpace friends; they also browse the site for new friends. Gone are the days when people exchanged phone numbers—today they exchange MySpace profiles.

Facebook, created by three roommates at Harvard in 2004, was originally designed to help Harvard students become familiar with other people living in their dorm units. Within one month, buzz about the site was so great that the creators expanded it to include students at Columbia, Stanford, and Yale. In 2005, the site had users at more than 800 colleges/universities—adding up to more than 2.8 million users. Like users at MySpace, Facebook is so integrated within the everyday lives of young adults that rather than exchanging phone numbers or e-mail addresses, they simply tell friends and acquaintances to "facebook" them. Students use Facebook to meet people attending the same schools, announce parties, and share class notes, among other things. Facebook users post profiles and acquire friends just like those at MySpace, and again, how many friends a user has can be a social status indicator.

With the popularity of sites such as MySpace and Facebook comes a new set of safety concerns. Many users post detailed private information and personal photos (often provocative) on their profiles, which can lead to unwanted attention. Some users actually post their whereabouts. These actions are raising red flags among the college/university administration and others who feel students may be putting themselves in danger of stalking or worse. Users of all social networking sites are advised to delete personal information such as addresses and cell phone numbers from their profiles. Facebook only allows individuals with .edu e-mail addresses to register—a requirement that would appear to limit access. Sites are stepping up their privacy measures, but the responsibility still rests with the users to protect themselves. The Internet and sites like MySpace and Facebook have opened up an entirely new social realm—most of which is harmless—but it is important to remember that with this new social access comes a new set of precautions. As long as users take safety into account, these sites are incredible resources.[56] ❖

# Q: Discussion Questions

1. Explain the popularity of social communication Web sites.

2. How do MySpace and Facebook make a profit?

3. What are the privacy issues associated with MySpace and Facebook?

basis.[62] To deter identity theft, the National Fraud Center wants financial institutions to implement new technologies, such as digital certificates, digital signatures, and biometrics—the use of fingerprinting or retina scanning.[63]

## Intellectual Property and Copyrights

In addition to protecting personal privacy, Internet users and others are concerned about protecting their rights to property they may create, including songs, movies, books, and software. Such intellectual property consists of the ideas and creative materials developed to solve problems, carry out applications, and educate and entertain others. Intellectual property is generally protected via patents and copyrights. The American Society for Industrial Security estimates that intellectual property and proprietary information losses in the United States total tens of billions of dollars per year.[64] This issue has become a global concern because of disparities in enforcement of laws throughout the world. In fact, the Business Software Alliance estimates that global losses from software piracy amount to $13 billion a year, including movies, music, and software downloaded from the Internet.[65]

U.S. copyright laws protect original works in text form, pictures, movies, computer software, musical multimedia, and audiovisual work. Owners of copyrights have the right to reproduce, derive from, distribute and publicly display, and perform the copyrighted works. Copyright infringement is the unauthorized execution of the rights reserved by a copyright

Shawn Fanning, the founder of Napster, was just a college student when he figured out a way to make music files sharable over the Internet. After Napster met its demise for violating copyright laws, Fanning launched Snocap .com, a service to help the music industry detect songs swapped illegally online.

holder. Congress passed the Digital Millennium Copyright Act (DMCA) in 1998 to protect copyrighted materials on the Internet and limit the liability of online service providers.

## Taxing the Internet?

An increasingly controversial issue in e-business is whether states should be able to levy a sales tax on Internet sales. The issue of collecting taxes on online purchases had been subject to a moratorium that went into effect in 2001. However, many states—facing huge budget deficits—have been lobbying for the right to charge a sales tax on Internet sales originating within their states. In 2005, the Sales Tax Simplification Agreement passed with the support of 18 states. The purpose of the agreement is to simplify the nation's varying state tax laws. Under this system, it is expected that companies who are not required by law to remit sales tax on Internet sales may voluntarily collect taxes.[66]

## The Dynamic Nature of Information Technology and E-Business

As we have pointed out in this chapter, information technology and e-business are having a major effect on the business world and thus your future career. Future leaders of businesses will need more than just a technical understanding of information technology; they will need a strategic understanding of how information technology and e-business can help make business more efficient and productive. Companies that depend on information technology as their core focus provide examples of how savvy managers can adapt to using our knowledge in this area. Companies such as UPS have found that information systems make their "bricks, mortar, and trucks" world come alive to provide

There is a wide variety of levels of information technology (IT) work, from help-desk call-center technician through chief information officer of a major corporation. People interested in technology can pursue careers in software and database development, telecommunications infrastructure, operations and end-user support, electronic commerce, and management. The main types of IT employers are large corporations and technology service providers such as Internet service providers, consultancies, dotcoms, and high-tech startups that operate independently from the Internet.

Although many IT professionals and specialists lost their jobs during the dot-com meltdown at the beginning of the century, demand is once again surging as companies begin to ramp up their IT hiring. Some areas of the United States have been identified as having particularly strong IT hiring markets. The west south-central states (Arkansas, Louisiana, Oklahoma, and Texas) are predicted to show an 8 percent hiring increase, while the east south-central states (Alabama, Kentucky, Mississippi, and Tennessee) are expected to experience a 19 percent increase. Although U.S. companies were expected to create 900,000 new IT jobs in 2001, about 425,000 were expected to remain unfilled because of a shortage of skilled workers. Employers have a higher demand for certain skills, such as network security and programming in Java and XML. Certain industries present a more dynamic market for IT professionals, including entertainment, food and beverage, health care, pharmaceuticals, and biotechnology.

The Internet contains a wealth of information on IT job prospects, outlook, salaries, and current openings. Some IT job Web sites are www.dice.com, www.hotjobs.com, and www.monster.com. People interested in a future in IT must be prepared to be flexible, adapt, and keep themselves up-to-date on current and expected changes in the world of information technology.

Listed here is the average annual salary for selected computer executives and professionals.

| | |
|---|---|
| Chief information officer | $128,430 |
| Chief technology officer | 128,164 |
| Internet-technology strategist | 98,811 |
| Product manager | 88,730 |
| Information security manager | 77,959 |
| Database administrator | 72,236 |
| Help-desk/technical support manager | 64,551 |
| Network administrator | 51,265 |
| Help-desk/technical support specialist | 43,735 [67] |

service to customers. Charles Schwab has made stock trading and obtaining securities information more efficient while providing significant savings to customers. Dell Computer and Cisco have found it possible to sell over half their products online. Many medium- and large-sized companies are changing the way they do business in response to the availability of new technologies that facilitate business in a changing world. Small businesses, too, can succeed by using information technology as leverage to implement appropriate strategies. In the future, manufacturing, retailing, health care, and even government will continue to adapt and use information technologies that will improve business operations. Today, technology presents a tremendous range of potential applications that can improve the efficiency of employees and companies while providing better service to customers. With technology changing on an almost daily basis, it is impossible to predict the long-term effect on the global world of business. ■

## CHECK OUT

www.mhhe.com/FerrellIM

for study materials including Interactive Exercises, Quizzes, iPod downloads, and video.

## Build Your Business Plan

**Managing Information Technology And E-business**

If you are considering developing a business plan for an **established** product or service, explore whether or not the product is currently sold on the Internet. If it is currently not being sold on the Internet, think about why that is the case. Can you think of how you might be able to overcome any obstacles and market this product over the Internet?

If you are thinking about introducing a **new** product or service, now is the time to think about whether you might want to market this product on the Internet. Remember you do not have to have a brick and mortar store to open your own business anymore. Perhaps you might want to consider click instead of brick!

Is **M** in you?

M IS McGRAW-HILL

start here.

**www.mhhe.com/FerrelIM**

●● learning **OBJECTIVES**

**LO1**   Define and examine the advantages and disadvantages of the sole proprietorship form of organization.

**LO2**   Identify two types of partnership, and evaluate the advantages and disadvantages of the partnership form of organization.

**LO3**   Describe the corporate form of organization, and cite the advantages and disadvantages of corporations.

**LO4**   Define and debate the advantages and disadvantages of mergers, acquisitions, and leveraged buyouts.

# OPTIONS FOR ORGANIZING BUSINESS

introduction    The legal form of ownership taken by a business is seldom of great concern to you as a customer. When you eat at a restaurant, you probably don't care whether the restaurant is owned by one person (a sole proprietorship), has two or more owners who share the business (a partnership), or is an entity owned by many stockholders (a corporation); all you want is good food. If you buy a foreign car, you probably don't care whether the company that made it has laws governing its form of organization that are different from those for businesses in the United States. You are buying the car because it is well made, fits your price range, or appeals to your sense of style. Nonetheless, a business's legal form of ownership affects how it operates, how much tax it pays, and how much control its owners have.

This chapter examines three primary forms of business ownership—sole proprietorship, partnership, and corporation—and weighs the advantages and disadvantages of each. These forms are the most often used whether the business is a traditional "bricks and mortar" company, an online-only one, or a combination of both. We also take a look at S corporations, limited liability companies, and cooperatives and discuss some trends in business ownership. You may wish to refer to Table 5.1 to compare the various forms of business ownership mentioned in the chapter.

 **LO1**

Define and examine the advantages and disadvantages of the sole proprietorship form of organization.

# SOLE PROPRIETORSHIPS

**Sole proprietorships,** businesses owned and operated by one individual, are the most common form of business organization in the United States. Common examples include many restaurants, barbershops, flower shops, dog kennels, and independent grocery stores. Sondra Noffel Biggs opened her own stationery store called Papel (Spanish for "paper") in a high-traffic shopping center in Memphis, Tennessee. Biggs operates the store as a sole proprietorship. Indeed, many sole proprietors focus on services—small retail stores, financial counseling, appliance repair, child care, and the like—rather than on the manufacture of goods, which often requires large amounts of money not available to small businesses.

Sole proprietorships are typically small businesses employing fewer than 50 people. (We'll look at small businesses in greater

> ● ● **Common examples include many restaurants, barbershops, flower shops, dog kennels, and independent grocery stores.**

detail in Chapter 6.) There are nearly 18 million sole proprietorships in the United States (72 percent of all businesses), but they account for just 4 percent of total business sales and 15 percent of total income (see Figure 5.1).[1]

## Advantages of Sole Proprietorships

Sole proprietorships are generally managed by their owners. Because of this simple management structure, the owner/manager can make decisions quickly. This is just one of many advantages of the sole proprietorship form of business.

**ease and cost of formation.** Forming a sole proprietorship is relatively easy and inexpensive. In some states, creating a sole proprietorship involves merely announcing the new business in the local newspaper. Other proprietorships, such as barbershops and restaurants, may require state and local licenses and permits because of the nature of the business. The cost of these permits may run from $25 to $100. No lawyer is needed to create such enterprises, and the owner can usually take care of the required paperwork.

Of course, an entrepreneur starting a new sole proprietorship must find a suitable site from which to operate the business. Some sole proprietors look no farther than their garage or a spare bedroom that they can convert into a workshop or office. Among the more famous businesses that sprang to life in their founders' homes are Google, Walt Disney, Dell, eBay, Hewlett-Packard, Apple Computer, and Mattel.[2] Computers, personal copiers, fax machines, and other high-tech gadgets have been a boon for home-based businesses, permitting them to interact quickly with customers, suppliers, and others. Many independent salespersons and contractors can perform their work using a notebook computer as they travel. E-mail and cell phones have made it possible for many proprietorships to develop in the services area.

**TABLE 5.1** Various Forms of Business Ownership

| Structure | Ownership | Taxation | Liability | Use |
|-----------|-----------|----------|-----------|-----|
| Sole Proprietorship | 1 owner | Individual income taxed | Unlimited | Individual starting a business and easiest way to conduct business |
| Partnership | 2 or more owners | Individual owners' income taxed | Somewhat limited | Easy way for two individuals to conduct business |
| Corporation | Any number of shareholders | Corporate and shareholder taxed | Limited | A legal entity with shareholders or stakeholders |
| S Corporation | Up to 75 shareholders | Taxed as a partnership | Limited | A legal entity with tax advantages for restricted number of shareholders |
| Limited Liability Company | Unlimited number of shareholders | Taxed as a partnership | Limited | Avoid personal lawsuits |

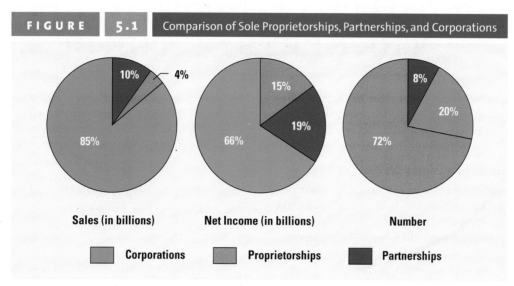

**Sales (in billions)**  **Net Income (in billions)**  **Number**

Corporations  Proprietorships  Partnerships

Source: U.S. Bureau of the Census, *Statistical Abstract of the U.S. 2003,* (Washington, D.C.: U.S. Government Printing Office, 2004), p. 459.

Internet connections also allow small businesses to establish Web sites to promote their products and even to make low-cost long-distance phone calls with voice over Internet protocol (VOIP) technology.

**secrecy.** Sole proprietorships make possible the greatest degree of secrecy. The proprietor, unlike the owners of a partnership or corporation, does not have to discuss publicly his or her operating plans, minimizing the possibility that competitors can obtain trade secrets. Financial reports need not be disclosed, as do the financial reports of publicly owned corporations.

government regulations—federal, state, and local—apply only to businesses that have a certain number of employees, and securities laws apply only to corporations that issue stock. Nonetheless, sole proprietors must ensure that they follow all laws that do apply to their business.

**taxation.** Profits from the business are considered personal income to the sole proprietor and are taxed at individual tax rates. The owner pays one income tax. Another tax benefit is that a sole proprietor is allowed to establish a tax-exempt retirement account or a tax-exempt profit-sharing account. Such

> ## Sole proprietorships have the most freedom from government regulation.

**distribution and use of profits.** All profits from a sole proprietorship belong exclusively to the owner. He or she does not have to share them with any partners or stockholders. The owner decides how to use the profits—for expansion of the business, for salary increases, or for travel to purchase additional inventory or find new customers.

**flexibility and control of the business.** The sole proprietor has complete control over the business and can make decisions on the spot without anyone else's approval. This control allows the owner to respond quickly to competitive business conditions or to changes in the economy.

**government regulation.** Sole proprietorships have the most freedom from government regulation. Many

accounts are exempt from current income tax, but payments taken after retirement are taxed when they are received.

**closing the business.** A sole proprietorship can be dissolved easily. No approval of co-owners or partners is necessary. The only legal condition is that all loans must be paid off.

## Disadvantages of Sole Proprietorships

What may be seen as an advantage by one person may turn out to be a disadvantage to another. The goals and talents of the individual owner are the deciding factors. For profitable businesses managed by capable owners, many of the following factors do not cause problems. On the other hand, proprietors starting out with little management experience and little money are likely to encounter many of the disadvantages.

**unlimited liability.** The sole proprietor has unlimited liability in meeting the debts of the business. In other words, if the business cannot pay its creditors, the owner may be forced to use personal, nonbusiness holdings such as a car or a home to pay off the debts. In a few states, however, houses and homesteads cannot be taken by creditors even if the proprietor declares bankruptcy. The more wealth an individual has, the greater is the disadvantage of unlimited liability.

**limited sources of funds.** Among the relatively few sources of money available to the sole proprietorship are a bank, friends, family, the Small Business Administration, or his or her own funds. The owner's personal financial condition determines his or her credit standing. Additionally, sole proprietorships may have to pay higher interest rates on funds borrowed from banks than do large corporations because they are considered greater risks. Often the only way a sole proprietor can borrow for business purposes is to pledge a car, a house, other real estate, or other personal assets to guarantee the loan. And if the business fails, the owner may lose the personal assets as well as the business. Publicly owned corporations, in contrast, can not only obtain funds from commercial banks but can sell stocks and bonds to the public to raise money. If a public company goes out of business, the owners do not lose personal assets.

**limited skills.** The sole proprietor must be able to perform many functions and possess skills in diverse fields such as management, marketing, finance, accounting, bookkeeping, and personnel. Business owners can rely on specialized professions for advice and services, such as accountants and attorneys. Musicians, for example, can turn to agents for assistance in navigating through the complex maze of the recording business. One startup firm specializing in this type of assistance for online musicians and bands is the Digital Artists Agency, which researches, markets, and cultivates online music talent in exchange for a commission on their online sales of music, tickets, and merchandise.[3] In the end, however, it is up to the business owner to make the final decision in all areas of the business.

**lack of continuity.** The life expectancy of a sole proprietorship is directly related to that of the owner and his or her ability to work. The serious illness of the owner could result in failure if competent help cannot be found.

It is difficult to arrange for the sale of a proprietorship and at the same time assure customers that the business will continue to meet their needs. For instance, how does one sell a veterinary practice? A veterinarian's major asset is patients. If the vet dies suddenly, the equipment can be sold but the patients will not necessarily remain loyal to the office. On the other hand, a veterinarian who wants to retire could take in a younger partner and sell the practice to the partner over time. And one advantage to the partnership is that not all the patients are likely to look for a new vet.

**lack of qualified employees.** It is usually difficult for a small sole proprietorship to match the wages and benefits offered by a large competing corporation because the proprietorship's level of profits may not be as high. In addition, there is little room for advancement within a sole proprietorship, so the owner may have difficulty attracting and retaining qualified employees. On the other hand, the trend of large corporations to downsize and outsource tasks has created opportunities for small business to acquire well-trained employees.

## Eliminating the Competition—That's No Bull

David Burke & Stephen Hanson

Business: Prime—David Burke's Primehouse Breeding Bull

Founded: 2006

Success: David Burke—chef and owner of restaurants davidburke & donatella, David Burke @ Bloomingdales, and David Burke's Primehouse—and his partner Stephen Hanson have invested $250,000 in a Black Angus bull named Prime. Taking part in a rising trend, this chef and his partner plan to breed their own cattle for David Burke's Primehouse in Chicago. Prime was purchased at the end of 2005 and currently lives on a ranch in Kentucky, where he is busily studding cattle that will, over time, give birth to the animals providing meat for David Burke's Primehouse. Apparently, one of the largest challenges chefs face is the competition among America's restaurants for top-quality meat. Providing one's own brand certainly eliminates the issue of competition. For quite some time, chefs have prided themselves on using unusual or specialized ingredients—using these unique ingredients as selling points, items the customers can't find anywhere else. Today, one of those specialized ingredients is meat that can't be found in other restaurants (and often meat with particular backgrounds), whether it be Dorset lambs, Dominique chickens, or rare Red Wattle pigs. Customers are drawn to the opportunities to savor unique dishes, and, of course, special ingredients allow chefs to justify charging higher prices for their dishes. Although it is too soon to know whether the investment in Prime will pay off, David Burke feels he will come out ahead by avoiding the rising cost of meat.[4] ❖

**taxation.** Although we listed taxation as an advantage for sole proprietorships, it can also be a disadvantage, depending on the proprietor's income. Under current tax rates, sole proprietors pay a higher marginal tax rate than do small corporations on income of less than $75,000. The tax effect often determines whether a sole proprietor chooses to incorporate his or her business.

  **LO2**

Identify two types of partnership, and evaluate the advantages and disadvantages of the partnership form of organization.

# PARTNERSHIPS

One way to minimize the disadvantages of a sole proprietorship and maximize its advantages is to have more than one owner. Most states have a model law governing partnerships based on the Uniform Partnership Act. This law defines a **partnership** as "an association of two or more persons who carry on as co-owners of a business for profit." Partnerships are the least used form of business organization, representing just 8 percent of U.S. businesses (see Figure 5.1). Moreover, partnerships account for only 10 percent of sales and 19 percent of income. They are typically larger than sole proprietorships but smaller than corporations.

## Types of Partnership

There are two basic types of partnership: general partnership and limited partnership. A **general partnership** involves a complete sharing in the management of a business. In a general partnership, each partner has unlimited liability for the debts of the business. For example, Cirque du Soleil grew from a group of Quebec street performers, who acted as partners, into a half-billion-dollar global company.[5] Professionals such as lawyers, accountants, and architects often join together in general partnerships.

A **limited partnership** has at least one general partner, who assumes unlimited liability, and at least one limited partner, whose liability is limited to his or her investment in the business. Limited partnerships exist for risky investment projects where the chance of loss is great. The general partners accept the risk of loss; the limited partners' losses are limited to their initial investment. Limited partners do not participate in the management of the business but share in the profits in accordance with the terms of a partnership agreement. Usually the general partner receives a larger share of the profits after the limited partners have received their initial investment

back. Popular examples are oil-drilling partnerships and real estate partnerships.

## Articles of Partnership

Articles of partnership are legal documents that set forth the basic agreement between partners. Most states require articles of partnership, but even if they are not required, it makes good sense for partners to draw them up. Articles of partnership usually list the money or assets that each partner has contributed (called *partnership capital*), state each partner's individual management role or duty, specify how the profits and losses of the partnership will be divided among the partners, and describe how a partner may leave the partnership as well as any other restrictions that might apply to the agreement. Table 5.2 lists some of the issues and provisions that should be included in articles of partnership.

## Advantages of Partnerships

Law firms, accounting firms, and investment firms with several hundred partners have partnership agreements that are quite complicated in comparison with the partnership agreement among two or three people owning a computer repair shop. The advantages must be compared with those offered by other forms of business organization, and not all apply to every partnership.

**TABLE 5.2** Issues and Provisions in Articles of Partnership

1. Name, purpose, location
2. Duration of the agreement
3. Authority and responsibility of each partner
4. Character of partners (i.e., general or limited, active or silent)
5. Amount of contribution from each partner
6. Division of profits or losses
7. Salaries of each partner
8. How much each partner is allowed to withdraw
9. Death of partner
10. Sale of partnership interest
11. Arbitration of disputes
12. Required and prohibited actions
13. Absence and disability
14. Restrictive covenants
15. Buying and selling agreements

Source: Adapted from "Partnership Agreement Sample," State of New Jersey, http://www.state.nj.us/njbusiness/start/biztype/partner/agreement_sample.shtml (accessed June 13, 2007).

**ease of organization.** Starting a partnership requires little more than drawing up articles of partnership. No legal charters have to be granted, but the name of the business should be registered with the state.

**availability of capital and credit.** When a business has several partners, it has the benefit of a combination of talents and skills and pooled financial resources. Partnerships

Friends since junior high, Ben Cohen and Jerry Greenfield initially began Ben & Jerry's Homemade Ice Cream as a partnership in 1978. The pair took a correspondence course in ice-cream making before founding the company in a renovated Vermont gas station.

Source: Linda Tischles, "Join the Circus," *Fast Company*, July 2005, pp. 53–58.

tend to be larger than sole proprietorships and therefore have greater earning power and better credit ratings. Because many limited partnerships have been formed for tax purposes rather than for economic profits, the combined income of all U.S. partnerships is quite low, as shown in Figure 5.1. Nevertheless, the professional partnerships of many lawyers, accountants, and investment banking firms make quite large profits. Goldman Sachs, a large New York investment banking partnership, earns several hundred million dollars in an average year.

**combined knowledge and skills.** Partners in the most successful partnerships acknowledge each other's talents and avoid confusion and conflict by specializing in a particular area of expertise such as marketing, production, accounting, or service. The diversity of skills in a partnership makes it possible for the business to be run by a management team of specialists instead of by a generalist sole proprietor. Service-oriented partnerships in fields such as law, financial planning, and accounting may attract customers because clients

may think that the service offered by a diverse team is of higher quality than that provided by one person. Larger law firms, for example, often have individual partners who specialize in certain areas of the law—such as family, bankruptcy, corporate, entertainment, and criminal law.

**decision making.** Small partnerships can react more quickly to changes in the business environment than can large partnerships and corporations. Such fast reactions are possible because the partners are involved in day-to-day operations and can make decisions quickly after consultation. Large partnerships with hundreds of partners in many states are not common. In those that do exist, decision making is likely to be slow.

**regulatory controls.** Like a sole proprietorship, a partnership has fewer regulatory controls affecting its activities than does a corporation. A partnership does not have to file public financial statements with government agencies or send out quarterly financial statements to several thousand owners, as do corporations such as Eastman Kodak and Ford Motor Co. A partnership does, however, have to abide by all laws relevant to the industry or profession in which it operates as well as state and federal laws relating to hiring and firing, food handling, and so on, just as the sole proprietorship does.

## Disadvantages of Partnerships

Partnerships have many advantages compared to sole proprietorships and corporations, but they also have some disadvantages. Limited partners have no voice in the management of the partnership, and they may bear most of the risk of the business while the general partner reaps a larger share of the benefits. There may be a change in the goals and objectives of one partner but not the other, particularly when the partners are multinational organizations. This can cause friction, giving rise to an enterprise that fails to satisfy both parties or even forcing an end to the partnership. Many partnership disputes wind up in court or require outside mediation. For example, a quarrel among the partners who owned the Montreal Expos baseball team moved to U.S. District Court after new general partner Jeffrey Loria moved the team to Florida and renamed it the Florida Marlins. Twelve of the team's limited partners sued Loria, accusing him of buying the Expos with the intent of moving the team, diluting their share in the team, and effectively destroying "the economic viability of baseball in Montreal."[6] In such cases, the ultimate solution may be dissolving the partnership. Major disadvantages of partnerships include the following.

**unlimited liability.** In general partnerships, the general partners have unlimited liability for the debts incurred by the business, just as the sole proprietor has unlimited liability for his or her business. Such unlimited liability can be a distinct disadvantage to one partner if his or her personal financial resources are greater than those of the others. A potential partner should check to make sure that all partners have comparable resources to help the business in time of trouble. This disadvantage is eliminated for limited partners, who can lose only their initial investment.

**business responsibility.** All partners are responsible for the business actions of all others. Partners may have the ability to commit the partnership to a contract without approval of the other partners. A bad decision by one partner may put the other partners' personal resources in jeopardy. Personal problems such as a divorce can eliminate a significant portion of one partner's financial resources and weaken the financial structure of the whole partnership.

**life of the partnership.** A partnership is terminated when a partner dies or withdraws. In a two-person partnership, if one partner withdraws, the firm's liabilities would be paid off and the assets divided between the partners. Obviously, the partner who wishes to continue in the business would be at a serious disadvantage. The business could be disrupted, financing would be reduced, and the

> # "All partners are responsible for the business actions of all others."

management skills of the departing partner would be lost. The remaining partner would have to find another or reorganize the business as a sole proprietorship. In very large partnerships such as those found in law firms and investment banks, the continuation of the partnership may be provided for in the articles of partnership. The provision may simply state the terms for a new partnership agreement among the remaining partners. In such cases, the disadvantage to the other partners is minimal.

Selling a partnership interest has the same effect as the death or withdrawal of a partner. It is difficult to place a value on a partner's share of the partnership. No public value is placed on the partnership, as there is on publicly owned corporations. What is a law firm worth? What is the local hardware store worth? Coming up with a fair value that all partners can agree to is not easy.

## As Collecting Declines, Online Auctions May Be the Answer

Interest in collecting, a widespread hobby for decades, is declining—causing many collectors to wonder what will happen to their collections when others inherit them. Children and young adults appear too caught up in everyday life and technology to become interested in collecting. Items such as comic books, baseball cards, and stamps, once popular collection items for children, are now collected by adults. A recent study by Unity Marketing estimates that out of the 37 or so million self-professed collectors, only 11 percent are younger than 36. For current collections to retain their value, a new generation of collectors must further the interest in collectible items.

Many collectors are concerned about the fates of their collections, not wanting them to be thrown or given away. A number of collector's societies are taking steps to make sure collections are treated properly. The International Sewing Machine Collector's Society, for example, contacts a member's family upon the death of that member in the hopes of passing the member's sewing machine(s) on to someone who will value it. The society has

good reason for doing this—when a member recently died, the family sold his sewing machines to a junk dealer for $200—only to discover that the society valued the machines at around $65,000. Due to a lack of interest and knowledge, many young people are unaware of the values of collected items. Some collector's society members are giving lectures to drum up new interest in their collectible items, whether they are toothpick holders or slide rules, but it's a tough sell. Harry Rinker, a collectibles researcher and avid collector, advises that collectors let go of any expectations regarding what will happen to their collections in the hands of the next generation. There is, however, another perspective.

Some experts advise collectors to view collecting as an entrepreneurial activity. eBay, the online auction site, has become a meeting point for collectors worldwide to find one another and to locate or exchange items. Collectors could either decide to sell their collections themselves at some point or advise their beneficiaries to do the same if they are not interested in keeping the collections they've inherited. There is no doubt that

collectors need to stay connected through online communities.

Linda Kruger, editor of *Collector's News*, predicts that perhaps at some point today's young people may be collecting "vintage" electronics such as cell phones, iPods, or MP3 players. However, it is impossible to predict the future value of items or future interest. Is collecting a thing of the past? We will have to wait and see.[7] ❖

**Q: Discussion Questions**

1. Why do you believe younger people are not interested in collecting?

2. Why is the Internet so important for operating a small collecting proprietorship?

3. What would you do if a family member gave you a collection of old coins?

● **CORPORATION** a legal entity, created by the state, whose assets and liabilities are separate from its owners

● **STOCK** shares of a corporation that may be bought or sold

● **DIVIDENDS** profits of a corporation that are distributed in the form of cash payments to stockholders

Selling a partnership interest is easier if the articles of partnership specify a method of valuation. Even if there is not a procedure for selling one partner's interest, the old partnership must still be dissolved and a new one created. In contrast, in the corporate form of business, the departure of owners has little effect on the financial resources of the business, and the loss of managers does not cause long-term changes in the structure of the organization.

**distribution of profits.** Profits earned by the partnership are distributed to the partners in the proportions specified in the articles of partnership. This may be a disadvantage if the division of the profits does not reflect the work each partner puts into the business. You may have encountered this disadvantage while working on a student group project: You may have felt that you did most of the work and that the other students in the group received grades based on your efforts. Even the perception of an unfair profit-sharing agreement may cause tension between the partners, and unhappy partners can have a negative effect on the profitability of the business.

**limited sources of funds.** As with a sole proprietorship, the sources of funds available to a partnership are limited. Because no public value is placed on the business (such as the current trading price of a corporation's stock), potential partners do not know what one partnership share is worth. Moreover, because partnership shares cannot be bought and sold easily in public markets, potential owners may not want to tie up their money in assets that cannot be readily sold on short notice. Accumulating enough funds to operate a national business, especially a business requiring intensive investments in facilities and equipment, can be difficult. Partnerships also may have to pay higher interest rates on funds borrowed from banks than do large corporations because partnerships may be considered greater risks.

### Taxation of Partnerships

Partnerships are quasi-taxable organizations. This means that partnerships do not pay taxes when submitting the partnership tax return to the Internal Revenue Service. The tax return simply provides information about the profitability of the organization and the distribution of profits among the partners. Partners must report their share of profits on their individual tax returns and pay taxes at the income tax rate for individuals.

**● ● LO3**

Describe the corporate form of organization, and cite the advantages and disadvantages of corporations.

## CORPORATIONS

When you think of a business, you probably think of a huge corporation such as General Electric, Procter & Gamble, or Sony because most of your consumer dollars go to such corporations. A **corporation** is a legal entity, created by the state, whose assets and liabilities are separate from its owners. As a legal entity, a corporation has many of the rights, duties, and powers of a person, such as the right to receive, own, and transfer property. Corporations can enter into contracts with individuals or with other legal entities, and they can sue and be sued in court.

Corporations account for 85 percent of all U.S. sales and 66 percent of all income. Thus, most of the dollars you spend as a consumer probably go to incorporated businesses (see Figure 5.1). There are almost 5 million corporations, but they account for only 20 percent of all U.S. businesses.[8] Not all corporations are mega-companies like General Mills or Ford Motor; even small businesses can incorporate. As we shall see later in the chapter, many smaller firms elect to incorporate as "S Corporations," which operate under slightly different rules and have greater flexibility than do traditional "C Corporations" like General Mills.

● ● **Corporations account for 85 percent of all U.S. sales and 66 percent of all income.**

Corporations are typically owned by many individuals and organizations who own shares of the business, called **stock** (thus, corporate owners are often called *shareholders* or *stockholders*). Stockholders can buy, sell, give or receive as gifts, or inherit their shares of stock. As owners, the stockholders are entitled to all profits that are left after all the corporation's other obligations have been paid. These profits may be distributed in the form of cash payments called **dividends.** For example, if a corporation earns $100 million after expenses and taxes and decides to pay the owners $40 million in dividends, the stockholders receive 40 percent of the profits in cash dividends. However, not all after-tax profits are paid to stockholders in dividends. In this example, the corporation retained $60 million of profits to finance expansion.

### Creating a Corporation

A corporation is created, or incorporated, under the laws of the state in which it incorporates. The individuals creating the corporation are known as *incorporators.* Each state has a specific procedure, sometimes called *chartering the corporation,* for incorporating a business. Most states require a minimum of three incorporators; thus, many small businesses can be and are incorporated. Another requirement is that the new corporation's name cannot be similar to that of another business. In most states, a corporation's name must end in "company," "corporation," "incorporated," or "limited" to show that the owners have limited liability. (In this text, however, the word *company* means any organization engaged in a commercial enterprise and can refer to a sole proprietorship, a partnership, or a corporation.)

The incorporators must file legal documents generally referred to as *articles of incorporation* with the appropriate state office (often the secretary of state). The articles of incorporation contain basic information about the business. The following 10 items are found in the Model Business Corporation Act, issued by the American Bar Association, which is followed by most states:

1. Name and address of the corporation.

2. Objectives of the corporation.

3. Classes of stock (common, preferred, voting, nonvoting) and the number of shares for each class of stock to be issued.

4. Expected life of the corporation (corporations are usually created to last forever).

5. Financial capital required at the time of incorporation.

6. Provisions for transferring shares of stock between owners.

7. Provisions for the regulation of internal corporate affairs.

8. Address of the business office registered with the state of incorporation.

9. Names and addresses of the initial board of directors.

10. Names and addresses of the incorporators.

Based on the information in the articles of incorporation, the state issues a **corporate charter** to the company. After securing this charter,

## Types of Corporations

If the corporation does business in the state in which it is chartered, it is known as a *domestic corporation.* In other states where the corporation does business, it is known as a *foreign corporation.* If a corporation does business outside the nation in which it incorporated, it is called an *alien corporation.* A corporation may be privately or publicly owned.

A **private corporation** is owned by just one or a few people who are closely involved in managing the business. These people, often a family, own all the corporation's stock, and no stock is sold to the public. Many corporations are quite large,

*Not all large corporations are publicly traded. Some, such as Levi Strauss, are privately owned.*

## " A corporation may be privately or publicly owned. "

the owners hold an organizational meeting at which they establish the corporation's bylaws and elect a board of directors. The bylaws might set up committees of the board of directors and describe the rules and procedures for their operation.

yet remain private, including Koch, the nation's largest private corporation. By acquiring Georgia-Pacific, Charles Koch turned his family business into the world's largest private corporation. Koch is an energy and natural resource business. There are no plans for Koch to become a public corporation, with Charles Koch owning 40 percent of the corporation's shares and stating that the company will be offered to the public "over my dead body." Prior to the Georgia-Pacific acquisition, Cargill was the largest private corporation and is now second to Koch.[9] Other well-known privately held companies include Publix Super Markets in the supermarket industry, L. L. Bean and Levi Strauss in the apparel industry, and PricewaterhouseCoopers and Ernst & Young in the accounting and financial services industries.[10] Privately owned corporations are not required to disclose financial information publicly, but they must, of course, pay taxes.

search engine, went public with an initial public offering in 2004.[12] Also, privately owned firms are occasionally forced to go public with stock offerings when a major owner dies and the heirs have enormous estate taxes to pay. The tax payment becomes possible only with the proceeds of the sale of stock. This happened to the brewer Adolph Coors Inc. When Adolph Coors died, his business went public and his family sold shares of stock to the public to pay the estate taxes.

On the other hand, public corporations can be "taken private" when one or a few individuals (perhaps the management of the firm) purchase all the firm's stock so that it can no longer be sold publicly. For example, the founder and CEO of Hollywood Video, Mark Wattles, took the video rental chain private in 2004 by buying up all the stock for $14 a share.[13] Taking a corporation private may be desirable when new owners want

> ## Privately owned corporations are not required to disclose financial information publicly, but they must, of course, pay taxes.

A **public corporation** is one whose stock anyone may buy, sell, or trade. Table 5.3 lists the largest U.S. corporations by revenues. Thousands of smaller public corporations in the United States have sales under $10 million. In large public corporations such as AT&T, the stockholders are often far removed from the management of the company. In other public corporations, the managers are often the founders and the major shareholders. Ford Motor Company, for example, was founded by Henry Ford; his great grandson William Clay Ford Jr. is chairman of the board of directors.[11] Publicly owned corporations must disclose financial information to the public under specific laws that regulate the trade of stocks and other securities.

A private corporation that needs more money to expand or take advantage of opportunities may have to obtain financing by "going public" through an **initial public offering (IPO)**, that is, becoming a public corporation by selling its stock so that it can be traded in public markets. For example, Google, the popular Internet

**TABLE 5.3** The Largest U.S. Corporations, Arranged by Revenues

| Rank | Company | Revenues (in billions of dollars) |
|------|---------|-----------------------------------|
| 1. | Wal-Mart | $351.139 |
| 2. | ExxonMobil | 347.254 |
| 3. | General Motors | 207.349 |
| 4. | Chevron | 200.567 |
| 5. | Conoco Phillips | 172.451 |
| 6. | General Electric | 168.307 |
| 7. | Ford Motor | 160.126 |
| 8. | Citigroup | 146.777 |
| 9. | Bank of America Corp. | 117.017 |
| 10. | American International Group | 113.194 |
| 11. | J.P. Morgan Chase & Co. | 99.973 |
| 12. | Berkshire Hathaway | 98.539 |
| 13. | Verizon Communications | 93.221 |
| 14. | Hewlett-Packard | 91.658 |
| 15. | International Business Machines (IBM) | 91.424 |
| 16. | Valero Energy | 91.051 |
| 17. | Home Depot | 90.837 |
| 18. | McKesson | 88.050 |
| 19. | Cardinal Health | 81.895 |
| 20. | Morgan Stanley | 76.688 |

Source: "*Fortune* 500: *Fortune*'s Annual Ranking of America's Largest Corporations," *Fortune*, http://money.cnn.com/magazines/fortune/fortune500/2007/full_list/index.html (accessed June 13, 2007).

to exert more control over the firm or they want to avoid the necessity of public disclosure of future activities for competitive reasons. Taking a corporation private is also one technique for avoiding a takeover by another corporation.

Two other types of corporations are quasi-public corporations and nonprofit corporations. **Quasi-public corporations** are owned and operated by the federal, state, or local government. The focus of these corporations is providing a service to citizens, such as mail delivery, rather than earning a profit. Indeed, many quasi-public corporations operate at a loss. Examples of quasi-public corporations include the National Aeronautics and Space Administration (NASA) and the U.S. Postal Service.

Like quasi-public corporations, **nonprofit corporations** focus on providing a service rather than earning a profit, but they are not owned by a government entity. Organizations such as the Children's Television Workshop, the Elks Clubs, the American Lung Association, the American Red Cross, museums, and private schools provide services without a

Google founders Larry Page and Sergey Brin were able to raise a whopping $1.66 billion via an initial public offering of the company's stock in 2004. The Google IPO was one of the largest in stock market history.

corporate officers, such as the president and the chief executive officer (CEO), who are responsible to the directors for the management and daily operations of the firm. The role and expectations of the board of directors took on greater significance after the accounting scandals of the early 2000s and the passage of the Sarbanes-Oxley Act.[14] As a result, most corporations have restructured how they compensate directors for their time and expertise in serving on a board.

Directors can be employees of the company (*inside directors*) or people unaffiliated with the company (*outside directors*). Inside directors are usually the officers responsible for running the company. Outside directors are often top executives from other companies, lawyers, bankers, even professors. Directors today are increasingly chosen for their expertise, competence, and

> ## "Taking a corporation private is also one technique for avoiding a takeover by another corporation."

profit motive. To fund their operations and services, nonprofit organizations solicit donations from individuals and companies and grants from the government and other charitable foundations.

## Elements of a Corporation

**the board of directors.** A **board of directors,** elected by the stockholders to oversee the general operation of the corporation, sets the long-range objectives of the corporation. It is the board's responsibility to ensure that the objectives are achieved on schedule. Board members are legally liable for the mismanagement of the firm or for any misuse of funds. An important duty of the board of directors is to hire

ability to bring diverse perspectives to strategic discussions. Outside directors are also thought to bring more independence to the monitoring function because they are not bound by past allegiances, friendships, a current role in the company, or some other issue that may create a conflict of interest. Many of the corporate scandals uncovered in recent years might have been prevented if each of the companies' boards of directors had been better qualified, more knowledgeable, and more independent. A survey by *USA Today* found that corporate boards have considerable overlap. More than 1,000 corporate board members sit on four or more company boards, and of the nearly 2,000 boards of directors, more than 22,000 board members are linked to boards of more than one company.[15] According to Phil Purcell, CEO of Morgan Stanley, "some director overlap is inevitable when shareholders demand the highest-caliber directors for their board."[16] This overlap creates the opportunity for conflicts of interest in decision making and limits the independence of individual boards of directors. For example, the telecommunications firm Verizon, which shares four board members with prescription-drug producer Wyeth, withdrew from nonprofit organization Business for Affordable Medicine, which had been criticized by Wyeth because of its stance on bringing generic drugs to market sooner.[17]

*Habitat for Humanity is a nonprofit, nondenominational Christian housing organization that builds simple, decent, affordable houses in partnership with those who lack adequate shelter. Chosen families work alongside volunteers to build their own home.*

**stock ownership.** Corporations issue two types of stock: preferred and common. Owners of preferred stock are

do not receive any dividends unless the preferred stockholders have already been paid. Dividend payments on preferred stock are usually a fixed percentage of the initial issuing price (set by the board of directors). For example, if a share of preferred stock originally cost $100 and the dividend rate was stated at 7.5 percent, the dividend payment will be $7.50 per share per year. Dividends are usually paid quarterly. Most preferred stock carries a cumulative claim to dividends. This means that if the company does not pay preferred-stock dividends in one year because of losses, the dividends accumulate to the next year. Such dividends unpaid from previous years must also be paid to preferred stockholders before other stockholders can receive any dividends.

Although owners of common stock do not get such preferential treatment with regard to dividends, they do get some say in the operation of the corporation. Their ownership gives them the right to vote for members of the board of directors and on other important issues. Common stock dividends may vary according to the profitability of the business, and some corporations do not issue dividends at all, but instead plow their profits back into the company to fund expansion.

Common stockholders are the voting owners of a corporation. They are usually entitled to one vote per share of common stock. During an annual stockholders' meeting, common stockholders elect a board of directors. Because they can choose the board of directors, common stockholders have some say in how the company will operate. Common stockholders may vote by *proxy,* which is a written authorization by which stockholders assign their voting privilege to someone else, who then votes for his or her choice at the stockholders' meeting. It is a normal practice for management to request proxy statements from shareholders who are not planning to attend the annual meeting. Most owners do not attend annual meetings of the very large companies, such as Westinghouse or Boeing, unless they live in the city where the meeting is held.

Common stockholders have another advantage over preferred shareholders. In most states, when the corporation decides to sell new shares of common stock in the marketplace, common stockholders have the first right, called a *preemptive right,* to purchase new shares of the stock from the corporation. A preemptive right is often included in the articles of incorporation. This right is important because it allows stockholders to purchase new shares to maintain their original positions. For

> ## "Common stockholders are the voting owners of a corporation."

a special class of owners because, although they generally do not have any say in running the company, they have a claim to any profits before any other stockholders do. Other stockholders

example, if a stockholder owns 10 percent of a corporation that decides to issue new shares, that stockholder has the right to buy enough of the new shares to retain the 10 percent ownership.

## Advantages of Corporations

Because a corporation is a separate legal entity, it has some very specific advantages over other forms of ownership. The biggest advantage may be the limited liability of the owners.

**limited liability.** Because the corporation's assets (money and resources) and liabilities (debts and other obligations) are separate from its owners', in most cases the stockholders are not held responsible for the firm's debts if it fails. Their liability or potential loss is limited to the amount of their original investment. Although a creditor can sue a corporation for not paying its debts, even forcing the corporation into bankruptcy, it cannot make the stockholders pay the corporation's debts out of their personal assets. Occasionally, the owners of a private corporation may pledge personal assets to secure a loan for the corporation; this would be most unusual for a public corporation.

**ease of transfer of ownership.** Stockholders can sell or trade shares of stock to other people without causing the termination of the corporation, and they can do this without the prior approval of other shareholders. The transfer of ownership (unless it is a majority position) does not affect the daily or long-term operations of the corporation.

**perpetual life.** A corporation usually is chartered to last forever unless its articles of incorporation stipulate otherwise. The existence of the corporation is unaffected by the death or withdrawal of any of its stockholders. It survives until the owners sell it or liquidate its assets. However, in some cases, bankruptcy ends a corporation's life. Bankruptcies occur when companies are unable to compete and earn profits. Eventually, uncompetitive businesses must close or seek protection from creditors in bankruptcy court while the business tries to reorganize.

**external sources of funds.** Of all the forms of business organization, the public corporation finds it easiest to raise money. When a corporation needs to raise more money, it can sell more stock shares or issue bonds (corporate "IOUs," which pledge to repay debt), attracting funds from anywhere in the United States and even overseas. The larger a corporation becomes, the more sources of financing are available to it. We take a closer look at some of these in Chapter 16.

**?**

**DID YOU KNOW?**

The first corporation with a net income of more than $1 billion in one year was General Motors, with a net income in 1955 of $1,189,477,082.[18]

**expansion potential.** Because large public corporations can find long-term financing readily, they can easily expand into national and international markets. And, as a legal entity, a corporation can enter into contracts without as much difficulty as a partnership.

## Disadvantages of Corporations

Corporations have some distinct disadvantages resulting from tax laws and government regulation.

**double taxation.** As a legal entity, the corporation must pay taxes on its income just like you do. When after-tax corporate profits are paid out as dividends to the stockholders, the dividends are taxed a second time as part of the individual owner's income. This process creates double taxation for the stockholders of dividend paying corporations. Double taxation does not occur with the other forms of business organization.

**forming a corporation.** The formation of a corporation can be costly. A charter must be obtained, and this usually requires the services of an attorney and payment of legal fees. Filing fees ranging from $25 to $150 must be paid to the state that awards the corporate charter, and certain states require that an annual fee be paid to maintain the charter.

**disclosure of information.** Corporations must make information available to their owners, usually through an annual report to shareholders. The annual report contains financial information about the firm's profits, sales, facilities and equipment, and debts, as well as descriptions of the company's operations, products, and plans for the future. Public corporations must also file reports with the Securities and Exchange Commission (SEC), the government regulatory agency that regulates securities such as stocks and bonds. The larger the firm, the more data the SEC requires. Because all reports filed with the SEC are available to the public, competitors can access them. Additionally, complying with securities laws takes time.

**employee-owner separation.** Many employees are not stockholders of the company for which they work. This separation of owners and employees may cause employees to feel that their work benefits only the owners. Employees without an ownership stake do not always see how they fit into the corporate picture and may not understand the importance of profits to the health of the organization. If managers are part owners but other employees are not, management–labor relations take on a different, sometimes difficult, aspect from those in partnerships and sole proprietorships. However, this situation is changing as more corporations establish employee stock ownership plans (ESOPs), which give shares of the company's stock to its employees. Such plans build a partnership between employee and employer and can boost productivity because they motivate employees to work harder so that they can earn dividends from their hard work as well as from their regular wages.

# OTHER TYPES OF OWNERSHIP

In this section we will take a brief look at joint ventures, S corporations, limited liability companies, and cooperatives—businesses formed for special purposes.

## Joint Ventures

A joint venture is a partnership established for a specific project or for a limited time. The partners in a joint venture may be individuals or organizations, as in the case of the international joint ventures discussed in Chapter 3. Control of a joint venture may be shared equally, or one partner may control decision making. Joint ventures are especially popular in situations that call for large investments, such as extraction of natural resources and the development of new products. Movie-Link, a joint venture of the film studios MGM, Paramount, Sony, Universal, and Warner Bros., was developed as a competitor to Netflix, the popular online movie-rental source.[19]

## S Corporations

An S corporation is a form of business ownership that is taxed as though it were a partnership. Net profits or losses of the corporation pass to the owners, thus eliminating double taxation. The benefit of limited liability is retained. Formally known as Subchapter S Corporations, they have become a popular form of business ownership for entrepreneurs and represent almost half of all corporate filings.[20] Accounting Systems, a Fort Collins, Colorado, accounting software firm, elected to

**Dow Corning, which makes over 7,000 silicon-based products, began as a joint venture between Corning Glass Works and Dow Chemical in 1943.**

incorporate as an S corporation to gain credibility from being incorporated, tax advantages, and limited liability. Advantages of S corporations include the simple method of taxation, the limited liability of shareholders, perpetual life, and the ability to shift income and appreciation to others. Disadvantages include restrictions on the number (75) and types (individuals, estates, and certain trusts) of shareholders and the difficulty of formation and operation.

## Limited Liability Companies

A limited liability company (LLC) is a form of business ownership that provides limited liability, as in a corporation, but is taxed like a partnership. Although relatively new in the United States, LLCs have existed for many years abroad. Professionals such as lawyers, doctors, and engineers often use the LLC form of ownership. Many consider the LLC a blend of the best characteristics of corporations, partnerships, and sole proprietorships. One of the major reasons for the LLC form of ownership is to protect the members' personal assets in case of lawsuits. LLCs are flexible, simple to run, and do not require the members to hold meetings, keep minutes, or make resolutions, all of which are necessary in corporations. For example, Segway, which markets the Segway Human Transporter, is a limited liability company.

## Cooperatives

Another form of organization in business is the cooperative or co-op, an organization composed of individuals or small businesses that have banded together to reap the benefits of belonging to a larger organization. Blue Diamond Growers, for example, is a cooperative of California almond growers; Ocean Spray is a cooperative of cranberry farmers. A co-op is set up not to make money as an entity but so that its members can become more profitable or save money. Co-ops are generally expected to operate without profit or to create only enough profit to maintain the co-op organization.

Many cooperatives exist in small farming communities. The co-op stores and markets grain; orders large quantities of fertilizer, seed, and other supplies at discounted prices; and reduces

# DESTINATION CEO

**Michelle Peluso—Travelocity.com** Last year more than 30 million households booked their vacations online. The revenue generated from this activity was about $53 billion. This is expected to double within the next five years. It is clear that online travel booking has become the norm. The video features a discussion with Michelle Peluso, who is the youngest CEO among the travel-related Internet portal businesses. She heads up Travelocity.com, which is a rapidly growing and successful Internet portal. Peluso comes to Travelocity through a most interesting route. She was educated at the Wharton School of Business then studied art history in Italy. After that, she was awarded a fellowship at Oxford where she studied philosophy and economics. She began a career with the World Bank in Africa prior to joining the BCG (Boston Consulting Group). She left BCG to assume a one-year White House Fellowship and was called back by BCG to consider an entrepreneurial startup in the travel industry. She has never looked back. Despite the short term drops post 9/11 (business declined by 70 percent), Travelocity.com has continued to move forward. Peluso attributes their success to her employees. According to Peluso, growth is a result of hard work and dedication.

## >>DISCUSSION QUESTIONS

1. How extensive is the travel industry through online portals?

2. What role did BCG play in assisting Peluso form her business?

3. What impact did 9/11 have on Travelocity's business?

>>To see the complete video about Michelle Peluso, go to our Web site at **www.mhhe.com/FerrellM** and look for the link to the Destination CEO videos.

● MERGER the combination of two companies (usually corporations) to form a new company

● ACQUISITION the purchase of one company by another, usually by buying its stock

costs and increases efficiency with good management. A co-op can purchase supplies in large quantities and pass the savings on to its members. It also can help distribute the products of its members more efficiently than each could on an individual basis. A

Ocean Spray is an agricultural cooperative owned by more than 650 cranberry growers in Massachusetts, Wisconsin, New Jersey, Oregon, Washington, British Columbia, and other parts of Canada. More than 100 Florida grapefruit growers are also part of the cooperative.

cooperative can advertise its members' products and thus generate demand. Ace Hardware, a cooperative of independent hardware store owners, allows its members to share in the savings that result from buying supplies in large quantities; it also provides advertising, which individual members might not be able to afford on their own.

 **L04**

Define and debate the advantages and disadvantages of mergers, acquisitions, and leveraged buyouts.

# TRENDS IN BUSINESS OWNERSHIP: MERGERS AND ACQUISITIONS

Companies large and small achieve growth and improve profitability by expanding their operations, often by developing and selling new products or selling current products to new groups of customers in different geographic areas. Such growth, when carefully planned and controlled, is usually beneficial to the firm and ultimately helps it reach its goal of enhanced profitability. But companies also grow by merging with or purchasing other companies.

A merger occurs when two companies (usually corporations) combine to form a new company. An acquisition occurs when one company purchases another, generally by buying most of its stock. The acquired company may become a subsidiary of the buyer, or its operations and assets may be merged with those of the buyer. For example, in 2006 Federated Department Stores decided to sell Lord & Taylor Stores, saying that the 180-year-old chain did not fit with its plans to promote Macy's and Bloomingdales. Federated did not want to sell Lord & Taylor to a rival department store.[22] A property development company, NRDC Equity Partners, purchased Lord & Taylor for $1.2 billion and promised not to change the stores. The buying company gains control of the property and assets of the other firm but also assumes its obligations. For example, Cingular Wireless outbid Vodafone Group to acquire AT&T Wireless Services for $47 billion.[23] Acquisitions sometimes involve the purchase of a division or some other part of a company rather than the entire company. The merger and acquisition frenzy seen in the late 1990s is slowing (see Table 5.4).

When firms that make and sell similar products to the same customers merge, it is known as a *horizontal merger,* as when Martin Marietta and Lockheed, both defense contractors, merged to form Martin Lockheed. Horizontal mergers, however, reduce the number of corporations competing within an industry, and for this reason they are usually reviewed carefully by federal regulators before the merger is allowed to proceed.

When companies operating at different but related levels of an industry merge, it is known as a *vertical merger.* In many instances, a vertical merger results when one corporation merges with one of its customers or suppliers. For example, if Burger King were to purchase a large Idaho potato farm—to ensure a ready supply of potatoes for its french fries—a vertical merger would result.

A *conglomerate merger* results when two firms in unrelated industries merge. For example, the purchase of Sterling Drug, a pharmaceutical firm, by Eastman Kodak, best-known for its films and cameras, represents a conglomerate merger because the two companies are of different industries.

When a company (or an individual), sometimes called a *corporate raider,* wants to acquire or take over another company, it first offers to buy some or all of the other company's stock at a premium over its current price in a *tender offer.* Most such offers are "friendly," with both groups agreeing to the proposed deal, but some are "hostile," when the second company does not want to be taken over. For example, Sanofi-Synthelabo, a French pharmaceutical corporation, made a hostile bid for Aventis, the French-German drug maker. Aventis ultimately accepted a higher, friendlier offer from Sanofi. The merged Sanofi-Aventis will become the world's third-largest pharmaceutical producer, after U.S.-based Pfizer and U.K.-based GlaxoSmithKline.[24]

To head off a hostile takeover attempt, a threatened company's managers may use one or more of several techniques. They

**TABLE 5.4**   Major Mergers and Acquisitions 2000–2006

Sprint and Nextel

Verizon and MCI

Kmart and Sears

Hewlett-Packard and Compaq

NBC Universal and Vivendi Universal

J.P. Morgan Chase and Bank One

Procter & Gamble and Gillette

Bank of America and Fleet Boston Financial

Cingular and AT&T Wireless

SBC and AT&T

Walt Disney Company and Pixar

Paramount and Dreamworks

Lucent and Alcatel

Source: http://en.wikipedia.org/wiki/Mergers_and_acquisitions (accessed June 7, 2006).

may ask stockholders not to sell to the raider; file a lawsuit in an effort to abort the takeover; institute a *poison pill* (in which the firm allows stockholders to buy more shares of stock at prices lower than the current market value) or *shark repellant* (in which management requires a large majority of stockholders to approve the takeover); or seek a *white knight* (a more acceptable firm that is willing to acquire the threatened company). In some cases, management may take the company private or even take on more debt so that the heavy debt obligation will "scare off" the raider. In the case of the initial hostile bid by Sanofi for Aventis, for example, Aventis initially instituted several measures to thwart the takeover attempt, including asking a rival Swiss firm, Novartis, to bid for Aventis. Only when Sanofi significantly raised its offer did Aventis's board of directors recommend that its stockholders accept the revised offer from Sanofi.[25]

In a **leveraged buyout (LBO),** a group of investors borrows money from banks and other institutions to acquire a company (or a division of one), using the assets of the purchased company to guarantee repayment of the loan. In some LBOs, as much as 95 percent of the buyout price is paid with borrowed money, which eventually must be repaid.

With the explosion of mergers, acquisitions, and leveraged buyouts in the 1980s and 1990s, some financial journalists coined the term *merger mania.* Many companies joined the merger mania simply to enhance their own operations by consolidating them with the operations of other firms. Mergers and acquisitions enabled these companies to gain a larger

● **LEVERAGED BUYOUT (LBO)** a purchase in which a group of investors borrows money from banks and other institutions to acquire a company (or a division of one), using the assets of the purchased company to guarantee repayment of the loan

## Heartland Farm Foods Co-op Helps Preserve Beef—and a Way of Life

Jim Farmer, a lifelong livestock producer, wants his son and two daughters to be able to carry on the family farm. To help achieve this goal, he formed the Heartland Farm Foods Co-op with about three dozen beef producers to turn 1,000 cattle a year into canned beef. The co-op form of organization is not unusual for small businesses that band together to obtain the benefits of a larger organization. The co-op is not set up to make money as an organization, but rather so that all the ranchers involved can become more profitable or in this case continue to maintain a lifestyle that they enjoy. In the face of intense competition from large commercial feedlots, Farmer's idea was to offer a different kind of product and to market and support it through the co-op, which has the support of the Missouri Beef Industry Council, the Missouri Department of Agriculture, and USDA Rural Development.

The co-op's canned, precooked ground and chunked beef products contain just one ingredient—beef, with no preservatives, not even salt. Any harmful bacteria are removed through a pressure-cooking process. Each animal yields 400 to 500 cans of federally inspected beef from cattle raised without steroids, hormone additives, or routine antibiotics. The precooked beef is targeted at outdoor enthusiasts—from hikers and hunters to anglers and campers. Thanks to a shelf life of two to five years, the cans can be stowed in tackle boxes or backpacks, or even stored in storm shelters in case of a disaster.

The co-op has constructed a 4,480-square foot plant on 10 acres to process the beef. Construction of this facility and first-year operating capital needs were estimated at approximately $750,000. Some of these expenses were partially offset by grants that the co-op received; co-ops that foster economic development in a region often receive grants or other financial support from state or federal development initiatives.

Currently, Heartland's canned beef is primarily available in north-central Missouri supermarkets and convenience stores and online at **www.heartlandfarmfoods.com.** Prices range from $2.69 to $3.99 on the Web site, although retailers sell the product for $4.99 per can. At this price, consumers surely demand a quality product, but Heartland believes the product's convenience and ingredients support sales. The co-op recently released five new products—Nacho Express, Zesty Beef'n Bean, Beef'n Bean Chili, Chili Con Queso, and Hearty Taco Beef—and is selling steaks to local restaurants and markets. Heartland's initiative offers an example of creativity in bringing back a product—canned meat—that was once a pantry staple before the era of refrigeration. The cooperative form of organization has made it possible for small ranchers to join together to make this product a reality.[21] ❖

**Q:   Discussion Questions**

1. Why did Heartland Foods employ a cooperative form of organization?

2. What are the advantages for ranchers who belong to the cooperative?

3. Can you think of any other industries where the cooperative form of business ownership would be beneficial?

Before you choose to accept or reject any job offer, whether it comes from a sole proprietorship, a partnership, or a corporation, it needs to be properly evaluated. Most organizations will not expect an immediate decision, so you will have time to consider issues regarding the organization, the job, compensation, and benefits.

Obtaining background information on the organization is important and doing so is generally easy. Factors to consider include the organization's business or activity, as well as its financial condition, age, size, and location. A public company's annual report contains this information and is usually available through the company's public relations office or the company's Web site. Press releases and company brochures or newsletters also can be helpful. Background information on many organizations is available at public libraries through reference directories such as *Dun & Bradstreet's Million Dollar Directory, Standard and Poor's Register of Corporations,* and *Thomas' Register of American Manufacturers.* There also are many sites on the Internet that offer company information, including *Hoover's Online* and the *Thomas Register.* Also, ask yourself whether the organization's

business or activity coincides with your interest and values and whether the organization is in an industry with favorable long-term prospects.

Consider the nature of the job offered. Does the work match your interests and make good use of your skills and abilities? Are you comfortable with the hours? Are there opportunities to learn new skills, increase your earnings, and rise to positions of greater responsibility and authority? Ask for an explanation of where the offered job fits into the organization and how you will contribute to overall organizational objectives.

In considering the salary offered, you should have a rough estimate of what the particular type of job should pay. Start with family or friends who may have similar jobs. Ask your college placement director about starting salaries in different industries and for applicants with qualifications such as yours. Consider cost-of-living differences if the job requires relocation to another city. Factor in the offered benefits as they add to base pay. Salary information by occupation can be found on the Web site of the Bureau of Labor Statistics.[26]

market share in their industries, acquire valuable assets, such as new products or plants and equipment, and lower their costs. Mergers also represent a means of making profits quickly, as was the case during the 1980s when many companies' stock was undervalued. Quite simply, such companies represent a bargain to other companies that can afford to buy them. Additionally, deregulation of some industries has permitted consolidation of firms within those industries for the first time, as is the case in the banking and airline industries.

Some people view mergers and acquisitions favorably, pointing out that they boost corporations' stock prices and market value, to the benefit of their stockholders. In many instances, mergers enhance a company's ability to meet foreign competition in an increasingly global marketplace. And, companies that are victims of hostile takeovers generally streamline their operations, reduce unnecessary staff, cut costs, and otherwise become more efficient with their operations, which benefits their stockholders whether or not the takeover succeeds.

Critics, however, argue that mergers hurt companies because they force managers to focus their efforts on avoiding takeovers rather than managing effectively and profitably. Some companies have taken on a heavy debt burden to stave off a takeover, later to be forced into bankruptcy when economic downturns left them unable to handle the debt. Mergers and acquisitions also can damage employee morale and productivity, as well as the quality of the companies' products.

Many mergers have been beneficial for all involved; others have had damaging effects for the companies, their employees, and customers. No one can say if mergers will continue to slow, but many experts say the utilities, telecommunications, financial services, natural resources, computer hardware and

software, gaming, managed health care, and technology industries are likely targets. ■

# CHECK OUT

## www.mhhe.com/FerrellM

# for study materials including Interactive Exercises, Quizzes, iPod downloads, and video.

## Build Your Business Plan

**Options For Organizing Business**  Your team needs to think about how you should organize yourselves that would be most efficient and effective for your business plan. The benefits of having partners include having others to share responsibilities with and to toss ideas off of each other. As your business evolves you will have to decide whether one or two members will manage the business while the other members are silent partners. Or perhaps you will all decide on working in the business to keep costs down, at least initially. However you decide on team member involvement in the business, it is imperative to have a written agreement so that all team members understand what their responsibilities are and what will happen if the partnership dissolves.

It is not too soon for you and your partners to start thinking about how you might want to find additional funding for your business. Later on in the development of your business plan you might want to show your business plan to family members. Together you and your partners will want to develop a list of potential investors in your business.

M
start here.

# SMALL BUSINESS ENTREPRENEURSHIP and FRANCHISING

## CHAPTER SIX

## Introduction

Although many business students go to work for large corporations upon graduation, others may choose to start their own business or find employment opportunities in small businesses with 500 or fewer employees. There are almost 25 million small businesses operating in the United States today.[1] Each small business represents the vision of its entrepreneurial owners to succeed by providing new or better products. Small businesses are the heart of the U.S. economic and social system because they offer opportunities and express the freedom of people to make their own destinies. Today, the entrepreneurial spirit is growing around the world, from Russia and China to Germany, Brazil, and Mexico.

● **ENTERPRENEUR-SHIP** the process of creating and managing a business to achieve desired objectives

● **SMALL BUSINESS** any independently owned and operated business that is not dominant in its competitive area and does not employ more than 500 people

● **SMALL BUSINESS ADMINISTRATION (SBA)** an independent agency of the federal government that offers managerial and financial assistance to small businesses

This chapter surveys the world of entrepreneurship and small business. First we define entrepreneurship and small business and examine the role of small business in the American economy. Then we explore the advantages and disadvantages of small-business ownership and analyze why small businesses succeed or fail. Next, we discuss how an entrepreneur goes about starting a small business and the challenges facing small business today. Finally, we look at entrepreneurship in larger businesses.

 **LO1**

Define entrepreneurship and small business.

# THE NATURE OF ENTREPRENEURSHIP AND SMALL BUSINESS

In Chapter 1, we defined an entrepreneur as a person who risks his or her wealth, time, and effort to develop for profit an innovative product or way of doing something. Entrepreneurship is the process of creating and managing a business to achieve desired objectives. Many large businesses you may recognize, including Levi Strauss and Co., Procter & Gamble, McDonald's, Dell Computers, Microsoft, and Federal Express, all began as small businesses based on the entrepreneurial visions of their founders. Some entrepreneurs who start small businesses have the ability to see emerging trends; in response, they create a company to provide a product that serves customer needs. For example, rather than inventing a major new technology, an innovative company may take advantage of a new technology to create markets that did not exist before, such as Amazon.com. Or they may offer something familiar but improved or repackaged, such as Starbucks did with its coffee shops. They may innovate by focusing on a particular market segment and delivering a combination of features that consumers in that segment could not find anywhere else (e.g. REI Outdoor Gear & Clothing for camping, hiking, backpacking, and more).[2]

Of course, smaller businesses do not have to evolve into such highly visible companies to be successful, but those entrepreneurial efforts that result in rapidly growing businesses become more visible with their success. Entrepreneurs who have achieved success, like Michael Dell and Bill Gates (Microsoft), are the most visible.

The entrepreneurship movement is accelerating with many new, smaller businesses emerging. Technology once available only to the largest firms can now be acquired by a small business. Printers, fax machines, copiers, voice-mail, computer bulletin boards and networks, cellular phones, and even overnight delivery services enable small businesses to be more competitive with today's giant corporations. Small businesses can also form alliances with other companies to produce and sell products in domestic and global markets.

## What Is a Small Business?

This question is difficult to answer because smallness is relative. In this book, we will define a small business as any independently owned and operated business that is not dominant in its competitive area and does not employ more than 500 people. A local Mexican restaurant may be the most patronized Mexican restaurant in your community, but because it does not dominate the restaurant industry as a whole, the restaurant can be considered a small business. This definition is similar to the one used by the Small Business Administration (SBA), an independent agency of the federal government that offers managerial and financial assistance to small businesses. On its Web site, the SBA outlines the first steps in starting a small business and offers a wealth of information to current and potential small business owners.

 **LO2**

Investigate the importance of small business in the U.S. economy and why certain fields attract small business.

## The Role of Small Business in the American Economy

No matter how you define small business, one fact is clear: Small businesses are vital to the soundness of the American economy. As you can see in Table 6.1, more than 99 percent of all U.S. firms are classified as small businesses, and they employ

**TABLE 6.1** Facts About Small Businesses

- Represent 99.7% of all employer firms.
- Employ half of all private sector employees.
- About 6–7% of the U.S. population is in the process of starting a business at any given time.
- 53% of new small businesses begin in the home with less than $10,000.
- Are responsible for 39% of GNP.
- Contribute 44% of all sales in the country.
- Are twice as innovative per employee as larger firms.

Source: "Small Business Facts," National Federation of Independent Business, http://www.nfib.com/object/smallBusinessFacts (accessed June 14, 2007); National Telecommunications and Information Administration, "Small Business Facts," http://www.ntia.doc.gov/opadhome/mtdpweb/sbfacts.htm (accessed June 14, 2007).

50 percent of private workers. Small firms are also important as exporters, representing 97 percent of U.S. exporters of goods and contributing 29 percent of the value of exported goods.[3] In addition, small businesses are largely responsible for fueling job creation and innovation. Small businesses also provide opportunities for minorities and women to succeed in business. Women-owned businesses total 10.6 million, employ 19.1 million, and contribute $2.46 trillion to the economy.[4] Between 1997 and 2004, the estimated growth rate in the number of women-owned firms was nearly twice that of all firms, while employment expanded at twice the rate and revenues kept pace with all firms.[5] In a survey by the Census Bureau, minority businesses grew to more than 4 million growing more than 31 percent over a five-year span of time. Hispanics own the most companies (1.6 million, for a 31 percent increase), African Americans second (1.2 million for a 45 percent increase), Asians third (1.1 million) and Native Americans and Alaska Natives own just over 200,000 businesses. In this same time period, the number of U.S. businesses overall grew 10 percent.[6] Consider the story of Tommy Hodinh, who came to the United States in 1972 as a Vietnamese refugee. After putting himself through college and working at IBM for 15 years, he decided to start his own business. Today, MagRabbit Inc., his logistics and transportation company, provides custom and highly complex logistics and transportation solutions. Services and custom critical logistics solutions are provided for Dell, Toyota, Boeing, Ford, DaimlerChrysler, General Motors, and the U.S. Military Surface Deployment and Distribution Command.[7] Hodinh himself has become a source of inspiration for many Asian Americans with an entrepreneurial bent.[8] According to the American Indian Report, Red Man Pipe and Supply Company, headquartered in Tulsa, Oklahoma, is the largest Native American owned business with annual sales of more than $540 million. The company, founded by Lewis Ketchum, a Delaware Tribe Native American Indian, today operates 62 store facilities and six sales offices. The company has received significant special recognition for the quality and care of their services including, ranking as the number-one minority business by *Minority Business News;* in 2002 and 2003, the Shell Oil Co. supplier diversity "Supplier of the Year"; the Houston Minority Business Council's "Supplier of the Year"; and the Oklahoma Minority Supplier Development Council's "Outstanding Minority Supplier of the Year"; the number-two minority business by "Minority Business News"; and finally, the Supplier Diversity Vendor of the Year award at the Marathon Oil Company Global Diversity Awards program.[9]

**job creation.** The energy, creativity, and innovative abilities of small-business owners have resulted in jobs for other people. In fact, in the last decade, between 60 to 80 percent of net new jobs annually were created by small businesses.[10] Table 6.2 indicates that 99.7 percent of all businesses employ fewer than 500 people.[11]

Many small businesses today are being started because of encouragement from larger ones. Many jobs are being created

**TABLE 6.2**  Number of Firms by Employment Size

| Firm Size | Number of Firms | Percentage of All Firms |
|---|---|---|
| 0–19 employees | 5,150,316 | 89.3 |
| 20–99 employees | 515,056 | 8.9 |
| 100–499 employees | 84,829 | 1.5 |
| 500 or more employees | 16,926 | 0.3 |

Source: U.S. Census Bureau, "Statistics about Business Size (including small businesses) from the U.S. Census Bureau," www.census.gov/epcd/www/smallbus.html (accessed June 14, 2007).

by big-company/small-company alliances. Whether through formal joint ventures, supplier relationships, or product or marketing cooperative projects, the rewards of collaborative relationships are creating many jobs for small-business owners and their employees. Some publishing companies, for example, contract out almost all their editing and production to small businesses. Elm Street Publishing Services is a small editing/ production house in Hinsdale, Illinois, that provides most services required to turn a manuscript into a bound book.

**innovation.** Perhaps one of the most significant strengths of small businesses is their ability to innovate and bring significant changes and benefits to customers. Small firms produce 55 percent of innovations. Among the important

*Kevin Plank, a walk-on college football player, hated how the cotton T-shirts under his uniform felt when they got wet. So he paid a tailor to stitch together some tees made of moisture-wicking fabric used to produce cycling shorts. Plank dubbed the creation "under armour" and lived in his grandmother's basement until he got Under Armour Inc. off the ground. Today, he is a multimillionaire.*

20th-century innovations by U.S. small firms are the airplane, the audio tape recorder, double-knit fabric, fiber-optic examining equipment, the heart valve, the optical scanner, the pacemaker, the personal computer, soft contact lenses, and the zipper. Paul Moller, an entrepreneur and inventor, may be working on one of the most important 21st century innovations: a flying car. Although currently still in the testing phase, Moller's SkyCar may one day help commuters avoid congested freeways. The car is currently being tested at Stanford University, tethered to a large Crane.[12]

The innovation of successful firms takes many forms. Small businessman Ray Kroc found a new way to sell hamburgers and turned his ideas into one of the most successful fast-food franchises in the world—McDonald's. Small businesses have become an integral part of our lives. James Dyson spent time from 1979 to 1984 developing a prototype of a dual-cyclone,

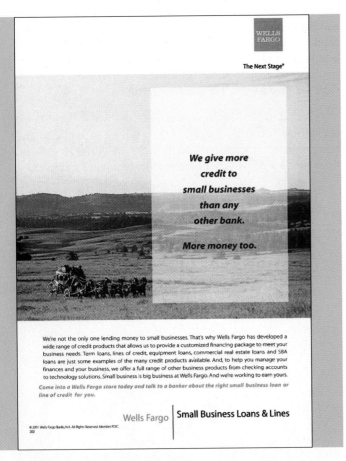

*Wells Fargo offers a number of different types of loans and lines of credit to small-business customers.*

bagless vacuum cleaner. As a matter of fact, he built more than 5,000 versions before manufacturing his G Force, which made the front cover of *Design* magazine in 1983. Today, the company outsells its leading rival, Hoover, by capturing 21 percent

of the U.S. dollars spent on upright vacuum cleaners versus 16 percent for Hoover. Dyson's vacuums sell for $400 to $600 each, whereas Hoover's sell for $69 to $389. Hoover still sells more overall units than does Dyson. Dyson's designs are featured in the Metropolitan Museum of Art, New York, Science Museum, London, and Victoria and Albert Museum, London, to name a few.[13] They provide fresh ideas and usually have greater flexibility to change than do large companies.

## Industries That Attract Small Business

Small businesses are found in nearly every industry, but retailing and wholesaling, services, manufacturing, and high technology are especially attractive to entrepreneurs because they are relatively easy to enter and require low initial financing. Small-business owners also find it easier to focus on a specific group of consumers in these fields than in others, and new firms in these industries suffer less from heavy competition, at least in the early stages, than do established firms.

### retailing and wholesaling.
Retailers acquire goods from producers or wholesalers and sell them to consumers. Main streets, shopping strips, and shopping malls are lined with independent music stores, sporting-goods shops, dry cleaners, boutiques, drugstores, restaurants, caterers, service stations, and hardware stores that sell directly to consumers. Retailing attracts entrepreneurs because gaining experience and exposure in retailing is relatively easy. Additionally, an entrepreneur opening a new retailing store does not have to spend the large sums of money for the equipment and distribution systems that a manufacturing business requires. All that a new retailer needs is a lease on store space, merchandise, enough money to sustain the business, a knowledge about prospective customers' needs and desires, the ability to use promotion to generate awareness, and basic management skills. Some small retailers are taking their businesses online. For example, Susan Brown, created the number-one baby product in the country, according to *American Baby* magazine. She created a donut-shaped pillow with an opening in one side called the "Boppy." The baby pillows are sold online at www.boppy.com, in Babies R Us and Pottery Barn Kids; although approached by Wal-Mart, Brown has decided not to discount the product in a desire to keep a more upscale feel. The Boppy has annual sales between $15 and $25 million.[14]

Wholesalers supply products to industrial, retail, and institutional users for resale or for use in making other products. Wholesaling activities range from planning and negotiating for supplies, promoting, and distributing (warehousing and transporting) to providing management and merchandising assistance to clients. Wholesalers are extremely important for many products, especially consumer goods, because of the marketing activities they perform. Although it is true that wholesalers themselves can be eliminated, their functions must be passed on to some other organization such as the producer, or another intermediary, often a small business. Frequently, small businesses are closer to the final customers and know what it takes to keep them satisfied. Some smaller businesses start out manufacturing but find their real niche as a supplier or distributor of larger firms' products.

### services.
Services include businesses that work for others but do not actually produce tangible goods. They represent one of the fastest growing sectors of the U.S. economy, accounting for 66 percent of the U.S. economy and employing roughly 70 percent of the workforce.[15] Real estate, insurance, and personnel agencies, barbershops, banks, television and computer repair shops, copy centers, dry cleaners, and accounting firms are all service businesses. Services also attract individuals—such as beauticians, morticians, jewelers, doctors, and veterinarians—whose skills are not usually required by large firms. Many of these service providers are also retailers because they provide their services to ultimate consumers.

### manufacturing.
Manufacturing goods can provide unique opportunities for small businesses. Texas Nameplate Company Inc. won the Malcolm Baldrige National Quality Award and is the smallest company to do so. The company, a privately held family business that produces custom nameplates, has been so successful because of careful cross-training of more than 80 percent of its employees to perform multiple jobs across departments; retaining customers, 70 percent of the company's top customers have been so for more than 10 years; and increasing profitability from 36 to 40 percent.[16] The award is designed to spur competitive business practices in American industry, and few companies with 500 or fewer employees have won the award since its inception in 1988. Small businesses can often customize products to meet specific customer needs and wants. Such products include custom artwork, jewelry, clothing, and furniture.

*Geek Squad employees vow to "fix any PC problem anytime, anywhere." The Geek Squad began as a one-man service firm in Minnesota in 1994. Founder Robert Stephens initially traveled by bicycle to and from service calls. Best Buy owns the firm today.*

**?**

**DID YOU KNOW?**

39 percent of high-tech jobs are in small businesses.[18]

### high technology.
High technology is a broad term used to describe businesses that depend heavily on advanced scientific and engineering knowledge. People who have been able to innovate or identify new markets in the fields of computers, biotechnology, genetic engineering, robotics, and other markets have become today's high-tech giants. Michael Dell, for example, started building personal computers in his University of Texas dorm room at age 19. His Dell Computer is now one of the leading PC companies in the world and the world's number-one direct-sale computer vendor with annual sales of more than $55 billion.[17] Apple Computers began in a garage. The Apple prototype was financed by the proceeds Steven Wozniak received from selling his Hewlett-Packard calculator and Steven Jobs got from selling his van. In general, high technology businesses require greater capital and have higher initial startup costs than do other small businesses. Many of them, nonetheless, started out in garages, basements, kitchens, and dorm rooms.

# DESTINATION CEO

**Be Your Own Boss**  Summary: Each year in the United States there are about 600,000 new startup small businesses and nearly an equal number of failures. This *BusinessWeek* TV segment introduces Shep and Ian Murray, the successful owners of Vineyard Vines. The two brothers started a few years ago by maxing out their credit cards for their business startup—manufacturing ties. They went door to door and were struggling. Today, gross sales will reach $20 million. They began with neckties but have expanded their lines to include totes, shirts, and belts. They emphasize the need for passion to carry through as a critical element in success. Further, the focus on building relationships should be the focus of activity, not "selling" their wares. Columbia University has an "entrepreneur in residence" in their business college. He notes that between 2001 and 2004, service startups are the most frequent new businesses. He also stresses the importance of passion as the first criterion of success.

## >>DISCUSSION QUESTIONS

1. What challenges did Shep and Ian Murray face in starting their business?

2. Why is passion to carry through so important to entrepreneurship?

3. What are the barriers and risks associated with entrepreneurship?

>>To see the complete video about Be Your Own Boss, go to our Web site at **www.mhhe.com/FerrellIM** and look for the link to the Destination CEO videos.

# ADVANTAGES OF SMALL-BUSINESS OWNERSHIP

There are many advantages to establishing and running a small business. These can be categorized as personal advantages and business advantages. Table 6.3 lists some of the traits that can help entrepreneurs succeed.

## Independence

Independence is probably one of the leading reasons that entrepreneurs choose to go into business for themselves. Being a small-business owner means being your own boss. Many people start their own businesses because they believe they will do better for themselves than they could do by remaining with their current employer or by changing jobs. They may feel stuck on the corporate ladder and that no business would take them

**TABLE 6.3**  Traits Needed to Succeed in Entrepreneurship

Neuroticism—helps entrepreneurs focus on details
Extroversion—facilitates network building
Conscientiousness—facilitates planning
Agreeableness—facilitates networking
Openness to new ideas

Source: Alex de Noble in Joshua Kurlantzick, "About Face," *Entrepreneur,* January 2004, www.entrepreneur.com/article/0,4621,312260,00.html.

seriously enough to fund their ideas. Sometimes people who venture forth to start their own small business are those who simply cannot work for someone else. Such people may say that they just do not fit the "corporate mold."

More often, small-business owners just want the freedom to choose whom they work with, the flexibility to pick where and when to work, and the option of working in a family setting. The availability of the computer, copy machine, business telephone, and fax machine has permitted many people to work at home. Only a few years ago, most of them would have needed the support that an office provides.

## The Buzz about Burt's Bees

In 1984, Roxanne Quimby was on her way to her waitressing job when she decided to stop at a roadside stand to buy some honey from beekeeper Burt Shavitz. She soon joined forces with Shavitz, and they began marketing the honey from Burt's bees to tourists and making candles and other products out of the beeswax. Quimby made handmade labels and traveled to craft fairs throughout her home state of Maine, marketing their products and closely observing customers' reactions to them. By applying her observations, Quimby learned to develop new products to satisfy a growing niche market for natural beauty products such as lip balm, soap, and baby products. By 1993, Burt's Bees was bringing in $3 million a year in sales, and Quimby and Shavitz (who has since retired and sold his share of the business to Quimby) decided to move their rapidly growing business to North Carolina. Within another 10 years, the firm had grown to nearly $60 million in sales and provided jobs for 200 full-time and 100 temporary workers.

These days Burt's Bees beauty and baby products are distributed through approximately 20,000 retail stores and natural food stores such as Whole Foods as well as online. Burt's Bees does not use advertising for its growing line of products, relying instead on word-of-mouth promotion from satisfied customers and an extensive sampling effort. Every month, Burt's Bees hosts special events at retail stores during which customers are invited to come and sample and learn about the company's products, giving them firsthand experience with the products.

When Roxanne Quimby first met Burt Shavitz, she was living a self-sustaining and uncompromising lifestyle in the Maine woods with her three children. While building Burt's Bees, Quimby applied her philosophies and values to the growing company—for example, eschewing wasteful packaging wherever possible, using the best ingredients available, and walking away from potentially lucrative discount store sales when a chain store company asked for concessions that violated her environmental sensibilities. Recently, the company signed an agreement with PETA (People for the Ethical Treatment of Animals) and is certifying with Leaping Bunny (The Coalition for Consumer Information on Cosmetics) against animal testing.

In 2003, Quimby sold 80 percent of Burt's Bees to New York investment firm AEA Investors for $179 million, although she retains 20 percent. Quimby has been using the proceeds toward creating a national park in her beloved Maine. Burt's Bees is now the top all-natural, earth-friendly manufacturer of personal care products and has been honored with a top spot in the *Triangle Business Journal* Fast 50 Awards.[19] ❖

## Q: Discussion Questions

1. Why do you think Burt's Bees was able to grow from a tiny company into a national distributor of personal-care products?

2. How has the firm's preference for natural ingredients and environmental consciousness affected its growth?

3. Do you think that Burt's Bees faces major competition from more traditional personal-care products from larger companies like Procter & Gamble?

## Costs

As already mentioned, small businesses often require less money to start and maintain than do large ones. Obviously, a firm with just 25 people in a small factory spends less money on wages and salaries, rent, utilities, and other expenses than does a firm employing tens of thousands of people in several large facilities. And, rather than maintain the expense and staff of keeping separate departments for accounting, advertising, and legal counseling, small businesses can hire other firms (often small businesses themselves) to supply these services as they are needed. Additionally, small-business owners can sometimes rely on friends and family members who volunteer to work to get out a difficult project in order to save money.

Small-business owners, such as dentists, know that maintaining a high-quality reputation is essential to their success.

## Flexibility

With small size comes the flexibility to adapt to changing market demands. Small businesses usually have only one layer of management—the owners. Decisions therefore can be made and carried out quickly. In larger firms, decisions about even routine matters can take weeks because they must pass through two or more levels of management before action is authorized. When McDonald's introduces a new product, for example, it must first research what consumers want, then develop the product and test it carefully before introducing it nationwide, a process that sometimes takes years. An independent snack shop, however, can develop and introduce a new product (perhaps to meet a customer's request) in a much shorter time.

## Focus

Small firms can focus their efforts on a few key customers or on a precisely defined market niche—that is, a specific group of customers. Many large corporations must compete in the mass market or for large market segments. Smaller firms can develop products for particular groups of customers or to satisfy a need that other companies have not addressed. For example, launched in 2006 in Indianapolis, Fatheadz focuses on producing sunglasses for people with big heads. To be an official "fathead" you need a ball cap size of at least 7⅝ and a head circumference above the ear of at least 23.5 inches. The idea arose when Rico Elmore was walking down the Las Vegas strip with his brother and realized that he had lost his sunglasses. He went to a nearby sunglass shop, and out of 300 pairs of glasses, he could not find one that fit. Customers include the entire starting line of the Indianapolis Colts, Rupert Boneham (of *Survivor* fame), and Tim Sylvia, former heavyweight title holder of Ultimate Fighting Championship.[20] By targeting small niches or product needs, small businesses can sometimes avoid fierce competition from larger firms, helping them to grow into stronger companies.

## Reputation

Small firms, because of their capacity to focus on narrow niches, can develop enviable reputations for quality and service. A good example of a small business with a formidable reputation is W. Atlee Burpee and Co., which has the country's premier bulb and seed catalog. Burpee has an unqualified returns policy (complete satisfaction or your money back) that demonstrates a strong commitment to customer satisfaction.

## ●● LO4

Summarize the disadvantages of small-business ownership, and analyze why many small businesses fail.

# DISADVANTAGES OF SMALL-BUSINESS OWNERSHIP

The rewards associated with running a small business are so enticing that it's no wonder many people dream of it. However, as with any undertaking, small-business ownership has its disadvantages.

## High Stress Level

A small business is likely to provide a living for its owner, but not much more (although there are exceptions as some examples in this chapter have shown). There are always worries about competition, employee problems, new equipment, expanding inventory, rent increases, or changing market demand. In addition to other stresses, small-business owners tend to be victims of physical and psychological stress. The small-business

● UNDERCAPITALIZA-
TION the lack of funds to
operate a business normally

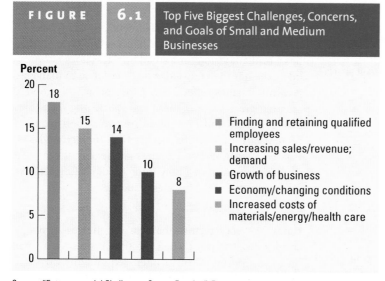

## FIGURE 6.1 Top Five Biggest Challenges, Concerns, and Goals of Small and Medium Businesses

**Percent**

- 18 — Finding and retaining qualified employees
- 15 — Increasing sales/revenue; demand
- 14 — Growth of business
- 10 — Economy/changing conditions
- 8 — Increased costs of materials/energy/health care

Source: "Entrepreneurial Challenges Survey Results," *Entrepreneur,* http://www.entrepreneur.com/encyclopedia/businessstatistics/article81812.html (accessed June 14, 2007).

five years.[21] Neighborhood restaurants are a case in point. Look around your own neighborhood, and you can probably spot the locations of several restaurants that are no longer in business.

Small businesses fail for many reasons (see Table 6.4). A poor business concept—such as insecticides for garbage cans (research found that consumers are not concerned with insects in their garbage)—will produce disaster nearly every time. Expanding a hobby into a business may work if a genuine market niche exists, but all too often people start such a business without identifying a real need for the goods or services. Other notable causes of small-business failure include the burdens imposed by government regulation, insufficient funds to withstand slow sales, and vulnerability to competition from larger companies. However, three major causes of small-business failure deserve a close look: undercapitalization, managerial inexperience or incompetence, and inability to cope with growth; roughly 90 percent of small business failures can be attributed to these faults.[22]

person is often the owner, manager, sales force, shipping and receiving clerk, bookkeeper, and custodian. Figure 6.1 shows the five biggest challenges and goals of small and medium-sized businesses. Many creative persons fail, not because of their business concepts, but rather because of difficulties in managing their business.

## High Failure Rate

Despite the importance of small businesses to our economy, there is no guarantee of small-business success. Roughly 90 percent of all new businesses fail within the first

**The failure rate for small businesses is very high.**

**undercapitalization.** The shortest path to failure in business is undercapitalization, the lack of funds to operate a business normally. Too many entrepreneurs think that all they need is enough money to get started, that the business can survive on cash generated from sales soon thereafter. But almost all businesses suffer from seasonal variations in sales, which make cash tight, and few businesses make money from the start. Many small rural operations cannot obtain financing within their own communities because small rural

## Alternative Outfitters Promotes High Fashion, Vegan Style

Jackie Horrick and Henny Hendra

Business: Alternative Outfitters

Founded: 2004

Success: The business has expanded to the point that the owners are looking to buy more warehouse space and to open a showroom.

In 2004, Jackie Horrick and Henny Hendra founded Alternative Outfitters—an online retail store featuring animal-free clothing, accessories, cosmetics, skin care products,

and shoes. The two are firmly committed to selling only cruelty-free products that also happen to be fashionable. The idea for Alternative Outfitters came about due to personal need. Years ago, Horrick, a vegetarian and a vegan, began shopping for shoes, bags, skin care products, cosmetics, and other items made without animal products. It was difficult for her to find the items she needed. Over time, Horrick began to realize that there were probably other individuals out there looking for the same items, and the concept for her

business was born. The company has been hugely successful in two short years. In 2005, Alternative Outfitters won its second PETA (People for the Ethical Treatment of Animals) Proggy Award and *VegNews* magazine's Veggie Award. The company and its products have been featured in *People, Lucky,* and *InStyle,* among others. In early 2006, the company was expanding beyond its warehouse space and considering both additional space and the possibility of opening a Pasadena, California–based showroom.[23] ❖

**TABLE 6.4** Most Common Mistakes Made by Startup Businesses

- Failing to spend enough time researching the business idea to see if it's viable.
- Miscalculating market size, timing, ease of entry, and potential market share.
- Underestimating financial requirements and timing.
- Overprojecting sales volume and timing.
- Making cost projections that are too low.
- Hiring too many people and spending too much on offices and facilities.
- Lacking a contingency plan for a shortfall in expectations.
- Bringing in unnecessary partners.
- Hiring for convenience rather than skill requirements.
- Neglecting to manage the entire company as a whole.
- Accepting that it's "not possible" too easily rather than finding a way.
- Focusing too much on sales volume and company size rather than profit.
- Seeking confirmation of your actions rather than seeking the truth.
- Lacking simplicity in your vision.
- Lacking clarity of your long-term aim and business purpose.
- Lacking focus and identity.
- Lacking an exit strategy.

Source: John Osher, in Mark Henricks, "What Not to Do," *Entrepreneur,* February 2004, www. entrepreneur.com/article/0,4621,312661,00.html.

banks often lack the necessary financing expertise or assets sizable enough to counter the risks involved with small business loans. Without sufficient funds, the best small-business idea in the world will fail.

*In 2001, Franson Nwaeze and Paula Merrell wanted to open a restaurant, but most lenders were skeptical of their lack of restaurant experience and collateral. When the husband-and-wife team learned that banks were much more willing to loan them money to buy a gas station, they purchased a Conoco station in Watauga, Texas, in 2003, and opened up a successful gourmet restaurant in one-half of it. Called Chef Point Café, the business's motto is "fill'er-up outside, fill'er-up inside."*

**managerial inexperience or incompetence.** Poor management is the cause of many business failures. Just because an entrepreneur has a brilliant vision for a small business does not mean he or she has the knowledge or experience to manage a growing business effectively. A person who is good at creating great product ideas and marketing them may lack the skills and experience to make good management decisions in hiring, negotiating, finance, and control. Moreover, entrepreneurs may neglect those areas of management they know little about or find tedious, at the expense of the business's success.

**inability to cope with growth.** Sometimes, the very factors that are advantages turn into serious disadvantages when the time comes for a small business to grow. Growth often requires the owner to give up a certain amount of direct authority, and it is frequently hard for someone who has called all the shots to give up control. Similarly, growth requires specialized management skills in areas such as credit analysis and promotion—skills that the founder may lack or not have time to apply. The founders of many small businesses, including those of Gateway and Dell Computers, found that they needed to bring in more experienced managers to help manage their companies through intense growing pains.

Poorly managed growth probably affects a company's reputation more than anything else, at least initially. And products that do not arrive on time or goods that are poorly made can quickly reverse a company's success. The biggest, immediate threats to small and mid-sized businesses include rising inflation, trade deficit and collapse of the dollar's value, energy and other supply shortages, excessive household and/or corporate debt, and the growing federal deficit.[24]

● ● **L05**

Describe how you go about starting a small business and what resources are needed.

# STARTING A SMALL BUSINESS

We've told you how important small businesses are, and why they succeed and fail, but *how do you go about* starting your own business? To start any business, large or small, you must first have an idea. Sam Walton, founder of Wal-Mart stores, had an idea for a discount retailing enterprise and spawned the world's largest retailing empire that changed the way traditional companies look at their business. Next, you need to devise a business plan to guide planning and development in the business. Finally, you must make decisions about form of ownership, the financial resources needed, and whether to buy an existing business, start a new one, or buy a franchise.

## The Business Plan

A key element of business success is a business plan—a precise statement of the rationale for the business and a step-by-step explanation of how it will achieve its goals. The business plan should include an explanation of the business, an analysis of the competition, estimates of income and expenses, and other information. It should establish a strategy for acquiring sufficient funds to keep the business going. Indeed, many financial institutions decide whether to loan a small business money based on its business plan. However, the business plan should act as a guide and reference document—not a shackle to limit the business's flexibility and decision making. Finally, the business plan should be revised periodically to ensure that the firm's goals and strategies can adapt to changes in the environment. Companies such as Benjamin Obdyke, a maker of roof vents and other building parts in Horsham, Pennsylvania, has created a culture of innovation and change. The company uses "idea management software" to allow employees to post ideas and comment on one another's suggestions. This process assists the company in creating new business ideas and plans, as well as saving roughly $100,000 per year.[25] The Small Business Administration Web site provides an overview of a plan for small businesses to use to gain financing. Appendix B presents a comprehensive business plan.

## Forms of Business Ownership

After developing a business plan, the entrepreneur has to decide on an appropriate legal form of business ownership—whether it is best to operate as a sole proprietorship, partnership, or corporation—and examine the many factors that affect that decision, which we explored in Chapter 5.

## Financial Resources

The old adage "it takes money to make money" holds true in developing a business enterprise. To make money from a small business, the owner must first provide or obtain money (capital) to start the business and keep it running smoothly. Even a small retail store will probably need at least $50,000 in initial financing to rent space, purchase or lease necessary equipment and furnishings, buy the initial inventory of merchandise, and provide working capital. Often, the small-business owner has to put up a significant percentage of the necessary capital. Few new business owners have the entire amount, however, and must look to other sources for additional financing.

equity financing. The most important source of funds for any new business is the owner. Many owners include among their personal resources ownership of a home or the accumulated value in a life-insurance policy or a savings account. A new business owner may sell or borrow against the value of such assets to obtain funds to operate a business. Additionally, the owner may bring useful personal assets—such as a computer, desks and other furniture, a car or truck—as part of his or her ownership interest in the firm. Such financing is referred to as *equity financing* because the owner uses real personal assets rather than borrowing funds from outside sources to get started in a new business. The owner can also provide working capital by reinvesting profits into the business or simply by not drawing a full salary.

Small businesses can also obtain equity financing by finding investors for their operations. They may sell stock in the business to family members, friends, employees, or other investors. When Tony Volk developed the pop-up turkey timer, he probably had no idea that he would one day sell around $100 million and be the only maker of the small, plastic gadget that pops out of the turkey at 180 degrees. The Volk pop-ups are embedded in 30 million of the 46 million turkeys consumed for Thanksgiving. To support the company's early growth, Tony had to convince his brother Henry to quit his job as an auditor and join the company. For more than 40 years, this family-run business has been a leader in innovative packaging and products.[26] Venture capitalists are persons or organizations that agree to provide some funds for a new business in exchange for an ownership interest or stock. Venture capitalists hope to purchase the stock of a small business at a low price and then sell the stock for a profit after the business has grown successful. A teenage dance club that only exists online has been a real hit with venture capitalists. Doppelganger raised $11 million in one year from venture capitalists. What's so attractive about the site? Users to the club enter a three-dimensional, virtual world with custom characters meant to replicate their real-world counterparts. Entry is free, but inside they encounter plenty of advertising from marketers. The only public advertiser that Doppelganger has acknowledged is Vivendi Universal's Interscope Records.[27] Individual venture capitalists are sometimes called *angels*. Increasingly, angels are banding together and pooling resources to reduce risk and increase the odds of finding the next Google or Amazon.com.[28] Although these forms of equity financing have helped many small businesses, they require that the small-business owner share the profits of the business—and sometimes control, as well—with the investors.

debt financing. New businesses sometimes borrow over half of their financial resources. Banks are the main suppliers of external financing to small businesses. On the federal

most important source of funds for any new business is the owner.

● **FRANCHISE** a license to sell another's products or to use another's name in business, or both    ● **FRANCHISER** the company that sells a franchise    ● **FRANCHISEE** the purchaser of a franchise

State and local agencies may guarantee loans, especially to minority businesspeople or for development in certain areas.

level, the Small Business Administration offers financial assistance to qualifying businesses. More detail on the SBA's loan programs can be found at the SBA Web site. They can also look to family and friends as sources for loans of long-term funds or other assets, such as a computer or an automobile, that are exchanged for an ownership interest in a business. In such cases, the business owner can usually structure a favorable repayment schedule and sometimes negotiate an interest rate below current bank rates. If the business goes bad, however, the emotional losses for all concerned may greatly exceed the money involved. Anyone lending a friend or family member money for a venture should state the agreement clearly in writing.

The amount a bank or other institution is willing to loan depends on its assessment of the venture's likelihood of success and of the entrepreneur's ability to repay the loan. The bank will often require the entrepreneur to put up *collateral,* a financial interest in the property or fixtures of the business, to guarantee

## Approaches to Starting a Small Business

### starting from scratch versus buying an existing business.

Although entrepreneurs often start new small businesses from scratch much the way we have discussed in this section, they may elect instead to buy an already existing business. This has the advantage of providing a network of existing customers, suppliers, and distributors and reducing some of the guesswork inherent in starting a new business from scratch. However, an entrepreneur buying an existing business must also deal with whatever problems the business already has.

### franchising.

Many small-business owners find entry into the business world through franchising. A license to sell another's products or to use another's name in business, or

> # Many small-business owners find entry into the business world through franchising.

payment of the debt. Additionally, the small-business owner may have to offer some personal property as collateral, such as his or her home, in which case the loan is called a *mortgage.* If the small business fails to repay the loan, the lending institution may eventually claim and sell the collateral (or the owner's home, in the case of a mortgage) to recover its loss.

Banks and other financial institutions can also grant a small business a *line of credit*—an agreement by which a financial institution promises to lend a business a predetermined sum on demand. A line of credit permits an entrepreneur to take quick advantage of opportunities that require a bank loan. Small businesses may obtain funding from their suppliers in the form of a *trade credit*—that is, suppliers allow the business to take possession of the needed goods and services and pay for them at a later date or in installments. Occasionally, small businesses engage in *bartering*—trading their own products for the goods and services offered by other businesses. For example, an accountant may offer accounting services to an office supply firm in exchange for computer paper and diskettes.

Additionally, some community groups sponsor loan funds to encourage the development of particular types of businesses.

both, is a **franchise.** The company that sells a franchise is the **franchiser.** Dunkin' Donuts, McDonald's, and Jiffy Lube are well-known franchisers with national visibility. The purchaser of a franchise is called a **franchisee.**

The franchisee acquires the rights to a name, logo, methods of operation, national advertising, products, and other elements associated with the franchiser's business in return for a financial commitment and the agreement to conduct business in accordance with the franchiser's standard of operations. Depending on the franchise, the initial fee to join a system varies. In addition, franchisees buy equipment, pay for training, and obtain a mortgage or lease. The franchisee also pays the franchiser a monthly or annual fee based on a percentage of sales or profits. In return, the franchisee often receives building specifications and designs, site recommendations, management and accounting support, and perhaps most importantly, immediate name recognition. Visit the Web site of the International Franchise Association to learn more on this topic.

The practice of franchising first began in the United States when Singer used it to sell sewing machines in the 19th century. It soon became commonplace in the distribution of goods in the automobile, gasoline, soft drink, and hotel industries. The concept of franchising grew especially rapidly during the 1960s, when it expanded to more diverse industries. Table 6.5 shows the 10 fastest growing franchises and the top 10 new franchises.

There are both advantages and disadvantages to franchising for the entrepreneur. Franchising allows a franchisee the opportunity to set up a small business relatively quickly, and because of its association with an established brand, a franchise outlet often reaches the breakeven point faster than an independent business would. Franchisees often report the following advantages:

- Management training and support.
- Brand-name appeal.
- Standardized quality of goods and services.
- National advertising programs.
- Financial assistance.
- Proven products and business formats.
- Centralized buying power.
- Site selection and territorial protection.
- Greater chance for success.[29]

However, the franchisee must sacrifice some freedom to the franchiser. Some shortcomings experienced by some franchisees include:

- Franchise fees and profit sharing with the franchiser.
- Strict adherence to standardized operations.
- Restrictions on purchasing.
- Limited product line.
- Possible market saturation.
- Less freedom in business decisions.[30]

Strict uniformity is the rule rather than the exception. Entrepreneurs who want to be their own bosses are often frustrated with a franchise.

## Help for Small-Business Managers

Because of the crucial role that small business and entrepreneurs play in the U.S. economy, a number of organizations offer programs to improve the small-business owner's ability to compete. These include entrepreneurial training programs and programs sponsored by the Small Business Administration. Such programs provide small-business owners with invaluable assistance in managing their businesses, often at little or no cost to the owner.

Entrepreneurs can learn critical marketing, management, and finance skills in seminars and college courses. In addition, knowledge, experience, and judgment are necessary for success in a new business. While knowledge can be communicated

and some experiences can be simulated in the classroom, good judgment must be developed by the entrepreneur. Local chambers of commerce and the U.S. Department of Commerce offer information and assistance helpful in operating a small business. National publications such as *Inc.* and *Entrepreneur* share statistics, advice, tips, and success/failure stories. Additionally, many urban areas—including Chicago; Jacksonville, Florida; Portland, Oregon; St. Louis; and Nashville—have weekly business journal/newspapers that provide stories on local businesses as well as on business techniques that a manager or small business can use.

Curves is for women only. It's not a fast-food franchise—it's a fast-exercise franchise.

**TABLE 6.5** Fastest Growing and Hottest New Franchises

| Top 10 Fastest Growing Franchises | Top 10 New Franchises |
|---|---|
| 1. Subway | United Shipping Solutions |
| 2. Jan-Pro Franchising International Inc. | Message Envy |
| 3. Dunkin Donuts | Super Suppers |
| 4. Coverall Cleaning Concepts | Dream Dinners Inc. |
| 5. Jazzercise Inc. | WineStyles Inc. |
| 6. Jackson Hewitt Tax Service | System4 |
| 7. RE/Max International Inc. | N-Hance |
| 8. CleanNet USA Inc. | Growth Coach, The |
| 9. Bonus Building Care | Instant Tax Service |
| 10. Jani-King | Snap Fitness Inc. |

Sources: "Fastest-Growing Franchises, 2007 Rankings," *Entrepreneur,* http://www.entrepreneur.com/franzone/fastestgrowing/index.html (accessed June 14, 2007); "Top New Franchises, 2007 Rankings," *Entrepreneur,*

http://www.entrepreneur.com/franchises/rankings/topnewfranchises-115520/2007, -1.html (accessed June 14, 2007).

The Small Business Administration offers many types of management assistance to small businesses, including counseling for firms in difficulty, consulting on improving operations, and training for owner/managers and their employees. Among its many programs, the SBA funds Small Business Development Centers (SBDCs). These are business clinics, usually located on college campuses, that provide counseling at no charge and training at only a nominal charge. SBDCs are often the SBA's principal means of providing direct management assistance.

The Service Corps of Retired Executives (SCORE) and the Active Corps of Executives (ACE) are volunteer agencies funded by the SBA to provide advice for owners of small firms. Both are staffed by experienced managers whose talents and experience the small firms could not ordinarily afford. SCORE has 10,500 volunteers at 389 U.S. locations and has served 7.2 million small businesses since 1964.[31] The SBA also has organized Small Business Institutes (SBIs) on almost 500 university and college campuses in the United States. Seniors, graduate students, and faculty at each SBI provide onsite management counseling.

Finally, the small-business owner can obtain advice from other small-business owners, suppliers, and even customers. A customer may approach a small business it frequents with a request for a new product, for example, or a supplier may offer suggestions for improving a manufacturing process. Networking—building relationships and sharing information with colleagues—is vital for any businessperson, whether you work for a huge corporation or run your own small business. Communicating with other business owners is a great way to find ideas for dealing with employees and government regulation, improving processes, or solving problems. New technology is making it easier to network. For example, some states are setting up computer bulletin boards for the use of their businesses to network and share ideas.

## Entrepreneurs Reinvent Pizza

Believe it or not, pizza—long an American food staple—has been losing popularity since 2000. A major contributor to the decline is America's growing interest in health. Those who fear carbohydrates don't want the crust; those who fear fat don't want the cheese, the oils, or the high-fat meats. So what is the pizza community doing to quell these fears and revive America's interest in pizza? Many pizzerias are moving away from fancy ingredients and large-sized pizzas and returning to the basics—focusing on quality ingredients rather than unique, abundant toppings. On the other hand, a few of the larger chains are trying out new-concept pizzas. Overall, the pizza industry is working hard to entice the pizza lover back.

Those pizzerias moving back to basics are paying attention to crust, sauce, and cheese—intending to present pizza as a pure, healthy meal. Along this line, restaurants such as American Flatbread don't even call their offerings pizza. Instead, at American Flatbread pizza is referred to as flatbread and made with organic flour and organic tomatoes. The company also uses only locally made mozzarella cheese and local meat. The company's franchisee agreement actually requires anyone owning an American Flatbread restaurant to use these ingredients. In addition to organic and fresh, local ingredients, artisanal-style pizzas are often considered healthier due to the thin crust. The transition has many pizzerias turning to Italy, the birthplace of pizza, for equipment and ingredients. Caputo, an Italian pizza flour company, had a 50 percent increase in U.S. sales in 2005, and GI. Metal, an Italian company selling pizza-making equipment, opened its first U.S. warehouse in 2005 due to demand for its products.

Taking another approach, Papa John's Pizza and Happy Joe's Pizza, two large chains, are working to open up a new pizza market. Both companies have launched breakfast pizzas at test locations. Breakfast pizzas are topped not with typical pizza ingredients but with scrambled eggs, bacon, and other breakfast fare. With pizza sales limping along and most sales occurring after 4 p.m., these chains see what they call Omelet Pizzas as an opportunity to hook an entirely new group of customers. Papa John's is currently testing Omelet Pizzas in downtown locations and focusing on corporate customers. Everyone agrees that selling breakfast pizzas will take time, but they feel it's worth a try.

Entrepreneurs interested in breaking into the casual dining restaurant industry should take a look at the artisanal pizza. Casual dining chains have been experiencing customer growth of about 8 percent annually—a highlight in the restaurant world right now. For an entrepreneur looking to launch a restaurant, pizza is a cost-effective choice. According to Dave Ostrander, a pizzeria consultant, the cost of pizza ingredients can easily be less than 25 percent of the menu price, allowing for a decent profit. Entrepreneurs already involved in the pizza industry are looking toward expansion—a possible indication that the downturn in the pizza market is about to shift.[32] ❖

## Q: Discussion Questions

1. Why is the pizza business a new opportunity for entrepreneurs?

2. How would you describe the new market for pizza for a startup small business?

3. Are there other food products similar to pizza that need reinventing to serve changing lifestyles and eating habits?

● ● **LO6**

Evaluate the demographic, technological, and economic trends that are affecting the future of small business.

# THE FUTURE FOR SMALL BUSINESS[33]

Although small businesses are crucial to the economy, they can be more vulnerable to turbulence and change in the marketplace than large businesses. Next, we take a brief look at the demographic, technological, and economic trends that will have the most impact on small business in the future.

## Demographic Trends

America's baby boom started in 1946 and ended in 1964. The earliest boomers are already past 50, and in the next few years, millions more will pass that mark. The boomer generation numbers about 76 million, or 28 percent of U.S. citizens.[34] This segment of the population is probably the wealthiest, but most small businesses do not actively pursue it. Some exceptions, however, include Gold Violin, which sells designer canes and other products online and through a catalog, and LifeSpring, which delivers nutritional meals and snacks directly to the customer. Industries such as travel, financial planning, and health care will continue to grow as boomers age. Many experts think that the boomer demographic is the market of the future.

Another market with huge potential for small business is the echo boomers, also called millennials or Generation Y. Born between 1977 and 1994, there are about 32 million people in the United States in this age group. Typically, they shop frequently and spend lavishly ($187 billion annually) on clothing, entertainment, and food.[35] Companies that have the most success with this group are ones that cater to the teens' and young adults' lifestyles. Some successful small businesses aimed at this market include Alien Workshop (designs and distributes skateboards and apparel), Burton Snowboards (manufactures snowboards and accessories), and Femme Arsenal (develops and distributes cosmetics).

Yet another trend is the growing number of immigrants living in the United States, about 35.2 million (legal and illegal immigrants).[36] That means that about one in every nine people living in the United States today was born in another country.[37] This vast number of people provides still another greatly untapped market for small businesses. Retailers who specialize in ethnic products, and service providers who offer bi- or multilingual employees, can find vast potential in this market. Table 6.6 ranks top cities in the United States for entrepreneurs.

## Technological and Economic Trends

Advances in technology have opened up many new markets to small businesses. Although thousands of small dot-coms

**TABLE 6.6** Top U.S. Cities for Entrepreneurs (Large Cities)

| | |
|---|---|
| 1. | Phoenix–Mesa, AZ |
| 2. | Charlotte–Gastonia–Rock Hill, NC/SC |
| 3. | Raleigh–Durham–Chapel Hill, NC |
| 4. | Las Vegas, NV/AZ |
| 5. | Austin–San Marcos, TX |
| 6. | Washington, DC–Baltimore, MD/VA/WV |
| 7. | Memphis, TN/AR/MS |
| 8. | Nashville, TN |
| 9. | Norfolk–Virginia Beach–Newport News, VA/NC |
| 10. | San Antonio, TX |

Source: "Hot Cities for Entrepreneurs," *Entrepreneur.com*, http://www.entrepreneur.com/bestcities/ (accessed June 14, 2007).

have failed, experts predict that Internet usage will continue to increase, and one of the hot areas will be the Internet infrastructure area that enables companies to improve communications with employees, suppliers, and customers.

Technological advances and an increase in service exports have created new opportunities for small companies to expand their operations abroad. Changes in communications and technology can allow small companies to customize their services quickly for international customers. Also, free trade agreements and trade alliances are helping to create an environment in which small businesses have fewer regulatory and legal barriers.

In recent years, economic turbulence has provided both opportunities and threats for small businesses. As large information technology companies such as Cisco, Oracle, and Sun Microsystems had to recover from an economic slowdown and an oversupply of Internet infrastructure products, some smaller firms found new niche markets. Smaller companies can react

*Sirius created value for a product and a market that didn't previously exist.*

quickly to change and can stay close to their customers. While many well-funded dot-coms were failing, many small businesses were learning how to use the Internet to promote their businesses and sell products online. For example, many arts and crafts dealers and makers of specialty products found they could sell their wares on existing Web sites, such as eBay. Service providers related to tourism, real estate, and construction also found they could reach customers through their own or existing Web sites.

Deregulation of the energy market and interest in alternative fuels and in fuel conservation have spawned many small businesses. Earth First Technologies Inc. produces clean-burning fuel from contaminated water or sewage. Southwest Windpower Inc. manufactures and markets small wind turbines for producing electric power for homes, sailboats, and telecommunications. Solar Attic Inc. has developed a process to recover heat from home attics to use in heating hot water or swimming pools. As entrepreneurs begin to realize that worldwide energy markets are valued in the hundreds of billions of dollars, the number of innovative companies entering this market will increase. In addition, many small businesses have the desire and employee commitment to purchase such environmentally friendly products. New Belgium Brewing Company received the U.S. Environmental Protection Agency and Department of Energy Award for leadership in conservation for making a 10-year commitment to purchase wind energy. The company's employees unanimously agreed to cover the increased costs of wind-generated electricity from the employee profit-sharing program.

The future for small business remains promising. The opportunities to apply creativity and entrepreneurship to serve customers are unlimited. While large organizations such as Wal-Mart, which has more than 1.8 million employees, typically must adapt to change slowly, a small business can adapt to customer and community needs and changing trends immediately. This flexibility provides small businesses with a definite advantage over large companies.

## ●● LO7

Explain why many large businesses are trying to "think small."

# MAKING BIG BUSINESSES ACT "SMALL"

The continuing success and competitiveness of small businesses through rapidly changing conditions in the business world have led many large corporations to take a closer look at what makes their smaller rivals tick. More and more firms are emulating small businesses in an effort to improve their own bottom line. Beginning in the 1980s and continuing through the present, the buzzword in business has been to *downsize,* or the even newer term is *right-size* to reduce management layers, corporate staff, and work tasks in order to make the firm more flexible, resourceful, and innovative like a smaller business. Many well-known U.S. companies, including IBM, Ford, Apple Computer, General Electric, Xerox, and 3M, have downsized to improve their competitiveness, as have German, British, and Japanese firms. Other firms have sought to make their businesses "smaller" by making their operating units function more like independent small businesses, each responsible for its profits, losses, and resources. Of course, some large corporations, such as Southwest Airlines, have acted like small businesses from their inception, with great success.

Trying to capitalize on small-business success in introducing innovative new products, more and more companies are attempting to instill a spirit of entrepreneurship into even the largest firms. In major corporations, intrapreneurs, like entrepreneurs, take responsibility for, or "champion," the development of innovations of any kind *within* the larger organization.[38] Often, they use company resources and time to develop a new product for the company. ∎

Business success is an outgrowth of knowledge and experience. All kinds of life experiences—as a family member, friend, student, employee, or consumer, or in sports or art—are valuable. "The things you know and love and see opportunities in—you ought to pick your business based on that," says Bill Gates, founder of Microsoft.

Because of financial constraints and the lack of experience, most college students cannot start a business immediately after graduation. However, the challenge in starting and running a successful business is to demonstrate good judgment. Someone with a B.S. degree, a $50,000 inheritance, and poor judgment will not succeed as an entrepreneur. On the other hand, a person with $2,000 in savings may end up wealthy because of good business judgment. Steve Jobs and Steve Wozniak started Apple Computer in a garage with only a few thousand dollars. Another high-tech entrepreneur, Michael Dell, started Dell Computers in his University of Texas dorm room. So great was the success of both Apple and Dell that IBM and other large corporations rushed to create new products to compete with them.

It is estimated that 80 percent of new jobs for college graduates will be found in small business. Therefore, knowing about successful small businesses may be the first step in assessing job opportunities. Along with this chapter, reading magazines such as *Inc.* or *Entrepreneur* can provide a good start in learning more about small business opportunities.[39]

## Build Your Business Plan

### Small Business, Entrepreneurship, and Franchising

Now you can get started writing your business plan! Refer to Guidelines for the Development of the Business Plan following Chapter 1, which provides you with an outline for your business plan. As you are developing your business plan keep in mind that potential investors might be reviewing it. Or you might have plans to go to your local Small Business Development Center for an SBA loan.

At this point in the process you should think about collecting information from a variety of (free) resources. For example, if you are developing a business plan for a local business, product or service you might want to check out any of the following sources for demographic information: your local Chamber of Commerce, Economic Development Office, Census Bureau, or City Planning Office.

Go on the Internet and see if there have been any recent studies done or articles on your specific type of business, especially in your area. Remember, you always want to explore any secondary data before trying to conduct your own research.

# the
# nature of
# management

**Introduction**  For any organization—small or large, for profit or nonprofit— to achieve its objectives, it must have equipment and raw materials to turn into products to market, employees to make and sell the products, and financial resources to purchase additional goods and services, pay employees, and generally operate the business. To accomplish this, it must also have one or more managers to plan, organize, staff, direct, and control the work that goes on.

This chapter introduces the field of management. It examines and surveys the various functions, levels, and areas of management in business. The skills that managers need for success and the steps that lead to effective decision making are also discussed.

● ● learning **OBJECTIVES**

**LO1** Define management, and explain its role in the achievement of organizational objectives.

**LO2** Describe the major functions of management.

**LO3** Distinguish among three levels of management and the concerns of managers at each level.

**LO4** Specify the skills managers need to be successful.

**LO5** Summarize the systematic approach to decision making used by many business managers.

## ●● LO1

Define management, and explain its role in the achievement of organizational objectives.

# THE IMPORTANCE OF MANAGEMENT

**Management** is a process designed to achieve an organization's objectives by using its resources effectively and efficiently in a changing environment. *Effectively* means having the intended result; *efficiently* means accomplishing the objectives with a minimum of resources. **Managers** make decisions about the use of the organization's resources and are concerned with planning, organizing, staffing, directing, and controlling the organization's activities so as to reach its objectives. Fred Franzia developed the fourth largest winery in the country by bucking industry trends and striving to produce the highest quality, lowest priced wines in the market. This family business is run out of a headquarters in a small, termite-infested building. This philosophy produced "Two Buck Chuck." Trader Joes started selling Franzia's wines for $1.99 ($3.99 outside of California), and the critics were amazed at its drinkability, with *Wine and Vines* picking the econo-wine over a $67 chardonnay.[1] Management is universal. It takes place not only in businesses of all sizes, but also in government, the military, labor unions, hospitals, schools, and religious groups—any organization requiring the coordination of resources.

Every organization, in the pursuit of its objectives, must acquire resources (people, raw materials and equipment, money, and information) and coordinate their use to turn out a final good or service. The manager of a local movie theater, for example, must make decisions about seating, projectors, sound equipment, screens, concession stands, and ticket booths. All this equipment must be in proper working condition. The manager must also make decisions about materials. There must be films to show, popcorn and candy to sell, and so on. To transform the physical resources into final products, the manager must also have human resources—employees to sell the tickets, run the concession stand, run the projector, and maintain the facilities. Finally, the manager needs adequate financial resources to pay for the essential activities; the primary source of funding is the money generated from sales of tickets and snacks. All these resources and activities must be coordinated and controlled if the theater is to earn a profit. Organizations must have adequate resources of all types, and managers must carefully coordinate the use of these resources if they are to achieve the organization's objectives.

## ●● LO2

Describe the major functions of management.

# MANAGEMENT FUNCTIONS

To coordinate the use of resources so that the business can develop, make, and sell products, managers engage in a series of activities: planning, organizing, staffing, directing, and controlling (Figure 7.1). Although we describe each separately, these five functions are interrelated, and managers may perform two or more of them at the same time.

## Planning

**Planning,** the process of determining the organization's objectives and deciding how to accomplish them, is the first function of management. Planning is a crucial activity, for it designs the map that lays the groundwork for the other functions. It involves forecasting events and determining the best course of action from a set of options or choices. The plan itself specifies what should be done, by whom, where, when, and how. When McDonald's CEO Jim Catalupo died suddenly of a heart attack in 2004, Charlie Bell took over as CEO and continued a three-year plan developed under Catalupo's leadership. Unfortunately, in November 2004 Bell learned that he had cancer and resigned, turning the position over to Jim Skinner.

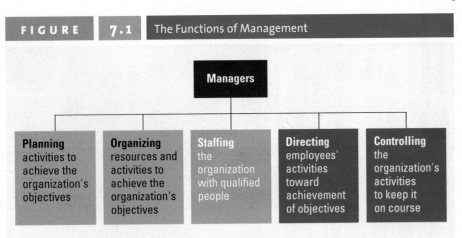

| **FIGURE** | **7.1** | The Functions of Management |

**Managers**

| **Planning** activities to achieve the organization's objectives | **Organizing** resources and activities to achieve the organization's objectives | **Staffing** the organization with qualified people | **Directing** employees' activities toward achievement of objectives | **Controlling** the organization's activities to keep it on course |

Bell later died in early 2005 and Skinner continued the work of both previous CEOs in an effort to revitalize the company. The plans called for remodels of current restaurants, an increased emphasis on service quality, as well as extending service hours and increased attention to offering nutritional menu items. The result for McDonald's has been positive, with same-store sales in the United States up for 36 consecutive months. In addition, the company's stock price is up more than 30 percent in the past two years.[3] All businesses—from the smallest restaurant to the largest multinational corporation—need to develop plans for achieving success. But before an organization can plan a course of action, it must first determine what it wants to achieve.

objectives. Objectives, the ends or results desired by the organization, derive from the organization's mission, which describes its fundamental purpose and basic philosophy. A photo lab, for example, might say that its mission is to provide customers with memories. To carry out its mission, the photo lab sets specific objectives relating to its mission, such as reducing development defects to less than 2 percent, introducing a selection of photo albums and frames for customers' use in displaying their photos, providing customers' proofs or negatives over the Internet, providing technical assistance, and so on. Herbal tea marketer Celestial Seasonings says that its mission is "To create and sell healthful, naturally oriented products that nurture people's bodies and uplift their souls."[4]

A business's objectives may be elaborate or simple. Common objectives relate to profit, competitive advantage, efficiency, and growth. Organizations with profit as a goal want to have money and assets left over after paying off business expenses. Objectives regarding competitive advantage are generally stated in terms of percentage of sales increase and market share, with the goal of increasing those figures. Efficiency objectives involve making the best use of the organization's resources. The photo lab's objective of holding defects to less than 2 percent is an example of an efficiency objective. Growth objectives relate to an organization's ability to adapt and to get new products to the marketplace in a timely fashion. The mission of Procter & Gamble is to continue to improve customers' quality of life through meaningful product research, development, and innovation. It took more than eight years and 180 researchers to develop the polymer that helps prevent diaper rash, resulting in happier and healthier babies. P&G spends nearly $2 billion on product research and development.[5] Other organizational objectives include service, ethical, and community goals. Cisco Systems was honored by the Points of Light "Awards for Excellence in Workplace Volunteer Programs" for their long-term commitment to volunteerism. Cisco's volunteerism program has a $1.2 million operating budget and more than $2 million in matching grants. Cisco operates the "Volunteer Connection" online tool that matches employees' skills with the needs of nonprofit organizations.[6] Objectives provide direction for all managerial decisions; additionally, they establish criteria by which performance can be evaluated.

plans. There are three general types of plans for meeting objectives—strategic, tactical, and operational. A firm's highest managers develop its strategic plans, which establish the long-range objectives and overall strategy or course of action by which the firm fulfills its mission. Strategic plans generally cover periods ranging from 2 to 10 years or even longer. They include plans to add products, purchase companies, sell unprofitable segments of the business, issue stock, and move into international markets. Faced with stiff competition, rising costs, and slowing sales, many companies are closing U.S. plants and moving production to factories abroad. For example,

**Objectives, the ends or results desired by the organization**

# El Pinto—A New Mexican Hot Spot

Jim and John Thomas

The Business: El Pinto Restaurant

Founded: 1962

Success: El Pinto is now the largest restaurant in the state of New Mexico.

Founded in Albuquerque, New Mexcio, in 1962, El Pinto Restaurant is touted as one of the best authentic New Mexican restaurants in the state. The restaurant's cuisine is based on family recipes and features El Pinto's famous chile salsas. Twins Jim and John Thomas purchased the restaurant from their parents in the early 1990s. During their first 10 years running the business, revenue grew from about $300,000 to $3.75 million a year—revenue that has continued to grow. El Pinto's real growth occurred when the brothers chose to bring their famous salsas to the retail market. The brothers invested about $310,000 into launching the salsas and recouped that amount in just three months. The brothers believe it is the quality of the salsas—priced above most of the competition—that is responsible for their retail success. The chile is all hand roasted, peeled, and packaged on the El Pinto restaurant site. The salsas are available in stores throughout the state of New Mexico and on the restaurant's Web site and have won second place Scovie awards at the Fiery Foods show and first place awards in multiple categories at the New Mexico State Fair. El Pinto was featured on ESPN's "Sports Center Across America" segment, a 50-states-in-50-days promotion in 2005, and a Wall Street Journal article, "The Search for the Perfect Nacho," in 2006. El Pinto continues to be one of the must stop spots in New Mexico.[2] ❖

Converse Inc. (sneaker maker), Lionel LLC (producer of model trains), and Zebco (fishing reel manufacturer) all stopped U.S. production in favor of Asian factories.[7] Strategic plans must take into account the organization's capabilities and resources, the changing business environment, and organizational objectives. Plans should be market-driven, matching customers' desire for value with operational capabilities, processes, and human resources.[8]

Tactical plans are short-range plans designed to implement the activities and objectives specified in the strategic plan.

These plans, which usually cover a period of one year or less, help keep the organization on the course established in the strategic plan. Because tactical plans permit the organization to react to changes in the environment while continuing to focus on the company's overall strategy, management must periodically review and update them. Declining performance or failure to meet objectives set out in tactical plans may be one reason for revising them. When ImClone Systems failed to gain approval for its anticancer drug Erbitux, the stock fell from $70 to the single digits. Former CEO and founder Sam Waksal was imprisoned for insider trading, and Martha Stewart served jail time for lying during the investigation. Six years after this hardship, ImClone has received approval from federal regulators for many of its cancer treatments and reported total revenue of $677.8 million. In a tactical plan to take advantage of the company's positive momentum, the company put itself on the marketplace to be sold for $4.5 to $5 billion. However, with increased competition from similar products to Erbitux and the failure of "reasonable" bids to materialize, Imclone shifted back from its planned sale.[9]

A retailing organization with a five-year strategic plan to invest $5 billion in 500 new retail stores may develop five tactical plans (each covering one year) specifying how much to spend to set up each new store, where to locate each new store, and when to open each new store. Tactical plans are designed to execute the overall strategic plan. Because of their short-term nature, they are easier to adjust or abandon if changes in the environment or the company's performance so warrant.

Operational plans are very short term and specify what actions specific individuals, work groups, or departments need to accomplish to achieve the tactical plan and ultimately the strategic plan. They may apply to just one month, week, or even day. For example, a work group may be assigned a weekly production quota to ensure there are sufficient products available to elevate market share (tactical goal) and ultimately help the firm be number one in its product category (strategic goal). Returning to our retail store example, operational plans may specify the schedule for opening one new store, hiring new employees, obtaining merchandise, training new employees, and opening for actual business.

Another element in planning is the idea of crisis management or contingency planning, which deals with potential disasters such as product tampering, oil spills, fire, earthquake, computer virus, or even a reputation crisis due to unethical or illegal conduct by one or more employees. Many mutual fund companies, for example, saw their reputations and business suffer as a result of a scandal in the industry when some companies allowed a few large clients special privileges in violation of federal regulations. At Putnam Investments, for example, customers withdrew $61 billion from the company's mutual funds and the company faced numerous lawsuits and federal and state charges of misconduct.[10] Businesses that have contingency plans tend to respond more effectively when problems occur than do businesses who lack such planning.

*"Only in winter can you tell which trees are truly green. Only when the winds of adversity blow can you tell whether an individual or a country has steadfastness."*

*John F. Kennedy*

The unforgettable events of September 11 united New Yorkers, the country and the world in ways terrorists could never imagine. For as long as this nation stands, its citizens will proudly venerate those who lost their lives that dreadful Tuesday as well as those who worked so tirelessly to rescue others.

We at Standard & Poor's offer our condolences to the families, friends and clients affected by this national tragedy. Throughout the world we rededicate ourselves to serve the communities in which we operate and to further an understanding and an appreciation for the democratic institutions that came under attack.

STANDARD & POOR'S

*A Division of The McGraw-Hill Companies*

*Companies that housed operations in and around the World Trade Center, many of them key players in the financial markets, had to rely on contingency plans after 9/11. Those that could, reassured clients and the world that operations would continue. Many took out patriotic, inspirational ads such as this one from Standard & Poor's.*

Many companies, including Ashland Oil, H. J. Heinz, and Johnson & Johnson, have crisis management teams to deal specifically with problems, permitting other managers to continue to focus on their regular duties. Some companies even hold regular disaster drills to ensure that their employees know how to respond when a crisis does occur. Crisis management plans generally cover maintaining business operations throughout a crisis and communicating with the public, employees, and officials about the nature of and the company's response to the problem. Communication is especially important to minimize panic and damaging rumors; it also demonstrates that the company is aware of the problem and plans to respond. The major hurricanes hitting the Gulf Coast region disrupted many business activities. The airlines were especially damaged when many Americans were reluctant to travel. Incidents such as this highlight the importance of tactical planning for crises and the need to respond publicly and quickly when a disaster occurs.

## Organizing

Rarely are individuals in an organization able to achieve common goals without some form of structure. Organizing is the structuring of resources and activities to accomplish objectives in an efficient and effective manner. Managers organize by reviewing plans and determining what activities are necessary to implement them; then, they divide the work into small units and assign it to specific individuals, groups, or departments. As companies reorganize for greater efficiency, more often than not, they are organizing work into teams to handle core processes such as new product development instead of organizing around traditional departments such as marketing and production.

Organizing is important for several reasons. It helps create synergy, whereby the effect of a whole system equals more than that of its parts. It also establishes lines of authority, improves communication, helps avoid duplication of resources, and can improve competitiveness by speeding up decision making. In an effort to reduce costs and improve efficiency, media giant Reuters Group PLC reorganized its product-based divisions into four key customer segments. The new business units are part of the company's strategy to get closer to clients using Internet technologies. The units focus on clients involved in financial products (sales and trading, enterprise solutions and research, and asset management), corporate products, and media products.[11] Because organizing is so important, we'll take a closer look at it in Chapter 8.

## Staffing

Once managers have determined what work is to be done and how it is to be organized, they must ensure that the organization has enough employees with appropriate skills to do the work. Hiring people to carry out the work of the organization is known as staffing. Beyond recruiting people for positions within the firm, managers must determine what skills are needed for specific jobs, how to motivate and train employees to do their assigned jobs, how much to pay employees, what benefits to provide, and how to prepare employees for higher-level jobs in the firm at a later date. These elements of staffing will be explored in detail in Chapters 10 and 11.

Another aspect of staffing is downsizing, the elimination of significant numbers of employees from an organization, which has been a pervasive and much-talked-about trend. Whether it is called downsizing, rightsizing, trimming the fat, or the new reality in business, the implications of downsizing have been dramatic. Ford Motor Company is in the process of implementing a major North American restructuring. The company will close at least 10 assembly and component plants and eliminate 25,000 to 30,000 hourly jobs within the next five years. Ford also eliminated top executive positions. The goal is to reverse a 10-year market share slide that the company has been experiencing.[12] Many firms downsize by outsourcing production, sales, and technical positions to companies in other countries with lower labor costs. Downsizing has helped numerous firms reduce costs quickly and become more profitable (or become profitable after lengthy losses) in a short period of time.

Downsizing, or laying off employees, obviously has a negative impact on the workers who lose their jobs. But the employees who keep their jobs suffer, too. They often feel bitter and insecure, and they resent having to take on the tasks their former co-workers used to do.

● ORGANIZING the structuring of resources and activities to accomplish objectives in an efficient and effective manner

● STAFFING the hiring of people to carry out the work of the organization

● DOWNSIZING the elimination of a significant number of employees from an organization

● **DIRECTING** motivating
and leading employees
to achieve organizational
objectives

● **CONTROLLING** the process of evaluating and correcting activities to keep the
organization on course

Downsizing and outsourcing, however, have painful consequences. Obviously, the biggest casualty is those who lose their jobs, along with their incomes, insurance, and pensions. Some find new jobs quickly; others do not. Another victim is the morale of the employees at downsized firms who get to keep their jobs. The employees left behind in a downsizing often feel more insecure, angry, and sad, and their productivity may decline as a result, the opposite of the effect sought. Managers can expect that 70 to 80 percent of those surviving a downsize will take a "wait-and-see" attitude and need to be led. Ten to 15 percent will be openly hostile or try to sabotage change in an effort to return to the way things were before. The remaining 10 to 15 percent will be the leaders who will try proactively to help make the situation work.[13] A survey of workers who remained after a downsizing found that many felt their jobs demanded more time and energy.[14]

After a downsizing situation, an effective manager will promote optimism and positive thinking and minimize criticism and fault-finding. Management should also build teamwork

jobs: They need to know that their employer values their ideas and input. Smart managers, therefore, ask workers to contribute ideas for reducing costs, making equipment more efficient, improving customer service, or even developing new products. This participation makes workers feel important, and the company benefits. For example, DaimlerChrysler AG's Chrysler Group is using a new online system called Dealer Scorecard. The "Scorecard" provides performance measurements along 37 different measures, covering all business activity from sales to financing and repair. Employee as well as dealership rewards are tied to exceptional service, and dealerships are able to recognize exemplary employee performance and employee deficiencies.[15] Recognition and appreciation are often the best motivators for employees. Employees who understand more about their effect on the financial success of the company may be motivated to work harder for that success, and managers who understand the needs and desires of workers can motivate their employees to work harder and more productively. The motivation of employees is discussed in detail in Chapter 10.

## Controlling

Planning, organizing, staffing, and directing are all important to the success of an organization, whether its objective is

## "Participation makes workers feel important, and the company benefits."

and encourage positive group discussions. Honest communication is important during a time of change and will lead to trust. Truthfulness about what has happened and also about future expectations is essential.

## Directing

Once the organization has been staffed, management must direct the employees. Directing is motivating and leading employees to achieve organizational objectives. All managers are involved in directing, but it is especially important for lower-level managers who interact daily with the employees operating the organization. For example, an assembly-line supervisor for Frito-Lay must ensure that her workers know how to use their equipment properly and have the resources needed to carry out their jobs, and she must motivate her workers to achieve their expected output of packaged snacks.

Managers may motivate employees by providing incentives—such as the promise of a raise or promotion—for them to do a good job. But most workers want more than money from their

earning a profit or something else. But what happens when a firm fails to reach its goals despite a strong planning effort? Controlling is the process of evaluating and correcting activities to keep the organization on course. Control involves five activities: (1) measuring performance, (2) comparing present performance with standards or objectives, (3) identifying deviations from the standards, (4) investigating the causes of deviations, and (5) taking corrective action when necessary.

Controlling and planning are closely linked. Planning establishes goals and standards for performance. By monitoring performance and comparing it with standards, managers can determine whether performance is on target. When performance is substandard, management must determine why and take appropriate actions to get the firm back on course. In short, the control function helps managers assess the success of their plans. When plans have not been successful, the control process facilitates revision of the plans. ExxonMobil has run ads indicating that peak oil demand is decades away. This message conflicts with ads that Chevron is running, indicating that world

# DESTINATION CEO

**T. Gary Rogers—Dreyer's** T. Gary Rogers started as a businessman early in life by delivering newspapers that earned him $30 per month. That early experience helped Rogers develop a sense of commitment and focus. Initially, Rogers thought that he would like to be an engineer. However, his education took him in a different direction. After completing his education at the University of California at Berkley, he enlisted in the Army for two years. When he returned from active duty, Rogers went on to the Harvard Business School. His early entrepreneurial adventures took him in the direction of the restaurant business. He opened five restaurants (called the Vintage House), but they failed.

He happened to meet the owner of Dreyer's Ice Cream at a time when the owner was struggling to get financing for a factory expansion. The bank would not finance the expansion, and Rogers asked whether he would consider selling the business. In 1974, Dreyer's had sold 150 million gallons of ice cream. T. Gary Rogers bought Dreyer's Ice Cream for $1 million in 1977, by raising $0.5 million in equity and $0.5 million in debt. Under his leadership, the company experienced rapid expansion and success. Twenty-five years after

purchasing Dreyer's Ice Cream for $1 million, he sold the business to Nestle's for $3.2 billion. Rogers observes that all of us have opportunities, but that success is determined by those who know how to seize them.

## >>DISCUSSION QUESTIONS

1. Which function(s) of management are most clearly identified in the video?

2. Dryer's increased in value from $1 million in 1977 to $3.2 billion 25 years later. What factors may account for this?

3. Did Rogers's engineering education contribute to his success as a businessman?

>>To see the complete video about T. Gary Rogers, go to our Web site at **www.mhhe.com/FerrellIM** and look for the link to the Destination CEO videos.

● **TOP MANAGERS** the president and other top executives of a business, such as the chief executive officer (CEO), chief financial officer (CFO), and chief operations officer (COO), who have overall responsibility for the organization

consumes two barrels of oil for every one that it finds. A strategy for dealing with concerns about depleting energy resources is for oil companies to invest in finding and developing new supplies of petroleum.[16]

The control process also helps managers deal with problems arising outside the firm. For example, if a firm is the subject of negative publicity, management should use the control process to determine why and to guide the firm's response.

# TYPES OF MANAGEMENT

All managers—whether the sole proprietor of a small video store or the hundreds of managers of a large company such as Paramount Pictures—perform the five functions just discussed. In the case of the video store, the owner handles all the functions, but in a large company with more than one manager, responsibilities must be divided and delegated. This division of responsibility is generally achieved by establishing levels of management and areas of specialization—finance, marketing, and so on.

## DID YOU KNOW?

Women represent only 15.7 percent of corporate officers and just 5.2 percent of all top earners.[19]

Distinguish among three levels of management and the concerns of managers at each level.

## Levels of Management

As we have hinted, many organizations have multiple levels of management—top management, middle management, and first-line, or supervisory management. These levels form a pyramid, as shown in Figure 7.2. As the pyramid shape implies, there are generally more middle managers than top managers, and still more first-line managers. Very small organizations may have only one manager (typically, the owner), who assumes the responsibilities of all three levels. Large businesses have many managers at each level to coordinate the use of the organization's resources. Managers at all three levels perform all five management functions, but the amount of time they spend on each function varies, as we shall see (Figure 7.3).

**top management.** In businesses, **top managers** include the president and other top executives, such as the chief executive officer (CEO), chief financial officer (CFO), and chief operations officer (COO), who have overall responsibility for the organization. Oprah Winfrey, for example, is the chief executive officer of Harpo Inc., which owns *O* magazine as well as the *Oprah Winfrey Show*. Circulation of *O* magazine fell just under 10 percent; however, advertising sales remain strong for the TV show, and a deal has been signed with XM satellite radio for three years for $55 million.[17] In public corporations, even chief executive officers have a boss—the firm's board of directors. With technological advances continuing and privacy concerns increasing, some companies are adding a new top management position—chief privacy officer (CPO). There are currently an estimated 2,000 CPOs in U.S. corporations, and that number is expected to rise over the next few years in response to growing concerns about privacy as well as new legislation such as the Sarbanes-Oxley Act. Among the companies that have appointed CPOs are American Express, Citigroup, Hewlett-Packard, Microsoft, and the U.S. Postal Service.[18] In government, top management refers to the president, a governor, or a mayor or city manager; in education, a chancellor of a university or a county superintendent of education.

| FIGURE | 7.2 | Levels of Management |
| --- | --- | --- |

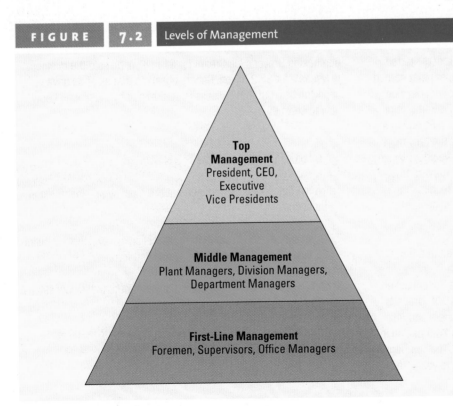

**Top Management**
President, CEO, Executive Vice Presidents

**Middle Management**
Plant Managers, Division Managers, Department Managers

**First-Line Management**
Foremen, Supervisors, Office Managers

Top-level managers spend most of their time planning. They make the organization's strategic decisions, decisions that focus on an overall scheme or key idea for using resources to take advantage of opportunities. They decide whether to add products, acquire companies, sell unprofitable business segments, and move into foreign markets. Top managers also represent their company to the public and to government regulators.

Given the importance and range of top management's decisions, top managers generally have many years of varied experience and command top salaries. In addition to salaries, top managers' compensation packages typically include bonuses, long-term incentive awards, stock, and stock options. Table 7.1 lists the 10 highest paid CEOs including bonuses, stock options and other compensation.

Some people question the pay disparity between top executives and U.S. workers. According to a recent report by United for a Fair Economy, the average executive now earns 431 times the average blue collar worker. According to the report, if the minimum wage had risen as fast as CEO pay since 1990, the lowest paid workers in the United States would be earning $23.03 an hour today, not $5.15 an hour.[20] Some CEOs, however, limit the level of compensation that they and other top managers can receive to minimize the disparity between the levels of employees and to show social responsibility with respect to their compensation. The chief executives of America's 500 biggest companies received a collective 38 percent pay raise in 2006, to $7.5 billion. This means the

average salary, benefits, and options package for chief executives of major corporations in the United States in 2006 was $15.2 million.[21]

Workforce diversity is an important issue in today's corporations. Effective managers at enlightened corporations have found that diversity is good for workers and for the bottom line. Putting together different kinds of people to solve problems often results in better solutions. Betsy Holden, CEO of Kraft Foods, said, "When we look at the composition of teams within our company, we have found that those with a variety

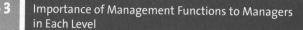

FIGURE 7.3 Importance of Management Functions to Managers in Each Level

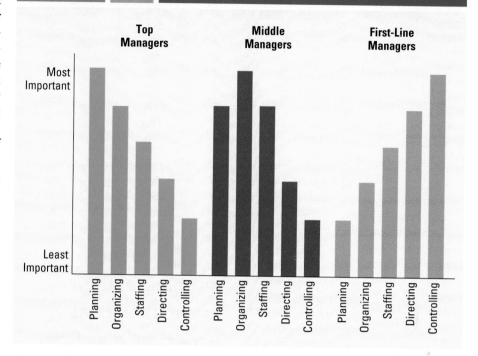

TABLE 7.1 The Ten Highest Paid CEOs

| Rank | CEO | Company | Total Compensation (dollars in thousands) |
|---|---|---|---|
| 1. | Steven Jobs | Apple | $646,600 |
| 2. | Ray Irani | Occidental Petroleum | 321,637 |
| 3. | Barry Diller | IAC/InteractiveCorp | 295,136 |
| 4. | William Folley II | Fidelity National Financial | 179,557 |
| 5. | Terry Semel | Yahoo! | 174,202 |
| 6. | Michael Dell | Dell | 153,228 |
| 7. | Angelo Mozilo | Countrywide Financial | 141,975 |
| 8. | Michael Jeffries | Abercrombie & Fitch | 114,638 |
| 9. | Kenneth Lewis | Bank of America | 99,802 |
| 10. | Henry Duques | First Data | 98,210 |

Source: Scott DeCarlo, "By the Numbers: America's Highest-Paid CEOs," *Forbes,* May 3, 2007, http://www.forbes.com/2007/05/03/ceo-executive-compensation-lead-07ceo-cx_sd_0503ceocompensationintro.html (accessed June 14, 2007).

supervise workers and the daily operations of the organization. They are responsible for implementing the plans established by middle management and directing workers' daily performance on the job. They spend most of their time directing and controlling. Common titles for first-line managers are foreman, supervisor, and office manager.

of perspectives are simply the most creative."[22] Managers from companies devoted to workforce diversity devised six rules that make diversity work (see Table 7.2). Diversity is explored in greater detail in Chapter 11.

**middle management.** Rather than making strategic decisions about the whole organization, middle managers are responsible for tactical planning that will implement the general guidelines established by top management. Thus, their responsibility is more narrowly focused than that of top managers. Middle managers are involved in the specific operations of the organization and spend more time organizing than other managers. In business, plant managers, division managers, and department managers make up middle management. The product manager for laundry detergent at a consumer products manufacturer, the department chairperson in a university, and the head of a state public health department are all middle managers. The ranks of middle managers have been shrinking as more and more companies downsize to be more productive.

**first-line management.** Most people get their first managerial experience as first-line managers, those who

## Areas of Management

At each level, there are managers who specialize in the basic functional areas of business: finance, production and operations, human resources (personnel), marketing, and administration.

**financial management.** Financial managers focus on obtaining the money needed for the successful operation of the organization and using that money in accordance with organizational goals. Among the responsibilities of financial managers are projecting income and expenses over a specified period, determining short- and long-term financing needs and finding sources of financing to fill those needs, identifying and selecting appropriate ways to invest extra funds, monitoring the flow of financial resources, and protecting the financial resources of the organization. A financial manager at Subway, for example, may be asked to analyze the costs and revenues of a new sandwich product to determine its contribution to Subway's profitability. All organizations must have adequate financial resources to acquire the physical and human resources that are necessary to create goods and services. Consequently, financial resource management is of the utmost importance.

**Most people get their first managerial experience as first-line managers**

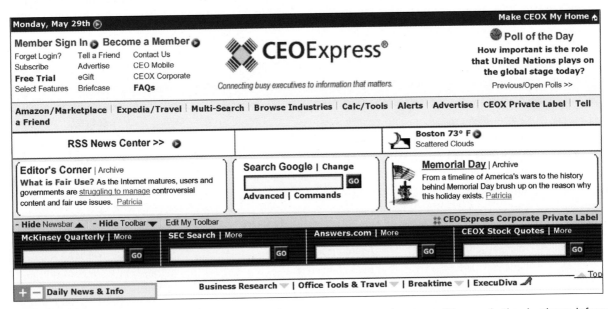

Top managers use online resources such as ceoexpress.com to gather economic, competitive, and other business information.

**TABLE 7.2** Six Rules That Make Diversity Work

| Rule | Action |
|---|---|
| 1. Search for the best | Invest time and money in "affirmative recruiting." |
| 2. Help newcomers fit in | Emphasize cooperation and teamwork. |
| 3. Educate everyone | Address employees' fears of change and discomfort with people from diverse backgrounds; encourage minority employees to express their views; encourage others to listen. |
| 4. Keep score | Hold managers accountable for diversity goals and progress. |
| 5. Sweat the details | Pay attention to the smaller differences in diverse employees and address concerns. |
| 6. See the future | Invest in potential employees of the future (e.g., develop programs that target minority groups in middle and high schools). |

Source: Annie Finnigan, "Different Strokes," *Working Woman,* April 2001, pp. 42–48.

● **PRODUCTION AND OPERATIONS MANAGERS** those who develop and administer the activities involved in transforming resources into goods, services, and ideas ready for the marketplace

● **HUMAN RESOURCES MANAGERS** those who handle the staffing function and deal with employees in a formalized manner

● **MARKETING MANAGERS** those who are responsible for planning, pricing, and promoting products and making them available to customers

## production and operations management.
**Production and operations managers** develop and administer the activities involved in transforming resources into goods, services, and ideas ready for the marketplace. Production and operations managers are typically involved in planning and designing production facilities, purchasing raw materials and supplies, managing inventory, scheduling processes to meet demand, and ensuring that products meet quality standards. Because no business can exist without the production of goods and services, production and operations managers are vital to an organization's success. At Pfizer Global Research, for example, Robert Swanson works as an associate director of logistics and supply chain management, which makes him responsible for transporting and caring for lab equipment, protective gear, chemicals, and maintenance and office supplies and shipping scientific documents, materials, and other equipment to other Pfizer facilities around the world.[23]

## human resources management.
**Human resources managers** handle the staffing function and deal with employees in a formalized manner. Once known as personnel managers, they determine an organization's human resource needs; recruit and hire new employees; develop and administer employee benefits, training, and performance appraisal programs; and deal with government regulations concerning employment practices. For example, some companies recognize that their employees' health affects their health care costs. Therefore, more progressive companies provide health care facilities and outside health club memberships, encourage proper nutrition, and discourage smoking in an effort to improve employee health and lower the costs of providing health care benefits. Pfizer of Canada and DaimlerChrysler's Windsor, Canada, Assembly Plant, launched a program called "Turn Up Your Heart." The goal of the program is to assess and reduce the risks of heart disease among both employees and retirees and to increase quality of life and productivity while reducing health care costs. The results of the program after one year were dramatic. Almost half of the participants lost an average 16 pounds, there was a 36 percent reduction in smoking (among those with high cardiovascular risks), and participants reduced their 10-year cardiovascular risk from "moderate" at the beginning of the program to "low risk" at its end. Business analysts indicate that DaimlerChrysler Canada could save more than $2 million in 10 years if this program were implemented across Canada.[24]

*Production managers oversee the activities that need to be done to transform the company's resources into quality goods and services in a timely manner.*

## marketing management.
**Marketing managers** are responsible for planning, pricing, and promoting products and making them available to customers through distribution. The marketing manager who oversees Sony televisions, for example, must make decisions regarding a new television's size, features, name, price, and packaging, as well as

plan what type of stores to distribute the television through and the advertising campaign that will introduce the new television to consumers. Within the realm of marketing, there are several areas of specialization: product development and management, pricing, promotion, and distribution. Specific jobs are found in areas such as marketing research, advertising, personal selling, retailing, telemarketing, and Internet marketing.

**information technology (IT) management.** Information technology (IT) managers are responsible for implementing, maintaining, and controlling technology applications in business, such as computer networks. Google, the online search engine, is one of the five most popular sites on the Internet and employs more than 5,500 employees, many of whom are IT managers. Google is the world's largest search engine as a result of partnerships with America Online, Netscape, and others. To maintain its creative and productive culture, Google employees have access to workout rooms, and roller hockey is played in the parking lot twice a week. The

entire business or a major segment of a business, such as the Cadillac Division of General Motors. Such managers coordinate the activities of specialized managers, which in the GM Cadillac Division would include marketing managers, production managers, and financial managers. Because of the broad nature of their responsibilities, administrative managers are often called general managers. However, this does not mean that administrative managers lack expertise in any particular area. Many top executives have risen through the ranks of financial management, production and operations management, or marketing management; but most top managers are actually administrative managers, employing skills in all areas of management.

 **LO4**

Specify the skills managers need to be successful.

# SKILLS NEEDED BY MANAGERS

Managers are typically evaluated as to how effective and efficient they are. Managing effectively and efficiently requires certain skills—leadership, technical expertise, conceptual skills,

> ## IT managers are also responsible for teaching and helping employees use technology resources efficiently through training and support.

Google Café provides healthy lunches and dinners for all staff.[25] One major task in IT management is securing computer systems from unauthorized users while making the system easy to use for employees, suppliers, and others who have legitimate reason to access the system. Another crucial task is protecting the systems' data, even during a disaster such as a fire. IT managers are also responsible for teaching and helping employees use technology resources efficiently through training and support. At many companies, some aspects of IT management are outsourced to third-party firms that can perform this function expertly and efficiently.

**administrative management.** Administrative managers are not specialists; rather they manage an

analytical skills, and human relations skills. Table 7.3 describes some of the roles managers may fulfill.

## Leadership

Leadership is the ability to influence employees to work toward organizational goals. Strong leaders manage and pay attention to the culture of their organizations and the needs of their customers. Table 7.4 offers some tips for successful leadership while Table 7.5 lists the world's 10 most admired companies and their CEOs. The list is compiled for *Fortune* magazine by executives and analysts who grade companies according to nine attributes, including quality of management. A survey of 150 senior executives indicated that 89 percent believe it is more challenging today to be a leader compared with five years ago.[26]

**TABLE 7.3** Managerial Roles

| Type of Role | Specific Role | Examples of Role Activities |
|---|---|---|
| Decisional | Entrepreneur | Commit organizational resources to develop innovative goods and services; decide to expand internationally to obtain new customers for the organization's products |
| | Disturbance handler | Move quickly to take corrective action to deal with unexpected problems facing the organization from the external environment, such as a crisis like an oil spill, or from the internal environment, such as producing faulty goods or services |
| | Resource allocator | Allocate organizational resources among different functions and departments of the organization; set budgets and salaries of middle and first-level managers |
| | Negotiator | Work with suppliers, distributors, and labor unions to reach agreements about the quality and price of input, technical, and human resources; work with other organizations to establish agreements to pool resources to work on joint projects |
| Informational | Monitor | Evaluate the performance of managers in different functions and take corrective action to improve their performance; watch for changes occurring in the external and internal environment that may affect the organization in the future |
| | Disseminator | Inform employees about changes taking place in the external and internal environment that will affect them and the organization; communicate to employees the organization's vision and purpose |
| | Spokesperson | Launch a national advertising campaign to promote new goods and services; give a speech to inform the local community about the organization's future intentions |
| Interpersonal | Figurehead | Outline future organizational goals to employees at company meetings; open a new corporate headquarters building; state the organization's ethical guidelines and the principles of behavior employees are to follow in their dealings with customers and suppliers |
| | Leader | Provide an example for employees to follow; give direct commands and orders to subordinates; make decisions concerning the use of human and technical resources; mobilize employee support for specific organizational goals |
| | Liaison | Coordinate the work of managers in different departments; establish alliances between different organizations to share resources to produce new goods and services |

Source: Gareth R. Jones and Jennifer M. George, *Essentials of Contemporary Management* (Burr Ridge, IL: McGraw-Hill/Irwin, 2004), p. 14.

Managers often can be classified into three types based on their leadership style. *Autocratic leaders* make all the decisions and then tell employees what must be done and how to do it. They generally use their authority and economic rewards to get employees to comply with their directions. *Democratic leaders* involve their employees in decisions. The manager presents a situation and encourages his or her subordinates to express opinions and contribute ideas. The manager then considers the employees' points of view and makes the decision. *Free-rein leaders* let their employees work without much interference. The manager sets performance standards and allows employees to find their own ways to meet them. For this style to be effective,

**TABLE 7.4** Seven Tips for Successful Leadership

- Build effective and responsive interpersonal relationships.
- Communicate effectively—in person, print, e-mail, etc.
- Build the team and enable employees to collaborate effectively.
- Understand the financial aspects of the business.
- Know how to create an environment in which people experience positive morale and recognition.
- Lead by example.
- Help people grow and develop.

Source: Susan M. Heathfield, "Seven Tips About Successful Management," What You Need to Know About.com (n.d.), http://humanresources.about.com/cs/managementissues/qt/mgmtsuccess.htm (accessed April 9, 2004).

**TABLE 7.5** World's Most Admired Companies and Their CEOs

| Company | Chief Executive Officer |
|---|---|
| General Electric | Jeffrey R. Immelt |
| Starbucks | James Donald |
| Toyota Motor | Katsuaki Watanabe |
| Berkshire Hathaway | Warren Buffett |
| Southwest Airlines | Gary Kelly |
| FedEx | Frederick Smith |
| Apple | Steve Jobs |
| Google | Eric Schmidt |
| Johnson & Johnson | William Weldon |
| Procter & Gamble | Alan Lafley |

Source: Adapted from "World's Most Admired Companies 2007," *Fortune*, http://money.cnn.com/magazines/fortune/mostadmired/2007/top20/index.html (accessed June 14, 2007).

employees must know what the standards are, and they must be motivated to attain the standards. The free-rein style of leadership can be a powerful motivator because it demonstrates a great deal of trust and confidence in the employee.

The effectiveness of the autocratic, democratic, and free-rein styles depends on several factors. One consideration is the type of employees. An autocratic style of leadership is generally needed to stimulate unskilled, unmotivated employees; highly skilled, trained, and motivated employees may respond better to democratic or free-rein leaders. On the other hand, employees who have been involved in decision making generally require less supervision than those not similarly involved. Other considerations are the manager's abilities and the situation itself. When a situation requires quick decisions, an autocratic style

of leadership may be best because the manager does not have to consider input from a lot of people. If a special task force must be set up to solve a quality-control problem, a normally democratic manager may give free rein to the task force. Many managers, however, are unable to use more than one style of leadership. Some are unable to allow their subordinates to participate in decision making, let alone make any decisions. Thus, what leadership style is "best" depends on specific circumstances, and effective managers strive to adapt their leadership style as circumstances warrant. Many organizations offer programs to develop leadership. Anne Mulcahy, chief operating officer and president of Xerox, has placed leadership development at the top of her agenda. She utilizes team meetings and retreats with up-and-coming managers to plan strategy and identify

## CEO Leads Burger King Recovery

Burger King, founded in Miami in 1954 by James McLamore and David Edgerton, serves almost 12 million customers per day worldwide. However, over the years the profits and success of Burger King restaurants have steadily declined. In 2004/2005, in an attempt to revitalize the company, a new CEO joined the team.

After seeing 10 CEOs pass through Burger King in 14 years, CEO number 11, Greg Brenneman, turned things around. This charismatic, driven CEO raised sales 6.8 percent in restaurants open over a year—the largest increase in more than 10 years. The company's market share improved after years of decline.

Although Brenneman has an MBA from Harvard Business School, he attributes much of his success to growing up on a Kansas farm. While growing up, Brenneman developed a strong work ethic. For him, days began at 6 a.m. and ended late in the evening. He spent those days manicuring golf courses, working at a furniture warehouse, and hoisting bales into haylofts. Those who have worked with him view him as intelligent, aggressive, and quick. Even Edgerton, co-founder of Burger King, feels Brenneman is the first CEO who listens to everyone.

In approaching the issues facing Burger King, Brenneman took the simple path. His

plan, called the "Go Forward Plan," existed on a single sheet of paper. His goals for the company were to earn money, bring in more customers/build enthusiasm in existing customers, and encourage BK employees. Among the changes he made to reach these goals are cutting the costs of building new Burger Kings and coming up with more ideas to take the company forward.

To cut the costs of building a new Burger King from $1.3 million to $970,000, Brenneman suggested making each new Burger King smaller. Research shows that many people currently order food to go, so the new Burger King prototype has about half the previous number of seats. The kitchens of these new stores are also smaller—making preparation more efficient. In addition, Brenneman wanted the new stores built with materials available at Home Depot. Doing all of this saved up to 50 percent on the price of land, which enabled franchisees to profit with greater speed.

When Brenneman took the helm of Burger King, the company had one project idea on the table. Now he is determined that there always be at least 30 project ideas in the works. Brenneman's first project was the Enormous Omelet Sandwich, which raised breakfast profits 20 percent.

Even given the challenges to be faced, employees and franchisees alike are rooting for the success of Burger King. The company still has a long way to go to return to the successful levels of the 1990s; in addition, Brenneman left the company after accomplishing many of his goals related to the recovery of the company. Burger King launched a successful public offering of its stock in 2006 and hired a new CEO, John Chidsey, to continue building a successful strategy for Burger King and to carry on Brenneman's leadership ideas.[27] ❖

## Q: Discussion Questions

1. How was Brenneman a strong leader in helping Burger King's recovery?

2. What areas of management do you think Brenneman emphasized to help Burger King reestablish itself as a fast-food leader?

3. What is the challenge for a new CEO when trying to ensure that Burger King continues to stay successful?

talent. Xerox managers have access to online tools designed to help them help themselves. Mulcahy was named among *Fortune* magazine's "Most Powerful Women in Business," along with the CEOs of Kraft Foods, eBay, PepsiCo, and Avon Products.[28]

## Technical Expertise

Managers need technical expertise, the specialized knowledge and training needed to perform jobs that are related to their area of management. Accounting managers need to be able to perform accounting jobs, and production managers need to be able to perform production jobs. Although a production manager may not actually perform a job, he or she needs technical expertise to train employees, answer questions, provide guidance, and solve problems. Technical skills are most needed by first-line managers and least critical to top-level managers.

Today, most organizations rely on computers to perform routine data processing, simplify complex calculations, organize and maintain vast amounts of information to communicate, and help managers make sound decisions. For this reason, most managers have found computer expertise to be an essential skill.

## Conceptual Skills

Conceptual skills, the ability to think in abstract terms, and to see how parts fit together to form the whole, are needed by all managers, but particularly top-level managers. Top management must be able to evaluate continually where the company will be in the future. Conceptual skills also involve the ability to think cre-

Norman Adami, named the CEO of Miller Brewing Co. in 2003, is credited with ending a 15-year sales decline at the company. One of the first moves Adami made when he assumed the post was to turn some unused space at the company's Milwaukee headquarters into "Fred's Pub," a bar named after the company's founder Frederick Miller. Although some people criticized the decision, Adami considered it a first step to motivating Miller's complacent workforce and a way of getting employees at all levels to talk to one another.

atively. Recent scientific research has revealed that creative thinking, which is behind the development of many innovative products and ideas, including fiber optics and compact disks, can be learned. As a result, IBM, AT&T, GE, Hewlett-Packard, Intel, and other top U.S. firms hire creative consultants to teach their managers how to think creatively.

## Analytical Skills

Analytical skills refer to the ability to identify relevant issues and recognize their importance, understand the relationships between them, and perceive the underlying causes of a situation. When managers have identified critical factors and causes, they can take appropriate action. All managers need to think logically, but this skill is probably most important to the success of top-level managers.

## Human Relations Skills

People skills, or human relations skills, are the ability to deal with people, both inside and outside the organization. Those who can relate to others, communicate well with others, understand the needs of others, and show a true appreciation for others are generally more successful than managers who lack human relations skills. People skills are especially important in hospitals, airline companies, banks, and other organizations that provide services. For example, at Southwest Airlines, every new employee attends "You, Southwest and Success," a day-long class designed to teach employees about

*Southwest Airlines has been able to successfully differentiate itself from its competitors by way of no-frills, low-price fares, and a highly diversified workforce. But Southwest also is known for its human relations skills. Humorous flight crews often crack jokes and pull gags on passengers.*

the airline and its reputation for impeccable customer service. All employees in management positions at Southwest take mandatory leadership classes that address skills related to listening, staying in touch with employees, and handling change without compromising values.

from within, however, can lead to problems: It may limit innovation. The new manager may continue the practices and policies of previous managers. Thus it is vital for companies—even companies committed to promotion from within—to hire outside people from time to time to bring new ideas into the organization.

Finding managers with the skills, knowledge, and experience required to run an organization or department is sometimes difficult. At Coca-Cola, for example, the board of directors agonized for months over the best choice to replace former CEO and chairman Douglas Daft upon his retirement. Their search marked the first time in the firm's history that it had sought new leadership from outside the company, although the board concentrated its search among executives experienced with well-known consumer brands.[29] Their ultimate choice wasn't exactly an outsider: E. Neville Isdell had risen through the ranks of Coca-Cola for more than 30 years before leaving to take the reins of another company.[30] For the first time in more than two decades, Americans drank fewer soft drinks than the previous year. Coca-Cola Classic sales fell 2 percent from the previous year, and strong leadership is needed to grow the core business and improve stock performance.[31] Specialized executive employment agencies—sometimes called headhunters, recruiting managers, or executive search firms—can help locate candidates from other companies. The downside is that even though outside people can bring fresh ideas to a company, hiring them may cause resentment among existing employees as well as involve greater expense in relocating an individual to another city or state.

Schools and universities provide a large pool of potential managers, and entry-level applicants can be screened for their

> # "Good managers are not born; they are made."

## WHERE DO MANAGERS COME FROM?

Good managers are not born; they are made. An organization acquires managers in three ways: promoting employees from within, hiring managers from other organizations, and hiring managers graduating from colleges.

Promoting people within the organization into management positions tends to increase motivation by showing employees that those who work hard and are competent can advance in the company. Internal promotion also provides managers who are already familiar with the company's goals and problems. Procter & Gamble prefers to promote managers from within, which creates managers who are familiar with the company's products and policies and builds company loyalty. Promoting

developmental potential. People with specialized management skills, such as those with an M.B.A. (Master of Business Administration) degree, may be good candidates.

Some companies offer special training programs for future potential managers. For example, Lehman Brothers Holdings Inc. financed a one-day run-through at the Marine Corps base at Quantico, Virginia, for M.B.A. candidates from the University of Pennsylvania's Wharton School of Business. In an effort to acquire leadership skills, student volunteers faced physically daunting tasks, including climbing an 18-foot wall with an 18-degree incline, crossing a rope 20 feet above the ground, crawling facedown under barbed wire through mud, and wading through a four-foot-deep stretch of 50-degree swampy water. The course challenged the students to stay composed in stressful situations, such as rescuing an "injured hostage" in an allotted time and carrying a 20-pound can of "ammunition" across a stream before advancing enemy troops arrived. According to the commanding officer, "The course is designed to take you beyond your self-imposed limits." Top business schools compete to produce the most sought-after graduates. The course at Quantico is designed to develop leadership skills, decisiveness, and teamwork, and Wharton hopes the "taste of life in the trenches" was a valuable experience for the students who participated.[32]

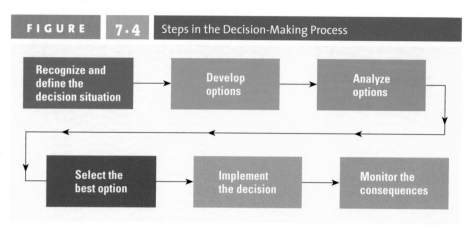

FIGURE 7.4 Steps in the Decision-Making Process

**L05**

Summarize the systematic approach to decision making used by many business managers.

# DECISION MAKING

Managers make many different kinds of decisions, such as hours of work, which employees to hire, what products to introduce, and what price to charge for a product. Decision making is important in all management functions and levels, whether the decisions are on a strategic, tactical, or operational level. A systematic approach using these six steps usually leads to more effective decision making: (1) recognizing and defining the decision situation, (2) developing options to resolve the situation, (3) analyzing the options, (4) selecting the best option, (5) implementing the decision, and (6) monitoring the consequences of the decision (Figure 7.4).

## Recognizing and Defining the Decision Situation

The first step in decision making is recognizing and defining the situation. The situation may be negative—for example, huge losses on a particular product—or positive—for example, an opportunity to increase sales.

## Little Tikes: Keeping It Simple Is the Best Decision

If you research almost any toy company or search toy shelves today, you will find technology being largely emphasized. One of the holdouts, a company actually determined *not* to focus on technology, is Little Tikes. Little Tikes, around since 1969, is known as the primary maker of large plastic toys. The company's philosophy is a simple one—let kids be kids. In other words, those at the company believe in encouraging imaginative play and creativity. In a competitive industry such as this, Little Tikes survives by sticking to this basic principle. The company has also avoided outsourcing its large items to China or Taiwan (popular sites used by toy manufacturers)—preferring to continue making them at their headquarters.

This simple approach to play appeals to parents who are becoming increasingly aware of the negative effects of technology on child development. It also seems to be in line with what children really want. The Little Tikes corporate site boasts a day care center also doing duty as a test lab for Little Tikes toys. Children consistently prefer the simple toys without all the literal bells and whistles. For example, a five-year-old at the center

was quick to point out his favorite toy—the Inside/Outside Cook 'n Grill Kitchen—but also quick to point out that he didn't like the cooking sounds made by the toy. A four-year-old at the center rejected the new Super Star Sing-Along Vanity (also a karaoke machine) in favor of a simple plastic workshop. Although she loves to use the workshop's plastic hammer, she wasn't interested in the Swirlin' Dust drill. Tests at the center overwhelmingly confirm that children prefer toys with which they can create their own play.

Everyone from executives on down is dedicated to preserving the simplicity of Little Tikes toys. Many parents know that plastic toys are simply more durable. The life expectancy of Little Tikes toys is high, making them hot items at garage sales where they sell for relatively high prices. One of the most popular toys—the Cozy Coupe, a red and yellow foot-propelled car—hasn't changed in 30 years, and it's still one of the best selling children's cars in the United States. More than 20 million Cozy Coupes have been purchased since its introduction in 1979. From time to time, the company does venture into

the high-tech market. Case in point—Little Tikes launched battery-powered, ride-on Hummers in 2004. The cars sold well for one year before sales stalled. Going back to basics, the company launched the super-low-tech inflatable Jumpn Slide Bouncer, and the item has been selling like crazy. If Little Tikes is lost in the "Stone Age," as some critics say, children and parents alike must feel the Stone Age is *the* place to be![33] ❖

**Q: Discussion Questions**

1. How has Little Tikes been so successful in making decisions about their products?

2. What types of skills are needed by managers at Little Tikes to stay attuned to parents and children's interest?

3. What type of leadership is needed to keep a company like Little Tikes on course to be successful?

> # AFTER DEVELOPING A LIST OF POSSIBLE COURSES OF ACTION, MANAGEMENT SHOULD ANALYZE THE PRACTICALITY AND APPROPRIATENESS OF EACH OPTION.

Situations calling for small-scale decisions often occur without warning. Situations requiring large-scale decisions, however, generally occur after some warning signals. Effective managers pay attention to such signals. Declining profits, small-scale losses in previous years, inventory buildup, and retailers' unwillingness to stock a product are signals that may warn of huge losses to come. If managers pay attention to such signals, problems can be contained.

Once a situation has been recognized, management must define it. Huge losses reveal a problem—for example, a failing product. One manager may define the situation as a product quality problem; another may define it as a change in consumer preference. These two definitions may lead to vastly different solutions to the problem. The first manager, for example, may seek new sources of raw materials of better quality. The second manager may believe that the product has reached the end of its lifespan and decide to discontinue it. This example emphasizes the importance of carefully defining the problem rather than jumping to conclusions.

## Developing Options

Once the decision situation has been recognized and defined, the next step is to develop a list of possible courses of action. The best lists include both standard courses of action and creative ones. As a general rule, more time and expertise are devoted to the development stage of decision making when the decision is of major importance. When the decision is of lesser importance, less time and expertise will be spent on this stage. Options may be developed individually, by teams, or through analysis of similar situations in comparable organizations. Creativity is a very important part of selecting the best option. Creativity depends on new and useful ideas, regardless of where the idea originates or the method used to create the ideas. The best option can range from a required solution to an identified problem to a volunteered solution to an observed problem by an outside work group member.[34]

## Analyzing Options

After developing a list of possible courses of action, management should analyze the practicality and appropriateness of each option. An option may be deemed impractical because of a lack of financial resources to implement it, legal restrictions, ethical and social responsibility considerations, authority constraints, technological constraints, economic limitations, or simply a lack of information and expertise to implement the option. For example, a small computer manufacturer may recognize an opportunity to introduce a new type of computer but lack the financial resources to do so. Other options may be more practical for the computer company: It may consider selling its technology to another computer company that has adequate resources or it may allow itself to be purchased by a larger company that can introduce the new technology.

When assessing appropriateness, the decision maker should consider whether the proposed option adequately addresses the situation. When analyzing the consequences of an option, managers should consider the impact the option will have on the situation and on the organization as a whole. For example, when considering a price cut to boost sales, management must consider the consequences of the action on the organization's cash flow and consumers' reaction to the price change.

## Selecting the Best Option

When all courses of action have been analyzed, management must select the best one. Selection is often a subjective procedure because many situations do not lend themselves to mathematical analysis. Of course, it is not always necessary to select only one option and reject all others; it may be possible to select and use a combination of several options.

## Implementing the Decision

To deal with the situation at hand, the selected option or options must be put into action. Implementation can be fairly simple or very complex, depending on the nature of the decision. Effective implementation of a decision to abandon a product, close a plant, purchase a new business, or something similar requires planning. For example, when a product is dropped, managers must decide how to handle distributors and customers and what to do with the idle production facility. Additionally, they should anticipate resistance from people within the organization (people tend to resist change because they fear the unknown). Finally, management should be ready to deal with the unexpected consequences. No matter how well planned implementation is, unforseen problems will arise. Management must be ready to address these situations when they occur.

## Monitoring the Consequences

After managers have implemented the decision, they must determine whether the decision has accomplished the desired result.

Without proper monitoring, the consequences of decisions may not be known quickly enough to make efficient changes. If the desired result is achieved, management can reasonably conclude that it made a good decision. If the desired result is not achieved, further analysis is warranted. Was the decision simply wrong, or did the situation change? Should some other option have been implemented?

If the desired result is not achieved, management may discover that the situation was incorrectly defined from the beginning. That may require starting the decision-making process all over again. Finally, management may determine that the decision was good even though the desired results have not yet shown up or it may determine a flaw in the decision's implementation. In the latter case, management would not change the decision but would change the way in which it was implemented.

# THE REALITY OF MANAGEMENT

Management is not a cut-and-dried process. There is no mathematical formula for managing an organization, although many managers passionately wish for one! Management is a widely

covering short-term goals and long-term objectives. Like a calendar, an agenda helps the manager figure out what must be done and how to get it done to meet the objectives set by the organization. Technology tools, such as personal digital assistants (PDAs) can help managers manage their agendas, contacts, and time.

Managers also spend a lot of time networking—building relationships and sharing information with colleagues who can help them achieve the items on their agendas. Managers spend much of their time communicating with a variety of people and participating in activities that on the surface do not seem to have much to do with the goals of their organization. Nevertheless, these activities are crucial to getting the job done. Networks are not limited to immediate subordinates and bosses; they include other people in the company as well as customers, suppliers, and friends. These contacts provide managers with information and advice on diverse topics. Managers ask, persuade, and even intimidate members of their network in order to get information and to get things done. Networking helps managers carry out

> ## Managers spend a lot of time establishing and updating an agenda of goals and plans for carrying out their responsibilities.

varying process for achieving organizational goals. Managers plan, organize, staff, direct, and control, but management expert John P. Kotter says even these functions can be boiled down to two basic activities:

1. Figuring out what to do despite uncertainty, great diversity, and an enormous amount of potentially relevant information, and

2. Getting things done through a large and diverse set of people despite having little direct control over most of them.[35]

Managers spend as much as 75 percent of their time working with others—not only with subordinates but with bosses, people outside their hierarchy at work, and people outside the organization itself. In these interactions they discuss anything and everything remotely connected with their business.

Managers spend a lot of time establishing and updating an agenda of goals and plans for carrying out their responsibilities. An agenda contains both specific and vague items,

their responsibilities. Andrea Nierenberg, independent business consultant and founder of Nierenberg Group Inc., has been called a "networking success story" by The Wall Street Journal. She writes three notes a day: one to a client, one to a friend, and one to a prospective client. She maintains a database of 3,000 contacts. However, she believes that it isn't how many people you know, but how many you have helped and who know you well enough to recommend you that really count. Opportunity can knock almost anywhere with such extensive networking. Grateful for numerous referrals to her friends, Nierenberg's dentist introduced her to a Wall Street executive who happened to be in the dentist's office at the same time as Nierenberg. She followed up on the meeting and later landed four consulting projects at the executive's firm.[37] Her clients include Citigroup, Time Inc., TIAA–CREF, Food Network, Coach, and Tiffany.[38]

Finally, managers spend a great deal of time confronting the complex and difficult challenges of the business world today. Some of these challenges relate to rapidly changing technology

If you've been reading business news over the last several years, you may be a bit skeptical about a career in management. Many companies have sharply reduced their management layers, especially at the middle level. However, management is, and will continue to be, one of the most crucial functions in the survival and growth of every business. Experts project that employment will increase by 21 million jobs—from 144 million to 165 million—between 2002 and 2012. Examples of areas where management jobs will continue to grow at faster-than-average rates include computer and information technology, education, medical and health services, human resources and labor, and marketing. Occupations in the health care and information technology sectors make up the fastest growing job segments. In the health care industry, for example, job growth will be driven by an aging population, insistence on better care, and breakthroughs in medical technology. The increase in health care workers is part of an overall trend of increasing employment in services, and service jobs in general are expected to increase 40 percent over the next decade. This larger workforce will require more managers to plan, organize, lead, and control their activities and ensure that they continue to increase productivity in the global marketplace.

The median annual salaries for management positions are shown below but, of course, actual salary ranges depend on numerous factors including size of employer, industry sector, and individual experience:

| | |
|---|---|
| Computer/IT managers | $85,240 |
| Marketing managers | $78,250 |
| Financial managers | $73,340 |
| Human resources/labor managers | $67,710 |
| Production/operations managers | $67,320 |
| Medical/health services managers | $61,370 |
| Administrative managers | $52,500 |

Companies will continue to recruit and offer positions to candidates with training and experience in how to manage capital and human resources. To secure a good job once you graduate, you must have realistic expectations and be adequately prepared to join the working world. This preparation means that you must set realistic goals, adopt positive attitudes, and learn to communicate your skills effectively.[36]

(especially in production and information processing), increased scrutiny of individual and corporate ethics and social responsibility, the changing nature of the workforce, new laws and regulations, increased global competition and more challenging foreign markets, declining educational standards (which may limit the skills and knowledge of the future labor and customer pool), and time itself—that is, making the best use of it. But such diverse issues cannot simply be plugged into a computer program that supplies correct, easy-to-apply solutions. It is only through creativity and imagination that managers can make effective decisions that benefit their organizations. ■

## CHECK OUT

www.mhhe.com/FerrellM

## for study materials including Interactive Exercises, Quizzes, iPod downloads, and video.

## Build Your Business Plan

### THE NATURE OF MANAGEMENT

The first thing you need to be thinking about is "What is the mission of your business? What is the shared vision your team members have for this business? How do you know if there is demand for this particular business? Remember, you need to think about the customer's *ability and willingness* to try this particular product.

Think about the various processes or stages of your business in the creation and selling of your product, or service. What functions need to be performed for these processes to be completed? These functions might include buying, receiving, selling, customer service and/or merchandising.

Operationally, if you are opening up a retail establishment, how do you plan to provide your customers with superior customer service? What hours will your customers expect you to be open? At this point in time, how many employees are you thinking you will need to run your business? Do you (or one of your partners) need to be there all the time to supervise?

are you **M**-powered?

**www.mhhe.com/FerrellM**      start here.

## learning OBJECTIVES

**LO1** Define organizational structure, and relate how organizational structures develop.

**LO2** Describe how specialization and departmentalization help an organization achieve its goals.

**LO3** Determine how organizations assign responsibility for tasks and delegate authority.

**LO4** Compare and contrast some common forms of organizational structure.

**LO5** Distinguish between groups and teams, and identify the types of groups that exist in organizations.

**LO6** Describe how communication occurs in organizations.

# Organization Teamwork AND Communication

**introduction** An organization's structure determines how well it makes decisions and responds to problems, and it influences employees' attitudes toward their work. A suitable structure can minimize a business's costs and maximize its efficiency. For these reasons, many businesses, such as Motorola, Apple Computer, and Hewlett-Packard, have changed their organizational structures in recent years in an effort to enhance their profits and competitive edge.

Because a business's structure can so profoundly affect its success, this chapter will examine organizational structure in detail. First, we discuss how an organization's culture affects its operations. Then we consider the development of structure, including how tasks and responsibilities are organized through specialization and departmentalization. Next, we explore some of the forms organizational structure may take. Finally, we consider communications within business.

chapter 8

# ORGANIZATIONAL CULTURE

One of the most important aspects of organizing a business is determining its organizational culture, a firm's shared values, beliefs, traditions, philosophies, rules, and role models for behavior. Also called corporate culture, an organizational culture exists in every organization, regardless of size, organizational type, product, or profit objective. For example, the organizational culture of the Marine Corps focuses on teamwork, often splitting into buddy teams and not working alone. The Marines drill into recruits to do the right thing whether its good for you or not, whether it is easy or hard.[1] A firm's culture may be expressed formally through its mission statement, codes of ethics, memos, manuals, and ceremonies, but it is more commonly expressed informally. Examples of informal expressions of culture include dress codes (or the lack thereof), work habits, extracurricular activities, and stories. Employees often learn the accepted standards through discussions with co-workers.

At Southwest Airlines, for example, new employees watch videotapes and attend training sessions that extol the company's policies, philosophies, and culture. This training encourages employees to have fun and to make flying exciting for their passengers. Such activities mark Southwest's culture as fun, casual, and friendly. Disneyland/Disney World and McDonald's have organizational cultures focused on cleanliness, value, and service. At Matsushita, employees sing a company song every morning that translates, "As individuals we will work to improve life and contribute to human progress." The company's president, Kunio Nakamura, also believes the highest paid employee should earn no more than 10 times the lowest paid employee. The effort to hire younger employees and more women is also affecting the Japanese firm's culture.[2] When such values and philosophies are shared by all members of an organization, they will be expressed in its relationships with stakeholders. However, organizational cultures that lack such positive values may result in employees who are unproductive and indifferent and have poor attitudes, which will be reflected externally to customers. Unethical cultures may have contributed to the misconduct at a number of well-known companies, such as Enron and WorldCom, at the turn of the century. At the *USA Today* newspaper, for example, an internal investigation into a reporter's plagiarized and fabricated stories identified the newspaper's organizational culture as one culprit in the scandal, which ultimately resulted in the resignation of the newspaper's editor. Investigators found that careless editing and management, the existence of a "star reporter" system, and a workplace environment of fear discouraged staff members from speaking out about their suspicions about the "Golden Boy" reporter's work.[3]

Organizational culture helps ensure that all members of a company share values and suggests rules for how to behave and deal with problems within the organization. The key to success in any organization is satisfying stakeholders, especially customers. Establishing a positive organizational culture sets the tone for all other decisions, including building an efficient organizational structure.

*Bill Gore, the founder of W. L. Gore & Associates, which makes Gore-Tex fabrics, wanted to instill a culture of innovation at the company. At W. L. Gore & Associates, there are no bosses. Employees are hired as "associates" and assigned to "sponsors" in the functional groups in which they work.*

● ● **LO1**

Define organizational structure, and relate how organizational structures develop.

# DEVELOPING ORGANIZATIONAL STRUCTURE

Structure is the arrangement or relationship of positions within an organization. Rarely is an organization, or any group of individuals working together, able to achieve common objectives without some form of structure, whether that structure is explicitly defined or only implied. A professional baseball team such as the Tampa Bay Devil Rays is a business organization with an explicit formal structure that guides the team's activities so that it can increase game attendance, win games, and sell souvenirs such as T-shirts. But even an informal group playing softball for fun has an organization that specifies who will pitch, catch, bat, coach, and so on. Governments and nonprofit organizations also have formal organizational structures to facilitate the achievement of their objectives. Getting people to work together efficiently and coordinating the skills of diverse individuals requires careful planning. Developing appropriate organizational structures is therefore a major challenge for managers in both large and small organizations.

An organization's structure develops when managers assign work tasks and activities to specific individuals or work groups and coordinate the diverse activities required to reach the firm's objectives. When Macy's, for example, has a sale, the store manager must work with the advertising department to make the public aware of the sale, with department managers to ensure that extra salespeople are scheduled to handle the increased customer traffic, and with merchandise buyers to ensure that enough sale merchandise is available to meet expected consumer demand. All the people occupying these positions must work together to achieve the store's objectives.

The best way to begin to understand how organizational structure develops is to consider the evolution of a new business such as a clothing store. At first, the business is a sole proprietorship in which the owner does everything—buys, prices,

● **ORGANIZATIONAL CHART** a visual display of the organizational structure, lines of authority (chain of command), staff relationships, permanent committee arrangements, and lines of communication

and displays the merchandise; does the accounting and tax records; and assists customers. As the business grows, the owner hires a salesperson and perhaps a merchandise buyer to help run the store. As the business continues to grow, the owner hires more salespeople. The growth and success of the business now require the owner to be away from the store frequently, meeting with suppliers, engaging in public relations, and attending trade shows. Thus, the owner must designate someone to manage the salespeople and maintain the accounting, payroll, and tax functions. If the owner decides to expand by opening more stores, still more managers will be needed. Figure 8.1 shows these stages of growth with three organizational charts (visual displays of organizational structure, chain of command, and other relationships).

Growth requires organizing—the structuring of human, physical, and financial resources to achieve objectives in an effective and efficient manner. Growth necessitates hiring people who have specialized skills. With more people and greater specialization, the organization needs to develop a formal structure to function efficiently. Consider Cirque du Soleil, which started in 1984 with 20 ambitious street artists. Today, with 3,000 employees and 40 nationalities, creativity and business must be balanced through some structure. Cirque returns 10 percent of its profits to employees, and the core team meets 10 times a year to recruit and keep the right people in a team-focused corporate culture.[4] As we shall see, structuring an organization requires that management assign work tasks to specific individuals and

> **Growth requires organizing—the structuring of human, physical, and financial resources to achieve objectives in an effective and efficient manner.**

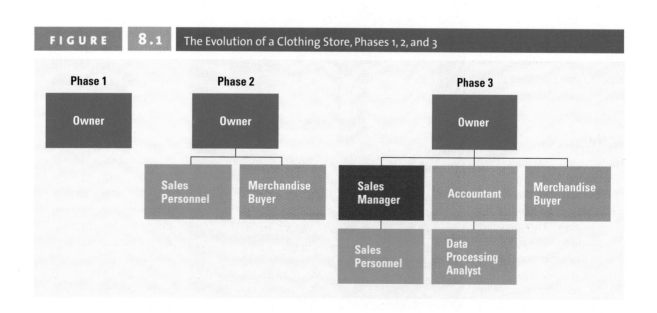

**FIGURE 8.1** The Evolution of a Clothing Store, Phases 1, 2, and 3

● **SPECIALIZATION** the division of labor into small, specific tasks and the assignment of employees to do a single task

## ●● **LO2**

Describe how specialization and departmentalization help an organization achieve its goals.

# ASSIGNING TASKS

For a business to earn profits from the sale of its products, its managers must first determine what activities are required to

departments and assign responsibility for the achievement of specific organizational objectives.

efficiently if they master just one task rather than all tasks. In *The Wealth of Nations,* 18th-century economist Adam Smith discussed specialization, using the manufacture of straight pins as an example. Individually, workers could produce 20 pins a day when each employee produced complete pins. Thus, 10 employees working independently of each other could produce 200 pins a day. However, when one worker drew the wire, another straightened it, a third cut it, and a fourth ground the point, 10 workers could produce 48,000 pins per day.[5] To save money and achieve the benefits of specialization, some companies outsource and hire temporary workers to provide key skills. Many highly skilled, diverse experience workers are available through temp agencies.[6]

> " **For a business to earn profits from the sale of its products, its managers must first determine what activities are required to achieve its objectives.** "

Adam Smith (1723–1790) is considered by many to be the founder of the economics profession. In his influential book The Wealth of Nations, Smith argued that specialization and trade are the source of much of a nation's wealth (or lack of it).

achieve its objectives. At Celestial Seasonings, for example, employees must purchase herbs from suppliers, dry the herbs and place them in tea bags, package and label the tea, and then ship the packages to grocery stores around the country. Other necessary activities include negotiating with supermarkets and other retailers for display space, developing new products, planning advertising, managing finances, and managing employees. All these activities must be coordinated, assigned to work groups, and controlled. Two important aspects of assigning these work activities are specialization and departmentalization.

## Specialization

After identifying all activities that must be accomplished, managers then break these activities down into specific tasks that can be handled by individual employees. This division of labor into small, specific tasks and the assignment of employees to do a single task is called specialization.

The rationale for specialization is efficiency. People can perform more

Specialization means workers don't waste time shifting from one job to another, and training is easier. However, efficiency is not the only motivation for specialization. Specialization also occurs when the activities that must be performed within an organization are too numerous for one person to handle. Recall the example of the clothing store. When the business was young and small, the owner could do everything; but when the business grew, the owner needed help waiting on customers, keeping the books, and managing other business activities.

Overspecialization can have negative consequences. Employees may become bored and dissatisfied with their jobs, and the result of their unhappiness is likely to be poor quality work, more injuries, and high employee turnover. Although some degree of specialization is necessary for efficiency, because of differences in skills, abilities, and interests, all people are not equally suited for all jobs. We examine some strategies to overcome these issues in Chapter 10.

## Departmentalization

After assigning specialized tasks to individuals, managers next organize workers doing similar jobs into groups to make them easier to manage. Departmentalization is the grouping of jobs into working units usually called departments, units, groups, or divisions. As we shall see, departments are commonly organized by function, product, geographic region, or customer (Figure 8.2). Most companies use more than one departmentalization plan to enhance productivity. For instance, many consumer goods manufacturers have departments for specific product lines (beverages, frozen dinners, canned goods, and so on) as well as departments dealing with legal, purchasing, finance, human resources, and other business functions. For smaller companies, accounting can be set up online, almost as an automated department. Accounting software can handle electronic transfers so you never have to worry about a late bill.[7] Many city governments also have departments for specific services (e.g., police, fire, waste disposal) as well as departments for legal, human resources, and other business functions. Figure 8.3 on page 172 depicts the organizational chart for the city of Corpus Christi, Texas, showing these departments.

● DEPARTMENTALIZA-
TION the grouping of jobs into working units usually called departments, units, groups, or divisions

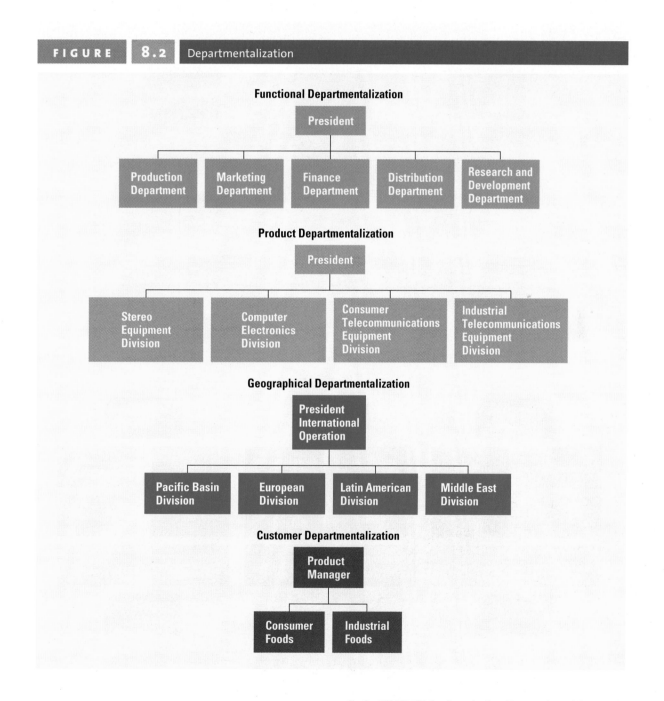

**FIGURE 8.2** Departmentalization

**Functional Departmentalization**

President
- Production Department
- Marketing Department
- Finance Department
- Distribution Department
- Research and Development Department

**Product Departmentalization**

President
- Stereo Equipment Division
- Computer Electronics Division
- Consumer Telecommunications Equipment Division
- Industrial Telecommunications Equipment Division

**Geographical Departmentalization**

President International Operation
- Pacific Basin Division
- European Division
- Latin American Division
- Middle East Division

**Customer Departmentalization**

Product Manager
- Consumer Foods
- Industrial Foods

**functional departmentalization.** Functional departmentalization groups jobs that perform similar functional activities, such as finance, manufacturing, marketing, and human resources. Each of these functions is managed by an expert in the work done by the department—an engineer supervises the production department; a financial executive supervises the finance department. This approach is common in small organizations. A weakness of functional departmentalization is that, because it tends to emphasize departmental units rather than the organization as a whole, decision making that involves more than one department may be slow, and it requires greater coordination. Thus, as business grow, they tend to adopt other approaches to organizing jobs.

**product departmentalization.** Product departmentalization, as you might guess, organizes jobs around the products of the firm. Procter & Gamble has global units,

**FIGURE 8.3** An Organizational Chart for the City of Corpus Christi

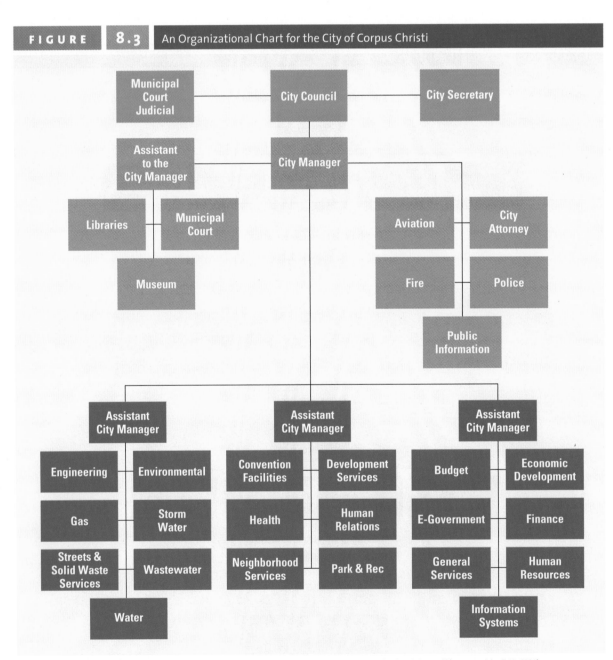

Source: "City of Corpus Christi Organizational Chart," City of Corpus Christi (n.d), http://cctexas.com/files/q10/organizationalchart.pdf (accessed April 13, 2004).

such as laundry and cleaning products, paper products, and health care products. Each division develops and implements its own product plans, monitors the results, and takes corrective action as necessary. Functional activities—production, finance, marketing, and others—are located within each product division. Consequently, organizing by products duplicates functions and resources and emphasizes the product rather than achievement of the organization's overall objectives. However, it simplifies decision making and helps coordinate all activities related to a product or product group. Kodak, for example, reorganized into special product groups devoted to areas such as digital cameras, online services, or photo kiosks. Chief operating officer Antonio Perez hopes this structure will improve communication between engineers and marketers to produce "breakthrough technology" and more rapid product introductions. The arrangement may be paying off: the company introduced six new digital cameras in one month.[8]

**geographical departmentalization.** Geographical departmentalization groups jobs according to geographic location, such as a state, region, country, or continent. FritoLay, for example, is organized into four regional divisions, allowing the company to get closer to its customers and respond more quickly and efficiently to regional

*At Peet's Coffee and Tea, the staff is provided in-depth product knowledge to serve their customers better than the competition.*

competitors. Multinational corporations often use a geographical approach because of vast differences between different regions. Coca-Cola, General Motors, and Caterpillar are organized by region. However, organizing by region requires a large administrative staff and control system to coordinate operations, and tasks are duplicated among the different regions.

**customer departmentalization.**  Customer departmentalization arranges jobs around the needs of various types of customers. Banks, for example, typically have separate departments for commercial banking activities and for consumer or retail banking. This permits the bank to address the unique requirements of each group. Airlines, such as British Airways and Delta, provide prices and services customized for either business/frequent travelers or infrequent/vacationing customers. Customer departmentalization, like geographical departmentalization, does not focus on the organization as a whole and therefore requires a large administrative staff to coordinate the operations of the various groups.

● ● **L03**

Determine how organizations assign responsibility for tasks and delegate authority.

# ASSIGNING RESPONSIBILITY

After all workers and work groups have been assigned their tasks, they must be given the responsibility to carry them out. Management must determine to what extent it will delegate responsibility throughout the organization and how many employees will report to each manager.

## Delegation of Authority

Delegation of authority means not only giving tasks to employees but also empowering them to make commitments, use resources, and take whatever actions are necessary to carry out those tasks. Let's say a marketing manager at Nestlé has assigned an employee to design a new package that is less wasteful (more environmentally responsible) than the current package for one of the company's frozen dinner lines. To carry out the assignment, the employee needs access to information and the authority to make certain decisions on packaging materials, costs, and so on. Without the authority to carry out the assigned task, the employee would have to get the approval of others for every decision and every request for materials.

● GEOGRAPHICAL DEPARTMENTALIZATION the grouping of jobs according to geographic location, such as state, region, country, or continent

● CUSTOMER DEPARTMENTALIZATION the arrangement of jobs around the needs of various types of customers

● DELEGATION OF AUTHORITY giving employees not only tasks, but also the power to make commitments, use resources, and take whatever actions are necessary to carry out those tasks

As a business grows, so do the number and complexity of decisions that must be made; no one manager can handle them all. Hotels such as Westin Hotels and Resorts and the Ritz-Carlton give authority to service providers, including front desk personnel, to make service decisions such as moving a guest to another room or providing a discount to guests who experience a problem at the hotel. Delegation of authority frees a manager to concentrate on larger issues, such as planning or dealing with problems and opportunities.

Delegation also gives a responsibility, or obligation, to employees to carry out assigned tasks satisfactorily and holds them accountable for the proper execution of their assigned work. The principle of accountability means that employees who accept an assignment and the authority to carry it out are answerable to a superior for the outcome. Returning to the Nestlé example, if the packaging design prepared by the employee is unacceptable or late, the employee must accept the blame. If the new design is innovative, attractive, and cost-efficient, as well as environmentally responsible, or is completed ahead of schedule, the employee will accept the credit.

The process of delegating authority establishes a pattern of relationships and accountability between a superior and his or her subordinates. The president of a firm delegates responsibility for all marketing activities to the vice president of marketing. The vice president accepts this responsibility and has the authority to obtain all relevant information, make certain decisions, and delegate any or all activities to his or her subordinates. The vice president, in turn, delegates all advertising activities to the advertising manager, all sales activities to the sales manager, and so on. These managers then delegate specific tasks to their subordinates. However, the act of delegating authority to a subordinate does not relieve the superior of accountability for the delegated job. Even though the vice president of marketing delegates work to subordinates, he or she is still ultimately accountable to the president for all marketing activities.

## Degree of Centralization

The extent to which authority is delegated throughout an organization determines its degree of centralization.

**centralized organizations.** In a centralized organization, authority is concentrated at the top, and very little decision-making authority is delegated to lower levels. Although decision-making authority in centralized organizations rests with top levels of management, a vast amount of responsibility for carrying out daily and routine procedures is delegated to even the lowest levels of the organization. Many government organizations, including the U.S. Army, the Postal Service, and the IRS, are centralized.

Businesses tend to be more centralized when the decisions to be made are risky and when low-level managers are not highly skilled in decision making. In the banking industry, for example, authority to make routine car loans is given to all loan managers, while the authority to make high-risk loans, such as for a large residential development, may be restricted to upper-level loan officers.

Overcentralization can cause serious problems for a company, in part because it may take longer for the organization as a whole to implement decisions and to respond to changes and problems on a regional scale. McDonald's, for example, was one of the last chains to introduce a chicken sandwich because of the amount of research, development, test marketing, and layers of approval the product had to go through.

*Bed, Bath & Beyond empowers its store managers who know their customers better than anyone else. Each manager selects about 70 percent of his or her store's merchandise, including linens, appliances, picture frames, and imported olive oil, to ensure they match that store's customers.*

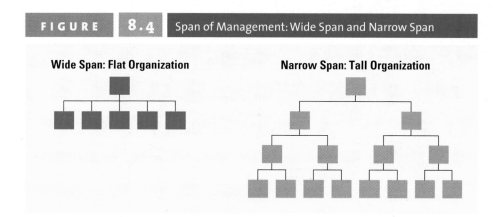

**FIGURE** **8.4** Span of Management: Wide Span and Narrow Span

**Wide Span: Flat Organization**

**Narrow Span: Tall Organization**

## decentralized organizations.

A decentralized organization is one in which decision-making authority is delegated as far down the chain of command as possible. Decentralization is characteristic of organizations that operate in complex, unpredictable environments. Businesses that face intense competition often decentralize to improve responsiveness and enhance creativity. Lower-level managers who interact with the external environment often develop a good understanding of it and thus are able to react quickly to changes.

Delegating authority to lower levels of managers may increase the organization's productivity. Decentralization requires that lower-level managers have strong decision-making skills. In recent years the trend has been toward more decentralized organizations, and some of the largest and most successful companies, including GE, Sears, IBM, and JCPenney, have decentralized decision-making authority. Nonprofit organizations benefit from decentralization as well. The Salvation Army, a charitable global organization with locations in 100 countries, is highly decentralized. The United States is divided into 50 territories and commands, and each is expected to finance all its activities through local fundraising efforts. The Salvation Army is successful in meeting its goal to help people, with a substantial portion of every $1 spent actually going toward this purpose.[10]

## Span of Management

How many subordinates should a manager manage? There is no simple answer. Experts generally agree, however, that top managers should not directly supervise more than four to eight people, while lower-level managers who supervise routine tasks are capable of managing a much larger number of subordinates. For example, the manager of the finance department may supervise 25 employees, whereas the vice president of finance may supervise only five managers. Span of management refers to the number of subordinates who report to a particular manager. A *wide span of management* exists when a manager directly supervises a very large number of employees. A *narrow span of management* exists when a manager directly supervises only a few subordinates (Figure 8.4). Wal-Mart, for example, operates with a much broader span of management in its Sam's Clubs and Wal-Mart Superstores than do the Dollar General and Family Dollar discount chains, which employ about four people per store.[11]

Should the span of management be wide or narrow? To answer this question, several factors need to be considered. A narrow span of management is appropriate when superiors and subordinates are not in close proximity, the manager has many responsibilities in addition to the supervision, the interaction between superiors and subordinates is frequent, and

## Sunrider—Communicating Health and Wealth Worldwide

Dr. Tei Fu Chen

Business: Sunrider International

Founded: 1982

Success: Sunrider International is currently operating in over 30 countries.

Sunrider International is currently one of the world's largest herbal food companies. Its entry into the health and wellness market was perfectly timed—herbal medicine, the balancing of body and mind, and acupuncture were all gaining mainstream popularity. Because of timing, the company has grown extremely fast and has had to overcome a number of hurdles. Born in Taiwan, Dr. Tei Fu Chen, Sunrider's founder, had been working for others and fighting to make ends meet after coming to the United States. Finally, in 1982, Chen purchased Natural Life—the small company he had been working for in Utah—and began creating new products based on thousands of years of Chinese herbal knowledge, thus turning the company into Sunrider. Having struggled for years to earn enough money, Chen chose to make his company a direct-selling, network marketing company (in which sales agents, called independent distributors, sell directly to consumers) in order to help others achieve their financial goals without working 24/7. Today, Sunrider has offices and distributors/customers in more than 30 countries, including Chen's native Taiwan. Much of the company's success can be attributed to the fact that to this day, Chen and the company have stayed true to their original belief—one built on more than 5,000 years of Chinese herbal knowledge—that with the right nutritional tools, the body has the ability to balance and regenerate itself.[9] ❖

problems are common. However, when superiors and subordinates are located close to one another, the manager has few responsibilities other than supervision, the level of interaction between superiors and subordinates is low, few problems arise, subordinates are highly competent, and a set of specific operating procedures governs the activities of managers and their subordinates, a wide span of management will be more appropriate. Narrow spans of management are typical in centralized organizations, while wide spans of management are more common in decentralized firms.

## Organizational Layers

Complementing the concept of span of management are **organizational layers,** the levels of management in an organization.

A company with many layers of managers is considered tall; in a tall organization, the span of management is narrow (see Figure 8.4). Because each manager supervises only a few subordinates, many layers of management are necessary to carry out the operations of the business. McDonald's, for example, has a tall organization with many layers, including store managers, district managers, regional managers, and functional managers (finance, marketing, and so on), as well as a chief executive officer and many vice presidents. Because there are more managers in tall organizations than in flat organizations, administrative costs are usually higher. Communication is slower because information must pass through many layers.

Organizations with few layers are flat and have wide spans of management. When managers supervise a large number of employees, fewer management layers are needed to conduct the organization's activities. Managers in flat organizations typically perform more administrative duties than managers in tall

 **A company with many layers of managers is considered tall**

organizations because there are fewer of them. They also spend more time supervising and working with subordinates.

Many of the companies that decentralized during the 1980s and 1990s also flattened their structures and widened their spans of management, often by eliminating layers of middle management. Many corporations, including Avon, AT&T, and Ford Motor Company, did so to reduce costs, speed decision making, and boost overall productivity.

## ●● L04

Compare and contrast some common forms of organizational structure.

# FORMS OF ORGANIZATIONAL STRUCTURE

Along with assigning tasks and the responsibility for carrying them out, managers must consider how to structure their authority relationships—that is, what structure the organization itself will have and how it will appear on the organizational chart. Common forms of organization include line structure, line-and-staff structure, multidivisional structure, and matrix structure.

## Line Structure

The simplest organizational structure, **line structure,** has direct lines of authority that extend from the top manager to employees at the lowest level of the organization. For example, a convenience store employee may report to an assistant manager, who reports to the store manager, who reports to a regional manager, or, in an independent store, directly to the owner (Figure 8.5). This structure has a clear chain of command, which enables managers to make decisions quickly. A mid-level manager facing a decision must consult only one person, his or her immediate supervisor. However, this structure requires that managers possess a wide range of knowledge and skills. They are responsible for a variety of activities

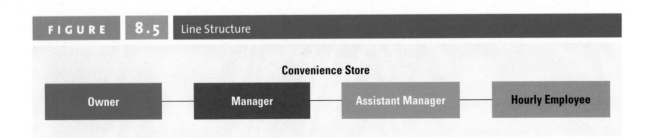

**FIGURE 8.5** Line Structure

**Convenience Store**

Owner — Manager — Assistant Manager — Hourly Employee

and must be knowledgeable about them all. Line structures are most common in small businesses.

## Line-and-Staff Structure

The **line-and-staff structure** has a traditional line relationship between superiors and subordinates, and specialized managers—called staff managers—are available to assist line managers (Figure 8.6). Line managers can focus on their area of expertise in the operation of the business, while staff managers provide advice and support to line departments on specialized matters such as finance, engineering, human resources, and the law. In the city of Corpus Christi (refer back to Figure 8.3), for example, assistant city managers are line managers who oversee groups of related departments. However, the city attorney, police chief, and fire chief are effectively staff managers who report directly to the city manager (the city equivalent of a business chief executive officer). Staff managers do not have direct authority over line managers or over the line manager's subordinates, but they do have direct authority over subordinates in their own departments. However, line-and-staff organizations may experience problems with overstaffing and ambiguous lines of communication. Additionally, employees may become frustrated because they lack the authority to carry out certain decisions.

## Multidivisional Structure

As companies grow and diversify, traditional line structures become difficult to coordinate, making communication difficult and decision making slow. When the weaknesses of the structure—the "turf wars," miscommunication, and working at cross-purposes—exceed the benefits, growing firms tend to restructure, often into the divisionalized form. A **multidivisional structure** organizes departments into larger groups called divisions. Just as departments might be formed on the basis of geography, customer, product, or a combination of these, so too divisions can be formed based on any of these methods of organizing. Within each of these divisions, departments may be organized by product, geographic region, function, or some combination of all three. General Motors, for example, operates with divisions structured around its well-known automotive brands (e.g., Chevrolet, Pontiac, and Buick). Within that structure, production and engineering tend to be centralized, while marketing is decentralized under each automotive division. Cadillac, however, operates as a more autonomous division with its own vice president and greater influence on design and engineering than that conferred on other divisions.[12]

Multidivisional structures permit delegation of decision-making authority, allowing divisional and department managers to specialize. They allow those closest to the action to make the decisions that will affect them. Delegation of authority and divisionalized work also mean that better decisions are made faster, and they tend to be more innovative. Most importantly, by focusing each division on a common region, product, or customer, each is more likely to provide products that meet the needs of its particular customers. However, the divisional structure inevitably creates work duplication, which makes it more difficult to realize the economies of scale that result from grouping functions together.

● **LINE-AND-STAFF STRUCTURE** a structure having a traditional line relationship between superiors and subordinates and also specialized managers—called staff managers—who are available to assist line managers

● **MULTIDIVISIONAL STRUCTURE** a structure that organizes departments into larger groups called divisions

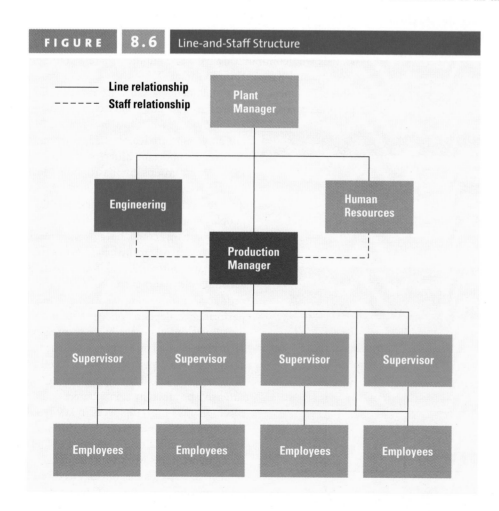

**FIGURE 8.6** Line-and-Staff Structure

— Line relationship
----- Staff relationship

Plant Manager

Engineering

Human Resources

Production Manager

Supervisor · Supervisor · Supervisor · Supervisor

Employees · Employees · Employees · Employees

to changes in the environment by giving special attention to specific projects or problems. However, they are generally expensive and quite complex, and employees may be confused as to whose authority has priority—the project manager's or the immediate supervisor's.

## Matrix Structure

Another structure that attempts to address issues that arise with growth, diversification, productivity, and competitiveness, is the matrix. A matrix structure, also called a project-management structure, sets up teams from different departments, thereby creating two or more intersecting lines of authority (see Figure 8.7). The matrix structure superimposes project-based departments on the more traditional, function-based departments. Project teams bring together specialists from a variety of areas to work together on a single project, such as developing a new fighter jet. In this arrangement, employees are responsible to two managers—functional managers and project managers. Matrix structures are usually temporary: Team members typically go back to their functional or line department after a project is finished. However, more firms are becoming permanent matrix structures, creating and dissolving project teams as needed to meet customer needs. The aerospace industry was one of the first to apply the matrix structure, but today it is used by universities and schools, accounting firms, banks, and organizations in other industries.

Matrix structures provide flexibility, enhanced cooperation, and creativity, and they enable the company to respond quickly

**L05**

Distinguish between groups and teams, and identify the types of groups that exist in organizations.

# THE ROLE OF GROUPS AND TEAMS IN ORGANIZATIONS

Regardless of how they are organized, most of the essential work of business occurs in individual work groups and teams, so we'll take a closer look at them now. Although some experts do not make a distinction between groups and teams, in recent years there has been a gradual shift toward an emphasis on teams and managing them to enhance individual and organizational success. Some experts now believe that highest productivity results only when groups become teams.[13]

Traditionally, a group has been defined as two or more individuals who communicate with one another, share a common identity, and have a common goal. A team is a small group whose members have complementary skills; have a common purpose, goals, and approach; and hold themselves mutually accountable.[14] All teams are groups, but not all groups are teams. Table 8.1 points out some important differences between them. Work groups emphasize individual work products, individual accountability, and even individual leadership. Salespeople working independently for the same company could be a work group. In contrast, work teams share leadership roles, have both individual and mutual accountability, and create collective work products. In other words, a work group's performance depends on what its members do as individuals, while a team's performance is based on creating a knowledge center and a competency to work together to accomplish a goal. To support sales of its extensive product lines, Procter & Gamble places teams of its employees in key retail customers' headquarters. For instance, Procter & Gamble teams assigned to Dollar General Stores work with the discount retailer to meet its customers' needs and even customize Procter & Gamble products to Dollar General's specification.[15]

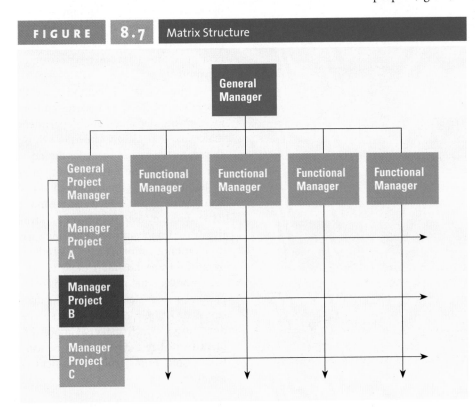

**FIGURE 8.7 Matrix Structure**

**TABLE 8.1**  Differences between Groups and Teams

| Working Group | Team |
|---|---|
| Has strong, clearly focused leader | Has shared leadership roles |
| Has individual accountability | Has individual and group accountability |
| Has the same purpose as the broader organizational mission | Has a specific purpose that the team itself delivers |
| Creates individual work products | Creates collective work products |
| Runs efficient meetings | Encourages open-ended discussion and active problem-solving meetings |
| Measures its effectiveness indirectly by its effects on others (e.g., financial performance of the business) | Measures performance directly by assessing collective work products |
| Discusses, decides, and delegates | Discusses, decides, and does real work together |

Source: Robert Gatewood, Robert Taylor, and O. C. Ferrell, *Management: Comprehension Analysis and Application,* 1995, p. 427. Copyright © 1995 Richard D. Irwin, a Times Mirror Higher Education Group, Inc., company. Reproduced with permission of the McGraw-Hill Companies.

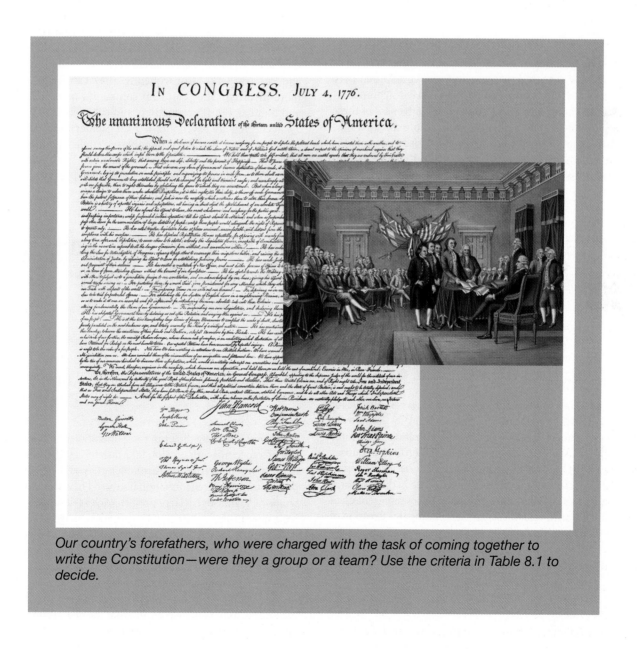

*Our country's forefathers, who were charged with the task of coming together to write the Constitution—were they a group or a team? Use the criteria in Table 8.1 to decide.*

The type of groups an organization establishes depends on the tasks it needs to accomplish and the situation it faces. Some specific kinds of groups and teams include committees, task forces, project teams, product-development teams, quality-assurance teams, and self-directed work teams. All of these can be *virtual teams*—employees in different locations who rely on e-mail, audio conferencing, fax, Internet, videoconferencing, or other technological tools to accomplish their goals. One survey found that almost 48 percent of workers have participated in virtual teams.[16]

## Committees

A committee is usually a permanent, formal group that does some specific task. For example, many firms have a compensation or finance committee to examine the effectiveness of these areas of operation as well as the need for possible changes. Ethics committees are formed to develop and revise codes of ethics, suggest methods for implementing ethical standards, and review specific issues and concerns.

competitiveness. In general, teams have the benefit of being able to pool members' knowledge and skills and make greater use of them than can individuals working alone. Team building is becoming increasingly popular in organizations, with 48 percent of executives indicating their companies had team-building training.[18] Teams require harmony, cooperation, synchronized effort, and flexibility to maximize their contribution.[19] Teams can also create more solutions to problems than can individuals. Furthermore, team participation enhances employee acceptance of, understanding of, and commitment to team goals. Teams motivate workers by providing internal rewards in the form of an enhanced sense of accomplishment for employees as they achieve more, and external rewards in the form of praise and certain perks. Consequently, they can help get workers more involved. They can help companies be more innovative, and they can boost productivity and cut costs.

According to psychologist Ivan Steiner, team productivity peaks at about five team members. People become less motivated and group coordination becomes more difficult after this size. Jeff Bezos, Amazon.com CEO, says that he has a "two-pizza

> **Teams are becoming far more common in the U.S. workplace as businesses strive to enhance productivity and global competitiveness.**

## Task Forces

A task force is a temporary group of employees responsible for bringing about a particular change. They typically come from across all departments and levels of an organization. Task force membership is usually based on expertise rather than organizational position. Occasionally, a task force may be formed from individuals outside a company. Such was the case in the task force selected by the Coca-Cola Company and the class representatives in a discrimination lawsuit filed against the company. Creation of the seven-member independent task force was one of the key elements in the settlement between the two parties. The task force will ensure the company's compliance with the settlement agreement and provide oversight of its diversity efforts.[17]

## Teams

Teams are becoming far more common in the U.S. workplace as businesses strive to enhance productivity and global

rule": If a team cannot be fed by two pizzas, it is too large. Keep teams small enough where everyone gets a piece of the action.[20]

**project teams.** Project teams are similar to task forces, but normally they run their operation and have total control of a specific work project. Like task forces, their membership is likely to cut across the firm's hierarchy and be composed of people from different functional areas. They are almost always temporary, although a large project, such as designing and building a new airplane at Boeing Corporation, may last for years.

Product-development teams are a special type of project team formed to devise, design, and implement a new product. Sometimes product-development teams exist within a functional area—research and development—but now they more frequently include people from numerous functional areas and may even include customers to help ensure that the end product meets the customers' needs. Motorola assembled a product development team to develop the Razr cell phone that revived their company.

The team grew to as many as 20 engineers (breaking the five team-member rule) that met daily at 4 p.m. in a conference room to discuss progress on a checklist of components. The Razr has sold almost as many units as the iPod.[21]

## quality-assurance teams.

Quality-assurance teams, sometimes called quality circles, are fairly small groups of workers brought together from throughout the organization to solve specific quality, productivity, or service problems. Although the *quality circle* term is not as popular as it once was, the concern about quality is stronger than ever. The use of teams to address quality issues will no doubt continue to increase throughout the business world.

## self-directed work teams.

A self-directed work team (SDWT) is a group of employees responsible for an entire work process or segment that delivers a product to an internal or external customer.[23] Sometimes called self-managed teams or autonomous work groups, SDWTs reduce the need for extra layers of management and thus can help control costs. For example, MySQL, a $40 million software maker, operates a worldwide workforce with no office. At MySQL people are matched with the technology task. The company relies on phone contact via Skype Internet voice communication. Voice communication is considered better than e-mail and helpful in building real contacts and understanding of tasks. One problem, though, is that a self-directed team does not end at the end of the day. It is always 8 a.m. somewhere for MySQL employees.[24]

SDWTs permit the flexibility to change rapidly to meet the competition or respond to customer needs. The defining characteristic of an SDWT is the extent to which it is empowered or given authority to make and implement work decisions. Thus, SDWTs are designed to give employees a feeling of "ownership" of a whole job. With shared team responsibility for work outcomes, team members often have broader job assignments and cross-train to master other jobs, thus permitting greater team flexibility.

● **QUALITY-ASSURANCE TEAMS (OR QUALITY CIRCLES)** small groups of workers brought together from throughout the organization to solve specific quality, productivity, or service problems

● **SELF-DIRECTED WORK TEAM (SDWT)** a group of employees responsible for an entire work process or segment that delivers a product to an internal or external customer

# PETCO Uses Communication and Teamwork to Create an Ethical Culture

PETCO Animal Supplies Inc. is the nation's number-two pet supply specialty retailer with more than 750 stores in 48 states and the District of Columbia. Its pet-related products include pet food; pet supplies; grooming products; toys; novelty items; vitamins; small pets such as fish, birds, other small animals (excluding cats and dogs); and veterinary supplies. PETCO, like most retailers, depends on teamwork and internal communication to reach its objectives.

Most organizations fear not discovering risk associated with operating their businesses. Regardless of the industry, there is concern that the public or a special interest group can uncover some activity that can immediately be used by critics and the mass media, competitors, or simply skeptical stakeholders to undermine a firm's reputation. Therefore, an ethical risk assessment is an important item included in most companies' ethics initiatives. A single negative incident can influence perceptions of a corporation's image and reputation instantly—and possibly for years afterward. Not all ethical concerns are of a company's making, and there are certainly those disgruntled antagonists who will distort the truth for their own self-interest. Because pets are such a strong emotional attachment for many, assessing risk of accusations in this industry is especially important. For all companies who sell pets, the question is not *if* there will be accusations but *when* the accusations are made, the company can respond rapidly enough to explain or correct the activities in question to mitigate possible negative perceptions. The important focus should be on a commitment to making the right decisions and to constantly assessing and dealing with the risks of operating a business.

PETCO has a comprehensive Code of Ethics, the main emphasis of which is that animals always come first. The care and well-being of animals is of paramount importance to PETCO, and the company wants to ensure that all the employees adhere to the Code of Ethics. One of PETCO's most important missions is to promote the health, well-being, and humane treatment of animals. It does this through its vendor selection programs, pet adoption programs, and its partnerships with animal welfare organizations.

All organizations in the retail area are subject to criticism and must work hard to maintain communication, providing assurance that employees follow ethical codes. PETCO accomplishes this through use of an ethics committee and by developing an ethical corporate culture. PETCO's Code of Ethics addresses all of the organizational risks related to human resources, conflict of interests, and appropriate behavior in the workplace. In the case of PETCO, a desire to do the right thing and to train all organizational members to communicate about ethical decisions ensures not only success in the marketplace but a significant contribution to society.[22] ❖

## Q: Discussion Questions

1. Why is an ethics committee so important in dealing with issues and dilemmas related to the sale of pet supplies and animals?

2. Why is internal communication so important in assessing risk and dealing with the resolution of ethical issues at PETCO?

3. Why is it important for all PETCO organizational members to learn to communicate about ethical issues rather than trying to resolve them independently?

# COMMUNICATING IN ORGANIZATIONS

Communication within an organization can flow in a variety of directions and from a number of sources, each using both oral and written forms of communication. The success of communication systems within the organization has a tremendous effect on the overall success of the firm. Communication mistakes can lower productivity and morale.

Alternatives to face-to-face communications—such as meetings—are growing thanks to technology such as voice-mail, e-mail, and online newsletters. At Matsushita, for example, company executives are required to file reports to president Kunio Nakamura by mobile e-mail and are provided an Internet-equipped mobile phone for that purpose.[26] Companies use intranets or internal computer networks to share information and to increase collaboration. Intranets help employees quickly find or view information, any time, subject to security provisions.[27] Capital One, IBM, Merrill Lynch, and Staples have been recognized as having some of the best intranets in corporate America.[28] At many companies, however, such communications technology has contributed to a state of information overload for employees, who spend more and more time managing e-mail. A growing problem is employees abusing e-mail. In some companies, up to 75 percent of e-mail messages are not business related.[29]

Experts say that managers must (1) plan how they will share important news, (2) repeat important information, and (3) rehearse key presentations. According to one study, 62 percent of executives think employees and companies benefit from fun and humor in communications and management style.[30]

## ?

### DID YOU KNOW?

People spend an average of one to one-and-a-half days per week in meetings.[25]

## Formal Communication

Formal channels of communication are intentionally defined and designed by the organization. They represent the flow of communication within the formal organizational structure, as shown on organizational charts. Traditionally, formal communication patterns were classified as vertical and horizontal, but with the increased use of teams and matrix structures, formal communication may occur in a number of patterns (Figure 8.8).

*Upward communication* flows from lower to higher levels of the organization and includes information such as progress reports, suggestions for improvement, inquiries, and grievances. *Downward communication* refers to the traditional flow of information from upper organizational levels to lower levels. This type of communication typically involves directions, the assignment of tasks and responsibilities, performance feedback, and certain details about the organization's strategies and goals. Speeches, policy and procedures manuals, employee handbooks, company leaflets, telecommunications, and job descriptions are examples of downward communication.

*Horizontal communication* involves the exchange of information among colleagues and peers on the

**Proud Past** In 24 years, The Home Depot has grown from an innovative concept – providing home improvement products and services – into the industry's home improvement leader. Our brand instills customer confidence and we continue to transform ourselves to more effectively meet customers' needs and aspirations. In 2003, this transformation yielded strong results driven by a focus on sales, service and execution.

**Bright Future** Today, our external focus on customers and the marketplace fuels our internal focus on improving the shopping experience in our stores. We are delivering more distinctive and innovative products and complementing our core capabilities by offering new services that extend our reach, and we are expanding into new markets. The powerful combination of The Home Depot's more than 1,700 locations and approximately 300,000 associates fulfills our brand promise:

You can do it. We can help.℠

At The Home Depot, we believe our associates are our competitive advantage. Attracting, motivating and retaining the best associates are top priorities. Our Store Manager Council provides effective two-way communication between company executives and our store leadership teams.

*Home Depot's organizational structure begins with CEO Frank Blake, to its "Store Manager Council," to its sales associates. The Store Manager Council provides the link for communication between the stores' sales associates and upper management.*

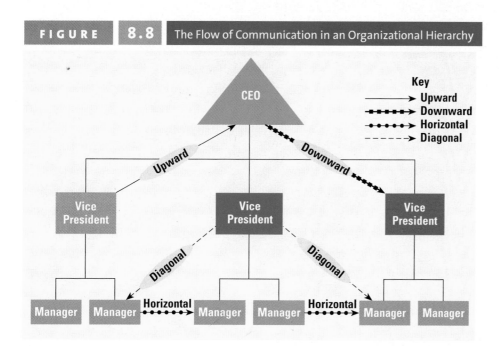

**FIGURE** | 8.8 | The Flow of Communication in an Organizational Hierarchy

same organizational level, such as across or within departments. Horizontal information informs, supports, and coordinates activities both within the department and with other departments. At times, the business will formally require horizontal communication among particular organizational members, as is the case with task forces or project teams.

With more and more companies downsizing and increasing the use of self-managed work teams, many workers are being required to communicate with others in different departments and on different levels to solve problems and coordinate work. When these individuals from different units and organizational levels communicate, it is *diagonal communication*. At OpenAir.

# Toyota's Growth: Slow and Steady

By all accounts, it looks as though Toyota is on its way to becoming the world's largest car company. The company has stated that it plans to increase its international car production by 10 percent in 2006, bringing it to a company high of 9.06 million. This means Toyota could easily fly past GM—the top producer since 1931. Interestingly, the fact that it may become number one poses some challenges for Toyota—a company with a humble corporate culture and a strong fear of creating backlash that might cause customers to shun its products. For the company, the goal to increase production is not about becoming number one but about meeting customer needs across the globe.

Toyota's motto has always been *jiwa-jiwa,* which means slow and steady in Japanese. The company has usually been late (from an industry perspective) producing new lines, such as the full-size pickup truck, but when it does produce, it gets rave reviews. Case in point, Honda was the first to produce the hybrid car on the U.S. market, but Toyota's Prius is now the standard for hybrids by which all other hybrids are measured. This slow-and-steady approach has served the company well; today, people in 170 countries can purchase Toyotas.

This new goal to increase production by 10 percent is a different approach for Toyota. It has also set itself a goal of having 15 percent of the market share in the next 10 years— bringing it up 5 percent from the 10 it currently holds. To achieve these goals, which Toyota's U.S. president Jim Press calls "spiritual targets," Toyota must open five new plants in the next 10 years—an ambitious project. Toyota's selling point has always been quality. Critics are questioning whether this fast growth is compromising that quality. Double the number of Toyotas were voluntarily recalled in 2005, and the company's competitors are gaining in quality surveys. By 2006, Toyota ranked fourth in overall quality, but its Lexus brand ranked second behind Porsche.

To Toyota, the car business is communication. Top executives and managers visit plants regularly, and employees at all levels are encouraged to talk to one another and solve problems though direct communication. Toyota has also been able to avoid layoffs in an industry plagued by them. It also makes sure plants continue flourishing. For example, when assembly of truck beds was assigned to a plant in Mexico, the plant that had been doing truck bed assembly was assigned an even more important project.

To keep up with production growth, Toyota is opening a plant for pickups in San Antonio, Texas, and an additional factory (it already has one) in Canada, and it is in the planning stages for plants in Russia, China, and Thailand. With all this growth, critics wonder if Toyota—used to slow and steady—can handle fast and chaotic. Obviously, the company is struggling to some degree with rapid growth, and it is showing in recalls and a decline in quality ranking. However, those at the top are still believers in Toyota's commitment to quality and are taking notice and making changes to fix recent mistakes. Regardless, Toyota's assent to number one appears assured.[31] ❖

## Q: Discussion Questions

1. Why is organizational structure important in developing internal communication at Toyota?

2. What type of organizational culture do you think Toyota is trying to create?

3. Why are quality teams so important in helping Toyota reach its objectives?

# DESTINATION CEO

**Julia Stewart—IHOP**     Restaurants are the largest employer in the United States next to the government and generate sales in excess of $1.8 billion annually. International House of Pancakes (IHOP) has become a full-service restaurant, providing far more than the breakfast pancakes that they are famous for, although they continue to serve more than 700 million pancakes each year. Julia Stewart, current CEO of IHOP, knows the restaurant business from the bottom up. She started out as a server in an IHOP restaurant when she was 16 years old.

Stewart majored in marketing in college and started her career in marketing in the restaurant industry. Early in her career, she had the personal goal of running a major business. To prepare more effectively for this goal, she left marketing to gain operations experience. She joined Taco Bell in the management development program, becoming first an assistant store manager where she learned how to operate a restaurant. She rose rapidly through the ranks to the position of vice president of franchising and licensing. After leaving Taco Bell, she assumed the position of vice president of international operations for Applebee's. After four years there, she assumed the CEO position at IHOP. Stewart attributes much

of her success to her early experiences at the lowest levels in the organization (server, bus person, cook, etc). She emphasizes the importance that immediate feedback plays as well as the impact of effective communications across broad stakeholder groups. Stewart states that it is an honor and a privilege to be CEO for 65,000 people.

## >> DISCUSSION QUESTIONS

1. What are the most important factors, according to Stewart, contributing to her success as CEO?

2. Was marketing or operations most important in preparing Stewart for her role as CEO?

3. Who is the largest employer in the United States? Who ranks number two?

>>To see the complete video about Julia Stewart, go to our Web site at **www.mhhe.com/FerrellM** and look for the link to the Destination CEO videos.

com Inc., all staff members meet every day at 9:30 a.m. to share information and anecdotes about customer calls from the previous day. No chairs are allowed, and everyone is encouraged to participate. COO Morris Panner says that the communication style "reemphasizes the fact that our company is based on collaboration."[32]

## Informal Communication Channels

Along with the formal channels of communication shown on an organizational chart, all firms communicate informally as well. Communication between friends, for instance, cuts across department, division, and even management–subordinate

## Monitoring Communications

Technological advances and the increased use of electronic communication in the workplace have made monitoring its use necessary for most companies. Failing to monitor employee's use of e-mail and the Internet can be costly. Chevron Corp. agreed to pay $2 million to employees who claimed that unmonitored, sexually harassing e-mail created a threatening environment for them.[33] Instituting practices that show respect for employee privacy but do not abdicate employer responsibility

> ## "Grapevines exist in all organizations. Information passed along the grapevine may relate to the job or organization, or it may be gossip and rumors unrelated to either."

boundaries. Such friendships and other nonwork social relationships comprise the *informal organization* of a firm, and their impact can be great.

The most significant informal communication occurs through the grapevine, an informal channel of communication, separate from management's formal, official communication channels. Grapevines exist in all organizations. Information passed along the grapevine may relate to the job or organization, or it may be gossip and rumors unrelated to either. The accuracy of grapevine information has been of great concern to managers.

Additionally, managers can turn the grapevine to their advantage. Using it as a "sounding device" for possible new policies is one example. Managers can obtain valuable information from the grapevine that could improve decision making. Some organizations use the grapevine to their advantage by floating ideas, soliciting feedback, and reacting accordingly. People love to gossip, and managers need to be aware that grapevines exist in every organization. Managers who understand how the grapevine works also can use it to their advantage by feeding it facts to squelch rumors and incorrect information.

are increasingly necessary in today's workplace. Several Web sites provide model policies and detailed guidelines for conducting electronic monitoring, including the Model Electronic Privacy Act on the American Civil Liberties Union site. ■

*Communication grapevines exist in every organization. Managers need to understand how they work if they want to use them to their advantage.*

Most business school students major in marketing, finance, accounting, management information systems, general management, or sales. Upon graduation, they generally expect to be hired by a company to do more of whatever it is they were trained to do as a student. For example, an accounting major expects to be an accountant. However, depending on the way the company is organized, the roles played by the employees will differ.

If you are hired by a large, divisionalized company, you might expect to practice your profession among many others doing the same or similar tasks. You are likely to learn one part of the business fairly well but be completely uninformed about other departments or divisions. A wise employee in this situation will learn to request occasional transfers to other divisions to learn all aspects of the corporation, thereby improving his or her usefulness to the company and promotion chances.

On the other hand, if you gain employment in a very small company or in one that is heavily decentralized, you may find that you are expected to do more than the tasks for which you were trained. In many small organizations, employees are often expected to wear many hats in order to make the organization more efficient. For example, it can come as a shock to an accounting graduate to discover that, in addition to accounting, he or she will also be doing bookkeeping, secretarial work and public relations.

Likewise, employees in larger organizations that make heavy use of teams and decentralized decision making may find that the company expects more of them than the skills learned in school. To be an effective team member, you may find that you will not only contribute your skills and expertise, but you will also be expected to learn some engineering, computer science, and marketing to be able to understand the needs and constraints of the other members of the team. Organizational flexibility requires individual flexibility, and those employees willing to take on new domains and challenges will be the employees who survive and prosper in the future.[34]

## CHECK OUT

www.mhhe.com/FerrellM

## for study materials including Interactive Exercises, Quizzes, iPod downloads, and video.

# Build Your Business Plan

## Organization, Teamwork, and Communication

Developing a business plan as a team is a deliberate move of your instructor to encourage you to familiarize yourself with the concept of teamwork. You need to realize that you are going to spend a large part of your professional life working with others. At this point in time you are working on the business plan for a grade, but after graduation you will be "teaming" with co-workers and the successfulness of your endeavor may determine whether or not you get a raise or a bonus. It is important that you be comfortable as soon as possible with working with others and holding them accountable for their contributions.

Some people are natural "leaders" and leaders often feel that if team members are not doing their work, they take it upon themselves to "do it all". This is not leadership, but rather micro-managing.

Leadership means holding members accountable for their responsibilities. Your instructor may provide ideas on how this could be implemented, possibly by utilizing peer reviews. Remember you are not doing a team member a favor by doing their work for them.

If you are a "follower" (someone who takes directions well) rather than a leader, try to get into a team where others are hard workers and you will rise to their level. There is nothing wrong with being a follower; not everyone can be a leader!

**M IS MOVING FORWARD**

are you **M**-powered?

www.mhhe.com/FerrellM

# MANAGING SERVICE (and) MANUFACTURING OPERATIONS

**Introduction** All organizations create products—goods, services, or ideas—for customers. Thus, organizations as diverse as Dell Computer, Campbell Soup, UPS, and a public hospital share a number of similarities relating to how they transform resources into the products we consume. Most hospitals use similar admission procedures, while Burger King and Dairy Queen use similar food preparation methods to make hamburgers. Such similarities are to be expected. But even organizations in unrelated industries take similar steps in creating goods or services. The check-in procedures of hotels and commercial airlines are comparable, for example. The way Subway assembles a sandwich and the way GMC assembles a truck are similar (both use automation and an assembly line). These similarities are the result of operations management, the focus of this chapter.

Here, we discuss the role of production or operations management in acquiring and managing the resources necessary to create goods and services. Production and operations management involves planning and designing the processes that will transform those resources into finished products, managing the movement of those resources through the transformation process, and ensuring that the products are of the quality expected by customers.

## ●● learning OBJECTIVES

**LO1**  Define operations management, and differentiate between operations and manufacturing.

**LO2**  Explain how operations management differs in manufacturing and service firms.

**LO3**  Describe the elements involved in planning and designing an operations system.

**LO4**  Specify some techniques managers may use to manage the logistics of transforming inputs into finished products.

**LO5**  Assess the importance of quality in operations management.

## LO1

Define operations management, and differentiate between operations and manufacturing.

# THE NATURE OF OPERATIONS MANAGEMENT

**Operations management (OM)**, the development and administration of the activities involved in transforming resources into goods and services, is of critical importance. Operations managers oversee the transformation process and the planning and designing of operations systems, managing logistics, quality, and productivity. Quality and productivity have become fundamental aspects of operations management because a company that cannot make products of the quality desired by consumers, using resources efficiently and effectively, will not be able to remain in business. OM is the "core" of most organizations because it is responsible for the creation of the organization's goods or services.

Historically, operations management has been called "production" or "manufacturing" primarily because of the view that it was limited to the manufacture of physical goods. Its focus was on methods and techniques required to operate a factory efficiently. The change from "production" to "operations" recognizes the increasing importance of organizations that provide services and ideas. Additionally, the term *operations* represents an interest in viewing the operations function as a whole rather than simply as an analysis of inputs and outputs.

Today, OM includes a wide range of organizational activities and situations outside of manufacturing, such as health care, food service, banking, entertainment, education, transportation, and charity. Thus, we use the terms **manufacturing** and **production** interchangeably to represent the activities and processes used in making *tangible* products, whereas we use the broader term **operations** to describe those processes used in the making of *both tangible and intangible products*. Manufacturing provides tangible products such as Hewlett-Packard's latest printer, and operations provides intangibles such as a stay at Wyndham Hotels and Resorts.

## The Transformation Process

At the heart of operations management is the transformation process through which **inputs** (resources such as labor, money, materials, and energy) are converted into **outputs** (goods, services, and ideas). The transformation process combines inputs in predetermined ways using different equipment, administrative procedures, and technology to create a product (Figure 9.1). To ensure that this process generates quality products efficiently, operations managers control the process by taking measurements (feedback) at various points in the transformation process and comparing them to previously established standards. If there is any deviation between the actual and desired outputs, the manager may take some sort of corrective action. All adjustments made to create a satisfying product are a part of the transformation process.

This transformation may take place through one or more processes. In a business that manufactures oak furniture, for example, inputs pass through several processes before being turned into the

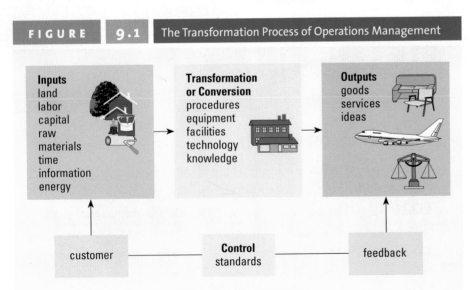

**FIGURE 9.1** The Transformation Process of Operations Management

**Inputs**
land
labor
capital
raw materials
time
information
energy

**Transformation or Conversion**
procedures
equipment
facilities
technology
knowledge

**Outputs**
goods
services
ideas

customer

**Control** standards

feedback

# DESTINATION CEO

**Gary Kusin—FedEx Kinko's** FedEx Kinko's is a business model that represents a one-stop comprehensive business services operation. Kinko's was known as the copy king but has expanded its services mix and product lines so that it competes with retailers such as Office Depot and Staples.

Gary Kusin, the current CEO of FedEx Kinko's, was profoundly influenced early in his life by Ross Perot. Kusin, like many college students during their early academic life, did not have a clear career goal. He did his undergraduate work at University of Texas at Austin. After graduating, he looked around and was impressed by successful businesspeople who all seemed to have one thing in common— an M.B.A. from the Harvard Business School. Kusin followed these role models and successfully completed his M.B.A. at Harvard. His work experience took him from working in the family furniture store at age 12 to his successful position as CEO of FedEx Kinko's. Prior to achieving this leadership position, he held the position of Vice President of Sanger Harris in the retail industry. He successfully navigated

a merger (Federated Department Stores) with their lead competitor (Laura Mercier), and then was finally bought out by Macy's. After his successful career as an executive in the retail sales industry, he assumed the CEO position at FedEx Kinko's.

## >>DISCUSSION QUESTIONS

1. What are the key competitive advantages of FedEx Kinko's?

2. What is the common thread that runs through Kusin's career path?

3. Who was Kusin's earliest role model?

>>To see the complete video about Gary Kusin, go to our Web site at **www.mhhe.com/FerrellIM** and look for the link to the Destination CEO videos.

final outputs—furniture that has been designed to meet the desires of customers (Figure 9.2). The furniture maker must first strip the oak trees of their bark and saw them into appropriate sizes—one step in the transformation process. Next, the firm dries the strips of oak lumber, a second form of transformation. Third, the dried wood is routed into its appropriate shape and made smooth. Fourth, workers assemble and treat the wood pieces, then stain or varnish the piece of assembled furniture. Finally, the completed piece of furniture is stored until it can be shipped to customers at the appropriate time. Of course, many businesses choose to eliminate some of these stages by purchasing already processed materials—lumber, for example—or outsourcing some tasks to third-party firms with greater expertise.

 **L02**

Explain how operations management differs in manufacturing and service firms.

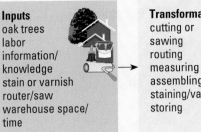

| FIGURE | 9.2 | Inputs, Outputs, and Transformation Processes in the Manufacture of Oak Furniture |

**Inputs**
oak trees
labor
information/ knowledge
stain or varnish
router/saw
warehouse space/ time

**Transformation**
cutting or sawing
routing
measuring
assembling
staining/varnishing
storing

**Outputs**
oak furniture

## Operations Management in Service Businesses

Different types of transformation processes take place in organizations that provide services, such as airlines, colleges, and most nonprofit organizations. An airline transforms inputs such as employees, time, money, and equipment through processes such as booking flights, flying airplanes, maintaining equipment, and

## IBM: A Strategic Transformation Toward Service

*Innovation* is perhaps the most used buzzword in the information technology (IT) industry today, and IBM, currently the world's largest IT company, has changed its entire company plan to focus on innovation—specifically its On Demand concept—by transferring its focus from computer hardware to computer services. The move to computer services poses serious challenges for IBM: The company has to be able to sell its premium services in the face of less expensive alternatives in an ever-expanding services market. However, with customers such as UPS, Procter & Gamble, Harry and David, and FedEx, it looks as though IBM is providing services businesses need.

IBM has long been one of IT's leaders and has acquired more than 22,000 patents in the past decade—more than the other 10 IT leaders combined. However, the 1990s were difficult years for IBM; the company had lost its draw for customers and its innovative edge. IBM began to rebound in the mid-1990s, and in 2003 decided to make some huge changes and refine its business model. The company phased out its presence in creating/selling hard disk drives, memory chips, and networking hardware. In perhaps its largest move, the company sold its Personal Computing Division to Lenovo, a computer company in China. For

IBM, having invented the hard disk drive and the DRAM chip and setting the standard in PCs, this was a difficult but necessary move. If a company wants to stay on top of its market, it must be constantly moving forward and reinventing its focus.

IBM restructured its business skills, assets, and delivery capabilities to meet the needs of clients wanting to blend information technology with business operations, and it set up all architecture and technologies for the On Demand Operating Environment (running a business in a way that makes it always ready to change) to run on open standards (not owned by a particular company)—giving clients the freedom to choose hardware platforms.

In 2005, IBM continued to make On Demand Business more tangible and even more focused on innovation. The company's goal has been execution. As part of IBM's On Demand focus, the company vowed to become more On Demand itself by creating a true global reach and utilizing the talent available worldwide and by giving authority and resources to those working in close contact with its clients. On Demand has allowed IBM—a company based in 170 countries with more than 350,000 employees and

670,000 stockholders—to become focused and in sync across the board.

Critics argue that there is nothing new to IT in On Demand, and others claim development has not gone far enough for On Demand to be truly functional. Regardless, IT companies such as Microsoft, Sun Microsystems, Hewlett-Packard, and Oracle (to name a few) are pursuing technology along the same lines. This tells developers and executives at IBM that they are certainly on the right track—setting the pace, and in the lead.[1] ❖

## Q: Discussion Questions

1. Why has IBM shifted from hardware to services for its customers?

2. How is IBM's transformation process different for On Demand services than it is for physical products such as computers?

3. Why do you think competition is viewing IBM's current service and technology solutions as important to pursue to maintain customer relationships?

training crews. The output of these processes is flying passengers and/or packages to their destinations. In a nonprofit organization like Habitat for Humanity, inputs such as money, materials, information, and volunteer time and labor are used to transform raw materials into homes for needy families. In this setting, transformation processes include fund-raising and promoting the cause in order to gain new volunteers and donations of supplies, as well as pouring concrete, raising walls, and setting roofs. Transformation processes occur in all organizations, regardless of what they produce or their objectives. For most organizations, the ultimate objective is for the produced outputs to be worth more than the combined costs of the inputs. The service sector represents approximately 80 percent of all employment in the United States, and the fastest growth of jobs is in service industries.[2]

Unlike tangible goods, services are effectively actions or performances that must be directed toward the consumers who use them. Consider Whole Foods, the all-natural grocery chain that is growing rapidly. By creating a fun shopping experience, Whole Foods turns the drudgery of grocery shopping into entertainment and pleasure (see Table 9.1).[3] Thus, there is a significant customer-contact component to most services. Examples of high-contact services include health care, real estate, tax preparation, and food service. At the world-renowned Inn at Little Washington, for example, food servers are critical to delivering the perfect dining experience expected by the most discriminating diners. Wait staff are expected not only to be courteous but also to demonstrate a detailed knowledge of the restaurant's offerings, and even to assess the mood of guests in order to respond to diners appropriately.[4] Low-contact services, such as online auction services like eBay, often have a strong high-tech component.

Fandango is a service business that provides moviegoers with advance tickets, show times, and movie information on the Internet, by telephone, and via personal wireless devices. Fandango customers can print their bar-coded tickets at home or work and bypass the box office.

**TABLE 9.1** How Whole Foods Makes Grocery Shopping Fun

| | |
|---|---|
| Candy Island | Dip a fresh strawberry in a flowing, chocolate fountain for $1.59 each. |
| Lamar Street Greens | Sit among the organic produce and have a salad handmade for you to enjoy with a glass of chardonnay. |
| Fifth Street Seafood | A version of Seattle's Pike Place Market; have any of 150 fresh seafood items cooked, sliced, smoked, or fried for instant eating. |
| Whole Body | A massage therapist works the kinks out with a 25-minute, deep-tissue massage for $50. |

Source: Bruce Horovitz, "A Whole New Ballgame in Grocery Shopping," *USA Today,* March 9, 2005, see also http://www.usatoday.com/money/industries/food/2005-03-08-wholefoods-cover-usat x.htm (accessed June 17, 2007)..

# "THE ACTUAL PERFORMANCE OF THE SERVICE TYPICALLY OCCURS AT THE POINT OF CONSUMPTION."

Regardless of the level of customer contact, service businesses strive to provide a standardized process, and technology offers an interface that creates an automatic and structured response. The ideal service provider will be high-tech and high-touch. JetBlue, for example, strives to maintain an excellent Web site; friendly, helpful customer contact; and satellite TV service at every seat on each plane. Thus, service organizations must build their operations around good execution, which comes from hiring and training excellent employees, developing flexible systems, customizing services, and maintaining adjustable capacity to deal with fluctuating demand.[5]

Another challenge related to service operations is that the output is generally intangible and even perishable. Few services can be saved, stored, resold, or returned.[6] A seat on an airline or a table in a restaurant, for example, cannot be sold or used at a later date. Because of the perishability of services, it can be extremely difficult for service providers to accurately estimate the demand to match the right supply of a service. If an airline overestimates demand, for example, it will still have to fly each plane even with empty seats. The flight costs the same regardless of whether it is 50 percent full or 100 percent full, but the former will result in much higher costs per passenger. If the airline underestimates demand, the result can be long lines of annoyed customers or even the necessity of bumping some customers off of an overbooked flight.

Businesses that manufacture tangible goods and those that provide services or ideas are similar yet different. For example, both types of organizations must make design and operating decisions. Most goods are manufactured prior to purchase, but most services are performed after purchase. Flight attendants at Southwest Airlines, hotel service personnel, and even the Tennessee Titans football team engage in performances that are a part of the total product. Though manufacturers and service providers often perform similar activities, they also differ in several respects. We can classify these differences in five basic ways.

### nature and consumption of output.

First, manufacturers and service providers differ in the nature and consumption of their output. For example, the term *manufacturer* implies a firm that makes tangible products. A service provider, on the other hand, produces more intangible outputs such as U.S. Postal Service delivery of priority mail or a business stay in a Hyatt hotel. As mentioned earlier, the very nature of the service provider's product requires a higher degree of customer contact. Moreover, the actual performance of the service typically occurs at the point of consumption. At the Hyatt, the business traveler may evaluate in-room communications and the restaurant. Toyota and other automakers, on the other hand, can separate the production of a car from its actual use. Manufacturing, then, can occur in an isolated environment, away from the customer. On the other hand, service providers, because of their need for customer contact, are often more limited than manufacturers in selecting work methods, assigning jobs, scheduling work, and exercising control over operations. At Toyota, for example, any employee who observes a problem can pull a cord and bring the assembly line to a stop to address the issue.[7] The quality of the service experience is often controlled by a service contact employee. However, some hospitals are studying the manufacturing processes and quality control mechanisms applied in the automotive industry in an effort to improve their service quality. By analyzing work processes to find unnecessary steps to eliminate and using teams to identify and address problems as soon as they occur, these hospitals are slashing patient waiting times, decreasing inventories of wheelchairs, readying operating rooms sooner, and generally moving patients through their hospital visit more quickly, with fewer errors, and at a lower cost.[8]

*Because services are perishable, service providers like ski areas offer less expensive tickets at night to stimulate demand.*

**uniformity of inputs.** A second way to classify differences between manufacturers and service providers has to do with the uniformity of inputs. Manufacturers typically have more control over the amount of variability of the resources they use than do service providers. For example, each customer calling Fidelity Investments is likely to require different services due to differing needs, whereas many of the tasks required to manufacture a Lincoln Navigator sport utility vehicle are the same across each unit of output. Consequently, the products of service organizations tend to be more "customized" than those of their manufacturing counterparts. Consider, for example, a haircut versus a bottle of shampoo. The haircut is much more likely to incorporate your specific desires (customization) than is the bottle of shampoo.

**uniformity of output.** Manufacturers and service providers also differ in the uniformity of their output, the final product. Because of the human element inherent in providing services, each service tends to be performed differently. Not all grocery checkers, for example, wait on customers in the same way. If a barber or stylist performs 15 haircuts in a day, it is unlikely that any two of them will be exactly the same. Consequently, human and technological elements associated with a service can result in a different day-to-day or even hour-to-hour performance of that service. The service experience can even vary at McDonald's or Burger King despite the fact that the two chains employ very similar procedures and processes. Moreover, no two customers are exactly alike in their perception of the service experience. Health care offers another excellent example of this challenge. Every diagnosis, treatment, and surgery varies because every individual is different. In manufacturing, the high degree of automation available allows manufacturers to generate uniform outputs and, thus, the operations are more effective and efficient. For example, we would expect every Movado or Rolex watch to maintain very high standards of quality and performance.

**labor required.** A fourth point of difference is the amount of labor required to produce an output. Service providers are generally more labor-intensive (require more labor) because of the high level of customer contact, perishability of the output (must be consumed immediately), and high degree of variation of inputs and outputs (customization). For example, Adecco provides temporary support personnel. Each temporary worker's performance determines Adecco's product quality. A manufacturer, on the other hand, is likely to be more capital-intensive because of the machinery and technology used in the mass production of highly similar goods. For instance, it would take a considerable investment for Nokia to make a digital phone that has a battery with longer life.

**measurement of productivity.** The final distinction between service providers and manufacturers involves the measurement of productivity for each output produced. For manufacturers, measuring productivity is fairly straightforward because of the tangibility of the output and its high degree of uniformity. For the service provider, variations in demand (e.g., higher demand for air travel in some seasons than in others), variations in service requirements from job to job, and the intangibility of the product make productivity measurement more difficult. Consider, for example, how much easier it is to measure the productivity of employees involved in the production of Intel computer processors as opposed to serving the needs of Prudential Securities' clients.

It is convenient and simple to think of organizations as being either manufacturers or service providers as in the preceding discussion. In reality, however, most organizations are a combination of the two, with both tangible and intangible qualities embodied in what they produce. For example, Porsche provides customer services such as toll-free hotlines and warranty protection, while banks may sell checks and other tangible products that complement their primarily intangible product offering. Thus, we consider "products" to include both tangible physical goods as well as intangible service offerings. It is the level of tangibility of its principal product that tends to classify a company as either a manufacturer or a service provider. From an OM standpoint, this level of tangibility greatly influences the nature of the company's operational processes and procedures.

Because health care is a service, perception of services is a challenge. Every diagnosis, treatment, and surgery varies because every individual is different.

● ● ● **L03**

Describe the elements involved in planning and designing an operations system.

# PLANNING AND DESIGNING OPERATIONS SYSTEMS

Before a company can produce any product, it must first decide what it will produce and for what group of customers. It must then determine what processes it will use to make these products as well as the facilities it needs to produce them. These decisions comprise operations planning. Although planning was once the sole realm of the production and operations department, today's successful companies involve all departments within an organization, particularly marketing and research and development, in these decisions.

## Planning the Product

Before making any product, a company first must determine what consumers want and then design a product to satisfy that want. Most companies use marketing research (discussed in Chapter 12) to determine the kinds of goods and services to provide and the features they must possess. Nissan, for example, conducted intensive market research before launching its first full-size pickup truck, the Titan. The company interviewed truck buyers about their likes and dislikes and sent researchers to drive competing trucks for a month to learn firsthand about how the large vehicles handle in a variety of situations.[9] Marketing research can also help gauge the demand for a product and how much consumers are willing to pay for it.

Developing a product can be a lengthy, expensive process. For example, in the automobile industry, developing the new technology for night vision, bumper-mounted sonar systems that make parking easier, and a satellite service that locates and analyzes car problems has been a lengthy, expensive process. Most companies work to reduce development time and costs. For example, through Web collaboration, faucet manufacturer Moen has reduced the time required to take an idea to a finished product in stores to just 16 months, a drop of 33 percent.[10] Once management has developed an idea for a product that customers will buy, it must then plan how to produce the product.

Within a company, the engineering or research and development department is charged with turning a product idea into a workable design that can be produced economically. In smaller companies, a single individual (perhaps the owner) may be solely responsible for this crucial activity. Regardless of who is responsible for product design, planning does not stop with a blueprint for a product or a description of a service; it must also work out efficient production of the product to ensure that enough is available to satisfy consumer demand. How does a lawn mower company transform steel, aluminum, and other materials into a mower design that satisfies consumer and environmental requirements? Operations managers must plan for the types and quantities of materials needed to produce the product, the skills and quantity of people needed to make the product, and the actual processes through which the inputs must pass in their transformation to outputs.

## Designing the Operations Processes

Before a firm can begin production, it must first determine the appropriate method of transforming resources into the desired product. Often, consumers' specific needs and desires dictate a process. Customer needs, for example, require that all 3/4-inch bolts have the same basic thread size, function, and quality; if they did not, engineers and builders could not rely on 3/4-inch bolts in their construction projects. A bolt manufacturer, then, will likely use a standardized process so that every 3/4-inch bolt produced is like every other one. On the other hand, a bridge often must be customized so that it is appropriate for the site and expected load; furthermore, the bridge must be constructed on site rather than in a factory. Typically, products are designed to be manufactured by one of three processes: standardization, modular design, or customization.

**standardization.** Most firms that manufacture products in large quantities for many customers have found that they can make them cheaper and faster by standardizing designs.

Online marketing surveys enable researchers to develop a database quickly with many responses at a relatively low cost.

**Standardization** is making identical, interchangeable components or even complete products. With standardization, a customer may not get exactly what he or she wants, but the product generally costs less than a custom-designed product. Television sets, ballpoint pens, and tortilla chips are standardized products; most are manufactured on an assembly line. Standardization speeds up production and quality control and reduces production costs. And, as in the example of the 3/4-inch bolts, standardization provides consistency so that customers who need certain products to function uniformly all the time will get a product that meets their expectations. As a result of its entry into the World Trade Organization, China promoted the standardization of agricultural production across the country; the nation saw a 17 percent increase in agricultural export productivity over a 10-month period as a result.[11]

## modular design.

**Modular design** involves building an item in self-contained units, or modules, that can be combined or interchanged to create different products. Personal computers, for example, are generally composed of a number of components—CPU case, motherboard, RAM chips, hard drives, floppy drives, graphics card, etc.—that can be installed in different configurations to meet the customer's needs. Because many modular components are produced as integrated units, the failure of any portion of a modular component usually means replacing the entire component. Modular design allows products to be repaired quickly, thus reducing the cost of labor, but the component itself is expensive, raising the cost of repair materials. Many automobile manufacturers use modular design in the production process. Manufactured homes are built on a modular design and cost $58,000, on average, compared with $267,000 for new site–built houses, including the land.[12]

## customization.

**Customization** is making products to meet a particular customer's needs or wants. Products produced in this way are generally unique. Such products include repair services, photocopy services, custom artwork, jewelry, and furniture, as well as large-scale products such as bridges, ships, and computer software. Although there may be similarities among ships, for example, builders generally design and build each ship to meet the needs of the customer who will use it. Delta Marine Industries, for example, custom-builds each luxury yacht to the customer's exact specifications and preferences for things like helicopter garages, golf courses, and swimming pools. The Seattle-based company has delivered 22 yachts longer than 100 feet since 1990.[14] Likewise, when you go to a printing shop to order business cards, the company must customize the cards with your name, address, and title.

## Planning Capacity

Planning the operational processes for the organization involves two important areas: capacity planning and facilities planning. The term **capacity** basically refers to the maximum load that an organizational unit can carry or operate. The unit of measurement may be a worker or machine, a department, a branch, or even an entire plant. Maximum capacity can be stated in terms of the inputs or outputs provided. For example, an electric plant might state plant capacity in terms of the maximum number of kilowatt-hours that can be produced without causing a power outage, while a restaurant might state capacity in terms of the maximum number of customers who can be effectively—comfortably and courteously—served at any one particular time. Honda Motor Company's Marysville, Ohio, plant, which produces the Accord sedan, Accord coupe, and Acura TL, has an annual production capacity of 440,000 vehicles.[15]

## Whoopie Pies Becomes a Whoppin' Business!

Amy Bouchard

The Business: Isamax Snacks

Founded: March 1994

Success: Amy Bouchard has gone from earning $1,900 per year to $1 million in 2005.

In the early 1990s, Amy Bouchard was looking for a way to earn money while staying at home with her children. For some time, Bouchard had been known among family and friends for her amazing whoopie pies—a traditional Maine dessert made with chocolate devil's food cake and vanilla cream filling. When her brother encouraged her to try selling them, she and her husband David decided to give it a shot. Bouchard began baking "Wicked Whoopies" in her home kitchen and delivering them by hand with her children. After awhile she began experimenting with different flavors such as strawberry, pumpkin, and oatmeal cakes and peanut butter and sweet raspberry cream fillings. A few years after beginning her business, success was such that Bouchard decided to move her operation to a commercial bakery site. The business tripled in size, and today the company makes 20 whoopie pie varieties along with muffins and cookies. In 2003, Wicked Whoopies were featured on the *Oprah Winfrey Show*—a stroke of luck that has helped to greatly expand Bouchard's business.[13] ❖

Efficiently planning the organization's capacity needs is an important process for the operations manager. Capacity levels that fall short can result in unmet demand, and consequently, lost customers. On the other hand, when there is more capacity available than needed, operating costs are driven up needlessly due to unused and often expensive resources. To avoid such situations, organizations must accurately forecast demand and then plan capacity based on these forecasts. Another reason for the importance of efficient capacity planning has to do with long-term commitment of resources. Often, once a capacity decision—such as factory size—has been implemented, it is very difficult to change the decision without incurring substantial costs.

**DID YOU KNOW?**

Hershey's has the production capacity to make 33 million Hershey's kisses per day or more than 12 billion per year.[16]

## Planning Facilities

Once a company knows what process it will use to create its products, it then can design and build an appropriate facility in which to make them. Many products are manufactured in factories, but others are produced in stores, at home, or where the product ultimately will be used. Companies must decide where to locate their operations facilities, what layout is best for producing their particular product, and even what technology to apply to the transformation process.

Many firms are developing both a traditional organization for customer contact as well as a virtual organization. Charles Schwab Corporation, a securities brokerage and investment company, maintains traditional offices and has developed complete telephone and Internet services for customers. Through its Web site, investors can obtain personal investment information and trade securities over the Internet without leaving their home or office.

**facility location.** Where to locate a firm's facilities is a significant question because, once the decision has been made and implemented, the firm must live with it due to the high costs involved. When a company decides to relocate or open a facility at a new location, it must pay careful attention to factors such as proximity to market, availability of raw materials, availability of transportation, availability of power, climatic influences, availability of labor, community characteristics (quality of life), and taxes and inducements. Inducements and tax reductions have become an increasingly important criterion in recent years. Kodak, for example, decided to invest $40 million in a photographic plant expansion in Windsor, Colorado, rather than at its Rochester, New York, headquarters after the Colorado Economic Development Commission offered $120,000 in cash incentives and $24,000 toward job training, and Colorado's Weld County agreed to $600,000 in property tax reductions (over 10 years) and concessions on building permits and inspection fees.[17] According to the Institute for Local Self-Reliance, Wal-Mart often receives millions of dollars in free roads, land, sewers, and tax abatements from local governments as incentives to locate new stores or distribution centers in certain areas.[18] The facility-location decision is complex because it involves the evaluation of many factors, some of which cannot be

*IBM ThinkPads were a smash hit when they first came out in the early 1990s. Unfortunately, IBM didn't plan for the high demand and couldn't produce all the machines consumers wanted.*

measured with precision. Because of the long-term impact of the decision, however, it is one that cannot be taken lightly.

**facility layout.** Arranging the physical layout of a facility is a complex, highly technical task. Some industrial architects specialize in the design and layout of certain types of businesses. There are three basic layouts: fixed-position, process, and product.

A company using a **fixed-position layout** brings all resources required to create the product to a central location. The product—perhaps an office building, house, hydroelectric plant, or bridge—does not move. A company using a fixed-position layout may be called a **project organization** because it is typically involved in large, complex projects such as construction or exploration. Project organizations generally make a unique product, rely on highly skilled labor, produce very few units, and have high production costs per unit.

Firms that use a **process layout** organize the transformation process into departments that group related processes. A metal fabrication plant, for example, may have a cutting department, a drilling department, and a polishing department. A hospital may have an X-ray unit, an obstetrics unit, and so on. These types of organizations are sometimes called **intermittent organizations,** which deal with products of a lesser magnitude than do project organizations, and their products they produce, the large number of units produced, and the relatively low unit cost of production.

Many companies actually use a combination of layout designs. For example, an automobile manufacturer may rely on an assembly line (product layout) but may also use a process layout to manufacture parts.

**technology.** Every industry has a basic, underlying technology that dictates the nature of its transformation process. The steel industry continually tries to improve steelmaking techniques. The health care industry performs research into medical technologies and pharmaceuticals to improve the quality of health care service. Two developments that have strongly influenced the operations of many businesses are computers and robotics.

Computers have been used for decades and on a relatively large scale since IBM introduced its 650 series in the late 1950s. The operations function makes great use of computers in all

> ## Every industry has a basic, underlying technology that dictates the nature of its transformation process.

are not necessarily unique but possess a significant number of differences. Doctors, makers of custom-made cabinets, commercial printers, and advertising agencies are intermittent organizations because they tend to create products to customers' specifications and produce relatively few units of each product. Because of the low level of output, the cost per unit of product is generally high.

The **product layout** requires that production be broken down into relatively simple tasks assigned to workers, who are usually positioned along an assembly line. Workers remain in one location, and the product moves from one worker to another. Each person in turn performs his or her required tasks or activities. Companies that use assembly lines are usually known as **continuous manufacturing organizations,** so named because once they are set up, they run continuously, creating products with many similar characteristics. Examples of products produced on assembly lines are automobiles, television sets, vacuum cleaners, toothpaste, and meals from a cafeteria. Continuous manufacturing organizations using a product layout are characterized by the standardized product

phases of the transformation process. **Computer-assisted design (CAD),** for example, helps engineers design components, products, and processes on the computer instead of on paper. **Computer-assisted manufacturing (CAM)** goes a step further, employing specialized computer systems to actually guide and control the transformation processes. Such systems can monitor the transformation process, gathering information about the equipment used to produce the products and about the product itself as it goes from one stage of the transformation process to the next. The computer provides information to an operator who may, if necessary, take corrective action. In some highly automated systems, the computer itself can take corrective action. At Dell's OptiPlex Plant, electronic instructions are sent to double-decker conveyor belts that speed computer components to assembly stations. Two-member teams are told by computers which PC or server to build, with initial assembly taking only three to four minutes. Then more electronic commands move the products (more than 20,000 machines on a typical day) to a finishing area to be customized, boxed, and sent to waiting delivery trucks. Although the plant covers 200,000 square feet, enough to enclose 23 football fields, it is managed almost entirely by a network of computers.[19]

Using flexible manufacturing, computers can direct machinery to adapt to different versions of similar operations. For example, with instructions from a computer, one machine can be programmed to carry out its function for several different versions of an engine without shutting down the production line for refitting.

Robots are also becoming increasingly useful in the transformation process. These "steel-collar" workers have become particularly important in industries such as nuclear power, hazardous-waste disposal, ocean research, and space construction and maintenance, in which human lives would otherwise be at risk. Robots are used in numerous applications by companies around the world. Many assembly operations—cars, television sets, telephones, stereo equipment, and numerous other products—depend on industrial robots. The Robotic Industries Association estimates that about 160,000 robots are now at work in U.S. factories, making the United States one of the two largest the users of robotics, second only to Japan.[20] Researchers continue to make more sophisticated robots, and some speculate that in the future robots will not be limited to space programs and production and operations, but will also be able to engage in

(CIM), a complete system that designs products, manages machines and materials, and controls the operations function. Companies adopt CIM to boost productivity and quality and reduce costs. Such technology, and computers in particular, will continue to make strong inroads into operations on two fronts—one dealing with the technology involved in manufacturing and one dealing with the administrative functions and processes used by operations managers. The operations manager must be willing to work with computers and other forms of technology and to develop a high degree of computer literacy.

## ●● LO4

Specify some techniques managers may use to manage the logistics of transforming inputs into finished products.

# MANAGING THE SUPPLY CHAIN

A major function of operations is supply chain management, which refers to connecting and integrating all parties or members of the distribution system to satisfy customers.[23] Also called logistics, supply chain management includes all the activities involved in obtaining and managing raw materials and component parts, managing finished products, packaging them, and getting them to customers. Sunny Delight had to quickly recreate its supply chain after spinning off from Procter & Gamble. This means it had to develop ordering, shipping, and billing, as well as warehouse management systems and

## "Robots are also becoming increasingly useful in the transformation process."

farming, laboratory research, and even household activities. Moreover, robotics are increasingly being used in the medical field. Voice-activated robotic arms operate video cameras for surgeons. Similar technology assists with biopsies, as well as heart, spine, and nervous system procedures. A heart surgeon at London Health Science Centre in Ontario uses a surgical robot to perform bypass operations on patients without opening their chests, except for five tiny incisions, while their hearts continue beating. More than 400 surgeons around the world currently use surgical robots with far fewer postoperative complications than encountered in conventional operations.[21] It is estimated that more than 150 hospitals in the United States use minimally invasive surgical robots for heart surgery.[22]

When all these technologies—CAD/CAM, flexible manufacturing, robotics, computer systems, and more—are integrated, the result is computer-integrated manufacturing

transportation, so it could focus on growing and managing the Sunny Delight brand.[24] The supply chain integrates firms such as raw material suppliers, manufacturers, retailers, and ultimate consumers into a seamless flow of information and products.[25] Some aspects of logistics (warehousing, packaging, distributing) are so closely linked with marketing that we will discuss them in Chapter 13. In this section, we look at purchasing, managing inventory, outsourcing, and scheduling, which are vital tasks in the transformation of raw materials into finished goods. To illustrate logistics, consider a hypothetical small business—we'll call it Rushing Water Canoes Inc.—that manufactures aluminum canoes, which it sells primarily to sporting goods stores and river-rafting expeditions. Our company also makes paddles and helmets, but the focus of the following discussion is the manufacture of the company's quality canoes as they proceed through the logistics process.

# Purchasing

**Purchasing,** also known as procurement, is the buying of all the materials needed by the organization. The purchasing department aims to obtain items of the desired quality in the right quantities at the lowest possible cost. Rushing Water Canoes, for example, must procure not only aluminum and other raw materials, and various canoe parts and components, but also machines and equipment, manufacturing supplies (oil, electricity, and so on), and office supplies to make its canoes. People in the purchasing department locate and evaluate suppliers of these items. They must constantly be on the lookout for new materials or parts that will do a better job or cost less than those currently being used. The purchasing function can be quite complex and is one area made much easier and more efficient by technological advances.

Not all companies purchase all the materials needed to create their products. Oftentimes, they can make some components more economically and efficiently than can an outside supplier. Coors, for example, manufactures its own cans at a subsidiary plant. On the other hand, firms sometimes find that it is uneconomical to make or purchase an item, and instead arrange to lease it from another organization. Some airlines, for example, lease airplanes rather than buy them. Whether to purchase, make, or lease a needed item generally depends on cost, as well as on product availability and supplier reliability.

# Managing Inventory

Once the items needed to create a product have been procured, some provision has to be made for storing them until they are needed. Every raw material, component, completed or partially completed product, and piece of equipment a firm uses—its **inventory**—must be accounted for, or controlled. There are three basic types of inventory. *Finished-goods inventory* includes those products that are ready for sale, such as a fully assembled automobile ready to ship to a dealer. *Work-in-process inventory* consists of those products that are partly completed or are in some stage of the transformation process. At McDonald's, a cooking hamburger represents work-in-process inventory because it must go through several more stages before it can be sold to a customer. *Raw materials inventory* includes all the materials that have been purchased to be used as inputs for making other products. Nuts and bolts are raw materials for an automobile manufacturer, while hamburger patties, vegetables, and buns are raw materials for the fast-food restaurant. Our fictional Rushing Water Canoes has an inventory of materials for making canoes, paddles, and helmets, as well as its inventory of finished products for sale to consumers. **Inventory control** is the process of determining how many supplies and goods are needed and keeping track of quantities on hand, where each item is, and who is responsible for it.

Operations management must be closely coordinated with inventory control. The production of televisions, for example, cannot be planned without some knowledge of the availability of all the necessary materials—the chassis, picture tubes, color guns, and so forth. Also, each item held in inventory—any type of inventory—carries with it a cost. For example, storing fully assembled televisions in a warehouse to sell to a dealer at a future date requires not only the use of space, but also the purchase of insurance to cover any losses that might occur due to fire or other unforeseen events.

Inventory managers spend a great deal of time trying to determine the proper inventory level for each item. The answer to the question of how many units to hold in inventory depends on variables such as the usage rate of the item, the cost of maintaining the item in inventory, the cost of paperwork and other

*When you think about UPS, you usually think of the nice drivers in brown uniforms and brown trucks who deliver packages around the world. In this ad, UPS promotes its "Supply Chain Solutions," its ability to solve logistics and distribution issues for companies, synchronizing "the movement of goods, information, and funds."*

procedures associated with ordering or making the item, and the cost of the item itself. Several approaches may be used to determine how many units of a given item should be procured at one time and when that procurement should take place.

**the economic order quantity model.** To control the number of items maintained in inventory, managers need to determine how much of any given item they should order. One popular approach is the **economic order quantity (EOQ) model,** which identifies the optimum number of items to order to minimize the costs of managing (ordering, storing, and using) them.

By tracking its sales in real time, 7-11 Japan manages its inventory on a minute-by-minute basis at each of its thousands of stores. Four times each day the stores receive fresh inventory, and at least three times a day employees rearrange the shelves, depending on what's selling well.

**just-in-time inventory management.** An increasingly popular technique is **just-in-time (JIT) inventory management,** which eliminates waste by using smaller quantities of materials that arrive "just in time" for use in the transformation process and therefore require less storage space and other inventory management expense. JIT minimizes inventory by providing an almost continuous flow of items from suppliers to the production facility. Many U.S. companies, including General Motors, Hewlett-Packard, IBM, and Harley Davidson, have adopted JIT to reduce costs and boost efficiency.

Let's say that Rushing Water Canoes uses 20 units of aluminum from a supplier per day. Traditionally, its inventory manager might order enough for one month at a time: 440 units per order (20 units per day times 22 workdays per month). The expense of such a large inventory could be considerable because of the cost of insurance coverage, recordkeeping, rented storage space, and so on. The just-in-time approach would reduce these costs because aluminum would be purchased in smaller quantities, perhaps in lot sizes of 20, which the supplier would deliver once a day. Of course, for such an approach to be effective, the supplier must be extremely reliable and relatively close to the production facility.

**material-requirements planning.** Another inventory management technique is **material-requirements planning (MRP),** a planning system that schedules the precise quantity of materials needed to make the product. The basic components of MRP are a master production schedule, a bill of materials, and an inventory status file. At Rushing Water Canoes, for example, the inventory-control manager will look at the production schedule to determine how many canoes the company plans to make. He or she will then prepare a bill of materials—a list of all the materials needed to make that quantity of canoes. Next, the manager will determine the quantity of these items that RWC already holds in inventory (to avoid ordering excess materials) and then develop a schedule for ordering and accepting delivery of the right quantity of materials to satisfy the firm's needs. Because of the large number of parts and materials that go into a typical production process, MRP must be done on a computer. It can be, and often is, used in conjunction with just-in-time inventory management.

## Outsourcing

Increasingly, outsourcing has become a component of supply chain management in operations. As we mentioned in Chapter 3, outsourcing refers to the contracting of manufacturing or other tasks to independent companies, often overseas. Many companies elect to outsource some aspects of their operations to companies that can provide these products more efficiently, at a lower cost, and with greater customer satisfaction. Delta Airlines, for example, contracts with Indian-based Wipro to handle its voice and data processing.[26] Many high-tech firms have outsourced the production of memory chips, computers, and telecom equipment to Asian companies.[27] The hourly labor costs in countries such as China and India are far less than in the United States, Europe, or even Mexico. These developing countries have improved their manufacturing capabilities, infrastructure, and technical and business skills, making them more attractive regions for global sourcing. On the other hand, the cost of outsourcing halfway around the world must be considered in decisions.[28] While information technology is often outsourced today, transportation, human resources, services, and even marketing functions can be outsourced. Our hypothetical Rushing Water Canoes might contract with a local janitorial service to clean its offices and with a local accountant to handle routine bookkeeping and tax-preparation functions.

Outsourcing, once used primarily as a cost-cutting tactic, has increasingly been linked with the development of competitive advantage through improved product quality, speeding up

technology. Outsourcing allows companies to free up time and resources to focus on what they do best and to create better opportunities to focus on customer satisfaction. Many executives view outsourcing as an innovative way to boost productivity and remain competitive against low-wage offshore factories. However, outsourcing may create conflict with labor and negative public opinion when it results in U.S. workers being replaced by lower-cost workers in other countries. According to a survey by Opinion Research Corporation, 69 percent of respondents believed that boycotting products and services from companies that actively send jobs overseas would influence companies.[29]

## Routing and Scheduling

After all materials have been procured and their use determined, managers must then consider the routing, or sequence of

> **Many executives view outsourcing as an innovative way to boost productivity and remain competitive against low-wage offshore factories.**

the time it takes products to get to the customer, and overall supply-chain efficiencies. Table 9.2 provides the world's top five outsourcing providers that assist mainly in the information

operations through which the product must pass. For example, before employees at Rushing Water Canoes can form aluminum sheets into a canoe, the aluminum must be cut to size. Likewise, the canoe's flotation material must be installed before workers can secure the wood seats. The sequence depends on the product specifications developed by the engineering department of the company.

Once management knows the routing, the actual work can be scheduled. Scheduling assigns the tasks to be done to departments or even specific machines, workers, or teams. At Rushing Water, cutting aluminum for the company's canoes might be scheduled to be done by the "cutting and finishing" department on machines designed especially for that purpose.

Many approaches to scheduling have been developed, ranging from simple trial and error to highly sophisticated computer programs. One popular method is the *Program Evaluation and Review Technique (PERT),* which identifies all the major activities or events required to complete a project, arranges them in a sequence or path, determines the critical path, and estimates the time required for each event. Producing a McDonald's Big Mac, for example, involves removing meat, cheese, sauce, and vegetables from the refrigerator; grilling the hamburger patties; assembling the ingredients; placing the completed Big Mac in its package; and serving it to the customer (Figure 9.3). The cheese,

**TABLE 9.2** The World's Top Five Outsourcing Providers

| Company | Services |
| --- | --- |
| IBM | Customer relationship management; human resources management; information and communication technology management |
| Capgemini | Customer relationship management; information and communication technology management; financial management |
| Hewlett-Packard | Information and communication technology management; financial management; imaging and printing |
| Sodhexo Alliance | Real estate and capital asset management; facility services |
| Accenture | Human resources management; information and communication technology management; financial management |

Source: "The 2007 Global Outsourcing 100," International Association of Outsourcing Professionals, http://www.outsourcingprofessional.org/content/23/152/1197/ (accessed June 17, 2007).

**FIGURE** **9·3** A Hypothetical PERT Diagram for a McDonald's Big Mac

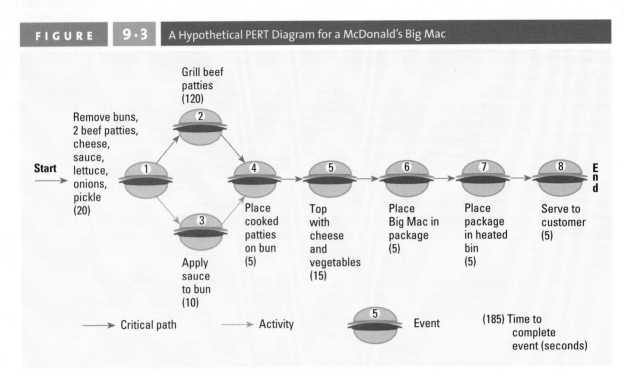

pickles, onions, and sauce cannot be put on before the hamburger patty is completely grilled and placed on the bun. The path that requires the longest time from start to finish is called the *critical path* because it determines the minimum amount of time in which the process can be completed. If any of the activities on the critical path for production of the Big Mac fall behind schedule, the sandwich will not be completed on time, causing customers to wait longer than they usually would.

# Preventing the Bump, Clogging, and Crazy Fares—Airlines Shape Up

Given the recent crises plaguing the airline industry, carriers are making changes and hoping to improve both their bottom lines and customer satisfaction. Frequent flier plans were used to retain customer loyalty regardless of ticket price. Use of the hub system allowed airlines to control key markets, and the formation of partnerships with international airlines was used to retain business customers. As a result, business travelers (often airlines' best customers) were continually charged more and vacation travelers were besieged with numerous restrictions. A first round of low-cost carriers sprouted up in the 1980s, only to go quickly out of business. This time around, low-cost carriers are flourishing, while large airlines are struggling to survive. To compete, large airlines are being forced to add flights and/or to offer comparable fares. To stay alive, airlines are also searching for additional service changes that they can use to save money and improve customer relations.

Although there are still many areas needing improvement, fewer travelers are being involuntarily bumped from flights today. How can the bump rate be declining while the booking rate is increasing? Apparently airlines have refined their overbooking techniques—the primary reason being improved information technology. Airlines are also seeing fewer no-shows. While travelers can still book flights without prepaying via travel agents, more and more customers are booking online—a move requiring prepayment. The majority of Web sales are for low-fare, nonrefundable tickets. The need for prepayment seems to result in fewer no-shows.

Also saving airlines money are new flight, boarding techniques. Airlines such as United, Delta, AirTran, and America West have gotten rid of the traditional back-to-front boarding technique in favor of new methods. United is now boarding travelers according to seat letter, boarding window, middle, and then aisle seats. A United spokesperson says the new method has cut boarding time down by about five minutes and is saving the company about $1 million annually. America West has followed suit, shaving about 2 minutes off the average 20-minute boarding process. AirTran boards travelers in the back four rows followed by the front four rows and the alternation continues until the flight is full. Delta follows a similar procedure—alternating between a few back rows, a few middle rows, and a few front rows.

Although airlines are making some changes to improve services as well as their own costs, most travelers still feel many more changes are needed and are interested to see which improvements come next.[30] ❖

## Q: Discussion Questions

1. What are airlines doing to improve the quality of service to passengers?

2. How is technology being used to enhance service quality?

3. How are routing and scheduling being used to improve productivity and service?

## L05

Assess the importance of quality in operations management.

# MANAGING QUALITY

Quality, like cost and efficiency, is a critical element of operations management, for defective products can quickly ruin a firm. Quality reflects the degree to which a good or service meets the demands and requirements of customers. Customers are increasingly dissatisfied with the quality of service provided by many airlines. There were thousands of air travel complaints last year (see Figure 9.4).[31] Determining quality can be difficult because it depends on customers' perceptions of how well the product meets or exceeds their expectations. For example, the fuel economy of an automobile or its reliability (defined in terms of frequency of repairs) can be measured with some degree of precision. Although automakers rely on their own measures of vehicle quality, they also look to independent sources such as the J. D. Power & Associates annual initial quality survey for confirmation of their quality assessment as well as consumer perceptions of quality. Many people were surprised when J. D. Power ranked Hyundai second behind only Toyota in terms of quality in 2004; for Hyundai executives, the news only substantiated the company's assessment of its long-running initiative to improve quality. However, it is more difficult to measure psychological characteristics such as design, color, or status. It is especially difficult to measure these characteristics when the product is a service. A company has to decide exactly which quality characteristics it considers important and then define those characteristics in terms that can be measured.

The Malcolm Baldrige National Quality Award is given each year to companies that meet rigorous standards of quality. The Baldrige criteria are (1) leadership, (2) information and analysis, (3) strategic planning, (4) human resource development and management, (5) process management, (6) business results, and (7) customer focus and satisfaction. The criteria have become a worldwide framework for driving business improvement. Six companies received the quality award last year: Sunny Fresh Foods Inc. (manufacturing), DynMcDermott Petroleum Operations (service), Park Place Lexus (small business), Richland College (education), Jenks Public Schools (education), and Bronson Methodist Hospital (health care).[32]

Quality is so important that we need to examine it in the context of operations management. Quality control refers to the processes an organization uses to maintain its established quality standards. Dieter Zetsche, DaimlerChrysler CEO, installed the "12 Gates of Quality" to overcome the company's reputation for inconsistent quality. When engineers, planners, marketers, and executives begin planning for a new car model, they must determine 12 benchmarks that must occur prior to the vehicle's launch and assign a deadline to each. Every department working on a project must meet the designated targets before the project can continue into the next phase.[33] Despite Zetsche's actions, a Mercedes costs $2,400 to $3,000 higher on average to produce per car than BMW.[34] The 2007 J. D. Power survey ranked Mercedes-Benz quality 5th compared to 25th in 2006, above BMW (21st), yet below Porsche, which was verified 1st for quality in 2007.[35]

Quality has become a major concern in many organizations, particularly in light of intense foreign competition and increasingly demanding customers. To regain a competitive edge, a number of firms have adopted a total quality management approach. Total quality management (TQM) is a philosophy that uniform commitment to quality in all areas of the organization will promote a culture that meets customers' perceptions of quality. It involves coordinating efforts

**QUALITY CONTROL** the processes an organization uses to maintain its established quality standards

**TOTAL QUALITY MANAGEMENT (TQM)** a philosophy that uniform commitment to quality in all areas of an organization will promote a culture that meets customers' perceptions of quality

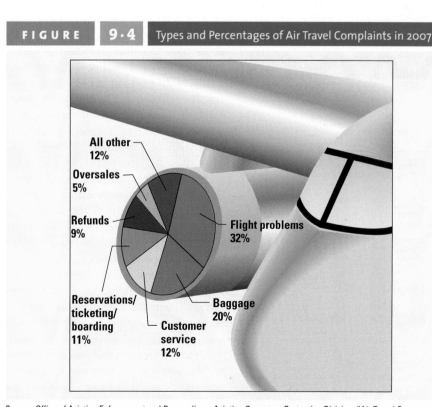

**FIGURE 9·4** Types and Percentages of Air Travel Complaints in 2007

All other 12%
Oversales 5%
Refunds 9%
Reservations/ticketing/boarding 11%
Customer service 12%
Baggage 20%
Flight problems 32%

Source: Office of Aviation Enforcement and Proceedings, Aviation Consumer Protection Division, "Air Travel Consumer Reports for 2007," June 2007, http://airconsumer.ost.dot.gov/reports/atcr07.htm (accessed June 17, 2007).

to improve customer satisfaction, increase employee participation and empowerment, form and strengthen supplier partnerships, and foster an organizational culture of continuous quality improvement. TQM requires continuous quality improvement and employee empowerment.

Continuous improvement of an organization's goods and services is built around the notion that quality is free; by

contrast, *not* having high-quality goods and services can be very expensive, especially in terms of dissatisfied customers.[36] A primary tool of the continuous improvement process is *benchmarking,* the measuring and evaluating of the quality of the organization's goods, services, or processes as compared with the quality produced by the best-performing companies in the industry.[37] Benchmarking lets the organization know where it stands competitively in its industry, thus giving it a goal to aim for over time.

Companies employing total quality management (TQM) programs know that quality control should be incorporated throughout the transformation process, from the initial plans to develop a specific product through the product and production facility design processes to the actual manufacture of the product. In other words, they view quality control as an element of the product itself, rather than as simply a function of the operations process. When a company makes the product correctly from the outset, it eliminates the need to rework defective products, expedites the transformation process itself, and allows employees to make better use of their time and materials. One method through which many companies have tried to improve quality is statistical process control, a system in which management collects and analyzes information about the production process to pinpoint quality problems in the production system.

Hyundai vehicles didn't win rave reviews in terms of quality when they were first produced. But in the early 2000s, a J. D. Power & Associates survey confirmed that the company had made great strides in its effort to improve the quality control in its manufacturing processes.

## Establishing Standards—ISO 9000

Regardless of whether a company has a TQM program for quality control, it must first determine what standard of quality it desires and then assess whether its products meet that standard. Product specifications and quality standards must be set so the company can create a product that will compete in the marketplace. Rushing Water Canoes, for example, may specify that each of its canoes has aluminum walls of a specified uniform thickness, that the front and back of each canoe be reinforced with a specified level of steel, and that each canoe contain a specified amount of flotation material for safety. Production facilities must be designed that can produce products with the desired specifications.

Quality standards can be incorporated into service businesses as well. A hamburger chain, for example, may establish standards relating to how long it takes to cook an order and serve it to customers, how many fries are in each order, how thick the burgers are, or how many customer complaints might be acceptable. Once the

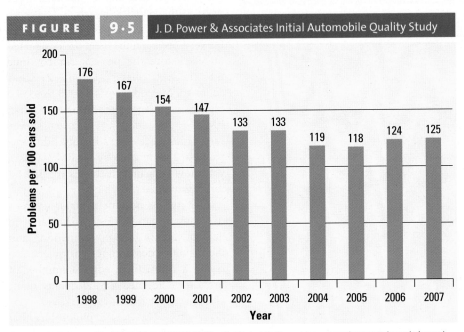

**FIGURE 9·5  J. D. Power & Associates Initial Automobile Quality Study**

Source: J. D. Power and Associates Report, 2007 Initial Quality Study, http://www.jdpower.com/corporate/news/releases/pressrelease.aspx?ID=2007088 (accessed June 17, 2007).

desired quality characteristics, specifications, and standards have been stated in measurable terms, the next step is inspection.

The International Organization for Standardization (ISO) has created a series of quality management standards—ISO 9000—designed to ensure the customer's quality standards are met. The standards provide a framework for documenting how a certified business keeps records, trains employees, tests products, and fixes defects. To obtain ISO 9000 certification, an independent auditor must verify that a business's factory, laboratory, or office meets the quality standards spelled out by the International Organization for Standardization. The certification process can require significant investment, but for many companies, the process is essential to being able to compete. Thousands of U.S. firms have been certified, and many more are working to meet the standards. Certification has become a virtual necessity for doing business in Europe in some high-technology businesses. ISO 9002 certification was established for service providers.

## Inspection

Inspection reveals whether a product meets quality standards. Some product characteristics may be discerned by fairly simple inspection techniques—weighing the contents of cereal boxes or measuring the time it takes for a customer to receive his or her hamburger. As part of the ongoing quality assurance program at Hershey Foods, all wrapped Hershey Kisses are checked, and all imperfectly wrapped kisses are rejected.[38] Other inspection techniques are more elaborate. Automobile manufacturers use automated machines to open and close car doors to test the durability of latches and hinges. The food-processing and pharmaceutical industries use various chemical tests to determine the quality of their output. Rushing Water Canoes might use a special device that can precisely measure the thickness of each canoe wall to ensure that it meets the company's specifications.

Organizations normally inspect purchased items, work-in-process, and finished items. The inspection of purchased items and finished items takes place after the fact; the inspection of work-in-process is preventive. In other words, the purpose of inspection of purchased items and finished items is to determine what the quality level is. For items that are being worked on—an automobile moving down the assembly line or a canoe being assembled—the purpose of the inspection is to find defects before the product is completed so that necessary corrections can be made.

## Sampling

An important question relating to inspection is how many items should be inspected. Should all canoes produced by Rushing Water be inspected or just some of them? Whether to inspect 100 percent of the output or only part of it is related to the cost of the inspection process, the destructiveness of the inspection process (some tests last until the product fails), and the potential cost of product flaws in terms of human lives and safety.

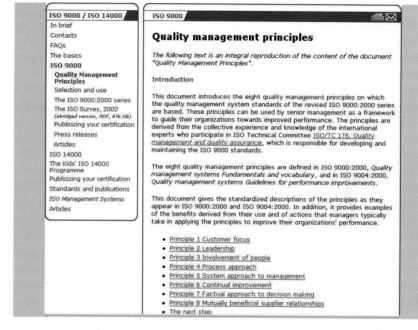

ISO 9000's principles of quality management. (From http://www.iso.ch/ isoen/iso9000-14000/iso9000/qmp.html)

Some inspection procedures are quite expensive, use elaborate testing equipment, destroy products, and/or require a significant number of hours to complete. In such cases, it is usually desirable to test only a sample of the output. If the sample passes inspection, the inspector may assume that all the items in the lot from which the sample was drawn would also pass inspection. By using principles of statistical inference, management can employ sampling techniques that assure a relatively high probability of reaching the right conclusion—that is, rejecting a lot that does not meet standards and accepting a lot that does. Nevertheless, there will always be a risk of making an incorrect conclusion—accepting a population that *does not* meet standards (because the sample was satisfactory) or rejecting a population that *does* meet standards (because the sample contained too many defective items).

Sampling is likely to be used when inspection tests are destructive. Determining the life expectancy of lightbulbs by turning them on and recording how long they last would

In an increasingly competitive global marketplace, quality becomes a key attribute on which companies can differentiate their products from competitors' in the minds and wallets of consumers. Quality has therefore become ever more important in all aspects of business, but particularly in production and operations management. More and more firms are adopting total quality management (TQM) programs to ensure that quality pervades all aspects of their businesses. Many firms are working to satisfy universal quality standards, such as ISO 9000, so that they can compete globally. This has created new career opportunities for students interested in working in TQM and other quality programs.

In the United States, many organizations—including 3M, Du Pont, Eastman Kodak, Kellogg, Union Carbide, and even the U.S. Department of Defense—have obtained ISO 9000 series certification and now require their suppliers to meet ISO 9000 quality standards as well. As a result, companies are experiencing difficulty recruiting graduates who understand the design and implementation of quality-improvement programs.

For these reasons, all students are encouraged to "think quality" when preparing for a business career. Even quality-oriented candidates in fields such as sales, finance, and human resources have the potential to play key roles in the integration of quality throughout their companies. For those who pursue advanced study in TQM in either an undergraduate or graduate program, the prospects for employment and career advancement in the field are promising. The median annual compensation for a quality assurance-control manager is $65,157.[39]

be foolish: There is no market for burned-out lightbulbs. Instead, a generalization based on the quality of a sample would be applied to the entire population of lightbulbs from which the sample was drawn. However, human life and safety often depend on the proper functioning of specific items, such as the navigational systems installed in commercial airliners. For such items, even though the inspection process is costly, the potential cost of flawed systems—in human lives and safety—is too great not to inspect 100 percent of the output. ■

**CHECK OUT**

www.mhhe.com/FerrellM

for study materials including Interactive Exercises, Quizzes, iPod downloads, and video.

# Build Your Business Plan

**Managing Service and Manufacturing Operations**
For your business you need to determine if you are providing raw materials that will be used in further production, or you are a reseller of goods and services, known as a retailer. If you are the former, you need to determine what processes you go through in making your product.

The text provides ideas of breaking the process into inputs, transformation processes and outputs. If you are a provider of a service or a link in the supply chain, you need to know exactly what your customer expectations are. Services are intangible so it is all the more important to better understand what exactly the customer is looking for in resolving a problem or filling a need.

are you **M**-powered?

M
start here.

# 10

# MOTIVATING the WORKFORCE

**introduction** Successful programs teach some important lessons about how to interact with and motivate employees to do their best. Because employees do the actual work of the business and influence whether the firm achieves its objectives, most top managers agree that employees are an organization's most valuable resource. To achieve organizational objectives, employees must have the motivation, ability (appropriate knowledge and skills), and tools (proper training and equipment) to perform their jobs. Ensuring that employees have the appropriate knowledge and skills and the proper training is the subject of Chapter 11; this chapter focuses on employee motivation.

We examine employees' needs and motivation, managers' views of workers, and several strategies for motivating employees. Managers who understand the needs of their employees can help them reach higher levels of productivity and thus contribute to the achievement of organizational goals.

## ●● learning OBJECTIVES

**LO1** Define human relations, and determine why its study is important.

**LO2** Summarize early studies that laid the groundwork for understanding employee motivation.

**LO3** Compare and contrast the human-relations theories of Abraham Maslow and Frederick Herzberg.

**LO4** Investigate various theories of motivation, including theories X, Y, and Z; equity theory; and expectancy theory.

**LO5** Describe some of the strategies that managers use to motivate employees.

## ● ● LO1

Define human relations, and determine why its study is important.

# NATURE OF HUMAN RELATIONS

What motivates employees to perform on the job is the focus of **human relations,** the study of the behavior of individuals and groups in organizational settings. In business, human relations involves motivating employees to achieve organizational objectives efficiently and effectively. The field of human relations has become increasingly important over the years as businesses strive to understand how to boost workplace morale, maximize employees' productivity and creativity, and motivate their ever more diverse employees to be more effective.

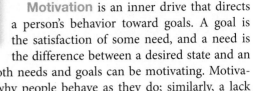

**DID YOU KNOW?**

Absenteeism costs a typical large company more than $3 million a year.[2]

Motivation is an inner drive that directs a person's behavior toward goals. A goal is the satisfaction of some need, and a need is the difference between a desired state and an actual state. Both needs and goals can be motivating. Motivation explains why people behave as they do; similarly, a lack of motivation explains, at times, why people avoid doing what they should do. A person who recognizes or feels a need is motivated to take action to satisfy the need and achieve a goal (Figure 10.1). Consider a person who feels cold. Because of the difference between the actual temperature and the desired temperature, the person recognizes a need. To satisfy the need and achieve the goal of being warm, the person may adjust the thermostat, put on a sweater, reach for a blanket, start a fire, or hug a friend. Human relations is concerned with the needs of employees, their goals and how they try to achieve them, and the impact of those needs and goals on job performance.

One prominent aspect of human relations is morale—an employee's attitude toward his or her job, employer, and colleagues. High morale contributes to high levels of productivity, high returns to stakeholders, and employee loyalty. Conversely, low morale may cause high rates of absenteeism and turnover (when employees quit or are fired and must be replaced by new employees). Table 10.1 outlines some of the direct and indirect expenses associated with low employee morale and turnover. The turnover cost for a fast-food employee is estimated at $500, whereas professional positions can cost up to 2.4 times the employee's annual salary. The highest cost to an organization for low morale comes from disgruntled or dissatisfied CEOs. CEO turnover has grown nearly 60 percent over the past decade.[1]

Respect, involvement, appreciation, adequate compensation, promotions, a pleasant work environment, and a positive

*Many employers now provide their workers with PDAs so they can stay on top of their e-mail while traveling or out of the office. In 2006, a Texas company went so far as to purchase PDAs for all 8,000 of its employees. The idea was to provide them with work updates and to boost their morale. What do you think might be some nonmotivating aspects of this scenario?*

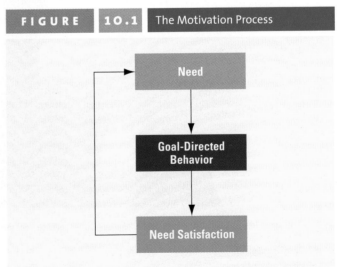

| FIGURE | 10.1 | The Motivation Process |

**TABLE 10.1** Negative Morale Results in Significant Turnover Costs

| Direct Expenses | Indirect Expenses |
| --- | --- |
| Severance package | Managers/co-workers time to engage in first and second interviews |
| Recruitment fees | Human resource management's time advising management and engaging in appropriate background checks |
| Advertising expenses | Management's time to recruit and train the new employee |
| Cost of screening/ pre-employment tests | Lost knowledge, skills, contacts, and possibly employees |
| Travel expenses | Exit interview cost |

Source: Adapted from "The High Cost of Turnover," PeopleLink Consulting, www.peoplelinkconsulting.com/article2.html (accessed June 11, 2007); and "The High Cost of Turnover," Ezine @rticles, John Bishop, www.ezinearticles.com/?The-High-Cost-of-Turnover&id=486954 (accessed June 11, 2007).

organizational culture are all morale boosters. Cognex Corporation, the leading provider of "computers that can see" and automate a wide range of manufacturing processes, believes in the power of creative compensation. At Google's California headquarters, employees are recognized and motivated in unique ways. Employees can receive haircuts in the parking lot through Onsite Haircuts. Employees also have access to organic food, laundry machines, a gymnasium, massages, volleyball court, bike repair, and onsite doctors. Workers who are new parents qualify for up to $500 in take-out food. Google increases employee loyalty and productivity through the creation of a work community unlike that of many other organizations.[3] Many companies offer a diverse array of benefits designed to improve the quality of employees' lives and increase their morale and satisfaction. As mentioned earlier, many companies offer reward programs to improve morale, lower turnover, and motivate employees. Some of the "best companies to work for" offer onsite day care, concierge services (e.g., dry cleaning, shoe repair, prescription renewal), domestic partner benefits to same-sex couples, and fully paid sabbaticals. Table 10.2 shows employee attitudes toward incentives.

**TABLE 10.2** Employee Attitudes toward Incentives

| Perception | Percent Who | |
| --- | --- | --- |
| | Agree | Disagree |
| Feel bonuses are something they are due | 77 | 23 |
| Feel bonuses have a negative impact if too small or not paid | 86 | 14 |
| Feel that bonuses are a part of the total compensation package | 60 | 40 |

Source: "2003 Incentive Federation Study Reveals Money Can't Buy Long-Term Motivation," ClariNet, September 8, 2003, http://quickstart.clari.net/qs_se/webnews/wed/cy/Bfl-incentive-federation.RPRg_DS8.html.

*New parents who work for Colgate-Palmolive get three additional weeks of paid leave in addition to the leave mandated by the Family Leave Act. Employees can also take advantage of onsite banking, a travel agency, and film processing at work.*

 **LO2**

Summarize early studies that laid the groundwork for understanding employee motivation.

# HISTORICAL PERSPECTIVES ON EMPLOYEE MOTIVATION

Throughout the 20th century, researchers have conducted numerous studies to try to identify ways to motivate workers and increase productivity. From these studies have come theories that have been applied to workers with varying degrees of success. A brief discussion of two of these theories—the classical theory of motivation and the Hawthorne studies—provides a background for understanding the present state of human relations.

## Classical Theory of Motivation

The birth of the study of human relations can be traced to time and motion studies conducted at the turn of the century by Frederick W. Taylor and Frank and Lillian Gilbreth. Their studies analyzed how workers perform specific work tasks in an effort to improve the employees' productivity. These efforts led to the application of scientific principles to management.

According to the classical theory of motivation, money is the sole motivator for workers. Taylor suggested that workers who were paid more would produce more, an idea that would benefit both companies and workers. To improve productivity, Taylor thought that managers should break down each job into its component tasks (specialization), determine the best way to perform each task, and specify the output to be achieved by a worker performing the task. Taylor also believed that incentives would motivate employees to be more productive. Thus, he suggested that managers link workers' pay directly to their output. He developed the piece-rate system, under which employees were paid a certain amount for each unit they produced; those who exceeded their quota were paid a higher rate per unit for all the units they produced.

We can still see Taylor's ideas in practice today in the use of mathematical models, statistics, and incentives. Moreover, companies are increasingly striving to relate pay to performance at both the hourly and managerial level. According to Marriott Hotels, roughly 40 percent of incentive planners choose an individual incentive to motivate and reward their employees. In contrast, team incentives are used to generate partnership and working together to accomplish organizational goals. The state of Washington offers teams 25 percent of the revenue generated (not to exceed $10,000) as the result of a continuous improvement or total quality process.[4] Figure 10.2 shows the percentages of companies giving incentives to employees to improve productivity.

More and more corporations are tying pay to performance in order to motivate—even up to the CEO level. The topic of executive pay has become controversial in recent years, and many corporate boards of directors have taken steps to link executive compensation more closely to corporate performance. In 2006, the average CEO's pay of a Standard & Poor's 500 company was $14.78 million, representing a 9.4 percent increase over the previous year. Excessive compensation packages were associated with departing CEOs of underperforming companies, including Home Depot's Robert Nardelli and Pfizer's Henry McKinnell—both of whom received more than

## The Joy of Working for a Grocery Store

Voted one of *Fortune* magazine's "Best 100 Companies to Work For" for nine straight years—number one in 2005 and number two in 2006—Wegmans Food Markets is loved by employees and customers alike. Located in New York, Pennsylvania, New Jersey, and Virginia, the 67-store Wegmans boasts more than $3 billion in annual sales and more than 32,000 employees. The company operates on an interesting and a somewhat backward motto—depending on your perspective: Employees first, customers second. Once you think about it, the logic behind the motto is clever—happy employees are more likely to go out of their way to ensure that customers are happy too.

Although many of us may think working at a grocery store would be a thankless, low-paying job—which it often is—life is different at Wegmans. At many grocery stores, annual turnover rates can reach nearly 100 percent. By comparison, about 20 percent of Wegmans employees have been with the company 10 years or more, and the company's turnover rate for full time employees is only 6 percent. What keeps Wegmans employees so happy? In addition to competitive benefits for both full- and part-time employees—including the traditional benefits plus scholarship opportunities, a Wegmans retirement plan in addition to a 401(k), adoption assistance, and numerous employee discounts—it's the fair salary and the respect for each person as an individual. Wegmans is a privately owned company, which allows it more freedom in where it spends its money. Some of this spending is used to be a good corporate citizen and create an ethical organizational culture.

Employees at Wegmans are allowed to do whatever it takes to create customer satisfaction without having to go higher up for approval. In some cases, this has taken the form of cooking a woman's Thanksgiving Day turkey at a Wegmans store because the one she purchased wouldn't fit in her oven or sending a chef to a customer's home in response to an SOS. While this may seem a bit extreme, a recent Gallup poll suggests that people who are emotionally connected to their grocery stores (and who wouldn't be emotionally connected to a store when its employees go so far out of their way?) spend up to 46 percent more. As proof, Wegmans received around 2,400 individual letters in one year in which the writers' begged Wegmans to build stores in their areas.

Even an ethical company such as Wegmans isn't without its share of issues and risks. In 2005, activists accused Wegmans of cruel animal treatment at their Wegmans Egg Farm. The New York State Police and the Wayne County District Attorney's office investigated the matter and acquitted Wegmans of any wrongdoing. In addition, in response Wegmans hired Dr. Joy Mench, professor of animal science at the University of California at Davis to consult with them on proper animal husbandry. The company also brings in a veterinarian from the Cornell University Poultry Diagnostic and Extension Service to monitor the health and well-being of the hens.

By all accounts, Wegmans does all it can to create happy, successful environments for both its employees and its customers. Almost anyone is sure to enjoy an ethical atmosphere filled with good food, abundant choices, responsible employees, and respect.[6] ❖

## Q: Discussion Questions

1. Do you think you would like to work for a supermarket like Wegmans? Why or why not?

2. What keeps Wegmans employees so happy?

3. How would you describe the Wegmans approach to employee motivation?

$200 million. Increasingly, shareholders and board members are becoming more involved in CEO accountability.[5]

Like most managers of the early 20th century, Taylor believed that satisfactory pay and job security would motivate employees to work hard. However, later studies showed that other factors are also important in motivating workers.

## The Hawthorne Studies

Elton Mayo and a team of researchers from Harvard University wanted to determine what physical conditions in the workplace—such as light and noise levels—would stimulate employees to be most productive. From 1924 to 1932, they studied a group of workers at the Hawthorne Works Plant of the Western Electric Company and measured their productivity under various physical conditions.

What the researchers discovered was quite unexpected and very puzzling: Productivity increased regardless of the physical conditions. This phenomenon has been labeled the Hawthorne effect. When questioned about their behavior, the employees expressed satisfaction because their co-workers in the experiments were friendly and, more importantly, because their supervisors had asked for their help and cooperation in the study. In other words, they were responding to the attention they received, not the changing physical work conditions. The researchers concluded that social and psychological factors could significantly affect productivity and morale. Medtronic, often called the "Microsoft of the medical-device industry," has a built-in psychological factor

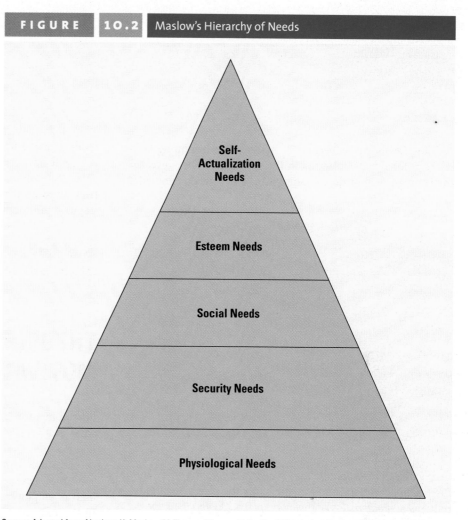

FIGURE 10.2 Maslow's Hierarchy of Needs

Source: Adapted from Abraham H. Maslow, "A Theory of Human Motivation," *Psychology Review* 50 (1943), pp. 370–396. American Psychology Association.

that influences employee morale. The company makes lifesaving medical devices, such as pacemakers, neurostimulators, and stents. New hires at Medtronic receive medallions inscribed with a portion of the firm's mission statement, "alleviate pain, restore health, and extend life." There is an annual party where people whose bodies function thanks to Medtronic devices give testimonials. Obviously, Medtronic employees feel a sense of satisfaction in their jobs. In a study investigating the impact of office temperature, when the office temperature dropped from 77 degrees to 68 degrees (a less comfortable temperature), typing mistakes increased by 74 percent and output dropped 46 percent.[7]

> ## Taylor believed that satisfactory pay and job security would motivate employees to work hard. However, later studies showed that other factors are also important in motivating workers.

The Hawthorne experiments marked the beginning of a concern for human relations in the workplace. They revealed that human factors do influence workers' behavior and that

*The employees who participated in the Hawthorne studies responded to the attention they received during the study and thereby improved their performance, not the changing of the physical characteristics of their workplace. Do you think the workers in this photo improved their pace or level of quality as this photo was taken?*

**TABLE 10-3** Country Comparison of Vacation Time: Time Off Can Improve Employee Motivation and Productivity

| Country/ Region | Minimum Paid Vacation Days | Paid Holidays | Total Time Off |
|---|---|---|---|
| Finland | 30 | 14 | 44 |
| Israel | 24 | 16 | 40 |
| France | 30 | 10 | 40 |
| Lithuania | 28 | 12 | 40 |
| Morocco | 21 | 19 | 40 |
| United Arab Emirates | 30 | 9 | 39 |
| Austria | 25 | 13 | 38 |
| Estonia | 28 | 10 | 38 |
| Malta | 24 | 14 | 38 |
| United States | 15 | 10 | 25 |

Source: http://money.cnn.com/2007/06/12/pf/vacation_days_worldwide/index.htm (accessed June 15, 2007).

managers who understand the needs, beliefs, and expectations of people have the greatest success in motivating their workers. Table 10-3 compares vacation time provided in various countries; vacation time has been shown to provide on incentive to improve productivity.

 **LO3**

Compare and contrast the human-relations theories of Abraham Maslow and Frederick Herzberg.

# THEORIES OF EMPLOYEE MOTIVATION

The research of Taylor, Mayo, and many others has led to the development of a number of theories that attempt to describe what motivates employees to perform. In this section, we will discuss some of the most important of these theories. The successful implementation of ideas based on these theories will vary, of course, depending on the company, its management, and its employees. It should be noted, too, that what worked in the past may no longer work today. Good managers must have the ability to adapt their ideas to an ever-changing, diverse group of employees.

## Maslow's Hierarchy of Needs

Psychologist Abraham Maslow theorized that people have five basic needs: physiological, security, social, esteem, and self-actualization. Maslow's hierarchy arranges these needs into the order in which people strive to satisfy them (Figure 10.2).[8]

Physiological needs, the most basic and first needs to be satisfied, are the essentials for living—water, food, shelter, and clothing. According to Maslow, humans devote all their efforts to satisfying physiological needs until they are met. Only when these needs are met can people focus their attention on satisfying the next level of needs—security.

Security needs relate to protecting yourself from physical and economic harm. Actions that may be taken to achieve security include reporting a dangerous workplace condition to management, maintaining safety equipment, and purchasing insurance with income protection in the event you become unable to work. Once security needs have been satisfied, people may strive for social goals.

Social needs are the need for love, companionship, and friendship—the desire for acceptance by others. To fulfill social

● **ESTEEM NEEDS** the need for respect—both self-respect and respect from others

● **SELF-ACTUALIZATION NEEDS** the need to be the best one can be; at the top of Maslow's hierarchy

● **HYGIENE FACTORS** aspects of Herzberg's theory of motivation that focus on the work setting and not the content of the work; these aspects include adequate wages, comfortable and safe working conditions, fair company policies, and job security

needs, a person may try many things: making friends with a co-worker, joining a group, volunteering at a hospital, throwing a party. Once their social needs have been satisfied, people attempt to satisfy their need for esteem.

Esteem needs relate to respect—both self-respect and respect from others. One aspect of esteem needs is competition—the need to feel that you can do something better than anyone else. Competition often motivates people to increase their productivity. Esteem needs are not as easily satisfied as the needs at lower levels in Maslow's hierarchy because they do not always provide tangible evidence of success. However, these needs can be realized through rewards and increased involvement in organizational activities. Until esteem needs are met, people focus their attention on achieving respect. When they feel they have achieved some measure of respect, self-actualization becomes the major goal of life.

Self-actualization needs, at the top of Maslow's hierarchy, mean being the best you can be. Self-actualization involves maximizing your potential. A self-actualized person feels that she or he is living life to its fullest in every way. For Stephen

about developing people for the long term, not just for their current job. Just over half of the employees believed their employers show them genuine care and concern.[9] Managers should learn from Maslow's hierarchy that employees will be motivated to contribute to organizational goals only if they are able to first satisfy their physiological, security, and social needs through their work.

## Herzberg's Two-Factor Theory

In the 1950s psychologist Frederick Herzberg proposed a theory of motivation that focuses on the job and on the environment where work is done. Herzberg studied various factors relating to the job and their relation to employee motivation

> # Maslow's theory maintains that the more basic needs at the bottom of the hierarchy must be satisfied before higher-level goals can be pursued.

King, self-actualization might mean being praised as the best fiction writer in the world; for actress Halle Berry, it might mean winning an Oscar.

Maslow's theory maintains that the more basic needs at the bottom of the hierarchy must be satisfied before higher-level goals can be pursued. Thus, people who are hungry and homeless are not concerned with obtaining respect from their colleagues. Only when physiological, security, and social needs have been more or less satisfied do people seek esteem. Maslow's theory also suggests that if a low-level need is suddenly reactivated, the individual will try to satisfy that need rather than higher-level needs. Many laid-off workers probably shift their focus from high-level esteem needs to the need for security. Almost 10,000 employees in 32 countries in business, government, and nonprofit organizations were surveyed for the Global Employee Relationship Report. Fifty percent of the respondents said they believe their organization cares

and concluded that they can be divided into hygiene factors and motivational factors (Table 10.4).

Hygiene factors, which relate to the work setting and not to the content of the work, include adequate wages, comfortable and safe working conditions, fair company policies, and job security. These factors do not necessarily motivate employees to excel, but their absence may be a potential source of dissatisfaction and high turnover. Employee safety and comfort are clearly hygiene factors.

Many people feel that a good salary is one of the most important job factors, even more important than job security and the chance to use one's mind and abilities. Salary and security, two of the hygiene factors identified by Herzberg, make it possible for employees to satisfy the physiological and security needs identified by Maslow. However, the presence of hygiene factors is unlikely to motivate employees to work harder.

Motivational factors, which relate to the content of the work itself, include achievement, recognition, involvement, responsibility, and advancement. The absence of motivational factors may not result in dissatisfaction, but their presence is likely to motivate employees to excel.

Many companies are beginning to employ methods to give employees more responsibility and control and to involve them more in their work, which serves to motivate them to higher levels of productivity and quality. L. L. Bean employees have tremendous latitude to satisfy customer's needs. One employee drove 500 miles from Maine to New York to deliver a canoe to a customer who was leaving on a trip. Disney has a similar commitment to empowering customers and making customers happy.[10]

Herzberg's motivational factors and Maslow's esteem and self-actualization needs are similar. Workers' low-level needs

**TABLE 10.4** Herzberg's Hygiene and Motivational Factors

| Hygiene Factors | Motivational Factors |
| --- | --- |
| Company policies | Achievement |
| Supervision | Recognition |
| Working conditions | Work itself |
| Relationships with peers, supervisors, and subordinates | Responsibility |
| Salary | Advancement |
| Security | Personal growth |

(physiological and security) have largely been satisfied by minimum-wage laws and occupational-safety standards set by various government agencies and are therefore not motivators. Consequently, to improve productivity, management should focus on satisfying workers' higher-level needs (motivational factors) by providing opportunities for achievement, involvement, and advancement and by recognizing good performance.

# Is It Possible Your Dog Could Increase Business Productivity?

In an age in which companies are cutting back health care benefits due to a sluggish economy, many employers are turning to low-cost perks to keep workers happy. In addition to perks such as gym and spa facilities and weight-loss programs, an increasing number of companies are actually allowing employees to bring their pets to work. A recent survey conducted by Dogster (an online dog forum) and Simply Hired indicates that two-thirds of all dog owners surveyed would work longer hours if allowed to bring their dogs to work. One-third claimed they would accept a 5 percent pay deduction if allowed to bring their dogs to work. Maybe this is because another survey indicated that 69 percent of dog owners view their dog as part of the family.

Having dogs and cats in the workplace can provide many benefits, including a more relaxed and flexible atmosphere, increased staff morale, and even increased employee retention. One company's spokesperson indicated that its pet policy gives employees individual flexibility and shows that the company respects employees enough to let them make choices about their work environment. The American Psychological Association has even honored companies such as Small Dog Electronics, a computer merchant with 27 employees, as psychologically healthy workplaces in part because of their pet-friendly policies. At this time, many pet-friendly companies (out of about 400 nationwide) have

50 or fewer employees, although a few *Fortune* 500 companies such as Amazon and Google have pet-friendly policies. At Planet Dog, a company allowing pets in the office daily, the company consists, so to speak, of 16 employees and 14 dogs.

A pet-friendly workplace can be a definite advantage in recruiting and retaining employees. Small Dog Electronics, for example, has boasted an employee turnover rate of 1 percent compared with its industry average of 11 percent. Even non–pet owners often appreciate the informal, flexible environments that characterize workplaces with pets. To some extent, being pet-friendly helps define a corporate culture—as it does at AutoDesk, a software provider. A Pet Products Manufacturers Association survey revealed that 73 percent of surveyed companies believed allowing pets at work increased productivity—compared with a 42 percent productivity increase due to business development or management training. Even when it is not possible for employees to bring pets to work every day, some companies allow them to bring their pets to work occasionally for short periods of time.

Many small businesses, particularly retailers, established pet-friendly policies out of personal necessity. Indeed many small retailers, such as antique dealers and bookstore owners, often have "store cats" or "store dogs" that are appreciated as much

by customers as by employees. Although law prohibits allowing pets in restaurants in the United States, many European restaurants allow customers to have their dogs right at their tables where food is served.

While bringing your pet to work can definitely improve morale, there are a few challenges. People with allergies or who are afraid of animals may get distracted from their jobs. Of course, there may be the concern that a dog may bite a person or another dog. However, research by attorneys at Ralston Purina found that lawsuits related to pets in the work environment are quite rare. As long as good judgment is used, allowing animals in the workplace appears to be a great move.[11] ❖

# Q: Discussion Questions

1. Why can a nonfinancial benefit such as being able to bring your dog to work motivate employees?

2. What type of businesses are appropriate for a pet-friendly workplace policy?

3. How do you personally feel about having other people's pets in an office where you work or store where you shop?

## L04

Investigate various theories of motivation, including theories X, Y, and Z; equity theory; and expectancy theory.

## McGregor's Theory X and Theory Y

In *The Human Side of Enterprise,* Douglas McGregor related Maslow's ideas about personal needs to management. McGregor contrasted two views of management—the traditional view, which he called Theory X, and a humanistic view, which he called Theory Y.

According to McGregor, managers adopting Theory X assume that workers generally dislike work and must be forced to do their jobs. They believe that the following statements are true of workers:

1. The average person naturally dislikes work and will avoid it when possible.
2. Most workers must be coerced, controlled, directed, or threatened with punishment to get them to work toward the achievement of organizational objectives.
3. The average worker prefers to be directed and to avoid responsibility, has relatively little ambition, and wants security.[12]

Managers who subscribe to the Theory X view maintain tight control over workers, provide almost constant supervision, try to motivate through fear, and make decisions in an autocratic fashion, eliciting little or no input from their subordinates. The Theory X style of management focuses on physiological and security needs and virtually ignores the higher needs discussed by Maslow.

The Theory X view of management does not take into account people's needs for companionship, esteem, and personal growth, whereas Theory Y, the contrasting view of management, does. Managers subscribing to the Theory Y view assume that workers like to work and that under proper conditions employees

3. People will commit to objectives when they realize that the achievement of those goals will bring them personal reward.
4. The average person will accept and seek responsibility.
5. Imagination, ingenuity, and creativity can help solve organizational problems, but most organizations do not make adequate use of these characteristics in their employees.
6. Organizations today do not make full use of workers' intellectual potential.[13]

Obviously, managers subscribing to the Theory Y philosophy have a management style very different from managers subscribing to the Theory X philosophy. Theory Y managers maintain less control and supervision, do not use fear as the primary motivator, and are more democratic in decision making, allowing subordinates to participate in the process. Theory Y managers address the high-level needs in Maslow's hierarchy as well as physiological and security needs. Today, Theory Y enjoys widespread support and may have displaced Theory X.

## Theory Z

Theory Z is a management philosophy that stresses employee participation in all aspects of company decision making. It was first described by William Ouchi in his book *Theory Z—How American Business Can Meet the Japanese Challenge.* Theory Z incorporates many elements associated with the Japanese approach to management, such as trust and intimacy, but Japanese ideas have been adapted for use

> ## Theory Z results in employees feeling organizational ownership.

will seek out responsibility in an attempt to satisfy their social, esteem, and self-actualization needs. McGregor describes the assumptions behind Theory Y in the following way:

1. The expenditure of physical and mental effort in work is as natural as play or rest.
2. People will exercise self-direction and self-control to achieve objectives to which they are committed.

in the United States. In a Theory Z organization, managers and workers share responsibilities; the management style is participative; and employment is long term and often lifelong. Theory Z results in employees feeling organizational ownership. Recent research has found that such feelings of ownership may produce positive attitudinal and behavioral effects for employees.[14] In a Theory Y organization, managers focus on assumptions about the nature of the worker. The two

**THEORY X** McGregor's traditional view of management whereby it is assumed that workers generally dislike work and must be forced to do their jobs

**THEORY Y** McGregor's humanistic view of management whereby it is assumed that workers like to work and that under proper conditions employees will seek out responsibility in an attempt to satisfy their social, esteem, and self-actualization needs

**THEORY Z** a management philosophy that stresses employee participation in all aspects of company decision making theories can be seen as complementary. Table 10.5 compares the traditional American management style, the Japanese management style, and Theory Z (the modified Japanese management style).

## Variations on Theory Z

Theory Z has been adapted and modified for use in a number of U.S. companies. One adaptation involves workers in decisions through quality circles. Quality circles (also called quality-assurance teams) are small, usually having five to eight members who discuss ways to reduce waste, eliminate problems, and improve quality, communication, and work satisfaction. Such quality teams are a common technique for harnessing the knowledge and creativity of hourly employees to solve problems in companies.

Even more involved than quality circles are programs that operate under names such as *participative management, employee involvement,* or *self-directed work teams.* Regardless of the term

Former Intel Corporation CEO Andy Grove declined the usual executive perks, choosing instead, for example, to work out of an interior cubicle at the company.

used to describe such programs, they strive to give employees more control over their jobs while making them more responsible for the outcome of their efforts. Such programs often organize employees into work teams of 5 to 15 members who are responsible for producing an entire product item. Team members are cross-trained and can therefore move from job to job within the team. Each team essentially manages itself and is responsible for its quality, scheduling, ordering and use of materials, and problem solving. Many firms have successfully employed work teams to boost morale, productivity, quality, and competitiveness.

## Equity Theory

According to **equity theory,** how much people are willing to contribute to an organization depends on their assessment of the fairness, or equity, of the rewards they will receive in exchange. In a fair situation, a person receives rewards proportional to the contribution he or she makes to the organization. However, in practice, equity is a subjective notion. Each worker regularly develops a personal input–output ratio by taking stock of his or her contribution (inputs) to the organization in time, effort, skills, and experience and assessing the rewards (outputs) offered by the organization in pay,

**TABLE 10.5** Comparison of American, Japanese, and Theory Z Management Styles

|  | American | Japanese | Theory Z |
|---|---|---|---|
| **Duration of employment** | Relatively short term; workers subject to layoffs when business slows | Lifelong; no layoffs | Long term; layoffs rare |
| **Rate of promotion** | Rapid | Slow | Slow |
| **Amount of specialization** | Considerable; worker develops expertise in one area only | Minimal; worker develops expertise in all aspects of the organization | Moderate; worker learns all aspects of the organization |
| **Decision making** | Individual | Consensual; input from all concerned parties is considered | Consensual; emphasis on quality |
| **Responsibility** | Assigned to the individual | Shared by the group | Assigned to the individual |
| **Control** | Explicit and formal | Less explicit and less formal | Informal but with explicit performance measures |
| **Concern for workers** | Focus is on work only | Focus extends to worker's whole life | Focus includes worker's life and family |

Source: Adapted from William Ouchi, *Theory Z—How American Business Can Meet the Japanese Challenge,* p. 58. © 1981 by Addison-Wesley Publishing Company, Inc. Reprinted by permission of Perseus Books Publishers, a member of Perseus Books, L.L.C.

benefits, recognition, and promotions. The worker compares his or her ratio to the input–output ratio of some other person—a "comparison other," who may be a co-worker, a friend working in another organization, or an "average" of several people working in the organization. If the two ratios are close, the individual will feel that he or she is being treated equitably.

Let's say you have a high-school education and earn $25,000 a year. When you compare your input–output ratio with that of a co-worker who has a college degree and makes $35,000 a year, you will probably feel that you are being paid fairly. However, if you perceive that your personal input–output ratio is lower than that of your college-educated co-worker, you may feel that you are being treated unfairly and be motivated to seek change. But, if you learn that co-worker who makes $35,000 has only a high-school diploma, you may feel cheated by your employer. To achieve equity, you could try to increase your outputs by asking for a raise or promotion. You could also try to have your co-worker's inputs increased or his or her outputs decreased. Failing to achieve equity, you may be motivated to look for a job at a different company. Table 10.6 shows how your income would need to vary by market to have the same quality of life. Inequity in real income can result in enormous dissatisfaction and employee turnover. You would need more than $200,000 to have the same quality of life in New York as you could have with an income of almost $89,000 in Houston.[15]

Because almost all the issues involved in equity theory are subjective, they can be problematic. Author David Callahan has argued that feelings of inequity may underlie some unethical or illegal behavior in business, such as the $600 billion a year stolen from companies by their own employees. Shoplifting alone is the cause of more than $10 billion a year in company losses.[16] Callahan believes that employees who do not feel they are being treated equitably may be motivated to equalize the situation by lying, cheating, or otherwise "improving" their pay, perhaps by stealing.[17] Managers should try to avoid equity problems by ensuring that rewards are distributed on the basis of performance and that all employees clearly understand the basis for their pay and benefits.

## Expectancy Theory

Psychologist Victor Vroom described expectancy theory, which states that motivation depends not only on how much a person wants something but also on the person's perception of how likely he or she is to get it. A person who wants something and has reason to be optimistic will be strongly motivated. For example, say you really want a promotion. And, let's say because you have taken some night classes to improve your skills, and moreover, have just made a large, significant sale, you feel confident that you are qualified and able to handle the new position. Therefore, you are motivated to try to get the promotion. In contrast, if you do not believe you are likely to get what you want, you may not be motivated to try to get it, even though you really want it.

 **L05**

Describe some of the strategies that managers use to motivate employees.

# STRATEGIES FOR MOTIVATING EMPLOYEES

Based on the various theories that attempt to explain what motivates employees, businesses have developed several strategies for motivating their employees and boosting morale and productivity. Some of these techniques include behavior modification and job design, as well as the already described employee involvement programs and work teams.

## Behavior Modification

Behavior modification involves changing behavior and encouraging appropriate actions by relating the consequences of behavior to the behavior itself. The concept of behavior modification was developed by psychologist B. F. Skinner, who showed that there are two types of consequences that can modify behavior—reward and punishment. Skinner found that

TABLE 10.6  Gross Salary Needed to Replicate $100,000 after Adjusting for Cost of Living

| City | Salary |
| --- | --- |
| New York | $205,426 |
| San Francisco | 179,034 |
| Los Angeles | 156,106 |
| San Diego | 149,384 |
| Washington, D.C. | 141,894 |
| Boston | 137,649 |
| Chicago | 126,929 |
| Seattle | 117,037 |
| Atlanta | 102,805 |
| Denver | 102,348 |
| Cleveland | 101,986 |
| Milwaukee | 101,478 |
| Phoenix | 97,976 |
| Dallas | 93,665 |
| Charlotte | 92,991 |
| Houston | 88,977 |

Source: Jeanne Sahadi, "Where the (Best) 6-Figure Jobs Are," CNNMoney. com, http://money.cnn.com/2006/07/13/pf/six_fig_farthest/index.htm (accessed June 15, 2007).

may lead to undesirable long-term side effects, such as employee dissatisfaction and increased turnover. In general, rewarding appropriate behavior is a more effective way to modify behavior.

behavior that is rewarded will tend to be repeated, while behavior that is punished will tend to be eliminated. For example, employees who know that they will receive a bonus, such as an expensive restaurant meal, for making a sale over $2,000 may be more motivated to make sales. Workers who know they will be punished for being tardy are likely to make a greater effort to get to work on time.

However, the two strategies may not be equally effective. Punishing unacceptable behavior may provide quick results but

## Job Design

Herzberg identified the job itself as a motivational factor. Managers have several strategies that they can use to design jobs to help improve employee motivation. These include job rotation, job enlargement, job enrichment, and flexible scheduling strategies.

### job rotation.

Job rotation allows employees to move from one job to another in an effort to relieve the boredom that is often associated with job specialization. Businesses often turn to specialization in hopes of increasing productivity, but there is a negative side effect to this type of job design: Employees become bored and dissatisfied, and productivity declines. Job rotation reduces this boredom by allowing workers to undertake a greater variety of tasks and by giving them the opportunity to learn new skills. With job rotation, an employee spends a specified amount of time performing one job and then moves on to another, different job. The worker eventually returns to the initial job and begins the cycle again.

Job rotation is a good idea, but it has one major drawback. Because employees may eventually become bored with all the jobs in the cycle, job rotation does not totally eliminate the problem of boredom. Job rotation is extremely useful, however, in situations where a person is being trained for a position that requires an understanding of various units in an organization. Some companies, such as Procter & Gamble, use job rotation to increase functional skills. For example, marketing employees may rotate from growing brands to declining brands, from established markets to new markets, or from global mega-brands to regional small brands.[18] Many executive training programs require trainees to spend time learning a variety of specialized jobs. Job rotation is also used to cross-train today's self-directed work teams.

### job enlargement.

Job enlargement adds more tasks to a job instead of treating each task as separate. Like job rotation, job enlargement was developed to overcome the boredom associated with specialization. The rationale behind this strategy is that jobs are more satisfying as the number of tasks performed by an individual increases. Employees sometimes enlarge, or craft, their jobs by noticing what needs to be done and then changing tasks and relationship boundaries to adjust. Individual orientation and motivation shape opportunities to craft new jobs and job relationships.[19] Job enlargement strategies have been more successful in increasing job satisfaction than have job rotation strategies. IBM, AT&T, and Maytag are among the many companies that have used job enlargement to motivate employees.

### job enrichment.

Job enrichment incorporates motivational factors, such as opportunity for achievement, recognition, responsibility, and advancement, into a job. It gives

*Nucor Corporation's 11,000-plus nonunion employees in Charlotte, North Carolina, don't see themselves as ordinary workers. There are no special benefits or compensation plans for executives, and the company's flat organizational structure encourages employees to adopt the mind-set of owner-operators.*

workers not only more tasks within the job but more control and authority over the job. Job enrichment programs enhance a worker's feeling of responsibility and provide opportunities for growth and advancement when the worker is able to take on the more challenging tasks. Hyatt Hotels Corporation and General Foods use job enrichment to improve the quality of work life for their employees. The potential benefits of job enrichment are great, but it requires careful planning and execution.

### flexible scheduling strategies.

Many U.S. workers work a traditional 40-hour workweek consisting of five 8-hour days with fixed starting and ending times. Facing problems of poor morale and high absenteeism as well as a diverse workforce with changing needs, many managers have turned to flexible scheduling strategies such as flextime, compressed work weeks, job sharing, part-time work, and telecommuting. Retention is critical in jobs such as information technology. A survey of more than 1,400 chief information officers revealed that 47 percent offer flexible schedules as a way to retain the best employees.[20]

**Flextime** is a program that allows employees to choose their starting and ending times, as long as they are at work during a specified core period (Figure 10.3). It does not reduce the total number of hours that employees work; instead, it gives employees more flexibility in choosing which hours they work. A firm may specify that employees must be present from 10:00 a.m. to 3:00 p.m. One employee may choose to come in at 7:00 a.m. and leave at the end of the core time, perhaps to attend classes at a nearby college after work. Another employee, a mother who lives in the suburbs, may come in at 9:00 a.m. to have time to drop off her children at a day care center and commute by public transportation to her job. Flextime provides many benefits, including improved ability to recruit and retain workers who wish to balance work and home life.

> **Flextime provides many benefits, including improved ability to recruit and retain workers who wish to balance work and home life.**

Customers can be better served by allowing more coverage of customers over longer hours. Workstations and facilities can be better utilized by staggering employee use. Communities experience reduced traffic at traditional "rush hours."[21]

Related to flextime are the scheduling strategies of the compressed workweek and job sharing. The **compressed workweek** is a four-day (or shorter) period in which an employee works 40 hours. Under such a plan, employees typically work 10 hours per day for four days and have a three-day weekend. The compressed workweek reduces the company's operating expenses because its actual hours of operation are reduced. It is also sometimes used by parents who want to have more days off to spend with their families.

**Job sharing** occurs when two people do one job. One person may work from 8:00 a.m. to 12:30 p.m.; the second person comes in at 12:30 p.m. and works until 5:00 p.m. Job sharing gives both people the opportunity to work as well as time to fulfill other obligations, such as parenting or school. Thirty percent of companies allow job sharing.[22] With job sharing, the company has the benefit of the skills of two people for one job, often at a lower total cost for salaries and benefits than one person working eight hours a day would be paid.

Two other flexible scheduling strategies attaining wider use include allowing full-time workers to work part time for a certain period and allowing workers to work at home either full or part time. Employees at some firms may be permitted to work part time for several months in order to care for a new baby or an elderly parent or just to slow down for a little while to "recharge their batteries." By 2020, 40 percent of U.S. workers will be caring for an aging parent, and employees are expected to demand benefits that reflect this major shift.[23] When the employees return to full-time work, they are usually given a position comparable to their original full-time position. Other firms are allowing employees to telecommute or telework (work at home a few days of the week), staying connected via computers, modems, and telephones. More than 45 million Americans work from home. Of those who work "at home," the average number of places these

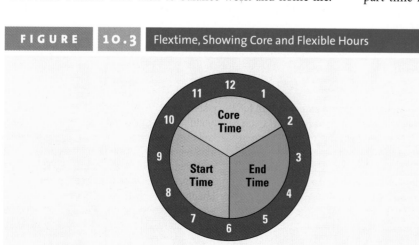

**FIGURE 10.3** Flextime, Showing Core and Flexible Hours

individuals work is 3.4, and these places can include home, car, and restaurant or coffee bar.[24] Although many employees ask for the option of working at home to ease the responsibilities of caring for family members, some have discovered that they are more productive at home without the distractions of the work-place. An assessment of 12 company telecommuting programs, including Apple, AT&T, and the state of California, found that positive productivity changes occurred. Traveler's Insurance Company reports its telecommuters to be 20 percent more productive than its traditional employees.[25] Other employees, however, have discovered that they are not suited for working at home. Human resource management executives are split as to whether telecommuting helps or hurts employees' careers. Thirty percent feel telecommuting helps their careers, while 25 percent feel that it hurts, whereas 39 percent feel it does nei-ther.[26] Still, work-at-home programs do help reduce overhead costs for businesses. For example, some companies used to maintain a surplus of office space but have reduced the surplus through employee telecommuting, "hoteling" (being assigned to a desk through a reservation system), and "hot-desking" (several people using the same desk but at different times).

Companies are turning to flexible work schedules to provide more options to employees who are trying to juggle their work duties with other responsibilities and needs. Preliminary results indicated that flexible scheduling plans increase job satisfaction, which, in turn, leads to increases in productivity. Some recent research, however, has indicated there are potential problems with telecommuting. Some managers are reluctant to adopt the practice because the pace of change in today's workplace is faster than ever, and telecommuters may be left behind or actu-ally cause managers more work in helping them stay abreast of changes. Some employers also worry that telecommuting work-ers create a security risk by creating more opportunities for computer hackers or equipment thieves. Some employees have found that working outside the office may hurt career advance-ment opportunities, and some report that instead of helping them balance work and family responsibilities, telecommuting increases the strain by blurring the barriers between the office and home. Co-workers call at all hours, and telecommuters are apt to continue to work when they are not supposed to (after regular business hours or during vacation time).[28]

Single working-parent families face a tough challenge in balancing work and home life. For single parents, business travel and other routine demands of a corporate career—including overtime and interoffice transfers—can turn life upside down. Sometimes single parents decline promotions or high-profile assignments to preserve time with their children. In some organizations, experts say, it may be assumed single-mom staffers can't handle new duties because of the responsibilities they're shouldering at home.

## Importance of Motivational Strategies

Motivation is more than a tool that managers can use to fos-ter employee loyalty and boost productivity. It is a process that affects all the relationships within an organization and influ-ences many areas such as pay, promotion, job design, training

## Lambert's Café Is on a Roll

Norman Ray Lambert and Family

The Business: Lambert's Café: The Only Home of "Throwed" Rolls

Founded: 1942

Success: The company serves more than 2 million throwed rolls per year.

Earl and Agnes Lambert, with just $1500 in their pockets, opened a small café that seated 41 people on March 13, 1942. The Lambert's Café soon became a quaint eatery known for its healthy servings. Norman Ray, Earl's son, took over the café upon his father's death in 1976. While handing out oven-fresh rolls dur-ing one busy lunch hour on May 26 of the same year, a hungry patron, out of arm's reach, told Norman to just throw him the @$%# thing. Thus was born the slogan, "If it doesn't say Lambert's, it's not . . . Throwed Rolls." Since then, Lambert's has been throwing rolls to thousands of diners who come from all over just to catch them and to fill up on extras like white beans and fried okra, which servers ladle on your plate free of charge. Lambert's now has two restaurants in Missouri and one in Alabama and seats nearly 1,300 people. The restaurant was featured on the Travel Channel's "Top Places to Pig Out," on which it was ranked number one. People from all over the country visit Lambert's once and keep returning.[27] ❖

In terms of satisfaction and motivation, where you live can be almost as important as where you work. Obtaining information about various cities can provide fodder for your job hunt and even help you decide to accept or reject a job offer. *Forbes* magazine conducts an annual survey of the "Best Places for Business and Careers." To develop its rankings, the magazine evaluates factors such as expenses related to labor, energy, taxes, and office space; the number of college graduates and Ph.D.'s in the area; job and income growth; migration patterns; crime rates; and culture and leisure activities (e.g., museums, theaters, golf courses, and sports teams). According to the magazine, the 10 best metropolitan areas to work in are listed in the next column.

Salary is certainly an important aspect in any job hunt. Various Web sites will estimate the salaries necessary to live equivalently in two different cities. According to the National Association of Realtors' Salary Calculator site (see e-Xtreme Surfing), if you currently have a job in Atlanta, Georgia, that pays $50,000, you will need a job that pays $76,698 in Boston to maintain your standard of living (calculated on May 6, 2004).[29]

| Rank | City | Population |
|------|------|-----------|
| 1. | Raleigh, North Carolina | 978,000 |
| 2. | Provo, Utah | 465,000 |
| 3. | Boise, Idaho | 560,000 |
| 4. | Des Moines, Iowa | 531,000 |
| 5. | Knoxville, Tennessee | 662,000 |
| 6. | Albuquerque, New Mexico | 813,000 |
| 7. | Durham, North Carolina | 462,000 |
| 8. | Fayetteville, Arkansas | 417,000 |
| 9. | Nashville, Tennessee | 1,438,000 |
| 10. | Olympia, Washington | 233,000 |

Source: Kurt Badenhausen (2007) "Best Places for Business and Careers," Forbes, April, 5, http://www.forbes.com/lists/2007/1/07bestplaces_all_slide.html?thisSpeed=30000, accessed October 24, 2007.

opportunities, and reporting relationships. Employees are motivated by the nature of the relationships they have with their supervisors, by the nature of their jobs, and by characteristics of the organization. Motivation tools, then, must be varied as well. Managers can further nurture motivation by being honest, supportive, empathetic, accessible, fair, and open. Motivating employees to increase satisfaction and productivity is an important concern for organizations seeking to remain competitive in the global marketplace. ■

# CHECK OUT

www.mhhe.com/FerrellM

for study materials including Interactive Exercises, Quizzes, iPod downloads, and video.

# Build Your Business Plan

**Motivating the Workforce** As you determine the size of your workforce, you are going to face the reality that you cannot provide the level of financial compensation that you would like to your employees, especially when you are starting your business.

Many employees are motivated by other things than money. Knowing that they are appreciated and doing a good job can bring great satisfaction to employees. Known as "stroking," it can provide employees with internal gratification that can be valued even more than financial incentives. Listening to your employees suggestions, involving them in discussions about future growth and valuing their input, can go a long way toward building loyal employees and reducing employee turnover.

Think about what you could do in your business to motivate your employees without spending much money. Maybe you will have lunch brought in once a week or offer tickets to a local sporting event to the employee with the most sales. Whatever you elect to do, you must be consistent and fair with all your employees.

Online exercises. Study material. iPod® content.

All in one place.

## ● ● learning OBJECTIVES

**LO1**  Define human resources management, and explain its significance.

**LO2**  Summarize the processes of recruiting and selecting human resources for a company.

**LO3**  Discuss how workers are trained and their performance appraised.

**LO4**  Identify the types of turnover companies may experience, and explain why turnover is an important issue.

**LO5**  Specify the various ways a worker may be compensated.

**LO6**  Discuss some of the issues associated with unionized employees, including collective bargaining and dispute resolution.

**LO7**  Describe the importance of diversity in the workforce.

# MANAGING HUMAN RESOURCES

**Introduction** Recruiting loyal and motivated employees are vital tasks in any organization. If a business is to achieve success, it must have sufficient numbers of employees who are qualified and motivated to perform the required duties. Thus, managing the quantity (from hiring to firing) and quality (through training, compensating, and so on) of employees is an important business function. Meeting the challenge of managing increasingly diverse human resources effectively can give a company a competitive edge in a global marketplace.

This chapter focuses on the quantity and quality of human resources. First we look at how human resources managers plan for, recruit, and select qualified employees. Next we look at training, appraising, and compensating employees, aspects of human resources management designed to retain valued employees. Along the way, we'll also consider the challenges of managing unionized and diverse employees.

## ●● LO1

Define human resources management, and explain its significance.

# THE NATURE OF HUMAN RESOURCES MANAGEMENT

Chapter 1 defined human resources as labor, the physical and mental abilities that people use to produce goods and services. **Human resources management (HRM)** refers to all the activities involved in determining an organization's human resources needs, as well as acquiring, training, and compensating people to fill those needs. Human resources managers are concerned with maximizing the satisfaction of employees and motivating them to meet organizational objectives productively. In some companies, this function is called personnel management.

HRM has increased in importance over the last few decades, in part because managers have developed a better understanding of human relations through the work of Maslow, Herzberg, and others. Moreover, the human resources themselves are changing. Employees today are concerned not only about how much a job pays; they are concerned also with job satisfaction, personal performance, leisure, the environment, and the future. Once dominated by white men, today's workforce includes significantly more women, African Americans, Hispanics, and other minorities, as well as disabled and older workers. Human resources managers must be aware of these changes and make the best of them to increase the productivity of their employees. Every manager practices some of the functions of human resources management at all times.

# PLANNING FOR HUMAN RESOURCES NEEDS

When planning and developing strategies for reaching the organization's overall objectives, a company must consider whether it will have the human resources necessary to carry out its plans. After determining how many employees and what skills are needed to satisfy the overall plans, the human resources department (which may range from the owner in a small business to hundreds of people in a large corporation) ascertains how many employees the company currently has and how many will be retiring or otherwise leaving the organization during the planning period. With this information, the human resources manager can then forecast how many more employees the company will need to hire and what qualifications they must have. HRM planning also requires forecasting the availability of people in the workforce who will have the necessary qualifications to meet the organization's future needs. The human resources manager then develops a strategy for satisfying the organization's human resources needs.

Next, managers analyze the jobs within the organization so that they can match the human resources to the available assignments. **Job analysis** determines, through observation and study, pertinent information about a job—the specific tasks that comprise it; the knowledge, skills, and abilities necessary to perform it; and the environment in which it will be performed. Managers use the information obtained through a job analysis to develop job descriptions and job specifications.

A **job description** is a formal, written explanation of a specific job that usually includes job title, tasks to be performed (for instance, waiting on customers), relationship with other jobs, physical and mental skills required (such as lifting heavy boxes or calculating data), duties, responsibilities, and working conditions. A **job specification** describes the qualifications necessary for a specific job, in terms of education (some jobs require a college degree), experience, personal characteristics (newspaper ads frequently request outgoing, hardworking persons), and physical characteristics. Both the job description and job specification are used to develop recruiting materials such as newspaper and online advertisements.

## ●● LO2

Summarize the processes of recruiting and selecting human resources for a company.

# RECRUITING AND SELECTING NEW EMPLOYEES

After forecasting the firm's human resources needs and comparing them to existing human resources, the human resources manager should have a general idea of how many new employees the firm needs to hire. With the aid of job analyses, management can then recruit and select employees who are qualified to fill specific job openings.

## Recruiting

**Recruiting** means forming a pool of qualified applicants from which management can select employees. There are two sources from which to develop this pool of applicants—internal and external.

Internal sources of applicants include the organization's current employees. Many firms have a policy of giving first consideration to their own employees—or promoting from within. The cost of hiring current employees to fill job openings is inexpensive when compared with the cost of hiring from external sources, and it is good for employee morale.

External sources consist of advertisements in newspapers and professional journals, employment agencies, colleges, vocational schools, recommendations from current employees, competing firms, unsolicited applications, and online. There are hundreds of Web sites where employers can post job openings and job seekers can post their résumés, including Monster.com, Hotjobs.com, and CareerBuilder .com. Employers looking for employees for specialized jobs can use more focused sites such as computerwork.com. Increasingly, companies can turn to their own Web sites for potential candidates: Nearly all of the *Fortune* 500 firms provide career Web sites where they recruit, provide employment information, and take applications. Using these sources of applicants is generally more expensive than hiring from within, but it may be necessary if there are no current employees who meet the job specifications or there are better-qualified people outside of the organization. Recruiting for entry-level managerial and professional positions is often carried out on college and university campuses. For managerial or professional positions above the entry level, companies sometimes depend on employment agencies or executive search firms, sometimes called *headhunters*, which specialize in luring qualified people away from other companies.

## Selection

**Selection** is the process of collecting information about applicants and using that information to decide which ones to hire. It includes the application itself, as well as interviewing, testing, and reference checking. This process can be quite lengthy and expensive. At Procter & Gamble, for example, the steps include the application, screening and comprehensive

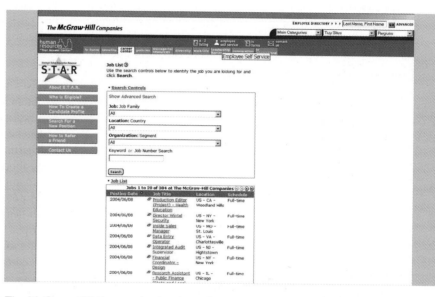

*The McGraw-Hill Companies has an online database of job offerings called "Strategic Talent Acquisition Resources," or STAR. STAR helps employees manage their careers by alerting them about future opportunities that match their experiences, captures all résumés in a common database so they can be shared nationwide, allows for electronic approvals, and eliminates all paper résumés.*

## Cuckoo for Cereality

Rick Bacher and David Roth

Business: Cereality

Founded: 2003

Success: With 65 percent repeat customers and the financial backing of Quaker, the company expects to be profitable in just a few years.

Although you probably buy your cereal at a supermarket, some customers get their Cheerios from four all-cereal cafés called Cereality.

David Roth and Rick Bacher opened the first Cereality in Arizona State University's Student Union, and they have plans for more cafés on campuses and in hospitals, train stations, arenas, airports, and office buildings across the United States. Why not? More than 95 percent of all Americans like cereal! Each Cereality café offers more than 30 varieties of brand-name hot and cold cereals, plus regular, flavored, or soy milk for about $3 a serving. In addition, the cafés offer a toppings bar with more than 45 toppings such as cherries and marshmallows as well as made-to-order cereal, yogurt blend smoothies ("Slurrealities"), and homemade breakfast bars. Cereality attracts customers with kitchen-style cabinets, employees dressed in pajamas and robes, and TVs playing cartoons day and night. Customers can store their custom concoctions in an onsite computer for their next visit or purchase select mixes. In addition to wearing pajamas at work, employees, known as "cereologists," are highly valued at Cereality, which offers competitive pay and benefits as well as fun, positive working environments.[1] ❖

> # MOST COMPANIES ASK FOR THE FOLLOWING INFORMATION BEFORE CONTACTING A POTENTIAL CANDIDATE: CURRENT SALARY, REASON FOR SEEKING A NEW JOB, YEARS OF EXPERIENCE, AVAILABILITY, AND LEVEL OF INTEREST IN THE POSITION.

interviews, day visits/site visits, and for those outside the United States, a problem-solving test. P&G attracts and retains high-quality employees.[2] Such rigorous scrutiny is necessary to find those applicants who can do the work expected and fit into the firm's structure and culture. If an organization finds the "right" employees through its recruiting and selection process, it will not have to spend as much money later in recruiting, selecting, and training replacement employees.

### the application.
In the first stage of the selection process, the individual fills out an application form and perhaps has a brief interview. The application form asks for the applicant's name, address, telephone number, education, and previous work experience. The goal of this stage of the selection process is to get acquainted with the applicants and to weed out those who are obviously not qualified for the job. Most companies ask for the following information before contacting a potential candidate: current salary, reason for seeking a new job, years of experience, availability, and level of interest in the position. In addition to identifying obvious qualifications, the application can provide subtle clues about whether a person is appropriate for a particular job. For instance, an applicant who gives unusually creative answers may be perfect for a position at an advertising agency; a person who turns in a sloppy, hurriedly scrawled application probably would not be appropriate for a technical job requiring precise adjustments. Many companies now accept online applications. The online application at Procter & Gamble is designed not only to collect biographical data but to create a picture of the applicant and how the person might contribute within the company. The Web site states that

there are no right or wrong answers and indicates that completion takes about 30 to 45 minutes. Applicants also must submit an electronic copy of their résumé.[3]

### the interview.
The next phase of the selection process involves interviewing applicants. Interviews allow management to obtain detailed information about the applicant's experience and skills, reasons for changing jobs, attitudes toward the job, and an idea of whether the person would fit in with the company. Furthermore, the interviewer can answer the applicant's questions about the requirements for the job, compensation, working conditions, company policies, organizational culture, and so on. A potential employee's questions may be just as revealing as his or her answers. Table 11.1 provides some insights on finding the right work environment. Figure 11.1 reveals mistakes candidates make in interviewing, while Table 11.2 lists some of the most common questions asked by interviewers.

### testing.
Another step in the selection process is testing. Ability and performance tests are used to determine whether an applicant has the skills necessary for the job. Aptitude, IQ, or personality tests may be used to assess an applicant's potential for a certain kind of work and his or her ability to fit into the organization's culture. One of the most commonly used tests is

**TABLE 11.1**   Interviewing Tips

1. Evaluate the work environment. Do employees seem to get along and work well in teams?
2. Evaluate the attitude of employees. Are employees happy, tense, or overworked?
3. Are employees enthusiastic and excited about their work?
4. What is the organizational culture, and would you feel comfortable working there?

Source: "What to Look for During Office Visits," Texas A&M Career Center, http://careercenter.tamu.edu/guides/interviews/lookforinoffice.html (accessed June 15, 2007).

**TABLE 11.2**   Top 10 Interview Questions

1. What are your weaknesses?
2. Why should we hire you?
3. Why do you want to work here?
4. What are your goals?
5. Why did you leave (or why are you leaving) your job?
6. When were you most satisfied with your job?
7. What can you do for us that the other candidate can't?
8. What are three positive things your last boss would say about you?
9. What salary are you seeking?
10. If you were an animal, which one would you want to be?

Source: Carole Martin, "Prep for the Top 10 Interview Questions," http://content.monster.com/articles/3479/17512/1/home.aspx (accessed June 15, 2007).

the Myers-Briggs Type Indicator. Myers-Briggs Type Indicator Test is used more than 2.5 million times each year according to a survey by *Workforce Management*. Although polygraph ("lie detector") tests were once a common technique for evaluating the honesty of applicants, in 1988 their use was restricted to specific government jobs and those involving security or access to drugs. Applicants may also undergo physical examinations to determine their suitability for some jobs, and many companies require applicants to be screened for illegal drug use. More than 40 million drug tests are conducted annually by employers, with less than 5 percent yielding a positive result.[4] Drug testing is common among government workers, companies that contract for the government, and in performance-critical industries such as airlines and construction work. Drug abuse in the United States costs approximately $180 billion in crime, productivity loss, health care, incarceration, and drug enforcement. This would represent around $600 cost for each person in the United States.[5] Some studies have shown that drug testing (1) does not increase productivity, (2) can foster resentment, and (3) may lead highly qualified people to avoid a company.[6] Indeed, the practice of drug testing has spawned a host of products intended to help applicants defeat the tests.[7] Like the application form and the interview, testing serves to eliminate those who do not meet the job specifications.

### reference checking.

Before making a job offer, the company should always check an applicant's references. Reference checking usually involves verifying educational background and previous work experience. Background checking is important because applicants may misrepresent themselves on their applications or résumés. ADP Screening and Selection Services, which conducts background checks for employers, reported that more than 50 percent of the applicants on whom it conducted background checks had presented false information about themselves on résumés or applications.[8] Consequently, reference checking is a vital, albeit often overlooked, stage in the selection process. Managers charged with hiring should be aware, however, that many organizations will confirm only that an applicant is a former employee, perhaps with beginning and ending work dates, and will not release details about the quality of the employee's work. Although some companies instruct their employees not to respond to additional questions in reference checking, Table 11.3 outlines the normal range of questions asked in checking employee supplied references.

| FIGURE | 11.1 | Mistakes Made in Interviewing |

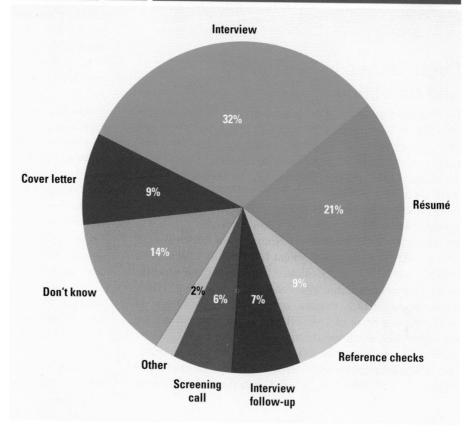

Source: *USA Today Snapshots,* January 4, 2006, p. 1B.

**TABLE 11.3** Potential Questions in Checking References

1. When did the employee work for the company?
2. Why did he or she leave?
3. What was the entry and departure salary?
4. What was the employee's position and job responsibilities?
5. Were there any other issues that affected job performance?
6. Did the employee get along well with co-workers and management?
7. Was the individual promoted while an employee?
8. How would you evaluate the employee's performance?
9. Did this employee supervise others? If so what was his or her management style, how effective were they?
10. How did this employee handle conflict, stress or pressure?
11. What was this employee's biggest accomplishment on the job?
12. Would you rehire this employee if the opportunity arose?
13. Can you describe this employee's ability to work in a team?
14. Is there anything that I have not asked that you would like to share?

Source: "Reference Check Questions," http://jobsearch.about.com/od/referencesrecommendations/a/refercheck.htm (accessed June 15, 2007).

## Legal Issues in Recruiting and Selecting

Legal constraints and regulations are present in almost every phase of the recruitment and selection process, and a violation of these regulations can result in lawsuits and fines. Therefore, managers should be aware of these restrictions to avoid legal problems. Some of the laws affecting human resources management are discussed here.

Because one law pervades all areas of human resources management, we'll take a quick look at it now. **Title VII of the Civil Rights Act** of 1964 prohibits discrimination in employment. It also created the Equal Employment Opportunity Commission (EEOC), a federal agency dedicated to increasing job opportunities for women and minorities and eliminating job discrimination based on race, religion, color, sex, national origin, or handicap. As a result of Title VII, employers must not impose sex distinctions in job specifications, job descriptions, or newspaper advertisements. The most common type of discrimination is race, followed by sex, disability, age, national origin, and religion. In 2006, the EEOC received more than 27,000 charges

**Be yourself.** Race. Ethnicity. Religion. Nationality. Gender. In the end, there's just one variety of human being. The individual. All six billion of us. **Be bullish.**

ml.com

*Merrill Lynch promotes diversity within its organization.*

of race discrimination with sexual harassment cases totaling more than 23,000.[9] The Civil Rights Act of 1964 also outlaws the use of discriminatory tests for applicants. Aptitude tests and other indirect tests must be validated; in other words, employers must be able to demonstrate that scores on such tests are related to job performance, so that no one race has an advantage in taking the tests. More than 40 years after passage of the Civil Rights Act, African Americans hold 8.2 percent of executive positions, Hispanics comprise 5 percent of the top positions, while women represent 15.7 percent of corporate officers.[10]

Other laws affecting HRM include the Americans with Disabilities Act (ADA), which prevents discrimination against disabled persons. It also classifies people with AIDS as handicapped and, consequently, prohibits using a positive AIDS test as reason to deny an applicant employment. The Age Discrimination in Employment Act specifically outlaws discrimination based on age. Its focus is banning hiring practices that discriminate against people between the ages of 49 and 69, but it also outlaws policies that require employees to retire before the age of 70. Generally, however, when companies need employees, recruiters head to college campuses, and when downsizing is necessary, many older workers are offered early retirement. AARP, the advocacy organization for people 50 and older, found that very few employers consider their companies one of the best for older workers. AARP mailed invitations to 10,000 companies for a chance to compete for a listing in *Modern Maturity* magazine as one of the "best employers for workers over 50." The 35-million-member organization received only 14 applications. Given that nearly 20 percent of the nation's workers will be 55 years old or over by 2015, many companies may need to change their approach toward older workers.[11] The Equal Pay Act mandates that men and women who do equal work must receive the same wage. Wage differences are acceptable only if they are attributed to seniority, performance, or qualifications. Women in full-time management and professional jobs average 73 percent of men's income, according to the Bureau of Labor Statistics.[12] African American women earn only 68 percent and Latinas 57 percent of what men earn. Asian and Pacific Islander American women earn less, too.[13]

## DEVELOPING THE WORKFORCE

Once the most qualified applicants have been selected and offered positions, and they have accepted their offers, they must be formally introduced to the organization and trained so they can begin to be productive members of the workforce. **Orientation** familiarizes the newly hired employees with fellow workers, company procedures, and the physical properties of the company. It generally includes a tour of the building; introductions to supervisors, co-workers, and subordinates; and the distribution of organizational manuals describing the organization's policy on vacations, absenteeism, lunch breaks, company benefits, and so on. Orientation also involves socializing the new employee into the ethics and culture of the new company.

Many larger companies now show videotapes of procedures, facilities, and key personnel in the organization to help speed the adjustment process.

● ● **L03**

Discuss how workers are trained and their performance appraised.

## Training and Development

Although recruiting and selection are designed to find employees who have the knowledge, skills, and abilities the company needs, new employees still must undergo training to learn how to do their specific job tasks. *On-the-job training* allows workers to learn by actually performing the tasks of the job, while *classroom training* teaches employees with lectures, conferences, videotapes, case studies, and Web-based training. Employee training expenses are increasing, as a percentage of payroll (up 2.2 percent), per employee (up 12.5 percent), and as a function of total hours of training (up 16 percent).[14] Development is training that augments the skills and knowledge of managers and professionals. Training and development are also used to improve the skills of employees in their present positions and to prepare them for increased responsibility and job promotions. Training is therefore a vital function of human resources management. Training and development plans are tailored to meet each employee's needs at Procter & Gamble. In addition to on-the-job training, the company offers one-on-one coaching from managers, peer mentoring, individualized work plans that outline key projects and highlight skills to sharpen, and formal classroom training conducted at the company's "Learning Center" in Cincinnati.[15]

## Assessing Performance

Assessing an employee's performance—his or her strengths and weaknesses on the job—is one of the most difficult tasks for managers. However, performance appraisal is crucial because it gives employees feedback on how they are doing and what they need to do to improve their performance. It also provides a basis for determining how to compensate and reward employees, and it generates information about the quality of the firm's selection, training, and development activities. Table 11.4 identifies 16 characteristics that may be assessed in a performance review.

Performance appraisals may be objective or subjective. An objective assessment is quantifiable. For example, a Westinghouse employee might be judged by how many circuit boards he typically produces in one day or by how many of his boards

**?**

**DID YOU KNOW?**

Internet-based training is expected to grow to be a $10.6 billion market by 2007.[16]

have defects. A Century 21 real estate agent might be judged by the number of houses she has shown or the number of sales she has closed. A company can also use tests as an objective method of assessment. Whatever method they use, managers must take into account the work environment when they appraise performance objectively.

When jobs do not lend themselves to objective appraisal, the manager must relate the employee's performance to some other standard. One popular tool used in subjective assessment is the ranking system, which lists various performance factors on which the manager ranks employees against each other. Although used by many large companies, ranking systems are unpopular with many employees. Qualitative criteria, such as teamwork and communication skills, used to evaluate employees are generally hard to gauge. Such grading systems have triggered employee lawsuits that allege discrimination in grade/ranking assignments. The charges were brought by older workers at Ford, by blacks and women at Microsoft, and by U.S. citizens at Conoco.[17]

Another performance appraisal method used by many companies is the 360-degree feedback system, which provides feedback from a panel that typically includes superiors, peers, and subordinates. Because of the tensions it may cause, peer appraisal appears to be difficult for many. However, companies that have success with 360-degree feedback tend to be open to learning and willing to experiment and

● **TRAINING** teaching employees to do specific job tasks through either classroom development or on-the-job experience

● **DEVELOPMENT** training that augments the skills and knowledge of managers and professionals

*More companies are providing their employees with training modules they can use when and where they need them. Cisco, for example, has 3,000 training VoDs (videos-on-demand) that can be downloaded off of the company's intranet on an as-needed basis.*

**TABLE 11.4**  General Performance Characteristics

**Communication ability**—effectiveness with which the employee presents accurate information both verbally and in writing.

**Relationships with others**—extent to which the employee establishes positive relationships with co-workers.

**Ability to work without supervision**—extent to which the employee can work by himself/herself; requiring very little supervision and being self-sufficient.

**Accuracy of work**—degree to which the employee makes mistakes or errors that require correction.

**Appearance**—physical appearance of the employee at work; cleanliness, grooming, neatness, and appropriateness of dress for the job.

**Cooperation**—extent to which the employee cooperates with supervisors, associates, and those for which work is performed.

**Dependability**—extent to which the employee can be relied upon to meet work schedules and fulfill job responsibilities and commitments.

**Use of work time**—how effectively and efficiently the employee uses his/her time to accomplish his/her job tasks (e.g., does not wait until the last minute to work on important projects).

**Meeting schedules**—extent to which the employee efficiently completes his/her work and effectively meets deadlines.

**Punctuality**—extent to which the employee is prompt in reporting for work and assignments/appointments at the specified time.

**Adaptability**—extent to which the employee can adapt to job or organizational changes.

**Willingness to learn**—extent to which the employee wants to learn about his/her job and asks intelligent questions about the job.

**Safety**—extent to which the employee follows established safety practices and corrects unsafe work practices on the job.

**Favorable job attitude**—extent to which the employee displays interest and enthusiasm for his/her work and takes pride in a job well done.

**Job knowledge**—extent to which the employee knows the details of the job and follows the job procedures.

**Quantity of work**—extent to which the employee produces an amount of acceptable work to meet schedules over which he/she has control.

**Quality of work**—extent to which the employee neatly, thoroughly, and accurately completes job assignments according to established standards of quality.

**Attendance**—concerns whether the employee is at work each day.

**Relationship with the public**—extent to which the employee establishes good relationships with the public (e.g., being courteous and helpful).

**Judgment**—quality of work-related decisions made by the employee.

Source: University of South Carolina, Division of Human Resources-Employee Relations Office, Employee Performance Management System, http://hr.sc.edu/relations/epms.html (accessed June 16, 2007).

> ## The results of a performance appraisal become useful only when they are communicated, tactfully, to the employee and presented as a tool to allow the employee to grow and improve in his or her position and beyond.

are led by executives who are direct about the expected benefits as well as the challenges.[18] For example, at AAH Pharmaceuticals, one of Great Britain's largest pharmaceutical companies, traditional one-on-one performance evaluations had resulted in conflict, and suggestions for improvements were not always accepted. When the company began to adopt a 360-degree appraisal approach, managers noticed that employees were more likely to accept criticism when it came from several different individuals.[19]

Whether the assessment is objective or subjective, it is vital that the manager discuss the results with the employee, so that the employee knows how well he or she is doing the job. The results of a performance appraisal become useful only when they are communicated, tactfully, to the employee and presented as a tool to allow the employee to grow and improve in his or her position and beyond. Performance appraisals are also used to determine whether an employee should be promoted, transferred, or terminated from the organization.

# DESTINATION CEO

**Jack Welch—Winning Advice** For two decades, Jack Welch was at the helm of the most admired company in the world—GE. Now that he is retired, he and his wife Susan, have written the book *Winning*.

Welch's secret for success, he says, is recruiting and hiring people who are smarter than he is and who have a lot of energy, those with an edge and who can be energized to pursue the goals of the company. Welch describes three categories of employees—the top performers, the middle 70 percent, and the "others." Success, he says is about maintaining the energy of the top performers. When asked how he motivates the middle 70 percent, he says that his approach is controversial. Welch maintains that it is important for that group to know what it takes for them to move up in the organization. Welch believes that it is important for all members of the organization to know where they stand. As for the "other" group, he says that more often than not, they will move on. Welch firmly believes that the job of the leader is to focus on the followers—not on your own success.

The most exciting thing about being a manager or a leader is helping people to grow and providing them the opportunity to change

their lives. The hardest part, he says, is letting people go. Overall, however, it is important that no one in the organization is ever surprised about their performance review. Constant feedback, letting people know where they stand, is the most important role of the manager. In short, Welch says that once you are a manager, "It's about them, not about you."

## >>DISCUSSION QUESTIONS

1. According to Welch, what is the most important aspect of being a leader?

2. How does Welch deal with the bottom group of employees in an organization?

3. What is the most exciting thing about being a boss, according to Welch?

>>To see the complete video about Jack Welch, go to our Web site at **www.mhhe.com/FerrellIM** and look for the link to the Destination CEO videos.

● ● **L04**

Identify the types of turnover companies may experience, and explain why turnover is an important issue.

## Turnover

Turnover, which occurs when employees quit or are fired and must be replaced by new employees, results in lost productivity from the vacancy, fees to recruit replacement employees, management time devoted to interviewing, and training costs for new employees. Some companies are able to manage their employees more effectively to minimize turnover. Costco's turnover rate is 17 percent overall and just 6 percent after one year of employment, costing the company $244 million per year, or $3,628 per employee. Wal-Mart's Sam's Club has a turnover rate of 44 percent (about the national average) and costs Sam's Club nearly $612 million per year, which is roughly $5,274 per employee.[20] One cause of turnover is job dissatisfaction: Office romances that do not work out create job dissatisfaction and contribute to turnover and can contribute to disruption of daily work activities (see Figure 11.2). Part of the reason for this detachment may be overworked employees as a result of downsizing and a lack of training and advancement opportunities.[21] Of course, turnover is not always an unhappy occasion when its takes the form of a promotion or transfer.

A promotion is an advancement to a higher-level job with increased authority, responsibility, and pay. In some companies and most labor unions, seniority—the length of time a person has been with the company or at a particular job classification—is the key issue in determining who should be promoted. Most managers base promotions on seniority only when they have candidates with equal qualifications: Managers prefer to base promotions on merit.

A transfer is a move to another job within the company at essentially the same level and wage. Transfers allow workers to obtain new skills or to find a new position within an organization when their old position has been eliminated because of automation or downsizing.

Separations occur when employees resign, retire, are terminated, or are laid off. Table 11.5 lists some guidelines for employees leaving the organization. Employees may be terminated, or fired, for poor performance, violation of work rules, absenteeism, and so on. Businesses have traditionally been able to fire employees *at will,* that is, for any reason other than for race, religion, sex, or age, or because an employee is a union organizer. However, recent legislation and court decisions now require that companies fire employees fairly, for just cause only. Managers must take care, then, to warn employees when their performance is unacceptable and may lead to dismissal. They should also document all problems and warnings in employees' work records. To avoid the possibility of lawsuits from individuals who may feel they have been fired unfairly, employers should provide clear, business-related reasons for any firing, supported by written documentation if possible. Employee disciplinary procedures should be carefully explained to all employees and should be set forth in employee handbooks.

Many companies have downsized in recent years, laying off tens of thousands of employees in their effort to become more productive and competitive. Motorola, for example, cut 7,500 jobs, which represented more than 11 percent of its 66,000 workforce. The company projected it would save $400 million from the layoffs.[22] In the last three years, some 300,000 U.S. jobs have been outsourced to overseas firms with lower labor costs.[23] Layoffs are sometimes temporary; employees may be brought back when business conditions improve. When layoffs are to be permanent, employers often help employees find

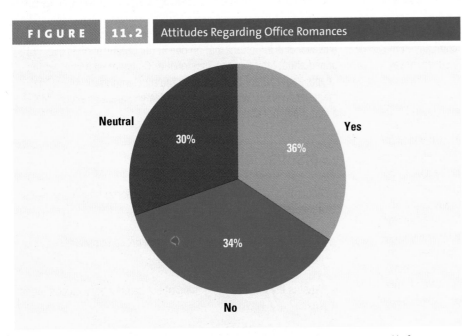

| FIGURE | 11.2 | Attitudes Regarding Office Romances |

Neutral 30%

Yes 36%

No 34%

Do you think that openly dating a co-worker would jeopardize your job security or advancement opportunities?

Source: "Workers Split on Office Romance," *USA Today Snapshots,* February 14, 2006, p. B1.

**TABLE 11.5** What to Avoid When Leaving Your Job

1. Don't use this as an opportunity to get emotional and say negative things about your boss or co-workers.
2. Don't damage or steal any company property, physical or intellectual.
3. Make sure that you secure the appropriate references before leaving.
4. Don't share negative sentiments with your replacement.
5. When interviewing for your next job, be careful not to be negative toward your previous employer.

Source: Adapted from Dawn Rosenberg McKay, "Things Not to Do When You Leave Your Job," http://careerplanning.about.com/od/jobseparation/a/leave_mistakes.htm (accessed June 16, 2007).

other jobs and may extend benefits while the employees search for new employment. Such actions help lessen the trauma of the layoffs.

A well-organized human resources department strives to minimize losses due to separations and transfers because recruiting and training new employees is very expensive. Note that a high turnover rate in a company may signal problems either with the selection and training process, the compensation program, or even the type of company. To help reduce turnover, companies have tried a number of strategies. Levi Strauss & Company, for example, provides emergency grants or loans of up to $1,000 to help employees confronted with a car that won't start, a sick child, or other unexpected financial hardship. Kraft Foods allows U.S. workers to share jobs, swap shifts, or to take annual vacations in one-hour increments to

**TABLE 11.6** Retention Considerations for Employers

1. Treat your employees as valued clients or customers
2. Keep your employees informed about the strategy and vision of the organization.
3. Strong retention strategies become strong recruiting advantages.
4. Retention is much more effective when you put the right person into the right job. Know the job, and try to understand your employees' motivation.
5. Money is important, but it is not the only reason people stay with an organization.
6. Employee committees to help develop retention strategies can be a valuable way to focus on key and relevant issues.
7. Management must believe in the value of retention strategies.
8. Recognition, in various forms, is a powerful retention strategy.
9. Remember, fun in the workplace is very important to many employees.
10. Know your competitors' benefit packages. Keep current and ahead of the pack to retain the best employees.

Source: Adapted from L. John Mason, "Top Ten Retention Strategies from the Stress Education Center, http://www.dstress.com/Retention.Art.htm (accessed June 16, 2007).

● **WAGE/SALARY SURVEY** a study that tells a company how much compensation comparable firms are paying for specific jobs that the firms have in common

● **WAGES** financial rewards based on the number of hours the employee works or the level of output achieved

help them deal with family emergencies. CVS offers simulated work experience to support new employees coming off welfare who have never held a traditional job.[24] Table 11.6 Shows considerations for owners and managers in retaining and motivating their employees.

 **LO5**

Specify the various ways a worker may be compensated.

# COMPENSATING THE WORKFORCE

People don't work for free, and how much they are paid for their work is a complicated issue. Also, designing a fair compensation plan is an important task because pay and benefits represent a substantial portion of an organization's expenses. Wages that are too high may result in the company's products being priced too high, making them uncompetitive in the market. Wages that are too low may damage employee morale and result in costly turnover. Remember that compensation is one of the hygiene factors identified by Herzberg.

Designing a fair compensation plan is a difficult task because it involves evaluating the relative worth of all jobs within the business while allowing for individual efforts. Compensation for a specific job is typically determined through a **wage/salary survey,** which tells the company how much compensation comparable firms are paying for specific jobs that the firms have in common. Compensation for individuals within a specific job category depends on both the compensation for that job and the individual's productivity. Therefore, two employees with identical jobs may not receive exactly the same pay because of individual differences in performance.

## Financial Compensation

Financial compensation falls into two general categories—wages and salaries. **Wages** are financial rewards based on the number of hours the employee works or the level of output achieved. Wages based on the number of hours worked are called time wages. A cook at Denny's, for example, might earn $5.15 per hour, the minimum wage. The minimum wage had been $5.15 for many years. President Bush signed legislation increasing the minimum wage a total of $2.10 over a three-year period. By the summer of 2008, a 70-cent increase makes the minimum wage $6.55 per hour, and the final increase of 70 cents will put the new minimum wage at $7.25 per hour by summer

**TABLE 11.7**  Managing the Workforce: Costco versus Wal-Mart

| | Costco | Wal-Mart |
|---|---|---|
| Number of employees | 86,900—U.S. | 1.3 million—U.S. |
| | 118,800—international | 1.9 million—international |
| Sales | $51.9 billion | $312.4 billion |
| Average hourly wage | $16.00 | $9.68 |
| Percent of employees covered by health plans | 82% | 48% |
| Turnover (per year) | 24% | 50% |
| Profits per employee | $13,647 | $11,038 (Sam's Club—a division of Wal-Mart) |

Sources: "Costco Employment," www.priceviewer.com/costco/costco_employment.htm (accessed April 20, 2006); Moira Herbst, "The Costco Challenge: An Alternative to Wal-Martization?, July 5, 2005, www.laborresearch.org/print/pgh?id=319 (accessed April 20, 2006); Wal-Mart, Annual Report 2006, http://media/corporate-ir.net/media_files/irol/11/112761/2006_annual_report.pdf (accessed April 20, 2006); Costco, "Company Profile," http://phx.corporate-ir.net/phoenix.zhtml?c_83830&p=irol-homeprofile (accessed April 20, 2006).

of 2009.[26] Roughly one-fourth of the U.S. workforce earns an income below the weighted poverty line for a family of four.[27] Table 11.7 compares wage and other information for Costco and Wal-Mart, two well-known discount chains. Time wages are appropriate when employees are continually interrupted and when quality is more important than quantity. Assembly-line workers, clerks, and maintenance personnel are commonly paid on a time-wage basis. The advantage of time wages is the ease of computation. The disadvantage is that time wages provide no incentive to increase productivity. In fact, time wages may encourage employees to do less than a full day's work.

To overcome these disadvantages, many companies pay on an incentive system, using piece wages or commissions. Piece wages are based on the level of output achieved. A major advantage of piece wages is that they motivate employees to supervise their own activities and to increase output. Skilled craftworkers are often paid on a piece-wage basis. At Longaberger, the world's largest maker of handmade baskets, weavers are paid per piece. The 2,500 workers produced 40,000 baskets a day, but productivity varied by as much as 400 percent among the weavers. A team of basket makers was assembled to try to improve productivity and reduce weaver downtime and the amount of leftover materials. After studying the basket makers for 19 days, the team's suggestions were implemented. The changes resulted in $3 million in annual savings for the company.[28]

# Ford: A New Perspective

Following in the wake of General Motors and alongside DaimlerChrysler, Ford Motor Company is downsizing and looking to restructure. This move came as Ford announced that it lost $1.6 billion (before taxes) on North American operations in 2005. The company has been declining in popularity for some time now, selling 4.7 percent fewer cars in 2005 than in the previous year. As an attempt to breathe life back into the automotive giant, Ford has said it will close 14 factories and cut around 30,000 jobs. The company plans to make these changes over the course of six years. As of now, five factories are set to close—other closures will be announced over time.

In addition to cutbacks, Ford plans to change its corporate culture. Mark Fields, leader of Ford's North American operations and the man partly responsible for turning around Ford at Mazda Corp. and Ford of Europe, says Ford needs to change the way it does business: Rather than continuing its conservative, stuck-in-a-rut ways, the company needs to become accountable and willing to change—to think like a small, startup company. Some of the changes the company plans to make are creating more hybrid cars, developing small cars that capture the consumers' interest and imagination, and reducing sticker prices so that they are in line with what consumers actually pay.

Although Ford has plans to improve its impact on the North American market, the company still has to deal with the impact this restructuring will have on its workers. Ford will be cutting about 25 percent of its 122,000 North American workforce, including a 10 percent cut in salaried positions and a 12 percent cut among executives. Cutting workers will cost Ford in a number of ways. In addition to the buyouts, attrition, layoffs, and reductions of contracts that Ford will have to deal with regarding salaried workers, Ford is going to have a tough job dealing with the United Auto Workers (UAW) union. Ford's unionized workers are covered by the JOBS Bank program. Under this program, workers whose jobs are cut still receive full pay and benefits. Unless Ford can get the UAW to agree to its cuts, Ford will not save money by closing factories and eliminating jobs. Ford's current contract with the UAW is up in 2007, and analysts point out that Ford's current move to downsize is only going to make 2007 negotiations more challenging.

Ford executives are confident that they can turn things around by 2008 and cite turnarounds in Mazda and Ford of Europe as proof that they're taking the correct steps to make this happen. Although Ford sees the optimistic promise of the future, workers in all but five factories must simply wait to find out if and when they will lose their jobs. The auto industry and the UAW will certainly have their eyes on Ford over the next few years.[25] ❖

## Q: Discussion Questions

1. Why is it so difficult to downsize by cutting the workforce at Ford?

2. Do you think Ford is being fair to its employees that it must lay off?

3. How can a company avoid layoffs in managing its workforce?

● COMMISSION an incentive system that pays a fixed amount or a percentage of the employee's sales

● SALARY a financial reward calculated on a weekly, monthly, or annual basis

● BONUSES monetary rewards offered by companies for exceptional performance as incentives to further increase productivity

● PROFIT SHARING a form of compensation whereby a percentage of company profits is distributed to the employees whose work helped to generate them

● BENEFITS nonfinancial forms of compensation provided to employees, such as pension plans, health insurance, paid vacation and holidays, and the like

The other incentive system, commission, pays a fixed amount or a percentage of the employee's sales. Karen Sabatini is an automobile salesperson at a Lincoln Mercury dealership in Garden City, Michigan, just 15 minutes away from Ford's world headquarters. In one year, Sabatini grossed almost $200,000, compared with $40,000 for the average auto salesperson. She earns $250–$300 for every Mercury and $350–$500 for every Lincoln she sells to a Ford employee. She makes $150–$225 on any sale to a non-Ford employee.[29] This method motivates employees to sell as much as they can. Some companies combine payment based on commission with time wages or salaries.

A salary is a financial reward calculated on a weekly, monthly, or annual basis. Salaries are associated with white-collar workers such as office personnel, executives, and professional employees. Although a salary provides a stable stream of income, salaried workers may be required to work beyond usual hours without additional financial compensation.

WHEN EMPLOYEES ARE HAPPY WITH THEIR 401(K) PLAN, IT SHOWS. They work harder and stay with you longer. We should know. As the nation's 401(k) leader, we've been helping growing businesses and their employees secure their financial futures for over 50 years. No wonder more companies choose The Principal® for their 401(k) plans.* Investment options, recordkeeping, loan services, plan member education and asset allocation—we've got what you need, plus personalized service and local support to make the process easy. What's not to love? If you'd like to hear what a 401(k) plan from The Principal can do for your employees, call 1-800-986-3343 (ext. 80080). One of our representatives will be happy to help, no matter what you're wearing. WE UNDERSTAND WHAT YOU'RE WORKING FOR℠

Principal Financial Group

www.principal.com

The Principal Financial Group promotes the advantages of its group benefits plan.

In addition to the basic wages or salaries paid to employees, a company may offer bonuses for exceptional performance as an incentive to increase productivity further. Many workers receive a bonus as a "thank you" for good work and an incentive to continue working hard. Many owners and managers are recognizing that simple bonuses and perks foster happier employees and reduce turnover. For example, the owner of Ticketcity.com, a small business in Austin, Texas, offers employees tickets to major events like the Super Bowl, Master's golf tournament, and even management retreats. The owner of a DreamMaker remodeling franchise in Peoria, Illinois, provides employees money to use toward new vehicles, takes them on staff outings to sporting games, and funds their retirement plans.[30]

Another form of compensation is profit sharing, which distributes a percentage of company profits to the employees whose work helped to generate those profits. Some profit-sharing plans involve distributing shares of company stock to employees. Usually referred to as ESOPs—employee stock ownership plans—they have been gaining popularity in recent years. One reason for the popularity of ESOPs is the sense of partnership that they create between the organization and employees. Profit sharing can also motivate employees to work hard, because increased productivity and sales mean that the profits or the stock dividends will increase. Many organizations offer employees a stake in the company through stock purchase plans, ESOPs, or stock investments through 401(k) plans. Employees below senior management levels rarely received stock options, until recently. Companies are adopting broad-based stock option plans to build a stronger link between employees' interests and the organization's interests. A study by professors at the Wharton School of the University of Pennsylvania found that companies that paid middle managers 20 percent more in options than comparable companies saw increased performance and stock prices that rose an average 5 percent faster a year. Similar results were seen in companies that paid technical specialists at least 20 percent more in options.[31] Table 11.8 provides the salary of college basketball coaches. Florida college basketball coach, Billy Donovan, won the 2007 NCAA National Championship and earned $1.6 million in annual salary.

## Benefits

Benefits are nonfinancial forms of compensation provided to employees, such as pension plans for retirement; health, disability, and life insurance; holidays and paid days off for vacation or illness; credit union membership; health programs; child care; elder care; assistance with adoption; and more. According to the Bureau of Labor Statistics, employer costs for employee compensation for civilian workers in the United

**TABLE 11.8** Salary of 15 College Basketball Coaches

| School | Coach | Salary | W−L | Percentage |
|---|---|---|---|---|
| Marquette University | Tom Crean | $1,655,819 | 163–84 | .660 |
| Vanderbilt University | Kevin Stallings | 1,339,643 | 142–105 | .575 |
| Duke University | Mike Krzyzewski | 1,200,000 | 702–199 | .779 |
| Northwestern University | Bill Carmody | 1,132,965 | 95–111 | .461 |
| Creighton University | Dana Altman | 937,714 | 257–140 | .647 |
| Boston College | Al Skinner | 592,093 | 194–117 | .624 |
| University of Dayton | Brian Gregory | 484,342 | 73–48 | .603 |
| University of Notre Dame | Mike Brey | 467,203 | 140–76 | .648 |
| Georgetown University | John Thompson, III | 449,054 | 132–71 | .650 |
| Baylor University | Scott Drew | 413,612 | 34–67 | .337 |
| Texas Christian University | Neil Dougherty | 379,487 | 65–80 | .448 |
| Syracuse University | Jim Boeheim | 377,387 | 724–249 | .744 |
| George Washington University | Karl Hobbs | 351,455 | 110–64 | .632 |
| DePaul University | Jerry Wainwright | 300,000 | 29–27 | .518 |
| Fordham University | Dereck Whittenburg | 264,043 | 35–54 | .393 |

Source: Andrew Heck, "March Madness: College Basketball Coaches Paid by Your Donations," March 6, 2007; http://www.charitynavigator.org/index.cfm/bay/content.view/cpid/568.htm, accessed (June 16, 2007).

States average $24.59 per hour worked. Wages and salaries account for approximately 71.4 percent of those costs, while benefits account for 28.6 percent. Legally required benefits (Social Security, workers' compensation, and unemployment insurance) average $1.96 per hour, or 8 percent of total compensation.[32] Such benefits increase employee security and, to a certain extent, their morale and motivation.

The Survey of Unit Employment Practices (SULEP) People Report found that, among 75 restaurant industry companies, the average rate of employee turnover in companies that offer basic health, dental, or retirement benefits is 109 percent, compared with 136 percent for companies that do not offer any benefits to their employees.[33] Table 11.9 lists some of the benefits Internet search engine Google offers its employees. Although health insurance is a common benefit for full-time employees, rising health care costs have forced a growing number of employers to trim this benefit. Microsoft, for example, recently reduced its prescription drug benefit, which had cost the company 16 percent of

**TABLE 11.9** Google' Employee Benefits

- Health care for employee and family, plus onsite physician and dental care at Google headquarters in Mountain View, California, and its engineering center in Seattle, Washington
- Vacation days and holidays, and flexible work hours
- Maternity and parental leave; new moms and dads are also able to expense up to $500 for take-out meals during the first four weeks they are home with their new baby
- Employee referral bonus program
- Employee assistance services for personal issues; child care referrals; answers to financial and legal questions
- Learning opportunities and tuition reimbursement
- Adoption assistance
- Google Child Care Center, just five minutes from Google headquarters in Mountain View
- Backup child care helps California parents when their regularly scheduled child care falls through
- Free shuttle service to several San Francisco, East Bay, and South Bay locations
- Fuel Efficiency Vehicle Incentive Program
- Employee discounts
- Onsite dry cleaning, plus a coin-free laundry room in the Mountain View office

Source: "Google Benefits," http://www.google.com/support/jobs/bin/static.py?page=benefits.html (accessed June 16, 2007).

its overall benefit budget, and now requires employees to pay $40 for brand-name prescription drugs for which a generic version is available. The company still provides many generous benefits, including free gym memberships and free drinks on the job.[34]

A benefit increasingly offered is the employee assistance program (EAP). Each company's EAP is different, but most offer counseling for and assistance with those employees' personal problems that might hurt their job performance if not addressed. The most common counseling services offered include drug and alcohol-abuse treatment programs, fitness programs, smoking cessation clinics, stress-management clinics, financial counseling, family counseling, and career counseling. EAPs help reduce costs associated with poor productivity, absenteeism, and other workplace issues by helping employees deal with personal problems that contribute to these issues. For example, exercise and fitness programs reduce health insurance costs by helping employees stay healthy. Family counseling may help workers trying to cope with a divorce or other personal problems better focus on their jobs.

● **LABOR UNIONS** employee organizations formed to deal with employers for achieving better pay, hours, and working conditions

● **COLLECTIVE BARGAINING** the negotiation process through which management and unions reach an agreement about compensation, working hours, and working conditions for the bargaining unit

themselves into labor unions to deal with employers and to achieve better pay, hours, and working conditions. Organized employees are backed by the power of a large group that can hire specialists to represent the entire union in its dealings with management. The United Auto Workers, for example, has considerable power in its negotiations with Ford Motor Company and General Motors. Unionized blue-collar workers make 54 percent more than their nonunionized counterparts and are twice as likely to have health insurance and pension plans.[35]

However, union growth has slowed in recent years, and prospects for growth do not look good. One reason is that most blue-collar workers, the traditional members of unions,

> ## "The most common counseling services offered include drug and alcohol-abuse treatment programs, fitness programs, smoking cessation clinics, stress-management clinics, financial counseling, family counseling, and career counseling."

Companies try to provide the benefits they believe their employees want, but diverse people may want different things. In recent years, some single workers have felt that co-workers with spouses and children seem to get "special breaks" and extra time off to deal with family issues. Some companies use flexible benefit programs to allow employees to choose the benefits they would like, up to a specified amount. Over the last two decades, the list of fringe benefits has grown dramatically, and new benefits are being added every year.

 **LO6**

Discuss some of the issues associated with unionized employees, including collective bargaining and dispute resolution.

# MANAGING UNIONIZED EMPLOYEES

Employees who are dissatisfied with their working conditions or compensation have to negotiate with management to bring about change. Dealing with management on an individual basis is not always effective, however, so employees may organize

have already been organized. Factories have become more automated and need fewer blue-collar workers. The United States has shifted from a manufacturing to a service economy, further reducing the demand for blue-collar workers. Moreover, in response to foreign competition, U.S. companies are scrambling to find ways to become more productive and cost efficient. Job enrichment programs and participative management have blurred the line between management and workers. Because workers' say in the way plants are run is increasing, their need for union protection is decreasing.

Nonetheless, labor unions have been successful in organizing blue-collar manufacturing, government, and health care workers, as well as smaller percentages of employees in other industries. In fact, 12.9 percent of all employed Americans are represented by a union.[36] Consequently, significant aspects of HRM, particularly compensation, are dictated to a large degree by union contracts at many companies. Therefore, we'll take a brief look at collective bargaining and dispute resolution in this section.

## Collective Bargaining

Collective bargaining is the negotiation process through which management and unions reach an agreement about compensation, working hours, and working conditions for the bargaining unit (Figure 11.3). The objective of negotiations is to reach agreement about a **labor contract,** the formal, written document that spells out the relationship between the union and management for a specified period of time, usually two or three years.

In collective bargaining, each side tries to negotiate an agreement that meets its demands; compromise is frequently necessary. Management tries to negotiate a labor contract that permits the company to retain control over things like work schedules; the hiring and firing of workers; production standards;

promotions, transfers, and separations; the span of management in each department; and discipline. Unions tend to focus on contract issues such as magnitude of wages; better pay rates for overtime, holidays, and undesirable shifts; scheduling of pay increases; and benefits. These issues will be spelled out in the labor contract, which union members will vote to either accept (and abide by) or reject.

Many labor contracts contain a *cost-of-living escalator clause (COLA),* which calls for automatic wage increases during periods of inflation to protect the "real" income of the employees. During tough economic times, unions may be forced to accept *givebacks*—wage and benefit concessions made to employers to allow them to remain competitive or, in some cases, to survive and continue to provide jobs for union workers.

## Resolving Disputes

Sometimes, management and labor simply cannot agree on a contract. Most labor disputes are handled through collective bargaining or through grievance procedures. When these processes break down, however, either side may resort to more drastic measures to achieve its objectives.

**labor tactics.** Picketing is a public protest against management practices and involves union members marching (often waving antimanagement signs and placards) at the employer's plant. Picketing workers hope that their signs will arouse sympathy for their demands from the public and from other unions. Picketing may occur as a protest or in conjunction with a strike.

Strikes (employee walkouts) are one of the most effective weapons labor has. By striking, a union makes carrying out the normal operations of a business difficult at best and impossible at worst. Strikes receive widespread publicity, but they remain a weapon of last resort. In California, members of the United Food and Commercial Workers (UFCW) went on strike against Albertson's, Ralph's, and Von's supermarkets after they failed to reach agreement on a new contract. The

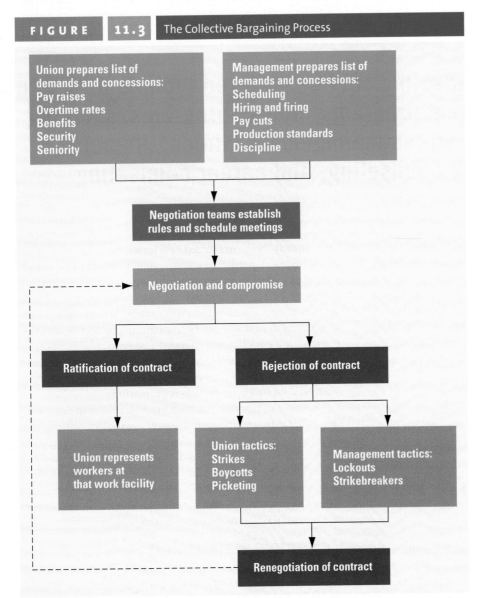

**FIGURE 11.3** The Collective Bargaining Process

Union prepares list of demands and concessions:
Pay raises
Overtime rates
Benefits
Security
Seniority

Management prepares list of demands and concessions:
Scheduling
Hiring and firing
Pay cuts
Production standards
Discipline

Negotiation teams establish rules and schedule meetings

Negotiation and compromise

Ratification of contract

Rejection of contract

Union represents workers at that work facility

Union tactics:
Strikes
Boycotts
Picketing

Management tactics:
Lockouts
Strikebreakers

Renegotiation of contract

● **LOCKOUT** management's version of a strike, wherein a work site is closed so that employees cannot go to work

● **STRIKEBREAKERS** people hired by management to replace striking employees; called "scabs" by striking union members

● **CONCILIATION** a method of outside resolution of labor and management differences in which a third party is brought in to keep the two sides talking

● **MEDIATION** a method of outside resolution of labor and management differences in which the third party's role is to suggest or propose a solution to the problem

● **ARBITRATION** settlement of a labor/management dispute by a third party whose solution is legally binding and enforceable

strike, which cost the companies millions of dollars in lost sales and the striking employees significant lost wages, ended when members agreed to ratify a new contract that gave them bonuses but required them to pay for health insurance for the first time.[37] The threat of a strike is often enough to get management to back down. In fact, the number of worker-days actually lost to strikes is less than the amount lost to the common cold.

A boycott is an attempt to keep people from purchasing the products of a company. In a boycott, union members are asked not to do business with the boycotted organization. Some unions may even impose fines on members who ignore the boycott. To gain further

*A strike by New York City's transit workers in the winter of 2005 shut down the transit system and left commuters battling their way home in the cold.*

support for their objectives, a union involved in a boycott may also ask the public—through picketing and advertising—not to purchase the products of the picketed firm.

**management tactics.** Management's version of a strike is the lockout; management actually closes a work site so that employees cannot go to work. Lockouts are used, as a general rule, only when a union strike has partially shut down a plant and it seems less expensive for the plant to close completely. In 2005, 22 major work stoppages involving 1,200 or more employees participating in strikes and lockouts idled 99,600 workers with 1.7 million lost workdays.

Strikebreakers, called "scabs" by striking union members, are people hired by management to replace striking employees. Managers hire strikebreakers to continue operations and reduce the losses associated with strikes—and to show the unions that they will not bow to their demands. Strikebreaking is generally a last-resort measure for management because it does great damage to the relationship between management and labor.

**outside resolution.** Management and union members normally reach mutually agreeable decisions without outside assistance. Sometimes though, even after lengthy negotiations, strikes, lockouts, and other tactics, management and labor still cannot resolve a contract dispute. In such cases, they have three choices: conciliation, mediation, and arbitration. Conciliation brings in a neutral third party to keep labor and management talking. The conciliator has no formal power over

union representatives or over management. The conciliator's goal is to get both parties to focus on the issues and to prevent negotiations from breaking down. Like conciliation, mediation involves bringing in a neutral third party, but the mediator's role is to suggest or propose a solution to the problem. Mediators have no formal power over either labor or management. With arbitration, a neutral third party is brought in to settle the dispute, but the arbitrator's solution is legally binding and enforceable. Generally, arbitration takes place on a voluntary basis—management and labor must agree to it, and they usually split the cost (the arbitrator's fee and expenses) between them. Occasionally, management and labor submit to *compulsory arbitration,* in which an outside party (usually the federal government) requests arbitration as a means of eliminating a prolonged strike that threatens to disrupt the economy.

## ●● L07

Describe the importance of diversity in the workforce.

# THE IMPORTANCE OF WORKFORCE DIVERSITY

Customers, employees, suppliers—all the participants in the world of business—come in different ages, genders, races, ethnicities, nationalities, and abilities, a truth that business has come

● **DIVERSITY** the participation of different ages, genders, races, ethnicities, nationalities, and abilities in the workplace

to label **diversity.** Understanding this diversity means recognizing and accepting differences as well as valuing the unique perspectives such differences can bring to the workplace.

## The Characteristics of Diversity

When managers speak of diverse workforces, they typically mean differences in gender and race. While gender and race are important characteristics of diversity, others are also important. We can divide these differences into primary and secondary characteristics of diversity. In the lower segment of Figure 11.4, age, gender, race, ethnicity, abilities, and sexual orientation

represent *primary characteristics* of diversity which are inborn and cannot be changed. In the upper section of Figure 11.4 are eight *secondary characteristics* of diversity—work background, income, marital status, military experience, religious beliefs, geographic location, parental status, and education—which *can* be changed. We acquire, change, and discard them as we progress through our lives.

Defining characteristics of diversity as either primary or secondary enhances our understanding, but we must remember that each person is defined by the interrelation of all characteristics. In dealing with diversity in the workforce, managers must consider the complete person—not one or a few of a person's differences.

> # Once dominated by white men, today's workforce includes significantly more women, African Americans, Hispanics, and other minorities, as well as disabled and older workers.

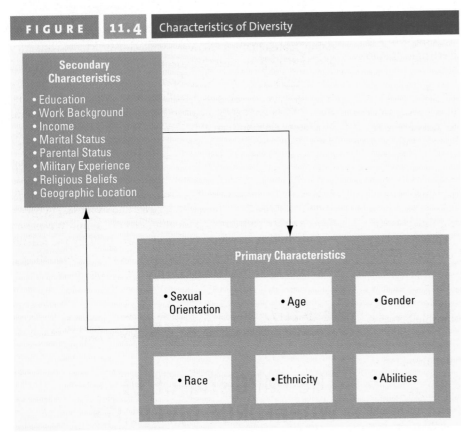

| FIGURE | 11.4 | Characteristics of Diversity |

**Secondary Characteristics**
- Education
- Work Background
- Income
- Marital Status
- Parental Status
- Military Experience
- Religious Beliefs
- Geographic Location

**Primary Characteristics**
- Sexual Orientation
- Age
- Gender
- Race
- Ethnicity
- Abilities

Source: Marilyn Loden and Judy B. Rosener, *Workforce America! Managing Employee Diversity as a Vital Resource,* 1991, p. 20. Used with permission. Copyright © 1991 The McGraw-Hill Companies.

## Why Is Diversity Important?

The U.S. workforce is becoming increasingly diverse. Once dominated by white men, today's workforce includes significantly more women, African Americans, Hispanics, and other minorities, as well as disabled and older workers. By 2010, women's share of the labor force will increase to 47.9 percent.[38] Table 11.10 presents some of the population data from the Census Bureau. It is estimated that within the next 50 years, Hispanics will represent 24 percent of the population, while African Americans and Asians/Pacific Islanders will comprise 15 percent and 9 percent, respectively.[39] These groups have traditionally faced discrimination and higher unemployment rates and have been denied opportunities to assume leadership roles in corporate America. Consequently, more and more companies are trying to improve HRM programs to recruit, develop, and retain more diverse employees to better serve their diverse customers. Some firms are providing special programs

**TABLE 11.10** Population by Race (in thousands)

| Ethnic Group | Total | Increase from 2000 to 2004 |
|---|---|---|
| Total population | 293,655.4 (100%) | 4.3% |
| White | 236,057.8 (80.4%) | 3.5 |
| Hispanic or Latino | 41,870.7 (14.5%) | 2.0 |
| Black or African American | 37,502.3 (12.8%) | 5.0 |
| American Indian and Alaska Native | 2,824.8 (1.0%) | 6.0 |
| Asian | 12,326.2 (4.2%) | 16.4 |
| Native Hawaiian and Other Pacific Islander | 505.6 (0.2%) | 9.3 |

Source: "Population by Race and Hispanic Origin: 2000 and 2004," U.S. Census Bureau, Population Estimates Program, April 1, 2000, and July 1, 2004, www.census.gov/population/pop-profile/dynamic/RACEHO.pdf (accessed May 15, 2006).

such as sponsored affinity groups, mentoring programs, and special career development opportunities. At US West, each manager's contributions to the company's diversity efforts are measured by a 16-point scorecard called the Diversity Accountability Tool. Managers use the scorecard to rate their own efforts to foster diversity and then explain their score in a meeting with the company's CEO. The manager receives an official diversity score that is one factor in determining the manager's annual bonus. Since the program was instituted, scores have jumped 60 percent.[40] Table 11.11 shows the top 10 companies for minorities according to a study by *Fortune*. Effectively managing diversity in the workforce involves cultivating and valuing its benefits and minimizing its problems.

## The Benefits of Workforce Diversity

There are a number of benefits to fostering and valuing workforce diversity, including the following:

1. More productive use of a company's human resources.

2. Reduced conflict among employees of different ethnicities, races, religions, and sexual orientations as they learn to respect each other's differences.

3. More productive working relationships among diverse employees as they learn more about and accept each other.

## Ursula Burns—She's No Carbon Copy!

There is no misunderstanding or underestimating Ursula Burns, Xerox's president of Business Group Operations and one of the company's most respected executives. A child of the projects in New York City, Burns began working at Xerox in 1980 as a summer intern after graduating with her master's degree in engineering from Columbia University. From there, she became executive assistant to a previous Xerox CEO, Paul Allaire. Now, as president of Business Group Operations, Burns heads engineering, product development, manufacturing, the supply chain, global purchasing, and research and development—just about everything. Those in her field speculate that she may be the natural successor to current CEO, Anne Mulcahy. There is no doubt that she is respected and knowledgeable in her field. In fact, she was recently featured in *Fortune* magazine's article, "Star Power: Meet 12 Executives Who Are Poised to Become the Next Great CEOs."

Burns's rise through the ranks has been no mistake or free ride; she has earned her position by taking risks along the way. As executive assistant to Paul Allaire, Burns attended a number of high-level meetings.

At one, held to discuss potential changes in the employee benefits policy, she raised her hand and let the executives in attendance know that not only were the policy changes not clear but that they sounded undesirable. Rather than being reprimanded for speaking out, Burns's comments were taken into consideration. Speaking out and receiving a positive response helped her approach her career with confidence. Although not being afraid to speak up is one of the traits Burns has used to good effect to get where she is today, she has also learned when to be quiet and let others do the talking—part of what makes her such a good leader.

Further evidence of Burns's willingness to take risks is the fact that in 2001, while Xerox looked into the face of bankruptcy, Burns managed one of the critical facets that ultimately resulted in the company's turnaround. She simultaneously facilitated a contract discussion with Xerox's unionized workers in Rochester, New York, while looking into the possibility of outsourcing those very jobs—a situation most people would never want to face. And Burns did this while recovering from emergency surgery.

Now Burns is spearheading projects to bring Xerox to the forefront of color printing, a sector accounting for about 35 percent of the company's revenue. She is also working toward growing the company's overall revenue by 5 percent, a more difficult challenge than it may appear to be. Although Burns, who is also the mother of two, may be viewed as successor to the CEO, she is content where she is and is happy to continue her career at Xerox for years to come.[41] ❖

## Q: Discussion Questions

1. How has Ursula Burns used her knowledge of technology to leverage her career with Xerox?

2. What do you think are Burns's personal characteristics that have made her so successful in her position at Xerox?

3. Why do you think *Fortune* magazine believes that Burns is poised to become a chief executive officer in the future?

4. Increased commitment to and sharing of organizational goals among diverse employees at all organizational levels.

5. Increased innovation and creativity as diverse employees bring new, unique perspectives to decision-making and problem-solving tasks.

6. Increased ability to serve the needs of an increasingly diverse customer base.[42]

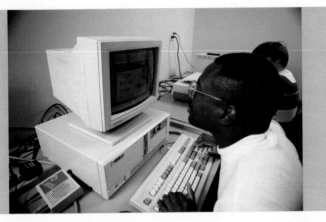

*Technology solutions can make the difference for the visually impaired, enabling them to operate computers and making the workplace more diverse.*

Companies that do not value their diverse employees are likely to experience greater conflict, as well as prejudice and discrimination. Among individual employees, for example, racial slurs and gestures, sexist comments, and other behaviors by co-workers harm the individuals at whom such behavior is directed. The victims of such behavior may feel hurt, depressed, or even threatened and suffer from lowered self-esteem, all of which harm their productivity and morale. In such cases, women and minority employees may simply leave the firm, wasting the time, money, and other resources spent on hiring and training them. When discrimination comes from a supervisor, employees may

**TABLE 11.11**  Top 20 Companies for Diversity

1. Bank of America
2. Pepsi Bottling Group
3. AT&T
4. The Coca-Cola Co.
5. Ford Motor Co.
6. Verizon Communications
7. Xerox Corporation
8. Consolidated Edison Co. of New York
9. JPMorgan Chase
10. PepsiCo
11. Wachovia
12. PricewaterhouseCoopers
13. Sodexho
14. Procter & Gamble
15. Blue Cross and Blue Shield of Florida
16. Novartis Pharmaceutical Corp.
17. Johnson & Johnson
18. Merck & Co.
19. Deloitte & Touche USA
20. Wells Fargo

Source: The 2007 Diversity Inc., "Top 50 Companies for Diversity," http://www.diversityinc.com/public/1595.cfm (accessed June 15, 2007).

*all* their diverse employees as well as the needs of the firm itself. They realize that the benefits of diversity are long term in nature and come only to those organizations willing to make the commitment. Most importantly, as workforce diversity becomes a valued organizational asset, companies spend less time managing conflict and more time accomplishing tasks and satisfying customers, which is, after all, the purpose of business.

## Affirmative Action

Many companies strive to improve their working environment through affirmative action programs, legally mandated plans that try to increase job opportunities for minority groups by analyzing the current pool of workers, identifying

> **"Companies that do not value their diverse employees are likely to experience greater conflict, as well as prejudice and discrimination."**

also fear for their jobs. A discriminatory atmosphere not only can harm productivity and increase turnover, but it may also subject a firm to costly lawsuits and negative publicity.

Astute businesses recognize that they need to modify their human resources management programs to target the needs of

areas where women and minorities are underrepresented, and establishing specific hiring and promotion goals along with target dates for meeting those goals to resolve the discrepancy. Affirmative action began in 1965 as Lyndon B. Johnson issued the first of a series of presidential directives. It was designed to

That's the big question everyone wants to know, whether considering future career options or a specific job in a particular company. While you're not likely to make as much as Donald Trump or Katie Couric, the potential for big bucks is out there, depending on your choice of career, the organization you ultimately work for, *and* how hard you are willing to work.

Experts suggest that you need to earn four times your age ($140,000/year for a 35-year-old, for example) if you want to be able to own a nice house and car, send your kids to college, stay ahead of inflation, and save for a comfortable retirement. Most people never come close to that yardstick, however. The median income for a full-time worker who has a bachelor's degree is $40,415 for women and $56,334 for men.

Clearly, some jobs pay a lot more than others. A CEO of a large corporation can earn millions in salary, benefits, and bonuses; while at the other end of the scale, a preschool teacher might earn just $12,000. Business management, engineers, health professionals, and technology specialists are all hot careers, in terms of both growth potential and pay.

Listed here are some human resource jobs and the median annual income for each:

| | |
|---|---|
| Labor relations manager | $107,900 |
| Compensation manager | $ 97,800 |
| Human resources manager | $ 91,400 |
| Benefits manager | $ 85,500 |
| Training manager | $ 78,200 |
| Payroll manager | $ 70,800 |

But for many people, money isn't everything. Remember Herzberg's motivation factors? Benefits, job security, desirable working hours, and a satisfying work environment are some of the factors that can help make up for a job that doesn't put you in the same tax bracket as Brad Pitt. The preschool teacher may find molding young minds for $12,000 just as satisfying as the challenge the millionaire CEO enjoys in running a company. And, with companies increasingly opting for limited pay raises in favor of bonuses tied to performance, people working in even fairly low-paying jobs can find themselves earning good money for hard work. The bottom line is that you have to decide what's important to you and go for it.[43]

make up for past hiring and promotion prejudices, to overcome workplace discrimination, and to provide equal employment opportunities for blacks and whites. Since then, minorities have made solid gains.

Legislation passed in 1991 reinforces affirmative action but prohibits organizations from setting hiring quotas that might result in reverse discrimination. Reverse discrimination occurs when a company's policies force it to consider only minorities or women instead of concentrating on hiring the person who is best qualified. More companies are arguing that affirmative action stifles their ability to hire the best employees, regardless of their minority status. Because of these problems, affirmative action became politically questionable in the mid-1990s. ∎

**CHECK OUT**

www.mhhe.com/FerrellM

for study materials including Interactive Exercises, Quizzes, iPod downloads, and video.

# Build Your Business Plan

**Managing Human Resources**  Now is the time to start thinking about the employees you will need to hire to implement your business plan. What kinds of background/skills are you going to look for in potential employees? Are you going to require a certain amount of work experience?

When you are starting a business you are often only able to hire part-time employees because you cannot afford to pay the benefits for a full time employee. Remember at the end of the last chapter we discussed how important it is to think of ways to motivate your employees when you cannot afford to pay them what you would like.

You need to consider how you are going to recruit your employees. When you are first starting your business, it is often a good idea to ask people you respect (and not necessarily members of your family) for any recommendations of potential employees they might have. You probably won't be able to afford to advertise in the classifieds, so announcements in sources such as church bulletins or community bulletin boards should be considered as an excellent way to attract potential candidates with little, if any, investment.

Finally, you need to think about hiring employees from diverse backgrounds. Especially if you are considering targeting diverse segments. The more diverse your employees, the greater the chance you will be able to draw in diverse customers.

# customer-driven marketing

12

## ● ● learning OBJECTIVES

**LO1** Define marketing and describe the exchange process.

**LO2** Specify the functions of marketing.

**LO3** Explain the marketing concept and its implications for developing marketing strategies.

**LO4** Examine the development of a marketing strategy, including market segmentation and marketing mix.

**LO5** Investigate how marketers conduct marketing research, and study buying behavior.

**LO6** Summarize the environmental forces that influence marketing decisions.

# Introduction

Marketing involves planning and executing the development, pricing, promotion, and distribution of ideas, goods, and services to create exchanges that satisfy individual and organizational goals. These activities ensure that the products consumers want to buy are available at a price they are willing to pay and that consumers are provided with information about product features and availability. Organizations of all sizes and objectives engage in these activities.

In this chapter, we focus on the basic principles of marketing. First we define and examine the nature of marketing. Then we look at how marketers develop marketing strategies to satisfy the needs and wants of their customers. Next we discuss buying behavior and how marketers use research to determine what consumers want to buy and why. Finally we explore the impact of the environment on marketing activities.

**LO1**

Define marketing and describe the exchange process.

# NATURE OF MARKETING

A vital part of any business undertaking, marketing is a group of activities designed to expedite transactions by creating, distributing, pricing, and promoting goods, services, and ideas. These activities create value by allowing individuals and organizations to obtain what they need and want. A business cannot achieve its objectives unless it provides something that customers value. McDonald's, for example, introduced an adult "Happy Meal" with a premium salad, water, exercise booklet, and a "stepometer" to satisfy adult consumers' desires to improve their eating habits and health.[1] But just creating an innovative product that meets many users' needs isn't sufficient in today's volatile global marketplace. Products must be conveniently available, competitively priced, and uniquely promoted.

Of all the business concepts covered in this text, marketing may be the hardest for organizations to master. Businesses try to respond to consumer wants and needs and to anticipate changes in the environment. Unfortunately, it is difficult to understand and predict what consumers want: Motives are often unclear; few principles can be applied consistently;

and markets tend to fragment, desiring customized products, new value, or better service.[2]

It is important to note what marketing is not: It is not manipulating consumers to get them to buy products they don't want. It is not just selling and advertising; it is a systematic approach to satisfying consumers. Marketing focuses on the many activities—planning, pricing, promoting, and distributing products—that foster exchanges.

## The Exchange Relationship

At the heart of all business is the exchange, the act of giving up one thing (money, credit, labor, goods) in return for something else (goods, services, or ideas). Businesses exchange their goods, services, or ideas for money or credit supplied by customers in a voluntary *exchange relationship,* illustrated in Figure 12.1. The buyer must feel good about the purchase, or the exchange will not continue. If your local dry cleaner cleans your nice suit properly, on time, and without damage, you will probably feel good about using its services. But if your suit is damaged or isn't ready on time, you will probably use another dry cleaner next time.

For an exchange to occur, certain conditions are required. As indicated by the arrows in Figure 12.1, buyers and sellers must be able to communicate about the "something of value" available to each. An exchange does not necessarily take place just because buyers and sellers have something of value to exchange. Each participant must be willing to give up his or her respective "something of value" to receive the "something" held by the other. You are willing to exchange your "something of value"—your money or credit—for compact discs, soft drinks, football tickets, or new shoes because you consider those products more valuable or more important than holding on to your cash or credit potential.

When you think of marketing products, you may think of tangible things—cars, stereo systems, or books, for example. What most consumers want, however, is a way to get a job done, solve a problem, or gain some enjoyment. You may purchase a Hoover vacuum cleaner not because you want a vacuum cleaner but because you want clean carpets. Starbucks provides coffee drinks at a premium price, providing convenience, quality, and an inviting environment. Therefore, the tangible product itself may not be as important as the image or the benefits associated with the product. This intangible "something of value" may be capability gained from using a product or the image evoked by it, such as "7 For all Mankind" jeans, which can sell for nearly $200.00 a pair.

●● **A business cannot achieve its objectives unless it provides something that customers value.**

**FIGURE 12.1** The Exchange Process: Giving Up One Thing in Return for Another

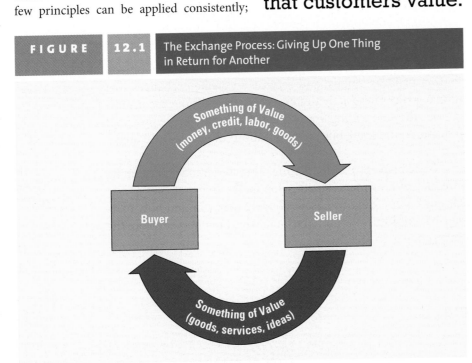

## Functions of Marketing

Marketing focuses on a complex set of activities that must be performed to accomplish objectives and generate exchanges. These activities include buying, selling, transporting, storing, grading, financing, marketing research, and risk taking.

**buying.** Everyone who shops for products (consumers, stores, businesses, governments) decides whether and what to buy. A marketer must understand buyers' needs and desires to determine what products to make available.

**selling.** The exchange process is expedited through selling. Marketers usually view selling as a persuasive activity that is accomplished through promotion (advertising, personal selling, sales promotion, publicity, and packaging).

**transporting.** Transporting is the process of moving products from the seller to the buyer. Marketers focus on transportation costs and services.

**storing.** Like transporting, storing is part of the physical distribution of products and includes warehousing goods. Warehouses hold some products for lengthy periods in order to create time utility. Consumers want frozen orange juice year-round, for example, although the production season for oranges is only a few months out of the year. This means that sellers must arrange cold storage for frozen orange juice concentrate all year.

**grading.** Grading refers to standardizing products and displaying and labeling them so that consumers clearly understand their nature and quality. Many products, such as meat, steel, and fruit, are graded according to a set of standards that often are established by the state or federal government.

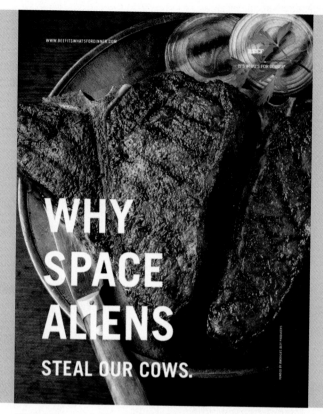

*Marketing can be used by industry groups to increase demand for their industry's product—like America's Beef Producers.*

**financing.** For many products, especially large items such as automobiles, refrigerators, and new homes, the marketer arranges credit to expedite the purchase.

**marketing research.** Through research, marketers ascertain the need for new goods and services. By gathering information regularly, marketers can detect new trends and changes in consumer tastes.

---

## Who Says You Have to Grow Up? Founding BigBadToyStore Inc.

Joel Boblit

Business: BigBadToyStore Inc.

Founded: 1999

Success: Joel Boblit has been able to turn a childhood hobby of collecting action figures into a more than $4 million dollar business (as of 2004).

After seeing how much Transformers (robot action figures from the 1980s) were selling for online, Joel Boblit began selling various nostalgic action figures himself. Selling action figures began as a hobby during college, but once Boblit graduated he began selling in earnest. BigBadToyStore.com was founded in 1999. The store specializes in vintage items such as figurines from the Star Wars movies and Teenage Mutant Ninja Turtles. Recently, Boblit has also begun selling numerous comic and movie items. Boblit attributes much of the success of BigBadToyStore.com to his parents, who financed his business and, in the beginning, put in more than 100 hours of work per week. Much of Boblit's success can be linked to the care he takes with customer service. Committed collectors of action figures value the packaging as much as the figures themselves; therefore, Boblit uses a grading system to identify the quality of the packaging. He also provides a premium packing service, promising an item will receive the utmost care when shipped. Customers can also make use of the "Pile of Loot" function—storing purchased items in a virtual storage bin until customers choose to have the items shipped; this reduces shipping costs for customers. With customers around the world and plans to begin distributing to approved retailers, BigBadToyStore.com appears to be a huge success.[3] ❖

**risk taking.** Risk is the chance of loss associated with marketing decisions. Developing a new product creates a chance of loss if consumers do not like it enough to buy it. Spending money to hire a sales force or to conduct marketing research also involves risk. The implication of risk is that most marketing decisions result in either success or failure.

## ●● LO3

Explain the marketing concept and its implications for developing marketing strategies.

## The Marketing Concept

A basic philosophy that guides all marketing activities is the marketing concept, the idea that an organization should try to satisfy customers' needs through coordinated activities that also allow it to

achieve its own goals. According to the marketing concept, a business must find out what consumers need and want and then develop the good, service, or idea that fulfills their needs or wants. The business must then get the product to the customer. In addition, the business must continually alter, adapt, and develop products to keep pace with changing consumer needs and wants. McDonald's,

often rejected these items. To remain competitive, the company must be prepared to add to or adapt its menu to satisfy customers' desires for new fads or changes in eating habits. Each business must determine how best to implement the marketing concept, given its own goals and resources.

Trying to determine customers' true needs is increasingly difficult because no one fully understands what motivates people to buy things. However, Estée Lauder, founder of her namesake cosmetics company, had a pretty good idea. When a prestigious store in Paris rejected her perfume in the 1960s, she "accidentally" dropped a bottle on the floor where nearby customers could get a whiff of it. So many asked about the scent that Galeries Lafayette was obliged to place an order. Lauder ultimately built an empire using then-unheard-of tactics like free samples and gifts with purchases to market her "jars of hope."[6]

Although customer satisfaction is the goal of the marketing concept, a business must also achieve its own objectives, such as boosting productivity, reducing costs, or achieving a percentage of a specific market. If it does not, it will not survive. For example, Dell could sell computers for $50 and give customers a lifetime guarantee, which would be great for customers but not so great for Dell. Obviously, the company must strike a balance between achieving organizational objectives and satisfying customer needs and wants.

To implement the marketing concept, a firm must have good information about what consumers want, adopt a consumer orientation, and coordinate its efforts throughout the entire organization; otherwise, it may be awash with goods, services, and ideas that consumers do not want or need. Successfully implementing the marketing concept requires that a business view customer value as the ultimate measure of work performance and improving value, and the rate at which this is done, as the

> ## According to the marketing concept, a business must find out what consumers need and want and then develop the good, service, or idea that fulfills their needs or wants.

as already mentioned, faces increasing pressure to provide more healthful fast-food choices; in addition to introducing its Go Active! Happy Meal, the company has eliminated supersized fries and soft drinks from its menu to address these concerns.[4] McDonald's was also the first fast-food chain to put nutritional information on its food packaging.[5] Over the years, the fast-food giant has experimented with healthier fare, but consumers

measure of success.[7] Everyone in the organization who interacts with customers—*all* customer-contact employees—must know what customers want. They are selling ideas, benefits, philosophies, and experiences—not just goods and services.

Someone once said that if you build a better mousetrap, the world will beat a path to your door. Suppose you do build a better mousetrap. What will happen? Actually, consumers are not likely to beat a path to your door because the market is too competitive. A coordinated effort by everyone involved with the mousetrap is needed to sell the product. Your company must reach out to customers and tell them about your mousetrap, especially how your mousetrap works better than those offered by competitors. If you do not make the benefits of your product widely known, in most cases, it will not be successful. Consider Apple's 116 retail stores in the United States and 8 international stores, which market computers and electronics in a way unlike any other computer manufacturer or retail store. The upscale stores, located in high-rent shopping districts, show off Apple's products in sparse, stylish settings to encourage consumers to try new things—like making a movie on a computer. The stores also offer special events like concerts and classes to give customers ideas on how to maximize their use of Apple's products.[8] You must also find—or create—stores willing to sell your mousetrap to consumers. You must implement the marketing concept by making a product with satisfying benefits and making it available and visible.

Orville Wright said that an airplane is "a group of separate parts flying in close formation." This is what most companies are trying to accomplish: They are striving for a team effort to deliver the right good or service to customers. A breakdown at any point in the organization—whether it be in production,

### the sales orientation.
By the early part of the 20th century, supply caught up with and then exceeded demand, and businesspeople began to realize they would have to "sell" products to buyers. During the first half of the 20th century, businesspeople viewed sales as the major means of increasing profits, and this period came to have a sales orientation. They believed the most important marketing activities were personal selling and advertising. Today some people still inaccurately equate marketing with a sales orientation.

### the marketing orientation.
By the 1950s, some businesspeople began to recognize that even efficient production and extensive promotion did not guarantee sales. These businesses, and many others since, found that they must first determine what customers want and then produce it rather than making the products first and then trying to persuade customers that they need them. Managers at General Electric first suggested that the marketing concept was a companywide philosophy of doing business. As more organizations realized

● MARKETING ORIENTATION an approach requiring organizations to gather information about customer needs, share that information throughout the firm, and use that information to help build long-term relationships with customers

> ## "Businesses today want to satisfy customers and build meaningful long-term relationships with them."

purchasing, sales, distribution, or advertising—can result in lost sales, lost revenue, and dissatisfied customers.

## Evolution of the Marketing Concept

The marketing concept may seem like the obvious approach to running a business and building relationships with customers. However, businesspeople are not always focused on customers when they create and operate businesses. Many companies fail to grasp the importance of customer relationships and fail to implement customer strategies. A recent survey indicated that only 46 percent of executives believe that their firm is committed to customers, but 67 percent of executives frequently meet with customers.[9] Our society and economic system have changed over time, and marketing has become more important as markets have become more competitive.

### the production orientation.
During the second half of the 19th century, the Industrial Revolution was well under way in the United States. New technologies, such as electricity, railroads, internal combustion engines, and mass-production techniques, made it possible to manufacture goods with ever increasing efficiency. Together with new management ideas and ways of using labor, products poured into the marketplace, where demand for manufactured goods was strong.

the importance of satisfying customers' needs, U.S. businesses entered the marketing era, one of marketing orientation.

A marketing orientation requires organizations to gather information about customer needs, share that information throughout the entire firm, and use that information to help build long-term relationships with customers. Top executives, marketing managers, nonmarketing managers (those in production, finance, human resources, and so on), and customers all become mutually dependent and cooperate in developing and carrying out a marketing orientation. Nonmarketing managers must communicate with marketing managers to share information important to understanding the customer. Consider the 115-year history of Wrigley's gum. In 1891 it was given away to promote sales of baking powder. Gum was launched as a product in 1893, and after four generations of Wrigley family CEOs, the company continues to reinvent itself and focus on consumers. In 2005 Wrigley launched 72 new products as well as purchasing Life Savers and Altoids.[10]

Trying to assess what customers want, difficult to begin with, is further complicated by the rate at which trends, fashions, and tastes can change. Businesses today want to satisfy customers and build meaningful long-term relationships with them. It is more efficient to retain existing customers and even increase the amount of business each customer provides the organization than to find new customers. Most companies' success depends on increasing the amount of repeat business. As we saw in Chapter 4, many companies are turning to technologies associated with customer-relationship management to help build relationships and boost business with existing customers.

Communication remains a major element of any strategy to develop and manage long-term customer relationships. By providing multiple points of interactions with customers—that is, Web sites, telephone, fax, e-mail, and personal contact—companies can personalize customer relationships.[11] Like many online retailers, Amazon.com stores and analyzes purchase data to understand each customer's interests. This information helps the retailer improve its ability to satisfy individual customers and thereby increase sales of books, music, movies, and other products to each customer.

The ability to identify individual customers allows marketers to shift their focus from targeting groups of similar customers to increasing their share of an individual customer's purchases.[12] Regardless of the medium through which communication occurs, customers should ultimately be the drivers of marketing strategy because they understand what they want. Customer relationship management systems should ensure that marketers listen to customers to respond to their needs and concerns and build long-term relationships.

 **LO4**

Examine the development of a marketing strategy, including market segmentation and marketing mix.

# DEVELOPING A MARKETING STRATEGY

To implement the marketing concept and customer relationship management, a business needs to develop and maintain a **marketing strategy,** a plan of action for developing, pricing, distributing, and promoting products that meet the needs of specific customers. This definition has two major components: selecting a target market and developing an appropriate marketing mix to satisfy that target market.

## Selecting a Target Market

A **market** is a group of people who have a need, purchasing power, and the desire and authority to spend money on goods, services, and ideas. A **target market** is a more specific group of consumers on whose needs and wants a company focuses its marketing efforts. Nike, for example, introduced a new line of golf clubs targeted at recreational golfers.[13]

Marketing managers may define a target market as a relatively small number of people, or they may define it as the total market (Figure 12.2). Rolls Royce, for example, targets its products at a small, very exclusive, high-income market—people who want the ultimate in prestige in an automobile. General Motors, on the other hand, manufactures vehicles ranging from the Aveo to Cadillac to GMC trucks in an attempt to appeal to varied tastes, needs, and desires. Likewise, the Gap, Inc., owns the Gap, Old Navy, Banana Republic, and Piperlime.

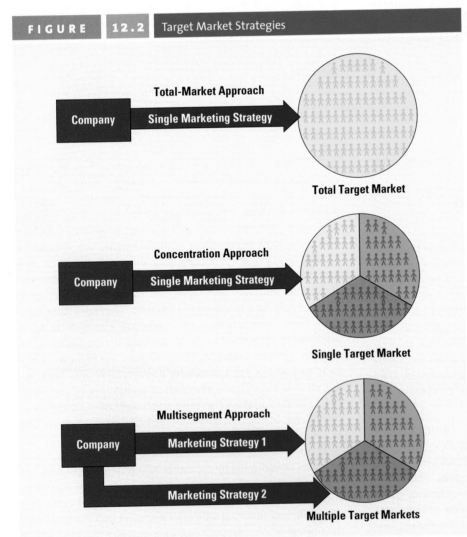

**FIGURE 12.2** Target Market Strategies

Total-Market Approach
Company → Single Marketing Strategy → Total Target Market

Concentration Approach
Company → Single Marketing Strategy → Single Target Market

Multisegment Approach
Company → Marketing Strategy 1 / Marketing Strategy 2 → Multiple Target Markets

Some firms use a total-market approach, in which they try to appeal to everyone and assume that all buyers have similar needs and wants. Sellers of salt, sugar, and many agricultural products use a total-market approach because everyone is a potential consumer of these products. Most firms, though, use market segmentation and divide the total market into groups of people who have relatively similar product needs. A market segment is a collection of individuals, groups, or organizations who share one or more characteristics and thus have relatively similar product needs and desires. Women are the largest market segment, with 51 percent of the U.S. population. In addition 11 million privately held companies are majority owned (50 percent or more) by women.[14] At the household level, segmentation can unlock each woman's

target markets so that they can develop a productive marketing strategy. Two common approaches to segmenting markets are the concentration approach and the multisegment approach.

**market segmentation approaches.** In the concentration approach, a company develops one marketing strategy for a single market segment. The concentration approach allows a firm to specialize, focusing all its efforts on the one market segment. Porsche, for example, focuses all its marketing efforts toward high-income individuals who want to own high-performance vehicles. A firm can generate a large sales volume by penetrating a single market segment deeply. The concentration

> # One market segment that many marketers are focusing on is the growing Hispanic population.

social, cultural, and stage in life to determine preferences and needs.[15] One market segment that many marketers are focusing on is the growing Hispanic population. In 2006 Hispanics spent more than $760 billion on things like clothes, cars, and electronics.[16] Staples gained a footing in the Hispanic market with a program called Exito Empressarial (Business Success) for small business owners. It is a seminar program to learn about accounting, taxes, and running a small business.[17] Table 12.1 shows the buying power and market share percentages of four market segments. Companies use market segmentation to focus their efforts and resources on specific

approach may be especially effective when a firm can identify and develop products for a particular segment ignored by other companies in the industry.

In the multisegment approach, the marketer aims its marketing efforts at two or more segments, developing a marketing strategy for each. Many firms use a multisegment approach that includes different advertising messages for different segments. Coca-Cola, for example, targets teenagers through its Coke Red Lounges, which are teen hangouts in shopping malls with exclusive music, movies, and videos, as well as lots of Coca-Cola products. And, in Britain, the soft-drink

**TABLE 12.1** Minority Buying Power by Race

| Category | Buying Power (billions) | | | | % Market Share | | | |
|---|---|---|---|---|---|---|---|---|
| | 1990 | 2000 | 2006 | 2011 | 1990 | 2000 | 2006 | 2011 |
| White | 3,816 | 6,231 | 8,159 | 10,479 | 89.4 | 86.7 | 85.7 | 84.7 |
| Black | 318 | 590 | 798 | 1,071 | 7.4 | 8.2 | 8.4 | 8.7 |
| American Indian | 19 | 39 | 53 | 73 | 0.5 | 0.5 | 0.6 | 0.6 |
| Asian | 116 | 268 | 426 | 621 | 2.7 | 3.7 | 4.5 | 5.0 |
| Multiracial | 0 | 58 | 86 | 119 | N/A | 0.8 | 0.9 | 1.0 |

Source: Jeffrey M. Humphreys, "The Multicultural Economy 2006," *GBEC* 66, no. 3. http://www.selig.uga.edu/forecast/GBEC/GBEC063Q.pdf (accessed June 17, 2007).

giant created a Web site where Internet surfers can mix their own music tracks.[19] Companies also develop product variations to appeal to different market segments. For example, in an effort to appeal to the growing number of children interested in gourmet cooking, Chef Revival U.S.A. launched a children's division that sells child-sized chef's hats, jackets, and kitchen pants in the same designs that a master chef would wear.[20] Many other firms also attempt to use a multisegment approach to market segmentation. The manufacturer of Raleigh bicycles uses a multisegment approach and has designed separate marketing strategies for racers, tourers, commuters, and children.

*Niche marketing* is a narrow market segment focus when efforts are on one small, well-defined segment that has a unique, specific set of needs. Catering to ice cream "addicts" and people who crave new, exotic flavors, several companies are selling ice cream on the Internet. This niche represents only a fraction of the $20.3 billion a year ice cream business, but online sales at some of the biggest makers increased 30 percent in just one year. Some of the firms focusing on this market are IceCreamSource.com, Nuts About Ice Cream, and Graeter's.[21]

For a firm to successfully use a concentration or multisegment approach to market segmentation, several requirements must be met:

1. Consumers' needs for the product must be heterogeneous.
2. The segments must be identifiable and divisible.

Expensive, custom-made motorcycles like those produced by Orange County Choppers Inc. appeal to niche market consumers.

3. The total market must be divided in a way that allows estimated sales potential, cost, and profits of the segments to be compared.
4. At least one segment must have enough profit potential to justify developing and maintaining a special marketing strategy.
5. The firm must be able to reach the chosen market segment with a particular market strategy.

# Iams Targets People Who Love Pets

Any company wanting to retain current customers and bring new customers in must be aware of trends and the changing needs of customers and be able to adapt accordingly. Companies also need to be willing to modify their products and marketing based on what the competition is doing. Iams, the successful retailer of Iams and Eukanuba pet products, is a good example of a company making the most of current trends to keep and attract customers.

These days, many pet owners treat their pets as additional family members and want to provide their pets with high-quality products. Procter & Gamble (P&G) and Iams, picking up on this trend, have begun marketing pet products mirroring products purchased and used by humans. For example, P&G now puts a tarter-control coating that comes from the technology used in the company's Crest toothpaste products on all adult pet food. This tarter-control coating was added to pet treats in 2006.

At one time, the Iams Company was focused primarily on pet nutrition. Now the focus has switched somewhat to one aimed at making pet owners happy by fulfilling their requests for fancy pet treats, sauces, and other items allowing them to spoil their pets. The company has made this shift as a result of surveying its customers. For example, customers were concerned about feeding cats in multicat households in which one cat might be overweight while another was not. As a result, the company created Multi-Cat—a cat food with ingredients aimed at reducing fat in heavy cats while still providing protein for lean cats. The company's Savory Sauce™ formulas for dogs are bottled just like our barbecue sauces or marinades. Among the flavors available are roasted turkey and pot roast. The sauces are fortified with vitamins, minerals, and antioxidants and low in calories and fat—sound familiar?

Iams's stiff competition is Nestlé's Purina and Wal-Mart's Ol'Roy, but, based on dollar sales, Iams is currently the number one national pet food brand. With research by Metamucil executives into the effects of fiber for pets, it looks as though innovation will continue for Iams and P&G. The company is also branching out into the areas of Iams Pet Imaging Centers, in partnership with ProScan, and pet health insurance, in partnership with Veterinary Pet Insurance Co. Iams Pet Imaging Centers are equipped with MRI (magnetic resonance imaging) machines that allow doctors to investigate health problems in pets without resorting to exploratory surgery.[18] ❖

**Q:** Discussion Questions

1. Describe Iams's target market.
2. Evaluate Iams's approach to targeting people who view their pets as family members.
3. Can you suggest other target markets that Iams could serve?

**bases for segmenting markets.** Companies segment markets on the basis of several variables:

1. *Demographic*—age, sex, race, ethnicity, income, education, occupation, family size, religion, social class. These characteristics are often closely related to customers' product needs and purchasing behavior, and they can be readily measured. For example, deodorants are often segmented by sex: Secret and Soft n' Dry for women; Old Spice and Mennen for men.

2. *Geographic*—climate, terrain, natural resources, population density, subcultural values. These influence consumers' needs and product usage. Climate, for example, influences consumers' purchases of clothing, automobiles, heating and air conditioning equipment, and leisure activity equipment.

3. *Psychographic*—personality characteristics, motives, lifestyles. Soft-drink marketers provide their products in several types of packaging, including two-liter bottles and cases of cans, to satisfy different lifestyles and motives.

4. *Behavioristic*—some characteristic of the consumer's behavior toward the product. These characteristics commonly involve some aspect of product use.

## Developing a Marketing Mix

The second step in developing a marketing strategy is to create and maintain a satisfying marketing mix. The **marketing mix** refers to four marketing activities—product, price, distribution, and promotion—that the firm can control to achieve specific goals within a dynamic marketing environment. (Figure 12.3) The buyer or the target market is the central focus of all marketing activities.

### DID YOU KNOW?

During its first year of operation, sales of Coca-Cola averaged just nine drinks per day for total first-year sales of $50. Today, Coca-Cola products are consumed at the rate of 1 billion drinks per day.[22]

**product.** A product—whether a good, a service, an idea, or some combination—is a complex mix of tangible and intangible attributes that provide satisfaction and benefits. A *good* is a physical entity you can touch.

A Porsche Cayenne, an Outkast compact disc, a Hewlett-Packard printer, and a kitten available for adoption at an animal shelter are examples of goods. A *service* is the application of human and mechanical efforts to people or objects to provide intangible benefits to customers. Air travel, dry cleaning, haircuts, banking, insurance, medical care, and day care are examples of services. *Ideas* include concepts, philosophies, images, and issues. For instance, an attorney, for a fee, may advise you about what rights you have in the event that the IRS decides to audit your tax return. Other marketers of ideas include political parties, churches, and schools.

A product has emotional and psychological as well as physical characteristics and includes everything that the buyer receives from an exchange. This definition includes supporting services such as installation, guarantees, product information, and promises of repair. Products usually have both favorable and unfavorable attributes; therefore, almost every purchase or exchange involves trade-offs as consumers try to maximize their benefits and satisfaction and minimize unfavorable attributes.

Products are among a firm's most visible contacts with consumers. If they do not meet consumer needs and expectations, sales will be difficult, and product life spans will be brief. The product is an important variable—often the central focus—of the marketing mix; the other variables (price, promotion, and distribution) must be coordinated with product decisions.

**price.** Almost anything can be assessed by a **price**, a value placed on an object exchanged between a buyer and a seller. Although the seller usually establishes the price, it may be negotiated between buyer and seller. The buyer usually exchanges purchasing power—income, credit, wealth—for the satisfaction or utility associated with a product. Because financial price is the measure of value

---

| FIGURE | 12.3 | The Marketing Mix: Product, Price, Promotion, and Distribution |

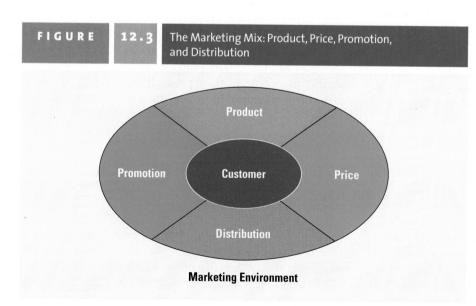

**Marketing Environment**

Although it offers upscale service, unlike many airlines, JetBlue was able to keep its costs and prices low, allowing it to capture market share and remain profitable during its first few years of operation.

commonly used in an exchange, it quantifies value and is the basis of most market exchanges.

Marketers view price as much more than a way of assessing value, however. It is a key element of the marketing mix because it relates directly to the generation of revenue and profits. Prices can also be changed quickly to stimulate demand or respond to competitors' actions. For example, a price war has developed in the market for high-speed Internet access, with prices for cable-modem service dropping below $20 a month in some areas.[23] McDonald's, Burger King, and other fast-food chains often use price changes to increase store traffic. For example, 99-cent Whoppers at Burger King and 99-cent Big Macs and Egg McMuffins may be offered for a limited time to increase sales, especially among heavy fast-food users.

distribution. Distribution (sometimes referred to as "place" because it helps to remember the marketing mix as the

when and where hunger strikes. McDonald's now operates more than 30,000 local restaurants serving 52 million people in more than 100 countries each day. More than 70 percent of McDonald's restaurants worldwide are owned and operated by independent local franchisees.[24] Intermediaries, usually wholesalers and retailers, perform many of the activities required to move products efficiently from producers to consumers or industrial buyers. These activities involve transporting, warehousing, materials handling, and inventory control, as well as packaging and communication.

Critics who suggest that eliminating wholesalers and other middlemen would result in lower prices for consumers do not recognize that eliminating intermediaries would not do away with the need for their services. Other institutions would have to perform those services, and consumers would still have to pay for them. In addition, in the absence of wholesalers, all producers would have to deal directly with retailers or customers, keeping voluminous records and hiring people to deal with customers.

promotion. Promotion is a persuasive form of communication that attempts to expedite a marketing exchange by influencing individuals, groups, and organizations to accept goods, services, and ideas. Promotion includes advertising, personal selling, publicity, and sales promotion, all of which we will look at more closely in Chapter 13.

The aim of promotion is to communicate directly or indirectly with individuals, groups, and organizations to facilitate exchanges. When marketers use advertising and other forms of promotion, they must effectively manage their promotional resources and understand product and target-market characteristics to ensure that these promotional activities contribute to the firm's objectives. For example, the *Bakersfield Californian*

> "The aim of promotion is to communicate directly or indirectly with individuals, groups, and organizations to facilitate exchanges."

"4 Ps") is making products available to customers in the quantities desired. McDonald's, for example, expanded distribution by opening restaurants in Wal-Mart stores and in Amoco and Chevron service stations. This practice permits the fast-food giant to share costs with its partners and to reach more customers

newspaper used text messaging on cell phones to target 15- to 24-year-olds in a cross-promotion with a local music store. The promotion allowed fans to vote for their favorite new CD listed in World Music's print ads, with participants gaining an opportunity to win gift certificates and other prizes.[25]

Most major companies have set up Web sites on the Internet to promote themselves and their products. The home page for Betty Crocker, for example, offers recipes, meal planning, the company's history, descriptions for its 200 products, online shopping for complementary items such as dinnerware, linens, and gifts, and the ability to print a shopping list based on recipes chosen or ingredients on hand in the consumer's kitchen. The Web sites for The Gap and Old Navy provide consumers with the opportunity to purchase clothing and other items from the convenience of their homes or offices. Some sites, however, simply promote a company's products but do not offer them for sale online.

 **L05**

Investigate how marketers conduct marketing research, and study buying behavior.

# MARKETING RESEARCH AND INFORMATION SYSTEMS

Before marketers can develop a marketing mix, they must collect in-depth, up-to-date information about customer needs. Marketing research is a systematic, objective process of getting information about potential customers to guide marketing decisions. Such information might include data about the age, income, ethnicity, gender, and educational level of people in the target market, their preferences for product features, their attitudes toward competitors' products, and the frequency with which they use the product. For example, Toyota's marketing research about Generation Y drivers (born between 1977 and 1994) found that they practically live in their cars, and many even keep a change of clothes handy in their vehicles. As a result of this research, Toyota designed its Scion as a "home on wheels" with a 15-volt outlet for plugging in a computer, reclining front seats for napping, and a powerful audio system for listening to MP3 music files, all for a $12,500 price tag.[26] Marketing research is vital because the marketing concept cannot be implemented without information about customers.

A marketing information system is a framework for accessing information about customers from sources both inside and outside the organization. Inside the organization, there is a continuous flow of information about prices, sales, and expenses. Outside the organization, data are readily available through

*Jones Soda's original distribution methods were as offbeat as the company's products. The beverages were initially placed in coolers in places like tattoo parlors, skate parks, and ski shops. Only later were the drinks available in more conventional outlets, like convenience stores.*

private or public reports and census statistics, as well as from many other sources. Computer networking technology provides a framework for companies to connect to useful databases and customers with instantaneous information about product acceptance, sales performance, and buying behavior. This information is important to planning and marketing strategy development.

Two types of data are usually available to decision makers. Primary data are observed, recorded, or collected directly from respondents. If you've ever participated in a telephone survey about a product, recorded your TV viewing habits for A. C. Nielsen or Arbitron, or even responded to a political opinion poll, you provided the researcher with primary data. Primary data must be gathered by researchers who develop a method to observe phenomena or research respondents. Many companies use "mystery shoppers" to visit their retail establishments and report on whether the stores were adhering to the companies' standards of service. Some use digital cameras and computer

**Secondary data** are compiled inside or outside the organization for some purpose other than changing the current situation. Marketers typically use information compiled by the U.S. Census Bureau and other government agencies, databases created by marketing research firms, as well as sales and other internal reports, to gain information about customers.

The marketing of products and collecting of data about buying behavior—information on what people actually buy and how they buy it—represents marketing research of the future. New information technologies are changing the way businesses learn about their customers and market their products. Interactive multimedia research, or *virtual testing,* combines sight, sound, and animation to facilitate the testing of concepts as well as packaging and design features for consumer products. Computerization offers a greater degree of flexibility, shortens the staff time involved in data gathering, and cuts marketing research costs. The evolving development of telecommunications and computer technologies is allowing marketing researchers quick and easy access to a growing number of online services and a vast database of potential respondents. Online research is set to grow from $1.3 billion to $4 billion in the next few years, according to a new report by Cambiar and GMI.[29] Many companies have created private online communities and research panels that bring consumer feedback into the companies 24 hours a day.

Look-Look.com is an online, real-time service that provides accurate and reliable information research and news about trendsetting youths ages 14 to 30. With this age group spending an estimated $140 billion a year, many companies are willing to shell out an annual subscription fee of about $20,000 for access to these valuable data. Look-Look pays more than 35,000 handpicked, prescreened young people from all over the world to e-mail the company information about their styles, trends, opinions, and ideas.[30]

Other companies are finding that quicker, less expensive online market research is helping them develop products faster and with greater assurance that the products will be successful. The CEO of Stonyfield Farm (maker of higher-priced yogurt) is convinced that Web feedback saved his company from a multimillion-dollar mistake. The online responses from 105 women caused the company to scrap the name originally planned for its new yogurt from YoFemme (which the respondents did not like) to YoSelf (to which the respondents voted yes).[31]

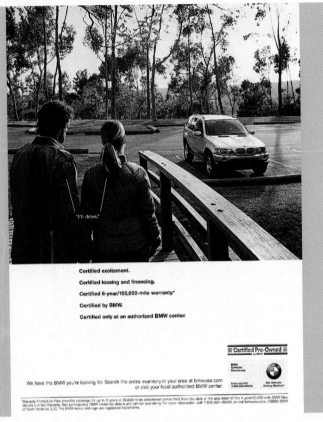

Certified excitement.

Certified leasing and financing.

Certified 6-year/100,000-mile warranty.*

Certified by BMW.

Certified only at an authorized BMW center.

≡ Certified Pre-Owned ≡

We have the BMW you're looking for. Search the entire inventory in your area at bmwusa.com or visit your local authorized BMW center.

*Market research can lead to a whole new market for your product. BMW targets a lower income consumer than its typical high-end one by selling "certified" used BMWs at a lower cost, but still with the BMW brand recognition and expectation.*

equipment to document their observations of store appearance, employee effectiveness, and customer treatment. These mystery shoppers provide valuable information that helps companies improve their organizations and refine their marketing strategies.[27] The state of Nebraska used focus groups as part of its effort to develop a formal marketing campaign. Among other things, focus groups suggested the state promote its history and natural beauty.[28] With surveys, respondents are sometimes untruthful in order to avoid seeming foolish or ignorant.

Some methods for marketing research use passive observation of consumer behavior and open-ended questioning techniques. Called ethnographic or observational research, the approach can help marketers determine what consumers really think about their products and how different ethnic or demographic groups react to them.

## BUYING BEHAVIOR

Carrying out the marketing concept is impossible unless marketers know what, where, when, and how consumers buy; marketing research into the factors that influence buying behavior helps marketers develop effective marketing strategies. **Buying behavior** refers to the decision processes and actions of people who purchase and use products. It includes

● **PERCEPTION** the process by which a person selects, organizes, and interprets information received from his or her senses

● **LEARNING** changes in a person's behavior based on information and experience

● **ATTITUDE** knowledge and positive or negative feelings about something

● **PERSONALITY** the organization ot an individual's distinguishing character traits, attitudes, or habits

● **SOCIAL ROLES** a set of expectations for individuals based on some position they occupy

the behavior of both consumers purchasing products for personal or household use as well as organizations buying products for business use. Marketers analyze buying behavior because a firm's marketing strategy should be guided by an understanding of buyers. People view pets as part of their families, and they want their pets to have the best of everything. Iams, which markets the Iams and Eukanuba pet food brands, recognized this trend and shifted its focus. Today, it markets high-quality pet food, fancy pet treats, sauces, and other items that allow pet lovers to spoil their pets.[32]

Both psychological and social variables are important to an understanding of buying behavior.

*Marketers like Benetton want their ads to appeal to a consumer's self-concept. "I'm like them, so I should buy their products."*

## Psychological Variables of Buying Behavior

Psychological factors include the following:

- **Perception** is the process by which a person selects, organizes, and interprets information received from his or her senses, as when hearing an advertisement on the radio or touching a product to better understand it.

- Motivation, as we said in Chapter 10, is an inner drive that directs a person's behavior toward goals. A customer's behavior is influenced by a set of motives rather than by a single motive. A buyer of a home computer, for example, may be motivated by ease of use, ability to communicate with the office, and price.

- **Learning** brings about changes in a person's behavior based on information and experience. If a person's actions result in a reward, he or she is likely to behave the same way in similar situations. If a person's actions bring about a negative result, however—such as feeling ill after eating at a certain restaurant—he or she will probably not repeat that action.

- **Attitude** is knowledge and positive or negative feelings about something. For example, a person who feels strongly about protecting the environment may refuse to buy products that harm the earth and its inhabitants.

- **Personality** refers to the organization of an individual's distinguishing character traits, attitudes, or habits. Although market research on the relationship between personality and buying behavior has been inconclusive, some marketers believe that the type of car or clothing a person buys reflects his or her personality.

## Social Variables of Buying Behavior

Social factors include **social roles,** which are a set of expectations for individuals based on some position they occupy. A person may have many roles: mother, wife, student, executive. Each of these roles can influence buying behavior. Consider a woman choosing an automobile. Her father advises her to buy a safe, gasoline-efficient car, such as a Volvo. Her teenaged daughter wants her to buy a cool car, such as a Pontiac GTO; her young son wants her to buy a Ford Explorer to take on camping trips. Some of her colleagues at work say she should buy a hybrid Prius to help the environment. Thus, in choosing which car to buy, the woman's buying behavior may be affected by the opinions and experiences of her family and friends and by her roles as mother, daughter, and employee.

example, buy *masa trigo,* a flour mixture used to prepare tortillas, which are basic to Mexican cuisine.

Other social factors include reference groups, social classes, and culture.

- **Reference groups** include families, professional groups, civic organizations, and other groups with whom buyers identify and whose values or attitudes they adopt. A person may use a reference group as a point of comparison or a source of information. A person new to a community may ask other group members to recommend a family doctor, for example.

- **Social classes** are determined by ranking people into higher or lower positions of respect. Criteria vary from one society to another. People within a particular social class may develop common patterns of behavior. People in the upper-middle class, for example, might buy a Lexus or a Cadillac as a symbol of their social class.

- **Culture** is the integrated, accepted pattern of human behavior, including thought, speech, beliefs, actions, and artifacts. Culture determines what people wear and eat and where they live and travel. Many Hispanic Texans and New Mexicans, for

## Understanding Buying Behavior

Although marketers try to understand buying behavior, it is extremely difficult to explain exactly why a buyer purchases a particular product. The tools and techniques for analyzing consumers are not exact. Marketers may not be able to determine accurately what is highly satisfying to buyers, but they know that trying to understand consumer wants and needs is the best way to satisfy them. In an attempt to better understand consumer behavior, Procter & Gamble sent video crews into about 80 households all around the world. The company, maker of Tide, Crest, Pampers, and many other consumer products, hoped to gain insights into the lifestyles and habits of young couples, families with children, and empty nesters. Participants were taped over a four-day period and were paid about $200–$250 a day. The behaviors caught on tape may lead the company to develop new products or change existing ones to better meet consumers' needs and give the company a competitive advantage over its rivals.[34]

## Using Technology to Mine Customer Opinions

Successful company marketers take the time to study and understand what they call consumer buying behavior—in other words, the behavior of customers buying a company's products for personal or household uses. Marketers pay attention to this behavior because how customers respond to a company's marketing strategies affect that company's success. They also aim to please customers and undertake research to discover what a company can do to satisfy its customers and keep them coming back. When marketers have a solid grasp on buying behavior, they can better predict how customers will react to marketing campaigns. A new strategy being used by large companies such as Citigroup, Johnson & Johnson, Pfizer, and Procter & Gamble is the use of online software to create large-scale focus groups. Companies that sell this software aim to help marketers listen to what their **customers want** rather than designing marketing campaigns based on generic strategies.

For years, companies have brought people together for traditional, face-to-face focus groups. In other words, a small group of people was brought together in a room to discuss products while people from the company

listened (often from another room) to what they had to say. The advantage to the new, large-scale focus groups is that you can reach a much larger audience—therefore, getting a much wider range of ideas and opinions. Perhaps this may create a more accurate picture of what the general public at large is looking for from a company. For example, for years Lego had been producing the same Lego sets based on feedback from traditional focus groups. The company created an online focus group involving 10,000 people—all Lego customers were invited via e-mail to participate in an online contest regarding new products—and the result was essentially brainstorming in cyberspace and customers suggesting departures from Lego's traditional toys.

Here is how this software works: In the instance of Lego, customers who had received e-mail invitations were part of an online "popularity contest" regarding new-product suggestions. Customers were shown lists of six proposed products at a time. They were asked to rank the toys they liked and, if they chose, offer their own ideas. The customer ideas were then filtered into the mix and sent to other customers to rank against Lego's proposed toys. The software filters

the selections shown to customers—those receiving the most votes early on most often appear later, and over time, the most popular ideas rise to the forefront.

Although there are many challenges regarding this new software and its uses (for example, some suggest online research may be skewed toward Internet users), online focus groups are much less expensive than the traditional version. At least for now, this new research method may be a good way to understand more about buying behavior.[33] ❖

**Q:** Discussion Questions

1. How can technology be used to determine consumer beliefs and opinions?

2. Compare face-to-face focus groups with online discussions for understanding consumer behavior.

3. What are the possible biases from using online research to assess consumer beliefs, opinions, and behavior?

# DESTINATION CEO

## Sharen Jester Turney—Victoria's Secret

Victoria's Secret is considered an Intimate Apparel Business. It averages about $4 billion in annual sales, has 1,000 stores, and mails approximately 4 million catalogs each year.

Sharen Jester Turney is the current president and CEO of Victoria's Secret Direct. She also holds the title of president and CEO of Limited Direct. Victoria's Secret is under the umbrella of the parent company Limited Brands. Turney's area of responsibility is the Internet and catalog sales division of Victoria's Secret. Turney grew up on a ranch near a small town in Oklahoma. She attended the University of Oklahoma, where she majored in business education and minored in public administration. As a pom pom girl at the university, she was able to travel and experience a much broader world than the small town in which she was raised. Her early career was started in the retail sales business with Byers, a part of the Federated companies. From there, she moved to Nieman Marcus and was promoted to CEO of Neiman Marcus Direct. When she joined Victoria's Secret, the only items available online were sleepwear. Today, all items are available online, and new sites have been launched such as the cosmetics line. Innovation is key to her success. Turney is responsible for

launching the very popular online Victoria's Secret fashion show. Under her leadership, the company has an unrelenting focus on the customer. The goal is to put yourself in the customer's position and to satisfy that need. Today, the Internet business accounts for as much in sales as does the catalog business.

### >>DISCUSSION QUESTIONS

1. What is the difference between Victoria's Secret Direct and the storefront Victoria's Secret?

2. What is the key focus on Victoria's Secret Direct in terms of customer satisfaction?

3. Which business generates more sales, Victoria's Secret Direct or the Victoria's Secret catalog?

>>To see the complete video about Sharen Jester Turney go to our Web site at **www.mhhe.com/FerrellM** and look for the link to the Destination CEO videos.

After a consumer group complained to federal regulators, fried-chicken giant KFC ended an ad campaign claiming that the company's chicken was healthy food.

## ●● LO6

Summarize the environmental forces that influence marketing decisions.

# THE MARKETING ENVIRONMENT

A number of external forces directly or indirectly influence the development of marketing strategies; the following political, legal, regulatory, social, competitive, economic, and technological forces comprise the marketing environment.

- *Political, legal, and regulatory forces*—laws and regulators' interpretation of laws; law enforcement and regulatory activities; regulatory bodies, legislators and legislation, and political actions of interest groups. Specific laws, for example, require that advertisements be truthful and that all health claims be documented.

- *Social forces*—the public's opinions and attitudes toward issues such as living standards, ethics, the environment, lifestyles, and quality of life. For example, social concerns have led marketers to design and market safer toys for children.

- *Competitive and economic forces*—competitive relationships, unemployment, purchasing power, and general economic conditions (prosperity, recession, depression, recovery, product shortages, and inflation).

- *Technological forces*—computers and other technological advances that improve distribution, promotion, and new-product development.

Marketing environment forces can change quickly and radically, which is one reason marketing requires creativity and a customer focus. For example, *Rolling Stone* magazine did a business analysis before entering the Chinese market. Unfortunately after a successful debut, the Chinese government had concerns about its license to publish in China. The success of *Rolling Stone* concerned other lifestyle and music magazines, and they informed the authorities that the license was not appropriate.[35] Because such environmental forces are interconnected, changes in one may cause changes in others. Consider that because of evidence linking children's consumption of soft drinks and fast foods to health issues such as obesity, diabetes, and osteoporosis, marketers of such products have experienced negative publicity and calls for legislation regulating the sale of soft drinks in public schools. When Morgan Spurlock saw an evening news story about two teenagers who unsuccessfully sued McDonald's for their poor health, he decided to make the movie *Super Size Me*. As director, he went on a supersized diet of fast food and gained 25 pounds, suffered from depression, and experienced heart pain.[36] Figure 12.4 indicates that the United States is the most overweight and obese nation in the world. More than 39 percent of the U.S. population over the age of 15 is obese, compared with only 1.6 percent of the population in Japan. However, there are 92 million obese people in the United States compared with 316 million in the rest of the world.[37] Some companies have

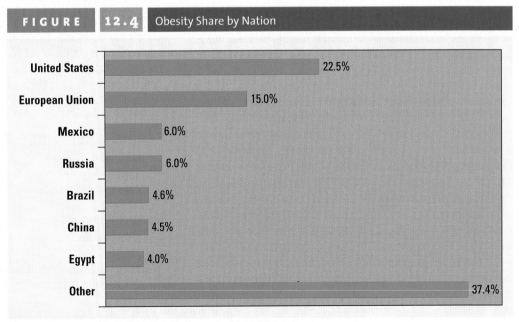

**FIGURE 12.4** Obesity Share by Nation

| Nation | Obesity Share |
|---|---|
| United States | 22.5% |
| European Union | 15.0% |
| Mexico | 6.0% |
| Russia | 6.0% |
| Brazil | 4.6% |
| China | 4.5% |
| Egypt | 4.0% |
| Other | 37.4% |

*Share of the world's obese population by nation. The United States has a nearly 23 percent share.*

Source: Bradley Johnson, "The Not-So-Skinny: U.S. Population Weighs In as the World's Most Obese," *Advertising Age*, May 15, 2006, p. 43.

FIGURE 12.5 The Marketing Mix and the Marketing Environment

**FIGURE** | **12.5** | The Marketing Mix and the Marketing Environment

Political, Legal, and Regulatory Forces

Social Forces

Product

Promotion

Customer

Price

Distribution

Technological Forces

Competitive and Economic Forces

Marketing Environment

responded to these concerns by reformulating products to make them healthier. Kellogg company is reformulating many of its popular children-targeted products (which account for 50 percent of its products) to make them more healthy. The goal is to cut sugar and fat to help fight childhood obesity. If brands such as Pop Tarts, Fruit Loops, Apple Jacks, or other products cannot be made more healthy while maintaining their same taste, the products will not be marketed to children under 12.[38] The fast-food industry's frantic race to cook up the first "better-for-you" french fry appears to have been won by Wendy's. The number-three fast-food chain announced that it will dump cooking oil for a blend of nonhydrogenated corn and soy oil containing next-to-no artery clogging trans fats.[39]

Although the forces in the marketing environment are sometimes called uncontrollables, they are not totally so. A marketing manager can influence some environmental variables. For example, businesses can lobby legislators to dissuade them from passing unfavorable legislation. Figure 12.5 shows the variables in the marketing environment that affect the marketing mix and the buyer. ∎

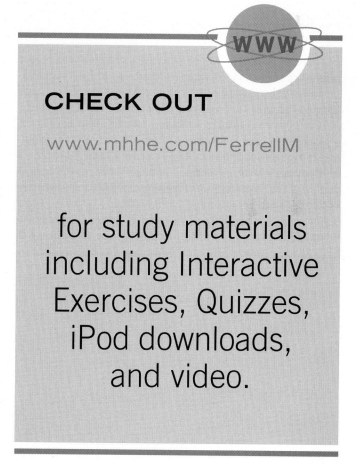

**CHECK OUT**

www.mhhe.com/FerrellM

for study materials including Interactive Exercises, Quizzes, iPod downloads, and video.

As you prepare to enter the workplace, you should be aware of how the environment is changing. A major part of your professional development will occur as a result of your ability to respond and adapt to some of these changes. One of the changes that exists today is that we are now living in a service economy. The focus on service means that the jobs available to you will probably require both good product knowledge and an ability to communicate well to customers about how the product can benefit them. Your skills in relating to others are critical to success in your career.

The increased focus on customer service presents opportunities for you in providing superior service to customers. Customer service involves providing what customers need in the best way possible so that they will keep coming back to your company for the products and services they need. Good customer service also helps attract new customers. Typical positions in this area will involve customer service training, customer service management, customer satisfaction, and the like. The average salary for a customer service manager is $57,200. Quality, another major movement, goes hand-in-hand with customer satisfaction. Keeping the company as the number-one choice among customers requires the constant improvement of products and service to ensure that they are of high quality.

To prepare yourself for a career in customer service and customer satisfaction, you may want to major in marketing with a minor in psychology or sociology. Also beneficial will be a class in consumer behavior, as it will enable you to better understand the purchasers.[40]

## Build Your Business Plan

**Customer Driven Marketing**  The first step is to develop a marketing strategy for your product or service. Who will be the target market you will specifically try to reach? What group(s) of people has the need, ability and willingness to purchsae this product? How will you segment customers within your target market? Segmenting by demographic and geographic variables are often the easiest segmentation strategies to attempt. Remember that you would like to have the customers in your segment be as homogeneous and accessible as possible. You might target several segments if you feel your product or service has broad appeal.

The second step in your marketing strategy is to develop the marketing mix for your product or service. Whether you are dealing with an established product or you are creating your own product or service, you need to think about what is the differential advantage your product offers. What makes it unique? How should it be priced? Should the product be priced below, above, or at the market? How will you distribute the product? And last but certainly not least, you need to think about the promotional strategy for your product.

What about the uncontrollable variables you need to be aware of? Is your product something that can constantly be technologically advanced? Is your product a luxury that will not be considered by consumers when the economy is in a downturn?

# dimensions *of* marketing strategy

**Introduction** Creating an effective marketing strategy is important. Getting just the right mix of product, price, promotion, and distribution is critical if a business is to satisfy its target customers and achieve its own objectives (implement the marketing concept).

In Chapter 12, we introduced the concept of marketing and the various activities important in developing a marketing strategy. In this chapter, we'll take a closer look at the four dimensions of the marketing mix—product, price, distribution, and promotion—used to develop the marketing strategy. The focus of these marketing mix elements is a marketing strategy that builds customer relationships and satisfaction.

## ● ● learning OBJECTIVES

**LO1**   Describe the role of product in the marketing mix, including how products are, developed, classified, and identified.

**LO2**   Define price and discuss its importance in the marketing mix, including various pricing strategies a firm might employ.

**LO3**   Identify factors affecting distribution decisions, such as marketing channels and intensity of market coverage.

**LO4**   Specify the activities involved in promotion, as well as promotional strategies and promotional positioning.

# THE MARKETING MIX

The key to developing a marketing strategy is maintaining the right marketing mix that satisfies the target market and creates long-term relationships with customers. To develop meaningful customer relationships, marketers have to develop and manage the dimensions of the marketing mix to give their firm an advantage over competitors. Successful companies offer at least one dimension of value that surpasses all competitors in the marketplace in meeting customer expectations. However, this does not mean that a company can ignore the other dimensions of the marketing mix; it must maintain acceptable, and if possible distinguishable, differences in the other dimensions as well.

Wal-Mart, for example, emphasizes price ("Save money, live better"). Procter & Gamble is well known for its promotion of top consumer brands such as Tide, Cheer, Crest, Ivory, Head & Shoulders, and Folgers. Domino's Pizza is recognized for its superiority in distribution after developing the largest home delivery pizza company in the world and its innovative new product introductions.

**DID YOU KNOW?**

Domino's Pizza delivery drivers cover 9 million miles a week delivering 400 million pizzas a year.[1]

●● LO1

Describe the role of product in the marketing mix, including how products are, developed, classified, and identified.

## PRODUCT STRATEGY

As mentioned previously, the term *product* refers to goods, services, and ideas. Because the product is often the most visible of the marketing mix dimensions, managing product decisions is crucial. In this section, we'll consider product development, classification, mix, life cycle, and identification.

### Developing New Products

Each year thousands of products are introduced, but few of them succeed. Coca-Cola has, in recent years, created or acquired thousands of new products, including acquiring Glacéau, maker of vitamin water. New products include Enviga green tea, Vault and Vault Zero energy soda, Full Throttle, and many variations and

> # The key to developing a marketing strategy is maintaining the right marketing mix that satisfies the target market and creates long-term relationships with customers.

*While he was attending Yale in 1966, Fred Smith, the founder of Federal Express, wrote a paper about his idea for the business. However, his professor said the concept would never fly. After watching how the U.S. military's logistics worked while serving in Vietnam, Smith later got FedEx off the ground.*

flavors of Dasani flavored water.[2] A firm can take considerable time to get a product ready for the market: It took more than 20 years for the first photocopier, for example. General Motors has trimmed the time required to develop and introduce a new vehicle model from four years to 18 months. The automaker released 29 new models, many with innovative designs, over a 16-month period.[3] Before introducing a new product, a business must follow a multistep process: idea development, the screening of new ideas, business analysis, product development, test marketing, and commercialization.

**idea development.** New ideas can come from marketing research, engineers, and outside sources such as advertising agencies and management consultants. Microsoft has a separate division—Microsoft Research—where scientists devise technology of the future. The division has more than 700 full-time employees who work in a university-like research atmosphere. Research teams then present their ideas to Microsoft engineers who are developing specific products. As we said in Chapter 12, ideas sometimes come from customers, too.

# DESTINATION CEO

**Isaac Larian—Father of Bratz** Isaac Larian immigrated to the United States from Iran in 1971. He founded the firm MBA Entertainment to manufacture fashion dolls for young girls. Many of Mattel's designers left that company to work for Larian on the development of the Bratz doll. Currently, MGA and Mattel are locked in a legal battle over this issue. This is the first doll to substantially cut into the "Barbie" doll market. MGA Entertainment went from a small company to one grossing hundreds of millions of dollars with the Bratz doll concept. The dolls are considered the "anti-Barbie" and feature modern fashion. MGA prides itself on continuously reinventing the product and pushing brand extensions such as consumer electronics for young girls. Larian continues to love the challenge.

## >>DISCUSSION QUESTIONS

1. What company is the major competitor of the Bratz doll?

2. What is the key marketing strategy associated with the Bratz doll?

3. According to the video, what is a brand extension for MGA?

>>To see the complete video about Issac Larian, go to our Web site at **www.mhhe.com/FerrellIM** and look for the link to the Destination CEO videos.

Other sources are brainstorming and intracompany incentives or rewards for good ideas. New ideas can even create a company. Las Vegas–based Shuffle Master, for example, grew out of entrepreneur Mark Breeding's card-shuffling machine. The Shuffle Master is on 12,000 of the 40,000 tables in casinos around the world.[4]

### new idea screening.

The next step in developing a new product is idea screening. In this phase, a marketing manager should look at the organization's resources and objectives and assess the firm's ability to produce and market the product. Important aspects to be considered at this stage are consumer desires, the competition, technological changes, social trends, and political, economic, and environmental considerations. Basically, there are two reasons new products succeed: They are able to meet a need or solve a problem better than products already available or they add variety to the product selection currently on the market. Bringing together a team of knowledgeable people including design, engineering, marketing and customers is a great way to screen ideas. Using the Internet to encourage collaboration is the next sea of innovation for marketers to screen ideas.[5] After many ideas were screened, Heinz Ketchup introduced Heinz kid-targeted Silly Squirts with three cool drawing nozzles to keep kids amused and entertained at dinner. In addition, Easy Squeeze upside-down bottles added to convenience.[6] Most new-product ideas are rejected during screening because they seem inappropriate or impractical for the organization.

### business analysis.

Business analysis is a basic assessment of a product's compatibility in the marketplace and its potential profitability. Both the size of the market and competing products are often studied at this point. The most important question relates to market demand: How will the product affect the firm's sales, costs, and profits?

### product development.

If a product survives the first three steps, it is developed into a prototype that should reveal the intangible attributes it possesses as perceived by the consumer. Product development is often expensive, and few product ideas make it to this stage. New product research and development costs vary. Adding a new color to an existing item may cost $100,000 to $200,000, but launching a completely new product can cost millions of dollars. The Coca-Cola Co. reduced the time and cost of product development research by 50 percent when it created an online panel of 100 teenagers and asked them how to remake its Powerade sports drink.[7] During product development, various elements of the marketing mix must be developed for testing. Copyrights, tentative advertising copy, packaging, labeling, and descriptions of a target market are integrated to develop an overall marketing strategy.

### test marketing.

Test marketing is a trial minilaunch of a product in limited areas that represent the potential market. It allows a complete test of the marketing strategy in a natural environment, giving the organization an opportunity to discover weaknesses and eliminate them before the product is fully launched. Consider Seasons 52, the latest concept restaurant developed by Darden Restaurants Inc., the world's largest casual dining company. Seasons 52 boasts a seasonally inspired menu with the freshest goods available served in a casual atmosphere. Seasons 52 targets those who are striving to live fit, active lives and are concerned about the quality and nutrition of their food. All menu items at Seasons 52 have fewer than 475 calories, significantly lower than competing restaurants, are nutritionally balanced, and are not fried. Darden is test marketing this restaurant concept in Florida and Georgia to experiment with variations in menu, advertising, and pricing and to measure the extent of brand awareness, brand switching, and repeat purchases resulting from these alterations in this concept restaurant.[8] ACNielsen assists companies in test-marketing their products. Figure 13.1 shows the permanent sites as well as custom locations for test marketing.

**FIGURE 13.1 ACNielsen Market Decisions**

**Market Decisions**
**Test Market Locations**

◆ Permanent Test Markets ("Data Markets")

★ Additional "Custom" Test Markets

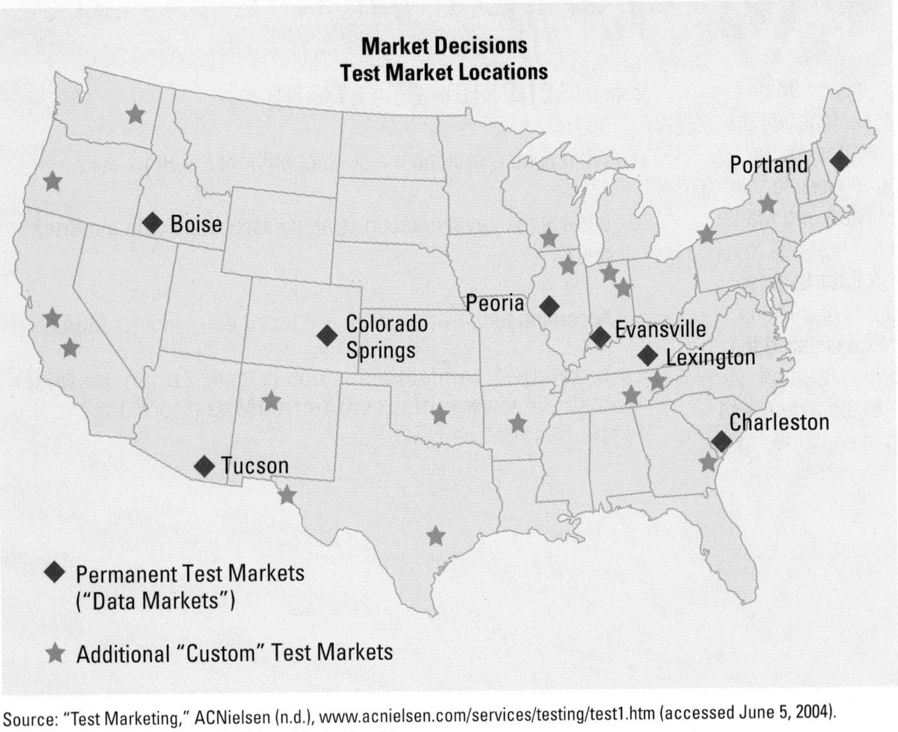

Source: "Test Marketing," ACNielsen (n.d.), www.acnielsen.com/services/testing/test1.htm (accessed June 5, 2004). Reprinted with permission of ACNielsen Market Decisions.

**commercialization.** Commercialization is the full introduction of a complete marketing strategy and the launch of the product for commercial success. During commercialization, the firm gears up for full-scale production, distribution, and promotion. When Procter & Gamble bought Gillette, it used its large distribution and retail network and spent more than $6 million for just two Super Bowl ads for the Fusion five-blade razor. It blanketed stores with 180,000 displays in the first week, coverage it took a year to achieve with the Mach3 razor in 1998. Once Fusion goes global, P&G's superior distribution will help speed its adoption in markets such as China and Eastern Europe, while its marketing expertise should help bolster Gillette's lagging shaving-prep business. The Fusion razor commands 30 percent higher prices than Mach3 products, which—at a time when Procter & Gamble cannot increase the prices on Tide or Crest—will boost earnings by $120 million and increase market share to 15 percent.[9]

## Classifying Products

Products are usually classified as either consumer products or business products. **Consumer products** are for household or family use; they are not intended for any purpose other than daily living. They can be further classified as convenience products, shopping products, and specialty products on the basis of consumers' buying behavior and intentions.

- *Convenience products,* such as eggs, milk, bread, and newspapers, are bought frequently, without a lengthy search, and often for immediate consumption. Consumers spend virtually no time planning where to purchase these products and usually accept whatever brand is available.

- *Shopping products,* such as furniture, audio equipment, clothing, and sporting goods, are purchased after the consumer has compared competitive products and "shopped around." Price, product features, quality, style, service, and image all influence the decision to buy.

- *Specialty products,* such as ethnic foods, designer clothing and shoes, art, and antiques, require even greater research and shopping effort. Consumers know what they want and go out of their way to find it; they are not willing to accept a substitute.

**Business products** are used directly or indirectly in the operation or manufacturing processes of businesses. They are usually purchased for the operation of an organization or the production of other products; thus, their purchase is tied to specific goals and objectives. They too can be further classified:

- *Raw materials* are natural products taken from the earth, oceans, and recycled solid waste. Iron ore, bauxite, lumber, cotton, and fruits and vegetables are examples.

- *Major equipment* covers large, expensive items used in production. Examples include earth-moving equipment, stamping machines, and robotic equipment used on auto assembly lines.

- *Accessory equipment* includes items used for production, office, or management purposes, which usually do not become part of the final product. Computers, fax machines, calculators, and hand tools are examples.

- *Component parts* are finished items, ready to be assembled into the company's final products. Tires, window glass, batteries, and spark plugs are component parts of automobiles.

- *Processed materials* are things used directly in production or management operations but not readily identifiable as component parts. Varnish, for example, is a processed material for a furniture manufacturer.

- *Supplies* include materials that make production, management, and other operations possible, such as paper, pencils, paint, cleaning supplies, and so on.

- *Industrial services* include financial, legal, marketing research, security, janitorial, and exterminating services. Purchasers decide whether to provide these services internally or to acquire them from an outside supplier.

*Milk is a convenience product. It is bought frequently by consumers for relatively quick consumption without their conducting a lengthy search.*

## Product Line and Product Mix

Product relationships within an organization are of key importance. A product line is a group of closely related products that are treated as a unit because of similar marketing strategy. At Colgate-Palmolive, for example, the oral-care product line includes Colgate toothpaste, toothbrushes, and dental floss. A product mix is all the products offered by an organization. Figure 13.2 displays a sampling of the product mix and product lines of the Colgate-Palmolive Company.

## Product Life Cycle

Like people, products are born, grow, mature, and eventually die. Some products have very long lives. Ivory Soap was introduced in 1879 and is still popular. In contrast, a new computer chip is usually outdated within a year because of technological breakthroughs and rapid changes in the computer industry. There are four stages in the life cycle of a product: introduction, growth, maturity, and decline (Figure 13.3). The stage a product is in helps determine marketing strategy. Figure 13.4

**FIGURE 13.2** Colgate-Palmolive's Product Mix and Product Lines

◄──────────── Product Mix ────────────►

| Oral Care | Personal Care | Household Care | Pet Nutrition |
|-----------|---------------|----------------|---------------|
| Toothpaste | Men's antiperspirant/deodorant | Dishwashing | Science diet |
| Toothbrushes | Women's antiperspirant/deodorant | Fabric conditioner | Prescription diet |
| Kids' products | Bar soap | Household cleaners | |
| Whitening products | Body wash | Institutional products | |
| Over the counter | Liquid hand wash | | |
| From the dentist | Toiletries for men | | |

(Product Lines)

Source: Colgate Products, http://www.colgate.com/app/Colgate/US/Corp/Products.cvsp (accessed June 17, 2007).

provides some real-world product examples of sales or unit growth over a 50-year period of time. Note that Tide continues on a solid growth pattern, while Buick may be in a decline stage. On the other hand, both Pepsi and Heinz have relatively flat sales over the past 20 years, but each company has introduced new products to sustain overall organizational sales. In the case of PepsiCo, the introduction of Aquafina, Starbucks Coffee drinks, as well as sports drinks have sustained the company in the growth of its beverage market.[10]

In the *introductory stage,* consumer awareness and acceptance of the product are limited, sales are zero, and profits are negative. Profits are negative because the firm has spent money on research, development, and marketing to launch the product. During the introductory stage, marketers focus on making consumers aware of the product and its benefits. When Procter & Gamble introduced the Tide Stainbrush to reach the 70 percent of consumers who pretreat stains when doing laundry, it employed press releases as well as television and magazine advertising to make consumers aware of the new product.[11] Sales accelerate as the product enters the growth stage of the life cycle.

In the *growth stage,* sales increase rapidly and profits peak, then start to decline. One reason profits start to decline during the growth stage is that new companies enter the market, driving prices down and increasing marketing expenses. Consider Apple's iPod, the most popular digital music player with more than 74 percent of the music player market. It sold 32 million iPods in 2005, and its iTunes music store has 83 percent of the U.S. market share for legal music downloads. iTunes has more than 20 million unique visitors a month.[12] During the growth stage, the firm tries to strengthen its position in the market by emphasizing the product's benefits and identifying market segments that want these benefits.

**FIGURE 13.3** The Life Cycle of a Product

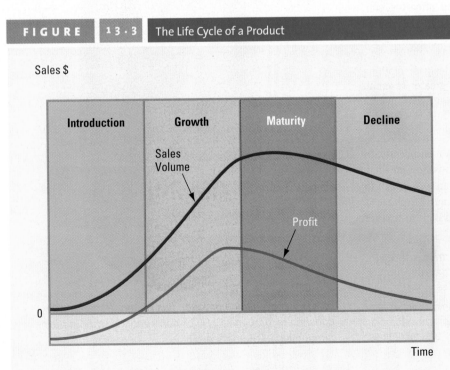

**FIGURE** **13.4** A Real-World Look at the Product Life Cycle

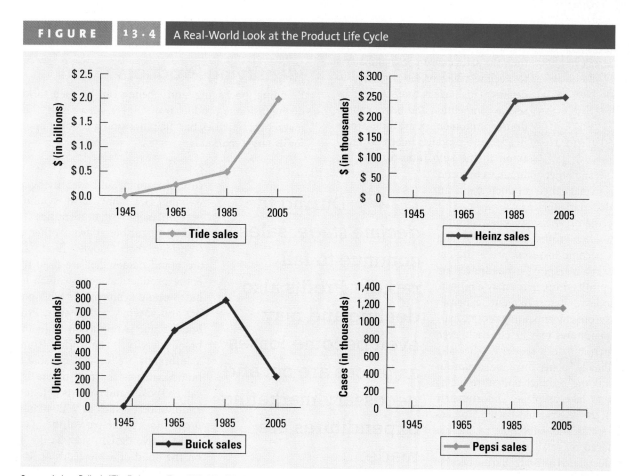

Source: Judann Pollack, "The Endurance Test, 1945–2005: We Map How Four Iconic Brands Have Changed with the Times," *Advertising Age,* November 14, 2005, p. 3.

# Snap, Crackle, and All Bran: Kellogg Pops Out New Products

Thanks to the vision of its founder, W. K. Kellogg, the Kellogg Company has been investing in international markets for almost 100 years. Due to this foresight, many international consumers consider Kellogg brands to be "of local origin." In 2005, Kellogg products were produced in 17 countries and sold in more than 180 countries. Kellogg International consists of Kellogg Europe, Kellogg Latin America, and Kellogg Asia Pacific.

Kellogg Europe grew 4 percent in 2004 and 2 percent in 2005. Kellogg's largest European area of business is the United Kingdom. "High-growth" regions are Italy and Spain, and business is growing in France. In the United Kingdom, popular products are *Special K* Lite Bites, *Frosties* Light, and yogurt-coated versions of *Special K* and *All-Bran*. A number of themed promotions and health challenges associated with various Kellogg products were successful marketing tools in Europe in 2004, given the region's current focus on health and wellness.

Growth in Latin America was at 11 percent for 2004 and again in 2005. In 2003, Kellogg's snack business doubled in Mexico, and the business continues to grow. In 2004, Kellogg

actually began building a manufacturing facility in Mexico devoted to producing cereals and snack foods. Business has also grown in Venezuela, Brazil, and the Caribbean. People in Latin America have a high rate of anemia, so in 2004 Kellogg continued its *Defensa K* campaign—promoting the nutritional value of Kellogg's products, especially iron content. Popular brands in Latin America are *Nutri-Grain, All-Bran, Choco Krispies* bars, and *Pop-Tarts*. Marketing campaigns with sports themes have been popular.

Asia Pacific showed a growth of 2 percent in 2004 and 1 percent in 2005. This is good news, as the environment in Australia has become more competitive and the South Korean cereal category was weak. To combat these pitfalls, Kellogg offered new varieties of cereals and bars in Australia and a new version of *Frosties* with less sugar in South Korea. The initial response to these introductions has been positive. Again, various campaigns run in Australia, India, and Japan focusing on health were successful.

In 2000, the company decided to invest money in its core global markets, rather than

working toward increasing its reach in new markets. As a result, Kellogg is now operating from a more stable foundation and is looking toward expansion. Those at Kellogg believe their company would be a very different place without the global groundwork set up by W. K. Kellogg. Ideas are shared and adapted around the world to make the Kellogg brands an international success.[13]❖

## Q: Discussion Questions

1. Why does Kellogg alter its products for different countries around the world?

2. Why do you think that many international consumers view Kellogg brands to be of local origin?

3. Can you think of a Kellogg's product item that should have global appeal with almost no modification?

Sales continue to increase at the beginning of the *maturity stage,* but then the sales curve peaks and starts to decline while profits continue to decline. This stage is characterized by severe competition and heavy expenditures. Automobiles are an example of a mature product; intense competition in the auto industry requires Toyota, GM, and other automakers to spend huge sums to make their products stand out in a crowded marketplace.

During the *decline stage,* sales continue to fall rapidly. Profits also decline and may even become losses as prices are cut and necessary marketing expenditures are made. As profits drop, firms may eliminate certain models or items. To reduce expenses and squeeze out any remaining profits, marketing expenditures may be cut back, even though such cutbacks accelerate the sales decline. Finally, plans must be made for phasing out the product and introducing new ones to take its place. Unfortunately for Mattel, the 48-year-old Barbie Doll has seen her status and sales slide as she has been replaced on retail shelves with more edgy products such as Bratz. Barbie became vulnerable from competition not only from Bratz but American Girl and the growth of toy sales in stores such as Wal-Mart and Target when they choose to allocate shelf space to products they considered more profitable.[14] Song

● ● **During the** *decline stage,* **sales continue to fall rapidly. Profits also decline and may even become losses as prices are cut and necessary marketing expenditures are made.**

airlines was pulled from the market after two years after its owner Delta went into bankruptcy.[15]

## Identifying Products

Branding, packaging, and labeling can be used to identify or distinguish one product from others. As a result, they are key marketing activities that help position a product appropriately for its target market.

**branding.** Branding is the process of naming and identifying products. A *brand* is a name, term, symbol, design, or combination that identifies a product and distinguishes it from other products. Consider that Google, iPod, and TiVo are brand names that are used to identify entire product categories, much like Xerox has become synonymous with photocopying and Kleenex with tissues. Protecting a brand name is important in maintaining a brand identity.[16] The world's 10 most valuable brands are shown in Table 13.1. The brand name is the part of the brand that can be spoken and consists of letters, words, and numbers—such as WD-40 lubricant. A *brand mark* is the part of the brand that is a distinctive design, such as the silver star on the hood of a Mercedes or McDonald's golden arches logo. A trademark is a brand that is registered with the U.S. Patent and Trademark Office and is thus legally protected from use by any other firm.

Two major categories of brands are manufacturer brands and private distributor brands. Manufacturer brands are brands initiated and owned by the manufacturer to identify products from the point of production to the point of purchase. Kellogg's, Sony, and Texaco are examples. Private distributor brands, which may be less expensive than manufacturer brands, are

*Prior to personal computers, typewriters were vital in home offices and businesses. What other goods do you think might be approaching the decline stages of their product life cycles?*

**TABLE 13.1**   The 10 Most Valuable Brands in the World

| Rank | Brand | Origin | 2006 Value ($ millions) |
|------|-------|--------|--------------------------|
| 1. | Coca-Cola | United States | $67,000 |
| 2. | Microsoft | United States | 56,926 |
| 3. | IBM | United States | 56,201 |
| 4. | GE | United States | 48,907 |
| 5. | Intel | United States | 32,319 |
| 6. | Nokia | Finland | 30,131 |
| 7. | Toyota | Japan | 27,941 |
| 8. | Disney | United States | 27,848 |
| 9. | McDonald's | United States | 27,501 |
| 10. | Mercedes-Benz | Germany | 21,795 |

Source: "The Top 100 Brands 2006," http://bwnt.businessweek.com/brand/2006/ (accessed June 17, 2007).

owned and controlled by a wholesaler or retailer, such as Kenmore appliances (Sears) and Sam's grocery products (Wal-Mart and Sam's Wholesale Club). The names of private brands do not usually identify their manufacturer. While private-label brands were once considered cheaper and poor quality, such as Wal-Mart's Ol'Roy dog food, many private-label brands are increasing quality and image and competing with national brands. Target hired architect Michael Graves to design its private-label products including kitchen appliances such as blenders and coffee pots. Martha Stewart designed a line of home fashions for K-Mart. Other firms such as JC Penney and Wal-Mart are also following the trend.[17] Manufacturer brands are fighting hard against private distributor brands.

Generic products like these appeal to consumers who are less concerned about quality and consistency but want lower prices.

Another type of brand that has developed is generic products—products with no brand name at all. They often come in plain, simple packages that carry only the generic name of the product—peanut butter, tomato juice, aspirin, dog food, and so on. They appeal to consumers who may be willing to sacrifice quality or product consistency to get a lower price.

Companies use two basic approaches to branding multiple products. In one, a company gives each product within its complete product mix its own brand name. Warner-Lambert, for example, sells many well-known consumer products—Dentyne, Chiclets, Listerine, Halls, Rolaids, and Trident—each individually branded. This branding policy ensures that the name of one product does not affect the names of others, and different brands can be targeted at different segments of the same market, increasing the company's market share (its percentage of the sales for the total market for a product). Another approach to branding is to develop a family of brands with each of the firm's products carrying the same name or at least part of the name. Gillette, Sara Lee, and IBM use this approach.

**packaging.** The packaging, or external container that holds and describes the product, influences consumers' attitudes and their buying decisions. A survey of over 1,200 consumers found that 40 percent are willing to try a new product based on its packaging.[18] It is estimated that consumers' eyes linger only 2.5 seconds on each product on an average shopping trip; therefore, product packaging should be designed to attract and hold consumers' attention.

A package can perform several functions including protection, economy, convenience, and promotion. Beverage manufacturers have been redesigning their bottles to make them more convenient for consumers and to promote them to certain markets. Scientists videotaped people drinking from different types of bottles and made plaster casts of their hands. They found that the average gulp is 6.44 ounces and that half the population would rather suck liquid through a pop-up top than drink it. Packaging also helps create an overall brand image. Coca-Cola's iconic bottle has been transformed into the shape of a round soccer ball at McDonald's corporation's 1,300 German outlets. The soccer ball–shaped bottle was used in association with World Cup meals; the bottle featured pictures of six soccer stars from leading national teams.[19]

**labeling.** Labeling, the presentation of important information on the package, is closely associated with packaging. The content of labeling, often required by law, may include ingredients or content, nutrition facts (calories, fat, etc.), care instructions, suggestions for use (such as recipes), the manufacturer's address and toll-free number, Web site, and other useful information. McDonald's introduced packaging that lets you know the nutritional value of Big Macs as well as other products. It was the first fast-food chain to adopt the initiative.[20] This information can have a strong impact on sales. The labels of many products, particularly food and drugs, must carry warnings, instructions, certifications, or manufacturers' identifications.

**product quality.** Quality reflects the degree to which a good, service, or idea meets the demands and requirements of customers. Quality products are often referred to as reliable, durable, easily maintained, easily used, a good value, or a trusted brand name. The level of quality is the amount of quality that a product possesses, and the consistency of quality depends on the product maintaining the same level of quality over time.

Quality of service is difficult to gauge because it depends on customers' perceptions of how well the service meets or exceeds their expectations. In other words, service quality is judged by consumers, not the service providers. A bank may define service quality as employing friendly and knowledgeable employees, but the bank's customers may be more concerned with waiting time, ATM access, security, and statement accuracy. Similarly,

**TABLE 13.2** Customer Satisfaction with Airlines

| Airline | 2007 Score | % Change from Previous Year |
|---|---|---|
| Southwest Airlines | 76 | 2.7 |
| All others | 75 | 1.4 |
| Continental Airlines | 69 | 3.0 |
| American Airlines | 60 | −3.2 |
| USAir Group | 61 | −1.6 |
| Northwest Airlines | 61 | 0 |
| Delta Airlines | 59 | −7.8 |
| United Airlines | 56 | −11.1 |

Source: The American Customer Satisfaction Index, http://www.theacsi.org/index.php?option=com_content&task=view&id=147&Itemid=155&i=Airlines (accessed June 17, 2007).

an airline traveler considers on-time arrival, on-board food service, and satisfaction with the ticketing and boarding process. The University of Michigan Business School's National Quality Research Center annually surveys customers of more than 200 companies and provides quarterly results for selected industries. The latest results showed that customer satisfaction rose to 73.5 (out of a possible 100) in nearly all industries covered by the survey, including utilities, hotels, telecommunications, airlines, express mail, and hospitals.[21] Table 13.2 shows the scores for major airlines and the percentage change from 2004. Services are becoming a larger part of international competition. As shown in Figure 13.5, people expect to receive the best service in restaurants.

The quality of services provided by businesses on the Internet can be gauged by consumers on such sites as ConsumerReports.org and BBBOnline. The subscription service offered by ConsumerReports. org provides consumers with a view of e-commerce sites' business, security, and privacy policies. BBBOnline is dedicated to promoting responsibility online. The Web Credibility Project focuses on how health, travel, advocacy, news, and shopping sites disclose business relationships with the companies and products they cover or sell, especially when such relationships pose a potential conflict of interest.[22] Quality can be associated with where the product is made. For example, "Made in U.S.A." labeling can be perceived as a different value and quality. As Table 13.3

*Coca-Cola's trademark varies from country to country. But the overall look is retained through use of similar letterforms and style, even with different alphabets.*

1. Arabic   5. Spanish
2. French   6. Chinese
3. Japanese 7. Hebrew
4. Thai     8. Polish

*Coca-Cola is the most valuable brand in the world.*

**TABLE 13.3** Perceived Quality and Value of Products Based on Country of Origin*

| | Made in U.S.A. | | Made in Japan | | Made in Korea | | Made in China | |
|---|---|---|---|---|---|---|---|---|
| | Value | Quality | Value | Quality | Value | Quality | Value | Quality |
| U.S. adults | 4.0 | 4.2 | 3.2 | 3.2 | 2.6 | 2.4 | 2.8 | 2.4 |
| Western Europeans | 3.3 | 3.4 | 3.5 | 3.5 | 2.8 | 2.4 | 2.9 | 2.4 |

*On a scale of 1 (low) to 5 (high).

Source: "American Demographics 2006 Consumer Perception Survey," *Advertising Age,* January 2, 2006, p. 9. Data by Synovate.

FIGURE 13.5 Where Customers Expect Best Service

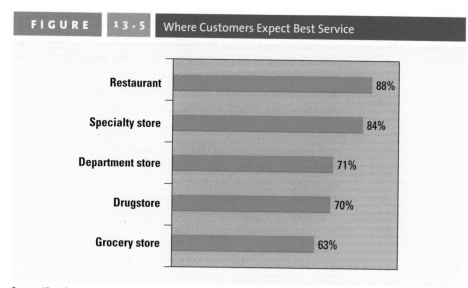

Source: "Best Service Expected at Restaurants," *USA Today Snapshots,* April 17, 2005. p. B4.

products or services from firms with good ethics. However, some types of consumers are increasingly "trading up" to more status-conscious products, such as automobiles, home appliances, restaurants, and even pet food, yet remain price-conscious for other products such as cleaning and grocery goods. This trend has benefited marketers such as Starbucks, Sub-Zero, BMW, and Petco—which can charge premium prices for high-quality, prestige products—as well as Sam's Clubs and Costco—which offer basic household products at everyday low prices.[25]

Price is a key element in the marketing mix because it relates directly to the generation of revenue and profits. McDonald's has increased profits with upscale items such as its $4.50 Cobb salad.[26] In large part, the ability to set a price depends on the supply of and demand for a product. For most products, the quantity demanded goes up as the price goes down, and as the price goes up, the quantity demanded goes down. Changes in buyers' needs, variations in the effectiveness of other marketing mix variables, the presence of substitutes, and dynamic environmental factors can influence demand. Consider that gas prices rose dramatically in 2006 in response to tightened petroleum supplies and increasing demand from China and the United States. Sales of large, less fuel-efficient sport utility vehicles began to decline as a result. Of course, price also depends on the cost to manufacture a good or provide a service or idea. A firm may temporarily sell products below cost

indicates, there are differences in the perception of quality and value between the U.S. consumers and Europeans when comparing products made in the United States, Japan, Korea and China.[23]

## ○ ● L02

Define price and discuss its importance in the marketing mix, including various pricing strategies a firm might employ.

# PRICING STRATEGY

Previously, we defined price as the value placed on an object exchanged between a buyer and a seller. Buyers' interest in price stems from their expectations about the usefulness of a product or the satisfaction they may derive from it. Because buyers have limited resources, they must allocate those resources to obtain the products they most desire. They must decide whether the benefits gained in an exchange are worth the buying power sacrificed. Almost anything of value can be assessed by a price. Many factors may influence the evaluation of value, including time constraints, price levels, perceived quality, and motivations to use available information about prices.[24] Indeed, consumers vary in their response to price: Some focus solely on the lowest price, while others consider quality or the prestige associated with a product and its price. As Figure 13.6 indicates, most consumers would pay higher prices for

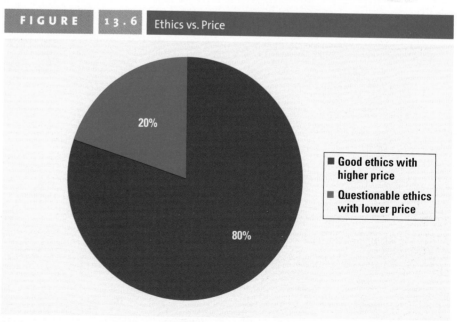

Source: "Ethics vs. Price," *USA Today Snapshots,* June 14, 2006, p. B1.

to match competition, to generate cash flow, or even to increase market share, but in the long run it cannot survive by selling its products below cost.

Price is probably the most flexible variable in the marketing mix. Although it may take years to develop a product, establish channels of distribution, and design and implement promotion, a product's price may be set and changed in a few minutes. Under certain circumstances, of course, the price may not be so flexible, especially if government regulations prevent dealers from controlling prices.

## Pricing Objectives

Pricing objectives specify the role of price in an organization's marketing mix and strategy. They usually are influenced not only by marketing mix decisions but also by finance, accounting, and production factors. Maximizing profits and sales, boosting market share, maintaining the status quo, and survival are four common pricing objectives.

## Specific Pricing Strategies

Pricing strategies provide guidelines for achieving the company's pricing objectives and overall marketing strategy. They specify how price will be used as a variable in the marketing mix. Significant pricing strategies relate to the pricing of new products, psychological pricing, and price discounting.

**pricing new products.** Setting the price for a new product is critical: The right price leads to profitability; the wrong price may kill the product. In general, there are two basic strategies to setting the base price for a new product. **Price skimming** is charging the highest possible price that buyers who want the product will pay. The $100 and higher market for jeans is growing rapidly. Companies such as True Religion, Rock & Republic, Citizens of Humanity, and 7 for All Mankind are sold at stores such as Saks Fifth Avenue and Barneys New York. True Religion experienced a sales increase of 41.8 percent over the previous year.[28] This strategy allows the company to generate much-needed revenue to help offset the costs of research and development. Conversely, a **penetration price** is a low price designed to help a product enter the market and gain market share rapidly. For example, when Industrias Añaños introduced Kola Real to capitalize on limited supplies of

## $180 for Levi's Jeans: Will They Buy It?

Levi Strauss & Co., known for its 501s and affordable prices, is attempting to break into the premium denim jean market. The company, which has been making jeans since the 1800s, wants to take part in the ever-growing $1 billion-plus market dominated by brands such as Earl Jeans, 7 for All Mankind, Citizens for Humanity, and True Religion. By launching a more aggressive marketing campaign, Levi's is hoping to get its Levi's Premium collection, selling for between $110 and $180, out there among the rest.

People in the fashion industry feel that Levi's reputation as a long-standing, reliable, inexpensive department store brand may hurt its chances in the high-end market. Women are the primary purchasers of high-end jeans, and Levi's has always been more of a men's jean. To compete, Levi's is going to have to prove that the Premium line has comparable quality and STYLE to the rest of the high-end brands out there.

To appeal to the fashion conscious, Levi's has linked with the Warhol Foundation to create a spring 2006 Premium collection based on the art of Andy Warhol. Andy Warhol wore

Levi's, and the company plans to capitalize on this. The company also threw an "underground" party in fall 2005 to promote its Ultimate boot-cut jeans with the help of cast members from "Desperate Housewives." More marketing like this will be key in introducing and selling the Premium jeans to high-end customers. Two new Levi's stores, located in Beverly Hills, California, and Georgetown in Washington, D.C., will market both the company's popular Red Tab collection and the Premium collection.

The Premium collection may contribute to a small portion of the company's revenue, but right now it is pushing the company's innovation. After seeing losses for several years, the company is seeing positive sales results in the premium market in Europe and Asia. Overall premium sales saw more than a 100 percent increase in 2004. Sally Singer of Vogue believes that if anyone can help Levi's break into the high-end market, Caroline Calvin—Levi's U.S. Creative Director—is the person to do it. The company will need to work directly with fashion magazines and convince trendy boutiques to carry their jeans, and to do so

they will have to talk up more than the company's heritage.

If Levi's can successfully compete in the high-end market and gain recognition for its Premium brand, this will most likely increase profitability in all segments of the Levi's market. And, of course, if Levi's popularity increases across the board, so does its revenue—the ultimate goal of any marketing strategy.[27] ❖

### Q: Discussion Questions

1. Why do you think that Levi's wants to charge premium prices for some of its products?

2. Who do you think is the target market for Levi's jeans that cost more than $100?

3. What will be the biggest obstacle in Levi's selling to an upscale, fashion-conscious market?

Coca-Cola and Pepsi Cola in Peru, it set an ultralow penetration price to appeal to the poor who predominate in the region. Kola Real quickly secured one-fifth of the Peruvian market and has since made significant gains in Ecuador, Venezuela, and Mexico, forcing larger soft-drink marketers to cut prices.[29] Penetration pricing is less flexible than price skimming; it is more difficult to raise a penetration price than to lower a skimming price. Penetration pricing is used most often when marketers suspect that competitors will enter the market shortly after the product has been introduced.

**psychological pricing.** Psychological pricing encourages purchases based on emotional rather than rational responses to the price. For example, the assumption behind *even/odd pricing* is that people will buy more of a product for $9.99 than $10 because it seems to be a bargain at the odd price. The assumption behind *symbolic/prestige pricing* is that high prices connote high quality. Thus the prices of certain fragrances are set artificially high to give the impression of superior quality. Some over-the-counter drugs are priced high because consumers associate a drug's price with potency.

**price discounting.** Temporary price reductions, or discounts, are often employed to boost sales. Although there are many types, quantity, seasonal, and promotional discounts are among the most widely used. Quantity discounts reflect the economies of purchasing in large volume. Seasonal discounts to buyers who purchase goods or services out of season help even out production capacity. Promotional discounts attempt to improve sales by advertising price reductions on selected products to increase customer interest. Often promotional pricing is geared to increased profits. On the other hand, many companies such as Wal-Mart, Home Depot, and Toys 'Я' Us have shunned promotional price discounts and, with everyday low pricing, are focusing more on relationships with customers. Polo killed its Polo jeans brand because the price of this product hurt its luxury image.[30] In the airline industry, low-cost airlines like JetBlue, AirTran, Frontier, and America West are competing head-to-head with the major airlines by offering sharply discounted fares. Additionally, Web sites like Priceline.com, Orbitz.com, and Travelocity.com help flyers find the lowest fares quickly, forcing airlines to become even more price competitive.

● ● **LO3**

Identify factors affecting distribution decisions, such as marketing channels and intensity of market coverage.

# DISTRIBUTION STRATEGY

The best products in the world will not be successful unless companies make them available where and when customers want to buy them. In this section, we will explore dimensions of distribution strategy, including the channels through which products are distributed, the intensity of market coverage, and the physical handling of products during distribution.

The publishers of the Harry Potter novels use a price skimming strategy. They set the price high when the book is first introduced, then lower the price significantly to maintain sales.

## Marketing Channels

A marketing channel, or channel of distribution, is a group of organizations that moves products from their producer to customers. Marketing channels make products available to buyers when and where they desire to purchase them. Organizations that bridge the gap between a product's manufacturer and the ultimate consumer are called *middlemen,* or intermediaries. They create time, place, and ownership utility. Two intermediary organizations are retailers and wholesalers.

Retailers buy products from manufacturers (or other intermediaries) and sell them to consumers for home and household use rather than for resale or for use in producing other products. Toys 'Я' Us, for example, buys products from Mattel and other manufacturers and resells them to consumers. Retailing usually occurs in a store, but the Internet, vending machines, mail-order catalogs, and entertainment, such as going to a Chicago Bulls basketball game, also provide opportunities for retailing. With more than 200 million Americans accessing the Internet, online sales were more than $80 billion in 2005. By bringing together an assortment of products from competing

● WHOLESALERS inter-mediaries who buy from producers or from other wholesalers and sell to retailers

producers, retailers create utility. Retailers arrange for products to be moved from producers to a convenient retail establishment (place utility). They maintain hours of operation for their retail stores to make merchandise available when consumers want it (time utility). They also assume the risk of ownership of inventories (ownership utility). Table 13.4 describes various types of general merchandise retailers.

Today, there are too many stores competing for too few customers, and, as a result, competition between similar retailers has never been more intense. In addition, retailers face challenges such as shoplifting, as indicated in Table 13.5. Further, competition between different types of stores is changing the nature of retailing. Supermarkets compete with specialty food stores, wholesale clubs, and discount stores. Department stores compete with nearly every other type of store including specialty stores, off-price chains, category killers, discount stores, and online retailers. Many traditional retailers, such as Wal-Mart and Macy's, have created online shopping sites to retain customers and compete with online-only retailers. One of the best-known online-only, or cyber, merchants is Amazon.com. Amazon offers millions of products from which to choose, all from the privacy and convenience of the purchaser's home. In some cases, Web merchants offer wide selections, ultra-convenience, superior service, knowledge, and the best products. More detail on the Internet's effect on marketing was presented in Chapter 4.

**TABLE 13.5** Stealing from Stores

| | |
|---|---|
| Shoplifters in United States | 23 million |
| Amount retailers lose per year | More than $10 billion |
| Percent of shoplifters who are adults | 75% |

Source: National Shoplifting Prevention Coalition, *USA Today,* "Stealing from Stores," March 10, 2006, p. A1.

○● **Although it is true that wholesalers can be eliminated, their functions must be passed on to some other entity, such as the producer, another intermediary, or even the customer.**

**Wholesalers** are intermediaries who buy from producers or from other wholesalers and sell to retailers. They usually do not sell in significant quantities to ultimate consumers. Wholesalers perform the functions listed in Table 13.6.

Wholesalers are extremely important because of the marketing activities they perform, particularly for consumer products. Although it is true that wholesalers can be eliminated, their functions must be passed on to some other entity, such as the producer, another intermediary, or even the customer. Wholesalers help consumers and retailers by buying in large quantities, then selling to retailers in smaller quantities. By stocking an assortment of products, wholesalers match products to demand.

**supply chain management.**
In an effort to improve distribution channel relationships among manufacturers and other channel intermediaries, supply chain management creates alliances between channel members. In Chapter 9, we defined supply chain management as connecting and integrating all parties or members of the distribution system to satisfy customers. It involves long-term partnerships

**TABLE 13.4** General Merchandise Retailers

| Type of Retailer | Description | Examples |
|---|---|---|
| Department store | Large organization offering wide product mix and organized into separate departments | Macy's, JCPenney, Sears |
| Discount store | Self-service, general merchandise store offering brand name and private brand products at low prices | Wal-Mart, Target |
| Supermarket | Self-service store offering complete line of food products and some nonfood products | Kroger, Albertson's, Winn-Dixie |
| Superstore | Giant outlet offering all food and nonfood products found in supermarkets, as well as most routinely purchased products | Wal-Mart Supercenters |
| Hypermarket | Combination supermarket and discount store, larger than a superstore | Carrefour |
| Warehouse club | Large-scale, members-only establishments combining cash-and-carry wholesaling with discount retailing | Sam's Club, Costco |
| Warehouse showroom | Facility in a large, low-cost building with large on-premises inventories and minimum service | Ikea |
| Catalog showroom | Type of warehouse showroom where consumers shop from a catalog and products are stored out of buyers' reach and provided in manufacturer's carton | Service Merchandise |

Source: William M. Pride and O. C. Ferrell, *Marketing: Concepts and Strategies,* 2008, p. 428. Copyright 2008 by Houghton Mifflin Company. Reprinted with permission.

Netflix has given Blockbuster a run for its money by delivering rental DVDs straight to viewers' homes. Some industry experts believe that to remain competitive, Netflix will eventually need to pursue a new distribution strategy of providing consumers with downloadable movies.

**TABLE 13.6**  Major Wholesaling Functions

| | |
|---|---|
| Supply chain management | Creating long-term partnerships among channel members |
| Promotion | Providing a sales force, advertising, sales promotion, and publicity |
| Warehousing, shipping, and product handling | Receiving, storing, and stockkeeping |
| | Packaging |
| | Shipping outgoing orders |
| | Materials handling |
| | Arranging and making local and long distance shipments |
| Inventory control and data processing | Processing orders |
| | Controlling physical inventory |
| | Recording transactions |
| | Tracking sales data for financial analysis |
| Risk taking | Assuming responsibility for theft, product obsolescence, and excess inventories |
| Financing and budgeting | Extending credit |
| | Making capital investments |
| | Forecasting cash flow |
| Marketing research and information systems | Providing information about market |
| | Conducting research studies |
| | Managing computer networks to facilitate exchanges and relationships |

Source: William M. Pride and O. C. Ferrell, *Marketing: Concepts and Strategies,* 2008, p. 389. Copyright 2008 by Houghton Mifflin Company. Reprinted with permission.

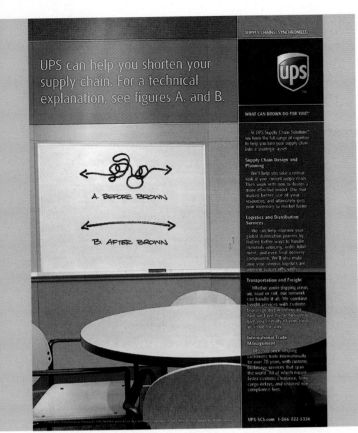

UPS runs a business-to-business ad showcasing its solutions for supply chain management.

among marketing channel members working together to reduce costs, waste, and unnecessary movement in the entire marketing channel in order to satisfy customers.[31] It goes beyond traditional channel members (producers, wholesalers, retailers, customers) to include *all* organizations involved in moving products from the producer to the ultimate customer. In a survey of business managers, a disruption in the supply chain was viewed as the number-one crisis that could decrease revenue.[32]

The focus shifts from one of selling to the next level in the channel to one of selling products *through* the channel to a satisfied ultimate customer. Information, once provided on a guarded,"as needed" basis, is now open, honest, and ongoing. Perhaps most importantly, the points of contact in the relationship expand from one-on-one at the salesperson–buyer level to multiple interfaces at all levels and in all functional areas of the various organizations.

**channels for consumer products.** Typical marketing channels for consumer products are shown in Figure 13.7. In Channel A, the product moves from the producer directly to the consumer. Farmers who sell their fruit and vegetables to consumers at roadside stands use a direct-from-producer-to-consumer marketing channel.

In Channel B, the product goes from producer to retailer to consumer. This type of channel is used for products such as college textbooks, automobiles, and appliances. In Channel C, the product is handled by a wholesaler and a retailer before it reaches the consumer. Producer-to-wholesaler-to-retailer-to-consumer marketing channels distribute a wide range of products including refrigerators, televisions, soft drinks, cigarettes, clocks, watches, and office products. In Channel D, the product goes to an agent, a wholesaler, and a retailer before going to the consumer. This long channel of distribution is especially useful for convenience products. Candy and some produce are often sold by agents who bring buyers and sellers together.

Services are usually distributed through direct marketing channels because they are generally produced *and* consumed simultaneously. For example, you cannot take a haircut home for later use. Many services require the customer's presence and participation: The sick patient must visit the physician to receive treatment; the child must be at the day care center to receive care; the tourist must be present to sightsee and consume tourism services.

**FIGURE 13·7** Marketing Channels for Consumer Products

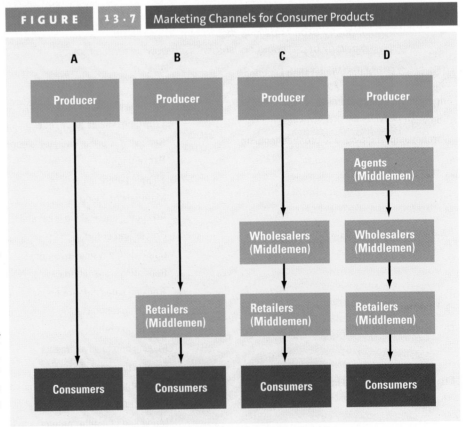

The use of online advertising is increasing. However, advertisers are demanding more for their ad dollars and proof that they are working. Certain types of ads are more popular than pop-up ads and banner ads that consumers find annoying. Also increasing in popularity are 6- to 11-minute made-for-the-Web ads called "advertainments." Produced, posted, and promoted by Ford, BMW, Diet Coke, and Absolut vodka, the movies feature a product as the star. One BMW movie features a man who drives difficult passengers (in one film, Madonna stars as a difficult, foul-mouthed celebrity) around in flashy BMWs and gives them the ride of their lives. The Ford advertainments feature a Ford vehicle in three different scenarios—the promise of a Ford Focus to a teenager if he can make the team; a shirtless teen boy lying on a Ford Focus, smoking and eyeing a nearby teen girl, and a young man who drives around in a Ford trying to save his goldfish.[35]

Infomercials—typically 30-minute blocks of radio or television air time featuring a celebrity or upbeat host talking about and demonstrating a product—have evolved as an advertising method. Toll-free numbers and Web site addresses are usually provided so consumers can conveniently purchase the product or obtain additional information. Although many consumers and companies have negative feelings about infomercials, apparently they get results.

## personal selling.

**Personal selling** is direct, two-way communication with buyers and potential buyers. For many products—especially large, expensive ones with specialized uses, such as cars, appliances, and houses—interaction between a salesperson and the customer is probably the most important promotional tool.

Personal selling is the most flexible of the promotional methods because it gives marketers the greatest opportunity to communicate specific information that might trigger a purchase. Only personal selling can zero in on a prospect and attempt to persuade that person to make a purchase. Although personal selling has a lot of advantages, it is one of the most costly forms of promotion. A sales call on an industrial customer can cost as much as $200 or $300.

There are three distinct categories of salespersons: order takers (for example, retail sales clerks and route salespeople), creative salespersons (for example, automobile, furniture, and insurance salespeople), and support salespersons (for example, customer educators and goodwill builders who usually do not take orders). For most of these salespeople, personal selling is a six-step process:

1. *Prospecting:* Identifying potential buyers of the product.
2. *Approaching:* Using a referral or calling on a customer without prior notice to determine interest in the product.
3. *Presenting:* Getting the prospect's attention with a product demonstration.
4. *Handling objections:* Countering reasons for not buying the product.
5. *Closing:* Asking the prospect to buy the product.
6. *Following up:* Checking customer satisfaction with the purchased product.

## publicity.

**Publicity** is nonpersonal communication transmitted through the mass media but not paid for directly by the firm. A firm does not pay the media cost for publicity and is not identified as the originator of the

*The Louisville Zoo advertises on this billboard to increase attendance.*

message; instead, the message is presented in news story form. Obviously, a company can benefit from publicity by releasing to news sources newsworthy messages about the firm and its involvement with the public. Many companies have *public relations* departments to try to gain favorable publicity and minimize negative publicity for the firm.

Although advertising and publicity are both carried by the mass media, they differ in several major ways. Advertising messages tend to be informative, persuasive, or both; publicity is mainly informative. Advertising is often designed to have an immediate impact or to provide specific information to persuade a person to act; publicity describes what a firm is doing, what products it is launching, or other newsworthy information, but seldom calls for action. When advertising is used, the organization must pay for media time and select the media that will best reach target audiences. The mass media willingly carry publicity because they believe it has general public interest. Advertising can be repeated a number of times; most publicity appears in the mass media once and is not repeated.

Advertising, personal selling, and sales promotion are especially useful for influencing an exchange directly. Publicity is extremely important when communication focuses on a company's activities and products and is directed at interest groups, current and potential investors, regulatory agencies, and society in general.

A variation of traditional advertising is buzz marketing, in which marketers attempt to create a trend or acceptance of a product. Companies seek out trendsetters in communities and get them to "talk up" a brand to their friends, family, co-workers, and others. Toyota, for example, parked its new Scions outside of raves and coffee shops, and offered hip-hop magazine writers the chance for test drives to get the "buzz" going about the new car.[36] Other marketers using the buzz technique include Hebrew National ("mom squads" grilled the company's hot dogs), Hasbro Games (fourth- and fifth-graders tantalized their peers with Hasbro's POX electronic game), and Chrysler (its retro PT Cruiser was planted in rental fleets). The idea behind buzz marketing is that an accepted member of a particular social group will be more credible than any form of paid communication.[37] The concept works best as part of an integrated marketing communication program that also includes traditional advertising, personal selling, sales promotion, and publicity.

*Sarah Jessica Parker's "Carrie Bradshaw" love of Manolo Blahnik shoes on Sex in the City was a publicity coup when Parker would also wear them to personal events.*

A related concept is viral marketing, which describes the concept of getting Internet users to pass on ads and promotions to others. For example, Ebrick offered special discounts to its shoppers and encouraged them to forward the deals to their friends and family.[38]

**sales promotion.** Sales promotion involves direct inducements offering added value or some other incentive for buyers to enter into an exchange. The major tools of sales promotion are store displays, premiums, samples and demonstrations, coupons, contests and sweepstakes, refunds,

and trade shows. In 2005, distribution of coupons increased 10 percent. Distribution now stands at more than 323 billion coupons. About 88 percent of these coupons were distributed via Sunday newspapers. However, the consumer response to coupon promotions fell to 3 billion coupons redeemed in 2005 from more than 3.8 billion redeemed in 2002.[39] Nearly 80 percent of all consumers use coupons.[40] Sales promotion stimulates customer purchasing and increases dealer effectiveness in selling products. It is used to enhance and supplement other forms of promotion. Test drives allow salespersons to demonstrate vehicles, which can help purchase decisions. Sampling a product may also encourage consumers to buy. PepsiCo, for example, used sampling to promote its Sierra Mist soft drink to reach more than 5 million potential consumers at well-traveled sites such as Times Square and Penn Station.[41] In a given year, almost three-fourths of consumer product companies may use sampling.

Sales promotions are generally easier to measure and less expensive than advertising. Although less than 2 percent of the 323 billion coupons distributed annually are redeemed, offering them in Sunday paper inserts is cheaper than producing a television commercial. Manufacturers typically pay about $7 per 1,000 inserts for a full page to reach 60 million homes, or nearly 60 percent of U.S. households.[42]

## Promotion Strategies: To Push or To Pull

In developing a promotion mix, organizations must decide whether to fashion a mix that pushes or pulls the product (Figure 13.8). A **push strategy** attempts to motivate intermediaries to push the product down to their customers. When a push strategy is used, the company attempts to motivate wholesalers and retailers to make the product available to their customers. Sales personnel may be used to persuade intermediaries to offer the product, distribute promotional materials, and offer special promotional incentives for those who agree to carry the product. Chrysler manufacturing plants operate on a push system. They assemble cars according to forecasts of sales demand. Dealers then sell to buyers with the help of incentives and other promotions.[43] A **pull strategy** uses promotion to create consumer demand for a product so that consumers exert pressure on marketing channel members to make it available. For example, when the Coca-Cola Company launched its new hybrid energy soda VAULT, the company gave away samples throughout the United States via sampling teams in VAULT-branded International CXTs, the world's largest production pickup trucks. They distributed ice-cold VAULT at concerts and targeted retail outlets, sporting events, and other locations.[44] Such sampling prior to a product rollout encourages consumers to request the product from their favorite retailer.

A company can use either strategy, or it can use a variation or combination of the two. The exclusive use of advertising indicates a pull strategy. Personal selling to marketing channel members indicates a push strategy. The allocation of promotional resources to various marketing mix elements probably determines which strategy a marketer uses.

## Objectives of Promotion

The marketing mix a company uses depends on its objectives. It is important to recognize that promotion is only one element of the marketing strategy and must be tied carefully to the goals of the firm, its overall marketing objectives, and the other elements of the marketing strategy. Firms use promotion for many reasons, but typical objectives are to stimulate demand, to stabilize sales, and to inform, remind, and reinforce customers.

Increasing demand for a product is probably the most typical promotional objective. Stimulating demand, often through advertising and sales promotion, is particularly important when a firm is using a pull strategy.

Another goal of promotion is to stabilize sales by maintaining the status quo—that is, the current sales level of the product. During periods of slack or decreasing sales, contests, prizes, vacations, and other sales promotions are sometimes offered to customers to maintain sales goals. Advertising is often used to stabilize sales by making customers aware of slack use periods. For example, auto manufacturers often provide rebates, free options, or lower-than-market interest rates to stabilize sales and thereby keep production lines moving during temporary slowdowns. A stable sales pattern allows the firm to run efficiently by maintaining a consistent level of production and storage and utilizing all its functions so that it is ready when sales increase.

An important role of any promotional program is to inform potential buyers about the organization and its products. A major portion of advertising in the United States, particularly in daily newspapers, is informational. Providing information about the availability, price, technology, and features of a product is very important in encouraging a buyer to move toward a purchase decision. Nearly all forms of promotion involve an attempt to help consumers learn more about a product and a company.

Promotion is also used to remind consumers that an established organization is still around and sells certain products that have uses and benefits. Often advertising reminds customers that they may need to use a product more frequently or in certain situations. Pennzoil, for example, has run television commercials reminding car owners that they need to change their oil every 3,000 miles to ensure proper performance of their cars.

Reinforcement promotion attempts to assure current users of the product that they have made the right choice and tells them how to get the most satisfaction from the product. Also, a company could release publicity statements through the news media about a new use for a product. Additionally, firms can have salespeople communicate with current and potential customers about the proper use and maintenance of a product—all in the hope of developing a repeat customer.

## Promotional Positioning

**Promotional positioning** uses promotion to create and maintain an image of a product in buyers' minds. It is a natural

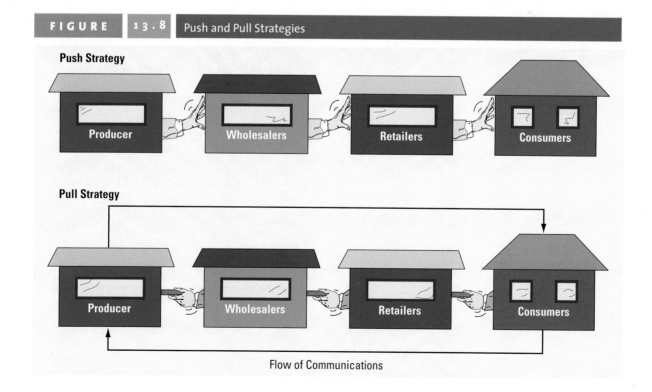

**FIGURE 13.8 Push and Pull Strategies**

Push Strategy

Producer — Wholesalers — Retailers — Consumers

Pull Strategy

Producer — Wholesalers — Retailers — Consumers

Flow of Communications

All organizations need people to perform marketing activities. Whether in manufacturing, financial services, health care, professional services, or nonprofit organizations, companies are constantly seeking individuals who can work to develop new products, use marketing research to stay on top of emerging trends, and, in general, create sales. Broad areas of opportunity in marketing include marketing research, sales, purchasing, advertising, retailing, and direct marketing. Employment of marketing, advertising, and public relations managers is expected to increase faster than average for all occupations through the year 2012. With between one-fourth and one-third of the civilian workforce in the United States employed in marketing-related jobs, it is clear that marketing offers many diverse career opportunities.

With increasing global and domestic competition and more complex products, students with marketing degrees will find excellent job prospects. Service and high-technology firms, in particular, are experiencing rapid growth and have a high demand for marketers to help develop, distribute, and promote new products. A bachelor's degree is generally necessary, but some higher-level positions require a master's or doctorate degree. Students with a bachelor's degree in marketing can expect to start out earning about $29,000, those with advertising degrees, $27,000. With experience and education, top-level advertising executives and marketing managers can expect to reach six-figure salaries, depending on the organization and how many people they supervise.

Listed below are starting salary ranges for selected marketing professionals.

| | |
|---|---|
| Brand/product manager | $57,000–$86,750 |
| Corporate marketing manager | $47,250–$74,500 |
| Ad agency marketing manager | $47,750–$75,000 |
| Advertising copywriter | $42,500–$59,000 |
| Media buyer | $41,500–$56,000 |
| Ad agency account executive | $38,250–$55,000[45] |

result of market segmentation. In both promotional positioning and market segmentation, the firm targets a given product or brand at a portion of the total market. A promotional strategy helps differentiate the product and make it appeal to a particular market segment. For example, to appeal to safety-conscious consumers, Volvo heavily promotes the safety and crashworthiness of Volvo automobiles in its advertising. Volkswagen has done the same thing with its edgy ads showing car crashes. Promotion can be used to change or reinforce an image. Effective promotion influences customers and persuades them to buy. ■

## CHECK OUT

www.mhhe.com/FerrellM

for study materials including Interactive Exercises, Quizzes, iPod downloads, and video.

## Build Your Business Plan

**DIMENSIONS OF MARKETING STRATEGY**   If you think your product/business is truly new to or unique to the market, you need to substantiate your claim. After a thorough exploration on the Web, you want to make sure there has not been a similar business/service recently launched in your community. Check with your Chamber of Commerce or Economic Development Office that might be able to provide you with a history of recent business failures. If you are not confident about the ability or willingness of customers to try your new product or service, collecting your own primary data to ascertain demand is highly advisable.

The decision of where to initially set your prices is a critical one. If there are currently similar products in the market, you need to be aware of the competitors' prices before you determine yours. If your product/service is new to the market, you can price it high (market skimming strategy) as long as you realize that the high price will probably attract competitors to the market more quickly (they will think they can make the same product for less), which will force you to drop your prices sooner than you would like. Another strategy to consider is market penetration pricing, a strategy that sets price lower and discourages competition from entering the market as quickly. Whatever strategy you decide to use, don't forget to examine your product/service's elasticity.

At this time you need to start thinking about how to promote your product. Why do you feel your product/service is different or new to the market? How do you want to position your product/service so customers view it favorably? Remember this is all occurring *within the consumer's mind.*

All in one place.

M start here.

## ● ● learning OBJECTIVES

**LO1**  Define accounting, and describe the different uses of accounting information.

**LO2**  Demonstrate the accounting process.

**LO3**  Examine the various components of an income statement to evaluate a firm's "bottom line."

**LO4**  Interpret a company's balance sheet to determine its current financial position.

**LO5**  Analyze financial statements, using ratio analysis, to evaluate a company's performance.

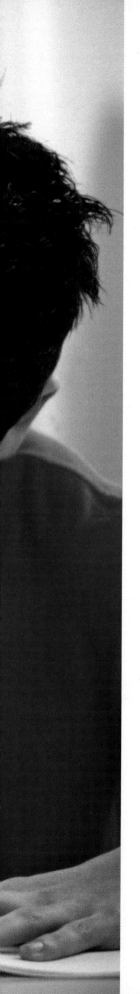

# ACCOUNTING & FINANCIAL STATEMENTS

**Introduction**    Accounting, the financial "language" that organizations use to record, measure, and interpret all of their financial transactions and records, is very important in business. All businesses—from a small family farm to a giant corporation—use the language of accounting to make sure they use their money wisely and to plan for the future. Nonbusiness organizations such as charities and governments also use accounting to demonstrate to donors and taxpayers how well they are using their funds and meeting their stated objectives.

This chapter explores the role of accounting in business and its importance in making business decisions. First, we discuss the uses of accounting information and the accounting process. Then, we briefly look at some simple financial statements and accounting tools that are useful in analyzing organizations worldwide.

## LO1

Define accounting, and describe the different uses of accounting information.

# THE NATURE OF ACCOUNTING

Simply stated, accounting is the recording, measurement, and interpretation of financial information. Large numbers of people and institutions, both within and outside businesses, use accounting tools to evaluate organizational operations. The Financial Accounting Standards Board has been establishing standards of financial accounting and reporting in the private sector since 1973. Its mission is to establish and improve standards of financial accounting and reporting for the guidance and education of the public, including issuers, auditors, and users of financial information. However, the accounting scandals at the turn of the century resulted when many accounting firms and businesses failed to abide by generally accepted accounting principles. More than 1,000 firms ultimately reported flaws in their financial statements between 1997 and 2002; in 2002 alone, a record 330 companies chose to restate their earnings to avoid further questions.[1] Consequently, the federal government has taken a greater role in making rules, requirements, and policies for accounting firms and businesses through the Securities and Exchange Commission's Public Company Accounting Oversight Board. For example, Ernst & Young, a leading accounting firm, was barred from undertaking new audit clients for six months as penalty for abusing the agency's auditor-independence rules.[2]

To better understand the importance of accounting, we must first understand who prepares accounting information and how it is used.

## Accountants

Many of the functions of accounting are carried out by public or private accountants.

**public accountants.** Individuals and businesses can hire a certified public accountant (CPA), an individual who has been certified by the state in which he or she practices

**?**

### DID YOU KNOW?

Corporate fraud costs are estimated at $600 billion annually.[5]

to provide accounting services ranging from the preparation of financial records and the filing of tax returns to complex audits of corporate financial records. Certification gives a public accountant the right to express, officially, an unbiased opinion regarding the accuracy of the client's financial statements. Most public accountants are either self-employed or members of large public accounting firms such as Ernst & Young, KPMG, Deloitte & Touche, and Pricewaterhouse Coopers, together referred to as "the Big Four." In addition, many CPAs work for one of the second-tier accounting firms that are about one-third the size of the Big Four firms, as illustrated in Table 14.1. The accounting scandals at the turn of the century, combined with more stringent accounting requirements legislated by the Sarbanes-Oxley Act, have increased job prospects for accountants and students with accounting degrees as companies and accounting firms hire more auditors to satisfy the law and public demand for greater transparency.[3]

With the demise of Arthur Andersen there have been concerns about one of the remaining Big Four accounting firms failing. The U.S. Chamber of Commerce published a report calling for regulators and policy makers to keep such an event from happening again to maintain competition and availability of accountants.[4]

A growing area for public accountants is *forensic accounting*, which involves analyzing financial documents in search of fraudulent entries or financial misconduct. Functioning as much like detectives as accountants, forensic accountants have been used since the 1930s. In the wake of the accounting scandals of the early 2000s, many auditing firms are rapidly adding or expanding forensic or fraud-detection services. Additionally, many forensic accountants root out evidence of "cooked books" for federal agencies like the Federal Bureau of Investigation or the Internal Revenue Service.

**TABLE 14.1** Leading Accounting Firms

| Company | Revenues ($ millions) |
|---|---|
| **"Big Four"** | |
| Ernst & Young | 21,986 |
| PricewaterhouseCoopers | 18,400 |
| Deloitte & Touche | 8,769 |
| KPMG | 4,700 |
| **Second-Tier Firms** | |
| Grant Thornton | 940 |
| BDO Sideman | 558 |
| Moss Adams | 229 |

Note: Prestige survey based ranking.

Source: "Top Accounting Firms—2007, Vault Top 40 Most Prestigious," http://europe.vault.com/nr/finance_rankings/accounting_rankings.jsp?accounting2006=2 (accessed June 18, 2007).

**Clarence Otis—Darden Restaurants**   About 30 years ago, Clarence Otis changed the name of his restaurant from the Green Frog to the Red Lobster. Today, it is the number-one seafood chain in the country. The same parent corporation, Darden Restaurants, owns the Olive Garden chain. Darden has more than 150,000 employees and nearly 1,500 restaurants.

At an early age, Otis had excellent guidance as his mother had very high expectations for him. His first job was a server in a full-service restaurant, where he learned the pressures associated with high expectations of customers. He attended Williams College as an undergraduate. From there, he returned to northern California to attend law school at Stanford. Otis returned to the East Coast, where he practiced corporate law in New York City with a focus on mergers and acquisitions. He found that he liked the financial aspects of the business better than the legal side. Otis changed his career to that of an investment banker. He moved to Darden in 1995 as treasurer. Eventually Otis became the CFO and advanced to the role of CEO.

Today, he sees a tremendous amount of growth potential for both the Red Lobster and Olive Garden chains. To remain relevant is the key. Both restaurants continue to evolve in concert with the guests' expectations. People who work for the Darden chains must be inspired and understand the corporate philosophy and its goals.

## >>DISCUSSION QUESTIONS

1. What prepared Clarence Otis for his position as CEO of Darden?

2. How extensive is Darden Restaurants in the United States?

3. According to Otis, what is the key area for success for employees at the Darden company?

>>To see the complete video about Clarence Otis, go to our Web site at www.mhhe.com/FerrelIM and look for the link to the Destination CEO videos.

The Association of Certified Fraud Examiners, which certifies accounting professionals as *Certified Fraud Examiners (CFEs)*, has grown to more than 40,000 members.[6]

## private accountants.

Large corporations, government agencies, and other organizations may employ their own private accountants to prepare and analyze their financial statements. With titles such as controller, tax accountant, or internal auditor, private accountants are deeply involved in many of the most important financial decisions of the organizations for which they work. Private accountants can be CPAs and may become certified management accountants (CMAs) by passing a rigorous examination by the Institute of Management Accountants.

## Accounting or Bookkeeping?

The terms *accounting* and *bookkeeping* are often mistakenly used interchangeably. Much narrower and far more mechanical than accounting, bookkeeping is typically limited to the routine, day-to-day recording of business transactions. Bookkeepers are responsible for obtaining and recording the information that accountants require to analyze a firm's financial position. They generally require less training than accountants. Accountants, on the other hand, usually complete course work beyond their basic four- or five-year college accounting degrees. This additional training allows accountants not only to record financial information, but to understand, interpret, and even develop the sophisticated accounting systems necessary to classify and analyze complex financial information.

## The Uses of Accounting Information

Accountants summarize the information from a firm's business transactions in various financial statements (which we'll look at in a later section of this chapter) for a variety of stakeholders, including managers, investors, creditors, and government agencies. Many business failures may be directly linked to ignorance of the information "hidden" inside these financial statements. Likewise, most business successes can be traced to informed managers who understand the consequences of their decisions. While maintaining and even increasing short-run profits is desirable, the failure to plan sufficiently for the future can easily lead an otherwise successful company to insolvency and bankruptcy court.

Basically, managers and owners use financial statements (1) to aid in internal planning and control and (2) for external purposes such as reporting to the Internal Revenue Service, stockholders, creditors, customers, employees, and other interested parties. Figure 14.1 shows some of the users of the accounting information generated by a typical corporation.

## internal uses.

Managerial accounting refers to the internal use of accounting statements by managers in planning and directing the organization's activities. Perhaps management's greatest single concern is cash flow, the movement of money through an organization over a daily, weekly, monthly, or yearly basis. Obviously, for any business to succeed, it needs to generate enough cash to pay its bills as they fall due. However, it is not at all unusual for highly successful and rapidly growing companies to struggle to make payments to employees, suppliers, and lenders because of an inadequate cash flow. One common reason for a so-called cash crunch, or shortfall, is poor managerial planning.

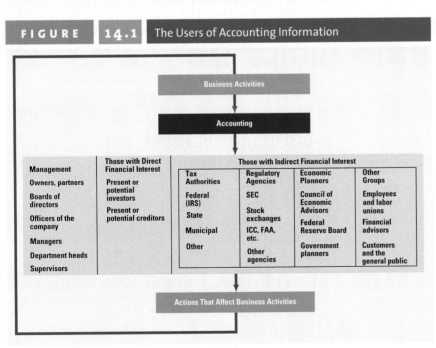

**FIGURE 14.1** The Users of Accounting Information

Source: Belverd E. Needles, Henry R. Anderson, and James C. Caldwell, *Principles of Accounting*, 4th edition.
Copyright © 1990 by Houghton Mifflin Company. Reprinted with permission.

Managerial accountants also help prepare an organization's **budget,** an internal financial plan that forecasts expenses and income over a set period of time. It is not unusual for an organization to prepare separate daily, weekly, monthly, and yearly budgets. Think of a budget as a financial map, showing how the company expects to move from Point A to Point B over a specific period of time. While most companies prepare *master budgets* for the entire firm, many also prepare budgets for smaller segments of the organization such as divisions, departments, product lines, or projects. "Top-down" master budgets begin at the top and filter down to the individual department level, while "bottom-up" budgets start at the department or project level and are combined at the chief executive's office. Generally, the larger and more rapidly growing an organization, the greater will be the likelihood that it will build its master budget from the ground up.

Regardless of focus, the major value of a budget lies in its breakdown of cash inflows and outflows. Expected operating expenses (cash outflows such as wages, materials costs, and taxes) and operating revenues (cash inflows in the form of payments from customers) over a set period of time are carefully forecast and subsequently compared with actual results. Deviations between the two serve as a "trip wire" or "feedback loop" to launch more detailed financial analyses in an effort to pinpoint trouble spots and opportunities.

**external uses.** Managers also use accounting statements to report the business's financial performance to outsiders. Such statements are used for filing income taxes, obtaining credit from lenders, and reporting results to the firm's stockholders. They become the basis for the information provided in the official corporate **annual report,** a summary of the firm's financial information, products, and growth plans for owners and potential investors. While frequently presented between slick, glossy covers prepared by major advertising firms, the single most important component of an annual report is the signature of a certified public accountant attesting that the required financial statements are an accurate reflection of the underlying financial condition of the firm. Financial statements meeting these conditions are termed *audited.* The primary external users of audited accounting information are government agencies, stockholders and potential investors, and lenders, suppliers, and employees.

Federal, state, and local governments (both domestic and overseas) require organizations to file audited financial statements concerning taxes owed and paid, payroll deductions for employees, and, for corporations, new issues of securities (stocks and bonds). Even nonprofit corporations and other

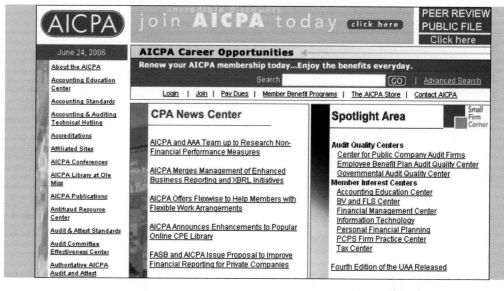

The American Institute of Certified Public Accountants (AICPA) is the premier national professional association for CPAs in the United States.
Source: Copyright © 2004 by the American Institute of Certified Public Accountants, Inc. Reprinted with permission.

*To stay in compliance with current disclosure procedures, most accountants purchase up-to-date software like that produced by SAS.*

nonbusiness organizations may be required to file regular financial statements. NASA, the federal space agency, has been criticized for not managing costs and for failing to adequately document them. PricewaterhouseCoopers, which audited the agency's financial statements, found numerous reporting errors and discrepancies as well as a $204 million line item labeled simply "Other" that the agency could not explain or support in a 2003 quarterly statement.[7] Like individuals, well-managed companies generally try to minimize their taxable income by using accepted accounting practices. Usually, accounting practices that reduce taxes also reduce reported profits. By reducing

taxes, the firm increases the cash available to the firm that can be used for many purposes, such as plant expansion, debt retirement, or repurchase of common stock.

A corporation's stockholders use financial statements to evaluate the return on their investment and the overall quality of the firm's management team. As a result, poor financial statements often result in changes in top management. Potential investors study the financial statements in a firm's annual report to determine whether the company meets their investment requirements and whether the returns from a given firm are likely to compare favorably with other similar companies.

## Did Coca-Cola Inflate Its Earnings?

Coca-Cola is the most valuable brand in the world. Founded in and successful since the late 1800s, it is now considered the largest beverage company in the world—with customers in more than 200 countries. Among the company's products are Coke, Diet Coke, Fanta, Sprite, and Dasani bottled water. The company has always made bringing in, satisfying, and keeping loyal customers a top priority and prided itself on its strong reputation.

Coca-Cola has long focused on social responsibility issues. The company has created a number of foundations focusing on education and community improvement. It is involved in issuing grants and scholarships both in the United States and internationally and is also concerned with preserving the environment and helping with the AIDS/HIV crisis in Africa. All of these contributions aid Coca-Cola in developing an emotional, trusting relationship with its customers.

Coca-Cola has been accused of channel stuffing. Channel stuffing occurs when the demand for a product is inflated because a company sends extra inventory to wholesalers or retailers at an unsustainable rate. This behavior can mislead investors and cause inflated earnings to be reported. Companies resort to channel stuffing to show a false increase in sales. Essentially, a company sends product to distributors and counts these shipments as sales—although the product often remains in warehouses or is later returned.

Many companies have recently been accused of channel stuffing, including Coca-Cola, Krispy Kreme Donuts Inc., Harley-Davidson Motorcycles, Clear One Communications, Symbol Technologies, Network Associates, Bristol-Myers, Taser International, and Intel.

Coca-Cola was accused of sending extra concentrate to Japanese bottlers from 1997 through 1999 in an effort to inflate its profit. The company was already under investigation due to a 2000 suit filed by a former employee that accused the company of fraud and improper business practices. In January 2004, former finance officials for Coca-Cola reported having come across statements of inflated earnings based on the company's shipping extra concentrate to Japan. Although the company has settled the allegations, the SEC (the Securities and Exchange Commission) did find that channel stuffing occurred. However, what Coca-Cola had done was to pressure bottlers into buying additional concentrate in exchange for extended credit. Therefore, the sales were technically considered legitimate.

To settle with the SEC, Coke agreed to avoid this behavior in the future. The company created an ethics and compliance office and is required to verify each financial quarter that it has not altered the terms of payment or extended special credit. The company also agreed to work to reduce the amount of concentrate held by international

bottlers. Although the company has settled with the SEC and the Justice Department, it still faced a shareholder lawsuit regarding channel stuffing in Japan, North America, Europe, and South Africa.

Despite a powerful focus on building and maintaining a strong, positive reputation and a key focus on social responsibility, Coca-Cola has found it difficult to balance ethics and responsibility to shareholders while coping with compliance with legal requirements on reporting earnings and maintaining the bottom line.[8] ❖

## Q: Discussion Questions

1. Why do you think Coke, accused of channel stuffing, possibly engaged in these activities to inflate quarterly earnings?

2. Coca-Cola is one of many companies accused of manipulating earnings. Why do you think it is possible to manipulate earnings under our existing accounting systems?

3. Why would a company with excellent, widely consumed brands not be able to achieve desired earnings as a responsible corporate citizen?

Banks and other lenders look at financial statements to determine a company's ability to meet current and future debt obligations if a loan or credit is granted. To determine this ability, a lender examines a firm's cash flow to assess its ability to repay a loan quickly with cash generated from sales. A lender is also interested in the company's profitability and indebtedness to other lenders. Short-term creditors focus on a firm's ability to pay off loans quickly; long-term lenders focus on profitability and indebtedness.

Labor unions and employees use financial statements to establish reasonable expectations for salary and other benefit requests. Just as firms experiencing record profits are likely to face added pressure to increase employee wages, so too are employees unlikely to grant employers wage and benefit concessions without considerable evidence of financial distress.

## ● ● LO2

Demonstrate the accounting process.

# THE ACCOUNTING PROCESS

Many view accounting as a primary business language. It is of little use, however, unless you know how to "speak" it. Fortunately, the fundamentals—the accounting equation and the double-entry bookkeeping system—are not difficult to learn. These two concepts serve as the starting point for all currently accepted accounting principles.

known as "goodwill," which in this case is Anna's reputation for preparing and delivering beautiful floral arrangements on a timely basis. Liabilities, on the other hand, are debts the firm owes to others. Among the liabilities of Anna's Flowers are a loan from the Small Business Administration and money owed to flower suppliers and other creditors for items purchased. The owners' equity category contains all of the money that has ever been contributed to the company that never has to be paid back. The funds can come from investors who have given money or assets to the company, or it can come from past profitable operations. In the case of Anna's Flowers, if Anna were to sell off, or liquidate, her business, any money left over after selling all the shop's assets and paying off its liabilities would comprise her owner's equity. The relationship between assets, liabilities, and owners' equity is a fundamental concept in accounting and is known as the accounting equation:

$$\text{Assets} = \text{Liabilities} + \text{Owners' equity}$$

## Double-Entry Bookkeeping

Double-entry bookkeeping is a system of recording and classifying business transactions in separate accounts in order to maintain the balance of the accounting equation. Returning to Anna's Flowers, suppose Anna buys $325 worth of roses on credit from the Antique Rose Emporium to fill a wedding order. When she records this transaction, she will list the $325 as a liability or a debt to a supplier. At the same time, however, she will also record $325 worth of roses as an asset

> ## Many view accounting as a primary business language.

## The Accounting Equation

Accountants are concerned with reporting an organization's assets, liabilities, and owners' equity. To help illustrate these concepts, consider a hypothetical floral shop called Anna's Flowers, owned by Anna Rodriguez. A firm's economic resources, or items of value that it owns, represent its assets—cash, inventory, land, equipment, buildings, and other tangible and intangible things. The assets of Anna's Flowers include counters, refrigerated display cases, flowers, decorations, vases, cards, and other gifts, as well as something

in an account known as "inventory." Because the assets and liabilities are on different sides of the accounting equation, Anna's accounts increase in total size (by $325) but remain in balance:

$$\text{Assets} = \text{Liabilities} + \text{Owners' equity}$$
$$\$325 = \$325$$

Thus, to keep the accounting equation in balance, each business transaction must be recorded in two separate accounts.

**ACCOUNTING CYCLE** the four-step procedure of an accounting system: examining source documents, recording transactions in an accounting journal, posting recorded transactions, and preparing financial statements

**JOURNAL** a time-ordered list of account transactions

**LEDGER** a book or computer file with separate sections for each account

In the final analysis, all business transactions are classified as either assets, liabilities, or owners' equity. However, most organizations further break down these three accounts to provide more specific information about a transaction. For example, assets may be broken down into specific categories such as cash, inventory, and equipment, while liabilities may include bank loans, supplier credit, and other debts.

Figure 14.2 shows how Anna used the double-entry bookkeeping system to account for all of the transactions that took place in her first month of business. These transactions include her initial investment of $2,500, the loan from the Small Business Administration, purchases of equipment and inventory, and the purchase of roses on credit. In her first month of business, Anna generated revenues of $2,000 by selling $1,500 worth of inventory. Thus, she deducts, or (in accounting notation that is appropriate for assets) *credits,* $1,500 from inventory and adds, or *debits,* $2,000 to the cash account. The difference between Anna's $2,000 cash inflow and her $1,500 outflow is represented by a credit to owners' equity, because it is money that belongs to her as the owner of the flower shop.

## The Accounting Cycle

In any accounting system, financial data typically pass through a four-step procedure sometimes called the **accounting cycle.** The steps include examining source documents, recording transactions in an accounting journal, posting recorded transactions, and preparing financial statements. Figure 14.3 shows how Anna works through them. Traditionally, all of these steps were performed using paper, pencils, and erasers (lots of erasers!), but today the process is often fully computerized.

**step one: examine source documents.** Like all good managers, Anna Rodriguez begins the accounting cycle by gathering and examining source documents—checks, credit-card receipts, sales slips, and other related evidence concerning specific transactions.

**step two: record transactions.** Next, Anna records each financial transaction in a **journal,** which is basically just a time-ordered list of account transactions. While most businesses keep a general journal in which all transactions are recorded, some classify transactions into specialized journals for specific types of transaction accounts.

**step three: post transactions.** Anna next transfers the information from her journal into a **ledger,** a book or computer program with separate files for each account. This process is known as *posting.* At the end of the accounting period (usually yearly, but occasionally quarterly or monthly), Anna prepares a *trial balance,* a summary of the balances of all the accounts in the general ledger. If, upon totalling, the trial balance doesn't (that is, the accounting equation is not in balance), Anna or her accountant must look for mistakes (typically an error in one or more of the ledger entries) and correct them. If the trial balance is correct, the accountant can then begin to prepare the financial statements.

**FIGURE 14.2** The Accounting Equation and Double-Entry Bookkeeping for Anna's Flowers

| | Assets | | | = Liabilities | | + Owners' Equity |
|---|---|---|---|---|---|---|
| | Cash | Equipment | Inventory | Debts to suppliers | Loans | Equity |
| Cash invested by Anna | $2,500.00 | | | | | $2,500.00 |
| Loan from SBA | $5,000.00 | | | | $5,000.00 | |
| Purchase of furnishings | –$3,000.00 | $3,000.00 | | | | |
| Purchase of inventory | –$2,000.00 | | $2,000.00 | | | |
| Purchase of roses | | | $325.00 | $325.00 | | |
| First month sales | $2,000.00 | | –$1,500.00 | | | $500.00 |
| Totals | $4,500.00 | $3,000.00 | $825.00 | $325.00 | $5,000.00 | $3,000.00 |

$8,325 = $5,325 + $3,000

$8,325 Assets = $8,325 Liabilities + Owners' Equity

**FIGURE** **14.3** The Accounting Process for Anna's Flowers

**Step 1:**
Source documents show that a transaction took place.

| Receipt |
| :---: |
| **Anna's Flowers** |

| July 7 Wedding floral arrangements | $500.00 |
| Consultation services | 250.00 |

**Step 2:**
The transaction is recorded in the journal.

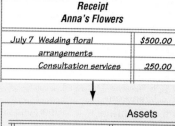

| Assets | |
| :---: | :---: |
| | Cash |
| July 7 Brown wedding | $750.00 |

**Step 3:**
The transaction is posted to the general ledger under the appropriate account (asset, liability, or some further breakdown of these main accounts).

| | | | | | | Balance | |
| :--- | :--- | :--- | :--- | :--- | :--- | :--- | :--- |
| Date | | Explanation | PR | Debit | Credit | Debit | Credit |
| 2007 | | | | | | | |
| July | 1 | | 1 | 2,000 | | 2,000 | |
| | 3 | | 1 | | 1,250 | | 1,250 |
| | 4 | | 1 | | | | |
| | 7 | Brown wedding | 1 | | 750 | | 750 |
| | 14 | | 1 | | | | |

**Step 4: At the end of the accounting period, the ledger is used to prepare the firm's financial statements.**

| Anna's Flowers |
| :---: |
| Income Statement |
| December 31, 2007 |

| | | |
| :--- | ---: | ---: |
| Revenues: | | |
| Net sales | | $123,850 |
| Consulting | | 73,850 |
| Total revenues | | $197,700 |
| Expenses: | | |
| Cost of goods sold | $72,600 | |
| Selling expenses | 37,700 | |
| General and admin. | 18,400 | |
| Other expenses | 5,600 | |
| Total expenses | | 134,300 |
| Net income | | $ 63,400 |

| Anna's Flowers |
| :---: |
| Balance Sheet |
| December 31, 2007 |

**Assets**
Current assets:

| | | |
| :--- | ---: | ---: |
| **Cash** | **$17,850** | |
| Accounts receivable | 10,200 | |
| Merch. Inventory | 8,750 | |
| Tot. assets | | $36,800 |
| Property and Equipment | | |
| Equipment | 11,050 | |
| Office building | 73,850 | |
| Tot. prop. & equip. | | 84,900 |
| Total assets | | $121,700 |

**Liabilities and Owner's Equity**
Current liabilities

| | | |
| :--- | ---: | ---: |
| Accounts payable | $12,600 | |
| Tot. cur. liabilities | | 12,600 |
| Long-term liabilities | | |
| Mortgage payable | | 23,600 |
| Total liabilities | | 36,200 |
| Owner's equity: | | |
| **Anna Rodriguez, capital** | | **$ 85,500** |
| Tot. liabilities and owners' equity | | $ 121,700 |

| Anna's Flowers |
| :---: |
| Annual Budget |
| for 2007 |

| | Sales | Consulting | Total |
| :--- | ---: | ---: | ---: |
| January | 10,500 | 4,500 | 15,000 |
| February | 10,000 | 5,500 | 15,500 |
| March | 10,800 | 5,700 | 16,500 |
| April | 10,100 | 6,050 | 16,150 |
| May | 12,000 | 6,000 | 18,000 |
| June | 12,100 | 6,250 | 18,350 |
| July | 13,000 | 6,600 | 19,600 |
| August | 9,950 | 6,000 | 15,950 |
| September | 9,700 | 6,200 | 15,900 |
| October | 9,900 | 7,000 | 16,900 |
| November | 8,500 | 7,150 | 15,650 |
| December | 7,300 | 6,900 | 14,200 |
| Annual | $123,850 | $73,850 | $197,700 |

## step four: prepare financial statements.

The information from the trial balance is also used to prepare the company's financial statements. In the case of public corporations and certain other organizations, a CPA must *attest,* or certify, that the organization followed generally accepted accounting principles in preparing the financial statements. When these statements have been completed, the organization's books are "closed," and the accounting cycle begins anew for the next accounting period.

# FINANCIAL STATEMENTS

The end results of the accounting process are a series of financial statements. The income statement, the balance sheet, and the statement of cash flows are the best-known examples of financial statements. These statements are provided to stockholders and potential investors in a firm's annual report as well as to other relevant outsiders such as creditors, government agencies, and the Internal Revenue Service.

It is important to recognize that not all financial statements follow precisely the same format. The fact that different organizations generate income in different ways suggests that when

**TABLE 14.2** Equivalent Terms in Accounting

| Term | Equivalent Term |
| --- | --- |
| Revenues | Sales |
| | Goods or services sold |
| Gross profit | Gross income |
| | Gross earnings |
| | Gross margin |
| Operating income | Operating profit |
| | Earnings before interest and taxes (EBIT) |
| | Income before interest and taxes (IBIT) |
| Income before taxes (IBT) | Earnings before taxes (EBT) |
| | Profit before taxes (PBT) |
| Net income (NI) | Earnings after taxes (EAT) |
| | Profit after taxes (PAT) |
| Income available to common stockholders | Earnings available to common stockholders |

it comes to financial statements, one size definitely does not fit all. Manufacturing firms, service providers, and nonprofit organizations each use a different set of accounting principles or rules upon which the public accounting profession has agreed. As we have already mentioned, these are sometimes referred to as *generally accepted accounting principles (GAAP).* Each country has a different set of rules that the businesses within that country are required to use for their accounting process and financial statements. Moreover, as is the case in many other disciplines, certain concepts have more than one name. For example, *sales* and *revenues* are often interchanged, as are *profits, income,* and *earnings.* Table 14.2 lists a few common equivalent terms that should help you decipher their meaning in accounting statements.

 **LO3**

Examine the various components of an income statement to evaluate a firm's "bottom line."

## The Income Statement

The question, "What's the bottom line?" derives from the income statement, where the bottom line shows the overall profit or loss of the company after taxes. Thus, the **income statement** is a financial report that shows an organization's profitability over a period of time, be that a month, quarter, or year. By its very design, the income statement offers one of the clearest possible pictures of the company's overall revenues and the costs incurred in generating those revenues. Other names for the income statement include profit and loss (P&L) statement or operating statement. A sample income statement

A passion for the business of **accounting.**

Grant Thornton LLP provides comprehensive accounting services such as financial statements to its clients.

with line-by-line explanations is presented in Table 14.3, while Table 14.4 presents the income statement of Starbucks. The income statement indicates the firm's profitability or income (the bottom line), which is derived by subtracting the firm's expenses from its revenues.

revenue. Revenue is the total amount of money received (or promised) from the sale of goods or services, as well as from other business activities such as the rental of property and investments. Nonbusiness entities typically obtain revenues through donations from individuals and/or grants from governments and private foundations. Starbucks' income statement (see Table 14.4) shows one main source of income: sales of Starbucks' products.

For most manufacturing and retail concerns, the next major item included in the income statement is the cost of goods sold, the amount of money the firm spent (or promised to

spend) to buy and/or produce the products it sold during the accounting period. This figure may be calculated as follows:

$$\text{Cost of goods sold} = \text{Beginning inventory} + \text{Interim purchases} - \text{Ending inventory}$$

Let's say that Anna's Flowers began an accounting period with an inventory of goods for which it paid $5,000. During the period, Anna bought another $4,000 worth of goods, giving the shop a total inventory available for sale of $9,000. If, at the end of

**TABLE 14.3** Sample Income Statement

The following exhibit presents a sample income statement with all the terms defined and explained.

| Company Name for the Year Ended December 31 | |
| --- | --- |
| Revenues (sales) | Total dollar amount of products sold (includes income from other business services such as rental-lease income and interest income). |
| Less: Cost of goods sold | The cost of producing the goods and services, including the cost of labor and raw materials as well as other expenses associated with production. |
| Gross profit | The income available after paying all expenses of production. |
| Less: Selling and administrative expense | The cost of promoting, advertising, and selling products as well as the overhead costs of managing the company. This includes the cost of management and corporate staff. One noncash expense included in this category is depreciation, which approximates the decline in the value of plant and equipment assets due to use over time. In most accounting statements, depreciation is not separated from selling and administrative expenses. However, financial analysts usually create statements that include this expense. |
| Income before interest and taxes (operating income or EBIT) | This line represents all income left over after operating expenses have been deducted. This is sometimes referred to as operating income because it represents all income after the expenses of operations have been accounted for. Occasionally, this is referred to as EBIT, or earnings before interest and taxes. |
| Less: Interest expense | Interest expense arises as a cost of borrowing money. This is a financial expense rather than an operating expense and is listed separately. As the amount of debt and the cost of debt increase, so will the interest expense. This covers the cost of both short-term and long-term borrowing. |
| Income before taxes (earnings before taxes—EBT) | The firm will pay a tax on this amount. This is what is left of revenues after subtracting all operating costs, depreciation costs, and interest costs. |
| Less: Taxes | The tax rate is specified in the federal tax code. |
| Net income | This is the amount of income left after taxes. The firm may decide to retain all or a portion of the income for reinvestment in new assets. Whatever it decides not to keep it will usually pay out in dividends to its stockholders. |
| Less: Preferred dividends | If the company has preferred stockholders, they are first in line for dividends. That is one reason their stock is called "preferred." |
| Income to common stockholders | This is the income left for the common stockholders. If the company has a good year, there may be a lot of income available for dividends. If the company has a bad year, income could be negative. The common stockholders are the ultimate owners and risk takers. They have the potential for very high or very poor returns because they get whatever is left after all other expenses. |
| Earnings per share | Earnings per share is found by taking the income available to the common stockholders and dividing by the number of shares of common stock outstanding. This is income generated by the company for each share of common stock. |

the accounting period, Anna's inventory was worth $5,500, the cost of goods sold during the period would have been $3,500 ($5,000 + $4,000 − $5,500 = $3,500). If Anna had total revenues of $10,000 over the same period of time, subtracting the cost of goods sold ($3,500) from the total revenues of $10,000 yields the store's **gross income or profit** (revenues minus the cost of goods sold required to generate the revenues): $6,500. For Starbucks, cost of goods sold was slightly more than $2.6 billion in 2005. Notice that Starbucks calls it cost of sales, rather than cost of goods sold. This is because Starbucks buys raw materials and supplies and produces drinks.

**expenses.** Expenses are the costs incurred in the day-to-day operations of an organization. Three common expense accounts shown on income statements are (1) selling, general, and administrative expenses; (2) research, development, and engineering expenses; and (3) interest expenses (remember that the costs directly attributable to selling goods or services are included in the cost of goods sold). Selling expenses include advertising and sales salaries. General and administrative expenses include salaries of executives and their staff and the costs of owning and maintaining the general office. Research and development costs include scientific, engineering, and marketing personnel and the equipment and information used to design and build prototypes and samples. Interest expenses include the direct costs of borrowing money.

The number and type of expense accounts vary from organization to organization. Included in the general and administrative category is a special type of expense known as **depreciation,** the process of spreading the costs of long-lived assets such as buildings and equipment over the total number of accounting periods in which they are expected to be used. Consider a manufacturer that purchases a $100,000 machine

**TABLE 14.4** Consolidated Statements of Earnings for Starbucks (in thousands, except earnings per share)

| Fiscal Year Ended | Oct 2, 2005 | Oct 3, 2004 | Sept 28, 2003 |
|---|---|---|---|
| Net revenues: | | | |
| Company-operated retail | $5,391,927 | $4,457,378 | $3,449,624 |
| Specialty: | | | |
| Licensing | 673,015 | 565,798 | 409,551 |
| Foodservice and other | 304,358 | 271,071 | 216,347 |
| Total specialty | 977,373 | 836,869 | 625,898 |
| Total net revenues | 6,369,300 | 5,294,247 | 4,075,522 |
| Cost of sales including occupancy costs | 2,605,212 | 2,191,440 | 1,681,434 |
| Store operating expenses | 2,165,911 | 1,790,168 | 1,379,574 |
| Other operating expenses | 197,024 | 171,648 | 141,346 |
| Depreciation and amortization expenses | 340,169 | 289,182 | 244,671 |
| General and administrative expenses | 357,114 | 304,293 | 244,550 |
| Subtotal operating expenses | 5,665,430 | 4,746,731 | 3,691,575 |
| Income from equity investees | 76,745 | 59,071 | 36,903 |
| Operating income | 780,615 | 606,587 | 420,850 |
| Interest and other income, net | 15,829 | 14,140 | 11,622 |
| Earnings before income taxes | 796,444 | 620,727 | 432,472 |
| Income taxes | 301,977 | 231,754 | 167,117 |
| Net earnings | $ 494,467 | $ 388,973 | $ 265,355 |
| Net earnings per common share—basic | $ 0.63 | $ 0.49 | $ 0.34 |
| Net earnings per common share—diluted | $ 0.61 | $ 0.47 | $ 0.33 |
| Weighted average shares outstanding: | | | |
| Basic | 789,570 | 794,347 | 781,505 |
| Diluted | 815,417 | 822,930 | 803,296 |

Source: *Starbucks 2005 Annual Report,* p. 40, available at www.starbucks.com/aboutus/Annual_Report_2005_part2.pdf (accessed June 28, 2006).

expected to last about 10 years. Rather than showing an expense of $100,000 in the first year and no expense for that equipment over the next nine years, the manufacturer is allowed to report depreciation expenses of $10,000 per year in each of the next 10 years because that better matches the cost of the machine to the years the machine is used. Each time this depreciation is "written off" as an expense, the book value of the machine is also reduced by $10,000. The fact that the equipment has a zero value on the firm's balance sheet when it is fully depreciated (in this case, after 10 years) does not necessarily mean that it can no longer be used or is economically worthless. Indeed, in some industries, machines used every day have been reported as having no book value whatsoever for over 30 years.

**net income.** Net income (or net earnings) is the total profit (or loss) after all expenses including taxes have been deducted from revenue. Generally, accountants divide profits into individual sections such as operating income and earnings before interest and taxes. Starbucks, for example, lists earnings before income taxes, net earnings, and earnings per share of outstanding stock (see Table 14.4). Like most companies, Starbucks presents not only the current year's results but also the previous two years' income statements to permit comparison of performance from one period to another.

**temporary nature of the income statement accounts.** Companies record their operational activities in the revenue and expense accounts during an accounting period. Gross profit, earnings before interest and taxes, and net income are the results of calculations made from the revenues and expenses accounts; they are not actual accounts. At the end of each accounting period, the dollar amounts in all the revenue and expense accounts are moved into an account called "Retained Earnings," one of the owners' equity accounts.

Revenues increase owners' equity, while expenses decrease it. The resulting change in the owners' equity account is exactly equal to the net income. This shifting of dollar values from the revenue and expense accounts allows the firm to begin the next accounting period with zero balances in those accounts. Zeroing out the balances enables a company to count how much it has sold and how many expenses have been incurred during a period of time. The basic accounting equation (assets = liabilities + owners' equity) will not balance until the revenue and expense account balances have been moved or "closed out" to the owners' equity account.

One final note about income statements: You may remember from Chapter 5 that corporations may choose to make cash payments called dividends to shareholders out of their net earnings. When a corporation elects to pay dividends, it decreases the cash account (in the assets category) as well as a capital account (in the owners' equity category). During any period of time, the owners' equity account may change because of the sale of stock (or contributions/withdrawals by owners), the net income or loss, or from the dividends paid.

 **LO4**

Interpret a company's balance sheet to determine its current financial position.

## The Balance Sheet

The second basic financial statement is the balance sheet, which presents a "snapshot" of an organization's financial position at a given moment. As such, the balance sheet indicates what the organization owns or controls and the various sources of the funds used to pay for these assets, such as bank debt or owners' equity.

The balance sheet takes its name from its reliance on the accounting equation: Assets *must* equal liabilities plus owners' equity. Table 14.5 provides a sample balance sheet with line-by-line explanations. Unlike the income statement, the balance sheet does not represent the result of transactions completed over a specified accounting period. Instead, the balance sheet is, by definition, an accumulation of all financial transactions conducted by an organization since its founding. Following long-established traditions, items on the balance sheet are listed on the basis of their original cost less accumulated depreciation, rather than their present values.

**TABLE 14.5**  Sample Balance Sheet

The following exhibit presents a balance sheet in word form with each item defined or explained.

| Typical Company December 31 | |
| --- | --- |
| Assets | This is the major category for all physical, monetary, or intangible goods that have some dollar value. |
| Current assets | Assets that are either cash or are expected to be turned into cash within the next 12 months. |
| Cash | Cash or checking accounts. |
| Marketable securities | Short-term investments in securities that can be converted to cash quickly (liquid assets). |
| Accounts receivable | Cash due from customers in payment for goods received. These arise from sales made on credit. |
| Inventory | Finished goods ready for sale, goods in the process of being finished, or raw materials used in the production of goods. |
| Prepaid expense | A future expense item that has already been paid, such as insurance premiums or rent. |
| Total current assets | The sum of the preceding accounts. |
| Fixed assets | Assets that are long term in nature and have a minimum life expectancy that exceeds one year. |
| Investments | Assets held as investments rather than assets owned for the production process. Most often the assets include small ownership interests in other companies. |
| Gross property, plant, and equipment | Land, buildings, and other fixed assets listed at original cost. |
| Less: Accumulated depreciation | The accumulated expense deductions applied to all plant and equipment over their life. Land may not be depreciated. The total amount represents in general the decline in value as equipment gets older and wears out. The maximum amount that can be deducted is set by the U.S. Federal Tax Code and varies by type of asset. |
| Net property, plant, and equipment | Gross property, plant, and equipment minus the accumulated depreciation. This amount reflects the book value of the fixed assets and not their value if sold. |
| Other assets | Any other asset that is long term and does not fit into the preceding categories. It could be patents or trademarks. |
| Total assets | The sum of all the asset values. |
| Liabilities and stockholders' equity | This is the major category. Liabilities refer to all indebtedness and loans of both a long-term and short-term nature. Stockholders' equity refers to all money that has been contributed to the company over the life of the firm by the owners. |
| Current liabilities | Short-term debt expected to be paid off within the next 12 months. |
| Accounts payable | Money owed to suppliers for goods ordered. Firms usually have between 30 and 90 days to pay this account, depending on industry norms. |
| Wages payable | Money owned to employees for hours worked or salary. If workers receive checks every two weeks, the amount owed should be no more than two weeks' pay. |
| Taxes payable | Firms are required to pay corporate taxes quarterly. This refers to taxes owed based on earnings estimates for the quarter. |
| Notes payable | Short-term loans from banks or other lenders. |
| Other current liabilities | The other short-term debts that do not fit into the above categories. |
| Total current liabilities | The sum of the preceding accounts. |
| Long-term liabilities | All long-term debt that will not be paid off in the next 12 months. |
| Long-term debt | Loans of more than one year from banks, pension funds, insurance companies, or other lenders. These loans often take the form of bonds, which are securities that may be bought and sold in bond markets. |

*(continued)*

**TABLE 14.5**   *(concluded)*

| | |
|---|---|
| Deferred income taxes | This is a liability owed to the government but not due within one year. |
| Other liabilities | Any other long-term debt that does not fit the preceding two categories. |
| Stockholders' equity | The following categories are the owners' investment in the company. |
| Common stock | The tangible evidence of ownership is a security called common stock. The par value is stated value and does not indicate the company's worth. |
| Capital in excess of par (a.k.a. contributed capital) | When shares of stock were sold to the owners, they were recorded at the price at the time of the original sale. If the price paid was $10 per share, the extra $9 per share would show up in this account at 100,000 shares times $9 per share, or $900,000. |
| Retained earnings | The total amount of earnings the company has made during its life and not paid out to its stockholders as dividends. This account represents the owners' reinvestment of earnings into company assets rather than payments of cash dividends. This account does not represent cash. |
| Total stockholders' equity | This is the sum of the preceding equity accounts representing the owner's total investment in the company. |
| Total liabilities and stockholders' equity | The total short-term and long-term debt of the company plus the owner's total investment. This combined amount *must* equal total assets. |

Balance sheets are often presented in two different formats. The traditional balance sheet format placed the organization's assets on the left side and its liabilities and owners' equity on the right. More recently, a vertical format, with assets on top followed by liabilities and owners' equity, has gained wide acceptance. Starbucks' balance sheet for 2004 and 2005 is presented in Table 14.6. In the sections that follow, we'll briefly describe the basic items found on the balance sheet; we'll take a closer look at a number of these in Chapter 16.

**assets.** All asset accounts are listed in descending order of *liquidity*—that is, how quickly each could be turned into cash. Current assets, also called short-term assets, are those that are used or converted into cash within the course of a calendar year. Thus, cash is followed by temporary investments, accounts receivable, and inventory, in that order. Accounts receivable refers to money owed the company by its clients or customers who have promised to pay for the products at a later date. Accounts receivable usually includes an allowance for bad debts that management does not expect to collect. The bad-debts adjustment is normally based on historical collections experience and is deducted from the accounts receivable balance to present a more realistic view of the payments likely to be received in the future, called net receivables. Inventory may be held in the form of raw materials, work-in-progress, or finished goods ready for delivery.

Long-term, or fixed assets represent a commitment of organizational funds of at least one year. Items classified as fixed include long-term investments, plant and equipment, and intangible assets, such as corporate "goodwill," or reputation, as well as patents and trademarks.

**liabilities.** As seen in the accounting equation, total assets must be financed either through borrowing (liabilities) or through owner investments (owners' equity). Current liabilities include a firm's financial obligations to short-term creditors, which must be repaid within one year, while long-term liabilities have longer repayment terms. Accounts payable represents amounts owed to suppliers for goods and services purchased with credit. For example, if you buy gas with a BP credit card, the purchase represents an account payable for you (and an account receivable for BP). Other liabilities include wages earned by employees but not yet paid and taxes owed to the government. Occasionally, these accounts are consolidated into an accrued expenses account, representing all unpaid financial obligations incurred by the organization.

**owners' equity.** Owners' equity includes the owners' contributions to the organization along with income earned by the organization and retained to finance continued growth and development. If the organization were to sell off all of its assets and pay off all of its liabilities, any remaining funds would belong to the owners. Not surprisingly, the accounts listed as owners' equity on a balance sheet may differ dramatically from company to company. As mentioned in Chapter 5, corporations sell stock to investors, who become the owners of the firm. Many corporations issue two, three, or even more different classes of common and preferred stock, each with different dividend payments and/or voting rights. Because each type of stock issued represents a different claim on the organization, each must be represented by a separate owners' equity account, called contributed capital.

## TABLE 14.6 Consolidated Balance Sheets for Starbucks (in thousands, except share data)

| Fiscal Year Ended | Oct 2, 2005 | Oct 3, 2004 |
|---|---|---|
| **Assets** | | |
| Current assets: | | |
| Cash and cash equivalents | $ 173,809 | $ 145,053 |
| Short-term investments—available-for-sale securities | 95,379 | 483,157 |
| Short-term investments—trading securities | 37,848 | 24,799 |
| Accounts receivable, net of allowances of $3,079 and $2,231, respectively | 190,762 | 140,226 |
| Inventories | 546,299 | 422,663 |
| Prepaid expenses and other current assets | 94,429 | 71,347 |
| Deferred income taxes, net | 70,808 | 63,650 |
| Total current assets | 1,209,334 | 1,350,895 |
| Long-term investments—available-for-sale securities | 60,475 | 135,179 |
| Equity and other investments | 201,461 | 167,740 |
| Property, plant and equipment, net | 1,842,019 | 1,551,416 |
| Other assets | 72,893 | 85,561 |
| Other intangible assets | 35,409 | 26,800 |
| Goodwill | 92,474 | 68,950 |
| Total Assets | $3,514,065 | $3,386,541 |
| **Liabilities and Shareholders' Equity** | | |
| Current liabilities: | | |
| Accounts payable | $ 220,975 | $ 199,346 |
| Accrued compensation and related costs | 232,354 | 208,927 |
| Accrued occupancy costs | 44,496 | 29,231 |
| Accrued taxes | 78,293 | 62,959 |
| Short-term borrowings | 277,000 | — |
| Other accrued expenses | 198,082 | 123,684 |
| Deferred revenue | 175,048 | 121,377 |
| Current portion of long-term debt | 748 | 735 |
| Total current liabilities | 1,226,996 | 746,259 |
| Deferred income taxes, net | — | 21,770 |
| Long-term debt | 2,870 | 3,618 |
| Other long-term liabilities | 193,565 | 144,683 |
| Shareholders' equity: | | |
| Common stock ($0.001 par value) and additional paid-in-capital—authorized, 1,200,000,000 shares; issued and outstanding, 767,442,110 and 794,811,688 shares, respectively, (includes 3,394,200 common stock units in both periods) | 90,968 | 956,685 |
| Other additional paid-in-capital | 39,393 | 39,393 |
| Retained earnings | 1,939,359 | 1,444,892 |
| Accumulated other comprehensive income | 20,914 | 29,241 |
| Total shareholders' equity | 2,090,634 | 2,470,211 |
| Total Liabilities and Shareholders' Equity | $3,514,065 | $3,386,541 |

Source: *Starbucks 2005 Annual Report,* p. 41, available at www.starbucks.com/aboutus/Annual_Report_2005_part2.pdf. (accessed June 28, 2006).

# The Statement of Cash Flow

The third primary financial statement is called the **statement of cash flow,** which explains how the company's cash changed from the beginning of the accounting period to the end. Cash, of course, is an asset shown on the balance sheet, which provides a snapshot of the firm's financial position at one point in time. However, many investors and other users of financial statements want more information about the cash flowing into and out of the firm than is provided on the balance sheet to better understand the company's financial health. The statement of cash flow takes the cash balance from one year's balance sheet and compares it to the next while providing detail about how the firm used the cash. Table 14.7 presents Starbucks' statement of cash flows.

The change in cash is explained through details in three categories: cash from (used for) operating activities, cash from (used for) investing activities, and cash from (used for) financing activities. *Cash from operating activities* is calculated

**TABLE 14.7** Starbucks Consolidated Statements of Cash Flows (in thousands)

| Fiscal Year Ended | Oct 2, 2005 | Oct 3, 2004 | Sept 28, 2003 |
|---|---|---|---|
| **Operating Activities** | | | |
| Net earnings | $494,467 | $388,973 | $265,355 |
| Adjustments to reconcile net earnings to net cash provided by operating activities: | | | |
| Depreciation and amortization | 367,207 | 314,047 | 266,258 |
| Provision for impairments and asset disposals | 20,157 | 13,568 | 7,784 |
| Deferred income taxes, net | (31,253) | (3,770) | (6,767) |
| Equity in income of investees | (49,633) | (31,801) | (21,320) |
| Distributions of income from equity investees | 30,919 | 38,328 | 28,966 |
| Tax benefit from exercise of nonqualified stock options | 109,978 | 63,405 | 36,590 |
| Net accretion of discount and amortization of premium on marketable securities | 10,097 | 11,603 | 5,996 |
| Cash provided/(used) by changes in operating assets and liabilities: | | | |
| Accounts receivable | (49,311) | (24,977) | (8,384) |
| Inventories | (121,618) | (77,662) | (64,768) |
| Accounts payable | 9,717 | 27,948 | 24,990 |
| Accrued compensation and related costs | 22,711 | 54,929 | 42,132 |
| Deferred revenue | 53,276 | 47,590 | 30,732 |
| Other operating assets and liabilities | 56,894 | 36,356 | 8,554 |
| Net cash provided by operating activities | 923,608 | 858,537 | 616,118 |
| **Investing Activities** | | | |
| Purchase of available-for-sale securities | (643,488) | (887,969) | (481,050) |
| Maturity of available-for-sale securities | 469,554 | 170,789 | 218,787 |
| Sale of available-for-sale securities | 626,113 | 452,467 | 141,009 |
| Acquisitions, net of cash acquired | (21,583) | (7,515) | (69,928) |
| Net additions to equity investments, other investments, and other assets | (7,915) | (64,747) | (47,259) |
| Net additions to property, plant and equipment | (643,989) | (412,537) | (377,983) |
| Net cash used by investing activities | (221,308) | (749,512) | (616,424) |
| **Financing Activities** | | | |
| Proceeds from issuance of common stock | 163,555 | 137,590 | 107,183 |
| Borrowings under revolving credit facility | 277,000 | — | — |
| Principal payments on long-term debt | (735) | (722) | (710) |
| Repurchase of common stock | (1,113,647) | (203,413) | (75,710) |
| Net cash provided/(used) by financing activities | (673,827) | (66,545) | 30,763 |

*(continued)*

| | | | | | |
|---|---|---|---|---|---|
| ● **RATIO ANALYSIS** calculations that measure an organization's financial health | ● **PROFITABILITY RATIOS** ratios that measure the amount of operating income or net income an organization is able to generate relative to its assets, owners' equity, and sales | ● **PROFIT MARGIN** net income divided by sales | ● **RETURN ON ASSETS** net income divided by assets | ● **RETURN ON EQUITY** net income divided by owner's equity; also called return on investment (ROI) | |

**TABLE 14.7** *(concluded)*

| | | | |
|---|---|---|---|
| Effect of exchange rate changes on cash and cash equivalents | 283 | 3,111 | 3,278 |
| Net increase in cash and cash equivalents | 28,756 | 45,591 | 33,735 |
| **Cash and Cash Equivalents** | | | |
| Beginning of period | 145,053 | 99,462 | 65,727 |
| End of period | $173,809 | $145,053 | $99,462 |
| **Supplemental Disclosure of Cash Flow Information** | | | |
| Cash paid during the year for: | | | |
| Interest | $ 1,060 | $ 370 | $265 |
| Income taxes | $227,812 | $172,759 | $140,107 |

by combining the changes in the revenue accounts, expense accounts, current asset accounts, and current liability accounts. This category of cash flows includes all the accounts on the balance sheet that relate to computing revenues and expenses for the accounting period. If this amount is a positive number, as it is for Starbucks, then the business is making extra cash that it can use to invest in increased long-term capacity or to pay off debts such as loans or bonds. A negative number may indicate a business that is still in a growing stage or one that is in a declining position with regards to operations.

*Cash from investing activities* is calculated from changes in the long-term or fixed asset accounts. If this amount is negative, as is the case with Starbucks, the company is purchasing long-term assets for future growth. A positive figure indicates a business that is selling off existing long-term assets and reducing its capacity for the future.

Finally, *cash from financing activities* is calculated from changes in the long-term liability accounts and the contributed capital accounts in owners' equity. If this amount is negative, the company is likely paying off long-term debt or returning contributed capital to investors. As in the case of Starbucks, if this amount is positive, the company is either borrowing more money or raising money from investors by selling more shares of stock.

 **LO5**

Analyze financial statements, using ratio analysis, to evaluate a company's performance.

# RATIO ANALYSIS: ANALYZING FINANCIAL STATEMENTS

The income statement shows a company's profit or loss, while the balance sheet itemizes the value of its assets, liabilities, and

owners' equity. Together, the two statements provide the means to answer two critical questions: (1) How much did the firm make or lose? and (2) How much is the firm presently worth based on historical values found on the balance sheet? Ratio analysis, calculations that measure an organization's financial health, brings the complex information from the income statement and balance sheet into sharper focus so that managers, lenders, owners, and other interested parties can measure and compare the organization's productivity, profitability, and financing mix with other similar entities.

As you know, a ratio is simply one number divided by another, with the result showing the relationship between the two numbers. Financial ratios are used to weigh and evaluate a firm's performance. Interestingly, an absolute value such as earnings of $70,000 or accounts receivable of $200,000 almost never provides as much useful information as a well-constructed ratio. Whether those numbers are good or bad depends on their relation to other numbers. If a company earned $70,000 on $700,000 in sales (a 10 percent return), such an earnings level might be quite satisfactory. The president of a company earning this same $70,000 on sales of $7 million (a 1 percent return), however, should probably start looking for another job!

Looking at ratios in isolation is probably about as useful and exciting as staring at a blank wall. It is the relationship of the calculated ratios to both prior organizational performance and the performance of the organization's "peers," as well as its stated goals, that really matters. Remember, while the profitability, asset utilization, liquidity, debt ratios, and per share data we'll look at here can be very useful, you will never see the forest by looking only at the trees.

## Profitability Ratios

Profitability ratios measure how much operating income or net income an organization is able to generate relative to its assets, owners' equity, and sales. The numerator (top number)

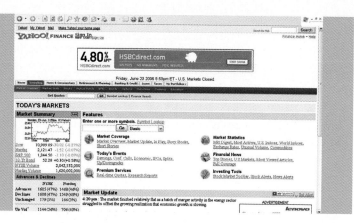

*You can look on Web sites like Yahoo! Finance under a company's "key statistics" link to find many of its financial ratios, such as its return on assets, return on equity, and current ratio. Other ratios require a closer look at a company's actual financial statements.*

used in these examples is always the net income after taxes. Common profitability ratios include profit margin, return on assets, and return on equity. The following examples are based on the 2005 income statement and balance sheet for Starbucks, as shown in Tables 14.4 and 14.6. Except where specified, all data are expressed in millions of dollars.

The profit margin, computed by dividing net income by sales, shows the overall percentage profits earned by the company. It is based solely upon data obtained from the income statement. The higher the profit margin, the better the cost controls within the company and the higher the return on every dollar of revenue. Starbucks' profit margin is calculated as follows:

$$\text{Profit margin} = \frac{\text{Net income}}{\text{Sales}} = \frac{\$494,467}{\$6,369,300} = 7.76\%$$

Thus, for every $1 in sales, Starbucks generated profits of almost 8 cents.

Return on assets, net income divided by assets, shows how much income the firm produces for every dollar invested in assets. A company with a low return on assets is probably not using its assets very productively—a key managerial failing. By its construction, the return on assets calculation requires data from both the income statement and the balance sheet.

$$\text{Return on assets} = \frac{\text{Net income}}{\text{Assets}} = \frac{\$494,467}{\$3,514,065} = 14.07\%$$

In the case of Starbucks, every $1 of assets generated a return of 14.07 percent, or profits of just over 14 cents.

Stockholders are always concerned with how much money they will make on their investment, and they frequently use the return on equity ratio as one of their key performance yardsticks. Return on equity (also called return on investment [ROI]), calculated by dividing net income by owners' equity, shows how much income is generated by each $1 the owners have invested in the firm. Obviously, a low return on equity means low stockholder returns and may indicate a need for immediate managerial attention. Because some assets may have been financed with debt not contributed by the owners, the value of the owners' equity is usually considerably lower than the total value of the firm's assets. Starbucks' return on equity is calculated as follows:

$$\text{Return on equity} = \frac{\text{Net income}}{\text{Equity}} = \frac{\$494,467}{\$2,090,634} = 23.65\%$$

For every dollar invested by Starbucks stockholders, the company earned a 23.65 percent return, or 23.65 cents per dollar invested. The reason the amount is higher than the return on assets is that owners' equity only accounts for about 60 percent of Starbucks' assets, while the other 40 percent is financed by debt.

## Asset Utilization Ratios

Asset utilization ratios measure how well a firm uses its assets to generate each $1 of sales. Obviously, companies using their assets more productively will have higher returns on assets than their less efficient competitors. Similarly, managers can use asset utilization ratios to pinpoint areas of inefficiency in their operations. These ratios (receivables turnover, inventory turnover, and total asset turnover) relate balance sheet assets to sales, which are found on the income statement.

The receivables turnover, sales divided by accounts receivable, indicates how many times a firm collects its accounts receivable in one year. It also demonstrates how quickly a firm is able to collect payments on its credit sales. Obviously, no payments mean no profits. Starbucks collected its receivables 33.4 times per year. The reason the number is so high is that most of Starbucks' sales are for cash and not credit.

$$\text{Receivable turnover} = \frac{\text{Sales}}{\text{Receivables}} = \frac{\$6,369,300}{\$190,762} = 33.39\times$$

Inventory turnover, sales divided by total inventory, indicates how many times a firm sells and replaces its inventory over the course of a year. A high inventory turnover ratio may indicate great efficiency but may also suggest the possibility of lost sales due to insufficient stock levels. Starbucks' inventory turnover indicates that it replaced its inventory nearly 12 times per year, or once per month.

$$\text{Inventory turnover} = \frac{\text{Sales}}{\text{Inventory}} = \frac{\$6,369,300}{\$546,299} = 11.66\times$$

**Total asset turnover,** sales divided by total assets, measures how well an organization uses all of its assets in creating sales. It indicates whether a company is using its assets productively. Starbucks generated $1.81 in sales for every $1 in total corporate assets.

$$\text{Total asset turnover} = \frac{\text{Sales}}{\text{Total assets}} = \frac{\$6,369,300}{\$3,514,065} = 1.81\times$$

## Liquidity Ratios

**Liquidity ratios** compare current (short-term) assets to current liabilities to indicate the speed with which a company can turn its assets into cash to meet debts as they fall due. High liquidity ratios may satisfy a creditor's need for safety, but ratios that are too high may indicate that the organization is not using its current assets efficiently. Liquidity ratios are generally best examined in conjunction with asset utilization ratios because high turnover ratios imply that cash is flowing through an organization very quickly—a situation that dramatically reduces the need for the type of reserves measured by liquidity ratios.

The **current ratio** is calculated by dividing current assets by current liabilities. Starbucks's current ratio indicates that for every $1 of current liabilities, the firm had $0.99 of current assets on hand. At first glance, this may appear troublesome. However, Starbucks has very little in accounts receivable and more than $300 million in cash and short-term marketable securities. They turn over their assets very quickly and are very liquid.

$$\text{Current ratio} = \frac{\text{Current assets}}{\text{Current liabilities}} = \frac{\$1,209,334}{\$1,226,996} = 0.99\times$$

The **quick ratio** (also known as the acid test) is a far more stringent measure of liquidity because it eliminates inventory, the least liquid current asset. It measures how well an organization can meet its current obligations without resorting to the sale of its inventory. In 2005, Starbucks had just 61 cents

invested in current assets (after subtracting inventory) for every $1 of current liabilities.

$$\text{Quick ratio} = \frac{\text{Current assets–Inventory}}{\text{Current liabilities}} = \frac{\$663,035}{\$1,226,996}$$
$$= 0.54\times$$

## Debt Utilization Ratios

**Debt utilization ratios** provide information about how much debt an organization is using relative to other sources of capital, such as owners' equity. Because the use of debt carries an interest charge that must be paid regularly regardless of profitability, debt financing is much riskier than equity. Unforeseen negative events such as recessions affect heavily indebted firms to a far greater extent than those financed exclusively with owners' equity. Because of this and other factors, the managers of most firms tend to keep debt-to-asset levels below 50 percent. However, firms in very stable and/or regulated industries, such as electric utilities, often are able to carry debt ratios well in excess of 50 percent with no ill effects.

The **debt to total assets ratio** indicates how much of the firm is financed by debt and how much by owners' equity. To find the value of Starbucks' total debt, you must add current liabilities to long-term debt and other liabilities.

$$\text{Debt to total assets} = \frac{\text{Total debt}}{\text{Total assets}} = \frac{\$1,423,401}{\$3,514,065} = 40.51\%$$

Thus, for every $1 of Starbucks' total assets, 40.5 percent is financed with debt. The remaining 59.5 percent is provided by owners' equity.

The **times interest earned ratio,** operating income divided by interest expense, is a measure of the safety margin a company has with respect to the interest payments it must make to its creditors. A low times interest earned ratio indicates that even a small decrease in earnings may lead the company into financial straits. Since Starbucks has more interest income than interest expense, it would appear that their times interest earned ratio is not able to be calculated by using the income statement. However, in the statement of cash flows in Table 14.7 on the second line from the bottom, we can see that Starbucks paid a little more than $1 million in interest expense, which was covered by income before interest and taxes 736 times. A lender would have very little concern about receiving interest payments.

$$\text{Times interest earned} = \frac{\text{Income before interest and taxes}}{\text{Interest expense}}$$

$$= \frac{\$780,615}{\$1,060} = 736.433$$

## Per Share Data

Investors may use **per share data** to compare the performance of one company with another on an equal, or per share, basis. Generally, the more shares of stock a company issues, the less income is available for each share.

**Earnings per share** is calculated by dividing net income or profit by the number of shares of stock outstanding. This ratio is important because yearly changes in earnings per share, in combination with other economywide factors, determine a company's overall stock price. When earnings go up, so does a company's stock price—and so does the wealth of its stockholders.

$$\text{Earnings per share} = \frac{\text{Net income}}{\text{Number of shares outstanding}}$$

$$= \frac{\$494,467}{789,570} = \$0.63 \quad 2005$$

$$= \frac{\$388,973}{794,347} = \$0.49 \quad 2004$$

We can see from the income statement and these calculations that Starbucks' basic earnings per share increased from $0.49 in 2004 to $0.63 in 2005. Notice that Starbucks lists diluted earnings per share of $0.47 for 2004 and $0.61 for 2005. You can see from the income statement that diluted earnings per share include more shares than the basic calculation; this is because diluted shares include potential shares that could be issued due to the exercise of stock options or the conversion of certain types of debt into common stock. Investors generally pay more attention to diluted earnings per share than basic earnings per share.

**Dividends per share** are paid by the corporation to the stockholders for each share owned. The payment is made from earnings after taxes by the corporation but is taxable income to the stockholder. Thus, dividends result in double taxation: The corporation pays tax once on its earnings, and the stockholder pays tax a second time on his or her dividend income. Starbucks has never paid a dividend, so the calculation of dividends per share does not apply in this case.

## Industry Analysis

We have used McDonald's as a comparison to Starbucks because there are no real national and international coffee houses that compete with Starbucks on the same scale. While McDonald's is almost four times larger than Starbucks in terms of sales, they both have a national and international presence

and to some extent compete for the consumer's dollars. Table 14.8 shows that while McDonald's earns more profit per dollar of sales, Starbucks earns more dollars per dollar of invested assets. This is because a Starbucks coffee shop is much less expensive to build and operate than a McDonald's. Both companies have very little accounts receivable relative to the size of their sales. McDonald's pushes off much of its inventory holding costs on its suppliers and so has much less inventory per sales dollar compared with Starbucks. Because McDonald's has very little inventory, its quick ratio and current ratios are almost the same and are much higher than Starbucks. This is of little consequence to the financial analyst because both companies have high times interest earned ratios, with Starbucks significantly higher than McDonald's. Starbucks earns less per share than McDonald's, but McDonald's pays a dividend and Starbucks does not. In summary, both companies are in good financial health, and it is hard to say which company is better managed. One thing for sure, if Starbucks could earn the same profit margin as McDonald's, they would improve their other profitability ratios dramatically. ■

**TABLE 14.8** Industry Analysis

| | Starbucks (SBUX) | McDonald's (MCD) |
|---|---|---|
| Profit margin | 7.76% | 12.72% |
| Return on assets | 14.97% | 8.68% |
| Return on equity | 23.65% | 17.18% |
| Receivable turnover | 33.39× | 25.71× |
| Inventory turnover | 11.66× | 139.19× |
| Total asset turnover | 1.81× | 0.68× |
| Current ratio | 0.99× | 1.45× |
| Quick ratio | 0.54× | 1.41× |
| Debt to total assets | 40.51% | 49.49% |
| Times interest earned | 736.43× | 11.29× |
| Earnings per share | $0.61 | $2.06 |
| Dividends per share | $0 | $0.67 |

By tracking and analyzing the financial data of 18 million-plus U.S. businesses, BizMiner.com is able to deliver industry analysis information to its online subscribers.

Perhaps no single area of business study offers better short- and long-term business opportunities than does accounting. Whether employed by private companies, public accounting firms, or government agencies, accountants probably learn and "know the numbers" of their organizations better than any other group of employees. If knowledge is power, then accountants are powerful people. And CPAs and CMAs, by virtue of their advanced study and higher prestige, are far and away the most powerful accountants.

Accountants prepare, analyze, and verify financial reports and taxes and monitor the systems that furnish this information to managers in all business, nonprofit, and government organizations. Management accountants are employed by private businesses to prepare, analyze, and interpret the financial information corporate executives need to make sound decisions. Public accountants and private internal auditors, on the other hand, specialize in the verification of corporate and personal financial records and in the preparation of tax filings. The increasing computerization of accounting means that accountants are frequently the most computer-literate employees not directly involved with the design and maintenance of an organization's computer systems.

As more states have increased the CPA collegiate hour requirement beyond 120 to 150 hours, the number of "accounting majors" meeting the new requirements has declined. With industry demand high and increasing, and the number of qualified accountants holding steady or even decreasing, accounting salaries (particularly for CPAs and CMAs) continue to rise from what are already high levels when compared with other business degrees.

According to Robert Half International, projected annual salaries for first-year accountants range from $35,750 to $42,500 at large public accounting firms, and from $29,500 to $38,250 at medium or small ones. In the corporate arena, first-year CMA salaries range from $28,500 to $39,750. In the fast-growing area of forensic accounting, starting salaries range from $25,000 to $40,000, but CFEs with several years' experience can earn $70,000 to as much as $150,000 in the private sector.[10]

**CHECK OUT**

www.mhhe.com/FerrellM

for study materials including Interactive Exercises, Quizzes, iPod downloads, and video.

## Build Your Business Plan

**Accounting and Financial Statements** After you determine your initial *reasonable selling price,* you need to estimate your sales forecasts (in terms of units and dollars of sales) for the first year of operation. Remember to be conservative and set forecasts that are more modest.

While customers may initially try your business, many businesses have seasonal patterns. A good budgeting/planning system allows managers to anticipate problems, coordinate activities of the business (so that subunits within the organization are all working toward the common goal of the organization), and control operations (how do we know whether spending is "in line").

The first financial statement you need to prepare is the income statement. Beginning with your estimated sales revenue, determine what expenses will be necessary to generate that level of sales revenue. Refer to Table 14.3 to assist you with this process.

The second financial statement you need to create is your balance sheet. Your balance sheet is a snapshot of your financial position in a moment in time. Refer to Table 14.5 to assist you in listing your assets, liabilities and owner's equity.

The last financial statement, the cash flow statement, is the most important one to a bank. It is a measure of your ability to get and repay the loan from the bank. Referring to Table 14.8, be as realistic as possible are you are completing it. Allow yourself enough cash on hand until the point in which the business starts to support itself.

**M**

start here.

# 15

# Money AND THE FINANCIAL SYSTEM

## Introduction

From Wall Street to Main Street—both overseas and at home—money is the one tool used to measure personal and business income and wealth. Not surprisingly, **finance** is the study of money: how it's made, how it's lost, and how it's managed. This chapter introduces you to the role of money and the financial system in the economy. Of course, if you have a checking account, automobile insurance, a college loan, or a credit card, you already have personal experience with some key players in the financial world.

We begin our discussion with a definition of money and then explore some of the many forms money may take. Next, we examine the roles of the Federal Reserve Board and other major institutions in the financial system. Finally, we explore the future of the finance industry and some of the changes likely to occur over the course of the next several years.

## ●● LO1

Define money, its functions, and its characteristics.

# MONEY IN THE FINANCIAL SYSTEM

Strictly defined, money is anything generally accepted in exchange for goods and services. Materials as diverse as salt, cattle, fish, rocks, shells, cloth, as well as precious metals such as gold, silver, and copper have long been used by various cultures as money. Most of these materials were limited-supply commodities that had their own value to society (for example, as a preservative or as jewelry). The supply of these commodities therefore determined the supply of "money" in that society. The next step was the development of "IOUs," or slips of paper that could be exchanged for a specified supply of the underlying commodity. "Gold" notes, for instance, could be exchanged for

*For centuries, people on the Micronesian island of Yap have used giant round stones, like the ones shown here, for currency. The stones aren't moved, but their ownership can change.*

gold, and the money supply was tied to the amount of gold available. While paper money was first used in North America in 1685 (and even earlier in Europe), the concept of *fiat money*—a paper money not readily convertible to a precious metal such as gold—did not gain full acceptance until the Great Depression in the 1930s. The U.S. abandoned its gold-backed currency standard largely in response to the Great Depression and converted to a fiduciary, or fiat, monetary system. In the United States, paper money is really a government "note" or promise, worth the value specified on the note.

## Functions of Money

No matter what a particular society uses for money, its primary purpose is to enable a person or organization to transform a desire into an action. These desires may be for entertainment actions, such as party expenses; operating actions, such as paying for rent, utilities, or employees; investing actions, such as buying property or equipment; or financing actions, such as for starting or growing a business. Money serves three important functions: as a medium of exchange, a measure of value, and a store of value.

**medium of exchange.** Before fiat money, the trade of goods and services was accomplished through *bartering*—trading one good or service for another of similar value. As any school-age child knows, bartering can become quite inefficient—particularly in the case of complex, three-party transactions involving peanut butter sandwiches, baseball cards, and hair barrettes. There had to be a simpler way, and that was to decide on a single item—money—that can be freely converted to any other good upon agreement between parties.

**measure of value.** As a measure of value, money serves as a common standard or yardstick of the value of goods and services. For example, $2 will buy a dozen large eggs and $25,000 will buy a nice car in the United States. In Japan, where the currency is known as the yen, these same transactions would cost about 200 yen and 2 million yen, respectively. Money, then, is a common denominator that allows people to compare the different goods and services that can be consumed on a particular income level. While a star athlete and a "burger-flipper" are paid vastly different wages, each uses money as a measure of the value of their yearly earnings and purchases.

**store of value.** As a store of value, money serves as a way to accumulate wealth (buying power) until it is needed. For example, a person making $500 per week who wants to buy a $500 computer could save $50 per week for each of the next 10 weeks. Unfortunately, the value of stored money is directly dependent on the health of the economy. If, due to rapid inflation, all prices double in one year, then the purchasing power value of the money "stuffed in the mattress" would fall by half. On the other hand, "mattress savings" buy more when prices fall as they did for more than 52 months in Hong Kong between 1999 and 2005.

# Characteristics of Money

To be used as a medium of exchange, money must be acceptable, divisible, portable, stable in value, durable, and difficult to counterfeit.

### acceptability.
To be effective, money must be readily acceptable for the purchase of goods and services and for the settlement of debts. Acceptability is probably the most important characteristic of money: If people do not trust the value of money, businesses will not accept it as a payment for goods and services, and consumers will have to find some other means of paying for their purchases.

### divisibility.
Given the widespread use of quarters, dimes, nickels, and pennies in the United States, it is no surprise that the principle of divisibility is an important one. With barter, the lack of divisibility often makes otherwise preferable trades impossible, as would be an attempt to trade a steer for a loaf of bread. For money to serve effectively as a measure of value, all items must be valued in terms of comparable units—dimes for a piece of bubble gum, quarters for laundry machines, and dollars (or dollars and coins) for everything else.

### portability.
Clearly, for money to function as a medium of exchange, it must be easily moved from one location to the next. Large colored rocks could be used as money, but you couldn't carry them around in your wallet. Paper currency and metal coins, on the other hand, are capable of transferring vast purchasing power into small, easily carried (and hidden!) bundles. Few Americans realize it, but more U.S. currency is in circulation outside the United States than within. Currently, about $725 billion of U.S. currency is in circulation, and the majority is held outside the United States.[1]

### stability.
Money must be stable and maintain its declared face value. A $10 bill should purchase the same amount of goods or services from one day to the next. The principle of stability allows people who wish to postpone purchases and save their money to do so without fear that it will decline in value. As mentioned earlier, money declines in value during periods of inflation, when economic conditions cause prices to rise. Thus, the same amount of money buys fewer and fewer goods and services. In some countries, particularly in Latin America, people spend their money as fast as they can in order to keep it from losing any more of its value. Instability destroys confidence in a nation's money and its ability to store value and serve as an effective medium of exchange. Ultimately, people faced with spiraling price increases avoid the increasingly worthless paper money at all costs, storing all of their savings in the form of real assets such as gold and land.

### durability.
Money must be durable. The crisp new dollar bills you trade at the music store for the hottest new CD will make their way all around town for about 20 months before

The decline of the value of the U.S. dollar against the euro and other important world currencies has made imports to the United States more expensive and exports from the United States less expensive.

## ?

**DID YOU KNOW?**

Experts estimate that more than $130 million in counterfeit U.S. bills is circulating around the world.[2]

being replaced (see Table 15.1). Were the value of an old, faded bill to fall in line with the deterioration of its appearance, the principles of stability and universal acceptability would fail (but, no doubt, fewer bills would pass through the washer!). Although metal coins, due to their much longer useful life, would appear to be an ideal form of money, paper currency is far more portable than metal because of its light weight. Today, coins are used primarily to provide divisibility.

### difficulty to counterfeit.
Finally, to remain stable and enjoy universal acceptance, it almost goes without saying that money must be very difficult to counterfeit—that is, to duplicate illegally. Every country takes steps to make counterfeiting difficult. Most use multicolored money, and many use specially watermarked papers that are virtually impossible to duplicate. Counterfeit bills represent less than

**TABLE 15.1** The Life Expectancy of Paper Currency

| Denomination of Bill | Life Expectancy (Years) |
| --- | --- |
| $ 1 | 1.8 |
| $ 5 | 1.3 |
| $ 10 | 1.5 |
| $ 20 | 2 |
| $ 50 | 4.6 |
| $100 | 7.4 |

Source: "How Currency Gets into Circulation," *Federal Reserve Bank of New York* (n.d.), www.newyorkfed.org/aboutthefed/fedpoint/fed01.html (accessed June 28, 2006); Barbara Hagenbaum, "Coins Cost More to Make Than Face Value," *USA Today*, May 10, 2007, http://www.usatoday.com/money/2006-05-09-penny-usat x.htm (accessed June 18, 2007).

**CHECKING ACCOUNT** money stored in an account at a bank or other financial institution that can be withdrawn without advance notice; also called a demand deposit

0.02 percent of the currency in circulation in the United States,[3] but it is becoming increasingly easier for counterfeiters to print money with just a modest inkjet printer. This illegal printing of money is fueled by hundreds of people who often circulate only small amounts of counterfeit bills. To thwart the problem of counterfeiting, the U.S. Treasury Department redesigned the U.S. currency, starting with the $20 in 2003, and the $50 in 2004, and the $10 in 2006. For the first time, U.S. money includes subtle colors in addition to the traditional green, as well as enhanced security features, such as a watermark, security thread, and color-shifting ink.[4] In 2006 the new Jefferson nickel was introduced, showing a profile of the nation's third president. Due to the increased price of metals, it costs 5.73 cents to make the 5 cent piece. President Lincoln was the first president to appear on a coin when the Lincoln penny was introduced in 1909.[5] As Figure 15.1 indicates it costs more than a penny to manufacture a penny, resulting in a call to discontinue it.

*While paper money and coins are the most visible types of money, the combined value of all of the printed bills and all of the minted coins is actually rather insignificant when compared with the value of money kept in checking accounts, savings accounts, and other monetary forms.*

## ●● **LO2**

Describe various types of money.

## Types of Money

While paper money and coins are the most visible types of money, the combined value of all of the printed bills and all of the minted coins is actually rather insignificant when compared with the value of money kept in checking accounts, savings accounts, and other monetary forms.

You probably have a **checking account** (also called a demand deposit), money stored in an account at a bank or other financial institution that can be withdrawn without advance notice. One way to withdraw funds from your account is by writing a *check*, a written order to a bank to pay the indicated individual or business the amount specified on the check from money already on deposit. Figure 15.2 explains the significance of the numbers found on a typical U.S. check. As legal instruments, checks serve as a substitute for currency and coins and are preferred for many transactions due to their lower risk of loss. If you lose a $100 bill, anyone who finds or steals it can spend it. If you lose a blank check, however, the risk of catastrophic loss is quite low. Not only does your bank have a sample of your signature on file to compare with a suspected forged signature, but you can render the check immediately worthless by means of a stop-payment order at your bank.

There are several types of checking accounts, with different features available for different monthly fee levels or specific minimum account balances. Some checking accounts earn interest (a small

| FIGURE | 15.1 | Cost to Produce a Penny |

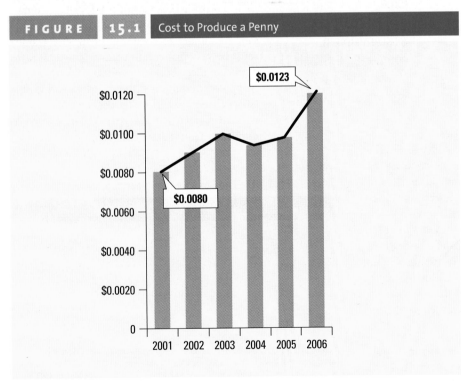

Source: *USA Today*, July 7, 2006, p. 2B.

percentage of the amount deposited in the account that the bank pays to the depositor). One such interest-bearing checking account is the *NOW (negotiable order of withdrawal) account* offered by most financial institutions. The interest rate paid on such accounts varies with the interest rates available in the economy but is typically quite low (ranging between 2 and 5 percent).

Savings accounts (also known as time deposits) are accounts with funds that usually cannot be withdrawn without advance notice and/or have limits on the number of withdrawals per period. While seldom enforced, the "fine print" governing most savings accounts prohibits withdrawals without two or three days' notice. Savings accounts are not generally used for transactions or as a medium of exchange, but their funds can be moved to a checking account or turned into cash.

Money market accounts are similar to interest-bearing checking accounts, but with more restrictions. Generally, in exchange for slightly higher interest rates, the owner of a money market account can write only a limited number of checks each

month, and there may be a restriction on the minimum amount of each check.

Certificates of deposit (CDs) are savings accounts that guarantee a depositor a set interest rate over a specified interval of time as long as the funds are not withdrawn before the end of the interval—six months, one year, or seven years, for example. Money may be withdrawn from these accounts prematurely only after paying a substantial penalty. In general, the longer the term of the CD, the higher is the interest rate it earns. As with all interest rates, the rate offered and fixed at the time the account is opened fluctuates according to economic conditions.

Credit cards allow you to promise to pay at a later date by using preapproved lines of credit granted by a bank or finance company. They are a popular substitute for cash payments because of their convenience, easy access to credit, and acceptance by merchants around the world. Indeed, it is difficult today to find stores (and even some governmental services, such as state license plate branches) that do not accept credit cards. The institution issuing the credit card guarantees

**FIGURE 15.2** A Check

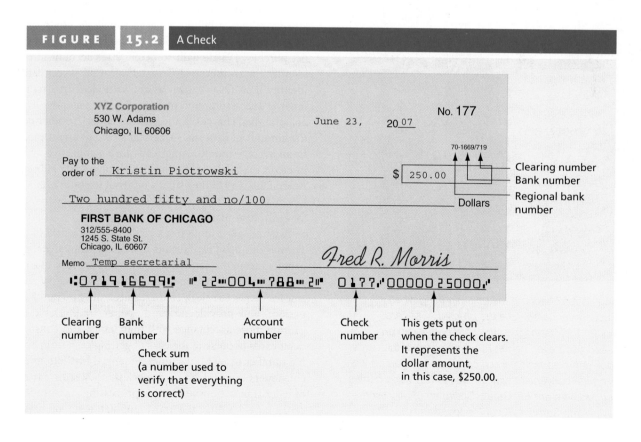

payment of a credit charge to merchants, less a small transaction fee, typically between 2 and 5 percent of the purchase, and assumes responsibility for collecting the money from the cardholder.

With few exceptions, credit cards allow cardholders great flexibility in paying off their purchases. Some people always pay off their monthly charges as they come due, but many others take advantage of the option of paying a stated minimum monthly amount with interest charges, based on yearly interest rates, added to the balance until it has been paid in full. For years, credit card companies lured clients with offers to lock in low fixed rates, sending the message for people who carry a balance on their card—and most people do—that there is no need to worry that the interest rate will rise without any warning. Today, more than half of all credit cards carry variable interest rates, a level that hadn't been reached since the 1990s. According to Bankrate.com, about 55 percent of all cards have variable rates, up from 38 percent in 2003.[6] Average annual fees for the privilege of carrying specific credit cards

## ● ● Two major credit cards— MasterCard and Visa—represent the vast majority of credit cards held in the United States.

are an important source of money for issuing banks and can sometimes reach $60 to $100 per year, although bank cards are increasingly available with no annual charge; reward cards generally charge a higher fee, which can be up to $200. Credit card issuers also charge a fee for converting from one nation's currency to another when the cardholder uses the card in another country.

Two major credit cards—MasterCard and Visa—represent the vast majority of credit cards held in the United States. More than half of the market is controlled by the industry's "Big Five"— Citigroup, MBNA, First USA, American Express, and Discover.[7] Banks are not the only issuers of credit cards. American Express has long been the dominant card company in the travel and entertainment market, with millions of cards outstanding. Unlike most bank cards, the original green American Express Card requires cardholders to pay their entire balances in full each month. However, American Express has expanded its card portfolio to include traditional credit cards.

Major department stores—Sears, JCPenney, Macy's, Saks Fifth Avenue, and others—offer their own credit cards to encourage consumers to spend money in their stores. Unlike the major credit cards discussed, these "private label" cards are generally accepted only at stores associated with the issuing company.

It is estimated that banks, credit card issuers, and retailers lose more than a billion dollars annually to credit card fraud, which includes lost or stolen cards, counterfeit cards, Internet purchases made with someone else's account number, and identity theft—the most devastating of all credit card frauds. Identity theft (also known as application or true name fraud) involves the assumption of someone else's identity by a criminal who then charges in the victim's name. Another concern is the amount of debt that Americans owe to credit card issuers. In an average month, Americans owe a collective $735 billion in credit card debt, while the British owe, $105 billion and the Australians, $19 billion. That works out to about $2,300 for each U.S. man, woman, and child; $1,616 for each Briton, and $950 for each Australian.[8]

A **debit card** looks like a credit card but works like a check. The use of a debit card results in a direct, immediate, electronic payment from the cardholder's checking account to a merchant or other party. While they are convenient to carry and profitable for banks, they lack credit features, offer no purchase "grace period," and provide no hard "paper trail." Debit cards are gaining more acceptance with merchants, and consumers like debit cards because of the ease of getting cash from an increasing number of ATM machines. Financial institutions also want consumers to use debit cards because they reduce the number of teller transactions and check processing costs. Indeed, debit cards have become the most popular form of payment for

Postepay cards may become the next big thing when it comes to consumer cards. Like the prepaid ATM cards parents buy for their teenagers, the card puts a cap on spending. Microsoft even began bundling some of the cards with its Xbox game consoles. Each card was charged up with cash, making it a convenient way for kids to buy Xbox games online. Pictured here are Bill Gates, Chairman of Microsoft (left), and Massimo Sarmi, CEO of Poste Italiane.

grocery and gasoline purchases and at "big-box" retailers like Best Buy.[9] Some cash management accounts at retail brokers like Merrill Lynch offer deferred debit cards. These act like a credit card but debit to the cash management account once a month. During that time, the cash earns a money market return.

Traveler's checks, money orders, and cashier's checks are other common forms of "near money." Although each is slightly different from the others, they all share a common characteristic: A financial institution, bank, credit company, or neighborhood currency exchange issues them in exchange for cash and guarantees that the purchased note will be honored and exchanged for cash when it is presented to the institution making the guarantee.

 **LO3**

Specify how the Federal Reserve Board manages the money supply and regulates the American banking system.

# THE AMERICAN FINANCIAL SYSTEM

The U.S. financial system fuels our economy by storing money, fostering investment opportunities, and making loans for new businesses and business expansion as well as for homes, cars, and college educations. This amazingly complex system includes banking institutions, nonbanking financial institutions such as finance companies, and systems that provide for the electronic transfer of funds throughout the world. Over the past 20 years, the rate at which money turns over, or changes hands, has increased exponentially. Different cultures place unique values on saving, spending, borrowing, and investing. The combination of this increased turnover rate and increasing interactions with people and organizations from other countries has created a complex money system. First, we need to meet the guardian of this complex system.

## The Federal Reserve System

The guardian of the American financial system is the **Federal Reserve Board,** or "the Fed," as it is commonly called, an independent agency of the federal government established in 1913 to regulate the nation's banking and financial industry. The Federal Reserve System is organized into 12 regions, each with a Federal Reserve Bank that serves its defined area (Figure 15.3). All the Federal Reserve banks except those in Boston and Philadelphia have regional branches. The Cleveland Federal Reserve Bank, for example, is responsible for branch offices in Pittsburgh and Cincinnati.

The Federal Reserve Board is the chief economic policy arm of the United States. Working with Congress and the president, the Fed tries to create a positive economic environment capable of sustaining low inflation, high levels of employment, a balance in international payments, and long-term economic growth. To this end, the Federal Reserve Board has four major responsibilities: (1) to control the supply of money, or monetary policy; (2) to regulate banks and other financial institutions; (3) to manage regional and national checking account procedures, or check clearing; and (4) to supervise the federal deposit insurance programs of banks belonging to the Federal Reserve System.

● **FEDERAL RESERVE BOARD** an independent agency of the federal government established in 1913 to regulate the nation's banking and financial industry

● **MONETARY POLICY** means by which the Fed controls the amount of money available in the economy

*With just a few simple words, U.S. Federal Reserve Board Chairman Ben Bernanke has the ability to affect monetary policy across the globe. Have you ever noticed the stock market on days in which he is supposed to make an announcement? Even days before or just after?*

**monetary policy.** The Fed controls the amount of money available in the economy through **monetary policy.** Without this intervention, the supply of and demand for money might not balance. This could result in either rapid price increases (inflation) because of too little money or economic recession and a slowdown of price increases (disinflation)

**FIGURE** **15.3** Federal Reserve System

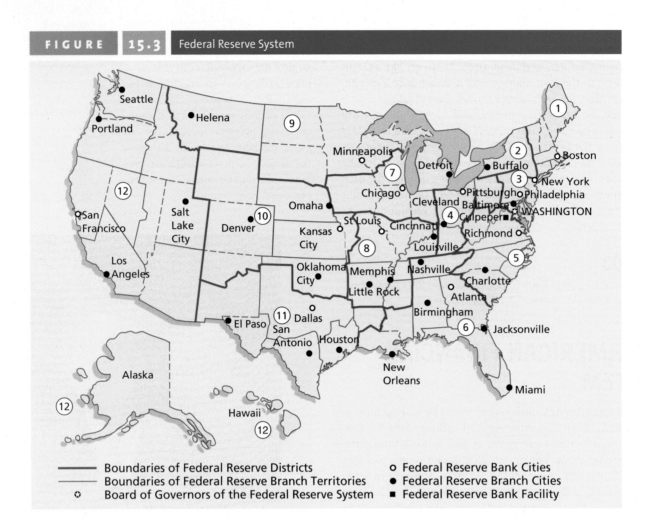

| | |
|---|---|
| ——— Boundaries of Federal Reserve Districts | ○ Federal Reserve Bank Cities |
| ——— Boundaries of Federal Reserve Branch Territories | ● Federal Reserve Branch Cities |
| ⊙ Board of Governors of the Federal Reserve System | ■ Federal Reserve Bank Facility |

because of too little growth in the money supply. In very rare cases (the depression of the 1930s) the United States has suffered from deflation, where the actual purchasing power of the dollar has increased as prices declined. To effectively control the supply of money in the economy, the Fed must have a good idea of how much money is in circulation at any given time. This has become increasingly challenging because the global nature of our economy means that more and more U.S. dollars

are circulating overseas. Using several different measures of the money supply, the Fed establishes specific growth targets which, presumably, ensure a close balance between money supply and money demand. The Fed fine-tunes money growth by using four basic tools: open market operations, reserve requirements, the discount rate, and credit controls (see Table 15.2). There is generally a log of 6 to 18 months before the effect of these charges shows up in economic activity.

**TABLE 15.2**  Fed Tools for Regulating the Money Supply

| Activity | Effect on the Money Supply and the Economy |
|---|---|
| Buy government securities | The money supply increases; economic activity increases. |
| Sell government securities | The money supply decreases; economic activity slows down. |
| Raise discount rate | Interest rates increase; the money supply decreases; economic activity slows down. |
| Lower discount rate | Interest rates decrease; the money supply increases; economic activity increases. |
| Increase reserve requirements | Banks make fewer loans; the money supply declines; economic activity slows down. |
| Decrease reserve requirements | Banks make more loans; the money supply increases; economic activity increases. |
| Relax credit controls | More people are encouraged to make major purchases, increasing economic activity. |
| Restrict credit controls | People are discouraged from making major purchases, decreasing economic activity. |

● OPEN MARKET OPER-
ATIONS decisions to buy
or sell U.S. Treasury bills
(short-term debt issued by
the U.S. government) and
other investments in the
open market

● RESERVE REQUIRE-
MENT the percentage of
deposits that banking institutions must hold in reserve

● DISCOUNT RATE the
rate of interest the Fed
charges to loan money to
any banking institution to
meet reserve requirements

● CREDIT CONTROLS the
authority to establish and
enforce credit rules for
financial institutions and
some private investors

Open market operations refer to decisions to buy or sell U.S. Treasury bills (short-term debt issued by the U.S. government; also called T-bills) and other investments in the open market. The actual purchase or sale of the investments is performed by the New York Federal Reserve Bank. This monetary tool, the most commonly employed of all Fed operations, is performed almost daily in an effort to control the money supply.

When the Fed buys securities, it writes a check on its own account to the seller of the investments. When the seller of the investments (usually a large bank) deposits the check, the Fed transfers the balance from the Federal Reserve account into the seller's account, thus increasing the supply of money in the economy and, hopefully, fueling economic growth. The opposite occurs when the Fed sells investments. The buyer writes a check to the Federal Reserve, and when the funds are transferred out of the purchaser's account, the amount of money in circulation falls, slowing economic growth to a desired level.

The second major monetary policy tool is the reserve requirement, the percentage of deposits that banking institutions must hold in reserve ("in the vault," as it were). Funds so held are not available for lending to businesses and consumers. For example, a bank holding $10 million in deposits, with a 10 percent reserve requirement, must have reserves of $1 million. If the Fed were to reduce the reserve requirement to, say, 5 percent, the bank would need to keep only $500,000 in reserves. The bank could then lend to customers the $500,000 difference between the old reserve level and the new lower reserve level, thus increasing the supply of money. Because the reserve requirement has such a powerful effect on the money supply, the Fed does not change it very often, relying instead on open market operations most of the time.

The third monetary policy tool, the discount rate, is the rate of interest the Fed charges to loan money to any banking institution to meet reserve requirements. The Fed is the lender of last resort for these banks. When a bank borrows from the Fed, it is said to have borrowed at the "discount window," and the interest rates charged there are often higher than those charged on loans of comparable risk elsewhere in the economy. This added interest expense, when it exists, serves to discourage banks from borrowing from the Fed.

● the Fed establishes and enforces banking rules that affect monetary policy and the overall level of the competition between different banks.

When the Fed wants to expand the money supply, it lowers the discount rate to encourage borrowing. Conversely, when the Fed wants to decrease the money supply, it raises the discount rate. The increases in interest rates that occurred in the United States from 2003 through 2006 were the result of more than 16 quarter-point (0.25 percent) increases in the Fed discount rate. The purpose was to keep inflation under control and to raise rates to a more normal level as the economy recovered from the recession of 2001. Not surprisingly, economists watch changes in this sensitive interest rate as an indicator of the Fed's monetary policy.

The final tool in the Fed's arsenal of weapons is credit controls—the authority to establish and enforce credit rules for financial institutions and some private investors. For example, the Fed can determine how large a down payment individuals and businesses must make on credit purchases of expensive items such as automobiles, and how much time they have to finish paying for the purchases. By raising and lowering minimum down payment amounts and payment periods, the Fed can stimulate or discourage credit purchases of "big ticket" items. The Fed also has the authority to set the minimum down payment investors must use for the credit purchases of stock. Buying stock with credit—"buying on margin"—is a popular investment strategy among individual speculators. By altering the margin requirement (currently set at 50 percent of the price of the purchased stocks), the Fed can effectively control the total amount of credit borrowing in the stock market.

**regulatory functions.** The second major responsibility of the Fed is to regulate banking institutions that are members of the Federal Reserve System. Accordingly, the Fed establishes and enforces banking rules that affect monetary policy and the overall level of the competition between different banks. It determines which nonbanking activities, such as brokerage services, leasing, and insurance, are appropriate for banks and which should be prohibited. The Fed also has the authority to approve or disapprove mergers between banks and the formation of bank holding companies. Increasingly, mergers between banks are crossing international waters. For example, Frances's BNP Paribas acquired United California Bank and Honolulu based BancWest Corp., while the

Royal Bank of Scotland, through its Citizens Financial Group subsidiary, purchased Pittsburgh's Mellon Financial and Philadelphia's Commonwealth Bancorp.[10] In an effort to ensure that all rules are enforced and that correct accounting procedures are being followed at member banks, surprise bank examinations are conducted by bank examiners each year.

### check clearing.

The Federal Reserve provides national check processing on a huge scale. Divisions of the Fed known as check clearinghouses handle almost all the checks written against a bank in one city and presented for deposit to a bank in a second city. Any banking institution can present the checks it has received from others around the country to its regional Federal Reserve Bank. The Fed passes on the checks to the appropriate regional Federal Reserve Bank, which then sends the checks to the issuing bank for payment. With the advance of electronic payment systems and the passage of the Check Clearing for the 21st Century Act (Check 21 Act), checks can now be processed in a day. The Check 21 Act allows banks to clear checks electronically by presenting an electronic image of the check. This eliminates mail delays and time-consuming paper processing.

### depository insurance.

The Fed is also responsible for supervising the federal insurance funds that protect the deposits of member institutions. These insurance funds will be discussed in greater detail in the following section.

## Banking Institutions

Banking institutions accept money deposits from and make loans to individual consumers and businesses. Some of the most important banking institutions include commercial banks, savings and loan associations, credit unions, and mutual savings banks. Historically, these have all been separate institutions. However, new hybrid forms of banking institutions that perform two or more of these functions have emerged over the last two decades. The following banking institutions all have one thing in common: They are businesses whose objective is to earn money by managing, safeguarding, and lending money to others. Their sales revenues come from the fees and interest that they charge for providing these financial services.

● ● **LO4**

Compare and contrast commercial banks, savings and loan associations, credit unions, and mutual savings banks.

### commercial banks.

The largest and oldest of all financial institutions are **commercial banks,** which perform a variety of financial services. They rely mainly on checking and savings accounts as their major source of funds and use only a portion of these deposits to make loans to businesses and individuals. Because it is unlikely that all the depositors of any one bank will want to withdraw all of their funds at the same time, a bank can safely loan out a large percentage of its deposits.

Today, banks are quite diversified and offer a number of services. Commercial banks make loans for virtually any conceivable legal purpose, from vacations to cars, from homes to college educations. Banks in many states offer *home equity loans,* by which home owners can borrow against the appraised value of their already purchased homes. Banks also issue Visa and MasterCard credit cards and offer CDs and trusts (legal entities set up to hold and manage assets for a beneficiary). Many banks rent safe deposit boxes in bank vaults to customers who want to store jewelry, legal documents, artwork, and other valuables. In 1999 Congress passed the Financial Services Modernization Act, also known as the Gramm-Leach-Bliley Bill. This act repealed the Glass Stegal Act, which was enacted in 1929 after the stock market crash and prohibited commercial banks from being in the insurance and investment

> # "banks are quite diversified and offer a number of services."

banking business. This puts U.S. commercial banks on the same competitive footing as European banks and provides a more level playing field for global banking competition. The stimulus for the Gramm-Leach-Bliley Bill was probably the merger of Citibank and Travelers Insurance. With its Salomon Smith Barney investment bank and brokerage units, Travelers Insurance, when combined with Citibank, became the largest financial services company in the United States. As commercial banks and investment banks have merged, the landscape has changed. Consolidation remains the norm in the U.S. banking industry. For example JPMorgan Chase completed a merger with Bank One in 2004, making it the second largest bank in the United States behind Citigroup. JPMorgan was created through a merger with Chase Manhattan Bank and JPMorgan, and Bank One acquired many Midwestern banks, with its biggest acquisition being First Chicago Corp.

## savings and loan associations.

**Savings and loan associations (S&Ls),** often called "thrifts," are financial institutions that primarily offer savings accounts and make long-term loans for residential mortgages. A mortgage is a loan made so that a business or individual can purchase real estate, typically a home; the real estate itself is pledged as a guarantee (called *collateral*) that the buyer will repay the loan. If the loan is not repaid, the savings and loan has the right to repossess the property. Prior to the 1970s, S&Ls focused almost exclusively on real estate lending and accepted only savings accounts. Today, following years of regulatory changes, S&Ls compete directly with commercial banks by offering many types of services.

Savings and loans have gone through a metamorphosis since the early 1990s, after having almost collapsed in the 1980s. Congress passed legislation that allowed more competition between banks and savings and loans. The problem was the owners and managers of the savings and loans did not know how to behave like a bank, and they did not have the products necessary to compete. Then, Congress passed laws in 1986 that took away many of the tax benefits of owning real estate, which caused investment in real estate to slow considerably and stimulated defaults that were spurred by a poor economy. Developers defaulted on loans, and the S&L managers who had lent the money for these high-risk ventures found themselves holding billions of dollars of virtually unsellable real estate properties.

Despite the efforts of the Federal Savings and Loan Insurance Corporation—which we discuss in more detail shortly—there were not enough funds to bail out the industry. Eventually, the insurance fund ran out of money, and Congress created the Resolution Trust Corporation (RTC) in 1989 to help the industry work its way out of trouble. At a cost of hundreds of billions of dollars, the RTC cleaned up the industry and, with its task completed, was dissolved by 1998.

## credit unions.

A **credit union** is a financial institution owned and controlled by its depositors, who usually have a common employer, profession, trade group, or religion. The Aggieland Credit Union in College Station, Texas, for example, provides banking services for faculty, employees, and current and former students of Texas A&M University. A savings account at a credit union is commonly referred to as a share account, while a checking account is termed a share draft account. Because the credit union is tied to a common organization, the members (depositors) are allowed to vote for directors and share in the credit union's profits in the form of higher interest rates on accounts and/or lower loan rates.

While credit unions were originally created to provide depositors with a short-term source of funds for low-interest consumer loans for items such as cars, home appliances, vacations, and college, today they offer a wide range of financial services. Generally, the larger the credit union, the more sophisticated its financial service offerings will be.

## mutual savings banks.

**Mutual savings banks** are similar to savings and loan associations, but, like credit unions, they are owned by their depositors. Among the oldest financial institutions in the United States, they were originally established to provide a safe place for savings of particular groups of people, such as fishermen. Found mostly in New England, they are becoming more popular in the rest of the country as some S&Ls have converted to mutual savings banks to escape the stigma created by the widespread S&L failures in the 1980s.

## insurance for banking institutions.

The **Federal Deposit Insurance Corporation (FDIC),** which insures individual bank accounts, was established in 1933 to help stop bank failures throughout the country during the Great Depression. Today, the FDIC insures personal accounts up to a

# From "Mom and Pop" to Giant Chain

Tom Monaghan

The Business: Domino's Pizza

Founded: 1960

Success: The company is currently bringing in more than $4 billion in annual sales.

In 1960, Tom Monaghan and his brother James bought Dominick's Pizza in Ypsilanti, Michigan, for $900. One year later, Tom Monaghan traded his Volkswagen Beetle for his brother's half of the business. Over the next 13 years, Monaghan worked 100 hours a week, seven days a week, and took just one six-day vacation to help grow his business. Along the way, he developed many innovative tools for the pizza industry such as dough trays, corrugated pizza boxes, and insulated pizza delivery bags. Domino's Pizza is also credited with creating the three-dimensional car-top sign and the spoodle (a cross between a spoon and a ladle). In 2004, Domino's was ranked the second largest pizza chain in the world. In 2006, Domino's has 8,000 locations in more than 55 countries, more than 140,000 employees, and more than $4 billion in annual sales. Tom Monaghan sold his interest in Domino's in 1999 for a reported $1 billion.[11] ❖

● **NATIONAL CREDIT UNION ASSOCIATION (NCUA)** an agency that regulates and charters credit unions and insures their deposits through its National Credit Union Insurance Fund

● **INSURANCE COMPANIES** businesses that protect their clients against financial losses from certain specified risks (death, accident, and theft, for example)

● **PENSION FUNDS** managed investment pools set aside by individuals, corporations, unions, and some nonprofit organizations to provide retirement income for members

maximum of $100,000 at nearly 8,000 FDIC member institutions.[12] While most major banks are insured by the FDIC, small institutions in some states may be insured by state insurance funds or private insurance companies. Should a member bank fail, its depositors can recover all of their funds, up to $100,000. Amounts over $100,000, while not legally covered by the insurance, are in fact usually covered because the Fed understands very well the enormous damage that would result to the financial system should these large depositors withdraw their money. The *Federal Savings and Loan Insurance Corporation (FSLIC)* insured thrift deposits prior to its insolvency and failure during the S&L crisis of the 1980s. Now, the insurance functions once overseen by the FSLIC are handled directly by the FDIC through its Savings Association Insurance Fund. The National Credit Union Association (NCUA) regulates and charters credit unions and insures their deposits through its National Credit Union Insurance Fund.

When they were originally established, Congress hoped that these insurance funds would make people feel secure about their savings so that they would not panic and withdraw their money when news of a bank failure was announced. The "bank run" scene in the perennial Christmas movie *It's a Wonderful Life,* when dozens of Bailey Building and Loan depositors attempted to withdraw their money (only to have the reassuring figure of Jimmy Stewart calm their fears), was not based on mere fiction. During the Great Depression, hundreds of banks failed and their depositors lost everything. The fact that large numbers of major financial institutions failed in the 1980s and 1990s—without a single major banking panic—underscores the effectiveness of the current insurance system. While the future may yet bring unfortunate surprises, most depositors go to sleep every night without worrying about the safety of their savings.

 **LO5**

Distinguish among nonbanking institutions such as insurance companies, pension funds, mutual funds, and finance companies.

## Nonbanking Institutions

Nonbank financial institutions offer some financial services, such as short-term loans or investment products, but do not accept deposits. These include insurance companies, pension funds, mutual funds, brokerage firms, nonfinancial firms, and finance companies. It may be a surprise to some, but General

## "a growing number of traditionally nonfinancial firms have moved onto the financial field."

**TABLE 15.3** Leading Diversified Financial Services Firms

| Company | Revenues (in Billions) |
| --- | --- |
| General Electric | $168.3 |
| Freddie Mac | 44 |
| American Express | 27.1 |
| Countrywide Financial | 24.4 |
| Marsh & McLennan | 12.1 |
| Aon | 10.3 |
| SLM | 8.7 |
| Ameriprise Financial | 8.1 |
| CIT Group | 6.9 |
| Thornburg Mortgage | 2.5 |

Source: "Fortune 500: Diversified Financial Companies," April 30, 2007, http://money.cnn.com/magazines/fortune/fortune500/2007/industries/Diversified_Financials/1.html (accessed June 18, 2007).

Electric Corporation's financial subsidiary, General Electric Capital Services (GECS) would rank as one of the top 10 largest U.S. banks with assets of $500 billion at the end of 2006.[13] Table 15.3 lists some other diversified financial services firms.

**diversified firms.** Recently, a growing number of traditionally nonfinancial firms have moved onto the financial field. These firms include manufacturing organizations, such as General Motors and General Electric, that traditionally confined their financial activities to financing their customers' purchases. GE, in particular, has been so successful in the financial arena that its credit subsidiary now accounts for more than 30 percent of the company's revenues and earnings. Not every nonfinancial firm has been successful with its financial ventures, however. Sears, the retail giant, once commanded an imposing financial network composed of real estate (Coldwell Banker), credit card (Discover Card), and brokerage (Dean Witter Reynolds) companies, but losses of hundreds of millions of dollars forced Sears to dismantle its network. The very prestigious brokerage firm Morgan Stanley acquired Dean Witter Discover, thus creating one of the largest investment firms in the country—in a league with Smith Barney and Merrill Lynch. Perhaps the moral of the story for firms like Sears is "stick to what you know."

## insurance companies.
Insurance companies are businesses that protect their clients against financial losses from certain specified risks (death, injury, disability, accident, fire, theft, and natural disasters, for example) in exchange for a fee, called a premium. Because insurance premiums flow into the companies regularly, but major insurance losses cannot be timed with great accuracy (although expected risks can be assessed with considerable precision), insurance companies generally have large amounts of excess funds. They typically invest these or make long-term loans, particularly to businesses in the form of commercial real estate loans.

## pension funds.
Pension funds are managed investment pools set aside by individuals, corporations, unions, and some nonprofit organizations to provide retirement income for members. One type of pension fund is the *individual retirement account (IRA),* which is established by individuals to provide for their personal retirement needs. IRAs can be invested in a variety of financial assets, from risky commodities such as oil or cocoa to low-risk financial "staples" such as U.S. Treasury securities. The choice is up to each person and is dictated solely by individual objectives and tolerance for risk. The interest earned by all of these investments may be deferred tax-free until retirement.

In 1997, Congress revised the IRA laws and created a Roth IRA. Although similar to a traditional IRA in that investors may contribute $3,000 per year, the money in a Roth IRA is considered an after-tax contribution. When the money is withdrawn at retirement, no tax is paid on the distribution. The Roth IRA is beneficial to young people who can allow a long time for their money to compound and who may be able to have their parents or grandparents fund the Roth IRA with gift money.

Most major corporations provide some kind of pension plan for their employees. Many of these are established with bank trust departments or life insurance companies. Money is deposited in a separate account in the name of each individual employee, and when the employee retires, the total amount in the account can be either withdrawn in one lump sum or taken as monthly cash payments over some defined time period (usually for the remaining life of the retiree).

Social Security, the largest pension fund, is publicly financed. The federal government collects Social Security funds from

# Allstate Helps Manage Financial Risks

Companies providing financial services are becoming increasingly important in our society and our economy. Customers value high-quality financial services, and Allstate goes above and beyond what is expected of them. The Allstate Corporation, the largest public personal insurance company in the United States, is one such service company. The company offers 13 lines of insurance including auto, property, life, and business. It also offers retirement, investment, and banking services. As of 2005, the company served about 17 million households and had offices in 49 U.S. states and in Canada. Allstate believes in bringing its customers value and prides itself on doing more than is expected of it in all areas—standing out in those of customer relationships and social responsibility.

Allstate is working hard to bring value to both customers and shareholders. The company believes strongly in acting ethically. In today's climate of corporate scandal, this is a valuable asset for the company and in building long-term shareholders. The company manages and invests its capital in an ethical manner, thereby providing shareholders with long-term financial stability. Allstate is also focusing on building long-term customers. In 2004, more than 1 million customers switched their auto insurance coverage to Allstate—now Allstate is working to make sure it keeps them. One way is by offering excellent claim management services. Doing this both strengthens the connection between the company and its customers (customers know and trust that Allstate will be there for them in times of need) and keeps costs low (helping the company). Allstate also focuses on streamlining its relationships with all individuals working with the company—employees and independent agents alike—so that they can then better provide clear, effective help to customers. The company members believe strongly in being good corporate citizens, which is an incredible value in and of itself.

The company also invests in municipal bonds and low-interest loans to support and grow urban neighborhoods. In addition, it is committed to helping the environment. At the company headquarters, lighting has been replaced both in and outside the buildings to cut down on energy consumption. The company is part of the Climate Resolve initiative—aimed at reducing greenhouse gas intensity. Employees who make use of public transportation are rewarded with subsidized tickets and complimentary shuttles to train stations. Allstate also works primarily with suppliers using recycled materials.

The 75-year-old Allstate comes to the aid of not only its customers but also the global community at large. Edward M. Liddy, chairman and chief executive officer, explains, "One of the most rewarding aspects of working at Allstate is to see the way our employees and agencies help others in a time of crisis. I know it is what we do as a business, but it's more than a business for Allstaters." This commitment rings true not only in times of disaster but in the day-to-day workings of the company and its relationships with its customers and shareholders.[14] ❖

## Q: Discussion Questions

1. What kind of financial services are provided by Allstate?

2. How is insurance related to managing financial resources?

3. What has Allstate done to develop the confidence of its customers through ethical and socially responsible activities?

payroll taxes paid by both employers and employees. The Social Security Administration then takes these monies and makes payments to those eligible to receive Social Security benefits—the retired, the disabled, and the young children of deceased parents.

## mutual funds.

A mutual fund pools individual investor dollars and invests them in large numbers of well-diversified securities. Individual investors buy shares in a mutual fund in the hope of earning a high rate of return and in much

**YOU SEE AN AGING GENERATION. WE SEE A GOLDEN OPPORTUNITY.**

Our perspective helps us spot growth opportunities ahead of the pack.

When our fund managers found a company developing a new treatment for the age-old problem of arthritis, they invested early in its stock. That company is now the world's largest biotech firm, and has been providing healthy returns for our fund shareholders.

Identifying an investment opportunity like this requires a unique perspective. Ours comes from using bottom-up research to identify companies with clear drivers of earnings growth. With one of the industry's largest research staffs committed to strong long-term performance without taking unnecessary risks, Franklin has been discovering growth opportunities with true potential for more than 50 years.

For details on how Franklin's perspective might benefit your portfolio, see your financial advisor, call 1-800-FRANKLIN, Ext. F853 or visit us at franklintempleton.com.

**FRANKLIN TEMPLETON INVESTMENTS**

< GAIN FROM OUR PERSPECTIVE® >

| FRANKLIN FLEX CAP GROWTH FUND Average Annual Total Returns 3/31/04 – Class A† | |
|---|---|
| 1-Year | 35.51% |
| 5-Year | 6.53% |
| 10-Year | 14.75% |

Before investing in Franklin Flex Cap Growth Fund, you should carefully consider the fund's investment goals, risks, charges and expenses. You'll find this and other information in the fund's prospectus, which you can obtain from your financial advisor. Please read the prospectus carefully before investing. Investment return and principal value will fluctuate so that your shares, when redeemed, may be worth more or less than the original cost. Performance data quoted includes the maximum 5.75% initial sales charge and represents past performance, which does not guarantee future results. More recent returns may differ from figures shown; for most recent month-end performance figures, please visit franklintempleton.com. The fund's focus on securities of California companies involves special risks including increased susceptibility to adverse economic or regulatory developments in that state. Smaller-company stocks have historically exhibited greater price volatility than larger-company stocks, particularly over the short term. Technology stocks can be highly volatile.

Holdings subject to change.

Franklin Templeton Distributions, Inc., One Franklin Parkway, San Mateo, CA 94403.

†The fund offers other share classes, subject to different fees and expenses, which will affect their performance. Prior to 6/3/98, fund shares were offered at a lower initial sales charge, thus actual returns may differ. Average annual total returns represent the average annual increase in value of an investment over the indicated periods and assume reinvestment of dividends and capital gains at net asset value.

*Mutual funds are considered an excellent method for investing for retirement.*

the same way as people buy shares of stock. Because of the large numbers of people investing in any one mutual fund, the funds can afford to invest in hundreds (if not thousands) of securities at any one time, minimizing the risks of any single security that does not do well. Mutual funds provide professional financial management for people who lack the time and/or expertise to invest in particular securities, such as government bonds. While there are no hard-and-fast rules, investments in one or

more mutual funds are one way for people to plan for financial independence at the time of retirement.

Like most financial institutions, mutual funds are regulated and in recent years have come under closer scrutiny because of a scandal precipitated by questionable activities at some fund companies. The Securities and Exchange Commission (SEC) is developing new rules and reforms "at warp speed" for the $7.5 trillion mutual-fund industry to curtail abuses that gave large traders an advantage over small investors. The problem stems from practices such as late trading and market timing—the rapid buying and selling of fund shares—which can lower the overall performance of a fund and result in higher costs for small investors.[15]

A special type of mutual fund called a *money market fund* invests specifically in short-term debt securities issued by governments and large corporations. Although they offer services such as check-writing privileges and reinvestment of interest income, money market funds differ from the money market accounts offered by banks primarily in that the former represent a pool of funds, while the latter are basically specialized, individual checking accounts. Money market funds usually offer slightly higher rates of interest than bank money market accounts.

## brokerage firms.

Brokerage firms buy and sell stocks, bonds, and other securities for their customers and provide other financial services. Larger brokerage firms like Merrill Lynch, Charles Schwab, and A. G. Edwards offer financial services unavailable at their smaller competitors. Merrill Lynch, for example, offers the Merrill Lynch Cash Management Account (CMA), which pays interest on deposits and allows clients to write checks, borrow money, and withdraw cash much like a commercial bank. The largest of the brokerage firms (including Merrill Lynch) have developed so many specialized services that they may be considered financial networks—organizations capable of offering virtually all of the services traditionally associated with commercial banks.

## finance companies.

Finance companies are businesses that offer short-term loans at substantially higher rates of interest than banks. Commercial finance companies make loans to businesses, requiring their borrowers to pledge assets such as equipment, inventories, or unpaid accounts as collateral for the loans. Consumer finance companies make loans to individuals. Like commercial finance companies, these firms require some sort of personal collateral as security against the borrower's possible inability to repay their loans. Because of the high interest rates they charge and other factors, finance companies typically are the lender of last resort for individuals and businesses whose credit limits have been exhausted and/or those with poor credit ratings. Major consumer finance companies include Household Finance and Wells Fargo. All finance companies—commercial or consumer—obtain their funds by borrowing from other corporations and/or commercial banks.

# Electronic Banking

Since the advent of the computer age, a wide range of technological innovations has made it possible to move money all across the world electronically. Such "paperless" transactions have allowed financial institutions to reduce costs in what has been (and what appears to continue to be) a virtual competitive battlefield. Electronic funds transfer (EFT) is any movement of funds by means of an electronic terminal, telephone, computer, or magnetic tape. Such transactions order a particular financial institution to subtract money from one account and add it to another. The most commonly used forms of EFT are automated teller machines, automated clearinghouses, and home banking systems.

automated teller machines. Probably the most familiar form of electronic banking is the automated teller machine (ATM), which dispenses cash, accepts deposits, and allows balance inquiries and cash transfers from one account to another. ATMs provide 24-hour banking services—both at home (through a local bank) and far away (via worldwide ATM networks such as Cirrus and Plus). Rapid growth, driven by both strong consumer acceptance and lower transaction costs for banks (about half the cost of teller transactions), has led to the installation of hundreds of thousands of ATMs worldwide. Table 15.4 presents some interesting statistics about ATMs.

automated clearinghouses. Automated clearinghouses (ACHs) permit payments such as deposits or withdrawals to be made to and from a bank account by magnetic computer tape. Most large U.S. employers, and many others worldwide, use ACHs to deposit their employees' paychecks directly to the employees' bank accounts. While direct deposit is used by only 50 percent of U.S. workers, nearly 100 percent of Japanese workers and more than 90 percent of European workers utilize it. The largest user of automated clearinghouses in the United States is the federal government, with 99 percent of federal government employees and 65 percent of the private workforce receiving their pay via direct deposit. And, more than 82 percent of all Social Security payments are made through an ACH system. In 2006, more than 2.3 billion business-to-business ACH payments were made.

The advantages of direct deposits to consumers include convenience, safety, and potential interest earnings. It is estimated that more than 4 million paychecks are lost or stolen annually, and FBI studies show that 2,000 fraudulent checks are cashed every day in the United States. Checks can never be lost or stolen with direct deposit. The benefits to businesses include decreased check-processing expenses and increased employee productivity. Research shows that businesses that use direct deposit can save more than $1.25 on each payroll check processed. Productivity could increase by $3 to $5 billion annually if all employees were to use direct deposit rather than taking time away from work to deposit their payroll checks.

Some companies also use ACHs for dividend and interest payments. Consumers can also use ACHs to make periodic (usually monthly) fixed payments to specific creditors without ever having to write a check or buy stamps. The estimated number of bills paid annually by consumers is 20 billion, and the total number paid through ACHs is estimated at only 7.5 billion. The average consumer who writes 10 to 15 checks each month would save $41 to $62 annually in postage alone.[16]

online banking. With the growth of the Internet, banking activities may now be carried out on a computer at home or at work, or through wireless devices such as cell phones and PDAs anywhere there is a wireless "hot point." Consumers and small businesses can now make a bewildering array of financial transactions at home or on the go 24 hours a day. Functioning much like a vast network of personal ATMs, computer networks such as America Online allow their subscribers to make sophisticated banking transactions, buy and sell stocks and bonds, and purchase products and airline tickets without ever leaving home or speaking to another human being. Many

**ELECTRONIC FUNDS TRANSFER (EFT)** any movement of funds by means of an electronic terminal, telephone, computer, or magnetic tape

**AUTOMATED TELLER MACHINE (ATM)** the most familiar form of electronic banking, which dispenses cash, accepts deposits, and allows balance inquiries and cash transfers from one account to another

**AUTOMATED CLEARINGHOUSES (ACHs)** a system that permits payments such as deposits or withdrawals to be made to and from a bank account by magnetic computer tape

**TABLE 15.4** ATM Fact Sheet

- An ATM costs between $9,000 and $50,000, depending on the functions it has been designed to perform.
- An ATM costs between $12,000 and $15,000 in annual maintenance costs, such as cash replenishment, servicing, telephone costs, and rent.
- The top five ATM owners are Bank of America, Cardtronics, JPMorgan Chase, U.S. Bancorp, and Wells Fargo.
- In 2006, there were 395,000 ATMs in the United States.
- Transactions at these machines totaled $10.1 billion.
- 26% of Americans prefer to bank via ATMs.
- The first ATM was in use in 1969 at the Chemical Bank in Long Island, NY.

Source: ATM Fact Sheet, 2007 ABA Issue Summary, American Bankers Association, http://www.aba.com/NR/rdonlyres/80468400-4225-11D4-AAE6-00508B95258D/45916/2ATMFacts.pdf (accessed June 18, 2007).

banks allow customers to log directly into their accounts to check balances, transfer money between accounts, view their account statements, and pay bills via home computer or other Internet-enabled devices. Computer and advanced telecommunications technology have revolutionized world commerce. In 2006, online banking customers grew by 27 percent, bringing the number of online banking customers to nearly 40 million.[17]

 **L06**

Investigate the challenges ahead for the banking industry.

## Challenge and Change in the Commercial Banking Industry

In the early 1990s, several large commercial banks were forced to admit publicly that they had made some poor loan decisions. Bank failures followed, including that of the Bank of New England, the third-largest bank failure in history. The vibrant economic growth in the 1990s substantially improved what had been a rather bleak picture for many financial institutions. Better management, combined with better regulation and a robust economy, saved commercial banks from the fate of the S&Ls. Indeed, low inflation rates meant low interest rates on deposits, and high employment led to very low loan default rates. Combined, these factors helped to make the 1990s one of the most profitable decades in the history of the banking industry.

The banking industry continued to change in the 2000s, and with the passage of the Gramm-Leach-Bliley Bill, banks are expected to continue their "urge to merge." Now that banks are allowed to offer insurance, brokerage, and investment banking services, there will be a hunt to find likely merger partners that will expand their customer reach and the services they are able to offer. On the other side of the coin, even as banks such as Bank of America continue to become national banks with offices in more than half the states, small community banks continue to start up to serve the customer who still wants personal service. The ability of these small banks to buy state-of-the-art technology from nonbank service providers allows them to offer Internet banking and many sophisticated services at competitive costs. They also provide a local face and service to the consumer who is more and more likely to be unwelcome at some large banks that cater to corporations and wealthy individuals.

CitiBank is one of the largest international banks in the world and has locations in Asia, Latin America, Europe, and of course North America. People living in Manila can use CitiBank's online banking services from abroad, and CitiBank customers can pay their bills on the Internet while traveling around the world in addition to having access to their money with their

## ING Direct Wants to Be Your Bank

ING Direct has become the largest Internet-based bank in the United States and one of the 40 largest banks nationwide by not acting like a traditional "brick-and-mortar" bank. As of 2004, ING Direct served more than 1.5 million customers in the United States and 8 million customers in Canada, Australia, France, Spain, Italy, United Kingdom, and Germany. In 2005, ING Direct added 1.2 million new customers—a 52 percent jump compared with 2004. ING Direct's U.S. operations are headquartered in Wilmington, Delaware—with innovative ING Direct cafés in Philadelphia, New York, Los Angeles, and Delaware, where you can drop by for coffee, call a sales associate, or visit INGdirect.com to learn about the bank and how to use it.

A subsidiary of the Amsterdam-based ING Group, ING Direct has built a reputation as an easy-to-use, reliable bank. It has rejected the notion of building branches with high-service contact on every corner; instead it exploits a range of technological innovations, making it possible to move money around the world electronically. It doesn't shower customers with free toasters and other gifts but rather offers them low-cost, simple banking products. It doesn't spend a lot of time coddling or directly interacting with its customers; such one-on-one service would be expensive and time-consuming. ING instead relies on paperless transactions, which reduce costs and improve speed, efficiency, and service to its clients. These cost reductions result, for example, in higher savings account APYs (annual percentage yields) that are, on average, 3 percent above the APYs offered by traditional banks.

To improve its success, ING studied the lifestyles and habits of its most profitable customers and applied what it learned to targeting prospects with similar behaviors. Its ideal customers are savings-minded parents, aged 30 to 50, who are comfortable using the Internet to order products and communicate with others about their buying experiences and what they've learned from searching Internet information resources. The average customer is comfortable but not wealthy, with average deposits of around $14,000.

ING Direct strives to carry out its theme of low-cost, simple transactions by letting savers open accounts with no fees, no minimums, and one of the best rates in the United States. Its mortgages include no application fees, a simple no-hassle application, and great rates that can save customers thousands of dollars on their mortgages compared with the 30-year fixed mortgages offered by traditional banks. The company now offers savings accounts, CDs, mortgage loans, home equity loans, and mutual funds.[18] ❖

**Q:** **Discussion Questions**

1. Why do you think online banking is becoming so popular?

2. Explain why a bank from the Netherlands has been so successful in getting such a large share of the U.S. online banking business.

3. Do you see any major obstacles for ING Direct in competing with U.S. banks in the future?

CitiBank ATM card. Banking will continue to become more international with large banks such as the Dutch ABN-AMRO bank continuing to acquire banking assets in the United States. For instance in Chicago, ABN-AMRO owns LaSalle Bank, and The Bank of Montreal owns The Harris Bank.

Indeed, the recent trend toward ever bigger banks and other financial institutions is not happening by chance alone. Financial services may be an example of a "natural oligopoly," meaning that the industry may be best served by a few very large firms rather than a host of smaller ones. As the largest U.S. banks merge into even larger international entities, they will erase the relative competitive advantages now enjoyed by the largest foreign banks. It is by no means implausible that the financial services industry of the year 2020 will be dominated by 10 or so internationally oriented "megabanks."

Rapid advances and innovations in technology are challenging the banking industry and requiring it to change. As we said earlier, more and more banks, both large and small, are offering electronic access to their financial services. ATM technology is rapidly changing, with machines now dispensing more than just cash. Online financial services, ATM technology, and bill presentation are just a few of the areas where rapidly changing technology is causing the banking industry to change as well. ∎

## CHECK OUT

www.mhhe.com/FerrellM

for study materials including Interactive Exercises, Quizzes, iPod downloads, and video.

## Build Your Business Plan

**Money and the Financial System**   This chapter provides you with the opportunity to think about money and the financial system and just how many new businesses fail every year. In some industries the failure rate is as high as 80 percent. One reason for such a high failure rate is the inability to manage the finances of the organization. From the start of the business, financial planning plays a key role. Try getting a loan without an accompanying budget/forecast of earnings and cash flow.

While obtaining a loan from a family member may be the easiest way to fund your business, it may cause more problems for you later on if you are unable to pay the money back as scheduled. Before heading to a lending officer at a bank, contact your local SBA center to see what assistance they might provide.

M IS MOMENTUM

M IS MCGRAW-HILL

are you M-powered?
www.mhhe.com/FerrellM

# Financial Management and Securities Markets

16

**introduction**     While it's certainly true that money makes the world go 'round, financial management is the discipline that makes the world turn more smoothly. Indeed, without effective management of assets, liabilities, and owners' equity, all business organizations are doomed to fail—regardless of the quality and innovativeness of their products. Financial management is the field that addresses the issues of obtaining and managing the funds and resources necessary to run a business successfully. It is not limited to business organizations: All organizations, from the corner store to the local nonprofit art museum, from giant corporations to county governments, must manage their resources effectively and efficiently if they are to achieve their objectives.

In this chapter, we look at both short- and long-term financial management. First, we discuss the management of short-term assets, which companies use to generate sales and conduct ordinary day-to-day business operations. Next we turn our attention to the management of short-term liabilities, the sources of short-term funds used to finance the business. Then, we discuss the management of long-term assets such as plant and equipment and the long-term liabilities such as stocks and bonds used to finance these important corporate assets. Finally, we look at the securities markets, where stocks and bonds are traded.

DESTINATION CEO

**Charles Schwab**   Thirty years ago, one man shook up the world of trading by cutting the brokerage fee in half. Charles Schwab created that new investment business model to make it possible for all people to invest in equities. Currently, Charles Schwab has $1 trillion in investments and is one of the largest firms in the industry. Schwab services approximately 7 million individual accounts.

Charles Schwab became interested in stocks at the age of 13. He was the son of a lawyer who helped him learn about trading, investments, and equities. He credits his father's guidance in helping drive him to his success. Schwab studied economics while in business school and got his feet wet in the industry as an analyst at 22 years of age. He founded an investment newsletter and learned the ups and downs of the markets. In 1974 and 1975, regulation came to the industry that had traditionally been the domain of the large, wealthy, and institutional investors. Schwab made it more accessible to the average individual. He started his firm with 10 employees. Growth of his firm came from aggressive advertising that cut the brokerage fees in half; today, those fees have been eliminated. Schwab turned the reigns over to another individual as CEO but

remained as chairman of the board. Within a few years, however, Schwab was unhappy about the direction that the firm was heading and returned as CEO. Currently, there is a new marketing campaign that centers around the concept of "talk to Chuck." Schwab is committed to the belief that the stock market is a good place for investments for all individuals, not just those who are affluent.

## >>DISCUSSION QUESTIONS

1. What was the key for Schwab's initial success?

2. What is the relative size of Charles Schwab as a company?

3. Discuss the new marketing campaign being launched by Schwab.

>>To see the complete video about Charles Schwab, go to our Web site at **www.mhhe.com/FerrellM** and look for the link to the Destination CEO videos.

# MANAGING CURRENT ASSETS AND LIABILITIES

Managing short-term assets and liabilities involves managing the current assets and liabilities on the balance sheet (discussed in Chapter 14). Current assets are short-term resources such as cash, investments, accounts receivable, and inventory. Current liabilities are short-term debts such as accounts payable, accrued salaries, accrued taxes, and short-term bank loans. We use the terms *current* and *short term* interchangeably because short-term assets and liabilities are usually replaced by new assets and liabilities within three or four months, and always within a year. Managing short-term assets and liabilities is sometimes called **working capital management** because short-term assets and liabilities continually flow through an organization and are thus said to be "working."

## Managing Current Assets

The chief goal of financial managers who focus on current assets and liabilities is to maximize the return to the business on cash, temporary investments of idle cash, accounts receivable, and inventory.

**managing cash.** A crucial element facing any financial manager is effectively managing the firm's cash flow. Remember that cash flow is the movement of money through an organization on a daily, weekly, monthly, or yearly basis. Ensuring that sufficient (but not excessive) funds are on hand to meet the company's obligations is one of the single most important facets of financial management.

Idle cash does not make money, and corporate checking accounts typically do not earn interest. As a result, astute money managers try to keep just enough cash on hand, called **transaction balances,** to pay bills—such as employee wages, supplies,

> ● **WORKING CAPITAL MANAGEMENT** the managing of short-term assets and liabilities
>
> ● **TRANSACTION BALANCES** cash kept on hand by a firm to pay normal daily expenses, such as employee wages and bills for supplies and utilities

## Hershey Foods: Melts in Your Mouth and May Melt Your Heart

Hershey Foods is the leading North American producer of quality chocolate and candy products, including much-loved brands such as Hershey's milk chocolate bar, Hershey's syrup, Hershey's cocoa, Almond Joy, Mr. Goodbar, Hershey's Kisses, Kit Kat, and Reese's peanut butter cups. A century after its founding, the company continues to operate by the values of its founder. Milton Hershey was born in 1857 and was of Pennsylvania Dutch descent. He became an apprentice to a candy maker in 1872, at age 15. By age 30, he had founded the Lancaster Caramel Company. After visiting the Chicago Exhibition in 1893, he became interested in a new chocolate-making machine. He sold his caramel factory and built a large chocolate factory in Derry Church, Pennsylvania, in 1905; the city was renamed Hershey in 1906. Hershey pioneered modern confectionery mass-production techniques by developing much of the machinery for making and packaging his milk chocolate products. The Hershey Foods Corporation as it exists today was organized under the laws of the state of Delaware on October 24, 1927, as a successor to the original business founded in 1894 by Milton Hershey. The company's stock was first publicly traded on December 1, 1927, and investors can still purchase shares today.

Milton Hershey was not only interested in innovative candy making; he also wanted to help the members of his community. An example of his concern for the community was the founding of a home and school for orphan children, the Hershey Industrial School (now called the Milton Hershey School) in 1909. Many of the children who attended the school became Hershey employees, including former Hershey chairman William Dearden (1976–1984). Today, the 10,000-acre campus houses and provides education for nearly 1,300 financially and socially disadvantaged children. Although Hershey remains a public corporation, the Milton Hershey School Trust, which financially supports the school, owns about 30 percent of Hershey Foods' total equity. The Milton Hershey School Trust also owns 100 percent of the Hershey Entertainment and Resort Company, which operates a number of Hershey's nonchocolate properties, including the Hershey Park theme park, the Dutch Wonderland theme park for younger children, the Hershey Hotel, the Hershey Lodge and Convention Center, the Hershey Bears minor league hockey team, Hershey's zoo, a four-course golf club, an outdoor sports stadium, and an indoor sports arena.

Because of Milton Hershey's original funding and the wise investment management by the trust managers, the assets of the Milton Hershey School Trust have grown to a value of more than $7 billion. Milton Hershey was a visionary in terms of using a public corporation to support his philanthropic dreams.[1] ❖

**Q: Discussion Questions**

1. Do you think that Milton Hershey made the right decision in leaving his foundation the controlling voting interest in the Hershey Foods Corporation?

2. Is Hershey Foods' example of founders willing stock for philanthropic purposes something that you believe that companies could do today? Why or why not?

3. Knowing that a large share of Hershey's profits support philanthropic causes, would you be more likely to purchase the company's stock?

and utilities—as they fall due. To manage the firm's cash and ensure that enough cash flows through the organization quickly and efficiently, companies try to speed up cash collections from customers.

To accelerate the collection of payments from customers, some companies have customers send their payments to a lockbox, which is simply an address for receiving payments, instead of directly to the company's main address. The manager of the lockbox, usually a commercial bank, collects payments directly from the lockbox several times a day and deposits them into the company's bank account. The bank can then start clearing the checks and get the money into the company's checking account much more quickly than if the payments had been submitted directly to the company. However, there is no free lunch: The costs associated with lockbox systems make them worthwhile only for those companies that receive thousands of checks from customers each business day.

Large firms with many stores or offices around the country, such as Household International (parent company of the well-known finance company, Household Finance), frequently use electronic funds transfer to speed up collections. Household Finance's local offices deposit checks received each business day into their local banks and, at the end of the day, Household's corporate office initiates the transfer of all collected funds to its central bank for overnight investment. This technique is especially attractive for major international companies, which face slow and sometimes uncertain physical delivery of payments and/or less-than-efficient check-clearing procedures.

More and more companies are now using electronic funds transfer systems to pay and collect bills online. It is interesting that companies want to collect cash quickly but pay out cash slowly. When companies use electronic funds transfers between buyers and suppliers, the speed of collections and disbursements increases to one day. Only with the use of checks can companies delay the payment of cash quickly and have a three- or four-day waiting period until the check is presented to their bank and the cash leaves their account.

**investing idle cash.** As companies sell products, they generate cash on a daily basis, and sometimes cash comes in faster than it is needed to pay bills. Organizations often invest this "extra" cash, for periods as short as one day (overnight) or for as long as one year, until it is needed. Such temporary investments of cash are known as marketable securities. Examples include U.S. Treasury bills, certificates of deposit, commercial paper, and Eurodollar loans. Table 16.1 summarizes a number of different marketable securities used by businesses and some sample interest rates on these investments as of June 23, 2006. The safety rankings are relative. While all of the listed securities are very low risk, the U.S. government securities are the safest.

Many large companies invest idle cash in U.S. Treasury bills (T-bills), which are short-term debt obligations the U.S. government sells to raise money. Issued weekly by the U.S. Treasury, T-bills carry maturities of between one week to one year. U.S. T-bills are generally considered to be the safest of all investments and are called risk free because the U.S. government will not default on its debt.

Commercial certificates of deposit (CDs) are issued by commercial banks and brokerage companies. They are available in minimum amounts of $100,000 but are typically in units of $1 million for large corporations investing excess cash. Unlike consumer CDs (discussed in Chapter 15), which must be held until maturity, commercial CDs may be traded prior to maturity. Should a cash shortage occur, the organization can simply sell the CD on the open market and obtain needed funds.

One of the most popular short-term investments for the largest business organizations is commercial paper—a written promise from one company to another to pay a specific amount

**TABLE 16.1** -Short-Term Investment Possibilities for Idle Cash

| Type of Security | Maturity | Seller of Security | Interest Rate 6/23/06 | Safety Level |
|---|---|---|---|---|
| Treasury bills | 90 days | U.S. government | 4.80% | Excellent |
| Treasury bills | 180 days | U.S. government | 5.05 | Excellent |
| Commercial paper | 30 days | Major corporations | 5.14 | Very good |
| CDs | 90 days | U.S. commercial banks | 5.40 | Very good |
| CDs | 180 days | U.S. commercial banks | 5.43 | Very good |
| Eurodollars | 90 days | European commercial banks | 5.48 | Good |

Source: http://research.stlouisfed.org/Fred2/series and www.bank.guarantygroup.com/corporate/services/eurodollarrates.

of money. Because commercial paper is backed only by the name and reputation of the issuing company, sales of commercial paper are restricted to only the largest and most financially stable companies. As commercial paper is frequently bought and sold for durations of as short as one business day, many "players" in the market find themselves buying commercial paper with excess cash on one day and selling it to gain extra money the following day.

Some companies invest idle cash in international markets such as the eurodollar market, a market for trading U.S. dollars in foreign countries. Because the Eurodollar market was originally developed by London banks, any dollar-denominated deposit in a non-U.S. bank is called a eurodollar deposit, regardless of whether the issuing bank is actually located in Europe, South America, or anyplace else. For example, if you travel overseas and deposit $1,000 in a German bank, you will have "created" a eurodollar deposit in the amount of $1,000. Since the U.S. dollar is accepted by most countries for international trade, these dollar deposits can be used by international companies to settle their accounts. The market created for trading such investments offers firms with extra dollars a chance to earn a slightly higher rate of return with just a little more risk than they would face by investing in U.S. Treasury bills.

## maximizing accounts receivable.

After cash and marketable securities, the balance sheet lists accounts receivable and inventory. Remember that accounts receivable is money owed to a business by credit customers. For example, if you charge your Shell gasoline purchases, until you actually pay for them with cash or a check, they represent an account receivable to Shell. Many businesses make the vast majority of their sales on credit, so managing accounts receivable is an important task.

Each credit sale represents an account receivable for the company, the terms of which typically require customers to pay the full amount due within 30, 60, or even 90 days from the date of the sale. To encourage quick payment, some businesses offer some of their customers discounts of between 1 to 2 percent if they pay off their balance within a specified period of time (usually between 10 and 30 days). On the other hand, late payment charges of between 1 and 1.5 percent serve to discourage slow payers from sitting on their bills forever. The larger the early payment discount offered, the faster customers will tend to pay their accounts. Unfortunately, while discounts increase cash flow, they also reduce profitability. Finding the right balance between the added advantages of early cash receipt and the disadvantages of reduced profits is no simple matter. Similarly, determining the optimal balance between the higher sales likely to result from extending credit to customers with less than sterling credit ratings and the higher bad-debt losses likely to result from a more lenient credit policy is also challenging. Information on company credit ratings is provided by local credit bureaus, national credit-rating agencies such as Dun and Bradstreet, and industry trade groups.

● EURODOLLAR MARKET a market for trading U.S. dollars in foreign countries

## optimizing inventory.

While the inventory that a firm holds is controlled by both production needs and marketing considerations, the financial manager has to coordinate inventory purchases to manage cash flows. The object is to minimize the firm's investment in inventory without experiencing production cutbacks as

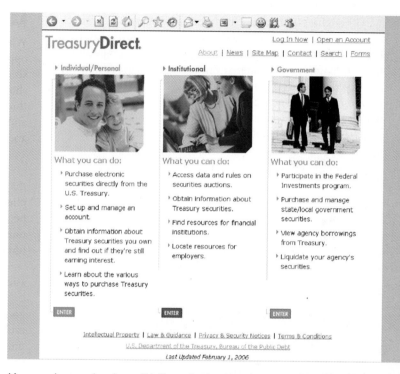

You can buy and redeem T-bills and other government securities directly from the U.S. Department of the Treasury at www.treasurydirect.gov.

a result of critical materials shortfalls or lost sales due to insufficient finished goods inventories. Every dollar invested in inventory is a dollar unavailable for investment in some other area of the organization. Optimal inventory levels are determined, in large part, by the method of production. If a firm attempts to produce its goods just in time to meet sales demand, the level of inventory will be relatively low. If, on the other hand, the firm produces materials in a constant, level pattern, inventory increases when sales decrease and decreases when sales increase. One way that companies are attempting to optimize inventory is through the use of radio frequency identification (RFID) technology.

The automobile industry is an excellent example of an industry driven almost solely by inventory levels. Because it is inefficient to continually lay off workers in slow times and call them back in better times, Ford, General Motors, and Chrysler try to set and stick to quarterly production quotas. Automakers typically try to keep a 60-day supply of unsold cars. During particularly slow periods, however, it is not unusual for inventories to exceed 100 days of sales. When sales of a particular brand fall far behind the average and inventories build up, production of that model may be canceled, as General Motors did with its Oldsmobile marque. Before eliminating a brand outright, however, automakers typically try to "jump-start" sales by offering rebates, special financing incentives, or special lease terms—all of which GM tried without success.

Although less publicized, inventory shortages can be as much of a drag on potential profits as too much inventory. Not having an item on hand may send the customer to a competitor—forever. Complex computer inventory models are frequently employed to determine the optimum level of inventory a firm should hold to support a given level of sales. Such models can indicate how and when parts inventories should be ordered so that they are available exactly when required—and not a day before. Developing and maintaining such an intricate

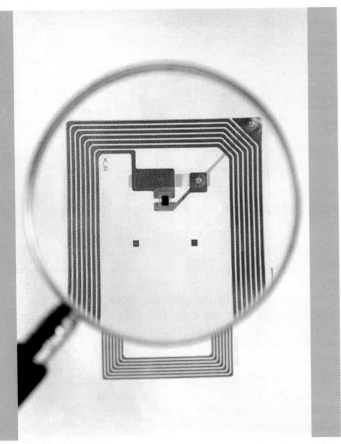

*Companies such as Wal-Mart are attempting to better manage their inventories by using radio-frequency-identification (RFID) tags. An RFID tag, which contains a silicon chip and an antenna, allows a company to use radio waves to track and identify the products to which the tags are attached—even after the products have left the store.*

production and inventory system is difficult, but it can often prove to be the difference between experiencing average profits and spectacular ones.

 **LO2**

Identify some sources of short-term financing (current liabilities).

## Managing Current Liabilities

While having extra cash on hand is a delightful surprise, the opposite situation—a temporary cash shortfall—can be a crisis. The good news is that there are several potential sources of short-term funds. Suppliers often serve as an important source through credit sales practices. Also, banks, finance companies, and other organizations offer short-term funds through loans and other business operations.

**accounts payable.** Remember from Chapter 14 that accounts payable is money an organization owes to suppliers for goods and services. Just as accounts receivable must be actively managed to ensure proper cash collections, so too must accounts payable be managed to make the best use of this important liability.

The most widely used source of short-term financing, and therefore the most important account payable, is trade credit—credit extended by suppliers for the purchase of their goods and services. While varying in formality, depending on both the organizations involved and the value of the items purchased, most trade credit agreements offer discounts to organizations that pay their bills early. A supplier, for example, may offer trade terms of "1/10 net 30," meaning that the purchasing organization may take a 1 percent discount from the invoice amount if it makes payment by the 10th day after receiving the bill. Otherwise, the entire amount is due within 30 days. For example, pretend that you are the financial manager in charge of payables. You owe Ajax Company $10,000, and it offers trade terms of 2/10 net 30. By paying the amount due within 10 days, you can save 2 percent of $10,000, or $200. Assume you place orders with Ajax once per month and have 12 bills of $10,000 each per year. By taking the discount every time, you will save 12 times $200, or $2,400, per year. Now assume you are the financial manager of Gigantic Corp., and it has monthly payables of $100 million per month. Two percent of $100 million is $2 million per month. Failure to take advantage of such trade discounts can, in many cases, add up to large opportunity losses over the span of a year.

**bank loans.** Virtually all organizations—large and small—obtain short-term funds for operations from banks. In most instances, the credit services granted these firms take the form of a line of credit or fixed dollar loan. A line of credit

● **SECURED LOANS** loans backed by collateral that the bank can claim if the borrowers do not repay them

● **UNSECURED LOANS** loans backed only by the borrowers' good reputation and previous credit rating

● **PRIME RATE** the interest rate that commercial banks charge their best customers (usually large corporations) for short-term loans

● **FACTOR** a finance company to which businesses sell their accounts receivable—usually for a percentage of the total face value

● **LONG-TERM (FIXED) ASSETS** production facilities (plants), offices, and equipment—all of which are expected to last for many years

is an arrangement by which a bank agrees to lend a specified amount of money to the organization upon request—provided that the bank has the required funds to make the loan. In general, a business line of credit is very similar to a consumer credit card, with the exception that the preset credit limit can amount to millions of dollars.

In addition to credit lines, banks also make secured loans—loans backed by collateral that the bank can claim if the borrowers do not repay the loans—and unsecured loans—loans backed only by the borrowers' good reputation and previous credit rating. Both individuals and businesses build their credit rating from their history of borrowing and repaying borrowed funds on time and in full. The three national credit-rating services are Equifax, TransUnion, and Experian. A lack of credit history or a poor credit history can make it difficult to get loans from financial institutions. The *principal* is the amount of money borrowed; *interest* is a percentage of the principal that the bank charges for use of its money. As we mentioned in Chapter 15, banks also pay depositors interest on savings accounts and some checking accounts. Thus, banks charge borrowers interest for loans and pay interest to depositors for the use of their money. In addition, these loans may include origination fees.

The prime rate is the interest rate commercial banks charge their best customers (usually large corporations) for short-term loans. While, for many years, loans at the prime rate represented funds at the lowest possible cost, the rapid development of the market for commercial paper has dramatically reduced the importance of commercial banks as a source of short-term loans. Today, most "prime" borrowers are actually small and medium-sized businesses.

The interest rates on commercial loans may be either fixed or variable. A variable, or floating-rate loan offers an advantage when interest rates are falling but represents a distinct disadvantage when interest rates are rising. Between 1999 and 2004, interest rates plummeted, and borrowers refinanced their loans with low-cost fixed-rate loans. Nowhere was this more visible than in the U.S. mortgage markets, where homeowners lined up to refinance their high-percentage home mortgages with lower-cost loans, in some cases as low as 5 percent on a 30-year loan. These mortgage interest rates had returned to 6.5 percent by mid-2006. Individuals and corporations have the same motivation: to minimize their borrowing costs.

**nonbank liabilities.** Banks are not the only source of short-term funds for businesses. Indeed, virtually all financial institutions, from insurance companies to pension funds, from money market funds to finance companies, make short-term loans to many organizations. The largest U.S. companies also actively engage in borrowing money from the eurodollar and commercial paper markets. As noted earlier, both of these funds' sources are typically slightly less expensive than bank loans.

In some instances, businesses actually sell their accounts receivable to a finance company known as a factor, which gives the selling organizations cash and assumes responsibility for collecting the accounts. For example, a factor might pay $60,000 for receivables with a total face value of $100,000 (60 percent of the total). The factor profits if it can collect more than what it paid for the accounts. Because the selling organization's customers send their payments to a lockbox, they may have no idea that a factor has bought their receivables.

Additional nonbank liabilities that must be efficiently managed to ensure maximum profitability are taxes owed to the government and wages owed to employees. Clearly, businesses are responsible for many different types of taxes, including federal, state, and local income taxes, property taxes, mineral rights taxes, unemployment taxes, Social Security taxes, workers' compensation taxes, excise taxes, and even more! While the public tends to think that the only relevant taxes are on income and sales, many industries must pay other taxes that far exceed those levied against their income. Taxes and employees' wages represent debt obligations of the firm, which the financial manager must plan to meet as they fall due.

 **LO3**

Summarize the importance of long-term assets and capital budgeting.

# MANAGING FIXED ASSETS

Up to this point, we have focused on the short-term aspects of financial management. While most business failures are the result of poor short-term planning, successful ventures must also consider the long-term financial consequences of their actions. Managing the long-term assets and liabilities and the owners' equity portion of the balance sheet is important for the long-term health of the business.

Long-term (fixed) assets are expected to last for many years—production facilities (plants), offices, equipment, heavy

● **CAPITAL BUDGET-
ING** the process of ana-
lyzing the needs of the
business and selecting the
assets that will maximize
its value

machinery, furniture, automobiles, and so on. In today's fast-paced world, companies need the most technologically advanced, modern facilities and equipment they can afford. Automobile, oil refining, and transportation companies are dependent on fixed assets.

Modern and high-tech equipment carry high price tags, and the financial arrangements required to support these investments are by no means trivial. Leasing is just one approach to financing. Obtaining major long-term financing can be challenging for even the most profitable organizations. For less successful firms, such challenges can prove nearly impossible. One approach is leasing assets such as equipment, machines,

future cash obligations more visible.[2] We'll take a closer look at long-term financing in a moment, but first let's address some issues associated with fixed assets, including capital budgeting, risk assessment, and the costs of financing fixed assets.

## Capital Budgeting and Project Selection

One of the most important jobs performed by the financial manager is to decide what fixed assets, projects, and investments will earn profits for the firm beyond the costs necessary to fund them. The process of analyzing the needs of the business and selecting the assets that will maximize its value is called **capital budgeting,** and the capital budget is the amount of money

> # Budgeting is not an exact process, and managers must be flexible when new information is available.

and buildings. In the case of leasing or not taking ownership but paying a fee for usage, potential long-term assets can be taken off the balance sheets as a debt. Still, the company has the asset and an obligation to pay money that is a contractual obligation. Leases are associated with $1.25 trillion off-the-balance-sheet obligations, and the Securities and Exchange Commission is considering changing accounting rules to make

budgeted for investment in such long-term assets. But capital budgeting does not end with the selection and purchase of a particular piece of land, equipment, or major investment. All assets and projects must be continually reevaluated to ensure their compatibility with the organization's needs. As Figure 16.1 indicates, financial executives believe most budgeting activities are occasionally or frequently unrealistic or irrelevant. If a particular asset does not live up to expectations, then management must determine why and take necessary corrective action. Budgeting is not an exact process, and managers must be flexible when new information is available.

## Assessing Risk

Every investment carries some risk. Figure 16.2 ranks potential investment projects according to estimated risk. When considering investments overseas, risk assessments must include the political climate and economic stability of a region. The decision to introduce a product or build a manufacturing facility in England would be much less risky than a decision to build one in the Middle East, for example.

Not apparent from Figure 16.2 are the risks associated with time. The longer a project or asset is expected to last, the greater its potential risk because it is hard

| FIGURE | 16.1 | How Reliable Is Budgeting and Planning? |

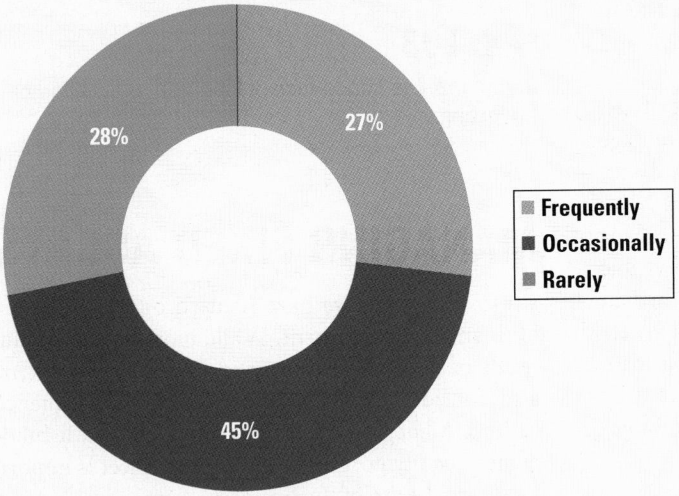

Legend:
- Frequently
- Occasionally
- Rarely

27%
28%
45%

How often is planning and budgeting information unrealistic or irrelevant?

Source: Don Durfee, "By the Numbers: Alternative Budgeting," *CFO,* June 2006, p. 28.

to predict whether a piece of equipment will wear out or become obsolete in 5 or 10 years. Predicting cash flows one year down the road is difficult, but projecting them over the span of a 10-year project is a gamble.

The level of a project's risk is also affected by the stability and competitive nature of the marketplace and the world economy as a whole. IBM's latest high-technology computer product is far more likely to become obsolete overnight than is a similar $10 million investment in a manufacturing plant. Dramatic changes in the marketplace are not uncommon. Indeed, uncertainty created by the rapid devaluation of Asian currencies in the late 1990s wrecked a host of assumptions in literally hundreds of projects world-wide. Financial managers must con-stantly consider such issues when making long-term decisions about the purchase of fixed assets.

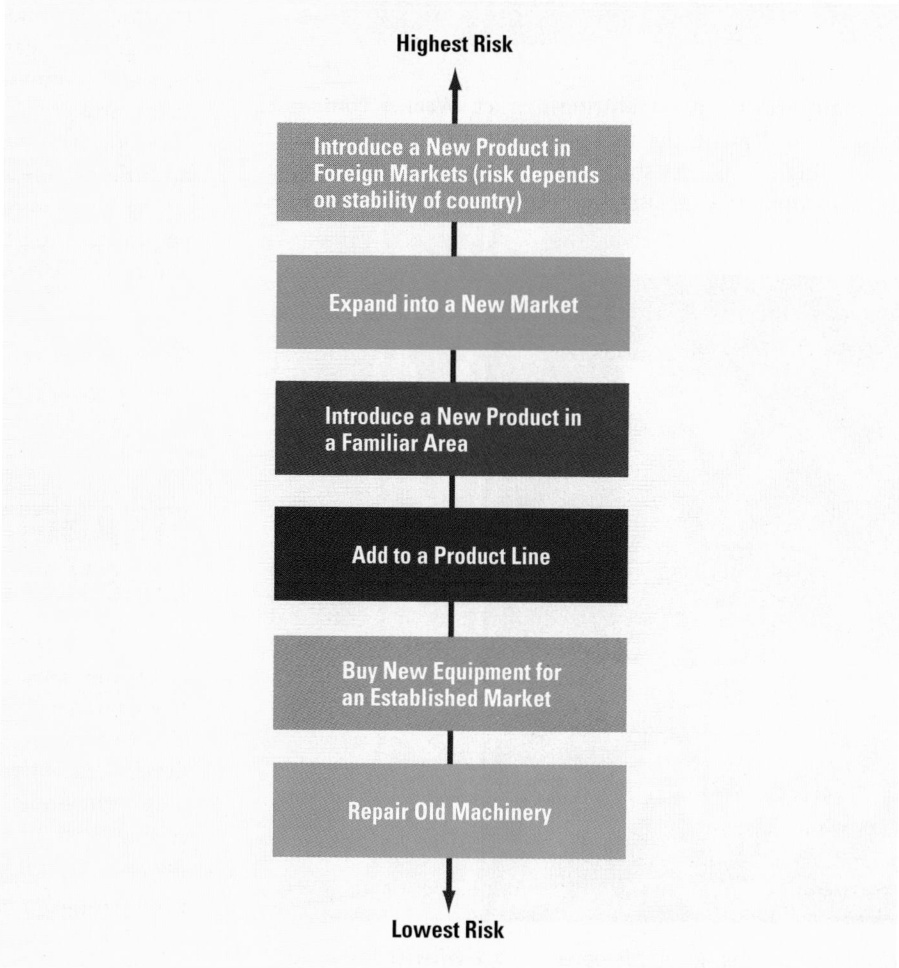

## Pricing Long-Term Money

The ultimate profitability of any project depends not only on accurate assump-tions of how much cash it will generate but also on its financing costs. Because a business must pay interest on money it borrows, the returns from any project must cover not only the costs of operat-ing the project but also the interest expenses for the debt used to finance its construction. Unless an organization can effec-tively cover all of its costs—both financial and operating—it will eventually fail.

Clearly, only a limited supply of funds is available for invest-ment in any given enterprise. The most efficient and profitable companies can attract the lowest-cost funds because they typi-cally offer reasonable financial returns at very low relative risks. Newer and less prosperous firms must pay higher costs to attract capital because these companies tend to be quite risky. One of the strongest motivations for companies to manage their finan-cial resources wisely is that they will, over time, be able to reduce the costs of their funds and in so doing increase their overall profitability.

In our free-enterprise economy, new firms tend to enter industries that offer the greatest potential rewards for suc-cess. However, as more and more companies enter an indus-try, competition intensifies, eventually driving profits down to average levels. The digital music player market of the early

**FIGURE 16.2** Qualitative Assessment of Capital Budgeting Risk

Highest Risk

Introduce a New Product in Foreign Markets (risk depends on stability of country)

Expand into a New Market

Introduce a New Product in a Familiar Area

Add to a Product Line

Buy New Equipment for an Established Market

Repair Old Machinery

Lowest Risk

2000s provides an excellent example of the changes in prof-itability that typically accompany increasing competition. When Apple introduced its iPod player, it earned very high returns, boosted by paid music downloads from its iTunes online service. Early on, Apple dominated the market with a 40 percent share of digital music player sales and 70 percent of legal paid music downloads. These high returns, coupled with the growing interest in music downloads, spurred com-peting firms like Dell, Samsung, Creative, and Rio Nitrus to introduce players with new features or lower prices. Creative, for example, markets a 40-gigabyte player for $200 less than the 40-gigabyte iPod. It is difficult to maintain market domi-nance in the consumer electronics industry for extended peri-ods of time. Some have even suggested that Apple spin off its iPod business through an initial public offering.[3] The same is true in the personal computer market. With increasing com-petition, prices have fallen dramatically since the 1990s. Even Dell and Gateway, with their low-cost products, have moved into other markets such as servers and televisions in order to maintain growth in a maturing market. Weaker companies have failed, leaving the most efficient producers/marketers scrambling for market share. The expanded market for personal computers dramatically reduced the financial returns generated by each dollar invested in productive assets. The "glory days" of the personal computer industry—the time in which fortunes could be won and lost in the space of an average-sized garage—have long since passed into history. Personal computers have essentially become commodity items, and profit margins for companies in this industry have shrunk as the market becomes mature and new PC versions do little to unleash new demand for the product. With sales falling and profits falling faster. Hewlett-Packard and Compaq merged to gain the economies of scale that saved money and created efficiencies.

## ●● L04

Specify how companies finance their operations and manage fixed assets with long-term liabilities, particularly bonds.

# FINANCING WITH LONG-TERM LIABILITIES

As we said earlier, long-term assets do not come cheap, and few companies have the cash on hand to open a new store across town, build a new manufacturing facility, research and develop a new life-saving drug, or launch a new product worldwide. To develop such fixed assets, companies need to raise low-cost, long-term funds to finance them. Two common choices for raising these funds are attracting new owners *(equity financing),* which we'll look at in a moment, and taking on long-term liabilities *(debt financing),* which we'll look at now.

Long-term liabilities are debts that will be repaid over a number of years, such as long-term bank loans and bond issues. These take many different forms, but in the end, the key word is *debt.* Companies may raise money by borrowing it from commercial banks or other financial institutions in the form of lines of credit, short-term loans, or long-term loans. Many corporations acquire debt by borrowing money from pension funds, mutual funds, or life-insurance funds.

Companies that rely too heavily on debt can get into serious trouble should the economy falter; during these times, they may not earn enough operating income to make the required interest payments (remember the times interest earned ratio in Chapter 14). In severe cases when the problem persists too long, creditors will not restructure loans but will instead sue for the interest and principal owed and force the company into bankruptcy.

## Bonds: Corporate IOUs

Aside from loans, much long-term debt takes the form of bonds, which are debt instruments that larger companies sell to raise

*Established firms like Apple have an edge when it comes to borrowing at a low cost to develop their products. Startup firms generally must pay more for their capital because lenders view them as being higher risk.*

*An IBM bond certificate.*

**TABLE 16.2** A Basic Bond Quote

| Bonds | Cur Yld | Vol | Close | Net Chg |
|---|---|---|---|---|
| ATT 8⅛ 22 | 7.9 | 121 | 102½ | .... |
| FordCr 6⅜ 08 | 6.4 | 45 | 100 | ⅛ |
| IBM 7½ 13 | 6.7 | 2 | 112 | +1½ |
| (1) (2) (3) | (4) | (5) | (6) | (7) |

(1) **Bond**—the name or abbreviation of the name of the company issuing the bond; in this case, IBM.

(2) **Annual Interest Rate**—the annual percentage rate specified on the bond certificate: IBM's is 7.5 percent so a $1,000 bond will earn $75 per year in interest.

(3) **Maturity date**—the bond's maturity date; the year in which the issuer will repay bondholders the face value of each bond; 2013.

(4) **Current yield**—percentage return from interest, based on the closing price (column 6); if you buy a bond with a $1,000 par value at today's closing price of 112.00 ($1,120) and receive $75 per year, your cash return will be 6.7 percent.

(5) **Volume**—the number of bonds trading during the day; 2.

(6) **Close**—the closing price; 112.00   112 percent of $1,000 per value or $1,120 per bond.

(7) **Change**—change in the price from the close of the previous trading day; IBM's went up 1½ percent of its $1,000 per value or $15.00 per bond.

long-term funds. In essence, the buyers of bonds (bondholders) loan the issuer of the bonds cash in exchange for regular interest payments until the loan is repaid on or before the specified maturity date. The bond itself is a certificate, much like an IOU, that represents the company's debt to the bondholder. Bonds are issued by a wide variety of entities, including corporations; national, state, and local governments; public utilities; and nonprofit corporations. Most bondholders need not hold their bonds until maturity; rather, the existence of active secondary markets of brokers and dealers allows for the quick and efficient transfer of bonds from owner to owner.

The bond contract, or *indenture*, specifies all of the terms of the agreement between the bondholders and the issuing organization. The indenture, which can run more than 100 pages, specifies the basic terms of the bond, such as its face value, maturity date, and the annual interest rate. Table 16.2 briefly explains how to determine these and more things about a bond from a bond quote, as it might appear in *The Wall Street Journal*. The face value of the bond, its initial sales price, is typically $1,000. After this, however, the price of the bond on the open market will fluctuate along with changes in the economy (particularly, changes in interest rates) and in the creditworthiness of the issuer. Bondholders receive the face value of the bond along with the final interest payment on the maturity date. The annual interest rate (often called the *coupon rate*) is the guaranteed percentage of face value that the company will pay to the bond owner every year. For example, a $1,000 bond with a coupon rate of 7 percent would pay $70 per year in interest. In most cases, bond indentures specify that interest payments be made every six months. In the preceding example, the $70 annual payment would be divided into two semiannual payments of $35.

## MySpace Makes Millions for Cofounders, DeWolfe and Anderson

Chris DeWolfe and Tom Anderson

Business: MySpace.com

Founded: 2003

Success: De Wolfe and Anderson sold MySpace.com to News Corp. for $580 million in 2005.

My Space.com has become the "it" cyberlocation for socializing. In October 2005, it was the fourth most viewed Web site on the Internet. When Chris DeWolfe and Tom Anderson created MySpace.com in 2003, they aimed the site at the music industry—hoping to create a site on which musicians could post bios, songs, and gig dates/locations and on which they could network. Although many musicians still use the site today, it has also become highly popular with the teenage/young adult crowd. MySpace works like this: You create a profile and then begin to acquire "friends"—people who join your networking group via your approval. Although no longer the primary focus, music is still a large part of MySpace culture. Popular bands such as Nine Inch Nails and R.E.M. are using MySpace to promote new music directly to fans. Recently, bands such as Hawthorne Heights and Hollywood Undead have launched successful careers, thanks in part to MySpace and the bands' "friends." In 2005, DeWolfe and Anderson sold MySpace to News Corporation/Rupert Murdoch for $580 million—an incredible sum for a two-year-old company. News Corp. has international interest in media outlets, including FOX TV, *The New York Post*, HarperCollins book publishing, and DirecTV. A News Corp. official was quoted as saying that MySpace .com is expected to bring the company a healthy profit of a few million dollars annually. Although they no longer own the company, DeWolfe and Anderson remain with the company as CEO and president, respectively.[4] ❖

● **UNSECURED BONDS** debentures, or bonds that are not backed by specific collateral

● **SECURED BONDS** bonds that are backed by specific collateral that must be forfeited in the event that the issuing firm defaults

● **SERIAL BONDS** a sequence of small bond issues of progressively longer maturity

● **FLOATING-RATE BONDS** bonds with interest rates that change with current interest rates otherwise available in the economy

● **JUNK BONDS** a special type of high interest-rate bond that carries higher inherent risks

In addition to the terms of interest payments and maturity date, the bond indenture typically covers other important areas, such as repayment methods, interest payment dates, procedures to be followed in case the organization fails to make the interest payments, conditions for the early repayment of the bonds, and any conditions requiring the pledging of assets as collateral.

## Types of Bonds

Not surprisingly, there are a great many different types of bonds. Most are unsecured bonds, meaning that they are not backed by specific collateral; such bonds are termed *debentures.* Secured bonds, on the other hand, are backed by specific collateral that must be forfeited in the event that the issuing firm defaults. Whether secured or unsecured, bonds may be repaid in one lump sum or with many payments spread out over a period of time. Serial bonds, which are different from

 **LO5**

Discuss how corporations can use equity financing by issuing stock through an investment banker.

# FINANCING WITH OWNERS' EQUITY

A second means of long-term financing is through equity. Remember from Chapter 14 that owners' equity refers to the owners' investment in an organization. Sole proprietors and partners own all or a part of their businesses outright, and their equity includes the money and assets they have brought into their ventures. Corporate owners, on the other hand, own stock or shares of their companies, which they hope will provide them with a return on their investment. Stockholders' equity includes common stock, preferred stock, and retained earnings.

> ## A second means of long-term financing is through equity.

secured bonds, are actually a sequence of small bond issues of progressively longer maturity. The firm pays off each of the serial bonds as they mature. Floating-rate bonds do not have fixed interest payments; instead, the interest rate changes with current interest rates otherwise available in the economy.

In recent years, a special type of high-interest-rate bond has attracted considerable attention (usually negative) in the financial press. High-interest bonds, or junk bonds as they are popularly known, offer relatively high rates of interest because they have higher inherent risks. Historically, junk bonds have been associated with companies in poor financial health and/or startup firms with limited track records. In the mid-1980s, however, junk bonds became a very attractive method of financing corporate mergers; they remain popular today with many investors as a result of their very high relative interest rates. But higher risks are associated with those higher returns (upward of 12 percent per year in some cases) and the average investor would be well-advised to heed those famous words: Look before you leap!

Common stock (introduced in Chapter 5) is the single most important source of capital for most new companies. On the balance sheet, the common stock account is separated into two basic parts—common stock at par and capital in excess of par. The *par value* of a stock is simply the dollar amount printed on the stock certificate and has no relation to actual *market value*—the price at which the common stock is currently trading. The difference between a stock's par value and its offering price is called *capital in excess of par.* Except in the case of some very low-priced stocks, the capital in excess of par account is significantly larger than the par value account. Table 16.3 briefly explains how to gather important information from a stock quote, as it might appear in *The Wall Street Journal* or on the NASDAQ Web site.

Preferred stock was defined in Chapter 5 as corporate ownership that gives the stockholder preference in the distribution of the company's profits but not the voting and control rights accorded to common stockholders. Thus, the primary advantage of owning preferred stock is that it is a safer investment than common stock.

All businesses exist to earn profits for their owners. Without the possibility of profit, there can be no incentive to risk investors' capital and succeed. When a corporation has profits left over after paying all of its expenses and taxes, it has the choice of retaining all or a portion of its earnings and/or paying them out to its shareholders in the form of dividends. Retained earnings are reinvested in the assets of the firm and belong to the owners in the form of equity. Retained earnings are an important source of funds and are, in fact, the only long-term funds that the company can generate internally.

When the board of directors distributes some of a corporation's profits to the owners, it issues them as cash dividend payments. But not all firms pay dividends.

Many fast-growing firms retain all of their earnings because they can earn high rates of return on the earnings they reinvest. Companies with fewer growth opportunities typically pay out large proportions of their earnings in the form of dividends, thereby allowing their stockholders to reinvest their dividend payments in higher-growth companies. Table 16.4 presents a sample of companies and the dividend each paid on a single

> ● RETAINED EARNINGS
> earnings after expenses and taxes that are reinvested in the assets of the firm and belong to the owners in the form of equity

TABLE 16.3   A Basic Stock Quote

| 1 | | 2 | 3 | 4 | 5 | 6 | 7 | 8 |
|---|---|---|---|---|---|---|---|---|
| Stock Price 52 Week | | | | | | | | |
| Hi | Low | Stock | Sym | Div | Yld. % | Vol | Close | Net Chg |
| 91.54 | 76.53 | Nike | NKE | 1.24 | 1.53 | 1,291,400 | 81.00 | 0.02 |
| 28.35 | 12.00 | Skechers USA | SKX | 0.00 | 0 | 1,256,900 | 24.11 | 0.36 |
| 41.01 | 26.23 | Timberland | TBL | 0.00 | 0 | 2,360,100 | 26.1 | −0.99 |
| 25.18 | 19.35 | Wolverine Worldwide | WWW | 0.30 | 1.29 | 550,900 | 23.33 | −0.29 |

1. The **52-week high and low**—the highest and lowest prices, respectively, paid for the stock in the last year; for Nike stock, the highest was $91.54 and the lowest price, $76.53.

2. **Stock**—the name of the issuing company. When followed by the letters "pf," the stock is preferred stock.

3. **Symbol**—the ticker tape symbol for the stock; NKE.

4. **Dividend**—the annual cash dividend paid to stockholders; Nike paid a dividend of $1.24 per share of stock outstanding.

5. **Dividend yield**—the dividend return on one share of common stock; 1.53%.

6. **Volume**—the number of shares traded on this day; 1,291,400.

7. **Close**—Nike's last sale of the day was for $81.00.

8. **Net Change**—the difference between the previous day's close and the close on the day being reported; Nike was up $0.02.

Source: Data from *The Wall Street Journal,* June 30, 2006. www.etrade.com/e/t/invest/performance

TABLE 16.4   Estimated Common Stock Price-Earnings Ratios and Dividends for Selected Companies

| Ticker Symbol | Company Name | Price Per Share | Dividend Per Share | Dividend Yield | Earnings Per Share | P-E Ratio |
|---|---|---|---|---|---|---|
| AXP | American Express | 52.31 | 0.60 | 1.15 | 2.91 | 17.98 |
| CPB | Campbell Soup | 37.01 | 0.72 | 1.95 | 1.97 | 18.79 |
| F | Ford Motor | 6.54 | 0.40 | 6.12 | −0.24 | N/A |
| GPS | GAP | 16.92 | 0.32 | 1.89 | 1.21 | 13.98 |
| HDI | Harley Davidson | 53.68 | 0.84 | 1.56 | 3.5 | 15.34 |
| HSY | Hershey Company | 55.24 | 0.98 | 1.77 | 2.07 | 26.69 |
| HD | Home Depot | 36.37 | 0.60 | 1.65 | 2.84 | 12.81 |
| MCD | McDonald's Corp. | 32.51 | 0.67 | 2.06 | 1.97 | 16.50 |
| PG | Procter & Gamble | 55.75 | 1.24 | 2.22 | 2.68 | 20.80 |
| LUV | Southwest Airlines | 16.17 | 0.018 | 0.11 | 0.65 | 24.88 |
| SBUX | Starbucks | 35.74 | 0.00 | 0.00 | 0.69 | 51.80 |

Source: Merrill Lynch On-Line, June 28, 2006, ending prices June 27, 2006.

share of stock. As shown in the table, when the dividend is divided by the price the result is the dividend yield. The dividend yield is the cash return as a percentage of the price but does not reflect the total return an investor earns on the individual stock. If the dividend yield is 3.1 percent on Campbell Soup and the stock price increases by 10 percent from $28.62 to $31.48, then the total return would be 13.1 percent. It is not clear that stocks with high dividend yields will be preferred by investors to those with little or no dividends. Most large companies pay their stockholders dividends on a quarterly basis.

## INVESTMENT BANKING

A company that needs more money to expand or take advantage of opportunities may be able to obtain financing by issuing stock. The first-time sale of stocks and bonds directly to the public is called a *new issue.* Companies that already have

### DID YOU KNOW?

If you bought one share of Microsoft stock when the company went public in 1986, it would be worth almost $8,000 today, after allowing for stock splits and adjustments.[5]

stocks or bonds outstanding may offer a new issue of stock to raise additional funds for specific projects. When a company offers its stock to the public for the very first time, it is said to be "going public," and the sale is called an *initial public offering.*

New issues of stocks and bonds are sold directly to the public and to institutions in what is known as the primary market—the market where firms raise financial capital. The primary market differs from secondary markets, which are stock exchanges and over-the-counter markets where investors can trade their securities with other investors rather than the company that issued the stock or bonds. Primary market transactions actually raise cash for the issuing corporations, while secondary market transactions do not.

Investment banking, the sale of stocks and bonds for corporations, helps such companies raise funds by matching people and institutions who have money to invest with corporations in need of resources to exploit new opportunities. Corporations usually employ an investment banking firm to help sell their securities in the primary market. An investment banker helps firms establish appropriate offering prices for their securities. In addition, the investment banker takes care of the myriad details and securities regulations involved in any sale of securities to the public.

Just as large corporations such as IBM, General Motors, and Microsoft have a client relationship with a law firm and an accounting firm, they also have a client relationship with an investment banking firm. An investment banking firm such as Merrill Lynch, Goldman Sachs, or Morgan Stanley can provide advice about financing plans, dividend policy, or stock repurchases, as well as advice on mergers and acquisitions. Many now offer additional banking services, making them "one-stop shopping" banking centers. When Chrysler merged with Daimler-Benz, both companies used investment bankers to help them value the transaction. Each firm wanted an outside opinion about what it was worth to the other. Sometimes mergers fall apart because the companies cannot agree on the price each company is worth or the structure of management after the merger. The advising investment banker, working with management, often irons out these details. Of course, investment bankers do not provide these services for free. They usually charge a fee of between 1 and 1.5 percent of the transaction. A $20 billion merger can generate between $200 and $300 million in investment banking fees. The merger mania of the late 1990s allowed top investment bankers to earn huge sums. Unfortunately, this type of fee income is dependent on healthy stock markets, which seem to stimulate the merger fever among corporate executives.

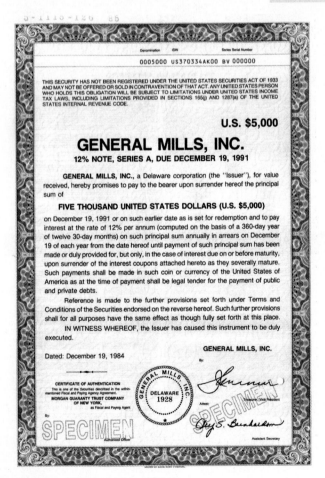

*A General Mills stock certificate.*

| **PRIMARY MARKET** the market where firms raise financial capital | **SECONDARY MARKETS** stock exchanges and over-the-counter markets where investors can trade their securities with others | **INVESTMENT BANKING** the sale of stocks and bonds for corporations | **SECURITIES MARKETS** the mechanism for buying and selling securities | **OVER-THE-COUNTER (OTC) MARKET** a network of dealers all over the country linked by computers, telephones, and Teletype machines |
| --- | --- | --- | --- | --- |

## LO6

Describe the various securities markets in the United States.

# THE SECURITIES MARKETS

Securities markets provide a mechanism for buying and selling securities. They make it possible for owners to sell their stocks and bonds to other investors. Thus, in the broadest sense, stocks and bonds markets may be thought of as providers of liquidity—the ability to turn security holdings into cash quickly and at minimal expense and effort. Without liquid securities markets, many potential investors would sit on the sidelines rather than invest their hard-earned savings in securities. Indeed, the ability to sell securities at well-established market prices is one of the very pillars of the capitalistic society that has developed over the years in the United States.

Unlike the primary market, in which corporations sell stocks directly to the public, secondary markets permit the trading of previously issued securities. There are many different secondary markets for both stocks and bonds. If you want to purchase 100 shares of Du Pont common stock, for example, you must purchase this stock from another investor or institution. It is the active buying and selling by many thousands of investors that establishes the prices of all financial securities. Secondary market trades may take place on organized exchanges or in what is known as the over-the-counter market. Many brokerage houses exist to help investors with financial decisions, and many offer their services through the Internet. One such broker is Paine Webber. Its site offers a wealth of information and provides educational material to individual investors.

## Stock Markets

Stock markets exist around the world in New York, Tokyo, London, Frankfort, Paris, and other world locations. The two biggest stock markets in the United States are the New York Stock Exchange (NYSE) and the NASDAQ market. There are other smaller markets such as the American Stock Exchange, the Chicago Stock Exchange, and exchanges in Philadelphia, Boston, Cincinnati, and Los Angeles.

Exchanges used to be divided into organized exchanges and over-the-counter markets, but during the last several years, dramatic changes have occurred in the markets. Both the NYSE and NASDAQ became publicly traded companies. They were previously not-for-profit organizations but are now for-profit companies. Additionally both exchanges bought or merged with electronic exchanges, the NYSE with Archipelago and the NAS-

*Large investment banking firms like Goldman Sachs arrange the sale of stocks for corporations worldwide. Pictured is the groundbreaking ceremony for the new $2.4 billion world headquarters in lower Manhattan.*

DAQ with Instinet. Electronic trading is faster and less expensive than floor trading (where brokers meet to transact business) and now accounts for most of the stock trading done worldwide.

In an attempt to expand their markets, NASDAQ acquired more than 25 percent of the London Stock Exchange in 2006, and the New York Stock Exchange countered by agreeing to merge with Euronext, a large European electronic exchange that trades options and futures contracts as well as common stock. Both the NYSE and NASDAQ have expanded their reach, their product line, and their ability to trade around the world. What we are witnessing is the globalization of the world's financial markets.

Traditionally, the NASDAQ market has been an electronics market, and many of the large technology companies such as Microsoft, Oracle, and Apple Computer trade on the NASDAQ market. The NASDAQ operates through dealers who buy and sell common stock (inventory) for their own accounts. The NYSE has traditionally been a floor-traded market, where brokers meet at trading posts on the floor of the New York Stock Exchange to buy and sell common stock. The brokers act as agents for their clients and do not own their own inventory. This traditional division between the two markets is becoming less significant as the exchanges become electronic.

## The Over-the-Counter Market

Unlike the organized exchanges, the over-the-counter (OTC) market is a network of dealers all over the country linked by computers, telephones, and Teletype machines. It has no central location. While many very small new companies are traded on the OTC market, many very large and well-known concerns trade there as well. Indeed, thousands of shares of the stocks of companies such as Apple Computer, Intel, and Microsoft are traded on the OTC market every day. Further, because most corporate bonds and all U.S. securities are traded over the counter, the OTC market regularly accounts for the largest total dollar value of all of the secondary markets.

## Measuring Market Performance

Investors, especially professional money managers, want to know how well their investments are performing relative to the market as a whole. Financial managers also need to know how their companies' securities are performing when compared with their competitors'. Thus, performance measures—averages and indexes—are very important to many different people. They not only indicate the performance of a particular securities market but also provide a measure of the overall health of the economy.

Indexes and averages are used to measure stock prices. An *index* compares current stock prices with those in a specified base period, such as 1944, 1967, or 1977. An *average* is the average of certain stock prices. The averages used are usually not simple calculations, however. Some stock market averages (such as the Standard and Poor's Composite Index) are weighted averages, where

the weights employed are the total market values of each stock in the index (in this case 500). The Dow Jones Industrial Average is a price-weighted average. Regardless of how constructed, all market averages of stocks move closely together over time.

Many investors follow the activity of the Dow Jones Industrial Average very closely to see whether the stock market has gone up or down. Table 16.5 lists the 30 companies that currently make

**TABLE 16.5**   The 30 Stocks in the Dow Jones Industrial Average

| | | |
|---|---|---|
| 3M | Du Pont | JPMorgan Chase |
| Alcoa | ExxonMobil | McDonald's |
| Altria | General Electric | Merck |
| American Express | General Motors | Microsoft |
| American International Group | Hewlett-Packard | Pfizer |
| AT&T | Home Depot | Procter & Gamble |
| Boeing | Honeywell | United Technologies |
| Caterpillar | IBM | Verizon |
| Citigroup | Intel | Wal-Mart |
| Coca-Cola | Johnson & Johnson | Walt Disney |

# Looks Like Pepsi's Taken the Fizz out of Coke

In the mid-1990s, analysts panned Pepsi in favor of Coke, claiming that Pepsi had thoroughly lost any competition with Coke in the beverage wars. Pepsi's profits had fallen 47 percent behind Coke's, and it had low stock market value. Pepsi and Coke have been rivals for more than 100 years, but, to everyone's surprise, in 2006 Pepsi, long the ridiculed underdog, pulled ahead of Coke in market value of its stock. Since 2000, Pepsi's profits have grown by more than 100 percent, and its stock has climbed while Coke's stock has remained flat over the past 10 years. What has made such a remarkable turn around possible?

Interestingly, Pepsi's rise has nothing to do with the sales of soda; today Coke still sells more of the fizzy beverage than Pepsi does. What Pepsi discovered was diversification, and it has served the company well. Knowing that they were losing the cola competition, Pepsi began looking elsewhere for profit opportunities. It began marketing bottled water and sports drinks before Coke did. As a result, Pepsi's Aquafina is ranked number one among bottled waters, and its Gatorade has a corner on 80 percent of the sports drink market. Pepsi has become successful by paying attention to consumer trends and moving along with those trends. In the 1990s, Coke

appealed to investors by claiming that customer brand loyalty would prevail in good times or bad; however, Coke and investors neglected to consider the possibility that consumers might begin moving away from soda all together.

Much of Pepsi's forethought may be attributed to its current CEO, Steve Reinemund. Reinemund has a reputation for thinking ahead to the future and for shifting as customer preferences shift. In 2000, Reinemund was responsible for the company's purchase of Sobe—gaining Pepsi a foothold in the "New Age" drink market that is growing in popularity. Thanks also to collaboration with Starbucks, Pepsi is expected to sell $300 million in Frappuccinos alone, making it a strong contender in the bottled coffee drink market.

As much as Pepsi is succeeding in the beverage arena, its greatest success lies within its Frito-Lay division. Currently, Frito-Lay has taken charge of 60 percent of the U.S. snack foods market. As a result, investors are beginning to view Pepsi as a food company that also happens to market drinks; it no longer makes sense even to compare Pepsi to Coke.

Since 2000, Pepsi's sales have increased by 33 percent. From 2002 through 2005, there

has been continual quarterly growth in sales and earnings per share. Of the company's brands, 16 of them bring in more than $1 billion a year each. Analysts expect Pepsi's operating profits to rise by 7.5 percent annually over the next five years, a prediction that brings Pepsi 2.5 percent above the rest of the industry and 1 percent above Coke. Ironically, while investors and analysts discount Coke as a rival to Pepsi, for those working at Pepsi, Coke is still the major competitive motivator, and you can pretty much bet on the fact that Coke is looking at how it can catch up with Pepsi. Some rivalries never end.[6] ❖

## Q: Discussion Questions

1. What do you think has driven Pepsi's stock prices?

2. Why have Coca-Cola stock prices been flat for the past 10 years?

3. How can Coca-Cola get its stock price to increase?

Practically every organization—whether in manufacturing, communications, finance, education, health care, or government—has one or more financial managers and/or financial analysts. Working under titles such as treasurer, controller, cash manager, or financial analyst, these financial managers and analysts prepare and interpret the financial reports required by organizations seeking to ensure that the resources under their control are optimally employed.

Financial management differs from accounting chiefly by its differential focus. By nature, accounting is based almost exclusively on summaries of past organizational transactions and prior account history. In contrast, financial management, despite its frequent reliance on many accounting statements, primarily looks forward. The question, "Where should we go from here?" could serve

as the creed of most financial analysis. Should a new project be implemented? Should a new stock issue be sold? Should dividends be increased? How should the firm invest its excess cash? These and countless other forward-looking questions are addressed by legions of financial managers and analysts every business day.

The employment of financial managers and analysts is expected to increase about as fast as the average for all occupations through the year 2012. Unfortunately, like other managerial occupations, the number of applicants for financial management positions is expected to exceed the number of job openings, resulting in increased competition for superior positions. However, those finding employment as financial managers are likely to enjoy considerable economic rewards. [8]

---

up the Dow. Although these companies are only a small fraction of the total number of companies listed on the New York Stock Exchange, because of their size they account for about 25 percent of the total value of the NYSE.

The numbers listed in an index or average that tracks the performance of a stock market are expressed not as dollars but as a number on a fixed scale. If you know, for example, that the Dow

Jones Industrial Average climbed from 860 in August 1982 to a high of 11,497 at the beginning of 2000, you can see clearly that the value of the Dow Jones Average increased more than 10 times in this 19-year period, making it one of the highest rate of return periods in the history of the stock market. With U.S. interest rates at modest levels and inflation at 30-year lows, many people think that as long as U.S. companies can continue to produce rising earnings, stock prices will continue to climb. If inflation rises and interest rates go up, and if corporate earnings slow down or decline, the market will most likely be in for a tumble.

A period of large increases in stock prices is known as a *bull market,* with the bull symbolizing an aggressive, charging market and rising stock prices. The bull market of the 1990s was one of the strongest on record, with the Dow Jones Industrial Average rising from 3,300 in April 1992 to over 11,000 in 2000. After going up another 5 percent, the market dropped in the early 2000, and was at about 13,600 in June 2007. A declining stock market is known as a *bear market,* with the bear symbolizing sluggish, retreating activity. When stock prices decline very rapidly, the market is said to *crash.* The worst point loss in history (684.81 points) occurred on September 17, 2001, after markets were closed for four days following the terrorist attacks on September 11 that destroyed the World Trade Center and portions of the Pentagon.[7] The stock market—and indeed all of American industry—occasionally stumbles, but it eventually returns to its long-term pattern of growth. (See Figure 16.3.)

For investors to make sound financial decisions, it is important that they stay in touch with business news, markets, and indexes. Of course, business and investment magazines, such as *BusinessWeek, Fortune,* and *Money,* offer this type of information. Many Internet sites, including the *CNN/Money, Business Wire, USA Today,* other online newspapers, and *PR Newswire,* offer this information, as well. Many sites offer searchable databases of information by topic, company, or keyword. However investors choose to receive and review business news, doing so is a necessity in today's market. Table 16.6 provides information about total shareholder return by industry over the past 10 years. ∎

*Smith Barney is one of the many dealers around the world that trade stocks in the over-the-counter (OTC) market.*

**TABLE 16.6** Annual Total Return to Shareholders by Industry

| | Revenues | % | 1 Year | % Growth in Profits | 5 Years | % Annual Growth in Profits |
|---|---|---|---|---|---|---|
| 1 | Securities | 44.1 | Packaging, containers | 96 | Wholesalers: diversified | 43.2 |
| 2 | Oil and gas equipment, services | 31.4 | Oil and gas equipment, services | 77.6 | Mining, crude-oil production | 41.2 |
| 3 | Internet services and retailing | 24.2 | Wholesalers: diversified | 61.4 | Health care: insurance and managed care | 34.2 |
| 4 | Commercial banks | 23.7 | Semiconductors and other electronic components | 56.1 | Insurance: P&C (stock) | 34 |
| 5 | Engineering, construction | 21.8 | Metals | 51 | Petroleum refining | 33.9 |
| 6 | Hotels, casinos, resorts | 17.1 | Securities | 46.6 | Health care: pharmacy and other services | 30 |
| 7 | Health care: insurance and managed care | 17 | Mining, crude-oil production | 46.4 | Publishing, printing | 29.2 |
| 8 | Mining, crude-oil production | 16.8 | Hotels, casinos, resorts | 46.3 | Hotels, casinos, resorts | 28.1 |
| 9 | Wholesalers: diversified | 16.8 | Engineering, construction | 37.3 | Securities | 27.1 |
| 10 | Telecommunications | 16.5 | Insurance: P&C (stock) | 34.1 | Oil and gas equipment, services | 27 |

Source: Top Industries: Fastest Growing Industries, *Fortune*, http://money.cnn.com/magazines/fortune/fortune500/2007/performers/industries/growthinrevenues/index.html (accessed June 18, 2007).

**FIGURE 16.3** Long-Term Performance of the Stock Market

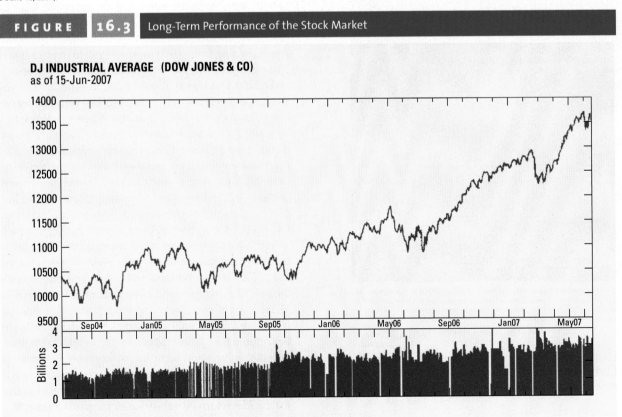

DJ INDUSTRIAL AVERAGE (DOW JONES & CO)
as of 15-Jun-2007

Source: http://finance.yahoo.com/q/bc?s=%5EDJI&t=2y&1=on&z=m&q=1&c= (accessed June 18, 2007).

## Build Your Business Plan

**Financial Management and Securities Market** This chapter helps you realize that once you are making money, you need to be careful in determining how to invest it. Meanwhile, your team should consider the pros and cons of establishing a line of credit at the bank.

Remember the key to building your business plan is to be realistic!!

## CHECK OUT

www.mhhe.com/FerrellM

# for study materials including Interactive Exercises, Quizzes, iPod downloads, and video.

## Chapter 1

1. Lorraine Woellert, "HP Wants Your Old PCs Back," *Business-Week*, April 10, 2006, pp. 82–83.

2. www.cummins.com, "Community Involvement Teams," Cummins Diesel, South Africa CIT, **www.cummins.com/cmi/content .jsp?siteId=1&langId=1033&menuId=82&overviewId=5&anchor Id=393&index=2&menuIndex=0** (accessed May 31, 2006).

3. Kemba J. Dunham, "The Jungle," *The Wall Street Journal*, May 1, 2001, p. B10; **www.diversitypipeline.org,** "About Us" (accessed May 31, 2006).

4. "The Home Depot Social Responsibility Report 2000," Home Depot (n.d.), **www.homedepot.com** (accessed August 27, 2001); "Preparing and Responding to Disasters," Home Depot (n.d.), **www.homedepot.com/HDUS/EN_US/corporate/corp_respon/ prepare_respond.shtml** (accessed March 5, 2004). "Rebuilding Hope and Homes: Mapping Our Impact" (n.d.), **http://rhh .homedepot.com/pc.htm** (accessed June 1, 2006).

5. "CEO of the Year: Jeff Potter, Frontier Airlines' 'Informal Nice Guy' Piloted Company Through Turbulent Times," *ColoradoBiz*, December 2005, pp. 19–23; Jeff Kass, "Frontier Goes Slow," *U.S. News & World Report*, November 7, 2005, pp. EE6–EE10, 3p, 3c; EBSCOHost Research Databases, **http://search.epnet .com/login.aspx?direct=true&db=aph&an=18698492** (accessed December 15, 2005).

6. Chris Isidore, "NASCAR Goes Hollywood," May 25, 2006, **http:// money.cnn.com/2006/05/26/commentary/column_sportsbiz/ sportsbiz/index.htm** (accessed June 1, 2006).

7. Riva Richmond, "Update-Google CEO: Rising Competition Is Expanding Market," May 31, 2006, **http://money.cnn.com/services/ tickerheadlines/for5/200605311542DOWJONESDJONLINE001020_ FORTUNE5.htm** (accessed June 1, 2006).

8. Julie Jargon, "McDonald's to Convene 'Global Mom's Panel,'" *Crain's Chicago Business*, May 9, 2006, **http://chicagobusiness. com/cgi-bin/news.pl?id=20536&bt=McDonalds+menu&arc= n&searchType=** (accessed June 1, 2006).

9. "Health and Wellness "(n.d.), **www.fritolay.com/fl/flstore/cgi-bin/ health_wellness.htm?** (accessed June 1, 2006).

10. **www.whymilk.com/celebrityarchive.htm** (accessed June 1, 2006).

11. Toddi Guttner, "In the Venture Drought, an Oasis," *Business-Week*, July 16, 2001, pp. 86E2, 86E4.

12. **www.magicjohnson.org/about_us.php,** accessed June 1, 2006; Earle Eldridge, "Rebuilding from Basketball Court to Boardroom," *USA Today.com*, November 7, 2004, **www.usatoday .com/money/companies/management/2004-11-07-magic_x.htm** (accessed June 1, 2006). Susan Berfield, with Diane Brady and Tom Lowry, "The CEO of Hip Hop," *BusinessWeek*, October 27, 2003, pp. 90–98.

13. James R. Healey, "Gasoline Supplies Likely to Shrink, Prices Rise," *USA Today*, February 26, 2004, p. 1B.

14. Michael McCarthy and Theresa Howard, "Universal Music Slashes CD, Cassette Prices," *USA Today*, September 4, 2003, p. 1B.

15. "Leading With Patents" in United States Patent and Trademark Office. *United States Patent and Trademark Office Performance and Accountability Report Fiscal Year 2006* (n.d.), **http://www. uspto.gov/web/offices/com/annual/2006/200 message director.html** (accessed May 29, 2007).

16. **http://www.Businessinafrica.net/news/southern_africa/43014htm** (accessed June 2, 2006) Business in Africa 5/2 May 26, 2006, "Zimbabwe Inflation Moves Towards 2000%.

17. "The Debt to the Penny," *Bureau of the Public Debt, United States Treasury* (n.d.), **http://www.treasurydirect.gov/NP/BPDLogin? application=np** (accessed May 29, 2007).

18. Christine McManus, "Bingham Hill Returns," *The Coloradoan*, November 11, 2005, p. D8, Kate Sander, "Rustic Blue Won Bingham Hill Its Fame; Now Company Delves into New Cheeses," Retail Watch—News and Marketing Ideas to Help Sell More Cheese, September 2, 2005, **www.cheesemarketnews.com/ articlearch/retailwatch/2005/rw02sept05.html** (accessed November 15, 2005); Kate Sander, "Bingham Hill Builds on Microbreweries' Success with Colorado 'Microcessery,'" Retail Watch—News and Marketing Ideas to Help Sell More Cheese, June 15, 2001, **www.cheesemarketnews.com/articlearch/retailwatch/2001/ rw13jul01.html** (accessed November 15, 2005); Anna Wolfe, "Bingham Hill Quadruples Production Capacity," Originally in *Gourmet News*, August 2005, **www.looksmartitalianfood.com/p/ articles/mi_qa4024/is_200508/ai_n14851846** (accessed November 15, 2005); Julie Gordon, "Churning Up Cheese," *MouCo News*, June 24, 2001, **http://mouco.com/newz/?m=200106** (accessed November 15, 2005); and Christine McManus, "Landlord Plans to Demolish Cheese Production Building," *Fort Collins Coloradoan*, February 10, 2006, p. D8.

19. "Women in the Labor Force, 1900–2002," *InfoPlease* (n.d.), **www .infoplease.com/ipa/A0104673.html** (accessed March 9, 2004).

20. Tom LaRocque, "Planet Bluegrass Liftoff," *coloradobiz*, 32, no. 10 (October 2005); **www.bluegrass.com;** Telluride Bluegrass Festival at **www.bluegrass.com/planet/telluride_bluegrass_festival .shtml;** RockyGrass Festival at **www.bluegrass.com/planet/rocky- grass_festival.shtml;** Celtic Festival at **www.bluegrass.com/planet/ mabon_festival.shtml;** Folks Festival at **www.bluegrass.com/ planet/folks_festival.shtml;** and Rocky Grass Academy at **www .bluegrass.com/rga/index.html** (all accessed January 10, 2005).

21. "The Hershey Company," Hoover's Guide to Business, **http:// www.hoovers.com/hershey/--ID__10722--/free-co-factsheet.xhtml** (accessed May 31, 2007); Hershey Company History, **http:// www.hersheys.com/discover/history/company.asp** (accessed May 31, 2007).

22. "Wal-Mart Stores Inc.," Hoover's Guide to Business, **http://www. hoovers.com/wal-mart/--ID__11600--/free-co-factsheet.xhtml** (accessed May 31, 2007).

23. "Stewart Convicted on All Charges," *CNNMoney*, March 5, 2004, **www.money.cnn.com;** "Martha Stewart Settles with SEC on Civil Charges," *The Wall Street Journal Online*, August 8, 2006, **http://online.wsj.com/article/SB115496196167028712.html? mod=home_whats_news_us** (accessed May 31, 2007).

24. Abby Schultz, "100 Best Corporate Citizens 2007," *Corporate Responsibility Officer*, Jan/Feb 2007, pp. 21–22, **http://www. thecro.com/?q=node/304** (accessed May 31, 2007).

25. Ronald Alsop, "Corporate Scandals Hit Home," *The Wall Street Journal*, February 18, 2004, **http://online.wsj.com.**

26. Census 2000 Supplementary Survey presented in *USA Today* Snapshot, *USA Today*, August 24, 2001, p. A1; Maggie Jones, "25 Hottest Careers for Women," *Working Women*, July 1995, pp. 31–33; "Reversing the Decline in Corporate Loyalty," PR Newswire (n.d.); Thomas A. Stewart, "Planning a Career in a World Without Managers," *Fortune*, March 20, 1994, pp. 72–80.

## Chapter 2

1. Greg Farrell, "Lay, Skilling Found Guilty," *USA Today,* May 26, 2006, pp. A1, B1; *The New York Times* coverage of the Enron trial, **www.nytimes.com/business/businessspecial3/index.html?adxnnl =1&adxnnlx=1147986237-z56Vd16RUkp6eHnHTTXBHw** (accessed May 18, 2006).

2. Ronald Alsop, "Corporate Scandals Hit Home," *The Wall Street Journal,* February 18, 2004, **http://online.wsj.com.**

3. Carrie Johnson, "Jury Acquits HealthSouth Founder of All Charges," June 29, 2005, p. A01, **www.washingtonpost.com/ wp-dyn/content/article/2005/06/28/AR2005062800560.html** (accessed June 2, 2006).

4. O. C. Ferrell, John Fraedrich, Linda Ferrell, *Business Ethics: Ethical Decision Making and Cases,* 6th ed. (Boston: Houghton Mifflin, 2005), p. 7.

5. David Callahan, as quoted in Archie Carroll, "Carroll: Do We Live in a Cheating Culture?" *Athens Banner-Herald,* February 21, 2004, **www.onlineathens.com/stores/022204/bus_20040222028 .shtml.**

6. Devon Leonard, "The Curse of Pooh," *Fortune,* January 20, 2003, pp. 85–92; "Pooh Suit against Disney Dismissed," *CNN,* March 29, 2004, **www.cnn.com.**

7. John Lyman, "Who Is Scooter Libby? The Guy Behind the Guy," *Center for American Progress.* October 28, 2005.

8. **http:en.wikipedia.org/wiki/Hwang_Woo-suk,** *Wikipedia* (accessed May 23, 2006).

9. "Colorado Places Barnett on Administrative Leave," *SI.com,* February 19, 2004, **http://sportsillustrated.cnn.com/.**

10. Mark Long, "Jimmy Johnson's Crew Chief Thrown Out of Daytona 500," StarTribune.com, February 13, 2006, **www.startribune .com/694/story/244568.html.**

11. Ferrell, Fraedrich, Ferrell, *Business Ethics.*

12. "National Business Ethics Survey 2005," "Survey Documents State of Ethics in the Workplace," and "Misconduct" Ethics Resource Center (n.d.), **www.ethics.org/nbes/2005/release.html** (accessed April 11, 2006).

13. Peter Lattman, "Boeing's Top Lawyer Spotlights Company's Ethical Lapses," *The Wall Street Journal,* Law Blog., Januray 30, 2006, **blogs.wsj.com/law/2006/01/31/boeings-top-lawyer-rips-into-his-company** (accessed March 31, 2006).

14. Janet Guyon, "Jack Grubman Is Back. Just Ask Him," *Fortune,* May 16, 2005. pp. 119–26.

15. "Three Ex-IBM Korea Officials Are Sentenced," *The Wall Street Journal,* February 18, 2004, **http://online.wsj.com.**

16. "Transparency International 2006 Corruption Perception Index," Transparency International, **www.transparency.org/policy_ research/surveys_indices/cpi/2006** (accessed June 1, 2007).

17. "Pens and Post-Its Among Most Pilfered Office Supplies, Says New Vault Survey," November 16, 2005. (**www.vault.com/nr/ newsmain.jsp?nr_page=3&ch_id=420&article_id=25720773** (accessed June 2, 2006).

18. David Whelan, "Only the Paranoid Resurge," *Forbes,* April 10, 2006.

19. Yuri Kageyama, "Mitsubishi Motors Says Massive Defect Cover-ups Were Intentional," *Boston Globe,* August 22, 2000, **www.boston.com;** "Mitsubishi Cover-up May Bring Charges," *Detroit News,* August 23, 2000, **www.det-news.com/2000/ autos/0008/23/b03-109584.htm.**

20. Michael Josephson. "The Biennial Report Card: The Ethics of American Youth." Josephson Institute of Ethics, press release, **www.josephsoninstitute.org/survey2004/** (accessed August 11, 2005).

21. "Teens Respect Good Business Ethics." *USA Today,* Snapshots, December 12, 2005, p. 13-1.

22. Marianne Jennings, "An Ethical Breach by Any Other Name," *Financial Engineering News.* January/February 2006.

23. "The 'Skinny Pills' Do Not Make You Skinny, Says the FTC," Federal Trade Commission, press release, February 4, 2004, **www.ftc.gov/opa/2004/02/skinnypill.htm.**

24. "Campaign Warns about Drugs from Canada," *CNN,* February 5, 2004, **www.cnn.com;** Gardiner Harris and Monica Davey, "FDA Begins Push to End Drug Imports," *The New York Times,* January 23, 2004, p. C1.

25. "Briefing: Tobacco Packaging and Labelling," Information Resource Center, **http://infolink.cancerresearchuk.org/publicpolicy/ briefings/prevention/tobacco.** Accessed July 31, 2006.

26. 2005 National Business Ethics Survey (Washington, D.C.: Ethics Resource Center, 2005), p. 43.

27. Susan Pullman, "Ordered to Commit Fraud, A Staffer Balked, Then Caved," *The Wall Street Journal,* June 23, 2003, **http:// online.wsj.com.**

28. Blake Morrison, "Ex-USA Today Reporter Faked Major Stories," *USA Today,* March 19, 2004, **www.usatoday.com/.**

29. Thomas M. Jones, "Ethical Decision Making by Individuals in Organizations: An Issue-Contingent Model," *Academy of Management Review* 2 (April 1991), pp. 371–73.

30. Sir Adrian Cadbury, "Ethical Managers Make Their Own Rules," *Harvard Business Review* 65 (September–October 1987), p. 72.

31. Ferrell, Fraedrich, and Ferrell, pp. 174–75.

32. Ethics Resource Center.

33. Ethics Resource Center, "2005 National Business Ethics Survey: Executive Summary" (n.d.), **www.ethic.org/nbes2005/ 2005nbes_summary.html** p. 29.

34. Richard Lacavo and Amanda Ripley, "Persons of the Year 2002— Cynthia Cooper, Coleen Rowley, and Sherron Watkins," *Time,* December 22, 2002, **www.time.com/personofth-year/2002.**

35. Ferrell, Fraedrich, and Ferrell, p. 13.

36. John Galvin, "The New Business Ethics," *SmartBusinessMag .com,* June 2000, p. 99.

37. Archie B. Carroll, "The Pyramid of Corporate Social Responsibility: Toward the Moral Management of Organizational Stakeholders," *Business Horizons* 34 (July/August 1991), p. 42.

38. "Social Responsibility," ChrevronTexaco (n.d.), **www.chevron- texaco.com/social_responsibility/** (accessed April 6, 2004).

39. Mary Miller, "A New Job Title to Love," *Business Ethics,* Summer 2001, p. 12.

40. Ferrell, Fraedrich, and Ferrell, pp. 13–19.

41. Rachel Emma Silverman, "On-the-Job Cursing: Obscene Talk Is Latest Target of Workplace Ban," *The Wall Street Journal,* May 8, 2001, p. B12.

42. "Nestlé Boss Starts an African Crusade," *The Sunday Times,* March 13, 2005, **www.timesonline.co.uk/article/0,,2095- 1522290,00.html;** "The Nestlé Coffee Report," *Faces of Coffee,* March 2004; Nestlé S.A., Public Affairs, **www.nestle.com/NR/ rdonlyres/4F893E04-4129-4E4C-92F1-91AF4C8C4738/0/2003_ Coffee_Report.pdf;** "The Nestlé Commitment to Africa,"

Africa Report, Nestlé, **www.nestle.com/Our_Responsibility/Africa+Report/Overview/Africa+Report.htm** (all accessed November 7, 2005).

43. "Business Discover the Value in Fighting AIDS," *Milwaukee Journal Sentinel*, March 14, 2004, via World Business Council for Sustainable Development, **www.wbcsd.org/Plugins/DocSearch/details.asp...**; Lucia Mutikani, "German Automakers Tackle S. Africa AIDS Scourge," Reuters News Service, as reported in *Forbes*, January 22, 2004, **www.forbes.com/business/newswire/2004/01/22/rtr1221795.html.**

44. Wendy Zellner, "No Way to Treat a Lady?" *BusinessWeek*, March 3, 2003, pp. 63–66.

45. Chad Terhune, "Jury Says Home Depot Must Pay Customer Hurt by Falling Merchandise $1.5 Million," *The Wall Street Journal*, July 16, 2001, p. A14.

46. Charales Haddad and Brian Grow, "Wait a Second—I Didn't Order That!" *BusinessWeek*, July 16, 2001, p. 45.

47. Amy's Ice Cream, **www.amysicecream.com** (accessed October 25, 2005); Renuka Rayasam, "Amy's Grows Up," *Austin American-Statesman*, September 29, 2005, **www.statesman.com**; Donna Fenn, "Alpha Dogs," "About Alpha Dogs," and "Chapter List," **www.donnafenn.com/book/chapter.asp** (accessed February 28, 2006).

48. Lauren Etter, "Earth Day: 36 Years on, Plenty of Concerns Remain," *The Wall Street Journal*, April 22–23, 2006, p. A7.

49. Lauren Etter, "Earth Day: 36 Years on, Plenty of Concerns Remain," *The Wall Street Journal*, April 22–23, 2006, p. A7.

50. John Yaukey, "Discarded Computers Create Waste Problem, *USA Today* (n.d.), **www.usatoday.com/news/ndsmon14.htm** (accessed October 13, 2000.)

51. Andrew Park, "Stemming the Tide of Tech Trash," *BusinessWeek*, October 7, 2002, pp. 36A–36F.

52. Alan K. Reichert, Marion S. Webb, and Edward G. Thomas, "Corporate Support for Ethical and Environmental Policies: A Financial Management Perspective," *Journal of Business Ethics* 25 (2000), pp. 53–64.

53. "Trend Watch," *Business Ethics*, March/April 2001, p. 8.

54. David & Lynch "Corporate America Warms to Fight Against Global Warming," *USA Today*, June 1, 2006, p. B1.

55. Amy Standen, "Bulging at the Waste," *Terrain*, Winter 2003, **www.ci.sf.ca.us/sfenvironment/articles_pr/2003/article/110003_2.htm.**

56. "GreenChoice: The #1 Green Power Program in America," Austin Energy (n.d.), **www.austinenergy.com/Energy%20Efficiency/Programs/Green%20Choice/index.htm** (accessed February 24, 2004).

57. "Certification," Home Depot (n.d.), **www.homedepot.com/HDUS/EN_US/corporate/corp_respon/certification.shtml** (accessed April 6, 2004).

58. "Yes, We Have No Bananas: Rainforest Alliance Certifies Chiquita Bananas," *AgJournal* (n.d.), **www.agjournal.com/story.cfm?story_id_1047** (accessed April 6, 2004).

59. "Charity Holds Its Own in Tough Times (Giving USA 2003: The Annual Report on Philanthropy for the Year 2002)," American Association of Fundraising Council, press release, June 2003, **http://aafrc.org/press_releases/trustreleases/charityholds.html.**

60. Mark Calvey, "Profile: Safeway's Grants Reflect Its People," *San Francisco Business Times*, July 14, 2003, **http://sanfrancisco.bizjournals.com/sanfrancisco/stories/2003/07/14/focus9.html.**

61. "About Avon," Avon (n.d.), **www.avoncompany.com/about/** (accessed February 25, 2004; "The Avon Breast Cancer Crusade," Avon (n.d.), **www.avoncompany.com/women/avoncrusade/** (accessed February 25, 2004).

62. "Take Charge of Education," Target (n.d.), **http://target.com/common/page.jhtml;jsessionid=GWORM5AQSLBLDLARAAVWW4FMCEACU1IX?content=target_cg_take_charge_of_education** (accessed February 25, 2004).

63. Susan Gains, "Holding Out Halos," *Business Ethics* 8 (March/April 1994), p. 21; Judith Kamm, "Ethics Officers: Corporate America's Newest Profession," *Ethics, Easier Said Than Done*, Summer 1993, Josephson Institute, p. 38; Robert Levering and Milton Moskowitz, *The 100 Best Companies to Work for in America* (New York: The Penguin Group, 1994), p. 123; Allynda Wheat, "Keeping an Eye on Corporate America," *Fortune*, November 24, 2002, pp. 44–45.

64. Tim Klusmann, "The 100 Best Corporate Citizens," *Business Ethics*, March/April 2000, p. 13.

## Chapter 3

1. Grainger David, "Can McDonald's Cook Again," *Fortune*, April 14, 2003, p. 122; McDonald's (n.d.), **www.mcdonalds.com/corp.html** (accessed March 22, 2004).

2. **http://www.starbucks.com/aboutus/company-fact-sheet-Feb06.pdf** (accessed May 24, 2006), Bruce Horovitz, "Starbucks Aims Beyond Lattes to Extend Brand," *USA Today*, May 19–21, 2006, pp. A1–A2.

3. Dexter Roberts and David Rocks, "China: Let a Thousand Brands Bloom," *BusinessWeek*, October 17, 2005, pp. 58, 60.

4. Nandini Lakshman, "Subcontinental Drift: More Westerners Are Beefing Up Their Resumes with a Stint in India," *BusinessWeek*, January 16, 2006, pp. 42–43.

5. "2006 Annual Trade Highlights, Dollar Change from Prior Year," *U.S. Census Bureau, Foreign Trade Statistics* (n.d.), **http://www.census.gov/foreign-trade/statistics/highlights/annual.html** (accessed June 7, 2007).

6. Dexter Roberts and David Rocks, "China: Let a Thousand Brands Bloom," *BusinessWeek*, October 17, 2005, pp. 58, 60.

7. "2006 Annual Trade Highlights, Dollar Change from Prior Year."

8. Ibid.

9. Roberts and Rocks, "China: Let a Thousand Brands Bloom."

10. J. Bonasia, "For Web, Global Reach Is Beauty—and Challenge," *Investor's Business Daily*, June 13, 2001, p. A6.

11. Chad Terhune, "U.S. Thirst for Mexican Cola Poses Sticky Problem for Coke," *The Wall Street Journal*, January 11, 2006, pp. A1, A10; Louise Chu, "Is Mexican Coke the Real Thing?" *The San Diego Union-Tribune*, November 9, 2004, **http://www.signonsandiego.com/uniontrib/20041109/news_1b9mexcoke.html** (accessed January 30, 2006); Madhusmita Bora, "Bottled Mexican Coca-Cola Offers a Sweet Taste of Home," *The Indianapolis Star*, indystar.com, May 5, 2005, **http://www.indystar.com/apps/pbcs.dll/article?AID=/20050505/LIVING/505050378** (accessed January 30, 2006).

12. Stan Beer, "Global Software Piracy Cost US$40 billion in 2006: BSA," *IT Wire*, May 15, 2007, **http://www.itwire.com.au/content/view/12171/53/** (accessed June 7, 2007).

13. Helene Cooper, "WTO Rules Against U.S.'s Quota on Yarn from Pakistan in Latest Textiles Setback," *The Wall Street Journal,* April 27, 2001, p. A4.

14. "WTO Panel Rules U.S. Duties on Canadian Lumber Are Illegal," *The Wall Street Journal,* March 22, 2004, **http://online.wsj.com.**

15. Julie Bennett, "Product Pitfalls Proliferate in Global Cultural Maze," *The Wall Street Journal,* May 14, 2001, p. B11.

16. Greg Botelho, "2003 Global Influentials: Selling to the World," *CNN,* December 9, 2003, **www.cnn.com.**

17. Slogans Gone Bad, **www.joe-ks.com/archives_apr2004/slogans_gone_bad.htm** (accessed June 6, 2006).

18. Sydney B. Leavens, "Father-Daughter Ad Breaks Latino Mold," *The Wall Street Journal,* p. B7.

19. Bonasia, "For Web Global Reach Is Beauty—and Challenge."

20. Joann Muller, "Parts for the Sensitive Car," *Forbes,* November 28, 2005, pp. 204, 206, 208; The Bosch Group, "Tradition," **www.bosch.com/content/language2/html/2919.htm,** "Public Spirit," **www.bosch.com/content/language2/html/2260.htm,** "Robert Bosch GmbH," **www.bosch.com** (all accessed February 27, 2006 and March 31, 2006).

21. Jim Hopkins, "Other Nations Zip by USA in High-Speed Net Race," *USA Today,* January 19, 2004, pp. 1B, 2B.

22. "What Is the WTO," World Trade Organization (n.d.), **www.wto.org** (accessed February 25, 2004).

23. "WTO: U.S. Steel Duties Are Illegal," *USA Today,* November 10, 2003, **http://usatoday.com.**

24. "Bush Ends Steel Tariffs," *CNNMoney,* December 4, 2003, **http://cnnmoney.com.**

25. Geri Smith and Cristina Lindblad, "Mexico: Was NAFTA Worth It?" *BusinessWeek,* December 22, 2003, pp. 66–72.

26. Bureau of the Census, *Statistical Abstract of the United States, 2003* (Washington D.C.: Government Printing Office, 2004), pp. 842–44, 852; "NAFTA: A Decade of Strengthening a Dynamic Relationship," U.S. Department of Commerce, pamphlet, 2003, available at **www.ustr.gov.**

27. **www.cia.gov/cia/publications/factbook/geos/ca.html** (accessed June 6, 2006).

28. "Canada-U.S. Trade Statistics," Canada Customs and Revenue Agency, September 2002, **www.ccra-adrc.gc.ca/newsroom/factsheets/2002/sep/stats-e.html.**

29. Washington Canadian Embassy, **www.dfait-maeci.gc.ca/can-am/washington/trade_and_investment/trade_partnership-en.asp** (accessed June 6, 2006).

30. U.S. Census Bureau, **www.census.gov/foreign-trade/balance/c2010.html#2006** (accessed June 6, 2006).

31. Smith and Lindblad, "Mexico: Was NAFTA Worth It?"; Cheryl Farr Leas, "The Big Boom," *Continental,* April 2001, pp. 85–94.

32. "Antecedents of the FTAA Process," Free Trade Area of the Americas (n.d.), **www.ftaa-alca.org/View_e.asp** (accessed February 25, 2004); "FTAA Fact Sheet," Market Access and Compliance, U.S. Department of Commerce (n.d.), **www.mac.doc.gov/ftaa2005/ftaa_fact_sheet.html** (accessed November 3, 2003).

33. "U.S.-Brazil Split May Doom Americas Free-Trade Zone," *The Wall Street Journal,* November 7, 2003, **http://online.wsj.com.**

34. "Archer Daniels to File NAFTA Claim Against Mexico," *Inbound Logistics,* October 2003, p. 30.

35. Smith and Lindblad "Mexico: Was NAFTA Worth It?"

36. "Europe in 12 Lessons," The Official EU Web site, **http://europa.eu/abc/12lessons/lesson_2/index_en.htm** (accessed June 7, 2007).

37. Stanley Reed, with Ariane Sains, David Fairlamb, and Carol Matlack, "The Euro: How Damaging a Hit?" *BusinessWeek,* September 29, 2003, p. 63; "The Single Currency," *CNN* (n.d.), **www.cnn.com/SPECIALS/2000/eurounion/story/currency/** (accessed July 3, 2001).

38. "Microsoft Hit by Record EU Fine," *CNN,* March 24, 2004, **www.cnn.com.**

39. **www.apec.org/content/apec/about_apec.html** (accessed June 6, 2006).

40. Smith and Lindblad, "Mexico: Was NAFTA Worth It?"

41. Clay Chandler, "China Is Too Darn Hot!" *Fortune,* November 10, 2003, pp. 39–40; Clay Chandler, "How to Play the China Boom," *Fortune,* December 22, 2003, pp. 141, 142.

42. David J. Lynch, "The IMF Is Tired . . . Fund Struggles to Reinvent Itself," *USA Today,* April 19, 2006. p. B1.

43. Brad Fishman, "International Trade Shows: The Smartest Ticket for Overseas Research," International Franchise Association (n.d.), **www.franchise.org/news/fw/april03c.asp** (accessed July 27, 2001).

44. Tim Annett, Yu Wong, and Deborah Creighton, "Understanding Outsourcing: An Online Journal Roundtable," *The Wall Street Journal,* March 1, 2004, **http://online.wsj.com.**

45. "Bank of America to Outsource 1,000 Jobs to India," [Albany] *Business Review,* February 18, 2004, **www.bizjournals.com/albany/stories/2004/02/16/daily18.html.**

46. Nick Easen, "Firms Get Savvy About Outsourcing," *CNNMoney,* February 18, 2004, **www.cnn.com.**

47. Walter B. Wriston, "Ever Heard of Insourcing?" commentary, *The Wall Street Journal,* March 24, 2004, p. A20.

48. "Bharti of India Will Outsource IT Needs to IBM," *The Wall Street Journal,* March 29, 2004, **http://online.wsj.com.**

49. Jason Bush, "GM: On the Road to Russia," *BusinessWeek,* January 19, 2004, p. 14.

50. "What We're About," NUMMI (n.d.), **www.nummi.com/co_info.html** (accessed February 26, 2004).

51. Joann Muller, "Global Motors," *Forbes,* January 12, 2004, pp. 62–68.

52. O. C. Ferrell, John Fraedrich, and Linda Ferrell, *Business Ethics,* 6th ed. (Boston: Houghton Mifflin, 2005), pp. 227–30.

53. Kim Jung Min, "Asian Company's Perfume Passes French Smell Test," *The Wall Street Journal,* March 19, 2004, **http://online.wsj.com.**

54. "Best Leaders; Entrepreneurs; Stewart Butterfield & Caterina Fake," *BusinessWeek,* December 19, 2005, p. 66; Katherine Mieszkowski, "The Friendster of photo sites," **www.salon.com,** December 20, 2004, **www.salon.com/tech/feature/2004/12/20/flickr/** (accessed January 18); "2005 Fast 50," "Reinventing a Category Whose Flashbulb Burnt Out," *FastCompany,* **www.fast-company.com/fast50_05/profile/index.html?stewart_butterfield718** (accessed January 18); "Flickr," *Wikipedia,* the free encyclopedia, **http://en.wikipedia.org/wiki/Flickr** (accessed January 18).

55. Vanessa O'Connell, "Exxon 'Centralizes' New Global Campaign," *The Wall Street Journal,* July 11, 2001, p. B6.

56. Export.gov, **www.export.gov/comm_svc/about_home.html**(accessed February 9, 2006), CIBER *Web,* **http://CIBERWEB.msu.edu** (accessed February 9, 2006).

57. Philip R. Cateora, *International Marketing,* 8th ed. (Homewood, IL: Richard D. Irwin, 1993), pp. 25–26; "NAFTA: Exports, Jobs, Wages, and Investment," *Business America,* October 18, 1993, p. 3; *VGM's Handbook of Business & Management Careers,* Annette Selden, ed. (Lincolnwood, IL: VGM Career Horizons, 1993), pp. 43–44.

## Chapter 4

1. Jac Chebatoris, "More Monkeyshines? Or the Real Deal?," *Newsweek,* February 6, 2006, p. 10; Paul Sexton, "Arctic Monkeys Earn Fastest-Selling U.K. Debut," *Billboard.com,* **www.billboard.com/bbcom/news/article_display.jsp?vnu_content_id=1001920504** (accessed February 9, 2006); "Arctic Monkeys Make Chart History," *BBC News,* **news.bbc.co.uk/go/pr/fr/-/1/hi/entertainment/4660394.stm** (accessed February 9, 2006); "Arctic Monkeys," *Wikipedia,* the free encyclopedia, **http://en.wikipedia.org/wiki/Arctic_Monkeys** (accessed February 28, 2006).

2. Catherine Yang, "Homeland Security Dept.," *BusinessWeek,* November 24, 2003, p. 85.

3. **www.cosmetics.com** (accessed June 6, 2006).

4. Roger W. Ferguson, Jr., "Remarks by Vice Chairman Roger W. Ferguson, Jr.," American Economic Association meeting, January 4, 2004, San Diego, California, available at **www.federalreserve.gov/boarddocs/speeches/2004/200401042/default.htm.**

5. Edward P. Lazear and Katherine Baicker, "America at Work," *The Wall Street Journal Online,* May 8, 2006, **http://online.wsj.com/article/SB114705083956846285-searchhtml?KEYWORDS=productivity+adds+to+GDP&COLLECTION=wsjie/6month,** (accessed June 6, 2006).

6. **www.autodesk.com/buzzsaw** (accessed June 6, 2006).

7. Alan Greenspan, "Remarks to the Economic Club of New York," January 13, 2000, Federal Reserve Board, available at **www.federalreserve.gov/boarddocs/speeches/2000/200001132.htm.**

8. "Data," *Webopedia,* October 28, 2003, **www.webopedia.com/TERM/D/data.html.**

9. "Anheuser Busch Goes Full Tilt," August 8, 2005, **www.anheuserbusch.com/news/tilt080805.htm** (accessed June 6, 2006).

10. "What Is OnStar?" OnStar (n.d.), **www.onstar.com** (accessed March 2, 2004).

11. "About IRI," Information Resources Inc. (n.d.), **www.infores.com/public/global/about/default.htm** (accessed April 23, 2004); "On-line Purchases of Consumer Packaged Goods on the Rise," study by Information Resources Inc., *DSN Retailing Today,* June 4, 2001.

12. Information Resources Inc, Company Overview, **http://us.infores.com/page/about/company_overview** (accessed June 8, 2006).

13. "How Duke Helps Students Connect," April 5, 2004, *BusinessWeek Online,* **www.businessweek.com/bschools/content/apr2006/bs2006045_8177.htm?campaign_id=search** (accessed June 6, 2006).

14. "Worldwide Internet Users Top 1 Billion in 2005," *Computer Industry Almanac Inc.,* January 4, 2006, **www.c-i-a.com/pr0106.htm** (accessed June 6, 2006).

15. Deborah Fallows, "How Women and Men Use the Internet," Pew/Internet, 2005, **http://www.pewinternet.org/PPF/r/171/report_display.asp,** (accessed June 6, 2006), Pew/Internet, "Home Broadband Adoption 2006," **http://www.pewinternet.org/PPF/r/184/report_display.asp,** (accessed June 6, 2006). "OECD Broadband Statistics to December 2006," Organization for Economic Co-operation and Development; December 2006, **http://www.oecd.org/document/7/0,2340,en_2649_34223_38446855_1_1_1_1,00.html** (accessed June 12, 2007).

16. "Spam Volume Hit Record High," *Marshall News,* February 21, 2007, **http://www.marshal.com/pages/newsitem.asp?article=135** (accessed June 12, 2007).

17. "Worldwide Internet Users Top 1 Billion in 2005," *Computer Industry Almanac Inc.,* January 4, 2006, **www.c-i-a.com/pr0106.htm** (accessed June 6, 2006).

18. "S&P500," *BusinessWeek,* April 5, 2004, p. 157.

19. Alex Veiga, "MTV Launches Online Music, Video Store, *Business Week Online,* May 15, 2006, **http://www.businessweek.com/ap/tech/D8HK11080.htm?campaign_id=search** (accessed June 6, 2006); **www.nyjobsource.com/realnetworks.html** (accessed June 6, 2006).

20. "Shaping the Future Mobile Information Society," International Telecommunication Union (n.d.), **www.itu.int/osg/spu/ni/future-movile** (accessed March 21, 2004).

21. Adam Wright, "Mobile Phones Could Soon Rival the PC as the World's Dominant Internet Platform," April 18, 2006, **http://www.ipsos-na.com/news/pressrelease.cfm?id=3049#** (accessed June 6, 2006).

22. "Japan's Camera Phone Craze Spreads to Funerals," *msnbc.com,* February 16, 2006, **http://www.msnbc.msn.com/id/11385672/** (accessed June 6, 2006).

23. **www.epicurious.com** (accessed June 7, 2006).

24. **www.bluetooth.com/bluetooth** (accessed June 7, 2006).

25. Bob Jordan, "Wireless Mesh Networks Boost Reliability," Network WorldFusion, November 10, 2003, **www.nwfusion.com/news/tech/2003/1110techupdate.html;** Alexander Linden, "Predicts 2004: Emerging Technologies," Gartner Research, December 12, 2003, **www4.gartner.com/DisplayDocument?doc_cd=118940.**

26. FCC Consumer Facts, "VoIP/Internet Voice," **www.fcc.gov/cgb** (accessed June 6, 2006).

27. "Wal-mart Leading the RFID Retail Revolution," *cnn.com,* May 22, 2006, **http://www.cnn.com/2006/TECH/05/22/rfid.retail.ap/index.html** (accessed June 6, 2006).

28. "Shaping the Future Mobile Information Society."

29. Jack Ewing, "How Otto Got an e-Commerce Head Start," *BusinessWeek Online,* May 9, 2006, **http://www.businessweek.com/globalbiz/content/may2006/gb20060509_889752.htm?campaign_id=search** (accessed June 14, 2006).

30. John Gaffney, "How Do You Feel about a $44 Tooth-Bleaching Kit?" *Business 2.0,* October 2001, p. 126; Stephanie Stahl and John Soat, "Feeding the Pipeline: Procter & Gamble Uses IT to Nurture New Product Ideas," *Information Week,* February 24, 2003, **www.informationweek.com/story/showArticle.jhtml;-jsessionid=4SA2EIBSJYSZCQSNDBGCKHY?articleID=8700568&pgno=1.**

31. "About DoubleClick," DoubleClick (n.d.), **www.doubleclick.com/us/about_doubleclick/** (accessed April 28, 2004); Julia Angwin, "DoubleClick Stays Two Steps Ahead of Rivals," *The Wall Street Journal,* April 26, 2001, p. B6.

32. 2006 Fortune 500, **http://money.cnn.com/magazines/fortune/fortune500/snapshots/69.html** (accessed June 14, 2006).

33. "To Our Shareholders," Amazon.com (n.d.), **http://media .corporate-ir.net/media_files/irol/97/97664/reports/8k_041103/ v89126exv99wl.htm** (accessed March 21, 2004).

34. Michael J. Mandel and Robert D. Hof, "Rethinking the Internet," *BusinessWeek,* March 26, 2001, p. 118.

35. Edward C. Baig, "Love Growing Strong on the Web, But Online-Dating Sites Fear Shakeout as They Vie to Win Customers' Hearts and Cash," *USA Today,* Feburary 14, 2005, p. B1; "Online Dating Market Hotter, Less Profitable for Biggies," *Marketing VOX —The Voice of Online Marketing,* October 12, 2004, **www.marketingvox.com/archives/2004/10/12/online_dating_ market_hotter_less_profitable_for_biggies/**" (accessed November 17, 2005); "During the Holidays, More Than a Third of Single Americans Feel Extra Pressure to Be in a Relationship," November, 17, 2005, found on Yahoo! Finance at **http://biz.yahoo.com/ prnews/051117/dath-046.html?.v=24&printer=1, says source is Match.com** (accessed November 19, 2005); Ellen Gamerman, "Mism@tched.com," *The Wall Street Journal,* April 1–2, 2006, pp. P1, P4.

36. Peter Passi, "Goodbye, Waiting Rooms," April 8, 2006, **http:// www.duluthsuperior.com/mld/duluthsuperior/news/14295747.htm** (accessed June 14, 2006).

37. Mandel and Hof, "Rethinking the Internet."

38. "How It Works," *The Wall Street Journal,* May 21, 2001, p. R8.

39. Mandel and Hof.

40. *BusinessWeek,* special supplement, February 28, 2000, p. 74.

41. "About Covisint," **www.covisant.com/about/** (accessed June 14, 2006).

42. Laura Rush, "E-Commerce Growth Will Impact SMBs," *InternetNews.com,* January 23, 2004, **www.internetnews .com/stats/article/php/3303241.**

43. Travel Industry Association of America, "Leading Travel Industry Consumer Survey Reports Significantly More Travelers Plan and Book Trips Online," November 16, 2005, **www.tia.org/pressmedia/ pressrec.asp?Item=689** (accessed June 14, 2006).

44. Tessa Romita. "Sky's the Limit for Airlines Online," *Business 2.com,* January 23, 2001, p. 4.

45. Adapted from Judy Strauss and Raymond Frost, *Emarketing,* 2nd ed. (Upper Saddle River, NJ: Prentice-Hall, 2001).

46. Adapted from William M. Pride and O.C. Ferrell, *Marketing,* 13th ed. (Boston: Houghton Mifflin, 2005).

47. **www.olay.com/clubolay/intro.htm** (accessed June 15, 2006).

48. O. C. Ferrell, Michael D. Hartline, and George H. Lucas, Jr., *Marketing Strategy* (Fort Worth, TX: Dryden, 2002), p. 97.

49. **www.salesforce.com/products/sales-force-automation.jsp, www .salesforce.com/partners/** (both accessed June 15, 2006).

50. Edward Prewitt, "How to Build Customer Loyalty in an Internet World," *CIO,* January 1, 2002, **www.cio.com/archive/010102/ loyalty_content.html.**

51. Eve M. Caudill and Patrick E. Murphy, "Consumer Online Privacy: Legal and Ethical Issues," *Journal of Public Policy & Marketing,* 19 (Spring 2000), pp. 7–12.

52. **www.truste.org/about/fact_sheet.php** (accessed June 16, 2006).

53. Better Business Bureau Online (n.d.), **www.bbbonline.org/** (accessed April 28, 2004).

54. Thomas Claburn, "Spam Made up 94% of all E-Mail in December," *InformationWeek,* January 29, 2007, **http://www .informationweek.com/showArticle.jhtml;jsessionid=4H4VB4FGN IKEWQSNDLRSKHSCJUNN2JVN?articleID=197001430** (accessed June 12, 2007).

55. Antone Consalves, "Auk Names Top, Spam Subjects for 2005, *Information Week,* December 28th , 2005, **www.informationweek .com/** (accessed August 2, 2006).

56. Rebecca Buckman, "Too Much Information? Colleges Fear Students Postings on Popular 'Facebook' Site Could Pose Security Risks," *The Wall Street Journal,* December 8, 2005, pp. B1, B4; "Chris DeWolfe & Tom Anderson, MySpace.com," Entrepreneurs, *BusinessWeek,* December 19, 2005, p. 66; Soraya Nadia McDonald, "Facebook Frenzy," *CBS News,* July 5, 2005, **http://www.cbsnews.com/stories/2005/07/05/tech/main706634 .shtml** (accessed January 27, 2006); Janet Kornblum, "Teens Hang Out at MySpace," *USA Today,* January 8, 2006, **www .usatoday.com/tech/news/2006-01-08-myspace-teens_x.htm** (accessed January 15, 2006).

57. Tim Hanrahan and Jason Fry, "Spammers, Human Mind Do Battle Over Spelling," *The Wall Street Journal,* February 9, 2004, **http://online.wsj.com.**

58. "EU Orders Anti-Spam Legislation," *CNN,* April 1, 2004, **www .cnn.com.**

59. "FTC Issues Annual List of Top Consumer Complaints: Identity Theft Complaints Again Top the List," February 7, 2007, **http:// www.ftc.gov/opa/2007/02/topcomplaints.shtm** (accessed June 12, 2007).

60. Andrea Chipman, "Stealing You," *The Wall Street Journal,* April 26, 2004, **http://online.wsj.com.**

61. Christine Dugas, "Identity Theft on the Rise," USA Today, May 11, 2001, p. 3B.

62. **http://en.wikipedia.org/wiki/identify.theft** (accessed June 16, 2006).

63. Jack McCarthy, "National Fraud Center: Internet Is Driving Identity Theft," *CNN,* March 20, 2000, **www.cnn.com.**

64. Juan Carlos Perez, "Biggest Security Threat? Insiders," *PC World,* October 2, 2002, **www.pcworld.com/news/article/0,aid, 105528,00.asp.**

65. Douglas Heingartner, "Software Piracy Is in Resurgence," New York Times News Service, *Naples Daily News,* January 20, 2004, **www.naplesnews.com/npdn/business/article/0,2071,- NPDN_14901_2588425,00.html.**

66. "States Approve Effective Date for Sales Tax Simplification Agreement," **www.govtech.net/news/news.php?id=94929#** (accessed June 15, 2006).

67. "Computer Executives and Professionals, *Career Journal,* **www .careerjournal.com/salaryhiring/industries/computers/20031125- computer-tab.html** (accessed April 29, 2004); "Tech Hiring: No Longer an Oxymoron," *BusinessWeek Online,* February 4, 2004, **www.businessweek.com/technology/content/feb2004/tc2004024_ 4516_tc044.htm;** Mark Watson, "Book Touts Memphis as Haven for IT Work," Commercial Appeal, September 9, 2001, pp. C1, C3; Mark Watson, "More IT Jobs on the Way, Study Says," *Commercial Appeal,* September 9, 2001, pp. C1, C3.

## Chapter 5

1. U.S. Bureau of the Census, *Statistical Abstract of the United States, 2003* (Washington, D.C.: U.S. Government Printing Office, 2004), p. 495.

2. Maggie Overfelt, "Start-Me-Up: The California Garage," *Fortune Small Business,* July/Aug. 2003, **www.fortune.com/fortune/small-business/articles/0,15114,475872,00.html.**

3. "1: Digital Artists Agency," Business 2.0, April 2004, p. 90.

4. Katy McLaughlin, "Why Some Chefs Are Having a Cow," The Wall Street Journal, February 25, 2006, p. 1; David Burke, Executive Chief, **www.davidburke.com** (accessed March 1, 2006).

5. Linda Tischles, "Join the Circus," Fast Company, July 2005, pp. 53–58.

6. Alexis Muellner, "Marlins Partners in Dispute, Still Want Rings," South Florida Business Journal, February 27, 2004, **www .bizjournals.com/southflorida/stories/2004/03/01/story5.html**.

7. Jeffrey Zaslow, "Who's Going to Want Grandma's Hoard of Antique Gnomes?" The Wall Street Journal, February 25–26, 2006, pp. A1, A12; **www.dincum.com/articles.html** (accessed June 12, 2006); **www.beryl-the-gnome.co.uk/alva.htm** (accessed June 12, 2006).

8. U.S. Census Bureau, Statistical Abstract.

9. Daniel Fischer, "Mr. Big," Forbes.com, March 13, 2006, **www .forbes.com/global/2006/0313/024_print.html** (accessed June 7, 2006).

10. "America's Largest Private Companies," Forbes, November 6, 2003, **www.forbes.com/maserati/privates2003/privateland.html.**

11. David Kiley, "Ford Family Celebrates 100 Years of Cars," USA Today, June 10, 2003, pp. 1B, 2B.

12. Kevin J. Delaney and Robin Sidel, "Google IPO Aims to Change the Rules," The Wall Street Journal, April 30, 2004, **http:// online.wsj.com.**

13. Merissa Marr, "Video Chain CEO to Take Company Private in Buyout," The Wall Street Journal, March 30, 2004, **http:// online.wsj.com.**

14. O. C. Ferrell, John Fraedrich, and Linda Ferrell, Business Ethics: Ethical Decision Making and Cases, 6th ed. (Boston: Houghton Mifflin, 2005), p. 84.

15. Matt Krantz, "Web of Board Members Ties Together Corporate America," USA Today, November 23, 2002, pp. 1B, 3B.

16. Emily Thornton and Aaron Pressman, "Phil Purcell's Credibility Crisis," BusinessWeek, March 21, 2005.

17. Krantz, "Web of Board Members."

18. Joseph Nathan Kane, Famous First Facts, 4th ed. (New York: The H. W. Wilson Company, 1981), p. 202.

19. Eric J. Savitz, "Movie Madness," Barron's, February 23, 2004, **http://online.wsj.com/barrons/.**

20. Robert D. Hisrich and Michael P. Peters, Entrepreneurship, 5th ed. (Boston: McGraw-Hill, 2002), pp. 315–16.

21. "Farmers Offering up Beef in a Can," CNN, March 22, 2004, **www.cnn.com/2004/US/Midwest/03/22/canned.beef.asp;** Him Suhr, "Farmers Form Canned-Beef Co-op," Courier-Journal, March 28, 2004, **www.courier-journal.com/business/news2004/ 03/28/E7-beefcan28-4323.html;** Jim Suhr, "Livestock Farmer Hopes Canned Beef Will Catch On," The Fort Collins Colora-doan, March 28, 2004, p. E2; Erica Coble, "Trading on Tradi-tion," March 2005, **www.rurdev.usda.gov/rbs/pub/mar05/value. htm** (accessed March 1, 2006); **www.heartlandfarmfoods.com; www.heartlandfarmfoods.com/Company.htm; www.heartlandfarm-foods.com/Catalog_Page%201.htm; www.heartlandfarmfoods.com/ Producers.htm** (all accessed March 1, 2006).

22. James Covert, "Federated to Sell Lord & Taylor Amid Focus on Other Brands," The Wall Street Journal, January 13, 2006, p. A11; "Lord & Taylor sold for $1.2 Billion," **detnews.com** assessed, August 3, 2006.

23. Roger O. Crockett, "How the Cingular Deal Helps Verizon," BusinessWeek, March 1, 2004, pp. 36–37.

24. "Aventis Accepts Higher, Friendly Sanofi Bid," Dow Jones Newswire, April 26, 2004, via The Wall Street Journal, **http:// online.wsj.com.**

25. Ibid.

26. U.S. Department of Labor, "Evaluating a Job Offer," 2004–05 Occupational Outlook Handbook, **http://stats.bls.gov/oco/ oco20046.htm** (accessed March 12, 2004).

## Chapter 6

1. **http://app1.sba.gov/faqs/faqindexall.cfm?areaid=24** (accessed June 1, 2006).

2. "The Power of Innovation," Inc. State of Small Business, 23, no. 7 (2001), p. 103.

3. "Small Business Statistics," Small Business Administration (n.d.), **www.sba.gov/aboutsba/sbastats.html** (March 16, 2004).

4. **http://www.onlinewbe.gov/about.htm/** (accessed May 25, 2006).

5. "Top Facts about Women-Owned Businesses," Bizwomen.com, **http://www.bizjournals.com/bizwomen/facts/topfacts.html** (accessed June 14, 2007).

6. Jim Hopkins, "Minority Businesses Boom," USA Today, July 29, 2005, p. B5.

7. "MagRabbit Secures Contract with U.S. Military Surface Deployment and Distribution Command," March 13, 2006, **http://finance.6abc.com/abc?ID=3140604&Account=wpvi&Page =NewsRead** (accessed June 3, 2006).

8. Joshua Kurlantzick, "About Face," Entrepreneur, January 2004, **www.entrepreneur.com/article/0,4621,312260,00.html.**

9. **http://www.red-man.com/dsp_rmps.cfm?wcid=55; http://www.native-american-bus.org/topTenBusinesses.html** (accessed June 3, 2006).

10. **http://app1.sba.gov/faqs/faqindexall.cfm?areaid=24** (accessed June 1, 2006).

11. "Statistics about Business Size (including Small Business)," U.S. Census Bureau, **www.census.gov/epcd/www/smallbus.html# EMpSize** (accessed May 3, 2004).

12. **www.molles.com/news** (accessed June 1, 2006); John D. Stoll, "Visions of the Future" The Wall Street Journal, April 17, 2006, P. R8.

13. Beth Carney, "Dyson Magic Carpet Ride," BusinessWeek Online, April 1, 2005, **www.businessweek.com/bwdaily/dnflash/apr2005/ nf2005041_8000_db016.htm?campaign_id=search** (accessed June 3, 2006); **www.dyson.com; www.dyson.com/nav/inpage-frame.asp?id=DYSON/HIST/MUSEUMS** (accessed June 3, 2006).

14. Sharon Silke Carty, "Simple Pillow Evolved into Multimillion-Dollar Baby," USA Today, January 9, 2006, p. 7B.

15. Peter Svensson, "U.S. Economy Grows at a Slower Pace," Washingtonpost.com, June 5, 2006, **www.washingtonpost.com/ wp-dyn/content/article/2006/06/05/AR2006060500376.html** (accessed June 5, 2006).

16. "2004 Malcolm Baldrige Award Winners, **www.nist.gov/publi-caffairs/releases/2004baldrigewinners.htm** (accessed June 5, 2006).

17. "Dell at a Glance," Dell (n.d.), **www1.us.dell.com/content/ top-ics/global.aspx/corp/background/en/facts?c=us&l =en&s =corp& section=000& ck=mn** (accessed May 4, 2004); **www.hoouess .com/dell/--ID_13193-/free-co-factsheet.xhtml** (accessed June 5, 2006).

18. "Small Business Statistics."

19. Susan Donovan, "How I Did It: Roxanne Quimby," *Inc.* January 2004, **http://pf.inc.com/magazine/20040101/howididit.html;** "Hands on Marketing: Roxanne Quimby, CEO of Burt's Bees, Feels the Best Way to Sell Her Products Is by Putting It in Your Hands," *Inc.* January 2004, **http://pf.inc.com/articles/2004/01/handsonmarketing.html;** "In Depth: Largest Triangle of Deals of 2003," *Triangle Business Journal,* February 6, 2004, **www.bizjournals.com/triangle/stories/2004/02/09/focus6.html;** "Our Story," Burt's Bees, **www.burtsbees.com** (accessed March 17, 2004); "About the Company," **www.burtsbees.com/webapp/wcs/stores/servlet/AboutTheCompany?langId=-1&storeId=10101&catalogId=10751;** "About Our Products" (accessed March 3, 2006); **www.burtsbees.com/webapp/wcs/stores/servlet/AboutOurProductsView?langId=-1&storeId=10101&catalogId=10751** (both accessed March 3, 2006); "Burt's Bees Names John Replogle as CEO and President," *PRNewswire,* January 19, 2006, **http://sev.prnewswire.com/retail/20060119/NYTH14019012006-1.html** (accessed March 3, 2006).

20. Dana Knight, "Big Headed Guy Gets a Big Idea for Sunglasses Business," *USA Today,* March 21, 2006, p. 4B; **www.fatheadz.com.** (accessed June 5, 2006).

21. "You're Not the Boss of Me Now," *Weekend Today,* October 21, 2005, **msnbc.msn.com/id/9762771/** (accessed June 5, 2006).

22. "Small Business Resource," **www.2-small-business.com** (accessed June 5, 2006).

23. Rodney Tanake, "Clothier a Favorite of Vegans, PETA Honors Pasadena 'Animal-Friendly' Firm," *Pasadena Star-News,* **www.pasadenastarnews.com, www.pasadenastarnews.com/search/ci_3386589** (accessed January 14, 2006); **www.alternativeoutfitters.com,** "About Us," **www.alternativeoutfitters.com/index.asp?PageAction=COMPANY;** "Alternative Outfitters News," **www.alternativeoutfitters.com/index.asp?PageAction=Custom&ID=10;** "Pasadena-based Alternative Outfitters Wins Second Straight National PETA Award," **www.alternativeoutfitters.com/index.asp?PageAction=Custom&ID=45;** "The 2005 Veggie Awards," **www.vegnews.com/veggieawards_2005.html** (all accessed January 12, 2006).

24. "Spring 2005 Interland Business Barometer," *USA Today,* Snapshots, October 26, 2005.

25. Diane Brady, "Ideas That Bloom," *BusinessWeek Online,* Spring 2006, **www.businessweek.com/magazine/content/06_12/b3976401.htm** (accessed June 5, 2006).

26. Robert Tomsho, "Ask the Volk Family: 30 Million Turkeys Can't Be Wrong," *The Wall Street Journal,* November 22, 2005, p. A1; **www.volkenterprises.com/about_us/index.html,** "About Us," (accessed June 5, 2006).

27. Alex Halperin, "A Virtual World Targets Teens," *BusinessWeek Online,* May 15, 2006, **www.businessweek.com/technology/content/may2006/tc20060515_945235.htm?campaign_id=search** (accessed June 5, 2006).

28. Susan McGee, "A Chorus of Angels," *Inc.,* January 2004, **www.inc.com/magazine/20040101/finance.html.**

29. Thomas W. Zimmerer and Norman M. Scarborough, *Essentials of Entrepreneurship and Small Business Management,* 4th ed. (Upper Saddle River, NJ: Pearson Prentice Hall, 2005), pp. 118–24.

30. Ibid.

31. Explore SCORE, **http://score.org/explore_score.html** (accessed May 25, 2006).

32. Katy McLaughlin, "Pizza's Next Act," *The Wall Street Journal,* January 14–15, 2006, pp. P1, P8; Bruce Horovitz, "Wake Up and Smell the Breakfast Pizza," *USA Today,* December 8, 2005, p. B1; Alison Arnett, "Making a Living One Slice at a Time," *The Boston Globe,* boston.com, July 7, 2004, **www.boston.com/ae/food/articles/2004/07/07/making_a_living_one_slice_at_a_time?pg=full** (accessed February 8, 2006).

33. Adapted from "Tomorrow's Entrepreneur," *Inc. State of Small Business,* 23, no. 7 (2001), pp. 80–104.

34. "The Boomer Stats," Baby Boomer HQ, **www.bbhq.com/bomrstat.htm** (accessed March 17, 2004).

35. Michael J. Weiss, "To Be About to Be," *American Demographics,* 25 (September 2003), pp. 29–36.

36. Center for Immigration studies, December 2005, "Immigrants at mid-decade," **www.cis.org/articles/2005/back1405.html** (accessed June 5, 2006).

37. "Current Numbers," Center for Immigration Studies (n.d.), **www.cis.org/topics/currentnumbers.html** (accessed May 5, 2004).

38. Gifford Pinchott III, *Intrapreneuring* (New York: Harper & Row, 1985), p. 34.

39. "How Can Somebody Not Be Optimistic?" *BusinessWeek/Reinvesting America* 1992, special issue, p. 185; Mark Memmott, "Cutbacks Create Fierce Undertow," *USA Today,* October 20, 1993, p. B1.

## Chapter 7

1. Kermit Pattison, "The Scourge of Napa Valley," *Inc.com,* May 2006, **www.inc.com/magazine/20060501/franzia.html** (accessed June 12, 2006).

2. Raymond Sokolov, "The Search for the Perfect Nacho," *The Wall Street Journal,* February 4–5, 2006, pp. P1, P7; Jeff Carlton, "El Pinto Caters to Sports Show," *The Albuquerque Tribune,* August 27, 2005, **www.abqtrib.com/albq/nw_local/article/0,2546,ALBQ_19858_4035352,00.html** (accessed March 10, 2006); Charles C. Poling, "Salsa Is Hot—Brief Article," *New Mexico Business Journal,* June 2000, **www.findarticles.com/p/articles/mi_m5092/is_5_24/ai_63841959** (accessed March 10, 2006); "Welcome to El Pinto Restaurant" **www.el-pinto.com** (accessed March 10, 2006); "The El Pinto Family," **www.elpinto.com/family.html,** (accessed March 10, 2006).

3. Marc Gunther, "Yoga…Soy…McDonald's," *Fortune,* May 17, 2006, **http://money.cnn.com/2006/05/17/news/companies/pluggedin_fortune/index.htm** (accessed June 12, 2006); **www.mcdonalds.com/corp/news/corppr/2004/cpr_11222004.html** McDonald's Press Resease, November 22, 2004 (accessed June 12, 2006).

4. "Our Mission," Celestial Seasonings, **www.celestialseasonings.com/whoweare/corporatehistory/mission.php** (accessed June 12, 2006).

5. Procter & Gamble R&D Mission, **www.pg.com/science/rdmission.jhtml** (accessed June 12, 2006).

6. Points of Light Foundation, "2005 Honorees," **www.pointsoflight.org/awards/workplace/CorpWinnerDetails.cfm?ID=88** (accessed June 12, 2006).

7. Kelly Kurt, "Tulsa Bids Zebco Fishing Reels Farewell," *Chicago Tribune,* March 11, 2001, section 5, p. 7.

8. G. Tomas, M. Hult, David W. Cravens, and Jagdish Sheth, "Competitive Advantage in the Global Marketplace: A Focus on Marketing Strategy," *Journal of Business Research* 51 (January 2001), p. 1.

9. "ImClone Stock Drops on Erbitux Outlook," *NewYorkBusiness.com,* June 7, 2007, **http://www.newyorkbusiness.com/apps/pbcs.dll/article?AID=/20070607/FREE/70607003/1045/breaking** (accessed June 14, 2007).

10. Christine Dugas, "Putnam Targets Its Cutthroat Culture," *USA Today,* April 15, 2004, pp. B1, B2.

11. **www.aboutreuters.com/productsinfo/** (accessed June 12, 2006).

12. Bryce Hoffman, "Ford Downsizing Will Cut Deeper Than Expected," *DetroitNews.com,* January 21, 2006, **www.detnews .com/apps/pbcs.dll/article?AID=/20060121/AUTO01/601210384** (accessed June 12, 2006).

13. John Shepler, "Managing After Downsizing," JohnShepler.com (n.d.), **www.johnshepler.com/articles/managedown.html** (accessed May 18, 2004).

14. "The Big Picture," *BusinessWeek,* July 16, 2001, p. 12.

15. "Chrysler Group: You Don't Know the Dealers Without a Scorecard," *Ward's Dealer Business,* May 31, 2006 **http://wardsdealer .com/dealers_scorecard/** (accessed June 12, 2006).

16. "ASPO-USA Response to Exxon Mobil Peak Oil Advertisement," March 3, 2006, Association for the Study of Peak Oil & Gas-USA, **www.aspo-usa.com/news.cfm?nd=1468** (accessed June 12, 2006).

17. "Oprah Signs with XM," February 9, 2006. **www.cbsnews.com/ stories/2006/02/09/entertainment/main1300447.shtml** (accessed June 12, 2006). Laura Petrecca, "Satellite-Radio Rivals Mine New Revenue Streams," *USA Today,* February 19, 2006, **www .usatoday.com/money/industries/technology/2006-02-19-satellite-radio_x.htm** (accessed June 12, 2006).

18. Steve Ulfelder, "Chief Privacy Officers: Hot or Not?" *Computer World,* March 15, 2004, **www.computerworld.com/securitytopics/ security/story/0,10801,91168p3,00.html;** Steve Ulfelder, "CPOs on the Rise?" *Computer World,* March 15, 2004, **www .computerworld.com/securitytopics/security/story/0,108 01,91166,00.html.**

19. "2002 Catalyst Census of Women Corporate Officers and Top Earners," Catalyst (n.d.), **www.catalystwomen.org/press_room/ factsheets/COTE%20Factsheet%202002.pdf.** (accessed April 9, 2004).

20. Sarah Anderson, John Cavanagh, Scott Klinger, and Liz Stanton, "Executive Excess 2005. Defense Contractors Get More Bucks for the Bang. 12th Annual CEO Compensation Survey," *Institute for Policy Studies, United for a Fair Economy,* August 30, 2005, **www.faireconomy.org/press/2005/EE2005_pr.html** (accessed June 13, 2006).

21. Scott DeCarlo, "Big Paychecks," *Forbes,* May 3, 2007, **http:// www.forbes.com/2007/05/03/ceo-executive-compensation-lead-07ceo-cx_sd_0503ceocompensationintro.html** (accessed June 14, 2007).

22. Annie Finnigan, "Different Strokes," *Working Woman,* April 2001, p. 44.

23. "Developing Colleagues with Passion," *Inbound Logistics,* April 2004, p. 14.

24. "Improved Health of Employees and Financial Bottom Line Demonstrated Through Innovative Pilot Program at Daimler Chrysler Canada's Windsor Assembly Plant," **www.pfizer.ca/eng-lish/newsroom/press%20releases.default.asp?** (accessed June 4, 2006).

25. "Corporate Information," **www.google.com/corporate/facts.html** (accessed June 12, 2006); "The Google Culture," **www.google. com/corporate/culture.html** (accessed June 12, 2006).

26. "Tougher to Be a Leader," *USA Today* Snapshot, March 6, 2006, p. B1.

27. Bruce Horovitz, "CEO Turns the Flame Up," *USA Today,* May 23, 2005; Elaine Walker, "Whopper of a Recovery?" *The Kansas City Star,* September 24, 2005; Kate MacArthur, "Franchisees Turn on Crispin's King," *Advertising Age,* October 24, 2005; "Greg Brenneman, Chairman and Chief Executive Officer, Burger King Corporation," Burger King Corporation, **www .bk.com/CompanyInfo/bk_corporation/executive_team/brenneman .aspx** (accessed November 8, 2005).

28. "Xerox Chairman & CEO Among 'Most Powerful Women in Business," **www.xerox.com/go/xrx/template/019b.jsp?view=Award-Announcement&id=NR_Award_Fortune_Most_Powerful_Women_ Business&Xcntry=USA&Xlang=en_US** (accessed June 12, 2006).

29. Chad Terhune and Joann S. Lublin, "Coca-Cola Considers 4 Outsiders as Search for New CEO Intensifies," *The Wall Street Journal,* April 9, 2004, **http://online.wsj.com.**

30. "Coca-Cola Names E. Neville Isdell Chairman and Chief Executive Officer Elect," Coca-Cola, press release, May 4, 2004, **www2.coca-cola.com/presscenter/pc_include/.**

31. Pallavi Gogoi, "Big Soda's Sticky End," *BusinessWeek Online,* May 4, 2006, **www.businessweek.com/investor/content/may2006/ pi20060504_428474.htm?campaign_id=search** (accessed June 12, 2006).

32. Kara Scannell, "The Few . . . The Proud . . . The M.B.A.s (?!)," *The Wall Street Journal,* June 5, 2001, pp. C1, C18.

33. Bruce Horovitz, "Little Tikes Proves Durable with Low-Tech Plastic Toys," *USA Today,* December 15, 2005, pp. B1, B2; "Toymakers Wonder How Much Tech Is Too Much," *USAToday .com,* June 2, 2004, **www.usatoday.com/tech/news/2004-06-02-high-tech-toys_x.htm** (accessed February 2, 2006).

34. Kerrie Unsworth, "Unpacking Creativity," *Academy of Management Review,* 26 (April 2001), pp. 289–97.

35. *Harvard Business Review* 60 (November–December 1982), p. 160.

36. Bureau of Labor Statistics, U.S. Department of Labor, *Occupational Outlook Handbook,* 2004–2005 ed., **www.bls.gov/ oco/home.htm** (accessed May 18, 2004); "The Fogelman News: Student Edition," *Special/Career Week,* 1995; Managing Your Career, The College Edition of the National Business Employment Weekly," *The Wall Street Journal,* Spring 1994; "A Unifi Survey of Total Compensation for Middle Management: 2000," PricewaterhouseCoopers LLP, Unifi Network Survey Unit, Westport, Conn., **www.careerjournal.com/salaries/ industries/middlemanagers/20010308-middle-tab.html** (accessed July 4, 2001).

37. Kris Maher, "The Jungle," *The Wall Street Journal,* May 29, 2001, p. B16.

38. **www.selfmarketing.com/about.html** (accessed June 12, 2006).

## Chapter 8

1. Michael O'Neill, "From Wharton to War," *Fortune,* June 12, 2006, pp. 105–108.

2. Benjamin Fulford, "The Tortoise Jumps the Hare," *Forbes,* February 2, 2004, pp. 53–56.

3. "USA Today Culture Enabled Fabrications, Report Says," *The Wall Street Journal,* April 22, 2004, **http://online.wsj.com.**

4. Telis Demos, "Cirque du Balancing Act," *Fortune,* June 12, 2006, p. 114.

5. Adam Smith, *Wealth of Nations* (New York: Modern Library, 1937; originally published in 1776).

6. Jyoti Thottam, "When Execs Go Temp," *Time,* April 26, 2004, pp. 40–41.

7. Chris Perttila, "Keep It Simple," *Entrepreneur,* February 2006, pp. 60–64.

8. Faith Arner, with Rachel Tiplady, "No Excuse Not to Succeed," *BusinessWeek,* May 10, 2004, pp. 96, 98.

9. "Sunrider—More Than Two Decades of Success," MLM.com's 50 Most Influential Companies, **www.mlm.com/mlm/user/mlmarticles** (accessed January 6, 2006); **www.sunrider.com** (accessed January 6, 2006); Sunrider International, "The Founders of Sunrider," **http://store.sunrider.com/SROpp/Founders.asp** (accessed January 6, 2006); "The Best Company," **http://store.sunrider.com/SROpp/Company.asp** (accessed January 6, 2006)

10. Susan Lee and Ashlea Ebeling, "Can You Top This for Cost-Efficient Management?" *Forbes,* April 20, 1998, pp. 207–12.

11. Robert Berner and Brian Grow, "Out-Discounting the Discounter," *BusinessWeek,* May 10, 2004, pp. 78–79.

12. Jerry Flint, "When Car Guys Ran GM," *Forbes,* April 19, 2004, p. 77.

13. Jon R. Katzenbach and Douglas K. Smith, "The Discipline of Teams," *Harvard Business Review* 71 (March–April 1993), pp. 111–20.

14. Ibid.

15. Berner and Grow, "Out-Discounting the Discounter."

16. Darryl Haralson and Adrienne Lewis, "USA Today Snapshots," *USA Today,* April 26, 2001, p. B1.

17. "Coca-Cola Task Force Named," PRNewswire, press release, July 2, 2001, via **www.prnewswire.com/cgi-bin/stories.pl?_ACCT=104&STORY=/www/story/07-02-01/0001525462&EDATE=.**

18. Julia Chang, "A View from the Top," *Sales & Marketing Management,* February 2004, p. 19.

19. Jerry Useem, "What's That Spell? TEAMWORK," *Fortune,* June 12, 2006, p. 66.

20. Jia Lynnyang, "The Power of Number 4.6," *Fortune,* June 12, 2006, p. 122.

21. Adam Lashinsky, "Razr's Edge," *Fortune,* June 12, 2006, pp. 124–126.

22. **www.petco.com** (accessed January 23–February 3, 2006); Chris Penttila, "Magic Markets" *Entrepreneur's Be Your Own Boss Magazine,* September 2004, **www.entrepreneur.com/article/0,4621,316866-2,00.html** (accessed January 23–February 3, 2006); Catherine Colbert, "PETCO Animal Supplies, Inc." *Hoovers,* **www.hoovers.com/petco-(holding)/--ID__17256--/free-co-factsheet.xhtml** (accessed January 23–February 3, 2006); CNN Money.com, *Fortune 500 2005,* **money.cnn.com/magazines/fortune/fortune500/snapshots/2154.html** (accessed January 23–February 3, 2006).

23. Richard S. Wellins, William C. Byham, and Jeanne M. Wilson, *Empowered Teams: Creating Self-Directed Work Groups That Improve Quality, Productivity, and Participation* (San Francisco: Jossey-Bass Publishers, 1991), p. 5.

24. Josh Kyatt, "The Soul of a New Team," *Fortune,* June 12, 2006. pp. 134–150.

25. Peg Kelly, "Vampire Meetings and How to Slay Them," *WebPro News,* January 7, 2003, **www.webpronews.com/articles/2003/0102pk.html.**

26. Fulford, "The Tortoise Jumps Over the Hare."

27. Wikipedia, "Intranet," **http://er.wikipedia.org/wiki/intranet** (accessed June 12, 2006).

28. Nielsen Norman Group Report, *Intranet Design Annual 2006: Ten Best Intranets of the Year,* **www.nngroup.com/reports/intranet/design/** (accessed June 12, 2006).

29. "Personal Use Abuse," *Internet Works* 66 (January 2003), **www.iwks.com.**

30. "New Products Add Fun and Humor to Employee Communications and Training," PRNewswire, press release, June 5, 2001, via **www.prnewswire.com.**

31. Chris Woodyard, "'Slow and Steady' Drives Toyota's Growth," *USA Today,* December 21, 2005, pp. 1B–2B; Dan Lienert, "Why Toyota Is Beating Ford," *Forbes.com,* **www.forbes.com/lifestyle/travel/2003/11/17/cx_dl_1117feat.html** (accessed January 30, 2006); "Toyota's New Corporate Ad Tells Story of Continued Growth and Investment in West Virginia," Primezone Newswire & Multimedia Distribution, January 23, 2006, **www.primezone.com/newsroom/news.html?d=92625** (accessed January 30, 2006).

32. Erika Germer, "Huddle Up," *Fast Company,* December 2000, p. 86.

33. "Privacy (Employee)," Business for Social Responsibility, **www.bsr.org/CSRResources/IssueBriefDetail.cfm?DocumentID=538** (accessed May 20, 2004).

34. Robert Gatewood, Robert Taylor, and O. C. Ferrell, *Management: Comprehension, Analysis, and Application* (Homewood, IL: Austen Press, 1995), pp. 361, 365–66.

## Chapter 9

1. *IBM Annual Report 2004,* pp. 1–7; "Understanding Our Company, An IBM Prosepctus," March 2005; "Fast Facts," IBM, **www-1.ibm.com/press/PressServletForm.wss?MenuChoice=fastfacts&TemplateName=ShowFastFactsList&Menichoice=fastfacts&ApplicationSequence=** (accessed November 8, 2005); Stephen Shankland, "IBM: On-Demand Computing Has Arrived," clnet news.com, November 14, 2003, **http://news.com.com/IBM+On-demand+computing+has+arrived/2100-7339_3-5106577.html** (accessed February 17, 2006); Martin LaMonica and Mike Ricciuti, "Reinventing IBM: The Evolution of On-Demand," *CNET News.com,* June 15, 2004, **http://insight.zdnet.co.uk/business/0,39020481,39157666,00.htm** (accessed February 17, 2006).

2. Valerie A. Zeithaml and Mary Jo Bitner, *Services Marketing,* 3rd ed. (Boston: McGraw-Hill/Irwin, 2003), p. 7.

3. Bruce Horovitz, "A Whole New Ballgane in Grocery Shopping," *USA Today,* March 9, 2005, p. B1.

4. Tahl Raz, "A Recipe for Perfection," *Inc.,* July 2003, pp. 36–38.

5. Leonard L. Berry, *Discovering the Soul of Service* (New York: The Free Press, 1999), pp. 86–96.

6. Zeithaml and Bitner, *Services Marketing,* pp. 3, 22.

7. Bernard Wysocki Jr., "To Fix Health Care, Hospitals Take Tips from the Factory Floor," *The Wall Street Journal,* April 9, 2004, **http://online.wsj.com.**

8. Ibid.

9. Jean Halliday, "Nissan Delves into Truck Owner Psyche," *Advertising Age,* December 1, 2003, p. 11.

10. Faith Keenan, "Opening the Spigot," *BusinessWeek e.biz,* June 4, 2001, **www.businessweek.com/magazine/content/01_23/b3735616.htm.**

11. "Agricultural Export Benefits from Standardized Production," China.org, December 24, 2003, **www.china.org.cn/english/2003/Dec/83203.htm.**

12. Sue Kirchhoff, "Manufactured Homes—and Their Owners—Gain New Respect," *USA Today,* August 8, 2005 p. 13.

13. Glenn Adams, "Maine Woman's Whoopie Pies Made a Whopping Business," *The Boston Globe,* **www.boston.com/ae/food/ articles/2005/12/25/maine_womans_whoopie_pies_made_a_ whopping_business/** (accessed January 13, 2006); "Wicked Whoopies by Isamax Snacks; How It All Started," **www.wicked-whoopies.com/info.php?ssidx=MzI2MS43Ng==** (accessed January 13, 2006).

14. Stanley Holmes, "Boats as Big as the Ritz," *BusinessWeek,* April 26, 2004, **www.businessweek.com.**

15. "Overview of Assembly," Honda (n.d.), **www.hondacorporate .com/america/index.html?subsection=manufacturing** (accessed May 13, 2004).

16. Hershey, "Hershey's Chocolate Kisses," (n.d.), **www.hersheys .com/products/kisses.shtml** (accessed April 21, 2004).

17. Gargi Chakrabarty, "Kodak Picks Weld," *Rocky Mountain News,* March 23, 2004, **www.rockymountainnews.com/drmn/cda/article_ print/1,1983,DRMN_4_2750621....**

18. "Good Jobs First—Shopping for Subsidies," *Spokare Spokesman Review,* May 2004, **http://walmartwatch.com/pdf/ad-nyt-042005-backup.pdf.** (accessed June 13, 2006).

19. Stacy Perman, "Automate or Die," *eCompany,* July 2001, p. 62.

20. "First Quarter 2006 Robot Sales Impacted by Downturn in Automotive Market," *Robotics Online,* May 3, 2006, **www. roboticsonline.com/public/articles/articlesdetails .cfm?id=2377.**

21. David Noonan, "The Ultimate Remote Control," *Newsweek,* via **www.msnbc.com/news/588560.asp** (accessed July 18, 2001).

22. Robot Assisted Heart Surgery: Information from Answers.com, **www.answers.com/topic/robot-assisted-heart-surgery** (accessed June 13, 2006).

23. O. C. Ferrell and Michael D. Hartline, *Marketing Strategy* (Mason, OH: South-Western, 2005), p. 215.

24. John Edwards, "Orange Seeks Agent," *Inband Logistics,* January 2006, pp. 239–242.

25. Ferrell and Hartline, *Marketing Strategy,* p. 215.

26. Jyoti Thottam, "Is Your Job Going Abroad?" *Time,* March 1, 2004, pp. 28–34.

27. Bruce Nussbaum, "Where Are the Jobs?" *BusinessWeek,* March 22, 2004, pp. 36–37.

28. Lisa H. Harington, "Balancing on the Rim," *Inband Logistics,* January 2006, pp. 168–170.

29. "Opinion Research Corporation, Survey of 1,012 Respondents," *USA Today Snapshots,* Public Influence on Outsourcing. October 4, 2005, p. B1.

30. Barbara DeLollis and Barbara Hansen, *USA Today,* "Airlines Give Fliers Fewer Chances to Do the Bump," December 20, 2005, p. 6B; Roger Yu, "Airlines Change How They Herd Us Aboard," *USAToday.com,* **www.usatoday.com/money/biztravel/2006-01-09-boarding-usatx.htm** (accessed January 31, 2006), "How Airlines Resisted Change for 25 Years and Lost," Susan Carey, October 5, 2004, SFGate.com, Scott McCartney, *The Wall Street Journal,* **http://sfgate.com/cgi-bin/article.cgi?file=/news/ archive/2004/10/05/financial1103EDT0070.DTL** (accessed January 31, 2006).

31. Office of Aviation Enforcement & Proceedings, *Air Travel Consumer Report,* February 2004, p. 39, via **http://airconsumer.ost .dot.gov/reports/2004/0402atcr.pdf.**

32. Moon Ihlwan, with Larry Armstrong and Michael Eldam, "Hyundai: Kissing Clunkers Goodbye," *BusinessWeek,* May 17, 2004, p. 45;"Six Organizations to Receive 2005 Presidential Award for Quality and Performance Excellence," November 22, 2005, **www.nist.gov/public_affairs/releases/2005baldridgewinners.htm** (accessed June 13, 2006).

33. James R. Healey and David Kiley, "Surprise, Chrysler Loves Its German Boss," *USA Today,* May 3, 2001, p. 2B.

34. Gail Edmondson, "Mercedes' New Boss Rolls Up His Sleeves," *BusinessWeek,* October 17, 2005, p. 56.

35. J. D. Power and Associates Report, 2007 Initial Quality Study, **http://www.jdpower.com/corporate/news/releases/pressrelease. aspx?ID=2007088** (accessed June 17, 2007).

36. Philip B. Crosby, *Quality Is Free: The Art of Making Quality Certain* (New York: McGraw-Hill, 1979), pp. 9–10.

37. Nigel F. Piercy, *Market-Led Strategic Change* (Newton, MA: Butterworth-Heinemann, 1992), pp. 374–385.

38. Hershey, "Hershey's Chocolate Kisses."

39. T. E. Benson, "Quality Goes International," *Industry Week,* August 19, 1991, pp. 54–57; A. F. Borthick and H. P. Roth, "Will Europeans Buy Your Company's Products?" *Business Credit,* November/December 1992, pp. 23–24; S. J. Harrison and R. Stupak, "Total Quality Management: The Organizational Equivalent of Truth in Public Administration Theory and Practice," *Public Administration Quarterly,* 6 (1992), pp. 416–29; C. W. L. Hart and P. E. Morrison, "Students Aren't Learning Quality Principles in Business Schools," *Quality Progress,* January 1992, pp. 25–27; D. Marquardt, "Vision 2000: The Strategy for the ISO 9000 Series of Standards in the 90's," *Quality Progress,* May 1991, pp. 25–31; "Manufacturing Professionals & Managers: Median Annual Total Income," *Career Journal* (n.d.), **www.careerjournal.com/salaryhiring/industries/ manufacturing/20030827-manu-tab.html** (accessed April 22, 2004).

## Chapter 10

1. John Bishop, "The High Cost of Turnover," Ezine @rticles, **www.ezinearticles.com/?The-High-Cost-of-Turnover&id=486954,** accessed June 11, 2007; Jeffrey Pfeffer, "CEO Turnover: The High Cost of Free Agency," *Harvard Business Online,* May 24, 2007, **www.conversationstarter.hbsp.com/2007/05/ceo_turnover_ the_high_cost_of_1.html,** accessed June 11, 2007.

2. "The Flip Side of Productivity," *Ceredian,* newsletter, Spring 2004, **www.ceredian.com/myceredian/article/1,2481,11337- =3923,00.html.**

3. "Haircuts Just One of Google's Employee Perks," *USA Today,* **http://www.usatoday.com/tech/news/2007-05-10-google-perks_ N.htm,** accessed June 11, 2007.

4. "Why Individual Incentives?" **http://marriott.com/incentives/ Travel.mi** (accessed June 20, 2006); "Teamwork Incentive Program," **www.secstate.wa.gov/productivityboard/tip.aspx** (accessed June 20, 2006).

5. AFL-CIO, "2006 Trends in CEO Pay," **http://www.aflcio.org/ corporatewatch/paywatch/pay/,** accessed June 11, 2007.

6. "The 100 Best Companies to Work For," "The Wegmans Way," *Fortune,* January 24, 2005, pp. 61–90; "Wegmans: Who We Are," **www.wegmans.com/about/jobs/who_we_are.asp** (accessed May 15, 2006); "Wegmans: Benefits," **www.wegmans.com/ about/jobs/benefits.asp** (accessed May 15, 2006); "Wegmans

Egg Farm," www.wegmans.com/news/flash/eggFarmUpdate_print-able.asp (accessed May 15, 2006).

7. "Comfort Means Productivity for Office Workers," October 20, 2004, www.ergoweb.com/news/detail.cfm?id=1004 (accessed June 20, 2006).

8. Abraham Maslow, *Motivation and Personality* (New York: Harper & Row, 1954).

9. "Global Workforce Study Ranks Employees Low on Loyalty, Commitment to Employers," *SHRM HR News,* September 25, 2000, www.shrm.org/hrnews/articles/default.asp?page=bna0925c.htm.

10. John Tschohl, "Empowerment: The Key to Customer Service," www.bizonline-content.com/BizResourceOnline/harris/display-article.asp?clientid=4&categoryid=4&id=54 (accessed June 21, 2006).

11. "Employers Reap Awards and Rewards for Psychologically Healthy Workplaces," *Employee Benefit News,* April 15, 2004, www.benefitnews.com/pfv.cfm?id=5832; Susan McCullough, "Pets Go to the Office," *HR Magazine* 43 (June 1998), pp. 162–68; "Pets Provide Relief to Workplace Stress," *BenefitNews Connect,* July 1, 2003, www.benefitnews.com/detail.cfm?id=4736; "Taking Your Best Friend to Work," *Toronto Star,* December 13, 2004, p. C11; "Working Like a Dog—Survey of Owners Reveals They Would Work More Hours or for Less Pay if They Could Bring Their Pooch to Work," *CNNMoney.com,* January 24, 2006, http://money.cnn.com/2006/01/24/news/funny/dog_work/index.htm?cnn=yes (accessed January 27, 2006); "Every Day Is 'Take Your Dog to Work Day' at Planet Dog," Press Releases, www.planetdog.com/Press.asp?id=6 (accessed January 27, 2006); Best Friends Survey taken March 27, and 30, 2006, of 1,000 registered voters, "All in the Family," *USA Today Snapshots,* June 21, 2006.

12. Douglas McGregor, *The Human Side of Enterprise* (New York: McGraw-Hill, 1960), pp. 33–34.

13. Ibid, pp. 47–48.

14. Jon L. Pierce, Tatiana Kostova, and Kurt T. Kirks, "Toward a Theory of Psychological Ownership in Organizations, *Academy of Management Review* 26, no. 2 (2001), p. 298.

15. Jeanne Sahadi, "Where the (Best) 6-Figure Jobs Are," *CNNMoney.com,* http://money.cnn.com/2006/07/13/pf/six_fig_farthest/index.htm (accessed June 15, 2007).

16. The National Association for shoplifting prevention, www.shopliftingprevention.org/The Issue.htm (accessed June 2, 2006).

17. Archie Carroll, "Carroll: Do We Live in a Cheating Culture?" *Athens Banner-Herald,* February 21, 2004, www.onlineathens.com/stories/022204/bus_20040222028.shtml.

18. "FAQs," Procter & Gamble (n.d.), www.pg.com/jobs/jobs_us/faqs/index.jhtml (accessed May 25, 2004).

19. Amy Wrzesniewski and Jen E. Dutton, "Crafting a Job: Revisioning Employees as Active Crafters of Their Work," *Academy of Management Review* 26, no. 2 (2001), p. 179.

20. Lynn Haber, "Enterprises Focus on Retaining Tech Talent," 2006, http://itmanagement.earthweb.com/article.php/3612016 (accessed June 21, 2006).

21. www.batma.org/bizsol.html (accessed June 21, 2006).

22. Adam Geller, "Employers Cut 'Work/Life' Programs," *Sun,* October 23, 2003, www.thesunlink.com/redesign/2003–10–23/business/290909.shtml.

23. Larry Muhammad, "Help for the Helpers," *[Louisville] Courier-Journal,* April 20, 2004, www.courier-journal.com/features/2004/04/20/helpers.html.

24. "Annual Survey Shows Americans Are Working from Many Different Locations Outside Their Employer's Office," October 4, 2005, www.workingfromanywhere.org/news/pr100405.htm (accessed June 21, 2006).

25. "Telecommuting Benefits Documented," www.telecommutect.com/content/benifits.htm (accessed June 21, 2006).

26. "HR Executives Split on Telecommuting," *USA Today,* March 1, 2006, p. B1.

27. Lambert's Café Web site, Fun Facts!, www.throwedrolls.com/fun_facts.html (accessed January 5, 2006); Jill Bock, "Lambert's Will Be Featured Sunday," *The Standard Democrat,* May 16, 2003, http://news.mywebpal.com/partners/865/public/news458408.html (accessed January 5, 2006); "Lambert's Cafe—The Only Home of Throwed Rolls,®" *Green Book,* sold at Lambert's Cafe in Foley, Alabama, on June 14, 2003.

28. Stephanie Armour, "Telecommuting Gets Stuck in the Slow Lane," *USA Today,* June 25, 2001, pp. 1A, 2A.

29. Kurt Badenhausen, "Closer to Home," *Forbes,* May 24, 2004, pp. 15, 151; "The Salary Calculator," Realtor.com, www.homefair.com/homefair/calc/salcalc.html (accessed May 6, 2004).

30. Dan Malachowski, "Wasted Time at Work Costing Companies Billions," Salary.com, www.salary.com/careers/layoutscripts/crel_display.asp?ser=Ser374part=Par555 (accessed June 22, 2006); Anne Fisher, "Be Smarter at Work, Slack Off," *Fortune,* March 17, 2006, money.cnn.com/2006/03/16/news/economy/annie/fortune_annie0317 (accessed June 27, 2006).

## Chapter 11

1. "It's Saturday Morning All the Time," *CNN,* November 4, 2005, www.cnn.com/2005/US/08/12/cereality/index.html (accessed March 1, 2006), Joann "Totally Cereal-ous: All-Cereal Restaurant," Louiglio, *The Fort Collins Coloradoan,* December 2004, pp. E1, E2; "A Cereal Store for Cereal (Seriously)," *Business 2.0,* October 2004, p. 42; "Carb Appeal," *Fortune Small Business,* October 2004, p. 28; Cereality, www.cereality.com; www.cereality.com/exp_stores.php; www.cereality.com/comp.php; www.cereality.com/comp_found.php; www.cereality.com/comp_jobs.php; www.cereality.com/comp_press.php (all accessed March 1, 2006); April Y. Pennington, "Morning Glory," *Entrepreneur,* March 2005, p. 168.

2. Procter & Gamble, "U.S. Recruiting process," www.pg.com/jobs/jobs_us/recruitblue/recprocess.jhtml (accessed July 5, 2006).

3. Ibid.

4. Adam Geller, "Cheating Is Employed in Worker Drug Tests," *Detroit News,* March 28, 2004, www.detnews.com/2004/business/0403/29/c04-105176.htm.

5. "The Cost of Substance Abuse," http://ezinearticles.com/?The-Cost-of-Substance-Abuse&id=311005 (accessed June 15, 2007).

6. Lewis L. Malby, "Drug Testing: A Bad Investment," *Business Ethics,* March/April 2001, p. 7.

7. Geller, "Cheating Is Employed in Worker Drug Tests."

8. "Resume Fraud Gets Slicker and Easier," *CNN,* March 11, 2004, www.cnn.com.

9. "Discrimination Charges in the U.S. Increase in 2006," *The Source* 1, no. 2 (June 2007), **http://www.hrc.pdx.edu/The_Source/DiscrimCharges.htm** (accessed June 15, 2007).

10. Annie Finnigan, "Different Strokes," *Working Woman,* April 2001, p. 42; Linda Tischler, "Where Are the Women?" *Fast Company,* February 2004, pp. 52–60.

11. Sue Shellenberger, "Work and Family," *The Wall Street Journal,* May 23, 2001, p. B1.

12. Jessica Seid, "10 Best-Paid Executives: They're All Men. And They're Making about 2 to 3 Times What the 10 Top-Earning Women Executives Do," *CNNMoney.com,* October 10 2006 (accessed June 16, 2007).

13. AFL-CIO, "It's Time for Working Women to Earn Equal Pay," **www.aflcio.org/issues/jobseconomy/women/equalpay/** (accessed May 31, 2006).

14. "Employee Training Expenditures on the Rise," *American Salesman* 49 (January 2004), p. 26.

15. "FAQs," Procter & Gamble (n.d.), **www.pg.com/jobs/jobs_us/faqs/index.jhtml** (accessed May 7, 2004).

16. "By The Numbers," DMN (n.d.), **www.avvideo.com/articles/viewarticle.jsp?id=22469** (accessed May 28, 2004).

17. Matthew Boyle, "Performance Reviews: Perilous Curves Ahead," *Fortune,* May 28, 2001, pp. 187–88.

18. Maury A. Peiperl, "Getting 360-Degree Feedback Right," *Harvard Business Review,* January 2001, pp. 142–48.

19. Nathalie Towner, "Turning Appraisals 360 Degrees," *Personnel Today,* February 2, 2004, p. 18.

20. "High Cost for Treating Employees Poorly," *InfoWorld,* December 17, 2006, **http://weblog.infoworld.com/openresource/archives/2006/12/high_cost_for_t.html** (accessed June 16, 2007).

21. Anne Fisher, "Workplace: Turning Clock Watchers into Stars," *Fortune,* March 8, 2004, **www.fortune.com.**

22. "Motorola to Cut 4,000 Additional Jobs," May 30, 2007, **http://money.cnn.com/2007/05/30/news/companies/bc.motorola.jobs.reut/index.htm** (accessed June 16, 2007).

23. Bruce Nussbaum, "Where Are the Jobs?" *BusinessWeek,* March 22, 2004, p. 37.

24. Aaron Bernstein and Louise Lee, "Smart Ways to Help Low-Wage Workers," *BusinessWeek,* April 21, 2004, **www.businessweek.com.**

25. Chris Woodyard, "Ford to Cut Jobs, Close Plants," USA Today, January 24, 2006, p. H1; Sharon Silke Carty and James R. Healey, "Ford Tries for a Positive Spin," *USA Today,* January 24, 2006, pp. 1B, 2B; Jeffrey McCracken and Joseph B. White, "Ford Will Shed 28% of Workers in North America," *The Wall Street Journal,* January 24, 2006, pp. A1, A16; Stephen Power and Neal E. Boudette, "Daimler to Cut Management by 20%," *The Wall Street Journal,* January 24, 2006, pp. A3, A18.

26. "Federal Minimum Wage Increase for 2007," Labor Law Center, May 26, 2007, **http://www.laborlawcenter.com/federal-minimum-wage.asp?gclid=CMi9i-qs4YwCFRlmWAodZ2ej6w** (accessed June 26, 2007).

27. "The Working Poor: We Can Do Better," *BusinessWeek,* May 31, 2004, **www.businessweek.com.**

28. David Kiley, "Crafty Basket Makers Cut Downtimes, Waste," *USA Today,* May 10, 2001, p. C1.

29. Ed Henry, "The Personal Touch," *Kiplinger's,* June 2001, p. 87.

30. Kemp Powers, "Happy Employees," *Fortune,* March 25, 2004, **www.fortune.com.**

31. Winston Wood, "Work Week," *The Wall Street Journal,* May 1, 2001, p. A1.

32. "Employer Costs for Employee Compensation—December 2003," Bureau of Labor Statistics, press release, February 26, 2004, **www.bls.gov/news.release/ecec.nr0.htm.**

33. Marilyn Odesser-Torpey, "The Benefits Advantage," *QSR* (n.d.), **www.qsrmagazine.com/issue/62/benefits.phtml** (accessed May 7, 2004).

34. "Microsoft Reins in Benefits," *Austin American-Statesman,* May 21, 2004, **www.statesman.com.**

35. Michelle Conlin and Aaron Bernstein, "Working . . . and Poor," *BusinessWeek,* May 31, 2004, **www.businessweek.com.**

36. "Union Members in 2003," Bureau of Labor Statistics, press release, January 21, 2004, **www.bls.gov/news.release/union2.nr0.htm.**

37. "5-Month Grocery Strike Draws to an End," *CNN,* March 1, 2004, **www.cnn.com.**

38. "Characteristics of the Civilian Labor Force, 1990–2010," *InfoPlease* (n.d.), **www.infoplease.com/ipa/A0904534.html** (accessed May 28, 2004).

39. Finnigan, "Different Strokes," p. 44.

40. Feliciano Garcia, "US West Has the Tool," *Fortune,* July 10, 2000, p. 198.

41. Betsy Morris, "Star Power, Ursula Burns, Xerox," *Fortune,* February 6, 2006, p. 57; Julie Rawe, "The Art of Talking Straight," *Time:* "2003 Global Influentials," *CNN.com,* **http://edition.cnn.com/SPECIALS/2003/global.influentials/stories/burns/** (accessed February 15, 2006), "Ursula M. Burns," *Forbes.com,* **http://msxml.infospace.com/_1_28PDU260HZC667__loctbox.bres/search/web/ursula%2Bburns/1/20/1/-/1/1/1/1/1/1/-/-/-/-/-/-/-/-/-/-/-/-/-/-/-/-/-/-/-/-/-/-/-/-/-/ursula%2Bburns/-/1/-/-/-/-/-/-/-/-/-/0/107/left** (accessed February 15, 2006).

42. Taylor H. Cox, Jr., "The Multicultural Organization," *Academy of Management Executives* 5 (May 1991), pp. 34–47; Marilyn Loden and Judy B. Rosener, *Workforce America! Managing Employee Diversity as a Vital Resource* (Homewood, IL: Business One Irwin, 1991).

43. "Human Resources Managers," *CareerJournal* (n.d.), **www.careerjournal.com/salaryhiring/industries/hr/20040127-hr-tab.html** (accessed May 7, 2004); "Median Annual Income, by Level of Education, 1990–2000, *InfoPlease* (n.d.), **www.infoplease.com/ipa/A0883617.html** (accessed May 7, 2004).

## Chapter 12

1. "McDonald's Adult Happy Meal Arrives," *CNN/Money,* May 11, 2004, **http://money.cnn.com** (accessed June 6, 2006).

2. "Winning Ideas in Marketing," *Fortune,* May 15, 1995, p. 201.

3. April Y. Pennington, "Not Just for Kids; Who Says Business Can't Be Fun? Not These Specialty Toy E-tailers," *Entrepreneur Magazine,* **www.entrepreneur.com/article/0,4621,325141,00.html** (accessed January 18, 2006); "Joel Boblit—Big Bad Toy Store (01–2005)," The Allspark, **www.allspark.com/modules.php?name=Content&pa=showpage&pid=12** (accessed January 18, 2006).

4. "McDonald's Adult Happy Meal Arrives."

5. Marguerite Higgins, "McDonalds Labels Nutrition," *The Washington Times,* October 26, 2005, **washingtontimes.com/business/ 20051025-102731-2213r.htm** (accessed June 16, 2006).

6. "Beauty Queen," *People,* May 10, 2004, p. 187.

7. Michael Treacy and Fred Wiersema, *The Discipline of Market Leaders* (Reading, MA: Addison Weslsey, 1995), p. 176.

8. Apple Annual Report 10-k, 2005.

9. "Customer Is King—Says Who," *Advertising Age,* April 15, 2006, p. 4.

10. Janet Adamy, "Father, Son and Gum," *The Wall Street Journal,* March 11–12, 2006, p. A1.

11. Venky Shankar, "Multiple Touch Point Marketing," American Marketing Association Faculty Consortium on Electronic Commerce, Texas A&M University, July 14–17, 2001.

12. **www.amazon.com** (accessed June 16, 2006).

13. Stephanie Kang, "The Swoosh Finds Its Swing, Targeting Weekend Golfers," *The Wall Street Journal,* April 8, 2004, p. B1.

14. Mary Lower, "5 Tips to Help Men Target Women Authentically," *Marketing News,* April 15, 2006, p. 9.

15. Allison Marr, "Household-Level Research Gives Clearer Picture," *Marketing News,* April 15, 2006, p. 18.

16. Univision Ad, *Advertising Age,* May 15, 2006.

17. Mya Frazier, "Staples Gains Footing in Hispanic Market," *Advertising Age,* April 3, 2006, p. 58.

18. Diane Brady, "Pets Are People, Too, You Know," *Business-Week,* November 28, 2005, p. 114; Business Editors, "The Iams Company Hires Dean of The Ohio State University's College of Veterinary Medicine," *Business Wire,* January 9, 2004, **www.findarticles.com/p/articles/mi_mOEIN/is_2004_Jan_9/ ai_112007046/print** (accessed December 5, 2005); "The Iams Company and ProScan Launch Iams Pet Imaging Center to Bring Life-Saving MRI Scans To Bay Area Dogs and Cats," **www.iamsco.com/en_US/jhtmls/iamsco/news/sw_in_News_page .jhtml?li=en_US&bc=C&pti=IN&ai=2933** (accessed January 22, 2006); "Iams Savor Sauce;™ Spoil Your Dog Healthy!" and "Top the Great Nutrition of IAMS with Two Great News Tastes," **www.iams.com/en_US/jhtmls/product/sw_ProductArtilcle-Description_page.jhtml?sc=&bc=I&li=en_US&pti=AD&qi=3924** (accessed February 22, 2006).

19. Dean Foust, with Brian Grow, "Coke: Wooing the TiVo Generation," *BusinessWeek,* March 1, 2004, p. 77.

20. Pooja Bhatia, "The Pint-Size Gourmet," *The Wall Street Journal,* April 27, 2001, pp. W1, W4.

21. Charles Passy, "Your Scoop Is in the Mail," *The Wall Street Journal,* May 25, 2001, pp. W1, W6.

22. The Coca-Cola Company, **www.questions.coca-cola.com/vrep/ CokeSay.htm** (accessed June 2, 2004).

23. Jon Swartz, "Price War Looms for High-Speed Net Access," *USA Today,* November 14, 2003, p. 1B.

24. "About McDonalds," **http://www.mcdonalds.com/corp/about.html** (accessed June 17, 2007).

25. "Californian' Targets Youth with Text Messaging," *Yahoo! News,* November 20, 2003, **http://news.yahoo.com.**

26. Michael J. Weiss, "To Be About to Be," *American Demographics* 25 (September 2003), pp. 29–36.

27. Heimer, "Mystery Shopper."

28. "Focus Groups in Nebraska Help Market Tourism," *Marketing News,* January 6, 2003, p. 5.

29. "Online Research Spending Predicted to Grow to $4 Billion," GMI press, June 14, 2005, **www.gmi-mr.com/press/release .php?p=2005–06–14** (accessed June 16, 2006).

30. Look-Look, **www.look-look.com** (accessed June 16, 2006).

31. Ibid.

32. Brady, "Pets Are People Too, You Know."

33. Allison Fass, "Collective Opinion, Forget the Up-Close Focus Group. Newfangled Software Lets Lego, Procter & Gamble and Others Mine Ideas from Tens of Thousands of Opinionated Customers," *Forbes,* November 28, 2005, pp. 76–79; "About Us," **www.informative.com/aboutUs.html** (accessed December 10, 2005); "Solutions and Services," **www.informative.com/ solutionsServices.html** (accessed December 10, 2005); "Customer Communities," **www.communispace.com/customer_c.htm** (accessed December 10, 2005); "The Communispace Difference," **www.communispace.com/difference.htm** (accessed December 10, 2005); "Technology and Services," **www.com-munispace.com/technology.htm** (accessed December 10, 2005).

34. Emily Nelson, "P&G Checks Out Real Life," *The Wall Street Journal,* May 17, 2001, p. B1.

35. Normandy Madden, " 'Rolling Stone' Smacks into Great Wall of China," *Advertising Age,* April 3, 2006, p. 8.

36. Karen Valby, "The Man Who Ate Too Much," *Entertainment Weekly,* May 21, 2004, p. 45.

37. Bradley Johnson, "The Not-So-Skinny: U.S. Population Weighs In as the World's Most Obese," *Advertising Age,* May 15, 2006, p. 43.

38. Anjali Cordeiro, "Kelloggs Retreats on Ads to Kids," June 14, 2007, **http://online.wsj.com/article/SB118177043343134415-search.html?KEYWORDS=obesity&COLLECTION=wsjie/6month** (accessed June 17, 2007).

39. Bruce Horovitz, "Wendy's Will Be 1st Foodie with Healthier Oil," *USA Today,* June 8, 2006, p. 1A.

40. "Customer Service Professionals, Average Base Salary," Career-Journal.com (n.d.), **www.careerjounral.com/salaryhiring/indus-tries/sales/20040223-customer-tab.html** (accessed May 11, 2004); Donna J. Yena, *Career Directions,* 2nd ed. (Burr Ridge, IL: Richard D. Irwin, 1993).

## Chapter 13

1. **www.dominos.com/Public-EN/site+Content/secondary/ inside+dominos/pizza+particulars/** (accessed June 14, 2006).

2. The Coca Cola Company, New Products, **www.thecoca-colacompany.com/presscenter/newproducts.html** (accessed June 17, 2007).

3. Steve Rosenbush, "At GM, Tech Is Steering," *BusinessWeek,* May 27, 2004, **www.businessweek.com.**

4. Amy Barrett, with Christopher Palmeri and Stephanie Anderson Forest, "Hot Growth Companies," *BusinessWeek,* June 7, 2004, pp. 86–90.

5. Brett Shevack, "Open Up to a New Way to Develop Better Ideas," *Point,* June 2006, p. 8.

6. Judann Pollack, "The Endurance Test, Heinz Ketchup," *Advertising Age,* November 14, 2005, p. 39.

7. Faith Keenan, "Friendly Spies on the Net," *BusinessWeek e.biz,* July 9, 2001, p. EB27.

8. Seasons 52, **www.seasons52.com** (accessed June 15, 2006).

9. William C. Symonds, "Gillette's New Edge: P&G Is Helping Pump Up the Fusion Razor," *BusinessWeek,* February 6, 2006, p. 44.

10. Judann Pollack, "The Endurance Test, 1945–2005: We Map How Four Iconic Brands Have Changed with the Times," *Advertising Age,* November 14, 2005, pp. 38–39.

11. "Tide Unveils Milestone in Fabric Care with New Tide Stainbrush," Procter & Gamble, press release, February 13, 2004>, **www.pg.com/news/.**

12. Allison Enright, "The Urge to Merge," *Marketing News,* March 15, 2006, pp. 9–10.

13. Kellogg Company, Annual Report 2004, "Staying on Track," pp. 14–17; Kellogg Company, "Kellogg Company Fact Sheet" and "Overview," **www.kelloggcompany.com/kelloggco/company_info/overview.html** (accessed November 7, 2005); Kellogg Company, "Kellogg Around the World," **www.kelloggcompany.com/kelloggco/kellogg_around_the_world/index.html** (accessed March 21, 2006); Kellogg Company, Annual Report 2005, "The Tiger Inside," pp. 8–9, 16–21.

14. T. L. Stanley, "Barbie Hits the Skids," *Advertising Age,* October 31, 2005, pp. 1, 33.

15. Rich Thomaselli, "Song Is Ending, but Delta Vows to Apply Its Marketing Lesson," *Advertising Age,* October 31, 2005, p. 4.

16. Eric Wellweg, "Test Time for TiVo," *Business2.0,* May 24, 2004, **www.business2.com.**

17. Michael Fielding, "Private-Label Brands Use New Tools to Compete," *Marketing News,* May 15, 2006, p. 11.

18. Alessandra Galloni, "Advertising," *The Wall Street Journal,* June 1, 2001, p. B6.

19. Dagmar Mussey, "Coke Bottle Shape-Shifts for World Cup in Germany," *Advertising Age,* May 29, 2006, p. 12.

20. Pallavi Gogoi, "McDonald's New Wrap," *BusinessWeek,* February 17, 2006, **www.businessweek.com/print/bwdaily/dnflash/feb2006/nf20060217_8329_db016.htm?chan=db** (accessed February 2006).

21. Ibid; "Customer Satisfaction's Continued Rebound Bodes Well for Uncertain Economy," **www.theacsi.org/press_releases/0206q4.htm** (accessed June 15, 2006).

22. Stephanie Miles, "Consumer Groups Want to Rate the Web," *The Wall Street Journal,* June 21, 2001, p. B13.

23. *"American Demographics 2006 Consumer Perception Survey,"* Advertising Age, January 2, 2006, p. 9. *Data by Synovate.*

24. Rajneesh Suri and Kent B. Monroe, "The Effects of Time Constraints on Consumers' Judgments of Prices and Products," *Journal of Consumer Research* 30 (June 2003), pp. 92 +.

25. Linda Tischler, "The Price Is Right," *Fast Company,* November 2003, pp. 83 +.

26. Steven Gray, "McDonald's Menu Upgrade Boosts Meal Prices and Results," *The Wall Street Journal,* February 18, 2006, p. A1.

27. Theresa Howard, "Levi's Charms Buyers Back," *USA Today .com,* October 24, 2004, **www.usatoday.com/money/advertising/adtrack/2004-10-21-levis_x.htm** (accessed November 18, 2005); Sarah Duxbury, "Levi's Planning Pair of Snazzy Denim Depots," *San Francisco Business Times,* May 9, 2005, **http://sanfrancisco.bizjournals.com/sanfrancisco/stories/2005/05/09/story6.html** (accessed November 18, 2005); Stephanie Thompson, "Levi's Struggles to Redefine Itself as a Premium-Denim Purveyor," *Advertising Age,* July 11, 2005, p. 12.

28. Reena Jana, "Riding Hip Jeans into New Luxury Market," January 22, 2007, **http://www.businessweek.com/innovate/content/jan2007/id20070122_366747.htm?chan=search** (accessed June 17, 2007).

29. David Luhnow and Chad Terhune, "Latin Pop: A Low-Budget Cola Shakes Up Markets South of the Border," *The Wall Street Journal,* October 27, 2003, pp. A1, A18.

30. Stephanie Thompson, "Polo Jeans Thrown in the Hamper," *Advertising Age,* June 5, 2006, p. 3.

31. O. C. Ferrell and Michael D. Hartline, *Marketing Strategy* (Mason, OH: South-Western, 2005), p. 215.

32. "Top Threats to Revenue," *USA Today,* February 1, 2006, p. A1.

33. Todd Wasserman, "Kodak Rages in Favor of the Machines," *BrandWeek,* February 26, 2001, p. 6.

34. David Sharp, "Spuds Go the Way of Salad: Right Out of the Package," *The Coloradoan,* August 28, 2005, p. E2; Naturally Potatoes, "About Naturally Potatoes," **www.naturallypotatoes.com/about.html** (accessed November 23, 2005) Naturally Potatoes, "Retail," **www.naturallypotatoes.com/retail.html** (accessed November 23, 2005).

35. Jefferson Graham, "Web Pitches, That's 'Advertainment'," *USA Today,* June 26, 2001, p. 3D.

36. Michael J. Weiss, "To Be About to Be," *American Demographics* 25 (September 2003), pp. 29–36.

37. Gerry Khermouch and Jeff Green, "Buzz Marketing," *Business-Week,* July 30, 2001, pp. 50–56.

38. Olga Kharif, "An Epidemic of 'Viral Marketing'," *BusinessWeek,* August 30, 2001, **www.businessweek.com.**

39. Donna L. Montaldo, "2005 Coupon Usage and Trends," *About,* **http://couponing.about.com/od/groceryzone/a/2005cp_usage_p.htm** (accessed June 16, 2006)

40. "September Is National Coupon Month," Promotion Marketing Association, press release, September 2, 2003, **www.couponmonth.com/pages/news.htm.**

41. Kate MacArthur, "Sierra Mist: Cie Nicholson," *Advertising Age,* November 17, 2003, p. S-2.

42. Renae Merle, "U.S. Slowdown Is Good News for Coupon Seller Valassis," *The Wall Street Journal,* May 1, 2001, p. B2.

43. Michelle Maynard, "Amid the Turmoil, A Rare Success at DaimlerChrysler," *Fortune,* January 22, 2001, p. 112.

44. "Coca-Cola North America Announces the Launch of VAULT," February 17, 2006, **www2.coca-cola.com/presscenter/newproducts_vault.html** (accessed June 16, 2006).

45. Bureau of Labor Statistics, U.S. Department of Labor, *Occupational Outlook Handbook,* 2004–2005 ed., **www.bls.gov/oco/ocos020.htm** (accessed June 7, 2004); "Advertising and Marketing Professionals Annual Average Starting Salary Range," CareerJournal.com (n.d.), **www.careerjournal.com/salaryhiring/industries/sales/20040109-adv-mrk-tab.html** (accessed May 12, 2004).

## Chapter 14

1. "Post-Enron Restatements Hit Record," *MSNBC,* January 21, 2003, **www.msnbc.com/news/862325.asp.**

2. "Break up the Big Four?" *CFO,* June 1, 2004, **www.cfo.com/article/1,5309,14007%7C%7CM%7C926,00.html.**

3. Ken Rankin, "Silver Linings: Scandals May Create Job Security for CPAs," *Accounting Today,* May 17–June 6, 2004, **www.webcpa.com.**

4. Laura Demars, "Protectionist Measures," *CFO,* March 2006, p. 18.

5. Kris Frieswick, "How Audits Must Change," *CFO,* July 2003, p. 44.

6. About—Association of Certified Fraud Examiners, **http://www.acfe.com/about/about.asp** (accessed June 18, 2007).

7. Kris Frieswick, "NASA,We Have a Problem," *CFO,* May 2004, pp. 54–64.

8. Stephen Taub, "SEC Probing Harley Statements," Abstract on Channel Stuffing, July 13, 2005, **http://web.lexis-nexis.com/universe/document** (accessed November 8, 2005); "Grand Jury to Investigate Coke on Channel Stuffing Allegations," *Atlanta Business Cronicle,* May 3, 2004, **http://atlanta.bizjournals.com/atlanta/stories/2004/05/03/daily2.html** (accessed November, 8, 2005); Betsy McKay and Chad Terhune, "Coca-Cola Settles Regulatory Probe; Deal Resolves Allegations by SEC That Firm Padded Profit by 'Channel Stuffing,'" *The Wall Street Journal,* **http://proquest.umi.com/pqdweb?did=823831501&siD=1&Fmt=3&clientId=2945&RQT=309&Vname=PQD** (accessed November 8, 2005); T.C. Doyle, "Channel Stuffing Rears Its Ugly Head," *VARBusiness,* May 6, 2003, **www.varbusiness.com/showArticle.jhtml;jsessionid=PCVHTC51ICHQOQSNDBCSKHSCJUMEKJVN?articleID=18823602** (accessed December 1, 2005).

9. "2005 Hot 100," *Entrepreneur Magazine,* **www.entrepreneur.com/hot100/listings/0,6868,296117-2005-0,00.html** (accessed January 15, 2006); SeamlessWeb, "About Us," **www2.seamlessweb.com/AtHome/AboutUs.m,** "Our Service," **www2.seamlessweb.com/AtHome/OurService.m** "In the News," **www2.seamlessweb.com/AtHome/InTheNews.m,** and "Who We Are," **www.seamlessweb.com/public/aboutus.html** (all accessed January 16, 2006); Cord Cooper, "Cuisine for Your Cubicle," *Investor's Business Daily,* May 2, 2005; "In the News," "EatNow for Net Takeout," *Philadelphia Business Journal,* November 21, 2005, **www.seamlessweb.com/public/news20.html** (accessed January 25, 2006).

10. "Accounting," *The Wall Street Journal's College Journal* (n.d.), **www.collegejournal.com/salarydata/accounting/** (accessed June 14, 2004); Peter Vogt, "Forensic Accounting Emerges as a Hot Field," *The Wall Street Journal's College Journal* (n.d.), **www.collegejournal.com/salarydata/accounting/20030410-vogt.html** (accessed June 14, 2004).

## Chapter 15

1. "How Currency Gets into Circulation," Federal Reserve Bank of New York (n.d.), **www.newyorkfed.org/aboutthefed/fedpoint/fed01.html** (accessed June 28, 2006).

2. Barbara Hagenbaugh, "It's Too Easy Being Green," *USA Today,* May 13, 2003, **www.usatoday.com/.**

3. Ibid.

4. "U.S. Unveils New $50 Note with Background Colors," Bureau of Engraving and Printing, U.S. Department of the Treasury, press release, April 26, 2004, **www.moneyfactory.com/newmoney/main.cfm/media/.**

5. Barbara Hagenbaugh, "In a Mint First, Jefferson Puts His Best Face Forward," *USA Today,* January 12, 2006, **www.usatoday.com/money/economy/2006-01-12-nickel_x.htm** (accessed June 28, 2006).

6. Jane J. Kim, "The Credit-Card Catapult," *The Wall Street Journal,* March 25–26, 2006, p. B1.

7. Emily Thornton, Heather Timmons, and Joseph Weber, "Who Will Hold the Cards," *BusinessWeek,* March 19, 2001, p. 90.

8. "Card Debt," Card Trak, May 2004, **http://cardweb.com/cardtrak/pastissues/may2004.html.**

9. David Breitkopf, "MasterCard, Pulse Report Wider Use of Debit Cards," *American Banker,* May 17, 2004, p. 5.

10. Ian Rowley, "Banking on U.S. Acquisitions," *CFO,* February 2003, pp. 79–80.

11. Domino's Pizza, "Company Overview," **http://phx.corporate-ir.net/phoenix.zhtml?c=135383&p=irol-homeProfile;** "Domino's Success Factors," **http://phx.corporate-ir.net/phoenix.zhtml?c=135383&p=irol-whydominos;** "Press Releases," "Domino's Pizza Delivers 8,000th Store!," **http://phx.corporate-ir.net/phoenix.zhtml?c=135383&p=irol-newsArticle&ID=808843&highlight=** (all accessed January 26, 2006); "Domino's Pizza," *Wikipedia,* the **http://en.wikipedia.org/wiki/Domino's_Pizza** (accessed January 26, 2006).

12. "FDIC: Statistics on Banking," FDIC, **www.fdic.gov/bank/statistical** (accessed June 10, 2004).

13. GE Capital homepage, **http://www.gecapital.com/** (accessed June 18, 2007).

14. Allstate Insurance Company, "About Allstate," "The Allstate Corporation at a Glance," **www.allstate.com/about/pagerender.asp?page=allstate_at_a_glance.htm** (accessed October 19, 2005); "Allstate CEO: Firms Should Be Politically Active," *USA Today,* July 18, 2005; Allstate Insurance Company, "Community Commitment," "The Allstate Foundation," **www.allstate.com/Community/PageRender.asp?Page=foundation.html** (accessed October 19, 2005); "Years Like 2004 Bring Out the Best in Allstate," *The Allstate Corporation Summary Annual Report 2004,* pp. 5–9.

15. Judith Burns, "Mutual Fund Reforms 'at Warp Speed'—SEC Chmn Donaldson," *The Wall Street Journal,* May 13, 2004, **http://online.wsj.com.**

16. NACHA, news release, April 23, 2001, **www.nacha.org/news/news/pressreleases/2001/PR042301b/pr042301b.htm** (accessed September 6, 2001).

17. Antone Gonsalves, "Online Banking Numbers Reflect Slowing Growth," *InternetWeek,* April 10, 2006, **http://www.informationweek.com/showArticle.jhtml?articleID=185300173** (accessed June 18, 2007).

18. ING Direct, "About Us," **http://home.ingdirect.com/about/corporate_content.html** (accessed June 8, 2004); ING Direct, "ING Direct Bank Does One Thing Noticeably Well, news release, March 7, 2004, **http://home.ingdirect.com/about/aboutus_news.html#03072004;** Matthew Swibel, "Where Money Doesn't Talk," *Forbes,* May 24, 2004, p. 176; ING Direct, "Products & Rates," **http://home.ingdirect.com/products/products.asp;** "About Us," "News," **http://home.ingdirect.com/about/about.asp?s=News** (both accessed March 9, 2006); Megan Johnston, "Five Questions to Ask Before You Bank Online," Money, April 1, 2005, **http://banking.about.com/gi/dynamic/offsite.htm?zi=1/XJ&sdn=banking&zu=http%3A%2F%2Fwww.business2.com%2Fb2%2Fweb%2Farticles%2F0%2C17863%2C692636%2C00.html** (accessed March 9, 2006); Shaheen Pasha, "Online Savings Accounts Duke It Out," *CNN/Money,* August 9, 2005, **http://money.cnn.com/2005/08/09/news/economy/highyield_online_savings/index.htm** (accessed March 9, 2006); "ING Direct Bank—A Review," Soothsayer, *Epinions.com,* January 21, 2001, updated October 27, 2005, **www.epinions.com/content_6747557508** (accessed March 9, 2006).

19. Department of Labor, Bureau of Labor Statistics, *Occupational Outlook Handbook 2004–2005,* **www.bls.gov/oco/oco5055.htm** (accessed June 1, 2004).

# Chapter 16

1. Hershey Trust, "About Hershey Trust Company" (n.d.), **www.hersheytrust.com/cornerstones/about.shtml** (accessed March 26, 2006); O. C. Ferrell, "Hershey Foods' Ethics and Social Responsibility," case developed for classroom use, Colorado State University, revised edition, 2004; Hershey Foods, "Frequently Asked Questions," (n.d.), **www.hersheyinvestorrelations.com/ireye/ir_site.zhtml?ticker5HSY&script51801** (accessed June 10, 2004), "Company History," **www.hersheys.com/discover/history/company.asp** (accessed March 27, 2006); William C. Smith, "Seeing to the Business of Fun: Franklin A. Miles Jr., Hershey Entertainment & Resorts Co.," *National Law Journal,* December 22, 2003, p. 8; "Funding the School Trust," **www.hersheys.com/discover/milton/fund_school_trust.asp** (accessed March 27, 2006).

2. Tim Reason, "Hidden in Plain Sight," *CFO,* August 2005, p. 59.

3. Alex Salkever, "It's Time for an iPod IPO," *BusinessWeek,* May 5, 2004, **www.businessweek.com.**

4. "Chris DeWolfe & Tom Anderson, MySpace.com," Entrepreneurs, *BusinessWeek,* December 19, 2005, p. 66; Janet Kornblum, "Teens Hang Out at MySpace," *USA Today,* January 8, 2006, **www.usatoday.com/tech/news/2006-01-08-myspace-teens_x.htm** (accessed January 15, 2006); Richard Siklos, "News Corp. to Acquire Owner of MySpace.com," *The New York Times,* July 18, 2005, **www.nytimes.com/2005/07/18/business/18cnd-newscorp.html?ei=5090&en=33422c62f772785c&ex=1279339200&partner=rssuserland&emc=rss&pagewanted=print** (accessed January 15, 2006).

5. "Company Research," *The Wall Street Journal,* **http://online.wsj.com** (accessed June 17, 2004); Selena Maranjian, "The Math of the Dow," Motley Fool, January 29, 2004, **http://netscape.fool.com/News/mft/2004.mft04012904.htm.**

6. Katrina Brooker, "The Pepsi Machine," *Fortune,* February 6, 2006, pp. 68–72; Pepsi Company Information, **www.pepsi.com/help/company_info/index.php** (accessed June 30, 2006); Coca-Cola, Our Company, **www2.coca-cola.com/ourcompany/index.html** (accessed June 30, 2006).

7. "Dow Data, 2000–2009," Dow Jones Indexes (n.d.), **www.djindexes/jsp/avgDecades.jsp?decade=2000** (accessed June 18, 2004).

8. Adapted from "Financial Managers," *Occupational Outlook Handbook, 2004–2005.* Bureau of Labor Statistics, U.S. Department of Labor, **www.bls.gov/oco/ocos010.htm** (accessed June 18, 2004).

# PHOTO CREDITS